TELEVISION
PRODUCTION

M c G R A W - H I L L   S E R I E S
I N   M A S S
C O M M U N I C A T I O N

CONSULTING EDITOR
BARRY L. SHERMAN

FOURTH EDITION

TELEVISION PRODUCTION

ALAN WURTZEL

JOHN ROSENBAUM
Roy H. Park School of Communications
Ithaca College

McGRAW-HILL, INC.

New York   St. Louis   San Francisco   Auckland   Bogotá   Caracas
Lisbon   London   Madrid   Mexico City   Milan   Montreal   New Delhi
San Juan   Singapore   Sydney   Tokyo   Toronto

FOR
SUSAN, JOANNA, AND CAROLINE WURTZEL

FOR
TONI, JENI, AND AARON ROSENBAUM

TELEVISION PRODUCTION

 This book is printed on recycled, acid-free paper containing 10% postconsumer waste.

1 2 3 4 5 6 7 8 9 0   DOC   DOC   9 0 9 8 7 6 5 4

ISBN 0-07-072158-0

Library of Congress Cataloging-in-Publication Data

Wurtzel, Alan.
   Television production / Alan Wurtzel, John Rosenbaum.—4th ed.
      p.   cm.—(McGraw-Hill series in mass communication)
   Includes bibliographical references.
   ISBN 0-07-072158-0
   1. Television—Production and direction.
2. Television—Equipment and supplies.   I. Rosenbaum, John.
II. Title.   III. Series.
PN1992.75.W8   1995   94-27230
791.45'0232—dc20

This book was set in Helvetica by CRWaldman Graphic Communications.
The editors were Hilary Jackson and James R. Belser;
the designer was Joan E. O'Connor;
the production supervisor was Louise Karam.
R. R. Donnelley & Sons Company was printer and binder.

ABOUT THE
AUTHORS

Alan Wurtzel (Ph.D., New York University) is experienced in all aspects of television and radio production. In addition to his production background, Dr. Wurtzel has been a media consultant, noted educator, and is currently a network television executive.

His writings have appeared in various textbooks, major scholarly journals, trade and industry publications, and in a variety of newspapers and magazines.

John Rosenbaum is Chairman of the Television-Radio Department in the Roy H. Park School of Communications at Ithaca College where he teaches courses in international communication as well as in audio and video production. He has produced and directed award-winning programs for public television; written and edited programs for radio; served as a consultant to local, state, and federal agencies for media arts and education; and authored articles for various publications. Professor Rosenbaum was educated at Penn State, Temple, and Columbia University, where he received the doctorate.

CONTENTS
IN BRIEF

CONTENTS

ix

PREFACE

It's startling to realize that almost twenty years ago I began writing the first edition of this book. My objective was to approach television production as I did in my classes: pragmatically, contemporarily, and oriented toward "the way it's done in the real world." Having worked in the production industry and having had the opportunity to meet many of the industry's top professionals, I wanted to bring to the student the skills and techniques which these individuals had acquired over years of hands-on experience.

Over the past twenty years, I've been especially gratified to see the growth of the book as it was adopted by hundreds of schools and universities, found readers in various countries throughout the world, and became a standard reference for the production industry. I've always believed that the greatest compliment for any author is to have an impact on one's field, so it has been especially gratifying to meet people working in the television industry who tell me they have read (and occasionally even enjoyed) the book.

It is a well-worn cliché that television production is a rapidly changing industry but over the past few years, the dynamics of change in television production have been truly stunning. The advances in miniaturization and digital equipment combined with the integration of computerization and sophisticated software have completely democratized the production process. Simply stated, there is very little today to differentiate the production capabilities of the largest network or production house with even the most modest production facility. Today, it's talent and ingenuity—not the cost of equipment—which are the most critical ingredients in production.

To reflect these trends, my co-author, John Rosenbaum, and I have completely revised the Fourth Edition. Previous readers will find major changes in both the book itself and in its overall organization. In addition to updating content, we've attempted to respond to the feedback I've received over the years. Many readers have graciously provided me with invaluable suggestions and helpful criticism. While I've learned that it's impossible to please everyone, I am grateful for the generosity of so many readers who took the time to offer me their reactions to the book. Many of their suggestions are reflected in this edition.

The Fourth Edition is based on the framework of the three previous versions of *Television Production* and to that extent I would like to thank the countless individuals, institutions, and companies who were of invaluable help to me in writing the various editions of this book. Although many changes have been incorporated into the Fourth Edition, we have strived to maintain the fundamental integrity of the book's original premise: to provide the reader with insight into how television production is "really done" by the professionals who have invented the various tools, methods, and techniques which make up the medium. Each of them proves the point that regardless of whatever changes may occur, the one constant which remains is the need for creative people who are able to use the tools available to communicate effectively through the television medium. Whether the medium involved is broadcast, cable, or the various multimedia applications which are rapidly emerging, technique and technology can never substitute for creativity and imagination.

After twenty years, significant change is inevitable in one's personal as well as professional life. In my case, over the time the book has been in print, I've been fortunate to have experienced rewarding professional opportunities, first as a college instructor and then as a network executive dealing with many aspects of television. But the most significant changes have occurred within my family. Coinciding with the Fourth Edition is our second daughter, Caroline, whose name now happily joins Susan and Joanna on the dedication page.

Alan Wurtzel

New Features

Those readers who are familiar with the Third Edition of *Television Production* will immediately notice that the Fourth Edition appears different structurally from the earlier version.

- **First**, the most apparent change is its new organization. The twenty-three chapters have been divided into six parts. This format separates a wealth of material into manageable units and introduces the reader to the complete production process in a logical sequence paralleling the stages of television production. At the same time, each part stands on its own and can be used in any appropriate order. Extensive cross-referencing within the chapters makes this possible.
- **Second**, the new organization places an emphasis on *teamwork* in the production process. To emphasize that television production is the prod-

uct of teamwork, all the "players" are introduced in Chapter 1, and the chapters on writing, producing, directing, and performing have been moved toward the front of the book. Our intent is to convey from the outset that each individual is important, and that the roles of all the production team members are interrelated.

- **Third**, a new chapter on aesthetics has been added (Chapter 2), followed by two expanded chapters on the practical application of aesthetic principles to television production (Chapters 3 and 4). These additions emphasize the creative talent and aesthetic skills essential for producing imaginative ideas, images, and sounds for the television medium.
- **Fourth**, all subjects have been updated and expanded to include contemporary technology and practice. The most notable expansions are in the sections on digital audio production, video imaging, computer graphics, and video editing.
- **Fifth**, all the figures have been enhanced. The line art has been redrawn and most of the photographs have been updated to provide clear and timely illustrations of the subjects in the text. The new design elements strengthen the use of the Fourth Edition as a pedagogical tool and as a standard reference in the field.

While there are major changes in the Fourth Edition, we have maintained the familiar, successful approaches taken in earlier versions of *Television Production.* First, the Fourth Edition remains pragmatic, with its main purpose being to bring the skills of professionals to students. We have added more "Tech Tips" from working professionals, expanded the behind-the-scenes narratives describing actual productions, and included illustrative examples from contemporary television programs and films. Second, the Fourth Edition remains accessible. It is written in a conversational style with the nontechnical reader in mind. All necessary technical terms are defined in the body of the text as well as in an extensive glossary. The Fourth Edition, therefore, serves both the novice and the more experienced reader.

Acknowledgments

The work on the Fourth Edition was the collaborative effort of a team that extended well beyond the co-authors. A multitude of individuals from coast to coast provided invaluable advice and assistance. While we can't single out each person, we do want to acknowledge those who made major contributions to the revision.

Noteworthy among the production personnel who were generous with their time and expertise were Mike Biltucci, KGTV, San Diego; Dennis Caulkins, WIXT, Syracuse; Eileen Courtney, KABC, Los Angeles; Sue Keenan and Alrod Rodriguez, WPLG, Miami; Tim Mays, WKYT, Lexington, Kentucky; Bob Rice, WMTW, Auburn, Maine; and Joe Coscia, Mike Jacobson, Ann Limongello, George Paul, Bob Reichblum, Jack Reilly, and David Schisgall, Capital Cities/ABC, New York.

Professional educators who contributed helpful criticism and insights were Robert Albers, Michigan State University; Steven Anderson, Virginia Polytechnic Institute; Alan Bloom, California State University, Los Angeles; Aaron Bor, California State University, Chico; Jim Carter, California University of Pennsylvania; Connie Coleman, Philadelphia University of the Arts; John Doolittle, American University; Prudence Faxon, California State Polytechnic, Pomona; Jeffrey Guterman, University of Pittsburgh, Bradford; Andrew Marko, Loyola University of Chicago; Robert Musberger, University of Houston; Alan Powell, Temple University; Suzanne Williams, Trinity University; and Donald Wylie, San Diego State University.

The Fourth Edition would not have taken form without the contributions of many individuals in the College Division at McGraw-Hill. Several who deserve special recognition are Hilary Jackson, for her patient editorial guidance; Louise Karam, for her overall production supervision; Jim Belser for his exquisite attention to detail; and Joan O'Connor, for her appealing design.

I also want to thank my students and colleagues at Ithaca College for their support, especially Provost Thomas C. Longin and Dean Thomas W. Bohn, who provided time in my schedule for this work.

Finally, I want to express my heartfelt gratitude to my circle of family and friends for their understanding and encouragement during my three years of work on the Fourth Edition. A commitment of this duration becomes a central event in one's personal as well as one's professional life. It can be fulfilled only through personal as well as professional motivation. In the end, the professional reward is important, but the personal satisfaction is greater still. I have been blessed with family and friends who recognize the importance of these things to me. Their abiding faith has carried me through.

John Rosenbaum

TELEVISION
PRODUCTION

PART ONE

If you were to ask ten different people to define "television," you would probably get ten different answers. For some, television is entertainment: dramatic programs, musical shows, or comedy. For others, television is news: international, national, and local news and special events. Others think of television in terms of sports: from coverage of Olympic games in exotic locations to local high school football games. For still others, television is closed-circuit systems used for internal communication in schools, hospitals, and industry. And for many more television is home video—the new family album of recorded memories such as graduations, vacations, and personal history.

Of course, television is all these things and more. Regardless of the size and complexity of a program, how it is produced and transmitted, or what its content is, all television has one thing in common: the use of the television medium to communicate messages and ideas to a viewing audience. To use the television medium effectively, you must learn many television production skills, both creative and technical.

Overall, our goal is to help you develop a conceptual eye, an appreciation of visual storytelling, *and* an understanding of the medium's technological underpinnings. We hope you will concentrate on all of them, for only in combination will this knowledge allow you to transfer your intentions (whether to entertain, inform, persuade, or provoke) onto videotape and ultimately to the minds of your viewers.

INTRODUCTION TO TELEVISION PRODUCTION

Television is a medium that requires a team of aesthetically sensitive and technically skilled individuals to communicate ideas and emotions to an audience. Television brings together a great many communication arts to produce its programming: the scriptwriter's command of dialogue, the actor's oratory power and subtle expression, graphic and makeup artists' subtle touches, the lighting director's control of shadow and texture, the set designer's environmental influence, the audio operator's skill in blending music and sound effects, and the presentational talents of editors, directors, and producers. Since you have chosen to read this book, we assume that you would like to join this team in one of these positions.

In the brief history of television, the combined contributions of these talents have created a very powerful medium. Today, television has become a central part of world culture, the home entertainment center, the campaigns of advertisers, and the training and informational campaigns of schools and corporations. In the home, families will remember the early years through videocassette libraries as well as through their photo albums.

As you develop your production skills, think about two interrelated ideas. First, use the medium *to honestly present both the facts and the emotions of your story.* Technological advances have invested the medium with a remarkable sense of realism. Satellites transmit instantaneous coverage of news events from almost any point in the world. Miniaturized, rugged cameras can be

3

strapped to downhill skiers to literally put the viewer in the race. Using chroma key, studio talent can describe the dangers of heart disease by "walking through" the chambers of the human heart videotaped through fiber optic tubes. And videotape, a revolutionary technology of the 1950s, allows production teams to juxtapose different events in time-distorting ways. This power to realistically construct what is always a television reality has significant impact on other people. As you work with your team members, invest your ethics and sense of responsibility in what you show and tell the audience.

Second, television is a cluster of technological tools *applied to a program concept.* It requires a thorough understanding of what the technology can do in the service of your ideas. You should be aware of the ways that changes in television technology are changing the ways television programs are produced. For example, today news studios are being built in which the cameras are mounted on tracks, the zoom and focus of the cameras are servocontrolled, and a sequence of shots can be programmed into a computer by the program's director. Since the camera can be "trained" to center on talent, standard production formats such as news and talk shows can be produced without camera operators. Computers have changed many facets of television production, from writing and graphics design to the techniques of post-production editing. With computers, it's now possible for even the most modest production facility to employ techniques which were previously available only to the largest networks and production facilities. In light of such technological advances, which are being replicated in virtually every area of production, we have elected to focus on how equipment functions in the service of ideas rather than on its operational idiosyncracies. You might consider the use of this same strategy as you read the book.

We will use this first chapter to provide you with a brief overview of the complete production process because television production encompasses a vast array of approaches, equipment, and techniques.

We start with behind-the-scenes descriptions of typical television productions. Then we look at the members of television production teams, and we conclude with a comparison of in-studio and on-location productions.

This brief overview will introduce you to the basic concepts that will be examined in more detail in following chapters.

FOUR BACKSTAGE STORIES

Some television productions are carefully rehearsed and taped in studios. Others are spontaneous and covered live on location. There also are variations that combine elements of each. The four backstage stories we are about to tell illustrate the variety of approaches to television production.

A Network SitCom

The large set bustles with the expectant hum of a live studio audience. The periphery of the stage is cluttered with chairs drawn together in tight circles and seemingly endless sheets of paper marked with changes in the script. Individuals known to millions every Thursday night are rehearsing, speaking and moving in familiar ways. More than one audience member leans to his or her neighbor and comments that the stars look smaller and more like real people than they do on the television at home.

At center stage is a precariously built three-walled kitchen, a series of 12-foot-high flats lashed together and stabilized with sandbags. Four color cameras, one mounted atop a large crane, peer into the set. A boom microphone extends its reach to the center breakfast table from the same direction as the camera assigned the master long shot. The other three cameras, working with close-ups and two shots, are positioned to avoid the boom and the shadow it throws from several of the forty-two lights hung from the floating grid suspended by cable 20 feet in the air. Silhouetted against the bright set lights are the four camera operators, the boom operator, three production assistants with thick stacks of cue cards, and the floor manager. All are wearing headphones with tiny "rabbit ears," the latest in wireless intercom systems.

A floor above the set and completely isolated from the laughter of the studio audience as they are "warmed up" by the patter of yet another production assistant sit the director, assistant director (AD), technical director (TD), audio technician, and producer. The room is dark except for the glow of television monitors and seemingly thousands of multicolored buttons and switches. The producer suggests yet another last-minute change. The director concurs and dispatches a production assistant to deliver a new shot sheet to Camera 1.

The technical director is seated before the "switching console" to the right of the director. The switcher is a multibutton device which permits the technical director to put any video source—cameras, film or slides, videotaped segments, or remote feeds—on the air. Each of these video sources is displayed on a row of black and white monitors facing the console where the technical director, program director, and other production personnel sit during the program. The technical director punches up each of the four cameras and checks their picture quality on the large color monitor labeled "line," which is adjacent to the row of black and white screens.

The audio technician, seated behind the audio console in a small booth at the end of the control room, checks the audio level of the audience's microphones and practices mixing their laughter under the boom microphone assigned to the set.

Completing his conference with the producer, the program's director returns to his chair next to the technical director and puts on his headphone. On the set, the floor manager hears the director say "Stand by" and announces to the studio floor and audience "Places, everyone. This will be a take." The cameras move to their assigned places, while the technicians and production staff on the studio floor quickly move behind the cameras, outside the circle of light.

The program director checks with everyone in the control room. The technical director and audio technician are ready. The video technicians, seated in their own booth at the other end of the control room, peer into their waveform monitors, make a last check on video levels and picture quality, and nod to the director. The assistant director pushes a button on the console and speaks into a small microphone to the videotape operator,

who is located on the floor below. "Roll tape," says the AD. Through the loudspeaker on the console comes the reply, "VTR rolling and up to speed." The machines are ready to record the show.

On the studio floor, the floor manager calls out "Quiet please. Tape is rolling" and holds a small slate, on which are written the program title, taping date, and scene and take numbers, in front of one of the cameras.

The program director reads the slate off the line monitor in the control room, calls for the technical director to fade to black, and calls out over the headsets, "Stand by. Ready to cue talent, and fade in on Camera 1. Cue talent, and fade in 1."

The floor manager, standing with upraised arm beside one of the cameras, hears the director's cue and quickly points to the star. Camera 1 starts to move in and talent speaks. The audience rustles in restless anticipation, shifting its gaze from the set to the studio monitors. The loudest laughers, muses the audio technician as she balances the audience response to the unfolding situation, usually are watching the screen and not the live action on the studio set. Charged by the live audience, but understating their expressions for the camera's red tally light, the actors respond to their three-walled world. The taping has begun.

A Cable Sports Remote

Located behind the gymnasium on a college campus is a small remote production truck. The final championship game of the basketball season will be broadcast live over a regional cable system. Upstairs, in the crowded gym, the program director is speaking to the play-by-play announcer. They are going over the details of the program's opening. Technicians are working on the shading of the cameras so that the cameras can be intercut without distracting changes in brightness level. A production assistant is down at the official's table double-checking the spelling of the players' names and their numbers on the official roster with the character generator operator's list. The camera operators and the director meet for the last time before the broadcast will begin.

Two of the camera operators go to their platforms on the right side of center court about 20 feet above the floor. The other two mobile cameras take up their positions under the two baskets. Each of the mobile cameras is equipped with a shotgun microphone for court sounds, and there is an omnidirectional mike located next to the announcer to pick up crowd noise. The announcer's headset with the attached microphone will keep his voice dominant no matter how enthusiastic the crowd becomes. The director, satisfied that all know their jobs, leaves the gym. The game will be broadcast live, and once it has begun, there will be no chance for changes or retakes.

The inside of the remote truck is a miniature control room. It is five minutes to air time, and the AD is on the telephone talking to the master control engineer. She has just finished previewing the promotional clips about the competing schools and the previously recorded interviews with the coaches that will be inserted during timeouts. Also before her is the list of commercials which will be rolled in from the downtown studio on cue.

A small monitor shows the program now being cablecast. The director enters and sits down, checking with the audio technician to be sure that the theme music for the opening is cued and ready. Camera 1 pulls back to a wide shot of the gymnasium and the character generator operator checks the preview monitor showing the opening title to be overlayed on Camera 1. Camera 2 presets its opening shot on the tipoff, framing the two centers. The AD begins the countdown: "Two minutes to air. Stand by."

Tension builds in the truck as the second hand sweeps toward air time. At thirty seconds to air, the program director calls out the time over the headset, "Thirty seconds to air. Ready to hit music, fade up on Camera 1, key the CG on 1, and cue announcer." The AD watches the clock and calls out, "Ten seconds to air. Nine, eight, seven . . . "

The off-air monitor shows the end of the last program. At exactly "straight-up," i.e., on the hour, an operator at the cable system master control room presses a button, and the feed from the remote truck replaces the ID slide on the off-air monitor.

As the shot from Camera 1 appears on the screen, the director calls out, "Hit the music, key CG, and cue announcer."

Framed on Camera 2, the centers prepare to shake hands. The director calls, "Ready to Take 2, and Take 2." The live program is ten seconds into its three-hour marathon.

A Local News Report

The news day begins at 9:30 A.M. at the story meeting, attended by the news director, two assistant news directors, and the assignment manager. The managing editor and bureau manager are on the speaker phone. The daybook of anticipated stories has been compiled in advance by the assignment manager, who is also ready for breaking stories. Reporters and photographers are assigned stories from the daybook for the 5:00, 5:30, and 6:00 P.M. segments of the station's ninety-minute newscast. It is number one in its market, based on ratings announced the day before by an independent research organization. The mood of the meeting is positive and calm. There still are almost seven hours before air time when the story meeting ends.

The big board behind the assignment desk shows the locations of each story being covered that day. Remote locations can be shown on-air live via satellite and microwave. The station also can originate live shots from its helicopter and a remotely-controlled camera mounted on top of the tallest building in the area. Most location stories are covered on videotape by reporters and photographers, who drive the five station vans to and from the locations.

This day one team is assigned to cover a story about school children visiting a locally-owned business. It will be a feature package in the six o'clock newscast.

By 11:00 A.M., when they leave the station, the reporter has used a newswire service to get the basic facts of the story, which she discusses with the photographer as they drive. On location, the reporter and photographer work closely, quickly planning interviews, standups, and cover shots to be edited that afternoon. Sometimes the photographer takes the initiative and suggests shots; other times the reporter does. They both seem aware of what needs to be done to help the other person do the best job.

The photographer shoots with a camera/recorder that combines a chip camera and a half-inch tape deck. The reporter uses a hand mike for interviews and simultaneously records them on a small audiocassette that she will use later while writing the story and choosing word-for-word sound bites. Her script must be detailed because it will be used for closed-captioning and translating into a second language. (See Figure 1-1.)

The on-mike voices are recorded on track 1 and natural sound on track 2. The photographer controls the audio levels manually and listens to them on a speaker built into the camera. An electronic signal called "SMPTE time code" also is recorded on the videocassette for use when the tape is edited.

Back at the station, the reporter begins writing the script at her desk. She uses a computer word-processing program that will feed the script to the news producer and the studio Tele-Promp-Ters. The computer also feeds printers to make paper copies for files and a rundown for the director.

About 2:00 P.M. there is a production meeting to plan the technical aspects of the newscast. The producer, director, and technical director verify the order of elements, times, and sources of video and audio. The producer notes that they must be prepared for a breaking story that may be aired live from a remote feed. The reporter does not attend the meeting because at this time she is busily writing the story. In addition to the footage re-

corded that morning, the reporter decides to use file footage from the station archives.

By 4:30 P.M. the reporter is ready to edit. The package will be recorded on an Edit Master videocassette that will be placed in the archives after it airs.

The reporter and the assigned editor work as a team to create a coherent aural and visual story that flows back and forth between standups, bites, cover shots, and voice-overs. The reporter records the voice-overs right in the editing room, reading from a laptop computer.

The reporter must provide a list of written names which will become the visual lower-third identification captions and the times they must appear in the package.

About 5:30 P.M. the reporter selects three excerpts that will be used early in the newscast as promos for the package. The editor quickly dubs them onto three different cassettes. Despite the fast approaching air time, the team works calmly and quickly to complete the package.

At 6:11 P.M. the editor takes the cued Edit Master to the feed room, where it quickly is loaded onto the scheduled VCR. Two minutes later the director calls for the cassette to roll and puts it on the air.

FIGURE 1-1 **On-Location Interview.**
The reporter records the interview on an audiocassette to use later when writing the script. (*Courtesy: WPLG-TV.*)

A Corporate Training Tape

As the last office worker leaves the building, he passes in the parking lot a five-person television crew, which begins unloading equipment from its production van, checks it by the security guard, and sets it up in the high-tech surroundings. The crew is about to work through the night to produce a series of training tapes which will be shown to all the new engineers who will be joining the firm. In addition to the technical crew, a producer-director is on hand to supervise the taping. The program's "talent" consists of experienced employees who will demonstrate how the various computer-aided design stations operate.

A few days earlier, the producer-director discussed the script with each of the participants and explained to them exactly what they were to do during the production. Long before the taping date, the producer-director carefully worked out a detailed shooting schedule and had done a site visit to be sure adequate power was available and that environmental noise and lighting could be controlled. To expedite the production, she has decided to shoot the footage out of sequence, so she now explains once again to both talent and the production crew how she expects to proceed throughout the shoot.

The first sequence that will be taped involves how to enter data into the design system. The producer-director walks the talent through each of their moves, while the camera operator and the audio technician watch the action closely. Once she is satisfied with their performance, the director calls for a rehearsal with camera, lighting, and audio. The rehearsal proceeds smoothly, and the director decides to go for a take. The camera operator's assistant holds a slate in front of the camera while the director calls out, "Roll tape." The tape operator confirms that the videotape is rolling up to speed and nods to the director. The director says, "Action," and the talent begin their preplanned moves. In the middle of the sequence, the camera operator suddenly calls out, "Boom in the shot," indicating that the boom microphone, which is held over talent's heads in order to pick up the sound of their voices, has become visible in the camera viewfinder. "Cut," calls the director, and the sequence is repeated.

At the end of the take, the director calls for a videotape playback as the cast and crew gather around a small television monitor to watch their work. While the tape plays back, the audio technician monitors the sound, using a pair of headsets, while the lighting director examines the screen closely to see if there are any lighting problems. The director is satisfied with the last take, and there are no technical problems, so the crew moves on to tape the next sequence.

Since the production crew is using only one camera, every cut to a new shot in order to show the action from a different angle must be accomplished by physically moving the camera to a new position while one of the talent repeats his or her movements for the new shot. As the graveyard shift of security guards comes on duty, the production unit completes the last take and begins to strike their equipment and pack up the production van.

Although the taping is complete, the producer-director's job has only begun. Back in the edit room, she must screen the raw footage to decide which take to use for each sequence. Sometimes no single take is completely satisfactory, but by combining a piece from one take with a piece from another, she is able to assemble a perfect sequence. "Let's see that sequence again, when his hand moves to the monitor," says the producer-director to the tape editor. The editor touches a few buttons, and the tape begins to show the performer's hand guiding the light pen. "If we cut in a close-up of the hand here," says the tape editor, "we can eliminate the jump cut and pick up the rest of the action from Take 4." The director nods approval as the editor begins to edit the tape at precisely the point they decided on.

Although it took only six or seven hours to videotape all the segments, it takes the producer a full week of ten-hour days inside the edit room to screen the footage, select the takes she wants to use, and then edit the pieces together into a final rough-cut.

Once the rough-cut version is completed, the producer-director turns her attention to the audio sound track. Sitting inside an audio studio, she works with the announcer, who reads the voice-over narration. "Pause for emphasis on that line," she says, and the announcer reads the copy over again until the director is satisfied. Once the narration recording is finished, the director works closely with the audio technician to select the music and sound effects that will be added to the final audio mix.

Having assembled all the audio elements, the producer-director returns to the postproduction room, and the delicate job of mixing the sound track begins. The original sound which was recorded during the location taping must be mixed with the narration, music, and sound effects. The process is laborious not only because the audio technician must perfectly balance all the sound elements together, but also because the entire audio must match the visual action on the television screen.

Finally, both the audio technician and the producer-director are satisfied with the audio mix, but the production is still not completed. The final step is to integrate the master videotape footage, which was used to produce the rough-cut workprint, with the audio, which was mixed into a composite track. To do this, the producer-director and the tape editor return to the postproduction room, where a computer-assisted editing system coordinates the sound and pictures into the completed master tape.

Over one hundred hours were required to shoot, edit, and postproduce the thirty-minute training tape. The master version is used to make dozens of videocassette copies of the program, which are shipped to each of the corporation's regional offices. Exactly one month after the production crew taped the sequences inside the office building, the first group of employees sits before a television monitor to watch a program which shows them, in an interesting and informative way, how to do their jobs better. Although the program may not have any Hollywood stars or the excitement of a basketball play-off game, and although it will be seen by an audience of only a few hundred, it is another example of the effective use of television production to communicate a message to a viewing audience. And the sponsors of the tape received exactly what they wanted, a product that could accurately and without complaint show a complex operation in painstaking detail.

The quick pace at which the new engineers learned their responsibilities more than paid for

the production costs, which in turn helped the production company buy the new paint box system to add flexibility to their graphics. No doubt the next project, an instructional videotape about home construction, will benefit from the new technology of the paint box system and by what the crew learned about design from the engineers on their last shoot.

No matter what type of program is being produced, there are four stages of television production.

FOUR STAGES OF TELEVISION PRODUCTION

The actual production of a show may take only thirty minutes, but this is only a small part of the overall production process. Long before anyone enters the studio or control room or arrives on location, the program must be carefully planned and many detailed preparations completed. This involves work in a number of different steps which can be divided into four separate stages: (1) preproduction planning, (2) setup and rehearsal, (3) production, and (4) postproduction. Of course, not every production will require work in each stage, nor is the same emphasis always given to each. For example, a live, daily news program will probably require little setup and rehearsal and no postproduction, while a complicated dramatic special which is videotaped in segments and assembled later through tape editing would operate in all four stages. Throughout this book we will discuss the operation of equipment and the actions of production personnel as they apply to each phase of the television production process. (See Figure 1-2.)

Preproduction Planning

The preproduction planning for a program may begin days, weeks, or even months before the actual production date. The more complicated and involved the production, the more preproduction time is necessary. This stage begins with research

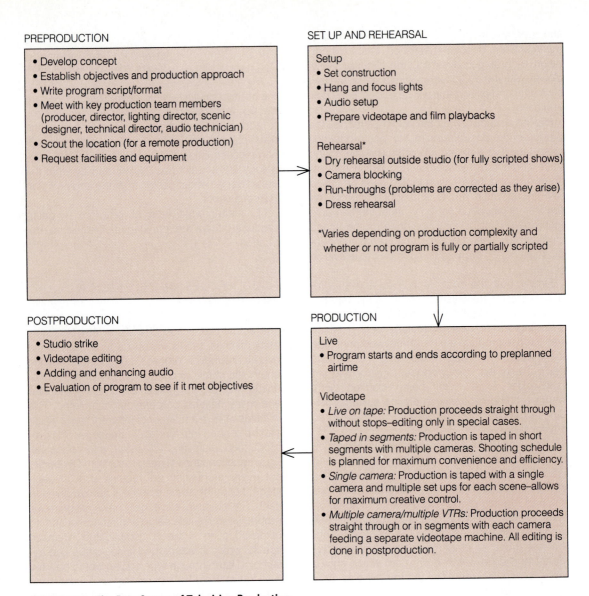

PREPRODUCTION

- Develop concept
- Establish objectives and production approach
- Write program script/format
- Meet with key production team members (producer, director, lighting director, scenic designer, technical director, audio technician)
- Scout the location (for a remote production)
- Request facilities and equipment

SET UP AND REHEARSAL

Setup
- Set construction
- Hang and focus lights
- Audio setup
- Prepare videotape and film playbacks

Rehearsal*
- Dry rehearsal outside studio (for fully scripted shows)
- Camera blocking
- Run-throughs (problems are corrected as they arise)
- Dress rehearsal

*Varies depending on production complexity and whether or not program is fully or partially scripted

POSTPRODUCTION

- Studio strike
- Videotape editing
- Adding and enhancing audio
- Evaluation of program to see if it met objectives

PRODUCTION

Live
- Program starts and ends according to preplanned airtime

Videotape
- *Live on tape:* Production proceeds straight through without stops–editing only in special cases.
- *Taped in segments:* Production is taped in short segments with multiple cameras. Shooting schedule is planned for maximum convenience and efficiency.
- *Single camera:* Production is taped with a single camera and multiple set ups for each scene–allows for maximum creative control.
- *Multiple camera/multiple VTRs:* Production proceeds straight through or in segments with each camera feeding a separate videotape machine. All editing is done in postproduction.

FIGURE 1-2 The Four Stages of Television Production.

and concept development, then the producer and director work with the writer to complete the script and to develop the overall production approach. The key members of the television team—producer, director, writer, TD, audio technician, lighting director, and scenic designer—meet to discuss the program and the part each will play.

Preproduction planning is essential for a successful show. Enormous difficulties can be avoided if the production has been planned out carefully in advance, with all key members of the team thoroughly aware of their contributions and areas of responsibility. It is much easier to correct a problem on paper during the preproduction stage than later when unanticipated difficulties can halt work in the studio, delay the production, and increase costs. Remember Murphy's law, which always seems to operate overtime in television: "If anything can go wrong, it will." There will always be problems even in the most carefully planned production, but producing a program without adequate preproduction is an invitation to disaster. (See Figure 1-3.)

TECH TIP The famous film director Alfred Hitchcock has been quoted as saying that for him, the actual production was the anticlimax of program creation. Once he had planned all the production elements—actor blocking, camera angles, sets, and lighting considerations—the actual filming was merely a mechanical exercise of translating his meticulous planning into a picture. While not everyone may agree with Hitchcock's definitive statement, the concept of thorough planning holds for television production. Preproduction, fully thought through, is the single most important, and creative, step in successful television.

Setup and Rehearsal

Setup Just prior to the actual production, the studio and control room must be prepared for the program. The amount of time allotted for setup will be determined during the preproduction planning

and usually depends on the program's complexity and the size of its budget. In order to maximize the amount of time available, all key members of the production team must know exactly what will be required and must carefully supervise their crews to accomplish the task. The various crews should try to work simultaneously, whenever possible. It is inefficient to have to wait until a set is completely finished and dressed by the stagehands before even beginning to hang lights or to wait until the lighting is completed before setting up microphones. (See Figure 1-4.)

While the studio floor is being set up for the production, a similar operation is occurring in the control room. The technical director must check on all external feeds from tape machines, film and slide projectors, electronic character generators, and remote locations. The audio technician has to prepare the audio console by patching in microphones and sound from videotape and film tracks, setting levels, and checking remote audio feeds and communication lines. The video technicians must electronically align each camera so that the cameras can provide the best possible pictures. Usually, most of the setup in the control room can

FIGURE 1-3 Preproduction Meeting.
Preproduction is the most important phase of television production.

FIGURE 1-4 Studio Setup.
During setup, crews must work together to save time.
(*Courtesy: Capital Cities/ABC, Inc.*)

studio and control room have been properly set up and prepared for the production, rehearsals can move into the studio. Since even on the largest shows the amount of rehearsal time is always limited, the director must carefully plan the use of out-of-studio and in-studio rehearsals.

It is during the in-studio rehearsal that all the production elements should finally come together: the set, costumes, and lighting; the music and sound effects; the camera shots; filmed and taped inserts; and so on. While the director works on perfecting performances and camera shots, the other key production team members must watch the operation of their individual areas and correct whatever problems arise. The audio technician may reposition a microphone; the lighting director might add another instrument to illuminate a dark area; the scenic designer may decide to move some furniture to have more space for a difficult camera shot.

During rehearsal, the producer carefully watches the program monitor, acting as a surrogate audience and making notes for suggested changes to improve both the aesthetic and the technical quality of the production. During a break, these notes are discussed with the director, performers, and production crew. (See Figure 1-5.)

Production

In the early days of television, before the development of videotape, all programming was produced live. The show started at the appropriate time and ran straight through until the end with no chance to stop or correct mistakes. This era of broadcasting was responsible for some classic stories, such as the "dead" body that crawled offstage while still on camera or the actor who, after blowing his lines throughout the entire program, turned to another "passenger" on the airplane set and said, in frustration, "This is where I get off." Whereupon he promptly walked off the airplane, ostensibly in midair.

The development of videotape has changed this, allowing the producer and director to correct major problems and offering far more flexibility in sequencing the production of program segments. With the advent of tape and tape-editing techniques, shows can be produced in a number of

proceed while the studio setup takes place on the studio floor.

A smooth and efficient setup is a crucial factor in the success or failure of a production. If too many details go unattended during the setup, they will have to be taken care of during rehearsal. Not only is this wasteful and inefficient, but it takes away valuable rehearsal time which is better spent in perfecting the performance and coordinating the various production elements into a smoothly operating team.

Rehearsal To save money and reduce pressure on valuable studio resources, early rehearsals often occur outside the studio. However, some in-studio rehearsal usually is required to coordinate the technical aspects of the production. Once the

different ways. We have divided them into two groups: live and videotaped for editing.

Live   For a program that is broadcast live, the production stage is the final phase in the production process. Most news programs, sports coverage, and other types of "immediate" programming are produced live. Sometimes a program may be produced "live on tape." While this may seem to be a contradiction in terms, it means that the program is produced in real time, as though it were live, but instead of being broadcast during production, the show is recorded on videotape for later broadcast. Tape is used essentially as a storage medium and permits the show to be produced at a more convenient time than the actual broadcast time. Only in the case of a serious blunder is the tape stopped and edited. Most talk programs and game shows are produced live on tape. (See Figure 1-6.)

Videotaping for Editing   The development of sophisticated videotape-editing techniques permits the use of tape not only as a storage medium but as a primary production tool like a camera or a microphone. Complex productions can be taped in short segments, which can be assembled

later through videotape editing. Sometimes, segments may not be taped in the exact order in which they will appear on the completed show but rather for the convenience of the production. On other occasions, a program may be taped in segments because some performers may not be available during the entire production period. In this case, all scenes involving a particular performer are taped at one time, and once they are completed to the director's satisfaction, the performer is released.

Taping in segments for later editing provides the program director with a high degree of creative control. Instead of the director and crew having to worry about the entire production, they can concentrate on each segment and, once that portion of the show is recorded and "in the can," move on to the next. Some productions are even taped with only one camera rather than with the more conventional multiple-camera technique. Shooting with a single camera, much like motion pictures, allows the director to concentrate on a very small part of the performance at any one time

FIGURE 1-5 Rehearsal. All production elements are practiced together during rehearsal. (*Courtesy: Capital Cities/ABC, Inc., and Ann Limongello.*)

FIGURE 1-6 Control Room in Production. The director calls the shots from the control room during production. (*Courtesy: Capital Cities/ABC, Inc.*)

and permits lighting, audio, and other production elements to be perfected and carefully controlled. Of course, this is a very costly and time-consuming technique, but some programs justify the additional expense involved.

Striking the Set After a live program or taping has been completed, the equipment and scenery is usually removed and the studio or location returned to its original condition. This task often is called "striking" the set, a term which has been borrowed from the theater.

The amount of time and effort required, and the crew members responsible for striking the set, varies from location to location. The most difficult and time-consuming strike follows a complex multicamera remote/location taping. Then everything has to be disconnected, packed, and loaded into vehicles. On the other hand, in a studio with a permanent set dedicated to one series—such as a daily newscast—little more may need to be done than to turn off the studio lights and monitors. The set, cameras, microphones, and other equipment may be left where they are in the studio because it would be inefficient to keep putting them away and setting them up again a short time later.

In a studio where a number of different programs may be taped each day—such as the typical college or university studio—the set should be disassembled and stored, cameras rolled to one side of the studio, cables "figure-eighted" neatly, and microphones and other equipment returned to storage after each program. The purpose of striking the studio like this is to leave it clear and ready to be set up for the next production.

In all cases, it's important to handle equipment carefully and leave the facilities and equipment the way you would like to find them at the beginning of your next production.

Postproduction

Programs that are produced on videotape for later editing require a postproduction phase. At this time, the director supervises the tape editing, selecting those takes or segments which are to be included in the final, edited version. Postproduction can be a simple matter of assembling a number of completed segments or a highly complicated procedure which adds special effects and computer graphics, and employs computers to help the director and tape editor combine hundreds of individual shots into the completed program.

One of the major advantages of postproduction is the creative control it offers the director in the selection of both shots and performances. It is possible to select the very best performance of both cast and crew from a number of different takes, literally building the show by assembling the best scene, shot, or even a performer's delivery of a single line. In many instructional or industrial productions, postproduction permits the addition of visual elements, such as graphics, film, or tape, to produce an even more effective presentation. Additional audio also can be added during postproduction to enhance or modify the existing sound track. (See Figure 1-7.)

THE TELEVISION TEAM

Television is a hybrid medium which has borrowed and adapted many techniques from the theatrical stage, motion pictures, and radio. Early television productions were often produced on a trial-and-error basis. Creative production staffs and technical crews worked together to explore the capabilities of the new medium, and as they worked, they developed many of the guidelines and practices used today. As producers and directors became more experienced, they constantly challenged engineers to develop more light-sensitive cameras, better lenses, newer and more flexible electronic effects, and more elaborate audio systems to permit them to expand and perfect their productions. The engineers quickly rose to the

challenge and, within a few short years, developed color television, videotape, and countless sophisticated electronic effects which have radically altered the way in which programs are produced.

Many changes have occurred in television production over the past fifty plus years, but one constant is the nature of television as a team operation that requires the skills and abilities of a variety of artists and craftspeople to produce the programming successfully. From the simplest program to the most complex, a television production is the sum total of the coordinated efforts of dozens of skilled individuals who make up the *television team.*

Perhaps Bob Lahendro, a talented director of such classic television programs as *All in the Family,* put it best when he said:

> I started in this business pulling cue cards and spent five years until I became a floor manager, assistant director, and then director. And while working at these various levels I was able to really appreciate every job that everyone was

FIGURE 1-7   **Postproduction Editing.**
In postproduction, the program segments are edited together. Additional graphic and audio elements can be added during postproduction. (*Courtesy: Capital Cities/ABC, Inc.*)

doing to make the show successful. No matter what your pay scale is or what your job is, you take a certain amount of pride in doing that job well. Television is a team effort and the entire team can make the director look good or make the director look bad. All it takes is one misplaced cue, a line not correctly picked up on audio, or one missed shot to ruin what could be a beautiful moment in a show. No matter how good a person may be in his job, unless everyone else puts out 100% effort, you won't look good and the program can't possibly be a success. If I've learned one thing about television, it's that the team approach is probably the single most important element in producing the kind of programs people will want to watch and that everyone can be proud to say they worked on.

A smoothly operating television team requires the integration of many different jobs, all performed and coordinated perfectly. In order to give you some understanding of the composition of the television team and to let you see how all the elements fit together in the production of a show, we provide here a brief description of some of the principal team members and their primary responsibilities.

The television team can be roughly divided into two groups: production *staff* members and production *crew* members. The production staff has primary responsibility for the program content and development and is composed of the producer, director, writer, and a variety of production assistants. Sometimes in terms of budgeting, these are called "above the line" positions. The production crew is made up of individuals who work primarily with the production hardware and equipment: the technical director, audio technician, camera operators, floor managers, and a variety of crew assistants and technicians. These jobs are sometimes referred to as "below the line" because they appear on a production budget in a separate category from the production staff.

To a certain extent, the division between staff and crew is arbitrary, since many jobs will invariably cross lines. For example, the director is considered to be a member of the production staff. In

some situations he or she may not actually operate any equipment. Other times the director may roll tapes, switch video, or operate other equipment. In either case, a good director must be as knowledgeable about the capabilities and limitations of the production hardware—cameras, microphones, lights, and the like—as about directing performers or selecting camera angles. Similarly, the production crew requires members with a great deal of creativity and ingenuity to help the program develop effectively. A good camera operator not only must understand the technical operation of the camera, but also must display a good sense of picture composition to frame and compose shots for the director. The graphic artist must render titles that are accurate and clear technically, and also attractive and expressive visually. There is little question that members of both the production staff and crew contribute the technical expertise, skillful artistry, creativity, and imagination needed to make a show a success.

Of course, each production job requires special skills and talents, and in most large studios they are performed by specialists. In many smaller operations, however, one person may be assigned to a number of different responsibilities. For example, it is not uncommon for the scene designer to also handle lighting or for the director to operate the switcher. However, for the sake of clarity, we will discuss each production position as a particular "role" with the understanding that it is possible and quite common for one individual to undertake a number of responsibilities during a production. (See Figure 1-8 on the following pages.)

The Production Staff

The Producer   The producer is responsible for the entire television production. He or she is the ultimate authority in charge of all production aspects from planning and writing of the script to final production and editing. Since the producer also must be concerned with program budgets and organizational matters, as well as with aesthetic decisions, in many large production studios the producer may have a number of associate producers for assistance.

The Director   The director is responsible for cre-

FIGURE 1-8 Members of the Production Team and Their Responsibilities.

Position	PREPRODUCTION	SETUP AND REHEARSAL	PRODUCTION	POSTPRODUCTION
Producer	Develop program concept. Develop production budget. Assign program's director. Work with writer on script. Approve director's approach, light design, and set design. Supervise and coordinate all preproduction planning.	Supervise overall production activities. Watch rehearsals as surrogate audience and make notes for changes or improvements. Keep production moving on time and within budget. Approve last-minute changes as they arise.	On live shows help director as needed. On taped shows work with director on which takes are usable.	Approve final edited version. Coordinate with station for promotion/publicity. Evaluate program to see if it met objectives.
Director	Participate in all preproduction meetings. Work with producer and writer in script development. Establish production approach in consultation with producer. Consult with lighting designer, set designer, audio technician and approve their various designs and approaches. Cast performers. Work out camera shots.	Rehearse performers. Rehearse camera shots in studio. Integrate all production elements into a coordinated show.	Execute production.	Supervise editing.
Writer	Work with producer and director in developing script or format. Revise script until approved.	Available for rewriting if necessary.		
Assistant Director	Help director in planning production approach.	Assist director during out-of-studio rehearsal. Ready camera shots and other cues during studio rehearsal.	Assist director by readying camera shots and other cues. Keep track of program timing. Roll in film or videotape segments.	Help director during editing. Keep track of timing during editing.
Technical Director (Switcher)	Consult with director and producer on necessary technical facilities.	Responsible for overall technical quality (if acting as technical director). Operate production switcher during studio camera rehearsals.	Operate production switcher.	Operate switcher during postproduction.

FIGURE 1-8 (*continued*) Members of the Production Team and Their Responsibilities.

Position	PREPRODUCTION	SETUP AND REHEARSAL	PRODUCTION	POSTPRODUCTION
Audio Technician	Consult with director and other key team members on production approach and necessary audio. Plan audio approach and necessary audio facilities. Prepare necessary audiotapes in advance.	Supervise audio crew in studio and control room preparation. Prepare audio control console. Check all microphones and balance audio sources.	Mix program audio.	Operate audio console during postproduction audio sweetening.
Scenic Designer	Consult with director, producer, and lighting designer on overall design. Develop set design approach and design settings.	Supervise set construction. Supervise activities of stagehands as set is erected in studio. Make necessary changes as problems develop during rehearsal.		
Lighting Designer	Consult with director, producer, and scenic designer on overall design approach. Develop lighting approach. Prepare lighting plot for production.	Supervise hanging and focusing of lighting instruments. Balance all instruments until proper illumination and effect are achieved. Make whatever changes are necessary as problems develop during studio rehearsal.	Coordinate all lighting cues. Operate lighting dimmer board.	
Graphic Artist	Consult with producer and writer on graphics needed. Design and prepare mechanical and electronic graphics.	Operate the character generator and electronic graphics if assigned. Available for making changes and additions during rehearsals.	Operate the character generator and electronic graphics if assigned. Available for making changes and additions during production.	Provides electronic graphics to be added during editing.

FIGURE 1-8 (*continued*) Members of the Production Team and Their Responsibilities.

Position	PREPRODUCTION	SETUP AND REHEARSAL	PRODUCTION	POSTPRODUCTION
Floor Manager		Responsible for all activities on studio floor. Serve as director's "eyes and ears" on floor during rehearsal and production. Responsible for props and costumes during rehearsal and production. Relay cues to talent as they come from director.	Relay all cues to talent.	
Camera Operators		Prepare cameras for production. Operate cameras during camera rehearsals.	Operate cameras during production.	
Video Technicians		Set up and align cameras for best picture. "Shade" cameras to control for variations in scene brightness. Help director to achieve special visual effects as necessary. Consult with lighting designer should illumination problems arise which affect camera operation.	Shade cameras during production.	

ating the look and sound of the production. To do this, the director oversees the performance of the on-air talent and coordinates the operation of the technical crew. A director's job is very complex and demanding and requires the ability to coordinate a tremendous number of different operations, often simultaneously. The director must watch several different camera shots; select the shot which will be sent over the air; direct the camera operators for their upcoming shots; listen to and cue the program audio; direct all production elements, including talent, cameras, audio, lighting, and so on; approve all art, graphic, and lighting designs; and make certain that the entire effect created is consistent with the producer's original concept of the production.

Assistant Director   The assistant director (AD) helps the program director by readying talent, cameras, and film or tape roll cues and by alerting other members of the production team to upcoming events. The AD also must keep careful track of the time for each program segment and for the overall production, making sure that the program begins and ends on time.

Production Assistant   The job of the production assistant (PA) often varies from program to program, but basically a PA's primary responsibility is to assist the producer, director, and other members of the production team. Usually, the PA works in the control room and helps the producer and director by taking notes; making necessary changes on all scripts when they occur; assisting the AD in timing the show; publishing scripts, script changes, and production forms; and keeping track of different program material such as films, tapes, and slides. Other times the PA will work on the studio floor, holding cue cards for talent or keeping track of the production by following the script and prompting performers should they forget their lines during rehearsal. Sometimes the PA is a "gofer" who takes care of whatever details require immediate attention (including such mundane tasks as "going for" coffee or sandwiches).

The Production Crew

Technical Director (Switcher)   The technical director (TD) sits next to the program director in front of a large bank of buttons and controls called the "switcher." The TD operates the switcher on the director's command, "punching up" whatever video source is called for onto the air. In some studios, the TD is also responsible for supervising the activities of the technical crew. In those studios where the TD's function is only to switch for the production, the position is sometimes referred to simply as the "switcher."

Audio Technician   The audio technician is responsible for the sound of a television production. During a show, the audio technician sits at a sound-control console mixing the various audio inputs from studio microphones, tape recorders, record turntables, film and videotape tracks, and remote feeds from outside the production studio. The audio technician must balance all the sound inputs together to create the mixed sound of the program.

In addition, the audio technician is responsible for planning the placement of microphones after consulting with the program's director. The audio technician supervises the operation of the audio crew and coordinates the setup of all audio equipment.

TECH TIP   In television's early days, engineers handled sound and video during a television production because the equipment was operationally very complex and prone to breakdown. Today, *engineers* mainly design and repair equipment. *Technicians* operate equipment and usually have troubleshooting skills. Technicians, or *operators*, can get the maximum performance from technology in the production setting but call an engineer when faced with a technical failure.

Scenic Designer   The scenic designer—sometimes called the "art director" or "set designer"—is responsible for devising the physical setting for a program. The scenic designer works closely with the program's director and the lighting designer in planning and executing the program's overall design. In some large productions, the "art director" also is responsible for the "look" of a show—from graphics style to set design. The scenic designer also supervises the stagehands and crew members who erect the set on the studio floor.

Lighting Designer The lighting designer plans and executes the lighting for a production. Much of the lighting designer's job takes place before the production enters the studio. The lighting designer consults with the director and plans a lighting approach that will complement the director's concept of the show. Lighting is a crucial production element not only because it provides the necessary illumination for the operation of the cameras, but also because it helps set the mood and tone of the program.

The lighting designer supervises the activities of the lighting crew in hanging and focusing the lighting instruments. During the production, the lighting designer is responsible for coordinating all lighting cues which may be necessary.

Graphic Artist In the past, television graphics were drawn or printed on cards, then shot by cameras. Today virtually all television graphics are computer-generated images created with desktop video tools, then shown directly on air. They may be two- or three-dimensional, still or animated. Graphic artists may preproduce computer artwork and titles, or actually operate computers and character generators during productions just like the audio and video technicians.

Floor Manager (Stage Manager) The floor manager (FM)—sometimes called a "stage manager" or "floor director"—is responsible for all operations on the studio floor. Since the program director operates from the control room, usually out of direct visual communication with the studio floor, the FM acts as the director's eyes, ears, and voice. He or she is responsible for seeing that everything on the floor goes smoothly and for cuing the performers by relaying the director's commands, which come over the headset.

Camera Operator The camera operator controls the television camera during a production. Studio cameras are mounted on pedestals, which are wheeled around the floor to set up different shots

and angles. Once the camera position is set, the camera operator composes, frames, and focuses shots using the camera controls. Although the camera operator receives shot instructions from the director via the headset, a good camera operator who exhibits a strong sense of composition and visualization is a valuable asset to a production.

Video Technician The video technician is responsible for the technical quality of the camera picture. Each studio camera has its own control unit, which enables the video technician to "ride levels," controlling for variations in scene brightness, contrast, color balance, and camera registration. Although the video technician concentrates primarily on the technical aspects of the picture, a good video technician can make an important contribution to a production by helping to achieve the desired visual effect through the manipulation of various "shading" controls.

Other Members of the Television Team

The list of jobs just described is by no means complete. We have purposely omitted material about many of the important members mentioned in Figure 1-8. These personnel, whom we will discuss in detail later, include writers, makeup and wardrobe personnel, and a host of technicians who operate videotape recorders and who repair and maintain the sophisticated and delicate production equipment. In order to keep this introduction from becoming too complicated, we will postpone describing these other functions until we have had a chance to describe the basic television production process.

THE TELEVISION STUDIO

Although a television program can be produced almost anywhere today, from a remote news location to a large athletic stadium, the television studio remains a common production environ-

(a)

(b)

FIGURE 1-9 Control Room
and Studio Floor.
(*a*) Video and audio inputs
are selected by the director
working in the studio control
room. (*b*) The cameras
operate on the studio floor.
(*Courtesy: Capital Cities/ABC,
Inc.*)

ment. Studios vary in size and complexity from the
immense, barnlike network complexes, which are
as large as a full city block, to the small, unpre-
tentious studios found at many closed-circuit in-
stallations. Regardless of their size and sophistication, all studios are made up of two areas:
(1) the *control room,* which is the operational nerve
center for the production, and (2) the *studio floor,*
where the production occurs. (See Figure 1-9.)

Control Room

The control room is where the program's director,
assistant director, technical director, audio technician, and video technician work. Producers and
production assistants also operate from the control room during rehearsals and production. Because the director and other crew members need
to talk during rehearsals and production, a control
room is needed that is separated from the studio.

The control room may be adjacent to the studio and separated by only a glass window, or it may be a mile away in a remote production control van.

As you walk into a control room, you will see a wall of monitors, each one displaying the output of a studio camera or other video source. If there are three cameras in the studio, there will be three camera monitors, each showing the picture from one of the cameras. Additional monitors show the video output of film or slide projectors, videotape machines, electronic character generators, and remote video feeds. Many broadcast control rooms also include an off-air monitor, which shows what the station is broadcasting over the air at the time.

Adjacent to the bank of black and white monitors are two large color monitors, one labeled "Preview" and the other labeled either "Line" or "Program." The line or program monitor shows the actual picture that is leaving the control room to be broadcast live or to be fed to videotape for recording. The preview monitor is used to check any picture or special video effect before it is actually sent out over the line. (See Figure 1-10.)

In the front of the monitor bank is a long table called the "production console." This is where the director, technical director, assistant director, and production assistants sit during a production. The director usually sits in the middle of the console

because all the monitors are clearly visible from that location. Seated next to the director is the technical director, who sits at the production switcher. By operating the switcher according to the director's commands, the technical director selects the video source displayed on the line monitor.

Seated on the other side of the director is the assistant director. Both the director and the AD wear intercom headsets so they can talk to various members of the production team who are out on the studio floor. The director and the AD have another intercom which permits them to talk with videotape operators or with film or slide projector technicians, who are often located in areas outside the production control room.

Some studio control rooms are built on two levels with a second long desk arranged one step up behind the production console. This is for the producer and various production assistants, and it gives them a good view of the monitor bank and the production operations without interfering with the director, who is seated below.

The audio technician and the audio control console are usually located to the side of the produc-

FIGURE 1-10 Using
Monitors in Production.
The director selects from
among the source monitors.
The program monitor shows
the actual program, and the
preview monitor is used to set
up video effects. (*Courtesy:
Capital Cities/ABC, Inc.*)

tion console area, often isolated behind a glass partition so the audio technician can listen to the audio mix or preview audio sources without interfering with the activities in the control room. Off to the side or to the rear of the control room are the camera control units which are used by the video technicians to regulate the camera pictures.

Although the preceding description is fairly typical, the configuration of a studio control room will vary from one facility to another. For example, in some operations the video technicians are located in an entirely separate area of the facility and communicate with the production team in the control room via an intercom system. While the exact layout will be different, the individual components found within a control room are common to all productions. Once you are familiar with their use and application, it will not be hard to orient to a slightly different control room.

Studio Floor

The studio floor is where the production actually occurs. During the days of radio it was important for directors and audio technicians located inside the control booth to have a direct view of the performers in the studio. This enabled the director to send hand signals to the performers while a production was in progress. However, since the television director is concerned only with the pictures on the monitors and the audio quality conveyed by the control room audio monitor, many newer studio facilities are built without a glass window separating the studio floor and the control room. In fact, some control rooms are located in New York while directing activities on studio floors in Los Angeles!

The studio floor is an open area that contains the television cameras, microphones, lighting equipment, sets, and, of course, performers and crew. The size of the studio floor will usually determine the complexity of the programming which is possible. The larger the studio, the more space for sets, performers, and equipment and the more flexible the operation. Smaller studios restrict equipment, technicians, and performers and tend to limit the size of the set and the number of performers that is practical. (See Figure 1-11.)

Located around the walls of the studio are various connector boxes to which cameras, microphones, and lighting equipment are connected. With so much activity taking place on the floor simultaneously, it is important to keep cables and wires to a bare minimum. (See Figure 1-12.)

The lighting equipment, hung above the studio floor, generates a considerable amount of heat, which is why most studios are equipped with powerful air conditioning to keep temperature levels down. The temperature is important both for personnel comfort and especially for the operation of delicate electronic equipment, which requires a fairly stable environment to function properly.

A well-planned studio facility will provide a large area adjacent to the studio floor for storing props, sets, and equipment. Otherwise, a portion of the studio floor must be used for storage, and this limits the amount of room available for the production. Oversized doors permit equipment and sets to be moved between the studio floor and the storage area.

Most studios employ large, soundproof doors, or "sound locks," that prevent extraneous noise from entering the studio, where it might be picked up by a sensitive microphone. A sign above the studio doors automatically lights whenever a microphone is "live" to warn that the studio is in operation.

Orson Welles, the actor and film director, once said, "A movie studio is the greatest toy a boy can have," and much the same can be said about a television studio. Although the studio and control room are fascinating places, they are also poten-

tially very dangerous. In the excitement of a production it is sometimes easy to forget that heavy lights are suspended overhead, high electrical current runs through equipment, and cables and wires are present everywhere. More than anything, it is important to treat the studio and equipment with a healthy measure of respect and to take care that performers, crew members, and production personnel are safeguarded at all times.

LOCATION/REMOTE PRODUCTION

Not all events we want to televise can be transported to a television studio. So if you can't take the event to the studio, you take the studio to the event for a location/remote, or "field" production.

Why Shoot on Location?

The answer to this question is self-evident for some remotes. A baseball game, a congressional hearing, a Thanksgiving Day parade all take place at a specific location, which is where television must go to cover them. The decision in these

Figure 1-12 **Studio Floor.** The smooth studio floor permits easy camera movement. Lights are suspended on battens attached to the ceiling, and mounted on floor stands. Cables and wires on the floor are kept to a minimum. (*Courtesy: Capital Cities/ABC, Inc.*)

cases is not whether to shoot on location, but whether to cover the event at all.

There are many other production situations, however, where the producer and director have a choice of shooting either inside the studio or out in the field. Commercials, entertainment programs, and industrial or instructional productions offer a wide choice of production approaches and locations. Why should a producer choose to produce a show either on location in the field or inside the studio? As with most other production decisions, the producer must weigh the advantages and disadvantages from both a creative and a technical perspective.

Advantages of Remote Production   A remote location offers realism, detail, and an atmosphere which is often impractical or impossible to recreate inside the studio. The producer of an industrial training tape on steel mill safety procedures could never duplicate the blast furnaces of a real mill inside the largest production studio. The producer of a commercial written to be shot on a busy city street could never hope to replicate New York's Fifth Avenue inside the studio. A musical program taped with the Rocky Mountains for a background offers a setting which not even the best scenic designer could ever build inside the studio.

Another advantage of remote production is that set design and construction are usually unnecessary. While the art director might dress a location setting or modify it slightly to suit the production's specific requirements, use of the existing background is one of the reasons for shooting on location in the first place. It also has been found that many performers—especially nonprofessionals—feel more comfortable working within their natural surroundings, so shooting on location often can result in better performances.

Finally, television viewers have come to expect a higher degree of realism and authenticity in virtually every aspect of television, from news and documentaries to entertainment and sports programming. Shooting on location is one way to enhance a production and add interest and excite-

ment, although even the most beautiful location will not compensate for a weak script or a poorly planned production.

Disadvantages of Remote Production   Before you contemplate shooting every production in the field, let us look at the other side of the coin. A television studio is a safe, comfortable, and well-equipped place to do a television show. It offers maximum production control over many different aspects of a production. It is soundproof, weatherproof, and lighttight and includes the equipment, electrical power, and physical space necessary to produce a television program. Studios also offer heating and air conditioning, bathrooms, telephones, and so many other items we take for granted that are not always available at a remote location.

To succeed, a remote production requires carefully detailed preplanning and coordination. A minor mistake or miscalculation on a studio production can turn into a major disaster if it occurs in the field. Even when the production is meticulously planned, however, it is still subject to such uncontrollable problems as weather, noise, and the usual set of difficulties we group under Murphy's law.

A Location as a Studio

As Shakespeare said, "All the world's a stage." Today all the world's also a television studio.

Technological changes have made audio and video equipment smaller, lighter, and more portable. Improved transmission links, especially satellites, make it possible for even the smallest station and production facilities to cover live events from distant locations. The result is a trend toward more field production for all types of television programs, from news and sports to music and drama. Knowing this, many organizations stage their events with television in mind. (See Figure 1-13 and Figure 1-14.)

Given the advantages and disadvantages of remote production, it basically still *is* television production. Therefore, the functions of remote equipment, the roles of team members, and the procedures followed during production—all are much the same on location and in the studio.

FIGURE 1-13 Satellite News Gathering (SNG). Local newscasts may incorporate live reports from great distances through the use of portable equipment and satellite news gathering (SNG) technologies, such as this SNG mobile unit. (*Courtesy: WLAS-TV.*)

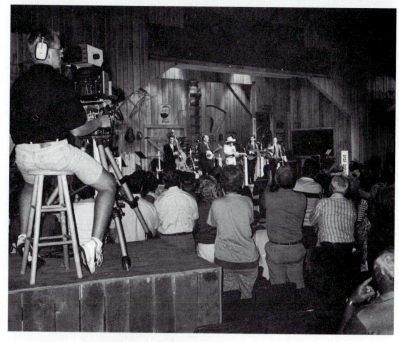

FIGURE 1-14 Remote Production. Remote events often are staged with television in mind.

SUMMARY

Television production operates in four separate stages: (1) preproduction planning, when the overall production concept and approach are developed and organized; (2) setup and rehearsal, when the studio and control room are prepared for the production and the program elements are rehearsed and coordinated; (3) production, which can be either live or on videotape; and (4) postproduction, when videotape is edited and additional video and audio material can be added to the edited master tape.

Television production is a team operation which requires the combined effort of dozens of skilled individuals to produce a program. The television team can be divided into two major groups: (1) the production staff, including the producer, director, assistant director, lighting director, scenic designer, and production assistants, who are concerned primarily with the program content and development, and (2) the production crew, including the technical director or switcher, the audio technician, video technicians, floor manager, camera operators, and the rest of the technical crew, who are primarily concerned with equipment operation.

The television studio complex is composed of two main areas: (1) the control room, which is the operational command center where program elements are directed and coordinated, and (2) the studio floor, where the production actually takes place.

By their nature, productions such as baseball games and parades must be shot in the field. Other productions may take place either in the studio or outside in the field, depending on the goals of the producer and director. Some productions, such as newscasts, take place both in the studio and in the field. Advantages of field production include realism, detail, atmosphere, and authenticity that would be difficult to recreate in the studio. Disadvantages include uncontrollable factors such as weather, noise, and things that may happen despite the most careful and thorough planning. Despite potential problems, the trend in television production has been out of the studio and into the field.

AESTHETICS IN VIDEOSPACE AND AUDIOSPACE

A television commercial shows a young tennis star in heated competition. He sprints left and right, smashing forehands and backhands with great skill and success. However, what he wears is just as noticeable as the way he plays. Instead of a traditional all-white tennis outfit, his shirt, shorts, shoes, and headband are brilliantly-colored. Even his shoulder-length hair is styled and streaked. He suddenly stops, turns to the camera, and asserts: "Image is everything."

Maybe this sports showman overstates the case. Indeed, the soundtrack of the commercial is intense and important, but there is little doubt that images have become ubiquitous in today's society. They are all around us on clothing, posters, billboards, and, of course, in film and television. Writer M. Schrage has said, "We are moving to a time when people will grope for the right image before they grope for the right word."

As images are used more and more to communicate, audiences need to know how to "read" visually in order to understand the meaning of visual messages. As communicators using a visual medium, television producers need to know what and *how* images mean, in order to plan effective visual communication. They also need to know how sound gives meaning to accompanying visual images. Rudolf Arnheim described the ability to combine seeing and thinking as *visual thinking*.

29

To help you begin thinking visually, and thinking of television as an art, this chapter briefly describes some basic principles of aesthetics as they may be applied in the visual arts. Then we describe the unique properties of video and audio, and how they may be used to create what we call *videospace* and *audiospace*. We hope these practical applications of aesthetic principles will help you use the technology of television to produce creative and effective visual messages that are honest and fair representations of reality, or create a new reality within the context of a story.

A BRIEF INTRODUCTION TO AESTHETICS

Aesthetics is a branch of philosophy that deals with beauty and art, and their relationship to reality. Early aestheticians focused on the traditional fine arts, such as painting and sculpture. They thought that the fine arts were different from everyday crafts. What artists did to produce great works of art was special—different from what people did day-to-day. Also, the way people responded to works of art was different from the way they experienced daily life.

But artists began enlarging their palettes, using materials from their life experiences as subjects and as media. For example, some artists stopped using brushes and threw paint—and other materials—directly onto their canvases. Others began using inflatable plastic and other new materials. Some critics called this kind of work "modern art" and "pop art" rather than fine art. Others said that it simply moved the fine arts closer to life. (See Figure 2-1.)

When television began, most people thought of it as a "vision box" bringing them "visual radio" and movies. The roots of the word "television" are word elements that mean "distant sight." Some people did see the potential of television to bring works of art out of distant museums and into millions of homes, but few people thought of television itself as a distinctive art form.

However, some early television producers, such as Ernie Kovacs, explored the new medium for its unique visual and auditory properties, like film artists had done before. As the technology of television became more accessible, "video art" paintings and sculpture began to be produced in experimental television studios.[1] (See Figure 2-2.)

Image and Reality

Today, television may be called many things, including a craft, a popular art, and even a fine art. Whatever it is labeled, any discussion of television's aesthetics must start with the relationship between television and reality. That is because images—both visual and auditory—are sensual experiences. The eye sees, the ear hears, and the brain registers the images and sounds.

As children we learned to recognize and associate meanings with shapes, sounds, and even colors. For example, researcher W. H. Nault reported that, "Children have learned many hue-associations before they ever learn to read maps; red is hot, blue is cold, green is grass, blue is water, etc."

However, television images are not reality. They only represent reality. It's like René Magritte's painting of a tobacco pipe titled *Ceci n'est pas une pipe*—This is not a pipe. After a moment's thought, the viewer gets it: of course, the painting of a pipe is not a pipe; it's a *painting* of a pipe. Television is like that Magritte painting—it's not actual reality, but an image of reality. It *represents* reality.

Because television is *representational*, its video and audio images can be manipulated. Therefore, the audience's *perception* of reality also may be manipulated. This capability places an enormous

---

[1] "Video art" is the term that may be used when discussing television as a fine art. Some say the comic Ernie Kovacs was commercial television's first and only video artist. From his start in 1950, Kovacs explored the unique formal properties of television's videospace and audiospace as the stages for his wacky comedy that later influenced programs such as *Rowan and Martin's Laugh In* and *Saturday Night Live*. The independent video art movement originated in the late 1960s, advanced by musician and avant-garde artist Nam June Paik, considered by some to be the George Washington of video art.

responsibility on television producers to represent reality honestly and fairly.

Applied Aesthetics

Applying aesthetic principles to create a work of art begins with our visual and auditory sense perceptions—seeing and hearing. We all have seen beautiful landscapes and people. We have heard beautiful sounds of nature. What makes them *beautiful*? Their shapes? Colors? What other features? In answering those questions, we are identifying the elements that comprise pleasing images to us. When we see paintings or photographs that are beautiful, is it because they con-

tain the same elements as nature? Because they intensify nature's reality? Because they contain elements that don't exist in nature? And what about everything on the continuum from beautiful to ugly?

For more than two thousand years aestheticians and artists have been asking "What is beauty?" and "What is art?" Not all people give the same answers because we are individuals in a diverse world, but there are some basic concepts that can help us organize the answers and then apply

(a)

(b)

FIGURE 2-1 **The Changing Subjects and Materials of the Fine Arts.**
The worldly subject of the modern work in mixed media contrasts with the lofty theme of the classic oil painting. (*Courtesy: Herbert F. Johnson Museum of Art, Cornell University, (a) David M. Solinger Fund, (b) Gift of Mr. & Mrs. Louis V. Keeler.*)

FIGURE 2-2 Video Art. In the late 1960s artists began to create works of art using the medium of television. The result looked very different from the standard broadcast television of the day.

some common aesthetic principles to the design of visual images.

DESIGN ELEMENTS

There are many ways to manipulate visual and auditory elements to create images. Traditional design elements that you should be familiar with include line, angle, shape, mass, space, texture, pattern, balance, and color. When dealing with the art of film and video, additional important elements include time, motion, and sound. The interactions between elements are also important design considerations. (See Figure 2-3.)

Line Lines surround us—from the straight lines of telephone poles to the jagged lines of our latest fender-bender. We can imagine lines, too. The equator is an imaginary line. So are the lines made by moving auto headlights on a dark road. Within an image, lines guide the eye of the viewer. They also may have a nonvisual effect. We may give lines meaning. Straight parallel lines may imply rigidity; curved lines, flexibility.

Angle Two more factors to consider are the angles of lines, their *horizontality* and *verticality*,

compared to the lines of the frame. Lines in an image that are parallel to the top and bottom or to the sides of the frame will appear more stable than *diagonal* lines, at angles to the frame. We perceive the horizon as a level, horizontal line and the walls of buildings as straight vertical lines. If the horizon or a building is shown at an angle, the image is more *dynamic*, implying action and change.

Shape Shapes are two-dimensional; they have width and height. As children we learned to recognize the natural shapes and geometric shapes of objects, even when we saw them as two-dimensional silhouettes. More difficult to recognize were objects with abstract shapes. As with lines, shapes can take on meaning. What does it mean to be square? Or well-rounded? (See Figure 2-4.)

Mass Like shape, mass helps us to recognize natural and geometric objects, but in this case the third dimension, depth, is added. A circle becomes a ball, and a square becomes a box. Abstract shapes that don't remind us of natural objects may look like different things to different people. One quality we assign to mass is *weight*; larger masses *look* heavier than smaller masses, even though that may not be true.

(a) *(b)*

(c) *(d)*

FIGURE 2-3 Lines and Angles.
The straight lines in (*a*) suggest rigidity; the curved lines in (*b*) imply flexibility. The lines parallel to the frame in (*c*) seem more stable than the diagonal lines in (*d*).

Space Space is the area within which the artwork is framed. If the area is a flat surface—such as a canvas or a television screen—the actual space is a two-dimensional plane, called *pictorial space*. In this case, one challenge for the artist may be to create the *illusion* of three-dimensional space. That may be done by carefully placing objects in the space to give it the appearance of natural perspective, or by creating the illusion of several flat *planes* at several distances, giving the space depth. Emptiness is perceived as *negative* space, or background holes. One perception of this space will be what is called the *figure-ground* relationship. Usually there is a tendency to see a main object (the figure), against a back-

ground (the ground). If the figure-ground relationship is not evident, it is called *ambiguous*. (See Figure 2-5.)

Texture Another way to make a flat surface appear to have depth is to show objects with surfaces that have texture. This effect is what artists call *modeling*. A gravel road, an eagle's feathers, a person's hair, a stucco wall—all have texture.

Pattern A repetitive design—whether found in nature or designed by an artist—will create an internal *rhythm* in an image. Patterns can be seen in different ways. A design element—such as shape, mass, or color—repeated in a regular pat-

33

(a)

(b)

FIGURE 2-4 Shape and Mass.
The two-dimensional shapes in (a) look flat, but the three-dimensional masses in (b) appear to have depth. The larger shapes and masses appear heavier in the frame.

(a)

(b)

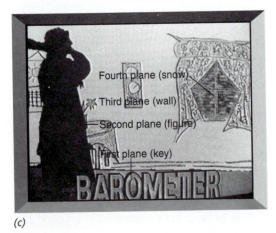

Fourth plane (snow)

Third plane (wall)

Second plane (figure)

First plane (key)

BAROMETER

(c)

(d)

34

(e)

FIGURE 2-5 Space, Depth, and the Figure-Ground Relationship.
Facing page: The illusion of depth can be created by (a) placing objects nearer and farther from the camera, (b) exaggerating perspective, or (c) establishing planes at different distances. The near object in (d) is called the *figure* and the background is considered the *ground*. In (e, above) the figure-ground relationship is ambiguous. Which shape appears in the foreground and which in the background?

(a)

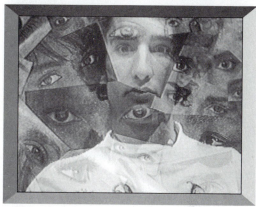

(b)

FIGURE 2-6 Texture and Pattern.
The texture of the material in (a) makes the flat surface of the television screen appear less smooth. The repetition of the pattern in (b) suggests order and unifies the image.

tern in the space may suggest order, but it also could suggest boredom, depending on the design. Repetition can give a sense of *unity* to an image, but may limit the *variety* of elements. (See Figure 2-6.)

Balance   Balance refers to the overall apparent steadiness or stability of an image. Our perceptions of balance come out of our own experiences, from the times when we struggled to keep our balance as we learned to walk. Balance or imbalance in an image results from the placement of elements. If one object is centered, or an equal number of similar objects are equidistant from the center, the image appears stable, and is said to have *symmetrical balance*. However, if the objects are not equidistant from the center, the image is said to be *asymmetrical*. Asymmetry in an image does not necessarily mean it will look unbalanced. Depending on the shapes, sizes, and colors of the objects, and their placement, the image may have *asymmetrical balance*.

Asymmetrical balance actually may look more interesting and pleasing than symmetrical balance. Classical painters used a design principle called the *Golden Mean* to achieve apparent balance that looked pleasing. (See Figure 2-7.)

Sometimes *imbalance* in an image is desirable to create an emotional effect, such as instability, tension, and the stress of outside forces.

Color   When light falls on an object, some of it is absorbed and some is reflected. The wavelengths

(a)

(b)

(c)

(d)

$$\frac{ab}{bc} = \frac{bc}{ac}$$

FIGURE 2-7 Balance.
Images with (*a*) symmetrical and (*b*) asymmetrical balance appear stable. The imbalance in (*c*) suggests stress and tension. The *Golden Mean* (*d*) was used by fine artists to create a pleasing sense of asymmetrical balance. (*Courtesy: Herbert F. Johnson Museum of Art, Cornell University, University Purchase Fund.*)

of light that are reflected are what we see as the object's color, or *hue*. The hue may look dull or vibrant, depending on its *saturation*, or chroma intensity. Greys are *achromatic*, or without color. Another quality of color is its *value*, or *brightness*—how much light is reflected. The brightness component of a television signal is called *luminance*.

When selecting different colors, remember that they affect each other. For example, one color surrounded by another color with a darker value will make the first one look lighter than it would appear by itself. There are several color "systems" or "wheels" that are helpful in selecting and mixing colors. The way painters mix colors is called *sub-*

tractive mixing. When the painter combines two colors, the second subtracts qualities from the first, and the result of the combination is a third color. In subtractive mixing, combining all the *primary colors* theoretically results in black. On the other hand, combining all the colors by *additive mixing* results in white. Additive mixing is done by shining different color lights on the same place, such as is done in the theater and in television. Color television cameras also work on the principle of additive mixing.

In addition to the visual effects of colors, designers need to know their psychological effects. For example, colors such as red and orange appear *warm* and exciting, while blue and green appear *cool* and relaxing. These feelings probably come from our perceptions and memories of nature's colors, such as red hot fires and cool relaxing days in green forests.

Figure 2-8 summarizes the visual effects of traditional design elements, and the potential nonvisual meanings that viewers may give to them.

In addition to the traditional design elements listed in Figure 2-8, when working with film and video, three other elements come into play—time, motion, and sound.

Time   Unlike paintings or sculpture, film and television have running times of limited duration. Therefore, controlling time is a concern of film and television producers. *Real time* can be slowed down or speeded up beyond physical reality. By changing between images, real time may also be condensed, expanded, repeated, or rendered im-

measurable. The result is *subjective time* in which pace is manipulated to create a desired feeling in the audience.

Motion   A still image such as a painting or photograph depicts a moment in time. It may imply motion and kinetic energy, and even suggest a past and future, but time is frozen in the image. Film and television, of course, can actually show movement—*primary movement* of subjects, *secondary movement* of cameras, and *tertiary movement* created by changes between images. The changes between images of objects in motion can make their movement appear smooth and continuous or interrupted and discontinuous.

FIGURE 2-8   **Visual Effects and Potential Nonvisual Meanings of Design Elements.**

Element	VISUAL EFFECTS	POTENTIAL NONVISUAL MEANINGS
Line	Marks off boundaries of spaces. Outlines shapes. Guides the viewer's eye to objects the designer wants to emphasize.	Implies degrees of rigidity or flexibility, calmness or excitement, hardness or softness, activity, speed, and power.
Angle	Establishes directions of lines—horizontal, vertical, or diagonal.	Implies the degree of stability or instability, strength, and effort. Implies a point of view.
Shape	Establishes the edges or outlines of objects in two-dimensional space.	Implies the degree of order or disorder, unity or opposition.
Mass	Adds the illusion of the third dimension, depth, to shapes.	Implies objects with weight. Placement implies relationships.
Space	Marked off by lines, shapes, and masses—whose placement adds the illusion of depth to spaces. Emptiness creates the illusion of negative space.	Implies sizes, distances, and degree of relationships between objects. The placement of objects in space implies spaces beyond the frame.
Texture	Establishes the surface quality of an object, how it would feel to the touch.	Implies a tactile sense from very smooth and cold to very rough and harsh.
Pattern	Repeats design elements and spaces in the image.	Implies that the repeated element is primary. Implies the degree of movement or rhythm, and feelings from boredom and monotony to evenness and uniformity.
Balance	Distributes design elements symmetrically or asymmetrically. Keeps the viewer's eye moving within the image.	Implies the degree of stability, from calm and steady to active and changeable, and unstable.
Color	Differentiates objects. Attracts attention to objects the designer wants to emphasize.	Implies mood, temperature, weight, strength, energy, and distance of objects and spaces. Symbolizes feelings about objects, places, and events.

Sound   Many of the design elements of visual images also describe elements of *auditory images*, or the pictures created in your mind by sounds. Shape, texture, pattern, balance, and color— all describe qualities of sound. Additional elements of sound include *pitch, loudness, dynamics,* and *timbre*. We will describe these elements in Chapter 7.

Of concern to film and television producers is the relationship between sound and picture. Sound can *parallel* picture or be in *counterpoint* to it. Most often the meaning of a picture will depend on the accompanying sound.

TELEVISION'S FORMAL VISUAL STRUCTURE

Artists have a variety of media with which to work. Painters may choose watercolors, oils, acrylics, or other pigments. They also may choose different types and sizes of surfaces on which to paint. Sculptors may work with bronze, marble, wood, concrete, or other materials. However, the television medium has a more formal visual structure that was set years ago by engineers and government regulators. We describe television technology in Chapter 11, but here we want to highlight

several key factors to consider when applying design principles to television.

Size   For years television sets have been relatively small, designed primarily for living room viewing. Even though it is common to see larger sets on the market today, and many public places have large-screen projection television, most sets still tend to be relatively small.

Shape   For many years the shape of television sets has been 4 units wide and 3 units high, called *television aspect ratio*. A new technical standard for High Definition Television (HDTV) sets the shape at 16 units wide and 9 units high, a ratio that makes HDTV pictures look more like motion picture film. However, many people will continue to use their old sets for years. (See Figure 2-9.)

Sharpness   If you look closely, you can see that television pictures are made up of horizontal lines, called *scanning* lines. (We will discuss video imaging thoroughly in Chapter 11.) Because the television image consists of a limited number of horizontal lines, it has limited *resolution*, or sharpness. The resolution of the HDTV picture is much sharper, approximating still and motion picture film. (See Color Plate 6.)

Contrast   *Contrast* refers to the differences between brightness levels or values, from the lightest

FIGURE 2-9   **The Changing Shape of the Television Screen.**
(*a*) Current television aspect ratio is 4 units wide and 3 units high. (*b*) High Definition Television (HDTV) has an aspect ratio of 16 units wide and 9 units high.

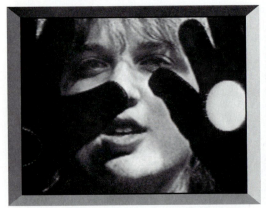

(*a*)   (*b*)

FIGURE 2-10 **Video Image Sources.**
Television images today may be a complex
combination of camera shots, digital video effects, and
computer paint systems.

production techniques in those areas in greater
detail.

VIDEOSPACE

When viewers have an opportunity to visit the set
of a favorite television program, most are invariably disappointed: the living room set which looks
so large on screen appears much smaller in real
life, the elegant furniture may be chipped or
cracked, the walls and doors appear flimsy and
frail, and the colors which look so vibrant and alive
on television seem faded and washed out. Usually, their faith is restored when they see the same
set on a television monitor. Magically, the room
reappears as its "normal" size, the walls look
strong and sturdy, and the colors are alive and
vital. (See Figure 2-11.)

This experience illustrates an essential concept
in television production which we call *videospace.*
Videospace means that the only measure of reality
for television viewers is what they see and hear
through the television receiver. A "real-life" event
that unfolds before the television cameras *does
not exist for viewers until that reality is translated
through the television medium* and onto their television sets.

Just as the proscenium arch on stage defines
the boundaries of reality for the theater audience,
videospace is the measure by which viewers
judge what exists on television. All the spatial relationships, all the sound cues, the appearance of
the performers, the total environment in which the
program takes place must be created and conveyed through the videospace. Videospace and
its aural counterpart, *audiospace,* really consist of
two interrelated components: the technical aspect
of the production and the aesthetic or creative elements. Together these create a reality for the
viewing audience.

Media consultant Tony Schwartz discusses this
idea in his book, *The Responsive Chord.* As
Schwartz puts it, "If we seek to communicate a
situation or event, our problem is not to capture
the reality of that situation but to record or create

to the darkest area in an image. The *contrast ratio*
of television images is about 30 to 1. This means
the number of different lighting values that can be
distinguished by the system is limited. As with
other elements, the contrast ratio is improved in
HDTV.

Imaging   In the early days of television the
source of all video images was the camera tube.
Today most sources involve computers in some
way, from digitized images to computer paint systems. This greatly enlarges the possibilities for image manipulation. (See Figure 2-10.)

One challenge facing you as a television producer is working effectively within the limitations
of television's formal visual (and auditory) structure. You will have to control many elements and
make many *production choices*, from framing
camera shots to mixing sounds. Making good
choices requires many technical and creative
abilities, including good aesthetic skills. If you
keep design principles in mind, your production
choices will demonstrate creative control, consistency, timeliness, and artistic unity. They will result
in visually effective programs, no matter what the
type—dramatic, persuasive, or informational.

In the remainder of this chapter we will highlight
some practical approaches for applying design
principles when you make production choices. In
later chapters of this text we will examine specific

FIGURE 2-11 Videospace.
The videospace is what viewers actually see on their television monitors, and often it appears very different from the set as seen in the studio.

stimuli that will affect the viewer in a manner similar to a viewer's experience in the real situation. What counts is not reality, as a scientist might measure it, but the ability to communicate the situation in a believable way." What Schwartz is pointing out is that the television team creates an *impression* of reality by *selecting* images and sounds for the viewer. The audience will reach different conclusions about the real-life event based on which pictures and sounds are presented to them.

It may seem paradoxical, but sometimes we must modify what actually exists in the television studio in order for the viewer to perceive it as "real." For example, an actor wearing television makeup may look rather odd in person but perfectly normal when seen on camera. Were he not wearing any makeup at all, his in-studio appearance would be quite normal, but his image on the screen would not look attractive or natural. Similarly, if we photograph a performer outside the studio on location under a bright, sunny sky, we may have to add artificial light to make her look natural on camera. The use of artificial illumination may seem superfluous, but the additional light is sometimes necessary to fill in the shadows on the performer's face and make her appear normal on screen.

These examples illustrate the application of the videospace concept to the television medium's technical capabilities and limitations. Quite often, because of the way in which television equipment operates, we must modify reality so that it will appear normal onscreen. The makeup and lighting we referred to earlier are necessary because of the technical limitations of the television camera. (See Figure 2-12.)

The other application of the videospace concept refers to its use to create an entirely new "reality" for the viewing audience. Sometimes we can use certain techniques to produce a reality in the videospace which actually does not exist. One commonly used technique is an electronic effect called "chroma key," in which two different video sources are electronically combined into a composite shot. Thus a sportscaster inside the studio can be electronically inserted into a wide shot of a football stadium. The illusion produced is as though the sportscaster is actually present at the stadium, when, in fact, that "reality" exists only in the videospace. The use of depth perspective in planning sets, lighting, and camera shots also can modify the viewer's perception of reality. A studio can be made to appear larger or smaller than it actually is through manipulation of the videospace.

Fill light

FIGURE 2-12 Lighting for the Camera.
Because of the technical limitation of the television camera, we often must vary television reality to make it appear "normal" onscreen. This reporter may look normal to the eye, but without additional fill lighting he would appear too dark.

CREATING THE VIDEOSPACE

For all intents and purposes, a television show begins with a blank screen. How you fill the screen—create the videospace—determines how the viewer perceives your program and the message you are trying to convey. Somerset Maugham, the author, once told an admirer, "Madame, all the words I can use in my stories can be found in that dictionary. It's just a matter of arranging them into the right sentences."

The television producer faces a similar situation. Just as every writer begins with the same set of words, all television producers start with essentially the same tools and techniques. There are only so many possible variations of camera shots or angles, only a limited number of lighting methods, just a few standard ways to change camera shots, only so many microphones and audio sources available, and so on. What separates one producer from another is how each uses the production elements which are available—how they are selected, combined, and integrated into the show. This is why you can give the identical program to two different people and you are likely to get two very different shows.

The Director and Production Choices

In effect, a television program is the sum total of the *director's* choices. Directing is a highly subjective art, which makes giving rules and guidelines difficult. Like other creative arts, directing is mostly about making choices within constraints of the medium. The director's choices influence the believability of the show, the emotional involvement of the audience, and whether the audience is bored or satisfied with the rate at which the information or plot is unveiled. Being able to recognize the choices open to you and knowing how to take advantage of them are two fundamental aspects of the art of directing.

There is a story about Mike Nichols—the highly acclaimed stage and film director—that illustrates the idea of a director faced with unlimited choices. Nichols had had a very successful stage career when he was assigned to direct his first film, *Who's Afraid of Virginia Woolf?* When he arrived at the studio for the first day of shooting, the first scene involved a simple matter of an actor coming in a door. As the story goes, the cinematographer asked Nichols how he wanted the performer to enter so the camera could be positioned. "Just have him come through the door," said Nichols. "No, no—you don't understand what I mean," said the cameraman. "Do you want to see the actor from a high angle, a low angle, in a wide shot, in a close-up? Should we pan with him or let him walk out of the frame? Does the camera dolly in or track along?" Coming directly from the stage, where things were a lot simpler, Mike Nichols was surprised to confront the many choices and decisions facing the film (or television) director.

Of course, stage directors also face many important decisions, but the television director's choices are particularly important because they determine what the viewer actually sees and hears. While the stage director works with the stage as a single proscenium arch, each new camera angle and shot length resets the television director's stage. As you become more proficient as a director, you learn to use this variable viewpoint to your advantage. However, in the early stages of the learning process, the number of choices can seem overwhelming. Nonetheless, you must become aware of the possibilities because reverting to a theater perspective misuses many of the creative opportunities available in the television medium.

Viewpoint

The many production decisions made by the director are obviously not determined by chance. The decisions are based on an overall approach, style, and concept which we define as the director's *viewpoint.* The director's viewpoint is shaped by the various creative and emotional responses the director has to the program's material. As long as the director views himself or herself simply as a neutral transmitter of events, there is no established approach to the show. In essence, a director must trust his or her instincts to "stand in" for the intended viewing audience, personalizing and bringing coherence to a program.

The process of directing involves a transfer of the director's emotional, intellectual, and creative values to the production. Without a viewpoint that is firmly established at the outset, it will be difficult for you to produce a unified program that realizes the production's overall objectives. It is easy to stray from the show's goals unless you have an image in your mind's eye to be used as a reference throughout planning, rehearsal, and production. Continually matching what transpires before the camera to his or her expectations guides the ongoing decisions a director makes as the show develops.

For example, ABC Sports describes its coverage of sporting events as "close-up and personal." It is a conscious effort by the producers and directors of ABC to show an event from a more intimate perspective than simply presenting detached reporting of the action on the playing field. Although the game is of primary importance, its story is told from a personal point of view, and the various camera shots of losers, as well as winners, and the many activities which surround the basic action give the productions a special look and feel, which conveys the network's established viewpoint.

TECH TIP   While much creative television undergoes constant change as it moves from script to tape, the changes usually are in methods, techniques, and production elements that better realize the director's viewpoint. A viewpoint that constantly changes usually reflects lack of planning or program objectives that were not properly clarified initially.

Do not think that viewpoint applies only to entertainment programs. An instructional show, for example, offers a variety of potential viewpoints, and it is up to the director to determine which approach to use. For instance, a chemistry experiment could be presented as an *expository,* step-by-step demonstration. Alternately, a more involving, but time-consuming *discovery* method could be used, and this would emphasize the audience's ability to predict the outcomes of each step in the process.

As another example, an interview program can explore social issues dispassionately or through heated argument. Cable News Network's *Crossfire* presents a very clear example of a director who has executed a confrontational viewpoint that effectively uses argument. Two hosts with diametrically opposed viewpoints invite two guests, also at polar extremes on a political or social issue, into a "crossfire." True to the show's name, questions from either host explode on the scene as each participant tries to shout down the opposition. In marked contrast, ABC's *David Brinkley Show* unfolds at a more "reasoned" pace as panelists take turns in addressing issues. The choice of panelists, visual pacing, and the way the audio operator is instructed to "ride gain" all establish the director's viewpoint in dealing with the interview show. While there are no ironclad rules for establishing a program's viewpoint, production elements must *complement* and enhance the program's objectives and *consistently* reflect a unified taste, style, and creativity.

Visualization

The television director works, in large part, with visual and auditory images. The director cannot reproduce reality as it exists; he or she *always* manipulates the representation of "reality" by creating images through the use of camera angles, lenses, and image effects. Before you can do this, however, you must be able to visualize the program in your mind's eye. This is not just an overall "image" of the show; it is every scene, every camera shot, every shot transition. In effect, you run the television show in your mind before you ever walk into the studio to direct it.

Learning to visualize takes much practice and concentration but, fortunately, no special equipment or supplies. Concentrate on seeing (and hearing) the show that you are planning to direct, and try to picture it in your mind's eye. Before long you will find it becomes easier and easier to actually "play" the show in your head. Until you can visualize the show in your imagination, you cannot begin to plan specific camera shots and performer blocking on paper.

TECH TIP Visualization can be practiced by decomposing daily events into a sequence of events rather than the "seamless" reality we typically experience. For example, present the critical elements in preparing breakfast using only six camera shots. Or visually describe an argument from the perspective of each of the persons involved in the disagreement. Without changing the dialogue, make the audience more sympathetic to one individual and then the other.

CAMERA SHOTS

One of the director's primary concerns is to develop the camera shots which convey the essence of what is happening to the viewing audience. Remember that the audience's only frame of reference is what the audience sees on the television screen and hears through the television speaker. What you show and how you show it are crucial factors in communicating to the audience.

Think about a stage play for a moment. While there are lots of tricks that stage directors use to focus your attention on what they feel is the most important aspect of the show at any particular time, there is nothing to stop your eyes from wandering from the actor who is speaking, for instance, to the actor who is listening or to look

across the background players or perhaps to concentrate on the stage furniture and props.

Unlike the theatrical audience, television viewers can see only what the director wants them to see. You decide what the audience can look at and, equally important, what the audience cannot look at. A good way to think about this is to show the viewers (1) what they *want* to see, (2) what they *need* to see, and (3) *when* they want and need to see it.

The audience knows—if only unconsciously—what it *wants* to see, but it is the director's job to decide what the audience needs to see and when they should see it. Take a scene with a young woman as she enters her apartment late at night. She walks into the door, flips on the switch, and her eyes widen in fear and astonishment. At this point the audience wants to see what she sees and wants to see it right away. But the director might decide that the audience should not see it immediately. Perhaps the show's suspense would be heightened if there were a pause between showing the woman's face and showing the cause of her fear and astonishment.

Quite often, of course, what the audience wants to see and needs to see is identical. Yet the director also must choose how to show it to the viewer. Should he or she use a wide shot or a close-up, a subjective angle, or a dolly shot? There are no rules here, because every situation presents its own set of possibilities or choices. You should remember how important it is to consider carefully what the audience sees, how they see it, and when they see it on screen as you develop your camera shots.

TECH TIP One way to become more sensitive to camera shots is to watch television with the sound turned off. Without the audio, you can concentrate on the visual presentation and watch how the director uses camera shots, lenses, angles, and movement to create the videospace and communicate to the audience.

The Shot

The shot is the basic visual element in a television

44

PART 1   IDEAS, IMAGES, AND SOUND

production. A *shot* is a single, continuous image taken by one camera. It can be as short as one-thirtieth of a second (the length of a single video frame) or as long as the length of an entire program. We almost never use a single shot for an entire program. Rather, we assemble a number of different shots together into a sequence to show the viewer the action from the best possible angle, distance, and viewpoint.

Developing Camera Shots

In every television program there are certain elements which are more important than others and which require the viewer's fullest attention in order to understand and enjoy the program. It is the director's job not only to develop camera shots in such a way that the viewers see what they want and need to see, but also to emphasize and punctuate those elements in the videospace which require audience attention. In order to do this, the director works with three related visual elements: (1) the size and content of the shot, (2) the camera angle, and (3) the movement of the camera or the subject in the shot.

Size and Content   What you decide to include in

the shot and what you decide to exclude are fundamental decisions which every director makes throughout a program. Visual emphasis is directly related to the size of the subject in the shot. As a shot tightens from a wide shot to a close-up, attention is focused because, by definition, a close-up excludes all other picture elements except the principal subject from the viewer's attention. As the shot widens out to include less of the principal subject and more of the background area, the principal subject becomes physically smaller and shares the videospace with other elements in the shot.

Because the close-up excludes all but a few critical visual elements, it concentrates emotional impact within the visual frame. On the other hand, wider shots present visual elements in *relationships,* which often can convey the reasons for the emotional impact of the close-up. (See Figure 2-13.)

Camera Angle   Certain camera angles convey specific impressions to the viewer. For example, a subject may be shot from below, in a *low-angle* shot, or from above, in a *high-angle* shot. A low-angle shot usually suggests a powerful and dominant subject, whereas a high-angle shot makes a subject appear less powerful and physically smaller. Besides serving in dramatic contexts, camera angle implies credibility and power in nonfictional situations as well. For example, political

FIGURE 2-13   Shot Size and Content.
(*a*) Close-ups emphasize the subject and often his or her emotional response to a situation. (*b*) Long shots include the environment and often are used to show relationships.

(*a*)

(*b*)

(a)

(b)

FIGURE 2-14 Camera Angle.
(a) Low camera angles often convey power, while (b) high camera angles "look down" on a subject, suggesting weakness.

consultants are careful to remind the director in charge of a televised presidential debate that their candidate must not be shot above eye level, conveying to the audience that this candidate may be weak and ineffective. (See Figure 2-14.)

Point of View A shot that places the camera's viewpoint within a scene rather than as an objective recorder existing outside the scene is *subjective.* Subjective points of view can involve audiences if used judiciously. In one classic episode of the *M*A*S*H* television series, the entire program is shot through the eyes of a wounded soldier. The subjective camera imparts an initial sense of disorientation, clouded pain, and unusual viewpoints of doctors moving needles and scalpels toward the body. Although we never once see the injured person, we know his experience and the pain of being shot better than if an objective camera graphically showed us the extent of his wounds.

Camera Movement Camera movement can help to create dominance or to establish visual emphasis in a shot. *Dollying,* moving the camera, differs from *zooming,* changing the focal length of the lens, in both impact and intent. For example, in *The Silence of the Lambs,* when Clarise Starling (Jodie Foster) is being stalked in the dark by the serial killer wearing night-vision goggles, the camera moves toward her, emphasizing the threat-

ening physical closeness of the psychopath and Starling's vulnerability. At another time, when Hannibal Lecter (Anthony Hopkins) begins intensely grilling Starling about her childhood memories, the camera zooms into extreme close-ups of their faces, bringing them closer figuratively, but not literally, representing how Lecter's malevolent questioning is an attempt to get into Starling's mind to destroy her psychologically. In both scenes, the camera movement and zooming intensify the action by bringing the audience visually closer to the actors. Camera moves, such as dollies, trucks, arcs, and pedestaling, are ways to focus audience attention where the director wants it. The speed of the movement is yet another method to vary audience attention—faster speeds create more attention than slower, more restrained movement.

TECH TIP As a general rule, dolly shots involve the viewer, while zooms direct or focus the viewer's attention. Because dolly shots require more effort—camera movement and follow focus—they are sometimes not used even when they are a more appropriate choice than a zoom.

Subject Movement We tend to direct our attention toward a moving object rather than toward one standing still. The director can use the effects of subject movement to focus audience attention. For example, frenzied movement in the crowd during a basketball tournament will pull the viewer's attention to that area of the stands and often precedes the director's choice of a close-up of a happy fan.

Additional Shot Elements   The use of lenses and optical effects as well as the use of "plastics"—the varied design elements, such as set, lighting, costumes, and makeup—are additional ways to build a shot and direct viewer attention.

LENSES AND OPTICAL EFFECTS   Lenses of varying focal lengths produce different perceptual effects. For example, a *wide-angle lens* takes a very wide shot, and a *long-focal-length lens* takes a narrow, close-up shot. Subject size and depth perspective are exaggerated by a wide-angle lens and compressed by a long-focal-length lens. The bustle and activity of a New York City local news show are introduced with the use of a long-focal-length lens. The pent-up energy of a college football team returning after halftime is reinforced with the wide-angle lens used from a low angle by the locker room door.

Focus also plays an important part in directing viewer attention in the videospace. If you have two subjects, each at a different distance from the lens, a shallow depth of field allows you to place one subject in focus and the other out of focus. Viewer attention initially will be aimed toward the in-focus portion of the screen. However, if movement then occurs in the out-of-focus image area, the viewer's attention will be drawn to the movement as the viewer tries to determine what the moving object is.

PLASTICS   Set design, lighting, costumes, make-up, graphics, and other similar art design considerations—often called "plastics"—are additional elements to use in creating the videospace and directing audience attention. Movement through set areas which are brightly illuminated in places but dark in others will hold a viewer's attention, since information is presented anew each time talent steps from the shadows. Using no set—as in a cameo or a limbo approach—rivets attention on

the foreground subject, since nothing in the background competes for viewer attention. A very busy and complicated set, on the other hand, may distract the viewer's attention away from foreground subjects.

AUDIOSPACE

You might think of the *audiospace* as the aural equivalent of the program's videospace. Just as the videospace serves as the audience's visual reality, what is heard over the speakers is the audience's only measure of aural reality. This means that the audio technician must evaluate the program audio for the way it ultimately will sound to the audience and not as it sounds inside the studio or even in the control room, where an expensive, high-quality monitoring system may misrepresent how the audience actually hears the sound.

Audiospace can be manipulated for a variety of special effects. There are many electronic and mechanical means of modifying or shaping sound in subtle or dramatic ways. In general, the audio should complement the video. Ideally, the two should interact so the combination of sound and picture presents a message that is more effective than either would convey individually. Sometimes this means that the audio should directly relate to the video. Other times the audio might be more effective as a counterpoint to the visual image. An example of the first case would be high-energy, uptempo music to accompany an edited montage of former professional athletes as we see them performing their greatest accomplishments. Taking the same example with an audio counterpoint, we might play a slow, moody, and sentimental ballad that would produce an interesting conflict between images of athletes in their prime and nostalgia of a time that has passed.

Naturally, these are creative decisions which must be made by both the director and the audio technician. The point is that audio is both a creative element in a production and a technical operation. A program that is planned only for video, with little, if any, consideration for the audio, is like a meal prepared with only half the necessary ingredients. Sound can play a very important role in any production, but only if you approach building the audiospace with the same care and planning as you would the videospace.

Naturally, everything about audio goes into building the audiospace. But there are two important concepts which go a long way in determining how the audience perceives the sound portion of the show: sound presence and sound perspective.

Sound Presence

As you walk toward a person who is speaking, the sound of his or her voice changes. The closer you get, the louder the voice sounds. The quality of the sound also changes as you approach the speaker; his or her voice becomes fuller and richer and appears to be closer. This characteristic is called *sound presence*. It is the *figure-ground* design principle applied to the auditory image. Sound presence is a function of the ratio of direct to indirect sound waves picked up by a microphone and is related to many audio elements, including the type of microphone you use, the room acoustics, and the volume of the sound source. (See Figure 2-15.) We will discuss these elements in detail in Chapter 10.

Sound presence plays an important part in how we perceive the audio of a show. When we want to attract a viewer's attention to a particular part of the videospace, we can use a number of lighting, lens, and camera-angle techniques to make a particular subject more dominant on screen. Sound presence offers a similar approach for the audio. A performer who is recorded with more sound presence sounds closer and more dominant than someone recorded with less sound presence.

One example of the way sound presence can affect an audience's perception is NBC's *The Tonight Show*. From the show's beginning in 1954, its hosts—from Steve Allen and Jack Paar to Johnny Carson and Jay Leno—have used ribbon mikes placed on the desks in front of them. The guests have been covered by a boom microphone suspended overhead. The ribbon mike produces a richer, warmer, and fuller sound than the boom mike. The result of the hosts using a ribbon microphone positioned nearby is that they have sounded "closer" to the audience than the guests and seemed dominant among the performers on the show.

Another program in which the principle of sound

presence is employed successfully is CBS's *Northern Exposure*. In this show the character Chris (and occasionally his brother Bernard) broadcasts from KBHR (K-Bear) radio, where a microphone is prominent just inches from his mouth. Chris (played by John Corbett) provides narrative links in the story line and commentary on it, often quoting philosophers, artists, and poets. The sound quality is intimate, contributing to the feeling that his thoughts are from the heart, spoken directly to each member of the audience. Attention is focused on Chris' words because of their

FIGURE 2-15 Sound Presence.
Sound presence is the quality of sound that corresponds to the nearness of a speaker and describes why a voice sounds warmer and more full in an intimate conversation than from across the room. Sound presence increases as the subject-to-mike distance decreases because the microphone receives more direct sound waves and fewer reflected waves.

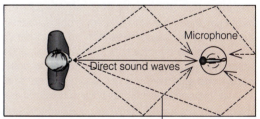

Distant Sound Presence   Reflected indirect sound waves

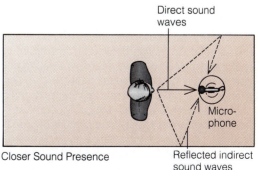

Closer Sound Presence   Reflected indirect sound waves

intimate sound presence and because of another principle called *sound perspective*.

Sound Perspective

Sound perspective refers to the relationship between the sound and the picture. Together, the sound presence and the image in the videospace determine the sound perspective. If you do not establish the proper relationship between the sound presence and the camera shot selected, the credibility of the program may suffer. When we see a tight close-up of a performer, we expect that the sound presence will be closer, fuller, and more intimate than the sound presence associated with a long shot.

Sometimes, sound perspective is created naturally by the television production process. When the director shoots an actor in a tight close-up, the boom operator can position the microphone very close to the speaker because the mike will not be visible in the shot. The sound will be perceived by the audience as coming from a relatively close distance and will complement the image. You might say that the sound presence of the audio is the same as the "visual presence" of the close-up shot. When the director cuts to a wide shot of the actor, the boom operator must boom up to make certain that the mike will not appear in the shot. This will increase the mike-to-subject distance and will change the sound presence. The audience will perceive the sound as coming from farther away, and the sound perspective will match the shot. In both instances, sound perspective has been maintained through the proper positioning of the boom.

Dramatic programs require a considerable amount of coordination between the program director and the audio crew because the sound perspective must change during the show. If you are producing a program where all the performers should be perceived as sounding equidistant from the viewer (a round-table discussion, for instance), it is important to create a sound presence for each performer that will convey this aural impression to the audience.

CREATING THE AUDIOSPACE

On many productions, the audio carries a significant part of the program message and deserves the director's attention as much as the visual portion of the show. Although the director leaves the actual audio production primarily in the hands of the audio operator, it is up to the director to establish how sound will be used in the show. This includes considering both the technical problems of audio pickup and reproduction and the creative uses of sound.

Sound Pickup

The audio technician must understand the basic program objectives before he or she can begin to plan how to pick up and reproduce the sound technically. If the program will require off-camera microphones, boom placement and talent blocking are as crucial to the audio technician as they are to the director and camera operators. Sometimes the director must modify certain shots or some actor blocking to pick up the audio better. If you are working on a remote production, audio considerations can become even more complex because of the difficult sound characteristics of your shooting location and the usual problems when shooting outside a soundproofed and controlled environment.

Even a relatively simple in-studio show that uses such on-camera microphones as lavalier or handheld mikes must consider audio. The audio technician needs to know if the talent will remain stationary or will move across the set. Also, must other individuals be miked, such as audience participants? On a demonstration show, can the talent move freely without audio problems?

The director who takes the time to discuss the program with the audio technician in advance can save an enormous amount of time and frustration later during rehearsal and production.

Controlling Sound Perspective

One of the important aesthetic audio considerations the director must keep in mind is the *sound perspective*. This refers to the quality of the sound and its relationship to the picture. (See above.) We would expect the sound perspective to suggest a more intimate sound presence when we shoot in close-up and to reflect less presence when we shoot in a wide shot. On some programs, the director may wish to alter sound perspective by manipulating the audio through special electronic effects to create the sound of a telephone voice, someone inside a cavernous, echo-producing environment, and so on.

Music and Sound Effects

Music and sound effects contribute enormously to the overall production. Selecting just the right piece of theme music, or a musical bridge is not easy and often takes a considerable amount of time. The right selection, however, used at the proper time, can result in a synergistic effect in which the audio and the video produce an impact greater than the sum of their parts.

Remember that music (like most sound) can be used to either *parallel* the video or provide a distinct *counterpoint* to the images onscreen. For example, in the film *Good Morning, Vietnam* zany disc jockey Adrian Cronauer (played by Robin Williams) welcomes his listeners to "another delightful day here in vacationland" with the familiar song "What a Wonderful World," performed by Louis Armstrong. At first the upbeat music parallels the images of a peaceful Vietnam morning, but as the scene turns violent, the song's cheerful lyrics stand in counterpoint to the destruction being shown, resulting in a cynical commentary on it. The possibilities are endless, but the effective marriage of sound and picture requires planning and a considerable amount of attention to audio elements.

Sound effects also provide important tools for the creative director. A phone rings and motivates the star to answer it. The sputtering of a race car engine cues the audience to accept the exasperated look on the driver's face in the next shot. The absence of sound also helps tell a story. One convention to convey the total involvement of an artist with her work uses an objective camera accompanied by loud music and insistent children clamoring for attention to show the world as it actually is. When the camera takes the subjective view of the artist absorbed in her work, the silence that accompanies the distorted faces of her nagging children expresses a different reality.

The Director and the Audio Mix

Be sure to listen to the audio mix not only prior to the production, but also after you have begun to integrate sound and picture. You may find that a well-balanced audio track sounds fine when you listen to it separately, but it just does not work when combined with the visuals. Once you can see and hear the effect of both sound and picture, you may have to remix or rebalance the sound to compensate for the combined impact that the video and audio create together.

TECH TIP As the TV's screen size has grown, the weak monophonic audio has become out of balance with the more dominant video. In today's improved audio environment, television directors must use the audio portion of a program to match the power of the available visual tools.

Remember that a program that has been beautifully shot and edited can be ruined by a poor audio track. While poor sound pickup or unintentional reverberations are usually obvious, the director also must listen for the more subtle audio elements, such as balance and perspective, which are essential in creating the audiospace. Ideally, sound and picture should complement each other to the extent that the resulting whole program which is seen and heard by the audience is greater than the sum of its component video and audio parts.

Videospace and audiospace must always be major considerations when planning and producing a program. The idea is to learn how to use them to convey the intended impression, mood, and overall message to the audience. Everything you do in television should be undertaken with the videospace and audiospace concepts in mind. You must learn to translate what you see and hear inside the studio or on location into how it will appear to, and be heard by, the audience. It does not matter how it looks or sounds in the studio, since the viewer's only measure of reality is what is seen and heard through the television receiver. If the videospace and audiospace you achieve create the proper mood and impression, establish the intended environment in which the production takes place, and complement the overall program objectives, then the production has moved a long way toward satisfying the basic goal of any program: to communicate ideas and messages to the audience successfully. The effective use of both videospace and audiospace will enable you to take full advantage of the many capabilities which the television medium has to offer.

SUMMARY

Television is an art form that represents reality through visual and auditory images. Aesthetic principles can guide the television producer in manipulating images to represent reality honestly and fairly or create a new reality with the context of a story. Aesthetic considerations in this process include design principles such as line, angle, shape, mass, space, texture, pattern, balance, color, time, motion, and sound. Auditory images are created by using similar principles. Additional elements of sound include pitch, loudness, dynamics, and timbre.

Television producers must work within limitations to develop good technical and aesthetic skills to be successful. Key limitations of television's formal visual structure are its size, shape, sharpness, contrast, and imaging sources. Television's auditory structure also has limitations.

The primary consideration in any production decision is the effective use of videospace and its sound counterpart, audiospace. Videospace and audiospace mean that the only measure of reality for the audience is what is seen and heard through the television receiver.

The director's viewpoint and visualization are controlling factors in constructing videospace and audiospace. Camera shots contain important elements in the videospace. Sound presence and perspective play important roles in audiospace, and how we perceive videospace.

Videospace and audiospace determine the context in which the audience perceives the program and the way in which visual and aural messages are understood.

W R I T I N G   F O R   T E L E V I S I O N

As we pointed out in Chapter 1, television is a team process in which individuals work together to communicate with an audience. One of the earliest collaborative efforts involves writing—taking a program idea and transforming it into words, sounds, and pictures.

Rarely in television is all the writing done by a single individual. The team members usually most involved in writing a script will be the producer, writer, and director. One of these individuals may perform more than one of these roles in a "hyphenated position" such as producer-writer, producer-director, or even producer-writer-director.

In some production situations—such as corporate communications or small broadcast stations—one individual may perform these three roles, then become the program editor too!

We will show in Chapter 4 that television is a producer's medium and that the idea for a program usually originates with the producer. As a producer-writer, after developing the program proposal he or she may also write the subsequent treatment and script, or the producer may bring in a writer to do that. The script usually includes an indication of the sounds and pictures, in addition to the words to be spoken, but the person who usually determines the shots and visual transitions is the director.

As described in Chapter 2, the director makes aesthetic choices between the shots to communicate *visually* to the audience. To help visualize the written script, the director may work with a graphic artist to produce a *storyboard* or *animatics*. This process of *picturization* may be thought of as *visual writing*. We will describe the roles of the director in Chapter 5 and the graphic artist in Chapter 16.

Other individuals also may contribute to the television script at the four stages of television production, depending on the type of program. For example, reporters usually write their own voice-overs for news reports. Talk show hosts may write their own introductions and questions. Sports announcers may write their own commentaries. Actors may even rewrite their lines at a final taping. Of course, live on-air talent may ad lib at any time. All these individuals contribute in their own ways to the writing of the television program. Therefore, in this chapter we concentrate on the *writing process* rather than the individual called the *writer*.

BEFORE YOU WRITE

How you go about writing a script for a television production depends in large part on the type of program you are writing for. Usually, an informational program is different from a drama, a commercial is different from an educational production. But there are some fundamental considerations which all productions share when it comes to writing. They deal with: (1) the *audience*, (2) the *purpose* of the production, and (3) the program's *approach*.

Audience

All writers must keep their intended audience in mind. Specifically, who is the target audience? Children? Adults? Men? Women? Viewers in their teens or viewers who are in their late fifties? Regardless of how broad or narrow your intended audience is, before you begin to write a single word or develop a visual concept you must consider your target audience. The words you use, the pictures you show, the sounds you include, the production techniques you employ—all are dictated in large part by your intended target audience. The basic content of a show will be quite different if it is designed for MTV than if it is designed for The Family Channel precisely because their audiences are so different.

Purpose

Before you start to write, another important consideration to keep in mind is the program's purpose. In other words, what is the point of the production? Why are we doing it? What are its objectives and goals? For example, a copywriter is told that the purpose of a planned public service announcement is to motivate students to register and vote. A corporate producer is told that the instructional objective of a particular program is to help employees complete their personnel forms accurately. A reporter is given a specific set of objectives in developing a story about how federal economic policy will impact on the daily lives of the viewers. Without a specifically defined set of objectives or purpose, the script can't possibly have a clear focus and the production is bound to be less effective.

Approach

Every writer must choose a particular way to approach his or her material when he or she begins a script. By "approach" we mean the framework you establish in which you set the structure and style of the program. For example, a newscast's approach is straightforward and clearly informational. But other productions can offer a wider range of choices. For example, an instructional program can be written with a "straight" approach but sometimes humor can be more effective in communicating the necessary ideas and concepts to the viewer. Again, this is where a consideration of the target audience and the program's purpose and objectives is necessary. Sometimes one audience is better reached through humor or parody while a straightforward approach works best for a different target audience.

There are situations where you have little choice for the approach. For example, if you are writing a script for a program in an established series, you will be expected to take the established approach which the viewer is familiar with. Other times the content itself will dictate a particular approach. A very serious topic—like a news program on child abuse or a story about an airline crash—hardly lends itself to a humorous approach.

On the other hand, some of the most memorable television programs have been created when risks have been taken. For example, former Monty Python John Cleese created an effective series of business training tapes by using humorous approaches to what otherwise might seem incredibly dry and boring subjects. Of course, advertising copywriters try to outdo each other in coming up with unexpected approaches. One of the most successful was the "Energizer Bunny," who "intrudes" on parody commercials that seem real at first. New technologies also have affected program approaches. For example, today it's not uncommon for slow-motion video, digital effects, canted camera angles, and music to be used in documentaries, with the result that they may look somewhat like music videos.

THE DRAMATIC UNDERSTRUCTURE OF TELEVISION PROGRAMS

As we discussed in Chapter 2, television has unique technical and aesthetic properties. These are the visual and auditory elements with which television producers must work. In addition, television programs have structures, or formats, within which producers must work. They have evolved

after being adapted, for the most part, from the theater, cinema, and radio.

Each television program has an understructure, or invisible framework that holds it together. The understructure is embedded in the *approach* and shaped to fit the duration of the program. The audience perceives the exterior of the structure as visual and auditory images—the words, sounds, and pictures. No matter how compelling the words, how resonant the sounds, and how brilliant the pictures, if they are not presented in some meaningful combination and sequence, the result will seem to have no clear purpose other than to occupy space and time.

Most television programs have a *dramatic* understructure—an organization of dramatic elements and action into *three acts*—the beginning, the middle, and the end. Even television programs such as newscasts and documentaries adhere to this dramatic understructure, even though they are not thought of as dramatic programming. In other words, virtually all television productions—whether commercials, news, instructional programs, or entertainment shows—must tell the viewer a coherent story.

Beginning

In all types of television productions the beginning, or opening, performs similar functions. It attracts the audience, establishes the program's subject and style, introduces the characters, and sets up the conflict or problem. The beginning can take a variety of forms—such as the lead in a news story, the introduction to a talk show, a teaser for a situation comedy, or the first few seconds of a commercial. In every case, the beginning must contain a *hook* to grab the viewer. ABC's Ted Koppel considers the "intro" to be one of the most important parts of *Nightline*.

Middle

The purpose of the middle, or body, of all programs is to hold and build interest in the program. That may be done in a drama by developing the characters, introducing new characters, adding complexity to the plot, or intensifying the conflict. Newscasts and talk shows may place stories in a certain order or use promos of upcoming stories to keep the audience tuned in. Commercials may include famous people, humor, music, and interesting shots to create a desire for the product, and to keep viewers from zipping to other channels. Sports contests, game shows, and awards programs have their own built-in drama, usually heightened by the announcers.

End

The program should end with a sense of closure for the audience. Even though many news stories run their course over several days, most newscasts place a human-interest story or humorous *kicker* at the end of the program for structural closure. The idea is to leave the audience feeling a little better than it would if the program ended instead with the latest disaster. Commercials usually end with an identification of the sponsor, and either an implication or direct appeal to the audience to purchase the product. Public Service Announcements usually end by giving a phone number or address and an appeal. Dramatic programs usually have some kind of resolution at the end of each episode, even if not all the subplots are wrapped up. A corporate training tape may end with a summary or a final step that completes a process.

Because television programs have a dramatic understructure, writing for television essentially involves storytelling in a hybrid form combining sound and picture.

WRITING AS STORYTELLING

The writer contributes to the process of delivering ideas to an audience through his or her word choices. Whether the writer's words are visualized in the form of an impassioned presidential speech, a bedroom conversation in an evening soap opera, or a sales pitch for computers during the halftime of the Super Bowl, the process is still *storytelling*. The big difference is that the writer's words do not stand alone but exist as only part of the story told on television.

In some ways, working with the television medium makes the storytelling function of the writer easier. If your assignment is to describe the process of welding, having the image of an acetylene torch at your disposal is a big advantage. On the other hand, the visual images of television can sometimes hamper the storytelling function of the writer. No doubt you have had the experience of seeing a favorite book of yours turned into a film or television program. At least once you probably have been disappointed when the director's imagination did not match your own and the characters or setting on the screen did not match the mental "picture" you were carrying around in your own head. This is the same problem you will encounter as a television writer. The only difference is that as the writer, you will have an opportunity to influence the director *before* the text is converted to audio and visual images.

There is no formula for successful storytelling on television. However, there are several elements that you usually will find in the understructure of a good dramatic story.

Story Idea   The first element is a good idea. You can get ideas many places, such as your own experiences, news reports, biographies, histories, movies, and other media. Today's audiences are attracted to "true" stories about real people and events. You could take a familiar story and put a new twist on it. That's how *Romeo and Juliet* became *West Side Story*. The story idea may be called the "concept" and expressed as a "logline," one sentence that generally describes the story and theme. For example, a logline could describe *Macbeth* as the story of a wife who persuades her husband to become the head of state by any means necessary.

Characters   Next, well-defined characters are needed. Know or invent their backgrounds. The characters must be special enough to get the audience to make emotional commitments to them, to love the heroes and hate the villains. Even if characters are aliens from outer space, like Mr. Spock, they must be believable within the "rules" of the story.

Franchise The third element, the franchise, is important in episodic series. The franchise is the situation that keeps the characters together from week-to-week. For example, the Huxtable family in *The Cosby Show*, the FYI show in *Murphy Brown*, and the town of Cicely in *Northern Exposure*,

Setting The fourth element is the setting. Take the audience to a place it would like to visit, such as Hawaii or Alaska. Locations near Los Angeles, such as Beverly Hills, also have practical attractions for production companies.

Plot Fifth on the list is a strong, clear plot. Open the story with an incident or dilemma that challenges the main characters. Then place obstacles and conflict in the characters' way to provide complications and tension. Unexpected twists and turns in the plot will heighten the audience's interest. Most dramas have multiple story lines. Others, such as *Murder, She Wrote*, have a main story line with subplots woven throughout it. Finally, resolve the story. It is true that slice-of-life stories in daytime "soaps" continue for weeks, but most stories in nighttime dramas have some degree of closure each week. The endings must be satisfying to the audience. That does not mean they always must be happy endings. An unhappy ending may be satisfying if it seems more inevitable and believable than a happy ending. Still, most stories on television—especially comedies—will end happily.

Theme Finally, ask yourself, "What does the journey teach the characters?" The answer will reveal the theme. It suggests the lesson the audience should learn in addition to being entertained.

In the program development process, the story will be written first in the form of a *treatment*.

WRITING THE TREATMENT

The *treatment* is a narrative description of what will happen in the program. It may be only two to four pages long for a brief training tape, or as much as seventy-five pages long for a feature film. (See Figure 3-1).

The producer may write the treatment or bring

in a writer for that purpose. The writer's job is to expand the program idea, or concept, while remaining faithful to the producer's program proposal.

The treatment is like a short story with much description and little dialogue. The writer describes the setting, introduces the characters, and works through the plot. The treatment should create excitement in the program and convey its style.

A good treatment is important for two reasons. First, it may be used to *pitch*, or sell, the concept to whoever must approve the production. Second, it will provide the inspiration and framework for the subsequent script.

WRITING SCRIPTS FOR TELEVISION

After the treatment is complete and the program is approved, the next step is to write the script. The development of a treatment into a script requires very special skills and talent. It also requires the ability to organize written material into a usable format, which takes practice and a clear understanding of the way a script is used in production. While we do not cover the purely creative aspects of writing in this chapter, we will discuss the basics of writing for television and describe the standard script formats that have been developed to organize a program's content for use in production.

The Script in Production

Writing scripts for television is not the same as writing for print media. Television involves the audience in a different way, through the relentless passage of time. A reader of a book can move along at his or her own speed, stop to reread a passage, or quickly skip over an uninteresting section. The television viewer cannot do any of these things and is locked into the presentation of the scriptwriter. To meet this added challenge, the scriptwriter must understand the medium's capabilities and limitations and be familiar with the basic techniques of television production.

```
                    Treatment

                    SpaceRaft

                        by

                   Lincoln Float


    Act I begins with our hero, Paul Riley, loafing in a hammock

in the back yard of his suburban home.  Paul, who appears to be

in his late twenties, is wearing a Phoenix Suns tee shirt,

cutoffs, and basketball sneakers.  As we hear the faint sound of

a distant jet, Paul opens his eyes, looks up, and sees the long,

white trail left by the jet across the clear, blue sky.

    Without warning, a small plane dives into Paul's view.  It

zooms straight toward him, but abruptly stops and hovers nearby

above the ground.  Strangely, it makes no sound.  Now we can see

it isn't a plane, but something that looks amusingly like a

four-person river raft with a dome over it.  Through the clear

dome Paul can see the pilot, dressed like an astronaut.  The

pilot motions to Paul as if to say, "Come aboard."  In a close-up

shot of Paul's face, we see his eyelids spring open.

    The scene cuts to a loud game of basketball on a driveway

court.  Paul is one of the players.  They don't notice a grey van

stop on the street and block the driveway.  Five men get out and

walk toward the players, who by now  have stopped their game.

The men are dressed casually, but look tense and nervous.  The

one who seems to be the leader asks, "Is Paul Riley here?"

Someone answers, "So who wants to know?"


                        1
```

FIGURE 3-1 Treatment.
The treatment tells the story, introduces characters, and describes the settings, as they will be seen and heard by the audience. Specific camera shots and other production choices usually are not indicated in the treatment.

We tend to think of writing for television as writing the lines delivered by performers, but this *dialogue* is only one part of the storytelling function engaged in by writers. In addition, the writer should think of his or her task as *issuing a set of instructions* that helps the director, set designer, performers, and other members of the television team bring the ideas, as a story, to the viewing audience.

The best way to understand what a writer does for television is to remember that whatever is written down as a script will be translated into sounds and images. The script is the basis for translating words into actions, as aural and visual representations. Above all else, the television scriptwriter must keep this in mind: The words of the script are delivered in actions, the actions of actors *and* the actions of the production team.

Although television scripts vary tremendously, all have the same purpose: to instruct the cast and crew *how to perform* during the planning, rehearsal, and production of a television program. Some scripts include word-for-word dialogue, specific camera shots, and staging instructions. Other scripts provide little more than an outline of the production routine. Regardless of the level of detail, successful scripts help to smoothly coordinate the activities of the members of the production team. One of the greatest demands made on a scriptwriter is that his or her work should be invisible to the audience; the television program must create its own immediate reality. Yet it is the script's responsibility to create the program by providing a strong framework and an explicit set of guidelines for the cast and crew to follow in production. Television scripts allow the talent and crew *to anticipate* how a production will unfold.

Write for Your Audience

If at all possible, know, and write for, your target audience. Obviously the style, tone, and complexity of a script for the children's show *Sesame Street* will be different from an instructional series aimed at university students. Although the difference in previous knowledge between young children and university students stands out, the writer always must begin with some inference about the audience's previous knowledge. If a show is targeted at novices, many experts will dismiss the program as "superficial," but if the program is couched at the expert level, the uninitiated viewers will find the show confusing. Network television generally presents programming for the "lay" audience. More specialized video production should consider more sophisticated language and a less leisurely style to effectively communicate more complex material.

The use of language and style also depends on the production situation. *Late Night with David Letterman* became popular because its style and language are appropriate for a particular audience that tunes in late at night. However, in a different production situation, such as a morning talk show, the same language, references, and jokes would fail even in the minds of the exact same audience.

Structure is also an important consideration. For example, it has been found that children do not

easily follow parallel action, flashbacks, or flashforwards. Even with adults, a writer must be careful never to get ahead of the audience's sophistication in structuring the show's format and development. For every *Moonlighting* and *Love and War*, that successfully have the actors "break the fourth wall" and speak directly to the audience, there are innumerable failed programs that confused audiences by violating their expectations of how the program would proceed.

A writer also must consider how much audience members share in common. For example, a news story about city government scandal aimed at a local audience could assume that most viewers are familiar with the mayor, the city council, and some of the surrounding cast of characters and events. The very same story would have to be written quite differently for a national network audience, since the writer could not assume that everyone watching would have the same background. More time would have to be spent introducing national viewers to local events and to the significant people involved to put the story into an understandable context.

Write for the Ear

Although television is a visual medium, all copy or dialogue in a script must be written for the ear, not for the eye. The viewers never read your script; they only listen to its delivery. Copy that might read well will not necessarily sound right when spoken by talent. As a general rule, always read your copy aloud, listening to how it sounds. It's also a good practice to have someone else read your copy aloud so you can hear how it sounds.

TECH TIP   Acting out copy is even more representative of how the audience will hear your words than reading aloud before a mirror. To be a visual medium means that language on television is heard in context, in the context of some location with physical presence. That location, which includes other people as well as the set, has a great influence on how your audience understands your language. Always imagine this level of visualization as you write.

Here are several techniques to keep in mind as you write copy for the ear to hear, not for the eye to see on the page:

Write Simply Strive for a relaxed, informal tone. Use 1- and 2-syllable words when possible. For example, "The police caught the suspect" sounds more natural than "The officers apprehended the perpetrator." Also use contractions as you would in a conversation. For example, if a friend asked "What's the weather like?" would you say "It is raining" or "It's raining"?

This is not to say that you should use slang or colloquial expressions for every script, but rather that you should avoid an overly formal writing style. Use language to call attention to the visual information. In a National Geographic special, "Look at the cloudless sky" communicates more comfortably than "There were no clouds in the sky." Formal language calls attention to itself rather than coming across as a natural part of television's multisensory experience.

TECH TIP One way to simplify your writing is to shun the *tions*. In other words, avoid turning verbs into nouns by adding "tion." For example, "He realized that he was right" is better than "He came to the realiza*tion* that he was right."

Write Clearly Avoid confusing statements, long first-person quotes, and involved statistics. The viewing audience must follow the script continuously and cannot review material once it has been presented, so try to establish a clear, logical presentation sequence. Do not cram too many facts, figures, names, or ideas into a few sentences. As a medium, television is better suited for creating impressions and understanding than for conveying detail.

Write Directly Keep your sentences simple, direct and to the point. A complex sentence structure is both difficult for talent to deliver effectively and hard for the audience to comprehend. Simple sentences introduce the subject before the verb. The structure helps the audience understand by progressively building a mental image. For example, "The halfback ran the 100-yard dash in ten seconds" allows the audience to first picture a man, then see him running, and finally see him cross a finish line after ten seconds. This more complex sentence, "A time of ten seconds was recorded by the halfback in the 100-yard dash" is much harder to visualize because the man does not "appear" until halfway through the sentence and you must then reach "backwards" into your memory to find out information about him.

Write Tightly Be concise. Use the fewest number of words you can to inform accurately and completely. Cut extraneous words and phrases out of sentences. For example: "He is in the process of making a statement at this very moment" could be tightened to "He's speaking now."

While there is no pat answer about how long sentences should be, just remember that someone will be *speaking* them and will have to breathe at the same time!

Write Actively Use vigorous verbs in active voice. For example, "In the ninth inning the game was won by the pitcher's home run" is not as active and exciting as "The pitcher slugged a home run and won the game in the ninth inning."

Present and present perfect tense verbs sound fresher than past tense, particularly when leading into news stories and news bites. For example, a news story that begins "A lost child is found" sounds fresher than "A lost child was found yesterday." However, when you begin a story in the present or present perfect tense, you will have to shift into past tense by the second or third sentence.

Write Fluently Make your copy flow. To increase flow and understanding, use transitions when you shift from one concept or story to another. The television writer has the advantage that changes between visual images can smooth out transitions.

Such familiar script approaches as flash-forwards, flashbacks, and parallel action require careful structuring to be effective. Since these techniques involve manipulating the passage of time, they must be handled with care by both the writer and the director to avoid totally confusing the audience. For example, flashbacks often are signaled by a visual convention such as a blurring of the image to suggest going back in time. Parallel action is used to convince the audience that several events are happening simultaneously. Usually, a common element is used in each of the parallel scenes to link them together. For example, a program that is trying to build suspense as a detective is driving to her office where a bomb is ticking might rely on a car radio and an office radio playing "Going to Wait for the Midnight Hour." The identical song providing audio background in both the car and office scenes indicates the actions are going on at the same time without needing dialogue to point this out.

TECH TIP One of the most helpful guides to clear, concise, and correct writing is Strunk and White's *The Elements of Style.*

Write for the Eye

It almost has become a cliché, but television *is* a visual medium. The television scriptwriter must be as comfortable working with images as with words. Understanding the best way to combine words and pictures and when to let one or the other carry the program's message is the essence of the scriptwriter's art. Often scriptwriting deals with very little spoken copy; the images may convey the message alone or in combination with appropriate sound effects or music. Since the writer must be as visually oriented as the director, it is no surprise that many television writers are "hyphenates," having combined responsibilities as a writer-director or writer-producer.

For some television programs, such as soap operas, the director will decide the camera shots during rehearsals. Therefore, the writer will write the copy, but leave the video column blank. However, many types of scripts must include both copy and pictures. In those cases, the writer must be a *visual storyteller.*

There are several ways to visualize a script. First, you can show the obvious. For example, in some straightforward programs—such as newscasts, documentaries, and talk shows—showing the person who is speaking may be an appropriate choice, especially for important statements such as a speech by a senator or a confession by a crook. The disadvantage is that simply showing

a person speaking for a long period of time gives the television look that has been called pejoratively the "Big Talking Head."

An obvious alternative is to show *what* the person is talking about. This approach can add visual interest, reinforce what is being said, and even communicate another level of meaning to the spoken words.

What can you do to go beyond the obvious choices as you visualize your script?

First, ask yourself if the pictures are telling as much of the story as they can. The television scripts of beginning writers often look like radio copy with pictures added later. Instead, start by imagining what your story would look like in a dream with no sound. How would it look before the sound is added?

Second, ask how much of your copy can be replaced by images that convey the same messages visually. Necessary spoken information might be repeated visually. Visual pauses could relieve monotony, provide transitions, heighten drama, reinforce points, and let the audience relax mentally for a moment.

Third, consider if your images always are *parallel* to sound and if there are any places where they could be in *counterpoint.* Parallel sound and picture communicate the same message and reinforce each other. However, when sound and picture are in counterpoint, they send different messages. The result is a third level of meaning. For example, we may see two characters who look outwardly calm, but a thunderstorm on the soundtrack may suggest a building tension between them. Music also can be parallel or in counterpoint to the picture. For example, happy times in a drama can turn tense and sinister with just a single chord change in the background music.

Fourth, ask if you have created settings that use the unique visual properties of the television medium. The tendency is to think of television production as taking place on a theater stage rather than the television screen. Remember that television production involves the creation of *videospace,* in which home may be an *electronic set,* instead of Kansas.

Fifth, ask if you can use graphics such as drawings, charts, and even text to reinforce the spoken copy. Do you suggest visual metaphors, signs, and symbols that have meaning in the program? Graphic images also can create more visual variety.

Sixth, on the other hand, ask yourself if your script has *too much* visualization. One tendency of beginning writers is to try to say too much and also to show too much in a program. A one-minute Public Service Announcement containing twenty still photographs may look hectic and cluttered. In a live three-camera studio production, it also may be impossible to get all twenty shots in one minute, without postproduction editing. Therefore, as you visualize your script, keep in mind the aesthetic and technical limitations of television production.

Consider Television's Aesthetic and Technical Production Capabilities

A script serves as a road map, or point of departure, for a television production. In the end, the viewing audience never sees the script; the viewers see only the program. Scripts should never be written as final, inalterable documents, but rather as flexible frameworks around which the production team works to build the videospace. There often is a tendency to overload the videospace with words and not let the visual images tell their own story. While "write less" generally is a good maxim, "show less" also should be considered by the scriptwriter. Experienced screenplay authors select their images carefully, recognizing that graphic visual detail is not always necessary or even desirable. For example, violence often can be more effectively conveyed with close-up reaction shots than with blood squibs. Quite apart from the role of the television censor, romance and intimacy often are better conveyed with a glance than with a touch. Finally, the scriptwriter needs to think about when images are too much "on point," or obvious. One criticism of many rock videos is that they spoonfeed predictable imagery to viewers that literally dictates to the viewers how they should perceive a song in their mind's eye. Sometimes it is better to rely on the imagination of viewers rather than the camera lens for visualization. A creative scriptwriter is able to balance words and images to provide just the right amount to clearly communicate with the audience while still allowing each individual to participate in creating the show's meaning.

TECH TIP   Natural-sounding television scripts avoid "radio writing." Radio writing refers to explicitly describing visual elements of the program. "Sit in the green chair by the door" helps a radio audience visualize the scene, but on television, "Sit over there" accompanied by a gesture is much more natural.

The television writer always must work within the production's own range of capabilities and limitations. When a writer has carefully constructed the videospace, it is not always easy for that writer to accept changes or revisions, especially when they are made for technical reasons. However, there are times when script changes are unavoidable because necessary equipment is unavailable, the budget will not cover the number of sets, locations, or performers indicated in the script, or a show is running long.

A common mistake of beginning scriptwriters is to write a script which requires resources that simply are not available. However, experienced writers often are able to overcome seemingly impossible limitations through the ingenious use of available production techniques. Where a naive writer might set a scene at the Super Bowl, a seasoned pro might change the setting to a living room where the television set, actually a monitor playing a football tape, was tuned to the game.

Time is a limitation which affects every scriptwriter. In the first place, most television scripts are written under serious time pressures. No matter whether you are writing a situation comedy, an episodic drama, a nightly news script, or an instructional presentation, there is rarely enough time to work at a leisurely pace. Time is also an important factor within a program, since the television scriptwriter usually is given a very inflexible time frame within which to present an idea or to communicate a message. Commercials are an obvious example where the writer has only ten, fifteen, thirty, or at most sixty seconds to deliver a sponsor's message. The existence of commercial messages forces a dramatic script to include multiple break points within the script. Ideally, these breaks will appear as natural transitions rather than plot-destroying interruptions.

Many other production situations also require a careful consideration of time. A theatrical play can run as long as the writer and director wish; a television drama must play with the time allocated to the production. A writer who has been asked for voice-over copy to accompany a silent film clip must produce material that runs the length of the available film. It is not uncommon to have twenty-seven seconds of script for only eighteen seconds worth of film. If talent speeds through the copy, it may be at the expense of the audience's comprehension. A stopwatch and the flexibility to approach the writing problem from a fresh perspective are as indispensable to a television scriptwriter as a word processor. Working within these many time limitations and still delivering an effective, high-quality script are the mark of a true professional.

TECH TIP Professional newscasters typically deliver 120 to 150 words per minute. Copy that is heavily punctuated with nonverbals and emotions, rather than straight information, cannot reliably be estimated with respect to number of words per minute. Remember to use the stopwatch during actual delivery of the lines. Clocking an isolated "stand-up" reading almost always underrepresents the true running time of the script.

Another mark of a professional scriptwriter is the presentation of his or her work formatted for use in television. A script consists of much more than the lines delivered by talent. It is the principle organizing document for the entire crew, and it must communicate with the creative and technical crews just as much as with the audience. Because of this, the form, as well as the content, of a script requires the attention of a scriptwriter.

DETAILED SCRIPT FORMAT

A detailed or complete script contains the spoken dialogue, sound and music information, the major visual elements which accompany the audio, and important production information, such as timing of segments and video and audio sources. The basic television script format, which, with minor

variations is used universally, is shown in Figure 3-2. Notice that the page is divided into a video column and an audio column and that the upper left hand corner indicates the page number, program title, and a "contact." The contact is an individual who can answer questions about the script and may be the show's writer, producer, or director.

The video column is left almost blank by the scriptwriter to leave room for the director's camera shot notations. However, important visual elements such as titles, graphics, special effects, and film or videotape inserts usually are typed in capital letters opposite the corresponding audio. The video column also may contain timing information. For example, the running time for a video insert would be enclosed in parenthesis next to its description. News directors use this information to manage the length of the newscast and to alert the anchors when they are about to reappear on camera after a remote segment.

The audio column contains the sound elements of the show. Each performer's dialogue is double-spaced with the speaker's name (or character if a drama) typed in capital letters. Sound effects and music cues are capitalized and underlined to separate them from spoken copy. Any other information which is not to be spoken (such as a performer's stage movements) is bracketed and typed in capital letters. This convention allows talent to avoid confusing spoken lines with instructions related to the production.

It is the rare script that does not undergo some change between the writer's original effort and actual production. For example, a late-breaking story might alter a newscaster's copy or the suggestions of an actor might prompt the rewriting of a dramatic scene. When a page of a script is revised, that page should be clearly marked "Revision" with the date (and occasionally the time if a newscast) of the revision. To make certain that everyone is using the same corrected version of the script, revision pages should be duplicated on paper of a different color than that used for the original script. Since revisions require page substitutions, original scripts should be written so that the material incorporates logical breaks. There-

```
Dimensions-Modern Dance
Carol Richards
Page 1
                                      AUDIO

VIDEO
                                      HOST
HOST SEEN IN CAMEO          Dance has long been one of the most
                            beautiful and interesting of the performing
                            arts.  In recent years its popularity has
                            increased tremendously with a wide range
                            of performances from classical ballet to
                            modern dance.  Yet for many people dance
                            remains somewhat intimidating.  Without
                            an understanding of what it is and where
                            it comes from it's hard to develop an
BACKGROUND LIGHT CUE AS     appreciation for the art.
CAMERA DOLLIES PAST HOST         Today with the help of the Modern Dance
INTO REHEARSING DANCER      Company, we'll explore the world of dance
                            in all of its multifaceted DIMENSIONS.
FILM OPENING (:30)          MUSIC:  THEME UP AND UNDER


                                 ANNOUNCER (V.O.)
                            DIMENSIONS. . . A weekly series on the
                            performing arts.  Today, "The World of Dance"
                            with the Modern Dance Company.  Here is
                            the host of DIMENSIONS, Carol Richards.
HOST AT INTERVIEW SET                 HOST
                            Good afternoon and welcome to DIMENSIONS.
```

FIGURE 3-2 **Detailed Script Format.** A detailed script format includes information about audio, video, and timing. The video column provides blank space for the director and other crew members to write production notes.

fore, dramas should be organized by scene for easy revision, and each story of a newscast should begin on a separate page.

TECH TIP Scripts used on camera should always be typed on pastel yellows, blues, greens, or pinks. Gray paper also is effective. White paper reflects too much light, blooms on camera, and is difficult for talent to read.

News Scripts

A news script is probably the most common type of television script, since every station prepares them daily. The news script must be written quickly, yet it also must be journalistically accurate. The news script also must be a nearly complete guide to the production process. Since few news programs have the luxury of rehearsals, it is very important for a news script to organize the information in a clear, concise package that can be followed easily.

News scripts are either typed on multisheet carbon packs or on word processors supported by high-speed copiers and collators. These production approaches allow all members of the crew and cast to have a copy of the script. If the production establishes a format, including margin size, type style, and the number of lines per page, it is easy to estimate a program's running time by counting pages of script. If thirty seconds of content are formatted per page, the director and talent can quickly estimate adjustments to a show's running time when late-breaking stories force a re-ordering of the newscast.

Each story should begin on its own separate

page, and each page should be labeled with a heading, or "slug," describing the story. One- or two-word descriptions such as "Arson," "Mayor defeated," or "Stock prices" usually are sufficient to identify the different stories. With each story as a separate "package" of pages, it is easy to drop or add a story as needed.

Remote Inserts   Although the in-studio anchor holds a newscast together, the use of remotely recorded tape inserts is an important part of the news script. On rare occasions, usually news coverage in other countries, remote footage will be received as film rather than video. Conventions have been developed to indicate in news scripts information about these remote inserts. The following examples refer to the news-script formats in Figure 3-3.

VOICE-OVER   A voice-over (VO) consists of narration read by in-studio talent while silent tape is fed from a videotape recorder. The notation in Figure 3-3*a* indicates (1) the number of the tape cut on the cassette, (2) the running time of the tape, (3) that no audio exists on the tape, and (4) the name of the talent who should read the voice-over. If the material is film rather than tape, it would be designated "FILM" to indicate the director should call the film chain rather than the VTR to play the remote segment.

SOUND-ON-TAPE   Sound-on-tape (SOT) indicates that the remote video cut includes its own sound track. Figure 3-3*b* shows (1) play cut 6 on the VTR, which includes sound-on-tape, (2) the running time of the videotape segment and that the sound on the tape should be played, and (3) the *outcue*, or the final words heard on the tape.

The outcue is especially important for sound-on-tape because it helps the director, switcher, and audio engineer make a smooth transition from the tape back to the in-studio newscaster. Unless the outcue is absolutely accurate, the cue can do more harm than good. The outcue and running time serve as a double-check that a transition is about to take place. If the outcue is sound rather than spoken dialogue, indicate it as follows: "OUTCUE: ' . . . why I intend to vote for it.' (APPLAUSE)."

A-ROLLING/B-ROLLING   If one remote source is inserted into another remote source, one of the two

tapes will be mounted on the A VTR and the other on the B VTR. The director will first "roll" the A VTR, insert the B roll, return to the A roll, and finally return to the in-studio talent. For A/B rolls, incues as well as outcues should be identified. Figure 3-3*c* indicates (1) the cut number on the A roll and that the B roll will be inserted, (2) the combined time of the A/B roll segment, (3) the start time and B-roll incue (which is the same as the A-roll outcue), (4) the time in the overall segment at which to return to tape A and the A-roll incue (the B-roll outcue), and (5) the final audio outcue for the entire tape insert. While it is easier to preassemble A/B rolls as single segments, last minute interviews or "live from the scene" footage make A/B rolls a practical necessity for all news shows.

Graphics and Chroma Key   The script also should indicate the use of lower-third supers, graphics, and chroma key. Since the script serves as a check for the pages provided by the character generator (CG) operator, the script must be accurate with respect to spelling, titles, and numbers. In Figure 3-3*d*, (1) "C/K" indicates the use of a chroma-key insert (the "STOCK EX SL" describes the C/K as a graphic slide featuring the stock exchange), and (2) "CG" represents character generator (the information in between the quotation marks is the word-for-word message which is to be displayed, in this case "DOW JONES 1837 UP 2").

Live on Remote   With the increase in satellite and microwave live feeds during a newscast, more of the newscast is delivered out of studio and in a semiscripted form. As presented in Figure 3-3*e*, (1) these segments are designated LOR (for live on remote) and typically include the remote newscaster's name and an estimated run time, and (2) the location of the next video source. These "handoffs" or outcues usually are not scripted, but often they rely on a standardized routine such as "Back to you, Alan."

Dramatic Scripts

Scripts for dramatic or comedy shows generally

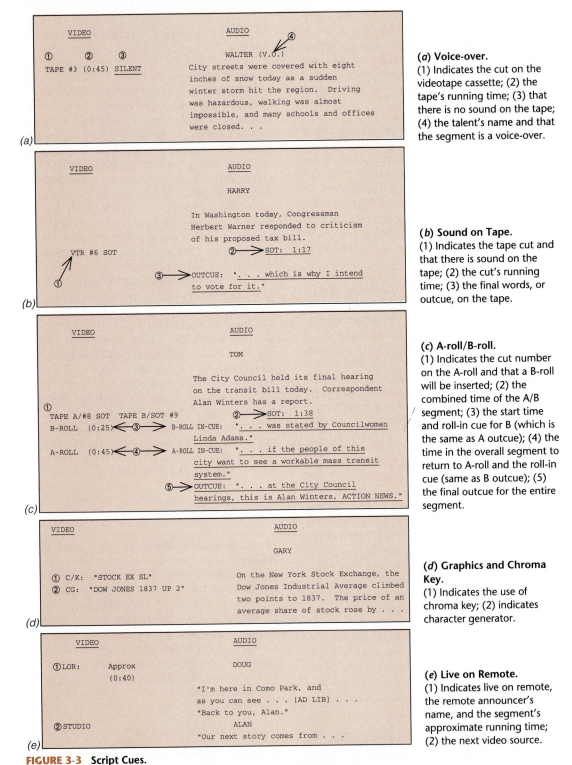

FIGURE 3-3 Script Cues.
The script cues illustrated here are useful for news and other program inserts.

follow the detailed script format. If the scriptwriter follows a standard margin and types the same number of lines per page, it is easy to estimate the running time of the script by counting pages. On the average, forty to forty-five television script pages run about a half hour of airtime. However, since type sizes and formats do vary, it is best for each writer to establish personal guidelines.

Commercials

Commercials also follow the detailed script format, but the visual column often is more elaborate. Since commercials usually run only fifteen or thirty seconds, visualization and timing are critical. Figure 3-4 presents a storyboarded script in which the shots are sketched to show visualizations more precisely.

Storyboarding is an important skill to develop. Commercial airtime can be staggeringly expensive, and clients rightfully are very demanding that their messages are executed for maximum impact. Since production costs easily can exceed one thousand dollars per second for national spots, ideas, in the form of storyboards, are screened carefully before beginning production. In addition to the presentation shown in Figure 3-4, storyboards often are presented as individual note cards or flip charts accompanied by the specific audio. By segmenting the commercial in this manner, individual shots can be changed without reworking the entire script.

Storyboarding is an excellent technique for developing commercial concepts and for removing unnecessary material. Every shot should be justifiable, and every camera change should be motivated to reveal important new material. If any frame in a storyboard fails either of these criteria, it should be removed and replaced with a more powerful substitute.

FILM-STYLE SCRIPT FORMAT

The two-column television script was devised for the director who must select shots from multiple cameras covering the action simultaneously from various angles. The single-camera, film-style production mode has become a practical option with the increased availability of EFP equipment and

precision postproduction editing. Some producers and directors now require programming intended for this production technique to be written in a film-style script format.

As you can see from the example in Figure 3-5, a film-style format is quite different from the two-column television script. Notably, the script is not divided into columns but rather into a series of scenes with the dialogue delivered by the various actors. Each scene is assigned a number and described as to time of day, location, and additional information to help create the overall atmosphere. A writer can establish considerable influence on the final product through the scene descriptions and the "look" implied by the settings and character sketches included.

This script format reflects the different demands of on-location shooting. With the script arranged film-style, the director easily can identify each individual scene and sequence the shooting of scenes by location, time of day, or the actors involved in a set of scenes. Also, since each scene is identified with its own unique number, the multiple angles from which a scene is shot for later editing are all slated with the same number. Postproduction editing requires this level of organization during production or it dissolves into time-consuming and costly confusion.

PARTIALLY SCRIPTED FORMATS

Not every television production lends itself to a completely detailed script. Sports events and live news coverage contain unpredictable events that cannot be fully scripted. Talk shows, interviews, and game shows cannot be scripted word-for-word. Instructional programs and demonstration shows sound stilted and boring when performers, especially nonprofessionals, attempt to follow a detailed script instead of talking in their own words.

Although word-for-word scripts do not work for these programs, scripts are still needed to provide the skeleton on which the program is built. The partially scripted format helps the production team

BDA
TV Script

Client	DELTA AIR LINES	City	DTW (MIA, TPA, PBI)	Spct No.	8100

Date 12/19/   Job No. D7-9188-9   Type   Length 30"

This Spot effective Jan. 16   It replaces   Remarks "CHEF"

KITCHEN SET. CHEF SHOWS
TRAY OF 12 BROILED STEAKS,
GARNISHED WITH PARSLEY, TO
CAMERA

CHEF: This is why every-
one's flying Delta to Florida
. . .my juicy steaks. . .
served on all mealtime nonstops
. . .in Tourist, too.

SOMMELIER INTERRUPTS WITH
BOTTLE OF CHAMPAGNE

SOMMELIER:
Hah! They fly Delta to
Florida for my fine champagne.

CHEF:
In tourist?

SOMMELIER NODS.

SOMMELIER:
And on <u>all</u> nonstops. . . daytime <u>and</u> Night Coach.

CUT TO ECU STEAK AS KNIFE
SLICES IT.

CHEF:
Ah, but you should <u>taste</u> my
steaks. . .choice, charbroiled
filet mignon.

80A-9

FIGURE 3-4 Storyboard.
The storyboard uses small sketches to convey important camera shots and angles.
Storyboards are essential elements of most prescripted programs and can save
considerable expense if used properly. (*Courtesy: Delta Air Lines.*)

anticipate what will be expected of them. By substituting a carefully developed format for a verbatim script, the director, talent, and production team have enough "feel" for the proper sequence of events to pull together a tight, integrated, and professional-looking production.

Rundown Sheet

A *rundown sheet* outlines the sequence of events from the top of the show to the final fade to black. Rundown sheets can be used on all productions,

but they are essential on semiscripted shows to forewarn the cast and crew of how the show is intended to unfold. Without this guidance, the subtle, unnoticed adjustments that allow the show to finish on time could not be made.

As you can see from the sample in Figure 3-6, a well-designed rundown sheet presents all the vital information about a production clearly and

```
    FADE IN:

1.  EXT. FRONT OF OFFICE BUILDING IN A DOWNTOWN CITY AREA - DAY    1.

    A taxi pulls up to the curb in front of the office building.
    KATE, an attractive young woman in her early 20's gets out of
    the cab and enters the building.

2.  INT. LOBBY AREA OF OFFICE BUILDING                             2.

    Camera picks up KATE as she walks through the building doors
    and enters the lobby.  She looks around a moment until she
    spots GARY, a business executive in his mid-30's who is standing
    near the elevators.  She walks over to him.

                        GARY
            Well, good morning!  I was afraid you
            weren't going to make it.

                        KATE
            I almost didn't.  You know, I'm
            not happy about this at all.

                        GARY
            Look, it's already been decided.  Now
            let's just do it and get it over with.
            Did you bring the papers?

                        KATE
            They're in my handbag.

                        GARY
            Okay.  Let's go.

    They walk over to an elevator and enter.  The elevator
    doors close behind them.

3.  INT. CONFERENCE ROOM - DAY                                     3.

    A large conference room.  The furnishings are modern, tasteful
    and obviously very expensive.  A secretary is arranging papers
    and pencils at each seat along the long table.  KATE and GARY
    enter.

                        SECRETARY
            Good morning, Mr. Johnson. . . Miss Kelly.

                        GARY
            Good morning, Grace.  I wonder if you
            wouldn't mind doing that later.  Miss
            Kelly and I have some important matters
            to discuss before the meeting begins.

                        SECRETARY
            Of course, Mr. Johnson.
```

FIGURE 3-5 Single-Camera Scripts.
Single-camera scripts include scene numbers to enable the director to schedule an efficient shooting sequence and to keep accurate track of each scene during planning and production. Each scene's location is described.

```
                    THE MORNING SHOW


                    Monday, January 29


  7:00:00    (0:20)   LOGO OPENING                    VTR

  7:00:20    (1:00)   BILL & SUSAN Intros.            HOMEBASE

  7:01:20    (5:00)   NEWS SEGMENT/Curtis             NEWS SET

  7:06:20    (1:00)   WEATHER/Roberts                 WEATHER BOARD

  7:07:20    (0:20)   UPCOME INTRO & COMML LEAD-IN    HOMEBASE

  7:07:40    (2:00)   COMMERCIAL #1                   VTR

  7:09:40    (0:15)   SUSAN: ENT. REVIEW INTRO        HOMEBASE

  7:09:55    (2:50)   MOVIE REVIEW                    VTR

  7:12:45    (7:30)   DRUNK DRIVING INTERVIEW/        LIV. ROOM SET

                      Bill and Rachel Warren

  7:20:15    (2:00)   COMMERCIAL #2                   VTR

  7:22:15    (4:00)   COOKING DEMO/Susan & Karen      KITCHEN SET

  7:26:15    (1:45)   SPORTS/Bill                     HOMEBASE

  7:28:00    (0:50)   Bill & Susan Goodbye and CREDITS   HOMEBASE/VTR

  7:28:50    (1:10)   STATION BREAK
```

FIGURE 3-6 Rundown Sheet.
A rundown sheet specifies the times for each segment, the talent involved, and the show's overall running time. Although the actual dialogue is not presented, the rundown sheet helps the director and talent stay within the show's time constraints.

concisely. Each segment shows the talent involved, where the action takes place (studio set, remote, from a VTR or film chain), and the segment's approximate running time. Rundown sheets should be produced and duplicated for every member of the production team.

Outline Scripts

Even though a show may be ad-libbed around an established format, it is a good idea to write the opening and the closing of the show to ensure a smooth beginning and ending. In addition, there are sometimes important segments within a production which need to be carefully presented, either because they contain important copy (such as a commercial) or because they are used as production cues (such as film or tape roll cues). In these instances, the *outline script* would contain both a word-for-word, detailed copy of important segments and a more general outline for loosely structured portions of the show.

As an example, take a typical demonstration program. The show is a series on home photog-

68

raphy with a professional host and guest photographers. As you can see from the example in Figure 3-7, the opening of the program is fully scripted to ensure a smooth and precise introduction. The middle section, where the demonstration takes place, is outlined loosely. The talent will have no trouble ad-libbing around the format, but the opening, closing, and commercial introductions (as well as important on-air plugs) are carefully written into the script.

The outline script frequently is used in news or sports coverage, where certain information for openings, closings, and breaks must be handled precisely. As you can see in Figure 3-8, this sports script has a specific opening, which is fully scripted. In addition, the roll cue for commercials, which are inserted from the home studio, is written as "With the score _____ to _____, we'll take a

brief time out for these commercial messages." This is an important production cue which must be delivered accurately in order to ensure smooth transitions from the remote feed to the home studio and back.

Interview Scripts

People often are surprised to learn that most talk or interview shows employ a staff of writers or producers. This does not mean that the interview seen on the air is scripted, but it does suggest that writing and research are necessary to make a difficult interview appear effortless on camera.

```
Fun with Photography
Tony Jordan
Page 1
        VIDEO                              AUDIO


FADE IN:


CLOSE-UP PHOTOGRAPHIC PRINT
AS IT SLOWLY DEVELOPS AND
THE IMAGE FORMS--PULL OUT
TO REVEAL HOST                             HOST
                                There's nothing more satisfying for a photographer
                                than to watch as the image slowly forms
                                on a print of a picture which you've taken,
                                developed, and printed.  It's one of the
                                most interesting and enjoyable parts of
                                photography.  By the time our program is
                                over you'll be able to develop your own
                                film, enlarge it, and print it in your own
                                home.  The Photographic Darkroom... our topic
                                today on "Fun With Photography."
OPENING FILM (:30)              MUSIC:  THEME UP AND UNDER


                                    ANNOUNCER (V.O.)
                                Introducing you to the fascinating world
                                of camera and pictures.  This is Fun With
                                Photography with your host, Tony Jordan.
                                            HOST
                                Hello, and welcome to Fun With Photography.
                                For most folks their role in photography
                                ends with the exposed roll of film.  They
                                drop it off at the local drugstore and a few
                                days later pick up their prints.  Sure it's
                                easy but if that's how you develop and print
```

FIGURE 3-7   Outline Script. An outline script fully scripts openings, closes, and important transitions such as intros to commercials, even though most of the show is ad-libbed. Outline scripts are commonly used in demonstration programs. Figure continues on page 70.

HOST (con't)

your pictures you're missing out on some
of the most creative aspects of picture taking.
But before we go any further, let's take a
look at a typical darkroom.

FOLLOW AS TONY POINTS   (TONY AD LIBS AS HE SHOWS:
OUT EQUIPMENT
                                    -Developing Tanks

                                    -Chemicals

                                    -Sinks

                                    -Enlarger

                                    -Print Trays
                                    HOST
VTR CUT #1 (1:45)   VTR ROLL CUE: Let's take a look and see how

                            to load the developing tank in the darkroom.

                            VTR SOUND TRACK (1:45).
                                    HOST
                            Once your film has been loaded into the
                            tank and you've secured the top cover you
                            can turn on the room lights again. The
                            next step is to prepare your chemicals.
                            (TONY AD LIBS AS HE PREPARES CHEMICALS ON TABLE)

FIGURE 3-7 Outline Script.
(continued)

Television programs cannot afford rambling, unfocused interviews for two reasons: (1) there is rarely enough time for irrelevant conversation, and (2) the viewing audience probably will not watch for long unless the conversation is interesting and to the point. This is why a talk show must be carefully organized.

An award-winning producer of the daily talk show *People Are Talking*, Alan Schroeder, describes the extensive preproduction planning that goes into each program: The process begins two to six weeks earlier with the selection of the topic. Then an associate producer scans the station's newspaper clipping file and runs a search on a computer database for timely information. The next few days the associate producer spends hours on the phone, talking with potential guests and trying to figure out if they would be good in a live, unrehearsed discussion.

When the guests are booked, the associate producer conducts individual *preinterviews* on the phone. Afterward, they are typed up, summarized, and given to the host, along with biographies of the guests. A preinterview often is the best way to structure a guest's appearance on a talk show. In a few minutes chatting with a guest, a writer or producer can pinpoint a number of good stories, interesting anecdotes, and issues that will form the basis of the host's on-camera questions.

However, preinterviews are not always possible. This may be the case with guests who appear to plug a book, movie, television show, or personal appearance and who arrive in town just prior to the production. In these situations, press releases, clipping files, computer searches, and other reference sources are the best way to research possible questions. Even professional and experienced hosts who write their own questions rely on

```
SATURDAY, JULY 16        BASEBALL GAME OF THE WEEK        OPENING OF TELECAST


                    VIDEO                          AUDIO
1.  VTR     BASEBALL OPENING                 SOT

            AT APPROX :18 FROM TOP ON TITLE FREEZE FRAME--MUSIC CONTINUES BG

                INSERT SLIDES                CUE ANNCE FROM MU
2.  INSERT SL:_____VS_____    AD LIB...THIS AFTERNOON......
                                        FROM_____THE_____
                                        VERSUS THE_____

                                        BROUGHT TO YOU BY...

3.  INSERT SL: CHRYSLER/PLYMOUTH        YOUR CHRYSLER PLYMOUTH DEALERS,
                                        WHO INVITE YOU TO BUY OR LEASE
                                        THE NEW CHRYSLER LE BARON...
                                        THE FIRST IN A TOTALLY NEW CLASS
                                        OF AUTOMOBILES.

                                        BY...

4.  INSERT SL: MILLER/LITE              LITE BEER.  EVERYTHING YOU ALWAYS
                                        WANTED IN A BEER...AND LESS.

                                        AND BY...

5.  INSERT SL: GILLETTE/DRY LOOK        GILLETTE...MAKERS OF THE DRY LOOK.
                                        #1 SPRAY FOR MEN.  AVAILABLE IN
                                        AEROSOL AND NEW PUMP SPRAY.
```

FIGURE 3-8 Program Opening Format. Program opening formats often introduce live remotes such as sports events. The scripted opening helps the program create an identity in the viewer's mind and makes sure important information, such as the show's sponsors or upcoming programs, is not forgotten. (*Courtesy: NBC Sports.*)

the preinterview scripts and research summaries provided by the staff writers and producers.

The audience who watches a talk show at home sees a program that appears spontaneous and effortless—just a group of people talking about an interesting topic. Little could they suspect the amount of planning and preproduction effort that is necessary to make it look so easy on the air.

SOFTWARE PROGRAMS FOR WRITERS

We have shown you some standard script formats in this chapter. Typing scripts in the proper formats can be long and tedious. Imagine how long it would take you to type a twenty-page film-style script like the one shown in Figure 3-5. Certainly longer than it would take to type a twenty-page

paper for an English class, even with footnotes. Fortunately, much of the tedium of typing scripts (and typing English papers) has been eliminated by *computer software programs*.

Some of the basic *word processors* that you might use to type a college paper also can be used for scriptwriting. Most will included a thesaurus, spelling and grammar checkers, and other helpful features. In addition, some standard features on word processors may be adapted to scriptwriting. For example, you may be able to format a split-page script using the column functions available on most processors. You also may be able to design your own *macros* that simplify formatting commands. However, script formats that look simple may be tricky to achieve on a basic word processing program.

To make the scriptwriting process simpler and easier, specialized programs called *script proces-*

FIGURE 3-9 **Script Processor.**
Script processors automatically put scripts into the
standard formats. (*Courtesy: Robert Schooley.*)

FIGURE 3-10 **News Software.**
Computer networks link the newsroom with the studio
control room. Scripts can be updated in seconds.
(*Courtesy: KGTV-TV.*)

FIGURE 3-11 **Storyboards and Animatics.**
Storyboards can be generated electronically and either
printed or transferred to videotape as animatics.
(*Courtesy: LAKE Compuframes, Inc.*)

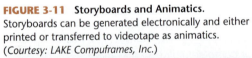

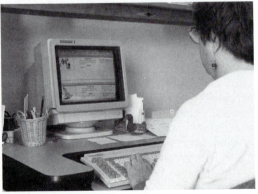

sors have been designed. (See Figure 3-9.) These
processors provide automatic script formatting
as you write. They also may be used in conjunction with other software, such as scheduling
programs.

One place where computers have had a great
impact is in television news, even in medium and
small markets. Today many news operations are
linked by LANs, or *Local Area Networks*. They
make it possible for the reporter to compose a
story on a word processor at his or her desk, then
send the story over the LAN to the producer's
desk, to printers, and even to the studio Tele-
Promp-Ter! (See Figure 3-10.) With some newsroom software, it's even possible for a reporter to
include coded identification keys (IDs) in the news
copy. The coded IDs then are downloaded directly into a character generator and ready to be
shown on air.

Reporters also are linked by computers to the
outside world. With a terminal at his or her desk,
a reporter may be able to search newspaper archives, government documents, and other electronic databases while writing a story.

There also are computer programs for writers
who need to include storyboards with their scripts.
(See Figure 3-11.) Writers may work with graphic
artists, using *desktop video* to create animated
storyboards called *animatics*. Desktop video is
discussed in Chapter 16.

SUMMARY

The television team members most involved in writing a script are the producer, writer, and director. Before they begin to write, they must know the program's purpose and audience. Writers choose an approach, or framework, for each program that fits a dramatic understructure of three acts.

Writing for television is a storytelling process. However, the process is modified because the words are presented within an audio and visual context. Therefore, in addition to the dialogue, the writer must provide instructions on how to present the words as sounds and images. The writer must communicate with the director and other members of the crew, as well as with the audience.

The treatment is a narrative description of what will happen in the program. It is written prior to the script. A television script includes the program's content, establishes the show's format, and organizes important production information so that it will be most useful in planning, rehearsal, and production.

The television writer must write for the ear to hear. Good television writing is simple, clear, direct, tight, active, and fluent. Copy must be written to sound natural. The audience never reads the script; it hears only the performer's delivery. The most effective television writing style is clear, simple, and concise and arranges information logically. The writer should use a style and approach which best suit the program's target audience, especially if the show is aimed at a specific and easily identifiable group. Finally, the television scriptwriter must be able to deal with the production limitations that exist. These include time problems, budget limitations, and production capability.

The television scriptwriter must have the skills and talents of a writer and a visualizer. Television is a visual medium, and the writer must deal with images, i.e., when they can stand alone and when they should oppose or complement the words. While writers should be encouraged to "write for the eye" and generally favor demonstration over excess verbal description, remember that overly explicit visuals sometimes can overpower the viewer's imagination to the detriment of the show.

Since a television script directs the actions of the entire crew during preproduction, rehearsal, and production, its form is as important as its content. The detailed script format includes specific dialogue, visual elements, and such additional audio as music and sound effects. It often is used on news, dramatic, documentary, and commercial productions. The film-style format is an alternative format that often is used for productions which are to be shot with a single camera.

Partially scripted formats are designed to encourage a show's natural spontaneity and still provide the needed structure of an established format. The amount of scripted material varies, but usually openings, closings, and important cue lines within the show are fully scripted. Rundown sheets and interview scripts help both performers and crew members anticipate and plan for upcoming events. This minimum level of organization is essential for professional on-air results.

Script processors and other computer software make it simple and easy to produce scripts and storyboards in standard formats.

PART TWO

Television production is a unique art requiring multitalented individuals who combine artistic ability, technical agility, and a sense of the television business. The individuals with the major responsibilities in the four stages of television production are the producer, director, and performer.

Unlike painters, who work directly with their tools, using brushes and paint to transform their visions into art, the ideas of television producers, directors, and performers must first be interpreted through electronic equipment that is operated by a production crew before they can appear in finished form. Another limitation in television production is that a program often must meet specific objectives and conform to a time limit. The way in which television producers must work would be akin to asking Picasso to create a painting without ever touching a brush and, instead, allowing the viewer to select the paints and canvas size on which Picasso creates.

The television producer, director, and performer must be able to translate the thoughts and visions in his or her imagination into the unique elements that make up videospace and audiospace. In addition, to achieve the desired results on the television screen, producers and directors must also be able to organize and manage the stages of production in which videospace and audiospace are created.

P R O D U C I N G
F O R   T E L E V I S I O N

It has been said that the theater is an actor's medium, film is a director's medium, and television is a producer's medium. These generalizations identify the person in each medium who is the focal point in the production process. While you may have a fairly good idea about what actors and film directors do, you may not be quite so sure about what television producers do.

The first thing to know about television producers is that there are different kinds of producers with different domains of responsibilities. Most producers are *staff producers*. These are regular employees of a network, station, or production organization who are responsible for developing and supervising program production. Staff producers at the three major networks usually are assigned to the news and sports divisions. At local stations and at production facilities, staff producers generally work on a wide variety of shows. The production staff working along with the producer also consists of regular employees. The show is invariably produced at the station or production organization's studios. While special equipment or personnel are hired from the outside when necessary, for the most part these shows are primarily in-house productions.

A slightly different breed of producer is the *independent producer,* an entrepreneur with a production company that sells programming to networks and stations. The independent producer assembles a creative "package," which he or she sells to a program buyer. The package consists of the program idea, the script, the director, the performers, and the production team. The show is produced at any facility, not necessarily the studios of the network or station that buys the show. Once the project is completed, the free-lance production team is dissolved and the members go their own ways. Independent producers are responsible for almost all network and syndicated entertainment shows.

Some very successful independent producers are Stephen J. Cannell (*Hunter* and *Wiseguy*), Stephen Bochco (*Hill Street Blues* and *L.A. Law*), and Marcy Carsey and Tom Werner (*The Cosby Show, Roseanne,* and *You Bet Your Life*). Independent producers may supervise a number of projects simultaneously. In this case, they serve as *executive producers,* who primarily develop and sell the initial idea. The day-to-day supervision on the studio set is handled by one of their subordinates, who is called a *line producer.* Local production houses often find their personnel functioning as independent producers as well, although their clients are more often corporations with communication needs than networks trying to fill prime time.

THE PRODUCER AS A RENAISSANCE PERSON

One reason for the producer's central role in television is the nature of the television business. Television requires a constant source of program material, and while many people are continually involved in producing specific television programs, most team members join a show only when their talents are needed, perform their jobs, and then leave the production once their contribution is over. Only the producer, and perhaps a few members of the producer's staff, actually stay with the show from its earliest inception until its ultimate broadcast or distribution. The producer must give a sense of continuity and unity to the production, since he or she is the one person who knows how all the different parts of the show will ultimately fit together.

The staff producer, or simply *the producer*, supervises everything from the first preproduction meeting to the last videotape edit. He or she is the person who ultimately is responsible for every aspect of the program—creative, technical, and commercial. "That means a producer needs to know a lot of things," says James A. DeVinney, who has won Emmys for his producing in the series *Wonderworks* and *Eyes on the Prize*. "But a producer doesn't have to know every single thing. Instead, a producer must know enough about everything to draw out what's needed from everyone to make the best show possible. That's part of the collaborative process."

While working in television clearly is a team effort, the producer is the leader in bringing the message to the audience. That requires the producer to have such a broad knowledge that he or she might be considered a kind of modern Renaissance person.

To provide this unity, the producer must be a leader and possess the authority, responsibility, and talent needed to plan the entire operation and make difficult decisions along the way. To fulfill this role, the television producer must know something about creative, organizational, and business aspects of television programming.

CREATIVE ASPECTS OF THE PRODUCER'S ROLE

A producer must be a creative individual—someone with a broad and varied background who is conscious of the world around him or her, sensitive to events, and able to undertake different responsibilities and varied program assignments. The producer must create a vision of the show—how it should look, how it should sound, and how it should communicate its message. Perhaps it is best summed up by producer James A. DeVinney, who says simply, "Vision is the main thing."

Unfortunately, neither vision nor creativity is easily taught. However, both bear a relationship to the diversity of one's experience and to the extent of one's preparedness. Knowing many different things allows you to "import" problem solutions from one kind of experience into a novel situation. Exhaustively researching a topic uncovers associations that may provide the framework for an idea that develops into an hour's television show. Broad backgrounds and extensive research protect you from unintentional meanings that become harmful to your intended message. Therefore, while we cannot teach you either creativity or vision, we can stress thorough preparation as a prerequisite to creative expression. This preparation extends to knowing your work, knowing the subject, and knowing the audience.

Knowing Your Work

First and foremost, the creative producer must be an effective communicator. You are dealing with people after all, and you must be able to convey ideas and enthusiasm to the production team so that each member can contribute his or her own creativity. You must motivate the unit, inspire, guide, and lead it, but most of all keep a group of diverse and sometimes temperamental people heading in the same direction toward a common goal. As one producer commented, "Producing is as much group psychology as it is television production." Remember, it is the production team that must ultimately turn your vision into a television reality. How well they do their jobs will affect the entire show and ultimately reflect on you as the producer.

Creativity requires translating a good mental concept into a good rendition in the videospace through the crew *and* the technology of television. Even though the producer may never dolly a camera, light a set, or edit a videotape, he or she must know enough about these and other production aspects to make intelligent decisions. A producer cannot earn the respect of the crew if he or she makes requests that cannot be fulfilled within the technical constraints of the medium. You also must know enough about every team member's job to understand and evaluate the contribution that each individual makes toward the entire production effort and to help you localize which production element needs attention when something in the videospace needs correcting. Finally, possessing this technical knowledge will help you

to understand the difficulty of the problems your crew solves for you so that your appreciation is genuine when the production team has been stretched to its limits and has met your demands.

Two early decisions based on the producer's knowledge of his or her work are as follows: (1) Should the show be produced inside the studio or on location? and (2) What specific production mode should be used: live, videotape, or film?

Studio versus Location   Quite often the show itself determines whether it is produced in the studio or outside on location. A baseball game, for instance, must be covered as a remote. Many other production situations, however, are not so clear-cut, and they offer the producer a number of shooting options. To use the studio or not depends on the type of show you are producing and the facilities, time, and money you have available for the production.

Studio work offers you maximum control over most production variables. Inside the studio you will not encounter cramped floor space, audio interference, weather problems, and the countless hassles that inevitably accompany location shooting. For these reasons, a studio show is usually less expensive than the same program shot on location, although there are exceptions to the rule.

However, some shows obviously benefit from outside production, especially those which require sets, props, or locations which cannot be duplicated easily in the studio. The new generation of portable production equipment has released the producer from the confines of the studio and made location shooting a realistic option. Certainly there is no way you could adequately recreate inside the studio the atmosphere of a romantic beachfront, a bustling factory, or a historical monument. However, location shooting generally increases both production costs and production time. As producer, you must decide if the trade-off in time, money, and inconvenience is worth the unique atmosphere and environment you can achieve with location shooting. Other considerations are the subject, purpose, audience, and format. Chapter 22 presents some of the specific considerations that apply to on-location production.

Producing Live   Going live is a unique combination of the very best and the very worst that television production has to offer. On the plus side is the immediacy that is available only on live television. Not only can this heighten audience interest, but the one-time-only aspect of a live show often inspires both cast and crew to superior performances because they know retakes are impossible. Since there is no postproduction on a live show, videotape recording and editing expenses are unnecessary, which eliminates postproduction costs.

On the other hand, a live show leaves no margin for error. Technical problems and production mistakes cannot be fixed by editing, and the producer generally has less control over a live production than over any other production mode. Of course, sometimes content automatically dictates whether or not a show is to be produced live. Events coverage, such as news or sports programs, are almost always produced live. Complex entertainment programs which do not require the immediacy of a live performance, are almost always recorded. If you have the option of producing live or on tape, consider the trade-offs involved. What is gained in immediacy and impact may be lost in the amount of control you can realistically expect to have over a live production.

Producing on Videotape   Videotape is by far the most commonly used production mode, and it offers the producer four different recording approaches: (1) live on tape, (2) recording in segments, (3) single camera/single VTR, and (4) multiple camera/multiple VTR. We will discuss the advantages and disadvantages of each technique in Chapter 21. Your recording approach should be based on the show's production requirements, the facilities available for production and editing, and the time and money you have to spend.

Producing on Film   With the exception of network prime-time entertainment shows and national commercials, few television programs are produced on film. Modern videotape equipment offers such increased production speed, versatility, and lower costs that most operations are only equipped with electronic gear. Nonetheless, the highest-quality "look" is still produced using motion picture film, and it must be considered for national market releases.

Knowing the Subject

As a producer of television you should be thinking about the videospace and how the story is told. However, if you ask a viewer what he or she saw on television last night, he or she will invariably describe the program content or subject. Since these are the individuals with whom your program is communicating, you too must think about program content. Program content develops from idea to execution.

Developing a Program Idea   Every program begins in a slightly different way. Some programs are assigned to producers because someone else wants it produced. For example, a local station may have sold a department store on the idea of sponsoring a series of one-hour musical programs featuring local talent. The task of developing the series concept and supervising its production is assigned to a producer. Or a station's management may wish to produce a public-affairs documentary program for a particular time slot and assigns the job to a staff producer. In corporate communications, a company may have a new product line and management asks the television production facility to prepare a program introducing it to regional sales representatives.

On other occasions, a producer may develop a show completely from scratch. Independent producers must do this continually by first trying to discern programming trends and then by developing shows which will meet the needs of potential sponsors. Also, a staff producer may simply come up with a good idea for a show or series that he or she tries to sell to management as a program possibility.

No matter how a program idea originates, the producer's job is to develop the initial concept, which usually begins as little more than a vague notion, into a viable and effective television production. To do this, the producer must move through a series of program-development steps. Although these steps may vary somewhat from program to program, for the most part, all shows travel along the same basic road from the initial idea to the completed production.

Researching the Idea   Once the producer has the basic idea for a show, the next step is to begin background research. If you are producing an informational program—a news, documentary, educational, or instructional show—the first step is a trip to the library to learn as much about the subject as possible. You also may conduct a computer search of an electronic database, such as Dialog, DataTimes®, or Nexus®. At the same time, you may wish to contact some content experts to help you focus on the important issues or to suggest additional sources for research. Local universities, public officials, professional associations, and consumer interest groups are all good resources for content specialists.

If you are producing a purely entertainment show, your research needs are somewhat different. This type of program depends largely on two important factors: (1) the script or "property" and (2) the talent. Often, one or both of these key ingredients give a program idea its audience appeal. Since the show hinges on your ability to come up with a group of acceptable performers and a worthwhile script or property, preliminary negotiations with the artists or their representatives is your first step. You will need to know immediately whether or not the talent and performance rights are available and, if so, whether you can afford to purchase them.

As you research the program concept, you must constantly ask yourself a key question: "Is this idea suitable for television and for my production situation?" Television is a visual medium and needs interesting and exciting pictures to make it most effective. Talking heads or relatively static scenes rarely play well on the screen. There are, however, some notable exceptions to this rule. Nothing could seem as nonvisual as some of the historic Congressional hearings, from the early Army-McCarthy hearings through Oliver North and Anita Hill/Clarence Thomas, yet the intense drama and impact of the hearings made them highly viewed, compelling television.

We usually think in terms of a large cast and as elaborate and realistic a set as possible for most

dramatic productions. Yet some highly dramatic shows are conceived so that the set is simple. For example, in one memorable episode of *Family Ties,* Michael J. Fox in his role as Alex Keaton moves about a cameo-lit stage as he talks to a psychiatrist about the death of a close friend. This very effective performance succeeded because it let the character work through his emotions for the audience without overly embellishing the story with elaborate skits or intricate dialogue. This does not mean that you can stand a performer on an empty set with only a blackboard and expect to produce a dazzling half hour on molecular biology. In general, look for a program idea that will lend itself to television's visual capabilities, but use your judgment in deciding when to break the rules for an exceptional idea that has the strength to maintain interest without the usual visual accompaniment.

Another important question is the extent of your production facility's resources. Some producers try to produce a show that requires the resources of Twentieth-Century Fox in a tiny studio with limited facilities. You must match your ideas with your available resources. This is not to say that you must always think small, just realistically. Given the talent, the facilities, and the means available, is your idea too ambitious to be produced well? On the other hand, what can you do to develop the show to take best advantage of television's unique qualities: its timeliness, its intimacy, and its ability to closely involve an audience in a program?

TECH TIP   The use of voice-over accompanied by panning and zooming cameras across existing photographs is one way to stretch visual resources and still produce an effective story or demonstration without elaborate studio facilities.

As the once vague program idea slowly begins to take shape, you must consider if the program topic is too broad or too narrow. A show that tries to cover too much ground can wind up sketchy and incomplete. At the same time, an idea that is too narrow or specific may turn dull and uninteresting because you have exhausted all there is to do or say about it. Also, ask yourself if you can present your program material successfully within the time allotted. Half an hour may be insufficient for some shows and too long for others.

An obvious, but often overlooked, rule is to try to work from your strengths. Some producers are more comfortable working primarily with informational programming, such as news and documentaries, whereas others may be better at dramatic or musical productions. A station also has particular strengths with respect to its facilities and resources. Maybe your station has the remote facilities and expertise to produce a regular sports series. Perhaps a local university has a number of renowned experts who could lend credibility to a talk show you are producing. A local station's strong point is often the fact that it can deal with *local* issues which are produced specifically to attract and interest an audience that simply cannot be served in the same way by the national networks regardless of their large production budgets. The point is to recognize your strengths and to try to use them whenever possible.

Every producer will tell you of the countless ideas that seemed so promising when they first came up, but which, after some background research, turned out to be totally uninteresting or unworkable. Never try to force an obviously "misfit" idea into a program. Rely on your judgment, research, and experience to tell you which ideas are suitable and which are not. The secret is to learn when to cut your losses and move on to another, perhaps more promising project or approach. The sooner you can make this important decision, the less time and expense you will waste on a program concept that simply will not work.

Knowing Your Audience

The fundamental reason for producing any show is, of course, to show it eventually to an audience. The audience's composition, program needs, and program preferences are important factors for the producer to consider at the very start of program development. Just as the public speaker selects his or her speaking approach for the audience to be addressed, so too must the producer develop a program with a *target audience* in mind. A target audience can be a rather small and specific group of people who are easily identified, or it can be a great mass of diverse individuals. Take the first instance, in which we can identify the audience. A health program, for instance, might be specifically produced to help teenagers to stop smoking. In this case, the producer knows the size and composition of the audience and can tailor the content and presentation of the program to be most effective for them.

Audience composition is not as easily defined for most broadcast programs, but even here we can begin to narrow it down somewhat. Are we producing for a national audience or for a local audience? Is the target audience mainly men, women, or children? What age? Obviously, there is a great difference in the producer's approach between the *Phil Donahue Show* and *Late Night with David Letterman*. Although they are both talk shows, the first is aimed primarily at older women, whereas the latter appeals to a younger and more contemporary audience. Novel, "off the cuff" production techniques work fine for the relaxed *Letterman* show but likely would confuse the daytime audience watching *Donahue*. As producer, therefore, you must always consider the composition of your audience and develop a show that you feel will best complement that audience's viewing needs and tastes.

Audience Research   A good producer relies heavily on his or her own instincts and experience in matching a program idea and approach to its audience. Still, "gut reactions" are not always reliable. Sometimes it is helpful to have more scientifically obtained data to use as an additional tool in analyzing audience program interests and attitudes.

Formative research techniques can be used to test specific program concepts or production approaches. The long-enduring and highly successful children's series *Sesame Street* is the product of years of elaborate audience research on children to learn the most effective ways to present material to young viewers. *Good Morning America,* a daily magazine show on ABC-TV, is another example of a show that was developed through extensive audience research. The results obtained from audience surveys and interviews played a significant role in the introduction of various program segments, the selection of regular talent for the show, and the development of kinds of program material that viewers indicated they most wanted to see. Most local news formats are designed in cooperation with program research consultants, who survey the audience in the market area and use the resulting data to develop a program style and approach that will best appeal to the station's target audience.

There is a lot of controversy over the value of various research methods for testing program concepts and audience attitudes. Some program executives make extensive use of the research data; others dismiss it as worthless. Of course, simply following a research-developed "recipe" will not guarantee you a successful show, but audience research that has been conducted, analyzed, and interpreted properly can be one of a number of useful factors that enter into program-development decisions. Figure 4-1 retraces the process for developing a program concept for television.

ORGANIZATIONAL ASPECTS OF THE PRODUCER'S ROLE

Creativity, even backed with thorough preparation, is not enough to succeed as a producer. Television is a complicated and technical medium that demands an efficient organizer to coordinate hundreds of different details. According to George Heinemann, an Emmy-winning producer, "Producing is 60 percent organization and 40 percent creativity." The point is that without the organizational ability, there is little chance you will be able to transform a creative concept into a successful television program. One of the earliest organizational elements involves writing a program proposal.

The Program Proposal

The proposal is a brief outline of the proposed program (or series) that is used by program executives in deciding whether or not to authorize you to begin production. (See Figure 4-2.)

Writing the Proposal
The proposal should reflect your knowledge of the job, content, and audience. It starts with a description of the basic

show idea, encompassing the general theme or story without details. This statement often is called the *concept*, or *premise*. Next the proposal should include the *format*, or production mode you have chosen. Finally, it should include any information which you think will help to sell the idea as unique. The last item, referred to as the program's *hook*, is often the most important because it can set your idea apart from similar ideas proposed by others. There just are not that many original ideas, and your project may be approved because you found a fresh, new angle to a standard format.

For example, when Gene Roddenberry was thinking about *Star Trek*, westerns were popular. He described his idea as a "*Wagon Train* to the stars," putting a new twist on a proven format. Other hooks might be a unique location, a popular celebrity as host, or a topic of widespread and intense audience interest. Beware of going too far in your proposal, however. Although a certain amount of "hype" is inevitable, program decision makers are intelligent and experienced executives who have heard on countless occasions why a proposed idea will make the world's greatest television show.

Proposals are required in broadcast television, where the program idea is "pitched" to a station or network buyer. In corporate or educational operations, you still should create a proposal to get your slant on the idea produced. Forcing yourself to sit down and develop a proposal will help you to better organize the program, to be more specific about the production's goals and objectives, and to communicate your concept to other production team members more effectively. If you cannot write out a clear and concise proposal, you have not adequately thought out the show.

The Production Book

While the proposal should convey all the fundamental information needed to plan your production, it lacks sufficient detail to be useful as an operational guide. The *production book* is a blueprint of the entire production process, and it offers in minute detail the who, what, when, where, and how of a production. When a producer, or his or

QUESTIONS TO ASK IN THE PROGRAM DEVELOPMENT PROCESS

1. Who is target audience?
   a. Demographics (age, gender, education, etc.)
   b. Is the audience homogeneous or heterogeneous?
2. Why should audience watch?
   a. Information, education, entertainment?
   b. To fulfill personal (relaxation, self-improvement, etc.) or organizational (training, corporate information, etc.) needs?
3. When should audience watch?
   a. Daytime, nighttime, prime time, class time, work time?
   b. Is material time-sensitive? (is material going to go "out of date" such as an election special or is the material of a long "shelf-life" such as a nature special?
4. How long should program be?
   a. Single topic series, or multipart program?
   b. Aired for half-hour, hour, or "miniseries" slot?
   c. Training module or integrate into class time?
5. What should audience watch?
   a. Is program assigned by station or organization, or is topic self-generated?
   b. Is topic of intense current interest (health, job, economy)?
   c. Is material historical or contemporary?
6. Where should ideas come from?
   a. Current media coverage (magazine, newspaper, other television).
   b. Library
   c. Interviews with subject experts
   d. Personal interest and knowledge
   e. Organization's "need to know" (e.g., new policies)
   f. Required by course content in educational setting.
7. How should program be produced?
   a. In-studio, remote, or a combination?
   b. Live or on-tape?
   c. How important is post-production editing?
   d. Single camera or multicamera?
8. What are production costs?
   a. Above-line and below-line estimates.
   b. Special prop or location costs
   c. Must transportation costs be considered?
   d. Are particular talent necessary to production at "any cost"?
9. Is the idea doable?
   a. Can you afford it?
   b. Are needed personnel available?
   c. Are facilities adequate?
   d. Do you have enough time?
   e. Can you obtain needed talent, program rights, special props and settings?
10. Can you sell the idea?
    a. Does treatment have hook to convince sponsors or decision makers?
    b. Will costs and efforts appear reasonable for benefits gained?
    c. Do you have research to back up your "gut feelings"?
    d. Can concept be visualized for benefit of decision makers?
11. How will you know if you've succeeded?
    a. Audience research (ratings and share)?
    b. Examination (training or educational material)?
    c. Call-ins (audience response)?
    d. Feedback forms (assessment of department heads, faculty or subject-matter experts).

FIGURE 4-1 Program Development Checklist. This checklist outlines a useful approach for developing an idea into a television program.

```
                    PROGRAM PROPOSAL
                          for
                       Job Fair
```

     The university's responsibility for placing its graduates is of great
importance to our students, their parents, our faculty, and the state
legislature. That "first job" is the number one priority of the nearly 8,600
students projected to graduate this Spring quarter. The three questions
uppermost in the mind of each of these graduates are: (1) What would it be
like to work in my chosen job field?, (2) What are the salary ranges offered
by the various employers in my field?, and (3) Where should I live?

     The informational program we are proposing will help answer these
questions for our graduating seniors. Job Fair, a three hour video program
will focus on the aerospace industry. It will be produced as a combination of
a 30-minute "on stage" presentation by our Career Exploration Office, a
90-minute series of short videotapes projected on the 20-foot screen in our
Student Union, and a 60-minute live audioconference with individuals
knowledgable about the aerospace industry. The union will be used for
one additional hour to answer follow-up questions from students and to coordinate
responses to requests for more information. Producing Job Fair will serve our
students most pressing need and further establish our university as a leader
in the use of telecommunications to provide student services.

     Six leading employers in the aerospace industry have been contacted and
each has agreed to furnish us with a 15-minute tape (provided on 3/4" U-Matic)
presenting their company and the job opportunities offered by it.
As importantly, each has agreed to join us in a one-hour panel session
conducted by audioconferencing on job opportunities in the aerospace
industry. Because of cost savings and the opportunity to explore a new
delivery mechanism for their recruitment efforts, these six corporations
have agreed to underwrite the audioconference costs that carry the panel
session. Our resource commitment is limited to renting the student union for
one day and some minimal "in house" costs associated with taping and
projecting the industry-provided tapes. We are asking for $1,300 to cover
the space rental, technical costs, and publicity associated with this project.

     We view this as an opportunity to pilot-test a novel concept that may
have broad application in furthering university-employer relations. Our
initial research (conducted in engineering classes) has indicated that
approximately 400 students would attend such a Job Fair if it were offered.
Our costs are very modest and the services provided our students are of
substantial benefit. Since the prospective employers also benefit, we feel
there is good potential for establishing a large scale, externally funded
program central to the mission of a Career Exploration Office in today's
recruitment environment. To assess this expectation, the College of
Engineering has agreed to support exit polling and follow-up interviews with
the participating corporations. In short, we are proposing a well-planned,
innovative use of video with a viable evaluation component.

FIGURE 4-2 **Program Proposal.**
A program proposal describes the basic idea, target audience, production approach,
and the unique concept that makes your program appealing to viewers.

her associate charged with keeping the production book up-to-date, is asked any question about the production, the answer should be available in this reference.

In addition to the proposal, the production book should include the treatment, the shooting script, complete budget information, and copies of all the various production forms, memos, and schedules which are written and distributed. A number of these essential schedules and production forms included in a production book are presented in the section on the producer in preproduction. For now, think of the production book as the "flesh and blood" of the producer's resolve to be well organized.

BUSINESS ASPECTS OF THE PRODUCER'S ROLE

The producer organizes a creative program concept within financial constraints. Whether the constraints are imposed by a television network, a local station, an independent production house, an educational institution, or your own limited financial wealth, the problems of allocating resources to produce your idea remain. Among the fundamental business aspects of the producer's role are (1) creating budgets, (2) selling your ideas, and (3) understanding contractual obligations.

Program Budgets

A *program budget* is a detailed estimate of the costs involved in producing your program. A program budget, like a household budget, is only as useful as the time and care you spend to develop it and how strictly you follow it. There are two important figures to keep in mind when you devise a budget: (1) how much money you estimate the show will cost to produce; and (2) how much money you expect to have available to produce it. Of course, the available funds must exceed the estimated costs. There is no point in attempting to produce a show unless you have enough money on hand to do the job right.

Most program budgets are divided into two sections: (1) *above-the-line costs,* which include all creative personnel, such as the costs of the producer, director, writer, and talent; and (2) *below-the-line costs,* which include the production expenses, such as the costs of personnel and technical facilities necessary to execute the production.

The sample budget in Figure 4-3 will give you an idea of how a production budget is broken down into specific categories. Sometimes a category such as "producer" includes not only an individual's salary but also staff and office expenses. The proportion of the above-line to below-line costs usually is about 45 percent of the total budget for above-the-line costs versus 55 percent for below-the-line costs. This will vary, however, depending on the particular show and its requirements. A program with expensive performers, writers, and directors will make the budget top-heavy. Shows that feature exotic locations or expensive production variables, such as sets or costumes, will inflate the below-line figure.

You will need to research your costs carefully to find out exactly what your expenses will be. All production studios have a *rate card,* which lists facilities and their costs on a per-hour and per-day basis. Various suppliers will quote you prices on such items as videotape, set construction materials, costumes, and special production equipment. If you are shooting on location, also figure in the costs of transportation, meals, and, if necessary, lodging. The trick in developing a budget is both determining *what* you need and for *how long* you will need it. You must accurately estimate the amount of time that will be spent in preproduction, rehearsal, production, and postproduction before you can figure your costs.

TECH TIP Television exposure is a valuable commodity, and you may be able to "trade out" for needed props, hotel accommodations, etc. by offering an on-air credit or "free" commercial air time. Although production budgets can be stretched considerably through trade-outs, be sure to check with station management for their approval before making any final trade-out arrangements, since they involve legal and regulatory concerns.

PROGRAM BUDGET

Program _____   Date Prepared _____

Producer _____

ABOVE-THE-LINE COSTS			
Item	Estimated Cost	Actual Cost	Under/Over
Producer			
Director			
Writer/Script			
Talent (a)			
(b)			
(c)			
(d)			
Music			
Office Overhead			
Miscellaneous (a)			
(b)			
(c)			
Pension & Welfare			
ABOVE LINE SUBTOTALS			
BELOW-THE-LINE COSTS			
Studio w/technicians			
Assistant Director			
Lighting Director			
Scenic Designer			
Set Construction			
(a) Supplies			
(b) Personnel			
Special Equipment (a)			
(b)			
(c)			
(d)			
Film Stock			
Videotape Stock			
Wardrobe			
Props			

FIGURE 4-3 Program Budget.
A budget must be accurate to be useful. It often is divided into above-line and below-line costs.
Figure continues on page 88.

Location Expenses			
(a) Food			
(b) Lodging			
(c) Transportation			
Graphics			
Videotape Editing & Postproduction			
Miscellaneous (a)			
(b)			
(c)			
(d)			
Contingency			
Union Benefits			
BELOW-THE-LINE SUBTOTALS			
ABOVE-THE-LINE SUBTOTALS			
PRODUCTION TOTALS			

The most essential part of developing a budget is to remember to include all the necessary items. Such additional expenses as pension and welfare payments for union employees and insurance and transportation costs must always be included in your budget. Once you have worked up all the items you think you will need, add another 10 or 15 percent for "contingencies." Remember Murphy's law: If something can go wrong, it will. The contingency pad will come in handy for emergencies or if you encounter some unexpected cost overruns.

It is difficult to overemphasize how important a role the budget plays in determining the final program. Although the budget may appear as only a series of numbers on a sheet of paper, in reality the budget determines—long before you ever enter the studio—exactly what you can or cannot do from a creative standpoint. Given a certain amount of money, it is up to the producer to allocate it intelligently. You can devote more money to providing increased production time in the studio, but the trade-off might be less editing time during postproduction. There is only one hard-and-fast rule about budgets: They are never large

enough. One of the producer's most difficult and important jobs is knowing where to spend—and where not to spend—so that the final product is as good as can possibly be accomplished given the limitations of the working budget.

At many smaller studios and stations, the producer's budget concentrates on expendable supplies and outside costs which are above and beyond normal salaries and overhead expenses. Small operations still require the producer to prepare a budget, since staff and production facilities assigned to one project are unavailable for other work assignments. Although such a budget consists mainly of "paper money," it gives the producer and station management a good idea of how much of the station's resources are expended on a particular program or project.

It is a good idea to develop an estimated budget before the production and an actual budget afterward to reflect the real costs of production. By comparing the two budgets, you can see where your estimates were significantly over or under the show's actual expenses. This information is helpful in preparing a more accurate budget the next time around.

Budgeting Software Computers have become invaluable to producers in preparing and updating budgets—as well as managing production schedules, making script revisions, and keeping up with other necessary paperwork.

Electronic spreadsheet programs such as *Excel* and *Lotus* 1-2-3- are invaluable aids in budgeting. Some programs have been designed specifically for film and television producers. Popular production software includes The Production Manager, Budget Master, and Movie Magic Budgeting. (See Figure 4-4.)

Computer programs allow you to ask "What if?" questions and recalculate budgets instantaneously. They also provide a standardized format to follow in subsequent productions. Using an electronic budgeting program will reduce the time it takes you to prepare your program proposals and make it much easier to update them as new elements enter the picture.

Selling Your Ideas

Once you have written the proposal and developed an estimated budget, you should be prepared to make a formal presentation to station management or to other executive decision makers who must give their approval before production can begin. The presentation is an opportunity

for you to expand on the information in the proposal and to convey personally your enthusiasm for the project. It also gives executives an opportunity to hear about the production directly from the producer and to raise any questions or objections. Quite often you, as a producer, are as much on display as your program idea. If you can show others that you have done your homework and are thoroughly prepared, you greatly improve the chances for approval. We cannot emphasize too much the importance of writing and presentational skills in producing for television.

It is quite possible that during the presentation a number of changes or revisions in the original idea will be requested. Your program budget may be too high; part of the show may not be completely acceptable; a production facility you expect to use may not be available. These problems are usually solved through compromise, but the one area on which to remain firm is the production budget. You may have added some extra expenses which are not essential and can be traded away during negotiations, but you also should have in your mind the rock-bottom figure that you think necessary to bring in a program of sufficient

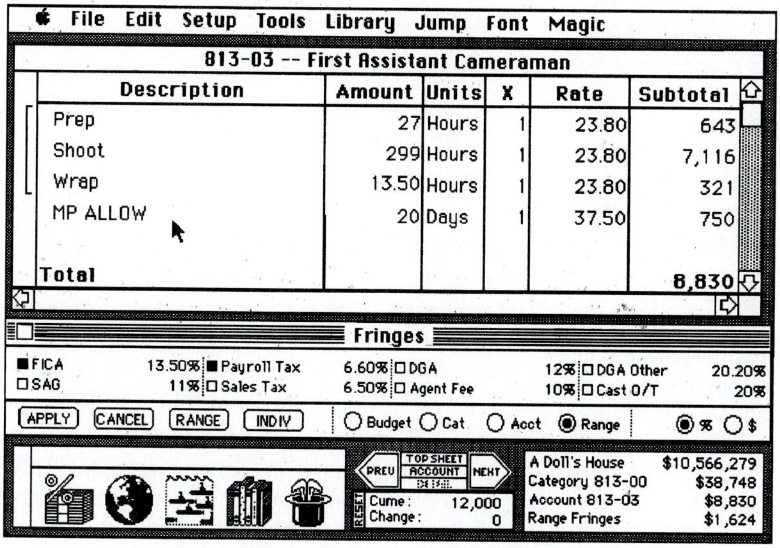

Movie Magic Budgeting (Mac Screen) • Detailed Account

FIGURE 4-4   Production Software.
Computer spreadsheets and production software have made it easier to prepare and keep track of budgets during production. (*Courtesy: Screenplay Systems.*)

quality. If you agree to a severe budget slash, you may have to totally revise your production concept or risk running out of money before the show is completed. Even if you can finish the show within the reduced budget, the shortcuts and compromises you may be forced to make can seriously damage production values. If you believe your budget is accurate and fair, stick with it. You will be better off not doing the show at all than risking an inferior production with an insufficient budget. Remember that the audience, the final decision maker, only sees the final program, and the audience does not care how little it cost to produce the show if it does not interest them.

TECH TIP   The producer should often *request* a presentation to more senior management rather than view it as an onerous obligation. Not only does management's approval "spread the risk," but it also involves management in the process. If you succeed, your subsequent presentations will be looked on more favorably.

Contractual Obligations

The creation of a television production involves working with many different people and creative or intellectual properties such as scripts, musical scores, and perhaps previously produced visual images. The contractual obligations that cover these important aspects of television production can involve large amounts of the producer's time. The following subsections describe some of the contractual obligations a producer must consider in bringing a product to the air.

Personnel   Even if your production is being conducted as a class project within a college or university studio, you should approach the relationships among crew members seriously. While there is seldom a need to be concerned with the legality of contractual obligations with members of your studio crew in a class project, the success of the team's effort still depends on crew members understanding their obligations and accepting re-

sponsibility for meeting them. In the case of talent who appear on camera, it is always a good idea, regardless of the scope of your program, to get signed model releases. And certainly when you find yourself working in professional environments, contracts with both crew and cast assume great importance.

At many stations and production facilities across the country, some of the staff and freelance positions are represented by unions or guilds which negotiate wage and working agreements with management. Since these contracts have a direct impact on both your program budget and the production operation, you ought to become familiar with some of the largest and most representative unions.

Talent Unions   Many above-line personnel belong to the following unions.

> *American Federation of Radio and Television Artists (AFTRA)*. This union represents radio and television talent (announcers, newscasters, reporters, sports commentators, singers, dancers, comedians) who appear on live or videotaped programs and commercials. AFTRA may also represent directors, assistant directors, and floor managers.

> *Screen Actors Guild (SAG)*. This union represents performers in all filmed television programs and commercials and on some videotaped productions as well. SAG agreements are in effect primarily in the major film production centers of Los Angeles and New York.

Both unions have a minimum wage for employees called *scale*. Of course, better-known or principal performers are commonly paid much more than scale. A major distinction in AFTRA salaries is between "under five" and "over five" performers. "Under five" performers are those who have less than five lines of dialogue, and their scale is lower than that for artists with more dialogue.

> *American Federation of Musicians (AFM)*. This union represents all musicians working in television production. The AFM is a national organization with various local chapters in the largest cities.

Directors' Guild of America (DGA). This union represents program directors, assistant directors, floor managers, and at some stations, production assistants in both film and television. In addition to stipulating scale wages for staff and free-lance directors, the DGA contract spells out working and travel conditions, fringe benefits, and the director's "creative rights" on a production.

Writers' Guild of America (WGA) represents television scriptwriters for live, tape, and television film production. In addition to basic wage agreements, the complex WGA contract stipulates the residual payment fees for reruns and specifies the "creative rights" and screen credits to which a writer is entitled.

Technical Unions Many below-line personnel are members of these unions. This is particularly true in New York and Los Angeles. Even as an independent producer in a secondary market, you may find yourself working with union personnel in commercial and dramatic productions for large market release.

National Association of Broadcast Employees and Technicians (NABET). NABET currently represents all NBC and ABC network technical personnel.

International Brotherhood of Electrical Workers (IBEW). The IBEW represents all CBS network technical personnel. Both NABET and IBEW also represent technicians at various stations throughout the country.

International Association of Theatrical and Stage Employees (IATSE). IATSE represents stage hands, carpenters, lighting grips, and some film crews at all three networks, as well as some television crew members at various stations.

Unions negotiate highly intricate agreements that specify each union's jurisdiction over equipment operation and working conditions. In addition to establishing basic wage and salary scales, the contracts stipulate overtime for extended work hours, the way in which employees can be scheduled, "penalty" fees for violating union work agreements, the timing of meal and rest breaks, and a host of other details.

Copyright Clearances

The performance rights to copyrighted audio and visual material are protected under the law. In order to use the material legally, the producer must arrange for permission from, and in many cases payment to, the copyright holders or their agents.

ASCAP and BMI Two major organizations—ASCAP (American Society of Composers, Authors and Publishers) and BMI (Broadcast Music Incorporated)—serve as clearinghouses for music performance rights. Virtually every tune that is written and performed is registered with one of these organizations, which, in turn, licenses all radio and television stations to use the music. The stations pay a yearly fee determined by the size and income of the station. The blanket fee permits the station to use any, or all, of the organization's musical catalogue during the year.

Production Music Music that is written and recorded especially for production use is also covered under copyright law. The purchase price of the record may not cover performance rights. It is best to check with the production music company to determine exact details about performance rights and fees.

At most operations, the producer is required to submit a music performance form after each show indicating all the ASCAP, BMI, and other music organizations' tunes used. These include not only major performances, but also theme, background, and incidental music. You can learn the organization which holds the rights by checking the record label.

Visual Material A number of organizations such as Black Star Photo work with a variety of visual artists to market their works. These photo libraries hold copyrights to still and motion images arranged by topic. For a fee, these visuals can be included in your television production. Other good sources of visuals are the Library of Congress and local historical societies. Other visual works are copyrighted by the creator independently. The copyright holder is referenced next to the © of a copyrighted work.

THE PRODUCER IN PRODUCTION

The role and personality of the producer are intimately involved in each of the four production stages, lend continuity to the entire show, and keep it moving toward the objectives outlined during the preproduction planning stages. The producer is naturally concerned with several important production decisions simultaneously, but in order to present these logically, we will have to deal with each one separately. Keep in mind, though, that in a real-life situation, events are rarely as well organized and as clear-cut as we have made them seem here.

Preproduction

Planning For the producer, preproduction planning is the busiest and most important part of the entire production. This is when the program concept is refined and focused, when the show's overall objectives are established and communicated to the production staff, and when the entire production effort is planned and coordinated. The better the job of planning and organizing now, the more smoothly will the production proceed.

During preproduction, the producer is concerned with countless details. Some are crucial; some are less important. At this point you must begin to delegate authority to your staff. You must naturally be fully involved in the important decisions about the script, the direction, the casting, and the budget, but let someone else order the coffee and doughnuts. As Bob Shanks, a network producer and program executive, has written, "There is a high risk of bruising necessary objectivity by getting too close to production. A producer must learn to protect his senses. The first

and best advice is to let other people do their jobs. If a producer is writing the jokes, mouthing the dialogue, painting the set, adjusting the lights, moving the props, and seating the audience, he is likely to develop calluses on his sensitivity. . . ."[1] As a producer, your most important function is to develop the program concept and then hire people you trust to do their jobs. There is simply too much to do for any one person to attempt it all. Veteran producer George Heinemann suggests that in the long run, the producer must be concerned primarily with those elements which will appear onscreen and affect what the audience sees. Select your production team carefully, explain what you want, and trust them to do their jobs for you. You will find that if you communicate your concept to others and give them the opportunity and freedom to contribute their ideas as well, you will wind up with a happier and more productive staff—and ultimately, a better show. As producer, you will be able to direct your attention to those production elements which most need your time during preproduction—the script, the director, casting, and preparing the production notebook.

The Program Script As discussed in Chapter 3, the foundation of every show is the program script. Of course, sports or events coverage has no detailed script, but you will still need someone to outline the production and to provide background material for the director and talent to use in formulating the coverage and on-camera commentary. Even on such ad-libbed interview programs as the *Tonight Show,* a staff of writers is assigned to research and preinterview guests and then to prepare a series of questions for the host to use on the air.

Because the script is so fundamental to the production, some producers prefer to write the show themselves. These "hyphenates" (so-called because of their title: writer-producer) are often found on comedy, dramatic, or documentary programs. If the producer does not write the script, then either a staff writer must be assigned to the production or a free-lance writer must be hired from the outside. If you are working on a program with historical, technical, or scientific subject mat-

[1]Shanks, Bob (1976). *The Cool Fire.* New York: Norton, p. 10.

ter, you also may wish to hire an outside content specialist who can serve as a consultant to the writer and producer. The job of the content specialist is to help develop the program's focus and to verify facts and information in the script.

A producer of an ongoing series which involves a number of different writers will sometimes develop a "writer's bible." This is a detailed explanation of the show's premise and objectives and a description of the major characters in the show. The "bible" serves as the writer's basic reference and eliminates the need for the producer to sit down with every new writer to explain the show's style and approach.

Almost every television script goes through a series of revisions and rewrites before it is produced. Even the best-written script may have problems with characterization, exposition, sequence, or style. Sometimes the writer's imagination may wind up costing more money than the budget will allow, and the producer will ask for certain scenes to be eliminated, for a number of different characters to be combined into a single role, or for an exotic location to be changed to one that is more accessible and less costly. At some stations and at the commercial networks the final script also must be approved by "program practices," which checks for offensive or inappropriate material and for possible legal problems.

Once the writer has responded to the producer's suggestions and has submitted a second draft, the producer may wish to hold a script conference with the writer, the director, and key production members. The director may offer some suggestions or point out potential production problems. The set and lighting designers can begin to use the script to formulate rough ideas on how to approach scenery and lighting. At this point be sure you have read through the script for running time. If it is too short, material must be added. If it is too long, the writer must make some cuts.

After the script revisions and "polishes" are completed, the final approved version becomes the shooting script. It is typed, duplicated, and distributed to the members of the production team. However, this does not mean that the script is not revised any further. Almost every show makes script changes throughout rehearsal and even into production, and the writer is often asked

to remain available for quick revisions. Some even set up a word processor in the studio so they can more easily work on the necessary rewrites during rehearsal and production.

Selecting a Director   Except for the producer, the program's director is the most important member of the production team. While the producer's job is to develop the idea and to supervise the production, the director must interpret and execute the producer's concept into the actual show. As the producer, you make an extremely important decision when you select a director for a production. Producer Norman Lear has said that the people he has selected to direct his various programs have each made a distinctive mark on the overall style and approach of every show.

The person you select to direct your show ought to be one with whom you can work closely and whose talents and abilities you trust and respect. The latter is particularly important because there will be times when the producer and director come into direct conflict over how to approach or interpret elements in the show. A good producer should always be open-minded about any suggestion, especially when it comes from the director. After all, the director is a creative and imaginative artist who might bring a fresher and more interesting perspective to the show than the one you had in mind.

As soon as the director joins the production, he or she becomes involved in almost all preproduction meetings, especially those dealing with the script, casting, and production. The director's first job is usually to read and carefully analyze the script, consider any potential production problems, and suggest possible solutions or script improvements. We will describe the complete directing process in Chapter 5.

Casting   Selecting talent for a production is always an important job, and this applies to nondramatic as well as dramatic roles. Casting even as deceptively simple a part as the narrator or on-camera teacher in an instructional production must be done with care. The talent onscreen will have to carry much of the show and contributes enormously to a program's success or failure. Good television talent is never easy to find. The performer must be comfortable in the role, be able to work on a studio set with all its distractions, and still relate well to the viewing audience.

Many variables enter into casting decisions: the availability of performers or actors, the costs of their salaries, and whether they look and sound "right" for the show. The director will usually assist the producer during casting, since he or she must ultimately work closely with the talent during rehearsal and production.

There are a number of ways to go about casting. If you can pay for performers, contacting talent agents is usually the best approach. These agencies generally profile their collection of talent and can provide photographs and the work experience of their artists. Advertising open auditions will usually produce a large number of eager applicants, but you must be prepared to spend time wading through countless try-outs before you find performers who are right for your program. If your budget is limited and you are unable to pay for talent, try some of the community theater groups and university drama departments, which often have a large pool of interested volunteers willing to trade their talent for television exposure.

Production Book   With the program script either finished or in final revision, the director assigned to the show, and work begun on various production elements, the producer must now coordinate the many complex operations that go into a television program. There is no way you can keep all this information in your head (even if you wanted to), so the producer must begin to work out production scheduling and organization on paper.

One reason producing may have appealed to you is the ability to work in a creative environment without the paper-pushing tedium associated with many desk jobs. However, the amount of information a producer must deal with and the communication and coordination between so many different people are so enormous that organizing on paper is the only practical way to get the job done. Paperwork is rarely fun, but if it is done care-

fully and accurately, it will save you much time and aggravation later on during rehearsal, production, and postproduction.

The *production book* is the producer's "bible," reference, and security blanket all rolled into a large loose-leaf binder. Most producers prefer to use a loose-leaf notebook so they can add or remove pages easily. Your production book should contain just about every piece of information you are likely to need about the show. What to include and how to arrange your production book is a matter of individual taste and habit, but most producers include the shooting script, complete budget information, and copies of all the various production forms, memos, and schedules which are written and distributed. The following schedules and production forms are examples of the kinds of material most often included in a production book. (See Figure 4-5.)

MASTER PRODUCTION SCHEDULE   The master production schedule is designed to give you an overview of the entire production. Every producer has a different method of outlining the master schedule. Some even prefer to mount it on a large bulletin board on the office wall and tack color-coded index cards on it for various activities. However, when you need to refer to it outside the production office, having a copy of the master schedule in your production book is a great convenience.

The master schedule includes every production operation which must be completed: what is to be done, who is to do it, when its completion is expected, and how it is to be integrated into the show. A television production involves many separate activities which proceed independently, but they must all come together precisely on schedule and in the proper sequence. Unless the set is constructed, lighting cannot be hung and focused. Pretaped insert segments must be produced and edited before they can be used in the actual production. Music, graphics, costumes, and props must all be ready by rehearsal time. The master schedule will help you to keep track of a large number of operations and to check on the show's progress and possible trouble spots before they become serious problems. (See Figure 4-6.)

CAST/CREW SHEET   As its name suggests, the cast/crew sheet is a complete listing of the names, phone numbers, and addresses of everyone in-

ELEMENTS OF A PRODUCTION BOOK

Master Production Schedule—provides overview of entire production

Cast/Crew List—lists names, phone numbers, and addresses of all involved in the show

Rehearsal Schedule—lists day, time, and location for all production rehearsals

Fax Sheet (Facilities sheet)—details all production facilities needed for show

Ops Sheet (operational schedule)—lists technical equipment and technical personnel needed for the show

Call Sheet—tells cast members where to be and when to be there for both rehearsal and production

Shooting Schedule—indicates the order in which specific scenes will be shot and the times scheduled for their completion

Release Forms and Permits—permission slips for copyright, parking, and other legal aspects of a production

FIGURE 4-5 Production Book.
The production book should contain all the necessary details to produce a show.

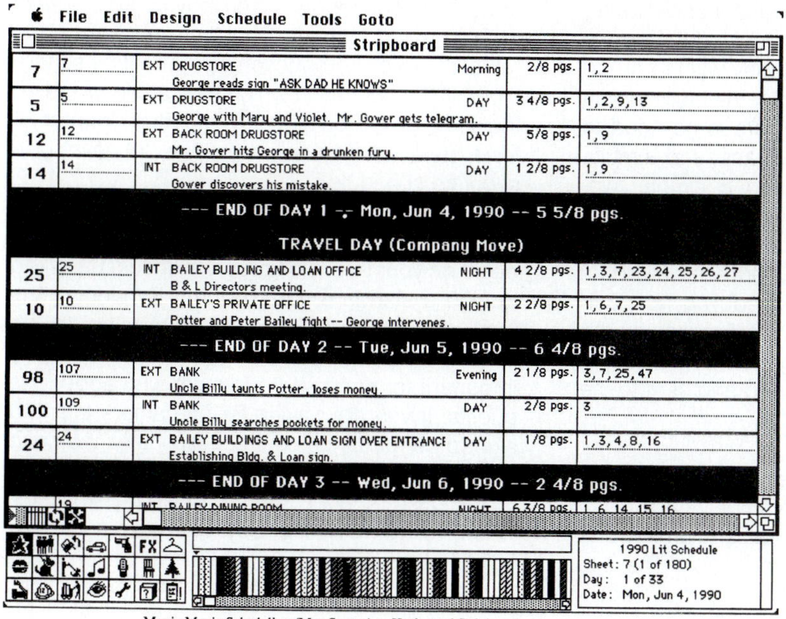

File Edit Design Schedule Tools Goto

Stripboard

7	7	EXT	DRUGSTORE	Morning	2/8 pgs.	1, 2
			George reads sign "ASK DAD HE KNOWS"			
5	5	EXT	DRUGSTORE	DAY	3 4/8 pgs.	1, 2, 9, 13
			George with Mary and Violet. Mr. Gower gets telegram.			
12	12	EXT	BACK ROOM DRUGSTORE	DAY	5/8 pgs.	1, 9
			Mr. Gower hits George in a drunken fury.			
14	14	INT	BACK ROOM DRUGSTORE	DAY	1 2/8 pgs.	1, 9
			Gower discovers his mistake.			

--- END OF DAY 1 -- Mon, Jun 4, 1990 -- 5 5/8 pgs.

TRAVEL DAY (Company Move)

25	25	INT	BAILEY BUILDING AND LOAN OFFICE	NIGHT	4 2/8 pgs.	1, 3, 7, 23, 24, 25, 26, 27
			B & L Directors meeting.			
10	10	EXT	BAILEY'S PRIVATE OFFICE	NIGHT	2 2/8 pgs.	1, 6, 7, 25
			Potter and Peter Bailey fight -- George intervenes.			

--- END OF DAY 2 -- Tue, Jun 5, 1990 -- 6 4/8 pgs.

98	107	EXT	BANK	Evening	2 1/8 pgs.	3, 7, 25, 47
			Uncle Billy taunts Potter, loses money.			
100	109	INT	BANK	DAY	2/8 pgs.	3
			Uncle Billy searches pockets for money.			
24	24	EXT	BAILEY BUILDINGS AND LOAN SIGN OVER ENTRANCE	DAY	1/8 pgs.	1, 3, 4, 8, 16
			Establishing Bldg. & Loan sign.			

--- END OF DAY 3 -- Wed, Jun 6, 1990 -- 2 4/8 pgs.

| 19 | | INT | BAILEY DINING ROOM | NIGHT | 6 3/8 pgs. | 1, 6, 14, 15, 16 |

1990 Lit Schedule
Sheet: 7 (1 of 180)
Day: 1 of 33
Date: Mon, Jun 4, 1990

Movie Magic Scheduling (Mac Screen) • Horizontal Stripboard

FIGURE 4-6 Scheduling Software.
Electronic scheduling software has made it easier to update the master production schedule. (*Courtesy: Screenplay Systems.*)

volved with the show. In the case of remote productions, it includes everyone's hotel address and phone number as well.

REHEARSAL SCHEDULE   The rehearsal schedule lists the day, time, and location for all production rehearsals. Usually, *dry rehearsals*—preliminary rehearsals without any cameras or costumes—are held outside the production studio in a rehearsal hall, an office, or some other rented space. That is why it is important to be specific about the location of each rehearsal session.

The schedule also should indicate which parts of the show will be covered during each rehearsal session and those cast/crew members expected to attend. You may not need everyone present if you intend to rehearse only a portion of the show during a rehearsal period. On complicated shows, the director may wish such key production team members as the assistant director, floor manager, and audio technician to attend a final dry rehearsal. (See Figure 4-7.)

FAX SHEET   The facilities, or "FAX," sheet is a detailed description of all the production facilities required for your show. The producer and director run down the FAX sheet and check off the equipment and technical personnel they wish to order. Of course, someone must pay for the facilities you request, so act reasonably. There is no need to ask for five cameras, a studio crane, and a multitrack audiotape recorder to do a simple two-person interview show. (See Figure 4-8.)

The information on the FAX sheet is needed by a number of different studio departments (production, engineering, traffic and scheduling, accounting, set and scenery, lighting, and so on), so the FAX sheet is often a multipage form. Each duplicate page is usually color-coded and sent to the appropriate department.

OPERATIONAL SCHEDULE   The operational schedule, or "ops sheet," as it is commonly called, is a rundown of the studio technical equipment and personnel assigned to the production. The ops sheet contains a description of every studio activity (setup, camera, blocking, taping), its scheduled time, the technical personnel required, the equipment that has been ordered on the FAX sheet, and any additional personnel, such as wardrobe, costumers, and makeup artists. The sample in Figure 4-9 will give you an idea of an ops sheet's content and layout.

CALL SHEET   The call sheet is generally reserved for cast members and indicates when and where they are expected both for rehearsal and for production. Be sure to consider makeup, costume, and transportation time when you work out your call sheet. For instance, if you want your performers in front of the camera by 9 A.M., you may need to call them for 8:15 A.M., so they have time to put on their makeup and costumes and still make the 9 A.M. camera call.

SHOOTING SCHEDULE   If your show is produced either live or live on tape, the shooting schedule is simply the program's rundown sheet, since everything occurs in normal sequence. However, if you are taping the program out of sequence, you must devise a shooting schedule to indicate the specific scenes which are to be shot and the day and the times for which they are scheduled. The shooting schedule should be arranged carefully to make the most efficient use of your cast, crew, and production facilities. You may be able to save both time and money on costly talent and on the rental of special production equipment by scheduling all the scenes in which they are involved on the same day. (See Figure 4-10.) (See Chapter 21 for a detailed discussion on how to develop a shooting schedule.)

RELEASE FORMS AND PERMITS   Everyone who appears on your television program should be asked to sign a standard release form. By signing the form, the individual grants permission to be photographed on television. This is especially important for nonpaid performers who appear as guests. If you are paying for on-camera talent, a signed performance contract eliminates the need for a release form.

You also should secure written permission whenever you utilize a copyrighted work such as still photographs, clips from films or television shows, illustrations, and so on. Even productions

REHEARSAL SCHEDULE

PRODUCTION TITLE: STARRY NIGHT

DIRECTOR: Robin Tellman

PRODUCER: William Rogers

Monday, Sept. 30th	9:00-12:00	Entire Cast Readthrough	REHEARSAL
	12:00-1:00	LUNCH BREAK	HALL #1
	1:00-2:30	BLOCK ACT I-Bill, Robert, Eileen, Paul	
	2:30-5:00	BLOCK ACT II-Bill, Eileen, Sandy, Karen	
Tuesday, Oct. 1	9:00-12:00	RUN THROUGH ACT I-Bill, Robert, Eileen, Paul	REHEARSAL
	12:00-1:00	LUNCH BREAK	HALL #1
	1:00-4:00	RUN THROUGH ACT II-Bill, Eileen, Sandy, Karen	
	4:00-5:00	RUN THROUGH COMPLETE SHOW-Entire Cast	
Wednesday, Oct. 2	STUDIO REHEARSAL-PRODUCTION STUDIO "C"		
	9:00-12:00	CAMERA BLOCK ACT I-Bill, Robert, Eileen, Paul	
	12:00-1:00	LUNCH BREAK	
	1:00-4:00	CAMERA BLOCK ACT II-Bill, Eileen, Sandy, Karen	
	4:00-5:00	NOTES-Entire Cast	
Thursday, Oct. 3	STUDIO REHEARSAL-PRODUCTION STUDIO "C"		
	9:00-12:00	RUN THROUGH ACT I-Bill, Robert, Eileen, Paul	
	12:00-1:00	LUNCH BREAK	
	1:00-3:00	RUN THROUGH ACT II-Bill, Eileen, Sandy, Karen	
	3:00-4:00	NOTES AND COSTUMES AND MAKEUP-Entire Cast	
	4:00-5:00	DRESS REHEARSAL	
	5:00-6:00	NOTES	

FIGURE 4-7 **Rehearsal Schedule.**
The rehearsal schedule lists location and time for all rehearsals and those cast
members who should attend.

PRODUCTION FACILITIES REQUEST FORM

Date: _____

Production: _____   Prod. Number _____

Producer: _____   Director: _____

Day/Date Requested: _____ Time From _____ to _____

FACILITIES   ( ) STUDIO SETUP/LIGHT ONLY   ( ) CONTROL ROOM ONLY   ( ) STUDIO & CONTROL

CAMERAS   Mounting   Lenses   Cable Length (if other than normal)
1. _____
2. _____
3. _____
4. _____

AUDIO

Microphones: (1) _____   (3) _____   (5) _____
(Type &
Number)   (2) _____   (4) _____   (6) _____

Boom: _____   Studio Flr Speaker _____   Other _____

TELECINE   (1) ( ) 35 mm Slide   ( ) 16 mm film   ( ) Super 8 mm

(2) ( ) 35 mm Slide   ( ) 16 mm film   ( ) Super 8 mm

( ) Interlock

VIDEOTAPE   Time From _____ to_____ RECORD   ( ) $1/2$-inch   ( ) 1 inch   ( ) $3/4$ cassette

Time From _____ to_____ PLYBK   ( ) $1/2$-inch   ( ) 1 inch   ( ) $3/4$ cassette

( ) TBC

MISCELLANEOUS
( ) Char. Gen

( ) Video Monitors (number and location) _____

( ) Other _____

_____

LOGGED _____ Engineering   _____ Production   _____ Traffic

OPERATIONAL SCHEDULE—"MUSICMAKERS"

THURSDAY, MARCH 18	STUDIO #1
LOAD-IN, SETUP, LIGHT	7:00 AM - 10:00 AM
ENGINEERING SETUP	10:00 AM - 10:00 AM
CAMERA BLOCK	10:30 AM - 12:30 PM
LUNCH BREAK	12:30 PM - 1:30 PM
CAMERA BLOCK	1:30 PM - 3:00 PM
NOTES & RESET, MAKEUP	3:00 PM - 3:30 PM
DRESS REHEARSAL	3:45 PM - 4:15 PM
NOTES & RESET, MAKEUP	4:15 PM - 5:00 PM
TAPE	5:00 PM - 5:30 PM
PICKUPS	5:30 PM - 6:00 PM
STRIKE	6:00 PM - 7:00 PM

ENGINEERING PERSONNEL   (7:00 AM - 7:00 PM)

1 TD	3 CAMERA OPERATORS
1 LIGHTING DESIGNER	2 CAMERA ASST/ASST FM
1 AUDIO	1 BOOM OPERATOR
1 VIDEO	

ENGINEERING EQUIPMENT   (STUDIO AT 7:00 AM)

3 CAMERAS ON PEDS

1 MOLE BOOM

(2) 1-INCH VTRs   (FAX ORDERED FROM 4:30 PM - 6:00 PM)

PRODUCTION PERSONNEL   (9:00 AM - 6:00 PM)

1 ASST DIRECTOR

1 FLOOR MANAGER

1 MAKEUP/WARDROBE/PROPS

FIGURE 4-9 **Ops Sheet.**
The ops sheet (operational schedule) lists the needed equipment and technical personnel.

FIGURE 4-8 **FAX Sheet.** (Facing page)
The FAX sheet (facilities schedule) details the production facilities needed for a show.

99

TITLE "The Dancers" TAPING SCHEDULE

PROD. NO' 5.32-11 PAGE 2 OF 8

DIRECTOR Robinson P.A. ______ A.D. ______ U.M. ______

DAY, DATE AND TIME	SCENE, SETUPS AND DESCRIPTION	D/N INT/EXT	LOCATION AND CAST	SET PIECES AND EQUIPMENT
MONDAY, JAN 29				
9:00 AM	SCENE #18-Dance Rehearsal	D/I	DANCE SCHOOL Robert Jill Martha All Dancers	LIGHTING MUST BE SETUP AND READY
9:45	SCENE #32-Robert & Jill Fight	D/I	DANCE SCHOOL Robert Jill	
10:30 A	SCENE #33-Jill & Martha Find Out	D/I	Jill Martha George	
12:00-1:00	LUNCH BREAK			
1:00 P	SCENE #35 Robert & Jill Together	D/E	OUTSIDE SCHOOL Robert Jill	REFLECTORS, BOOSTER LIGHT, TAXI & SUITCASES
2:30	SCENE #1-Jill Arrives at Dance School	D/E	OUTSIDE Jill Martha	TAXI-Same Lighting
3:00 P	SCENE #1A-Dancers outside School	D/E	Dancers-	Same Lighting

FIGURE 4-10 Shooting Schedule.
The shooting schedule indicates specific scenes to be shot and the dates and times of shooting. An efficient shooting schedule considers performer and location availabilities, necessary sets, and the requirements of the shooting script.

designed only for closed-circuit distribution are subject to limitations on the use of copyright material. Before you plan to make a slide from an illustration in a book or use a clip from a film which is available, make certain the proper permission has been obtained, and always file a release form to protect yourself should any question arise later.

Most cities require a production unit to obtain a police permit before shooting on remote locations. This does not apply to news crews (who already have a police press pass), but to more elaborate production crews that will be working in a public area for an extended period of time. The permit authorizes you to shoot on public property, provides a parking area for your production vehicles, and sometimes includes police assistance for traffic and crowd control. Check local regulations for the permit requirements in your area.

The details that concern producers during preproduction will vary, depending on several factors, such as the type of program, whether it is live or on tape, and whether it is in the studio or on location. For example, a field producer will need to conduct a site survey and may have to obtain a location agreement and public permit to be able to shoot at a specific location. A news producer may have to arrange for remote equipment, such as a cellular phone or satellite uplink for a live feed. We will take a closer look at video field production in Chapter 22.

Production Meetings   Throughout the entire preproduction phase, the producer is involved in a countless series of production meetings. Often these include only the producer, director, and a key production team member to discuss a specific area of the production, such as set design, the script, or casting.

A number of preproduction meetings, however, must be larger and should include all the key production team members. This is when the various facets of a production must be integrated so that all subsequent planning and execution will be based on the overall program objectives, which are understood by the entire production team.

Of course, some regularly scheduled programs require fewer production meetings because everyone's role has been defined over a period of time. A show that is produced completely from scratch would naturally require more meetings, since everyone is essentially working on the project for the first time.

Regardless of how many or how few production meetings are scheduled, some meeting of the minds among the key production team members is absolutely essential to ensure a coordinated and cohesive effort once the project moves into the setup and rehearsal and production stages.

Setup and Rehearsal

As the production moves into the setup and rehearsal stage, the producer's emphasis shifts from attention to specific details toward the

broader task of integrating all the production elements. By this time, specific production details are covered mainly by the production team members working in their respective areas: The director rehearses the cast and prepares the camera shots; the audio technician designs the audio pickup for the show; the scenic designer supervises the construction of the set; and so on.

The actual rehearsal is a crucial time when the show should begin to take shape. Before long it will be too late to make any major changes in the production, so the producer must watch each run-through with a critical eye. This is when he or she must become the "surrogate audience," watching and reacting to the program as the viewer would. As rehearsals continue, the producer watches the line monitor and makes copious notes on all the production aspects that need attention. These include the direction and camera shots, performances, sets and lighting, costumes and makeup, audio, music, and sound effects. Between run-throughs, the producer gives notes to the appropriate team members. Use discretion, however, in when and how to give notes. The first rough camera run-through is hardly the time to expect perfection, and the entire production team is better left alone until everyone settles down a bit.

While the producer watches the program monitor, he or she also must keep an eye on the studio clock. It is not uncommon for a director and cast to become so engrossed in a particular problem that they spend far too much time on what is basically a minor part of a much larger show. If your director lingers at one point in the production for too long, discreetly remind him or her to keep moving and to return to the problem later as time permits. You ought to have some idea of how much the director should accomplish—so many script pages, a number of scenes, and so on—during each rehearsal session so you do not wind up with a show that has been only half-rehearsed.

By the end of the rehearsal stage, the program should begin to look and sound the way the producer had envisioned it. During the final run-through before dress rehearsal, look carefully and critically at the entire production. To give you an idea of the kinds of things a producer looks for during a final run-through, here is how Paul Rauch ran a notes session with his key production personnel from *Another World*.

The program is a one-hour weekday drama produced in segments on tape. Since it is a continuing series, the entire production team works together closely every day, so everyone involved is already familiar with the show and with the program's basic objectives.

As producer, Rauch busies himself with a variety of details and problems during the morning, turning his attention specifically to the day's show at run-through time. He watches from his office on a conventional television receiver. By not watching from the control booth, he avoids its distractions and is able to gauge more realistically the program's impact on a home audience.

As the run-through proceeds, Rauch jots down many notes and suggestions on virtually every aspect of the show. His eye is critical, picking up subtle problems or inconsistencies which would probably have gone unnoticed by most viewers, yet taken as a whole, his comments and suggestions improve the entire production.

At one point Rauch noticed that the lighting in a scene appeared too intense on an actor, and he asked the lighting director to correct it. The background area of another set appeared too dark, and this also was noted. Rauch wanted one character to use a hand prop for some added business during a scene. Since the character was a wealthy businessman, it was decided to use a copy of the *Wall Street Journal*. A boom shadow appeared during an actor's cross to a chair, and this was noted for both audio and lighting. A variety of notes concerning performances was given to the program's director. Some covered minor nuances in voice or inflection; others were more substantial changes, such as a better way to establish a relationship between two characters. Costume problems were noted, and Rauch ordered an actress playing a scene in a garden to wear gardening gloves as she trimmed flowers. The dialogue in one scene read unconvincingly, and Rauch asked for a rewrite. Even a musical bridge between scenes did not escape his critical ear.

Rauch opted for a lighter and less orchestrated version than the one that had been played on the run-through.

Some members of the production team who were not directly involved in the run-through viewed the show with the producer in his office and received their notes immediately. Others, such as the director and the audio technician, were given notes after the run-through was completed. The key personnel then went off to meet with their respective crew members, while the director conveyed both Rauch's notes and his own suggestions to the performers.

Needless to say, *Another World* is a very special sort of show: a one-hour drama produced at a network studio five times a week. The notes from a producer will be different on a musical program, a news show, a sports event, or an instructional production, but the intent is the same: to keep on top of everything that appears onscreen and to serve as a substitute audience by evaluating the production as the viewer would.

The dress rehearsal is crucial for any prerehearsed program because it is an exact replica of the air show the audience will see. Any major changes you want to make in the show must be done before dress; otherwise, there will be no time to try them out before the actual production. Most production changes create a domino effect. A change in one actor's blocking can affect the camera shot, the lighting, the position of the boom microphone, the audio, and so on down the line. Naturally, a serious problem must be corrected regardless of when you see it, but a problem of this magnitude should have been spotted much earlier and corrected long before the dress rehearsal.

Some producers like to videotape the dress rehearsal, believing that it keeps the production crew and the performers more finely tuned and results in sharper performances. The extra tape footage is also helpful during editing, particularly if someone has turned in a one-time-only performance that you are lucky enough to have recorded during the dress rehearsal.

Production

According to George Heinemann, "during the production a good producer is the loneliest guy [*sic*] in the world. That's because if you've done your job properly, you get the feeling you're in the way since all the major decisions were made long before now."

Of course, there are some notable exceptions to this rule, particularly in live news, special-events, and sports programming, where the producer must make split-second decisions continuously the whole time the program is on the air. For most preplanned shows, however, by production time the producer's job is essentially over; the show is now in the hands of the director and the production crew. The producer is still there, of course, but more to give encouragement than for anything else. By this time the show you see on the line monitor should be the realization of what you saw in your mind's eye so much earlier, before all the meetings, the paperwork, the negotiations, the deadlines—a concept that has come to life in the videospace on screen.

Postproduction

Postproduction often involves the producer in more than just completion of the actual program. Of course, a show must be edited, but the producer is also concerned with such activities as promotion and publicity to ensure the largest possible audience for the show and with analyzing the audience response to the program to determine how well it was received and how close it came to satisfying the producer's initial production objectives.

Editing   Many producers prefer to leave the preliminary editing decisions to the director. This is generally a good idea, since the director probably shot the show with an editing strategy specifically in mind. The producer always should view the rough-cut, however, and make any comments or suggestions before the program is edited into the final version. Needless to say, there are some producers who insist on playing a more direct role in editing and others who leave the job entirely in the director's hands. This decision depends on your own judgment, how much "creative" editing is involved, and the amount of time you can spend in the edit room.

Promotion and Publicity   Even the best produced program is not worth much unless there is an audience to see it. Closed-circuit producers of educational or industrial shows usually do not

have to worry about promotion because they have a "captive" audience for which the program was originally produced, but broadcast programs are an entirely different story. The producer, along with the station or network, must try to publicize and promote the show so that as many viewers as possible are made aware of its air date and time.

Larger stations and the national networks all have promotion and publicity departments responsible for promoting upcoming programs. Usually the producer is asked to consult with the promotion department to suggest possible publicity angles and to help in the development of the promotional campaign. At smaller operations with no promotion department, you may have to take on the promotion and publicity chores yourself.

PRESS RELEASE   One way to publicize a show is through a press release sent to all radio and television newspaper and magazine editors within the broadcast area. Editors need a constant supply of copy material, and a well-written and interesting release about your show stands a good chance of being included as a feature or news item in a column.

The release should contain all the essential information about your show: its title, the air date and time, the channel, a brief summary of the show's content, and the names of principal performers and guests. It is also a good idea to work up some interesting production sidelights which make good copy. Anything different or unique about the show ought to be included. For instance, a press release about an upcoming sports remote might discuss the extraordinary preparation that went into the show, any special new production techniques that will be employed, and the number of cameras, miles of cables used, and so on.

Plan on sending out your press releases as early as possible. Daily newspaper deadlines are pretty flexible, but most magazines and newspaper TV supplements have deadlines that may be weeks or months in advance of your air date. If you are unsure about specific deadlines, call and find out. A press release is a great promotional opportunity, since it costs nothing for the print space and can help to generate audience interest and curiosity about your show.

PRINT AND BROADCAST ADVERTISING

A television program can be advertised and marketed just as any other product. Print advertising space can be purchased in newspapers, magazines, and even on billboards and posters. You also can produce radio and television commercials and purchase broadcast advertising time on local stations. Buying advertising space and time is expensive, though, and many smaller stations do not have the money necessary to run extensive advertising campaigns. Sometimes you can work out a trade-out where advertising space or time is exchanged for other services. Another possibility is to tie in a program's promotion with its sponsor's regular advertising efforts.

PROMOTIONAL SPOTS

An on-air promotional spot, or "promo," as it is commonly called, is an announcement that you produce for your own station. The spot is run in the place of a paid commercial, and it promotes your program. The advantage of a promo spot is that it costs you nothing. However, at most stations a "sustaining" promo will be replaced with a paying commercial if the sales department can sell the air time to a sponsor.

Variations on the promo are voice-over announcements which are run over the ending credits of other shows and shared-ID graphics which are used during station breaks to identify the station and to promote the show.

Audience Evaluation

In the final analysis, it is the audience that determines whether a program is a success or a failure. The criteria you use in evaluating the audience's response to your show can vary, however, depending on your specific production situation or the program's objectives. The size of the audience is often crucial in broadcast television, but noncommercial public stations are generally less concerned with audience size. Closed-circuit instructional or informational programs usually use entirely different program evaluation criteria from those used by broadcast television. These programs are produced with a specific audience and with particular objectives in mind. How effective the production was in teaching a process or in conveying information becomes the means for evaluating this style of program's success or failure.

You can learn about an audience's reaction to your show in a number of ways. Some are more formal and objective measures, such as program ratings and postviewing tests or interviews. Other types of audience feedback are more informal, such as letters, phone calls, advertiser response, and word-of-mouth.

PROGRAM RATINGS

Program ratings provide you with an estimate of the size of your viewing audience. Because they are only estimates (it is impossible to hook up every television set to a computer), they are subject to variation and error, particularly when the rating figures for two competing shows are very close.

Ratings can tell you only the size and the composition of your audience. They cannot tell you how much the audience enjoyed your show, whether or not they understood and appreciated what you were trying to communicate, whether they paid much attention, or even if they watched your show at all. The rating simply means that a certain number of television sets were tuned to a particular show at a particular time. (In fact, during a congressional hearing on ratings some years ago, it was learned that a woman with a ratings meter on her set kept the television on all day to entertain her dog while she was at work. The ratings company assumed that whatever shows the set was tuned to also were being watched by some 50,000 other television homes!) With all their faults, however, ratings have proved to be fairly reliable estimates of audience size, and until a better system comes along, they will remain the industry standard for audience measurement.

Most local and national ratings are conducted and reported by two major organizations: the A.C. Nielsen Company and the ARBITRON Company. They send regular ratings reports to their paying subscribers, who include local television stations, national networks, advertisers and ad agencies, and independent program producers.

The ratings book reports two important figures for every show: (1) the program rating and (2) the program's share.

Rating The program *rating* is a percentage of all television households tuned to a program from among all the television households who potentially could tune in. As an example, say we have a sample of 100 television homes included in our rating survey, and out of the 100, some 20 households are tuned to your program. The rating would be 20/100 = 20 percent, or a rating of 20 (the percent sign is always dropped when reporting a ratings figure). (See Figure 4-11.)

It may have occurred to you that the size of the rating figure depends not only on the popularity of the show, but also on the number of people who are actually watching television at the time. Naturally, you would expect more people to watch television at nine o'clock at night than at nine o'clock in the morning. Regardless of a show's popularity, the rating figure of a mediocre evening program will invariably be higher than the rating figure of a highly successful daytime program. In order to account for this difference among the number of available viewers and to permit us to make comparisons between programs that are broadcast at different times of day, we must use the second important program rating figure, the *share*.

Share *Share* is short for *share of audience*. Unlike the program rating, which is a percentage of homes watching from among all those with television sets, the share is calculated as the percentage of those households watching a show from among all homes that are using television at the time. (See Figure 4-11.)

Now look at our sample again. There are still the same 20 households turned to our show, but assume that only 60 percent, or 60 households, are actually using television (this figure is often referred to as the "HUT"—households using television). To calculate the share, we divide the total HUT by the number of households tuned to a show, or 20/60 = 33 percent, or a 33 share (remember, drop the percent sign). If your show was competing directly against two other programs, the 33 share would be a respectable portion of the total audience. Since all the program shares added together for each time period always equal 100, we can use the share to provide an indication of a show's relative popularity against direct competition in its particular time slot.

Overall program ratings and shares are important, but they tell only a part of the story. A ratings

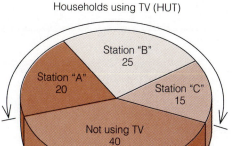

Households using TV (HUT)

SAMPLE SIZE = 100 Television Homes

Rating

Station "A" $\frac{20}{100}$ = 20

Station "B" $\frac{25}{100}$ = 25

Station "C" $\frac{15}{100}$ = 15

Total HUT = 60

Share

Station "A" $\frac{20}{60}$ = 33

Station "B" $\frac{25}{60}$ = 42

Station "C" $\frac{15}{60}$ = 25

100 (Note: Total shares always equal 100%)

FIGURE 4-11 **Program Rating and Share.** The rating represents the proportion of people watching television from among all people who own television sets, whether or not they are watching at the time. The share represents the proportion of the audience watching a program from among all people watching television at that time. Naturally, a program's rating is always smaller than its share.

report also breaks down the audience for a show into its *demographics*—various age, sex, and income groupings—which are helpful in determining a show's audience appeal, planning its future development, and buying advertising time. (See Figure 4-12.)

POSTVIEWING EVALUATION TESTS It is rarely difficult to learn the size and composition of a closed-circuit educational or industrial program audience, since all you need do is count heads to find

Nielsen NATIONAL TV AUDIENCE ESTIMATES — EVE. THU. APR. 7

TIME	7:00	7:15	7:30	7:45	8:00	8:15	8:30	8:45	9:00	9:15	9:30	9:45	10:00	10:15	10:30	10:45
HUT	49.8	51.8	53.7	56.3	59.2	61.5	62.5	63.9	64.7	65.8	65.1	64.3	61.6	60.6	58.5	56.7

ABC TV — BYRDS OF PARADISE / PRIMETIME LIVE / MATLOCK THE CONSPIRACY (R)(PAE)

HHLD AUDIENCE% & (000); 74% AVG. AUD. 1/2 HR; SHARE AUDIENCE %; AVG. AUD. BY 1/4 HR

	8:00	8:15	9:00	9:15	9:30	9:45	10:00	10:15	10:30	10:45
HHLD% (000)	8.7 / 12.2	8,200	9.1*	10.4 / 13.3	9,800	11.0*	14.3 / 13,470	14.5*
share	14	8.4	14*	16	15*	17*	27.3	14.1*	23*	25*
1/4 hr	8.4	8.4 / 8.9	9.3	9.5	10.2	10.8	13.8	14.4	14.3	14.7

CBS TV — CHRISTY / EYE TO EYE W. C. CHUNG / TRAPS

	8:00	8:15	8:30	9:00	9:15	9:45	10:00	10:15	10:30	10:45
HHLD% (000)	12.8 / 17.0	12,060	13.2*	10.4 / 15.3	9,800	10.5*	9.4 / 13.7	8,850	9.7*
share	20	12.4*	21*	16	14*	16*	9.1*	9.5*	17*
1/4 hr	12.1	12.6	13.2	13.1	10.6	10.1	10.5	9.1	9.6	9.8

DATELINE NBC-SPL

NBC TV — MAD ABOUT YOU-THU. / WINGS / SEINFELD (R) / FRASIER (R) / DATELINE NBC-SPL

	8:00	8:15	8:30	9:00	9:30	9:45	10:00	10:15	10:30	10:45
HHLD% (000)	12.6 / 15.1	11,870	15.1 / 17.3	14,220	19.4 / 27.8	18,270	17.9 / 20.1	16,860	12.2 / 19.1	11,490	11.1*
share	21	12.4*	24	30	28	21	19*
1/4 hr	11.9	13.4	14.5	15.7	19.0	19.9	18.2	17.7	13.6	11.6	10.5

FOX TV — SIMPSONS (R) / SINBAD SHOW / IN LIVING COLOR / HERMAN'S HEAD

	8:00	8:15	8:30	9:00	9:15	9:30	9:45
HHLD% (000)	9.7 / 12.7	9,140	8.6 / 10.2	8,100	7.0 / 4.3	6,990	5.7 / 7.2	5,370
share	16	16	14	11	9
1/4 hr	8.8	10.6	8.7	8.6	7.1	6.9	5.5	6.0

	7:00	7:45	8:00	8:30	9:00	9:30	10:00	10:15	10:30
INDEPENDENTS (INCLUDING SUPERSTATIONS EXCEPT TBS) — AVERAGE AUDIENCE / SHARE AUDIENCE %	13.0 (+F) / 26	13.9 (+F) / 25	6.6 / 11	7.0 / 11	6.6 / 10	6.6 / 10	11.8 / 19	10.4 (+F) / 18
PBS — AVERAGE AUDIENCE / SHARE AUDIENCE %	1.7 / 3	1.9 / 3	2.5 / 4	2.2 / 4	2.5 / 4	2.8 / 4	2.2 / 4	1.9 / 3
CABLE ORIG. (INCLUDING TBS) — AVERAGE AUDIENCE / SHARE AUDIENCE %	10.2 (+F) / 20	11.6 (+F) / 21	12.5 / 21	12.9 / 20	13.1 / 20	14.2 / 22	14.5 (+F) / 24	13.3 (+F) / 23
PAY SERVICES — AVERAGE AUDIENCE / SHARE AUDIENCE %	1.2 / 2	1.5 / 3	2.4 / 4	2.5 / 4	2.9 / 4	3.0 / 5	3.3 / 5	2.9 / 5

U.S. TV Households: 94,200,000

For an explanation of symbols, See page B.

FIGURE 4-12 Rating Books.

Rating books describe the numbers and demographics of the audience watching television shows. Rating books are important for setting advertising rates and determining which shows are renewed and which are canceled. (*Courtesy: A. C. Nielsen Co.*)

out who and how many people are watching. What is frequently more important in this situation is to discover how effective a program has been in communicating a skill or in conveying information to the audience. Even some broadcast programs with similar instructional objectives—such as *Sesame Street* or the *Electric Company*—will not find these answers in the program ratings. They must be discovered through postviewing evaluation tests.

You will probably need the help of an instructional development specialist in the design and administration of postviewing tests or questionnaires. You must first outline the basic objectives—in other words, what it is you want the audience to learn or take away from the show they have just seen. The specialist will develop a test instrument or questionnaire designed to record these concepts and to provide you with data that can be used to evaluate how effective your show was in meeting its objectives.

Sometimes the best way to evaluate the effectiveness of a training production is to analyze subsequent audience performance. Do sales figures show a rising trend after the sales staff has seen a motivational television production? Do premed college students' test scores show a significant improvement after viewing a series of supplemental programs on biology? Has the number of work-related accidents decreased after employees saw a tape on safety procedures? Not only can a careful study of performance data and test scores help you to find out the usefulness of the program as a whole, but it also can help you to identify specific

segments which may have proved more or less effective than others.

INFORMAL AUDIENCE FEEDBACK   Phone calls, letters, and the audience response to advertisers' commercials constitute more informal audience feedback. There are even some "computer bulletin boards" devoted to the exchange of viewer comments about such regular programs as daytime soap operas. All stations receive both letters and phone calls in which viewers register their approval or their dislike for particular programs. Of course, the trend of letters and calls can sometimes be biased by a highly vocal and visible minority, but many writers and callers are sincere both in their criticism and in their praise. Paying attention to various calls and letters and noting the overall trend of such messages can give you some interesting perspectives on viewer reactions to your show.

Another informal way to gauge the impact of a program on an audience is through audience response to advertisers' messages. The number of sales or the response to offers that were advertised on commercials can be carefully followed. Audience response to an advertiser's message often has nothing to do with the program itself, but a sizable reaction or a successful sales campaign suggests a substantial and attentive audience.

SUMMARY

The producer is the individual who is ultimately responsible for every element—both creative and technical—that goes into a television production. The producer must be familiar with all aspects of television production in order to supervise the production team and to make the maximum use of every production capability. A successful producer combines creativity, organizational efficiency, and business acumen. The organizational ability is essential to realize the creative idea in the financially constrained television medium.

The producer is responsible for the development of the program idea. Whether the concept was originally assigned to the producer or developed to fill an existing programming need, the producer must take the initial concept through a series of program development steps which include (1) analyzing audience needs and tastes, (2) researching the program idea for content and production feasibility, (3) determining the production mode—whether the show is produced in the studio or on location, live, on tape, or on film, (4) developing the program outline or treatment, and (5) preparing the program budget.

The producer is one of the few production team members who is directly involved in each of the four production stages. The preproduction stage is the busiest and most important for the producer, since this is when the program concept is developed and the show's approach and production are planned and organized. The script serves as the foundation for every show, and it is usually one of the producer's earliest concerns. The script can be written either by the producer or by a writer working closely with the producer.

After all necessary changes and revisions are made, the final draft becomes the shooting script. Another crucial preproduction concern for the producer is hiring the director, who must ultimately interpret and execute the producer's concept. Both the producer and director work closely on script revisions, casting, and production approaches. To help the producer organize the various elements which must go into the show, the production notebook is put together. The notebook is a collection of all necessary production information, including (1) the shooting script, (2) master production schedule, (3) cast/crew listing, (4) rehearsal schedules, (5) FAX sheets, (6) operational schedules, (7) call sheets, and (8) shooting schedules or rundown sheets.

During the rehearsals, the producer's most important function is to serve as a substitute audience, watching and critically analyzing the show as it appears on the program monitor. During rehearsals, the producer confers with the key production team members and hands out notes concerning all production elements that need attention. Changes must be made early enough in rehearsal so that they do not completely upset the performers or production crew. The dress rehearsal—a replica of the show as it will appear on the air—should always be run before actual production.

Once into the production stage, the producer turns the show over to the director and production crew. If the producer has done his or her homework during the earlier stages of production, there really is not much for him or her to do, since the production should look and sound as the producer envisioned it early in preproduction.

The producer's postproduction activities include approving the final edited videotape version of the program, working on promotion and publicity to attract the largest audience possible, and evaluating the audience's response to the show. For broadcast programs, two widely used measures of audience reaction are the program's rating and share. Other objective measures of audience response are postviewing evaluation tests and observation of audience performance on a job or task which the show addressed. More informal, but useful audience feedback can include phone calls, letters, and response to ads that appeared on the show.

108

DIRECTING FOR TELEVISION

The television director must function on two levels. The first level—the aesthetic—has already been discussed in Chapter 2. Visualizing the program and making the right series of choices at the right time, however, are only a part of the director's responsibilities. In this chapter we will discuss the second aspect of the director's job—the transformation of ideas and concepts into actual sounds and pictures.

A good director is involved in virtually every facet of a production. Every chapter in this book mentions the director because it is impossible to discuss any particular aspect of production without including the individual who must integrate the many diverse production elements to create a program. In this chapter we will see how the director plans, organizes, and supervises the production team and uses production techniques to create a television program.

THE DIRECTOR AND THE PRODUCTION TEAM

It is sometimes easy to lose sight of the fact that all the equipment used in a production must be operated by *people,* and it is the crew that plays a large part in any program's success or failure.

"You're only as good, only as effective, as the people you have with you," says Dwight Hemion, one of the top directors in television. "It's a big team effort and you've got to respect the crew, get to know them, give them the feeling that they are contributing a great deal to the production—because they are." Among successful directors, the importance of the team is a vital ingredient. "The director may work with actors and plan out the shots," says Bob LaHendro, a director of such programs as the classic *All in the Family,* "but when you come down to it you need that crew behind you working as a team. To get that kind of working attitude where everyone is pulling for the show simply demands that you, as director, respect everyone else's contribution. They like you, you like them, and there is mutual trust and respect. That way when you ask the crew to go above and beyond they'll do it willingly."

Even the most experienced directors make mistakes from time to time, but a production unit that works closely together can "save" each other through close teamwork and cooperation. If you and your crew have a mutual respect, you will avoid the experience of an arrogant young director who arrived on the set of a variety show one day. "I just wanted to let you know," said the director as he met the crew, "that I'm in charge here and I expect all of you to do exactly as you are told—no more, no less." Later, when the show went on the air—live in those days—the director told one of the cameras to dolly in on a female singer. As the camera began the move, the director's attention was diverted from the air monitor as

he set up the next shot. When he glanced back, he was horrified to see the camera continue to dolly past the singer, through the curtain, and all the way to the rear of the set. "What do you think you're doing!" he shrieked over the intercom PL system. "I followed your directions exactly," replied the camera operator. "You said, 'Dolly in,' you didn't say to stop."

Another point to remember when dealing with the crew is to know and respect each person's capabilities and limitations. You are never going to find the "perfect" crew, so learn to make the best use of the one you have. Put your best operator on the camera with the toughest job. Do not ask an inexperienced camera operator to accomplish intricate moves and maneuvers which you know he or she cannot do.

Because the director is so closely involved in a production, it is easy to forget that the crew may not be as familiar with the program. Even the best crew member cannot do a great job unless he or she knows what is expected. A short meeting with the crew just prior to rehearsal can help to familiarize them with the show and give everyone a better idea of what you expect them to do. A crew that knows what is to come and what is expected of them will feel more comfortable, work more confidently, and do a better job than a crew that is unfamiliar with the project and uncertain of what the director expects from them.

DIRECTOR COMMANDS

A visitor to a busy control room would probably wonder about the strange series of commands issued by the program's director: "Ready one on the cross. Take one and zoom in. Insert the graphic and ready to wipe to a split of one and three. Ready to roll VTR. Dissolve to the effect, roll VTR." To the uninitiated, the words and phrases may seem strange and almost unintelligible as the director spews them out in a steady stream of chatter. In reality, though, each of these commands refers to a specific production operation and is followed by the production crew during rehearsal and production. Because everything moves so quickly during production, the director must be able to communicate to the crew accurately, quickly, and efficiently.

The director can communicate with members of

the production team in several ways. First, the director is in contact with camera operators and other members of the production team through a headphone intercom system, sometimes called a "private line" or "PL." Second, the director may use a "Stage" mike connected to a studio speaker to communicate simultaneously with performers and crew members not wearing PL headsets. Third, on some live programs, such as sports or news coverage, the director may use an *interruptible foldback* (IFB) device, which is an unobtrusive earpiece worn by the performer. Pushing a button in the control room permits the director to talk directly to the performer, even while he or she is on-camera. Directors must be cautious using the IFB system because it is hard for a performer to talk while listening to another voice giving instructions at the same time.

In each chapter of this book we give the basic terminology associated with the equipment and production techniques covered. These terms—with a few variations—have become standard within the television industry, and they enable the director and the production team to communicate quickly and accurately. Although the director can communicate immediately with anyone on the crew who is wearing a headset connected to the PL system, during rehearsal and production, the director speaks primarily to the camera operators, the technical director (video switcher), the floor manager, and the audio technician.

Camera Commands

The director will probably speak to the camera operators more than to any other production team members in order to set up shots, perfect the framing and composition, and direct camera movement while the shot is on the air.

Here are the guidelines in giving camera commands:

1 *Give a "ready" whenever possible.* Before you punch up a camera on the air or ask the camera to execute a move, try to give a "standby," or "ready," cue. The camera operator will know to hold the shot still as soon as he or she hears the "ready." It is also a good idea to ready a camera move. For example, "Camera 1—ready to pan right with the host." This is particularly important when the on-camera subject

is about to make a major move, such as getting up from a chair, sitting down, or crossing the set. Although it is not always possible to give a "ready" on a spontaneous and unscripted show, try to give one whenever you can.

2 *Call each camera by number.* You ought to know each camera operator's name, but ignore names while you are calling shots. What if you have two camera operators named Susan? Also, other team members listening over the PL may not know the camera operators by name but will be able to easily identify the cameras by number.

3 *Preface the command with the camera number.* Say "Camera 2, pan right to the door," not "Pan right to the door, Camera 2." Prefacing the command with the camera number will alert the proper camera operator to pay attention and prevent the other camera operators from making unintentional moves. It also will help the switcher, audio engineer, and floor manager, since camera operations can affect their jobs.

4 *Remember the difference in pan and tilt commands and the resulting movement on screen.* When you pan right, you move the image onscreen to the left. When you tilt up, you move the image onscreen down. Be sure to consider the onscreen effect of the pan or tilt before you give the command.

5 *Be specific in your commands.* While you should use as few words as possible, do not eliminate specific references which will help the camera operators to get their shots. For instance, on a three-person interview show, the command "Camera 1, zoom in" is too vague. Instead, say "Camera 1, zoom in to a close-up of the host." The same applies to pans, tilts, dollies, and so on. Rather than say "Pan right," say "Pan right to a two-shot." The more specific your commands, the faster and more accurately the camera operator can get the shots for you.

Switcher Commands

At some studios, the director operates the

switcher during production. At other facilities, switching is performed by someone else, who operates the switching console on the program director's command. Even if you will operate the switcher yourself, get into the habit of giving verbal switching commands. If you do not, the production crew members listening to the PL for directions will not know about a video transition until it has already happened onscreen.

Here are guidelines for giving switcher commands:

1 *Give a "ready" before each transition.* A warning before each switching cue is helpful to the switcher, as well as to the camera operators. Try to give the "ready" cue just before the actual transition. A "ready" that comes too soon can be forgotten, and a "ready" that comes too late gives the switcher too little time to prepare. It is particularly important to give the switcher advance warning on such complex transitions as dissolves, wipes, or inserts, which require a preset before the transition can be performed.

2 *Be specific.* The more specific your commands, the less chance there is for error. If, for example, you want to insert one camera source over another picture, say "Ready to insert Camera 1 over Camera 3. Fade in insert." Remember to specify how you want the insert to appear, since an effect can usually be "popped in," "faded in," or "wiped in."

3 *Indicate the speed of a fade, dissolve, or wipe.* Use your voice or a hand motion to indicate how fast or slow you want to see the transition onscreen. A verbal countdown is even more precise and can help the audio technician, who may have to accompany the visual transition with an audio fade or segue.

4 *Give the switcher advance warning on complicated effects.* The commands "fade," "dissolve," "super," "insert," "key," or "wipe," should always remind you that the switcher must preset a number of video sources before the transition or effect can be produced. Especially on chroma keys or inserts, where clipping levels must be established, try to give as much advance notice as possible so the effect can be set up and checked on the preview monitor.

5 *Economize on command words.* Rather than saying, "Ready to cut to Camera 1 . . . Cut to Camera 1," say "Ready to take 1 . . . Take 1." Fewer words take less time and reduce the chance of confusion. Since cuts are the most often used transition, you might arrange with the switcher and camera operators to consider a "ready" without further qualification to be a straight cut. For example, "Ready 2 . . . Take 2" (a cut), but "Ready dissolve to 2 . . . Dissolve to 2" (a dissolve).

6 *In a sequence of commands, cue the switcher last.* Since the switcher is positioned next to the director in the booth, he or she usually needs less time to react to a command than other production team members, who must receive the cue through the PL or the floor manager. Therefore, if you must give a sequence of commands such as "Open mikes, cue talent, fade in on Camera 3," give the cues in the following order: (1) to audio, (2) to talent, and (3) to the switcher. This also will reduce the chance of fading up on a performer who might have missed the floor manager's cue.

Other Director Commands

Most of the other commands given by the director during the show involve the floor manager, the talent, and such areas as audio, lighting, telecine, and videotape. We will cover many of these commands in later chapters. In this chapter we will discuss some of the talent and floor manager commands, since they are given frequently by the director during rehearsal and production.

Talent and Floor Manager Commands The cue to start talking or to begin some other action is the most common command given by the director, usually through the floor manager. The same rules mentioned above apply equally to cuing talent:

1 *Be precise.* Say "Cue Tom," *not* "Cue him."
2 *Be economical.* Say "Cue Anne," *not* "Tell Anne to start talking."
3 *Be specific.* Say "Show the host five minutes remaining," *not* "Show him the time."

Avoid giving talent a "cold" cue without any

preparation. Talent "ready" cues are always important, especially when you are coming out of a prerecorded tape, commercial, station break, or other out-of-studio segment. Have the floor manager inform talent how much time is left until the show comes back to the studio. A silent hand countdown from the floor manager is helpful in smoothing the transition, since it gives talent a more precise idea of time remaining. The countdown is particularly important when the performer must lead into a film or videotape, which requires a precise preroll cue.

Often the floor manager will convey time signals to help talent gauge how much time is remaining in a segment or in the overall show. Be sure that the floor manager and the talent have coordinated all time signals before production. There is a big difference between "five minutes left in the program" and "five minutes left before you begin to wrap up the show." Confusion here can result in a program ending early or running late. The director should also ask talent the kinds of time signals and other cues he or she needs and then be sure to deliver them during the production.

TECH TIP The consistency and accuracy with which the director uses commands sets the level of professionalism for a production session. In addition to using the correct commands with adequate warning, the director's tone of voice should establish authority not dominance, control not panic.

ASSISTANT DIRECTOR

By now it should be apparent that a director is awfully busy during rehearsal and production. The director must set up and call camera shots; check for framing and composition; cue talent; follow the script; listen to the audio; watch all line, preview, and camera monitors; cue other production elements, such as audio, VTR, and film; and keep track of the program's time. In addition to all this, the director must constantly evaluate the performances and the interaction of sound and picture to be certain of accomplishing the production's preset goals and objectives.

Audio Commands In many television productions, the audio technician will be expected to take

initiative without being given each cue directly. For example, when a news director cuts back to the studio anchor from a field report, the director may not cue the audio technician to open the anchor's microphone and turn off the reporter's mike. The director may expect the audio technician to do that automatically. Therefore, the audio technician must listen carefully to the content of the program to be ready to change sound sources quickly without being cued.

How much initiative the audio technician takes will depend on the standard practices at a station, the format of a program, and the preproduction arrangements made by the director. If there are any doubts, the director should clear them up with the audio technician before the show begins.

Here are a few considerations for directors when giving audio commands during productions:

1   Microphones should always be opened before the talent is cued by saying, "Ready to open mike and cue talent . . . Open mike and cue talent." Obviously, the microphone must be turned on before the talent begins speaking in order for the audience to hear every word right from the start.

2   When audio cues are given before video cues, openings and transitions are tighter. For example, to make sure a performer begins speaking immediately when he or she appears on air, say "Ready to open mike, ready to cue talent, ready to take 1 . . . Open mike, cue talent, take 1." The talent will begin speaking right away, instead of staring blankly, without speaking, waiting for the cue to be given.

3   It must be made clear to the audio technician whether a videotape insert is silent or has sound. If it has a soundtrack, say "Ready to take and *track* videotape . . . Take and *track* it."

At times when several cues need to be given simultaneously, a single command may be prearranged by the director. For example, at the beginning of a program the audio technician, a camera operator, the lighting director, the video switcher, and talent may need to be cued at exactly the same time. In that case, prearrange one clear, brief command for everyone.

There is no doubt that the director can use some help in doing all this, and this is where the *assistant director* (called the *associate director* in some facilities) comes in. An assistant director (AD) is not always used at all production facilities, but if you have the opportunity to work with one, you will find the job of directing to be a lot easier. The director is still responsible for the entire production; but having someone to help keep track of time, ready cues, and even preset camera shots enables the director to concentrate more fully on what is happening now without having to worry too much about what is to come.

Exactly what the AD does during production depends pretty much on the program's director. Some directors give the AD enormous responsibility; others use the AD sparingly. Ideally, the AD and director should form a closely coordinated team where each complements the other. Usually the AD is responsible for (1) timing the show and individual segments, (2) readying upcoming cues, and (3) presetting camera shots.

Timing the Show

Time is one of the most important and difficult variables to work with during a production. Even if a show is to be videotaped in segments and edited later, accurate timing during production will avoid bringing in a show that is far too long or much too short for the time allotted. Accurate timing during production also will ensure a tightly produced show that looks better onscreen.

Calculating Time   It is not hard to calculate time, but you must think in terms of minutes and seconds. Adding or subtracting time requires a base of sixty (sixty seconds = one minute) instead of the usual ten. For example, say we are given the following segment times to add together:

1	Intro segment	0:35
2	Opening tape	1:00
3	Interview	4:15
4	Demonstration	2:40

To calculate the total time, first add all the seconds and divide the total by sixty, keeping the remainder in seconds. Then add all the minutes, and carry over the total number of minutes from the seconds column. The result is the total time (8:30) in minutes and seconds. For those who feel uncomfortable even with these simple calculations, you can buy an inexpensive pocket calculator which is programmed to figure time without the need for any conversion into seconds and minutes.

Backtiming   Often the director must know how much time remains in a program. In order to *backtime* the show, you will need to know both the present time and the program's end time. Then subtract the present time from the end time to find out how much time remains. For example, say we are 23:30 into a show that is scheduled to end at 28:50. To find remaining time:

```
  28:50  (show's end time)
− 23:30  (present time)
   5:20  (time remaining to end of show)
```

You can check your calculations quickly, because the time remaining plus the present time should equal the show's end time.

Backtiming calculations also allow you to determine the *dead-roll* time for a record, audiotape, videotape, or film. Dead-rolling means the sound is faded all the way down when it is started so it is not heard until the sound source is faded up later. Say you have recorded a musical theme that runs 3:45 and your show ends at 58:30. To find the time the music must dead-roll, subtract the theme's running time from the end time.

```
  58:30  (end time)
−  3:45  (theme running time)
  54:45  (dead-roll time)
```

The tape should be dead-rolled at 54:45 into the show. It will end precisely at 58:30. By the way, notice that in order to subtract the time we had to "borrow" sixty seconds from the minute side to subtract the seconds. Again, adding the calculated dead-roll time plus the theme running time should always equal the show's total running time.

Estimating Running Time   Knowing the running

	PROGRAM TIMING SHEET	ESTIMATED	RUN THRU	DRESS	AIR/TAPE
1	OPENING	:30	:30	:30	:30
2	INTRO	1:30	2:15/+ :45	1:45/+ :15	1:40/+ :10
3	INTERVIEW w/SALLY	5:00	4:45/− :15	5:00/	5:00
4	DEMONSTRATION #1	6:30	7:00/+ :30	6:45/+ :15	6:45/+ :15
5	INTERVIEW w/BILL	4:15	4:00/− 15	4:15/	4:00 − :15
6	DEMONSTRATION #2	8:30	1:15/+ 1:45	9:30/+ 1:00	9:00/+ :30
7	CLOSE & CREDITS	2:15	2:00/− :15	1:30/− :45	1:35

TOTAL 28:30 OVER by 2:15 OVER :15

Labels above table:
- Segment times as originally planned
- PROGRAM TIMING SHEET
- Segment time
- Times from first rehearsal
- Amount over/under from estimate
- Segment times from dress
- Actual times during production

FIGURE 5-1 Program Timing Sheet.
The program timing sheet allows the director or assistant director to keep track of a program's timing and to identify those segments of a show which are running too long or too short.

time as the show progresses is always helpful and avoids unpleasant surprises at the end of the show when you find there is too much (or too little) time remaining. Although segments should be timed during rehearsals and each segment's running time should be indicated on the program's rundown sheet, these times will vary once the performers get into the studio and the director starts to call shots. Using a timing sheet such as the one in Figure 5-1 can help you keep track of each segment's time. In the left-hand column is the estimated time; the first column is used to record the actual running time during the first rehearsal; the next column is used for the second rehearsal; and so on. Next to each time is a space where the AD can mark how much over or under the segment is running. It is easy to tell the director how much the actual running time deviates from the estimated time so that minor timing corrections can be made

throughout the show rather than waiting to make a major correction at the end of the show.

TECH TIP Variable crawl rates on character-generated ending credits are useful for avoiding dead air time or missing credits. If possible, establish a "normal" air time for the credits of some round number, such as sixty seconds. Then cutting the crawl rate in half adds one minute to show time, while doubling the crawl rate saves thirty seconds.

Timing and Countdowns Accurate timing is important in almost every production, so get into the habit of starting your stopwatch when the segment begins onscreen or as soon as the film or VTR material appears. Often a director or AD must use a number of stopwatches simultaneously. One might indicate total program running time, while another is used to time the individual segments.

Some directors prefer to have the AD give the verbal countdown when going in and out of prerecorded material. This way the director can concentrate on his or her cues while the production team hears the AD counting down over the PL system.

TECH TIP   A $15 "jogger's" watch is a valuable tool for a television director. The face of a jogger's watch will display clock time, program time, and backtime simultaneously, keeping the director "running" on schedule.

Postproduction Timing   During postproduction, the director can use the SMPTE time code to get accurate timing of the individual takes that will be used to make up the final program. SMPTE time code is an eight-digit number with two digits assigned to hours, minutes, seconds, and frames. It is recorded on the videotape to facilitate accurate editing. Remember that the rightmost pair of digits represent frames and that thirty frames of video equal one second of clock time.

Videotape Take Sheets   On productions which are videotaped for postproduction editing, the AD may be asked to keep track of each take as well as timing the segments. The take sheet includes the scene and take number of every take to permit accurate identification during editing. Some ADs find it convenient to combine the take sheet information and timing information onto one piece of paper.

If the AD is responsible for tracking each take, he or she must be certain that the floor manager has the proper scene and take number on the slate before every recording.

"Ready" Cues

The AD can help the director by supplying "ready" cues for audio, lighting, film, VTR rolls, announcer, and talent. Usually, the AD supplies the "ready" cue, but it is still the director who cues the music, effect, tape roll, and so on at the precise time it is to occur.

Presetting Camera Shots

On a fully scripted or semiscripted show, where a specific sequence of shots is planned, the AD can be used to set up the next camera shot for the director. To do this, the AD must copy the director's shooting script, shot by shot. During rehearsal and production, the AD stays one shot ahead of the director and readies each upcoming shot. The director will usually touch up the framing and composition before punching-up the shot on the air. Using the AD to preset shots allows the director to concentrate completely on the on-air camera composition and the timing of the video transitions rather than on the mechanical operation of alerting cameras for their upcoming shots.

Having the AD preset shots is a great convenience as long as the AD and director do not work at cross-purposes. Too much talk over the PL will make everyone's directions impossible to understand, so the AD must learn to fit in his or her commands between those of the director. The shot or action on the air always takes precedence over anything that is to come.

THE FLOOR MANAGER

The floor manager (or stage manager) is a central figure on the production team. The floor manager conveys the director's commands and relays cues to talent and other personnel, is responsible for checking on props and costumes, holds cue cards or follows along with the script, and generally oversees the operation on the studio floor. For talent, the floor manager serves as the basic communication link between the director in the booth and performers on the floor. Floor managing also can be an excellent way to learn the basics of directing.

Floor Manager Cues   During rehearsal and while the studio mikes are off during production, the floor manager can convey signals and cues verbally to the entire studio floor. Once the mikes are live and the cameras are shooting, the floor manager gives all cues to talent silently.

HAND CUES   A series of hand signals has been developed for some of the common direction and time cues. Obviously, these cues are given silently while the show is on the air. Figure 5-2 shows each

FIGURE 5-2 **The Floor Manager Communicates Silently with Talent Using Hand Cues.**

CUE	MEANING	HAND SIGNAL
Stand by	Show or sequence is about to start.	Stand next to the camera which talent should speak to. Hand and arm upraised.

| **Cue** | Start talking or begin action. | Upraised hand is pointed to talent. |

| **Cut** | Stop talking or stop action. | Draw hand across throat in a cutting motion. |

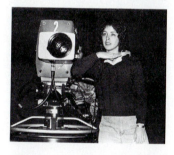

| **Stretch** | Slow down. There is too much time remaining. | Pull hands apart as though pulling taffy. Amount of stretching is indicated by relative distance of hands as cue is relayed. |

510

(Continued)

CUE	MEANING	HAND SIGNAL
Speed up	Talk faster. Accelerate the action. Not much time is left.	Rotate hand and arm clockwise in a circle above head. Speed of rotation indicates relative urgency and the amount of time remaining.

CUE	MEANING	HAND SIGNAL
OK	Everything is fine. Keep on doing/talking as you are.	Make a circle with thumb and forefinger.

CUE	MEANING	HAND SIGNAL
Thirty seconds to go	Thirty seconds left in show or segment.	Make a "T" with both hands.

CUE	MEANING	HAND SIGNAL
Fifteen seconds to go/wrap up	Fifteen seconds left in show or segment. Wrap up whatever you are doing.	Grabbing motion into a fist.

(Continued)

CUE	MEANING	HAND SIGNAL
Back up	Step back. Move away from microphone.	Pushing motion with both hands.

Come closer	Move toward camera. Move closer to microphone.	Palms facing floor manager with both arms toward FM.

Speak more softly	Tone down. Speak more softly. You are too loud.	Palm raised to mouth.

Speak up	Speak up. You are talking too softly. We cannot hear you well.	Cup ear with hand.

(Continued)

CUE	MEANING		HAND SIGNAL
Speak or look toward this camera	This is the camera you should be looking at. This is camera that is on the air.		Hand point to on-air camera. A waving motion from one camera to the other can be used to wave talent from the camera which is currently on-air to another which the director wants to punch up.

hand signal, how to give the cue, and what each means.

Hand cues must always be given clearly and forcefully. You need not wind up like a baseball pitcher before delivering a cue, but you must not underplay it either. It is the floor manager's responsibility to move to a position where the talent can see the cue without having to move his or her head or eyes noticeably on-camera. If the performer is speaking directly to the camera, the cue should be given next to the take lens of the camera that is on the air.

Talent should never overtly acknowledge a cue. Even the slightest nod of the head or wave of the hand will be visible on-camera. Usually the floor manager can tell if you have received the cue. If you do wish to acknowledge the cue, however, the least noticeable method is simply to blink your eyes slightly longer than usual.

Although the floor manager must establish eye contact when sending a cue, too much eye contact between the floor manager and performers when there are no signals is harmful. Some performers are distracted or unnerved, and others may begin talking to the floor manager rather than to the camera.

WRITTEN CUES   Some performers, particularly those who are unfamiliar with television, prefer using written cues. These are brief words printed in large type on hand-held cards. The floor manager flashes the card instead of a hand signal to relay the cue. (See Figure 5-3.)

Written cues are often easier to see and understand than a hand cue, and there is less chance for confusion about what a hand signal means. Such common cues as "Commercial," "Station break," or a series of time cues ("One minute," "Thirty seconds," and so on) are easily prepared. The only real disadvantage with written cues is that the floor manager must carry them during production. Hand cues, on the other hand, can be given as soon as the command is received from the control room.

COUNTDOWNS   A countdown into and out of program segments helps the performer make a smooth transition and sharpens the production's timing and precision. Whenever microphones are closed and the director is about to cue talent to begin, the floor manager should give a loud "Stand by" and tell everyone on the floor how much time remains until the cue.

As an example, say a program is about to finish a commercial and return to the studio. The floor manager yells out at the right time, "Stand by. Coming back in fifteen seconds." This alerts talent and crew alike to prepare for the cue. At ten seconds, the floor manager says, "Ready in ten seconds. Coming up on Camera 2." Directing talent to the proper camera will help to avoid confusion and a possible miscue. The floor manager should call out time, in seconds, from ten seconds down. At five seconds, the floor manager must also begin a hand countdown just next to the take lens of Camera 2. The last audible count should be

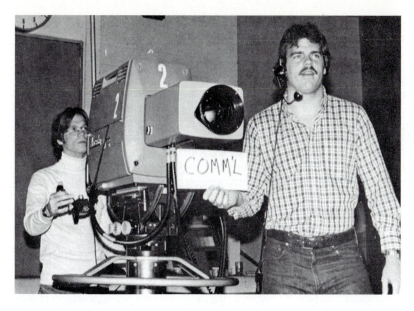

FIGURE 5-3 Written Cues. Written cues sometimes communicate more easily than hand cues, especially for nonprofessional talent.

"Three" with "Two, one, and cue" given silently in case the audio technician opens the mikes early. (See Figure 5-4.)

To count down into a closely timed segment, the floor manager should give the final five-second count with hand signals as he or she hears the time cues from the AD or director in the booth. The hand countdown is always given next to the take lens of the air camera, so talent can watch it while still maintaining eye contact with the audience.

THE DIRECTOR IN PREPRODUCTION

Production is certainly the most exciting time for the director, but without the proper preproduction planning, the production stage can be a disaster. Because crew and facilities time is too valuable to waste, the director must know what is needed and how to accomplish it long before rehearsal and production begin.

As director Bob LaHendro says, "I've found that if you do your homework and know what you want before you go into the studio, everything moves along much more quickly. The crew is happier because they know what you expect from them, it gives the performers more confidence, and if you've planned everything out, it just makes for a much smoother and more productive day."

Production that takes place outside the studio at a remote location demands the same amount of preproduction planning by the director, if not more. Inside the studio you will find a perfect working environment and all the equipment you need; on location, if you have not planned what to bring along and how it will be used, there is no way for you to get the job done properly. Regardless of where your production takes place—inside the studio or on location—preproduction planning is an essential part of the director's job. It is impos-

FIGURE 5-4 Floor Manager's Countdown Cues. Countdown cues are used for smooth transitions in and out of commercial breaks and other video inserts.

sible to overstate the importance of the preproduction stage to an effective and efficient production.

TECH TIP   While each production will differ somewhat, prepare to spend about 70 percent of your time in preproduction. The remaining 30 percent, divided among rehearsal, production, and postproduction, can be much more efficiently used than trying to "save" a poorly preproduced package.

The Director and the Producer

Sometimes the director also doubles as the program's producer; at other times the director works with a producer in developing the concept, planning the production, and interpreting the script into a show. In Chapter 4 we discussed the many details which the director and producer must handle during preproduction. Rather than repeat them here, we will just emphasize that the most important aspect of preproduction is for the director and producer to agree on the director's basic interpretation and approach to the show. Once this is done, most other problems can be solved. If the producer and director do not agree on interpretation at this point in the show, you may find yourselves in conflict over fundamental concepts during rehearsal and production, which will result in frustration, damaged egos, a confused cast and crew, and ultimately, a bad show.

During the initial preproduction period, the director will meet with the scriptwriter to iron out final script details and with the set and lighting designers to work out the setting and lighting. This should be done as early as possible because the director's most essential tools during preproduction planning are (1) the floorplan and (2) the script.

Floorplan

The *floorplan* is an overhead view of the set, which should always be drawn to scale. Using the floorplan, the director can plot camera shots, performer movements, and the positions of production equipment. (See Figure 5-5.)

Take a careful look at the studio layout as it is represented on the floorplan. You are interested as much in the off-set production areas as in the on-camera set because the cameras, additional equipment, and crew must have enough room to work during the production.

Begin by roughing out where you intend to position major pieces of equipment, such as cameras, boom microphones, video monitors, and so on. You will need the approximate dimensions of each piece of studio equipment in order to determine the amount of space needed. You are fooling yourself if you plot the equipment on paper as being smaller than it really is. The reality of the situation will become painfully obvious once you arrive in the studio and find insufficient room for your equipment to operate.

If it looks as though you will need more production room than you have available, consider reworking the location of the set in the studio to give you more flexibility. For example, on a show where you need a very wide cover shot, position the set so your cameras can dolly back as far as possible. On those productions where lateral camera movement is of primary importance, position the set to give you maximum horizontal working space. Remember that it is easy to experiment with the best set and equipment positions on paper as long as everything has been drawn to scale. Once the set is constructed in position in the studio, there is not much you can do to correct a serious problem.

TECH TIP   The various elements of a television production are so interrelated that few last-minute changes can be called "minor." Modification of one production element may require relighting, reblocking, and reworking which cameras take which shots. This can exasperate the crew and add undesirable uncertainty to the performance of talent.

Remote Floorplans   If you will be producing all or part of your production at a remote location, a

FIGURE 5-5   Floorplan. (Facing page)
The floorplan is a two-dimensional drawing as seen from above the studio floor. It should include the perimeter of the studio, all set pieces, and the boom and camera locations. They should be drawn to scale, usually with ¼-inch equal to 1 foot.

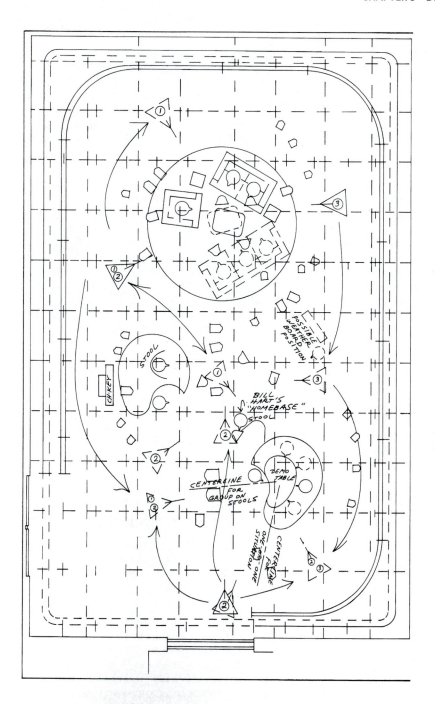

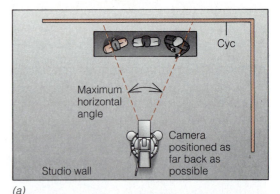

(a)

(b)

floorplan of the various areas where you will be shooting will help you to plan your camera positions and to work out shots before you arrive for production. Of course, few locations have ready-made floorplans, but you should take the time to visit the location, measure the space dimensions of the shooting area, and draw a floorplan as close to scale as possible. For more information, see Chapter 22.

Horizontal Camera Angles   Under most circumstances, you will not have any trouble getting close-up shots with your cameras. The combination of powerful zoom lenses and the ability to move the camera in for a close-up will usually permit you to shoot as tight as you wish. What is often more critical, however, is the maximum width you can expect from your widest cover shot. Unless the camera can photograph everything you must include in a wide shot, you will encounter some serious shooting problems.

As an example, consider a panel discussion with a large number of participants. The director wants the middle camera to be able to shoot a cover shot of the entire set. As you can see in Figure 5-6, when the camera is moved back as far as it can physically move, and zoomed out all the way to its widest shot, the horizontal camera angle is not wide enough to include the entire set. To get the desired shot, the set must be repositioned and the camera lens must be changed. We will discuss camera lenses, angles of view, and calculating horizontal camera angles in detail in Chapters 12 and 13. Knowing what your widest possible shot will be in advance is a great help in planning the positions of sets, talent, and cameras, and in avoiding unexpected surprises when you begin to work in the studio.

The Script

The program's script is the foundation for your show. Although some programs are produced with a partially detailed script and some are produced with virtually no script at all, for now let us assume that you are working with a complete

FIGURE 5-6   Set Placement for Shooting Requirements.
Use the horizontal-angle formula for lenses and a copy of the studio floorplan to establish set placements and shooting requirements of a production. (*a*) Here the horizontal angle of the lens is not wide enough to include the entire set as it has been positioned in the studio. (*b*) By changing the set's location, the director can capture the desired three-shot even in the small studio.

script, since the director's approach is essentially the same regardless of the program format or the amount of script detail. As the director reads through the script and begins to work with it, he or she must deal with four related stages: (1) read-through, (2) performer blocking, (3) camera shots, and (4) marking the script.

Read-through   Work with two copies of the script. Set one aside and do not mark it during preproduction or rehearsal. Use the other to plan your directing approach. Transfer your final thinking to the fresh script, emphasizing clarity and legibility. This is the script you will use during actual taping, and it must be interpretable at a glance.

As soon as you receive the original script, read it thoroughly, not just once, but a number of times. Each time you read the script you will likely find new ideas and possibilities which you should jot down on a pad or in the margin of the script. As you continue to read, try to visualize the show as you would like it to appear onscreen. At the same time, listen to the words. Does the dialogue sound natural or stilted? Do the lines make sense, or are they confusing? Are there any serious production problems in the script which need to be corrected: Do some scenes contain production difficulties, such as the need to cover many actors, an action sequence, or some very tight action in close-up? As you continue to read the script, your visualization will become more defined and focused as the overall program and point of view begin to crystallize in your mind.

Performer Blocking   Once you have become familiar with the script and have developed your point of view, you can begin to work out some tentative performer blocking. Where do we first see the talent? How and when do performers or actors move during the show? These are considerations that apply not only to dramatic programs but to any production where talent appears on-camera. Of course, the blocking you develop now is tentative. Once you begin talent rehearsals, you will undoubtedly revise or completely change some of the blocking to accommodate the artists, as well as camera shots and other production problems.

As you block out performer or actor moves, use your floorplan to help you to visualize the set and the relationship of the actor or performer to cameras, microphones, monitors, and so on. Do not worry too much about the exact camera shots at this point, but try to keep the approximate camera positions in mind so you do not trap yourself by moving performers or actors into positions where they cannot be easily photographed by the cameras.

Developing Camera Shots   Once you have established the basic performer blocking, you can go back to your script and floorplan to work out camera shots. The idea is to visualize the overall traffic pattern of moving talent, cameras, and

equipment, in addition to considering the camera shots themselves. As a director, you must plan your talent and camera blocking so the talent meets the camera at the right place at the right time to produce the shot you want. Of course, these shots are bound to change during the course of rehearsals and production, but they do provide you with a starting point. All this preplanning paperwork is demanding and requires considerable time and concentration, but the time spent with paper and pencil on preproduction will pay off later during rehearsals and production.

In Chapter 2 we discussed the various aesthetic considerations that determine the director's choice of camera shots. Now we will concentrate on how to get those shots which you need on the air. As you begin to work out camera shots, try to establish the basic shot and camera position. Do not worry too much at this point exactly what size the shot will be. Whether a camera shoots a subject in a close-up, a medium close-up, or a medium-wide shot does not matter much, since the camera operator need only zoom in or out from the camera position to vary the shot size. What is important is the camera-to-subject positioning and the overall sequence of camera shots and angles. Once these have been established, it is relatively easy to change a particular shot's size and visual emphasis.

As you develop your camera shots, there are some basic points to keep in mind. These include adherence to the action axis, cross-shooting when possible, and planning sufficient time to break a camera from one area of the studio to another.

ACTION AXIS   Remember to consider the action axis when planning your talent and camera blocking so that you do not inadvertently change screen direction or create a disturbing jump cut. A jump cut occurs when changing between shots in which the subject is framed slightly differently, and the subject appears to "jump" in the picture.

CROSSING SHOTS   Usually the most favorable and effective shot of a performer is one taken from a position that is relatively straight-on. Profile shots are rarely flattering, and because we see little of the talent's face, a great deal of expression and communication can be lost. In order to shoot straight-on, try to cross your cameras as indicated in Figure 5-7. Crossing camera shots is also called "cross shooting."

BREAKING A CAMERA   Often a camera must "break," from one area of the set to another, and the director must realistically estimate the amount of time necessary for the camera operator to break and set up the next shot. Underestimating the time may result in your needing a shot and calling for it before it is ready. Overestimating the amount of

necessary time may result in your planning fewer shots than you can get and possibly missing a shot that you need. As you plan camera breaks and set design, remember the concept of video-space. All the audience sees is what you show them onscreen, so you easily can position a camera card stand just off the set at a distance approximately equal to the camera-to-subject distance of the main action. This reduces the length of time the camera operator needs to focus and compose the next shot. The faster the camera operator can get you the shot, the sooner it will be available for you to use.

Marking the Script   As you work out camera shots, they must be indicated on your copy of the script. Each director usually develops an individual method for marking a script, but regardless of

FIGURE 5-7   Cross-Shooting.
Shooting subjects straight-on results in profile shots (*a*) which are usually unflattering and prevent the viewer from seeing the subject's face clearly, while cross-shooting (*b*) results in more pleasing full-face images of the subjects.

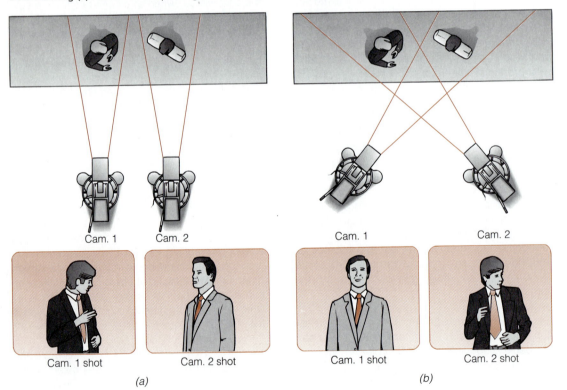

Cam. 1   Cam. 2   Cam. 1   Cam. 2

Cam. 1 shot   Cam. 2 shot   Cam. 1 shot   Cam. 2 shot

(*a*)   (*b*)

SYMBOL	MEANING
C1 ———————————	Camera number. Written alone symbol indicates a take to the camera. The line is used to indicate precisely on what word or action the cut should occur.
WS	Wide shot
MS	Medium shot
MCU	Medium close-up
CU	Close-up
ECU	Extreme close-up
2-SHT	Two-shot
3-SHT	Three-shot
OS	Over-the-shoulder shot
FG-BG John/Mary	Foreground/Background shot (Names used to specify subjects)
ROLL Q	Roll cue (for film or VTR)
Q	Cue
ANNC	Announcer
SOF/SOT	Sound on film/Sound on tape
SFX	Special effect
C/K	Chroma key
NSRT	Insert
✕ or DIS	Dissolve
X to	Actor cross (movement to new position while on camera)

FIGURE 5-8 **Director's Script Markings.**
All directors develop their own method of indicating camera shots and other production cues on the program script. The symbols and script markings presented here and on the following two pages can be adapted to your own style.

how you indicate shots and cues, the objective is clarity, legibility, and economy. You will need to follow your markings during the fast-paced activities in rehearsal and production, so make all script notations readable at a glance. A sloppy or illegible script is hard to follow and increases your chance of losing your place at a critical point in the show.

Figure 5-8 lists some of the common director shorthand symbols and their meanings. It is a good idea to write directions in pencil, since you will be able to erase and make changes more eas-

ily than if you write in ink. If you have time between rehearsals and production, you should completely transfer your cues and shots onto your clean copy of the program script.

TECH TIP Many directors, especially when working on live shows, will slash lines through a page of script once it has been shot. This prevents accidentally duplicating similar news stories or inadvertently inserting a completed page of script into an upcoming scene.

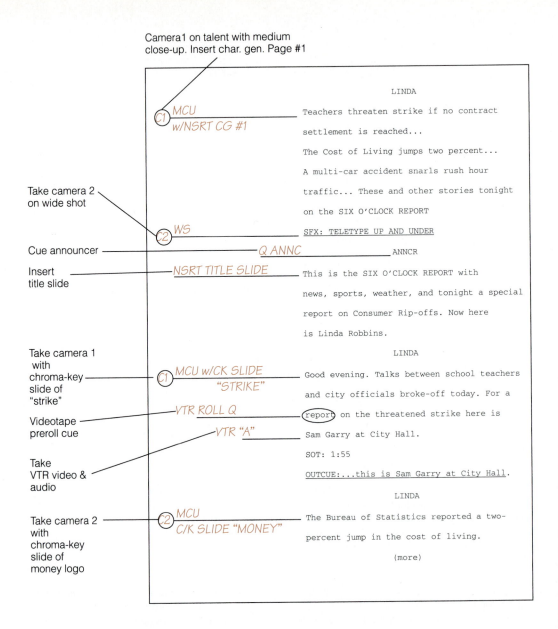

Camera1 on talent with medium close-up. Insert char. gen. Page #1

C1 MCU
w/NSRT CG #1

LINDA

Teachers threaten strike if no contract

settlement is reached...

The Cost of Living jumps two percent...

A multi-car accident snarls rush hour

traffic... These and other stories tonight

on the SIX O'CLOCK REPORT

Take camera 2 on wide shot

C2 WS

SFX: TELETYPE UP AND UNDER

Cue announcer — Q ANNC

ANNCR

Insert title slide — NSRT TITLE SLIDE

This is the SIX O'CLOCK REPORT with

news, sports, weather, and tonight a special

report on Consumer Rip-offs. Now here

is Linda Robbins.

Take camera 1 with chroma-key slide of "strike"

C1 MCU w/CK SLIDE "STRIKE"

LINDA

Good evening. Talks between school teachers

and city officials broke-off today. For a

Videotape preroll cue — VTR ROLL Q

report on the threatened strike here is

Take VTR video & audio

VTR "A"

Sam Garry at City Hall.

SOT: 1:55

OUTCUE:...this is Sam Garry at City Hall.

Take camera 2 with chroma-key slide of money logo

C2 MCU
C/K SLIDE "MONEY"

LINDA

The Bureau of Statistics reported a two-

percent jump in the cost of living.

(more)

CAMERA SHOTS Camera shots are the most common script notation and are written on the blank "video" side of the script. Indicate the camera number, the type of shot, and the subject being photographed. If the camera must move, zoom, or rack focus during the shot, include these directions as well.

TALENT MOVEMENT Remind yourself of major talent moves so you can alert the camera operators and other crew members before the move occurs.

UPCOMING READIES AND CUES Note important readies and cues, such as a camera break, a film

128

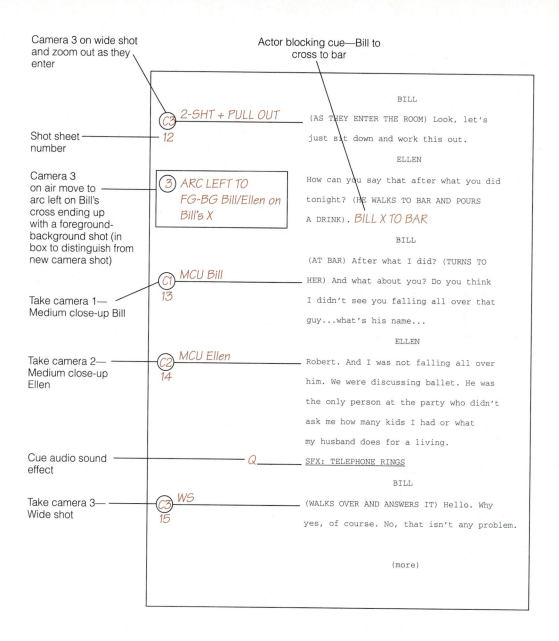

Camera 3 on wide shot and zoom out as they enter

Actor blocking cue—Bill to cross to bar

Shot sheet number

Camera 3 on air move to arc left on Bill's cross ending up with a foreground-background shot (in box to distinguish from new camera shot)

Take camera 1— Medium close-up Bill

Take camera 2— Medium close-up Ellen

Cue audio sound effect

Take camera 3— Wide shot

C3 2-SHT + PULL OUT
12

③ ARC LEFT TO FG-BG Bill/Ellen on Bill's X

C1 MCU Bill
13

C2 MCU Ellen
14

Q

C3 WS
15

BILL

(AS THEY ENTER THE ROOM) Look, let's

just sit down and work this out.

ELLEN

How can you say that after what you did

tonight? (HE WALKS TO BAR AND POURS

A DRINK). BILL X TO BAR

BILL

(AT BAR) After what I did? (TURNS TO

HER) And what about you? Do you think

I didn't see you falling all over that

guy...what's his name...

ELLEN

Robert. And I was not falling all over

him. We were discussing ballet. He was

the only person at the party who didn't

ask me how many kids I had or what

my husband does for a living.

SFX: TELEPHONE RINGS

BILL

(WALKS OVER AND ANSWERS IT) Hello. Why

yes, of course. No, that isn't any problem.

(more)

or VTR roll, a talent cue, or dead-pot time in your script. Bracketing these directions will help to differentiate between a "ready" and an on-air cue or command. Remember: mark your script with shorthand symbols. Don't write everything you say on the script or it will become cluttered and confusing.

STORYBOARD NOTES Some directors like to make small drawings to remind them of a particular visual composition. These notes are conveniently made on the blank page opposite the script page.

PREPARING SHOT SHEETS On a fully scripted show, you may wish to prepare shot sheets for each camera. A *shot sheet* is a description of every camera's shots listed in order from beginning to end. (See Figure 5-9.) You can use the shot sheets in a number of ways. If you never intend to vary the preset shot sequence, each camera operator can simply go to the next shot once the camera's tally lights go off. This makes shot setup virtually automatic, but it does cut down on the director's flexibility to cut between cameras spontaneously during a scene. Once the director has cut from a camera, the operator will automatically move on to the next shot.

If you are working with an AD, the assistant director can use the shot sheets to ready each camera shot by number alone. This eliminates extraneous chatter over the PL system, since it is a lot faster to say "Camera 3, shot 17" than "Camera 3, close-up of the host and follow to the door."

Probably the most flexible way to use shot sheets is to tell cameras to remain on each shot until they are released by the director or AD. Then, if your cutting pattern between cameras is slightly different from what you had planned, the cameras will still be holding their shots. Once the director releases the cameras, however, they can set up their next shot immediately, since it is indicated on the shot sheet.

Obviously, shot sheets are not of much use on an unscripted show, where the director and camera operators must respond to unexpected situations, but when you are able to plan all shots in advance, shot sheets can be an enormous help to a busy director and a great comfort to the camera operator.

Production Meetings

Throughout the preproduction stage the director is involved in a series of production meetings. Some of these are often long and intensive sessions in which each program element is carefully planned with the key production personnel. Other meetings are less formal but still enable the director to make certain that everyone involved with the show understands the program's objectives and their individual contribution to the production effort.

One crucial production meeting takes place in the studio just prior to rehearsal and production. This is when the director assembles the crew for a five- or ten-minute orientation. It is unlikely the crew members know much about your production, so this brief introduction can answer a number of questions at one time. A few minutes of explanation to everyone at this point can avoid countless later frustrations for the director. Because the crew will understand what is to happen, and why, it is in a better position to make a more meaningful contribution to the production.

SETUP AND REHEARSAL

The director is usually not closely involved with the actual studio setup once these functions can be handled by the production team following the director's prepared instructions. Nevertheless, the director should always take the time to check on

FIGURE 5-9   Camera Shot Sheets.
An easy way to make up camera shot sheets is to type them in rows on one sheet of paper. Each row can be cut out and clipped or taped to the appropriate camera.

Camera 1	Camera 2	Camera 3
1-Lake	2-Bridge	3-Trees
4-Stream	5-Waterfall	6-Canoeists
7-Woodland (fall)	8-Woodland (winter)	9-Woodland (spring)

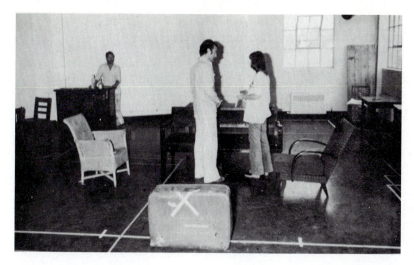

FIGURE 5-10 **Dry Rehearsal.**
A dry rehearsal takes place out of the studio. In this economical environment, the performers work out characterization, line delivery, and movement. Tape on the floor and various pieces of furniture can be used in the dry rehearsal hall to indicate studio set pieces and space limitations to help the performers prepare for the studio rehearsal.

the progress of the setup and approve the final set construction, lighting, and equipment.

The rehearsal stage is a demanding time for the director because this is when the various production elements must be coordinated and integrated into a television program. Exactly how the director approaches rehearsals will depend, in large part, on the particular show and the production mode being used. You already know that a program can be produced in a variety of ways, ranging from a live broadcast, where the director must work with the performers and crew in real time, to the single-camera/single-VTR film-style approach, where every shot is individually set up, lit, rehearsed, and videotaped before moving on to the next. The particular production mode will obviously influence the director's rehearsal approach. A director who uses a segmented or a shot-by-shot approach can concentrate on small portions of the show, perfecting and taping each one before going to the next. A show that is to be produced live or live-on-tape must be rehearsed in its entirety because that is how it must ultimately be produced.

Dry Rehearsal

The earliest rehearsal sessions take place outside the studio in a rehearsal hall. This is when the performers and director first assemble to read through the script and to discuss the production. Since no production facilities are used, these sessions are called *dry rehearsals*.

A dry rehearsal period is always used in dramatic, musical, or comedy shows, but it is often necessary in nonentertainment productions as well. An instructional or demonstration program needs rehearsals as much as any other type of program. A series of dry rehearsals in an office or large room will help the in-studio rehearsals and production of any show proceed more smoothly.

Once the initial read-throughs are completed and the necessary script changes are made, the director begins to work out talent blocking. Although you may be working in a room without sets or props, you can use tables, chairs, and other available furniture to suggest the actual set pieces and their relative positions. Some directors mark the exact dimensions of the set with masking tape to give the performers or actors a more accurate idea of their working area. However you simulate the studio set, try to keep your talent moving in an area that closely approximates the size of the actual setting. (See Figure 5-10.)

The director should give the performers some idea of where each camera will be positioned, how far the boom will extend to cover performers or actors, when they must hit their marks exactly, and so on. As you begin to take talent through the pre-planned blocking, you are likely to find some situations in which your early ideas are not working and others when someone comes up with improvements.

Dry rehearsal should be a time of innovation and experimentation. Although you want to keep the rehearsal proceeding on schedule, this is also when you can afford to be most flexible in trying out new ideas and alternative approaches. By the end of the dry rehearsal, both director and talent should be satisfied with the basic blocking. If you expect the performers or actors to have their lines memorized, give them an exact date when you want them to be "off book." If you will be using cue cards or other prompting devices, have them available so talent can practice working with them. This is particularly important for nonprofessional performers who are unfamiliar with using cue cards or prompters.

Studio Rehearsal

Studio rehearsal is a crucial time for the director. In too little time with too much to accomplish, the director must establish the shooting sequence, integrate all production elements, and at the same time maintain an objective eye and ear for the creative aspects of the program. Juggling both the technical matters and aesthetic judgments is not easy, and the time pressures, which all directors encounter, compound the difficulty. The secret is to use your rehearsal time as efficiently as possible: Have a plan worked out in advance, establish a rough rehearsal schedule of what must be accomplished by what time, and try not to get blocked by a minor problem that may take too much time away from the overall production.

The studio rehearsal generally proceeds through three phases: (1) camera blocking, (2) run-throughs, and (3) dress rehearsal.

Camera Blocking   The director has already established the talent blocking during dry rehearsal. Now is the time to determine the shots, angles, and positions for each camera. Camera blocking can be tedious and repetitious, especially for talent. The director should warn performers or actors of what to expect. Advise them to avoid expending all their energy in blocking and to save it for the dress rehearsal and actual production. If you are working with performers or actors who are inexperienced with television, explain what is happening so they will understand why they are asked to repeat a move over and over.

Some directors like to block cameras from the control booth; others prefer to work directly on the studio floor. The floor approach has an advantage in that the director can communicate easily to everyone involved and can see any problems instantly as they occur. If the director wears a PL headset connected to the switcher in the control room, any of the cameras can be punched up on the studio monitor as the blocking proceeds.

If you are working with a tightly scripted show, your shots already are established for every camera. If you are working on a semiscripted or unscripted production, give each camera an idea of its primary shooting responsibilities. For example, in an interview situation, Camera 2, which is positioned in the center, might be assigned to maintain a fairly wide shot and to cover the host, while Cameras 1 and 3 might be told to photograph whomever on the panel is talking.

Do not spend a lot of time during camera blocking perfecting the framing and composition of every shot; that will come later. For now, simply establish the camera's basic shot to be sure that, first, the camera operator understands what is to be photographed and, second, that the camera is in position to shoot the subject.

Camera Run-throughs   Once the camera shots, angles, and positions are established, the director can begin to run through the actual show. Understandably, the earliest run-throughs proceed much more slowly than normal, as production problems are encountered and resolved. The director should try to speed up the pacing of the run-through as soon as possible, though, until the production is moving along at close to normal speed. Only then will problems in pacing or with blocking moves of cameras and talent become apparent. It is a good idea to direct most run-throughs from the control booth, since the director can watch all camera monitors simultaneously and also can begin to work with the rest of the production team on their cues and operations.

The run-through usually flows in a start-and-stop manner in the beginning, with the director stopping to correct problems as they develop, backing up a little, and moving on until the next problem occurs. Once you have run through the entire production at least once and corrected what appear to be the major problems, successive run-throughs should become increasingly smooth as everyone starts to coordinate their operations.

The director is naturally concentrating on technical matters at this point but should not forget to keep an eye on the performances as well. Remind performers or actors of the necessity to remain as consistent as possible in their movements and voice projection and to be careful in handling graphics or other objects that are to be shot in close-up.

GIVING NOTES   After each rehearsal period is over, the director should give out suggestions, criticisms, and changes in the form of notes. If you have a production assistant available to jot down notes as they occur to you during rehearsal, you will not have to stop to write them down yourself. Otherwise, make some indication in your script so you will not forget your comments once the rehearsal is over. A good director hands out notes discreetly. Constant criticism of cast or crew will not necessarily result in superior performances. The note session should be a combination of the director's thoughts and the production team's feedback. Remember, the source of a good suggestion is unimportant; if the suggestion improves the show, it will make the director look better.

Dress Rehearsal   It is impossible to overestimate the importance of a dress rehearsal. The dress is the final chance for everyone to do the show before it is actually produced. If you never have a dress rehearsal—a complete show from start to finish—your air show will actually be the dress. Whatever problems might have been solved earlier will be a part of the production. Naturally, not all shows have a dress, but even a spontaneous and unscripted program can rehearse the opening, the closing, and some of the segments within the show.

The dress should include every element that will appear on the final production, including credits, music, sound effects, lighting cues, film, VTR inserts, and so on. Some directors like to tape the dress rehearsal, since there are times when the best performances of both cast and crew occur in dress, not in the actual air show. If you will be doing videotape editing, you can combine the best

performances from the dress and air shows into a superior production.

PRODUCTION

Strange as it may seem, in most artistic endeavors the actual production effort is almost anticlimatic. All the real work and planning are poured into the preproduction and rehearsal periods. If the preparation was done properly, the production itself will flow smoothly. A symphony conductor spends hours carefully analyzing the musical score to develop a point of view and a style. Then he or she enters into hours of intensive rehearsal as he or she molds the members of the orchestra into an ensemble unit, shaping, coloring, and building the sound. By the time of the actual performance, replicating what has already been achieved during planning and practice is the task at hand.

It is much the same for the television director. After so much time in preproduction and rehearsal, the actual production usually leaves little to be discovered. Of course, a live program poses its greatest challenges during the actual broadcast. Even so, the director already should have decided on the basic approach, the camera coverage, and how to use all the production equipment and techniques available. (See Figure 5-11.)

The Psychology of Directing

Directing—like sex—is one of those activities which must be experienced to be fully appreciated. We have only scratched the surface here, but regardless of how much reading you do about television directing, there is no substitute for the actual experience.

Before you sit in the director's chair, however, there are some points you ought to consider, which we will call the "psychology of directing." First, remember that the director is the leader of the production team. Consciously or unconsciously, the team relies on the director for guidance and for support. A director who appears to be in command will convey that feeling to the cast and crew. A director who appears tentative and uncertain will communicate this insecurity, which can result in a nervous and unsure performance. A good director is open with the crew, solicits suggestions and advice, but is also capable of making a firm decision when necessary.

When you sit in the director's chair, you must be the *director,* not the *directed.* Beginning directors are often overwhelmed by the barrage of information thrust on them—watching the camera monitors, following the script, listening to the audio, tracking the time, cuing shots and talent, watching the show on the line monitor, and trying to maintain some sort of objective perspective of the entire production. If you are not careful, these many elements can begin to run out of your control, forcing you to respond to events that have already occurred rather than to make things happen at your command. It is almost like Frankenstein's monster, who turns on its creator. Instead of the director controlling the show, the show controls the director. All the director can do in such a situation is to hold on and try to stay with the rapidly increasing momentum of a production gone out of control.

How do you avoid this? It is easier said than done, and a lot of it will come with practice and experience. One way to start is to develop the idea that everything which happens should occur because you, as director, want it to happen. The minute you feel control slipping away (it happens to every director at one time or another), realize what is happening and try to recover by slowing the pace, by going to a wide shot and staying there until you find your place, and by mentally composing yourself. Much like Hemingway's characters, a good director exhibits "grace under pressure."

When Things Go Wrong

Even on the most carefully planned show things are bound to go wrong sooner or later. A camera suddenly goes dead on a live broadcast, the film projector jams in the middle of a crucial insert, or an actor blows lines, upsetting your carefully prepared shot sequence. You cannot avoid these situations, but you can learn to develop the right attitude to deal with them.

"One thing I've learned," says John Litvack, a director of CBS-TV's *Guiding Light,* "is that nobody out there watching the show has a copy of your shooting script. There's not one viewer that knows you should have been on Camera 2 when you were on Camera 3." Quite often a mistake that seems so obvious to you goes completely unnoticed by the average viewer. And even when mistakes are obvious, getting excited or upset about them will not correct the problem. A calm director who thinks ahead quickly can respond to a problem with minimal damage to the show.

If you are videotaping a production, you might take a ten-minute break after a disaster has forced you to stop shooting. Sometimes all it takes is a break in the tension to help everyone (including the director) relax and recharge. Rather than push everyone to the limit, call a short break; it can be

FIGURE 5-11   Director in Production.
During production, the director calls shots from the monitors, not from the pages of the script. The script serves as a guide and reference, but the monitors show the all important videospace as seen by the viewers.

the most effective medicine for a hypertense production team.

Consider the Team

One final point is to consider the effort of the production team. It is easy to forget the enormous concentration and physical energy expended by everyone working on a show. Be sure to give rest breaks from time to time even if you are under time pressure. A refreshed crew and cast will invariably turn in a better performance. Finally, remember to thank everyone once the production is over. Regardless of how well or poorly the show ran, a "thank you" is a small courtesy that is always largely appreciated.

POSTPRODUCTION

The director's primary role in postproduction is to supervise the editing of videotaped shows. There are times when the editing is a simple assembly of various segments into a completed production. Other editing sessions may involve the elaborate editing of individual shots to build each sequence and then the assembly of each sequence into the final show. We discuss video editing fully in Chapter 23.

Viewing the Footage

The director's first job is to sit down and watch all the recorded footage that was marked "good" or "maybe" on the production take sheets. If you can make a work copy of the footage on ¾-inch or ½-inch tape, you will be able to view your tape off-line under less expensive and less distracting conditions. If you are editing with time code, you can begin to write down possible edit points as you view.

Screen the footage critically but with an open mind. First impressions in the control room can be deceiving. You may think, for instance, that there is nothing worthwhile in the dress rehearsal footage while you are in the booth only to find when viewing the recording later that there is a lot of strong material that can be used. Although you need not spend time viewing takes that were labeled "no good," do not throw them away yet. You

may still be able to use a shot or a short segment from a bad take even though the entire sequence was unsatisfactory.

TECH TIP   Do not get locked into thinking of a continuous shot as something which cannot be broken up in postproduction. Sometimes a superior beginning linked to a fluffed close can be saved by inserting a cutaway after the good beginning and returning to a usable close from another take.

It is a good idea to use a fresh copy of the script as an editing script. Make notes about the types of shots on both sides of a potential edit point to avoid producing a jump cut or a poor visual match. It is to be hoped that you will have recorded some protection, or cover shots, reactions, and pickups which can be used to smooth out difficult video transitions during editing.

Do not concentrate only on the picture, but listen carefully to the audio as well. Poor audio can be as good a reason to reject a take as a poorly framed shot. If you are working with multitrack audio recorders and postproduction audio mixing, start to think how you will be mixing the audio with the picture. The final audio mix is usually done when the video has been edited together, but considering both audio and video simultaneously will give you more control over both production elements.

Finally, remember that as you edit the show you may inadvertently alter the pacing of the shots. After you have completed editing a series of shots or segments, go back and view the entire sequence straight through with an eye on the pacing to make certain it remains consistent with the rest of the show.

COMMON DIRECTING SITUATIONS

The term *television production* applies to a wide variety of programming ranging from commercial broadcasting to educational and industrial closed-circuit communications. Yet, from the director's point of view, it is possible to group all programs into four major production categories: (1) fully scripted programs, (2) semiscripted programs, (3) unscripted programs, and (4) remote production. In this section we will discuss some of the most common programs within these four categories and show some of the directorial considerations for programming within each of the four. Our purpose is not to give you a detailed "recipe" to follow, since that is technically impossible and aesthetically undesirable, but rather to give you some idea of the director's role in working with various types of programs and to point out similarities and differences among the most common directing situations.

Fully Scripted Programs

As the name suggests, for shows in this category, the director uses a detailed script with specific dialogue and action that is rehearsed completely before production. The most common types of fully scripted shows are newscasts, dramatic or comedy shows, and musical programs.

Newscasts   The newscast has become a staple of broadcast and cable television. Although the newscast is fully scripted—insofar as the newscasters read from a prepared script—owing to time limitations, it is often produced without a complete rehearsal. The standard operations, such as the use of chroma key, lower-third graphic inserts, and film and VTR rolls, are done so often that once the pattern has been established, there is little need for daily rehearsals with an experienced production team.

The important factor in a newscast is to establish the basic operating procedures which are used day after day. It does not matter which graphic is actually used or which visual is chroma-keyed onto the screen. As long as the crew is able to perform the operation smoothly, the program will have a polished and precise on-air look. Any change in program format or a major change in the talent or production crew is a good time to schedule some rehearsals and run-throughs until the director is satisfied that the team is well coordinated again. News can occur so quickly at times that director and crew must work largely on instinct and habit when deadlines run close to air time. As long as the production has an established and workable production format, the director can handle the fastest-breaking news with little difficulty.

Here are some of the important points a newscast director should consider:

1   Make certain everyone knows and understands the preroll cue time that is used for VTR inserts. Confusion here can result in disastrous introductions and transitions.

2   Assign someone on the production team to check all graphics (on slide, camera card, or electronic still store) before the broadcast. The electronic graphics or CG operator usually fills this role. If no one is available, leave yourself enough time to check them for accuracy and correct sequencing.

3   Use the format sheet or daily rundown sheet to preview all videotape clips. Check for the proper sequence and to make sure that the running time, indicated on both the rundown sheet and the script, is accurate.

4   If you will be A- or B-rolling videotape, be sure you know the right cues and times for switching sound or video from one VTR to the other.

5   Look ahead to the next series of major events. Have some alternative plans in mind in the event of such unexpected problems as failure of the live remote feed or bad audio from the on-site reporter.

6   Timing is critical on a newscast because of the number of short VTR segments, the A- and B-rolling operation, which requires precision coordination of sound and picture; and the unexpected flow of news events, which can cause instant changes in a previously planned newscast. Whether you work with an AD or keep time yourself, you must be able to time all program segments accurately and to calculate running time, program time, and dead-pot time quickly and efficiently.

Drama and Comedy   Although drama and comedy may appear to be quite different types of programs, from the director's perspective the two can be approached in much the same way. The director assigned to either must read the program's script until he or she is sufficiently familiar with it to develop the approach and point of view that will be used to interpret the writer's script into pictures and sound.

Once the director is familiar with the script, he or she can begin to work out camera and talent blocking. The particular shots are determined by the director's point of view and interpretation of the script and characters.

In any dramatic or comedy show, the actors are of paramount importance. Although you are using television technology to convey the performance to a viewing audience, the play comes from the actors. The director must do whatever is necessary to make the actors feel comfortable, so that they can deliver the best possible performance. During the early dry rehearsals, the director should encourage the give and take of ideas, suggestions, and changes from the cast. This will help to make the actors feel more at ease with their dialogue and blocking and can result in a better overall show.

Timing—in terms of both actor performance and cutting from shot to shot—is an essential ingredient in both comedy and drama. Unless the director is able to meet the actor at the right place, at the right time, and with the right shot, the dramatic or comic moment that is being so carefully developed can be completely lost. The choice of shot, angle, and other aesthetic factors must never be casually decided in comedy or drama, but should be carefully selected to complement the script and the performances. Remember too that there are times when a simple reaction shot at the right moment or a nonverbal expression shot in close-up can be more powerful and revealing than pages of dialogue.

Musical Programs   Musical production situations vary in complexity from a relatively simple tune sung within a daily variety program to an elaborate opera performed by a full cast and symphonic orchestra. Musical programs can be difficult at times because they do not always have a written script with lines and action to follow. If you will be directing the performance of a singer or a group, you can transcribe the lyrics to use as the basic shooting script. For musical breaks between lyrics, indicate the solo instrument and the number of bars played between the lyrics.

TECH TIP   If you are to direct such classical works as symphonic or chamber music, you might use an actual musical score as the script. If you cannot read music notation, have a musician help follow the score for you. Simply indicate your shots on the score itself, and follow the notation as you would follow conventionally written dialogue.

How much you can do with a musical group in terms of shots depends in large part on how the performers are arranged on the studio set. Before deciding on any setting, consult the group to discuss its performance. Some musicians may have to be physically close together or at least maintain a line of sight so they can follow each other as they play. Work out a staging arrangement that will offer you some interesting pictorial composition with strong foreground and background elements. Avoid a setting in which important members of a group are in positions where the cameras cannot shoot them easily during the show.

Once you know the specific selections to be performed, listen to the music repeatedly until you begin to visualize what you want to show the audience. Make certain that the arrangement you are using to plan your shots is identical to the one that will be performed. A different arrangement might require a radical alteration of your planned shot sequence.

Avoid the common pitfall of scheduling too many shots for any musical number. Music that is being performed can go much faster than you might imagine while listening to a tape in your office. It is better to underestimate the number of shots you can comfortably use and to add more later than to have overplanned shots only to find that your shooting sequence is in a shambles when the cameras cannot get the shots in the time they have available.

TECH TIP   When planning musical programs, check the volume on the PL communication system. Music is often loud when performed—this applies to all music and groups short of a classical guitarist—and the volume can overpower a weak PL system, making director's commands unintelligible to camera operators.

Semiscripted Programs

A semiscripted show follows a definite program format, or rundown, but does not use a script containing word-by-word dialogue. Semiscripted programs are frequently used in instructional or demonstration-type programs, where the sequence of events is planned prior to production, but the actual dialogue is spontaneous within the preset format. Although semiscripted programs do not use a complete script, much of the show can still be thoroughly planned and rehearsed prior to production.

Demonstration and Instructional Shows The program format category of demonstration and instructional shows spans a wide range from the familiar cooking and gardening shows to instructional closed-circuit programming used in many schools, universities, and industries.

Generally, the demonstration and instructional show is produced in one of two ways. In the first approach, the talent speaks directly to the viewer. In the second approach, the talent is accompanied by a host or interviewer who acts as a substitute audience, asking questions, clarifying points, and providing emphasis where necessary. The advantage of the latter approach is that an experienced host can help nonprofessional talent by handling all the technical chores, such as timing, receiving cues, and remembering which of the cameras is on the air at a particular time.

Most demonstration and instructional programs use a fully scripted opening and close but only a detailed rundown sheet for the middle sections of the show. Even though talent may not need a complete set of cue cards, it is a good idea to put the outline of the show on a cue card so the talent will not alter the planned sequence of events once you are into production. Experts may know what they want to say, but they can easily confuse the order of events, which can ruin your camera blocking and shot sequence.

A demonstration can usually be covered by assigning at least one camera to shoot talent while another camera shoots a close-up of the action. This way you can vary the size of the talent shot from wide to close-up while still following the demonstration easily on the other camera.

Shooting effective close-ups takes some planning and coordination between director and talent. Make certain talent knows which camera will shoot the close-ups, and remain consistent with your shots. Instruct talent on the best angle to hold the objects for the most effective close-up shot. A studio monitor placed nearby, within sight of talent, can help performers to coordinate their moves with the camera operators. (See Figure 5-12.)

Talk and Variety Programs The talk and variety show is a potpourri of interviews, music, and features. Such shows are either partially or completely unscripted but rely on a very precise rundown sheet, which carefully outlines and times each program segment. The director uses the rundown sheet as a guide and tries to preset camera shots beforehand. Usually, musical segments and complex demonstrations are rehearsed before production.

For interview or talk segments, most directors develop a standard format that is followed on every show. On a three-camera production, for example, the middle camera might be used to cover a wide shot of the panel. One of the side cameras could cross-shoot whoever is talking at any given time, and the other side camera could be used to cross-shoot the opposite side of the panel. Once the basic shooting pattern is established, the director relies heavily on the camera operators to get their shots as automatically as possible.

Unscripted Programs

The term is somewhat misleading because even an *unscripted* show contains certain segments which are planned prior to production. In addition, most unscripted programs follow some sort of rundown sheet, which indicates the basic structure of the show and the ways openings, closing, and transitions are to be produced. Since this is the case, the open, close, and some of the internal sequences can be practiced and rehearsed prior to production.

Special News Coverage Special news events, such as election returns, extraordinary legislative sessions, parades, and rallies, are examples of

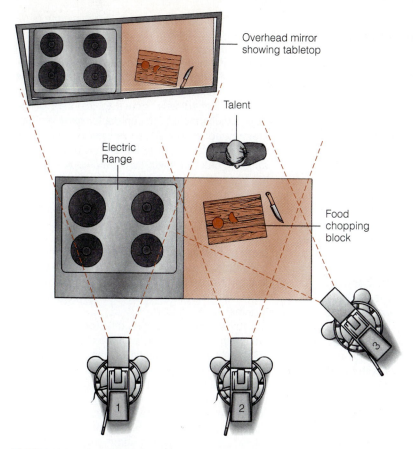

FIGURE 5-12 **Demonstration Program.**
This setup for a cooking demonstration shows effective camera use to cover the program. Camera 2 primarily shoots the performer and varies the shot size as requested by the director. Talent is instructed to speak to Camera 2. Camera 3 shoots primarily close-ups of the demonstration on the tabletop. Talent is instructed to "cheat" objects and graphics toward Camera 3 whenever they must be covered in close-up. Camera 1 shoots the demonstration as it appears in the overhead mirror, which is suspended directly above the demonstration table.

unscripted coverage. However, certain aspects of these programs can be planned and rehearsed to establish a production *pattern* for the director, crew, and talent. Again, the idea is to work out the use of cameras and equipment in the production, not to worry about specific content. Naturally, openings, closings, and transitions can all be rehearsed prior to air time.

Since the director is busy directing what is usually a live broadcast, the producer must take an active role during the production by alerting the director to the most important events and coordinating the various facets of the production. For example, on election returns, the producer should watch the different stories unfold and tell the director which story (and, therefore, which cameras, locations, talent, and so on) to cut to next. The same is true for any special news coverage. On many large preplanned events, the organizer of the event will usually hold an advance press conference to give details concerning the sequence of the event, anticipated running times, and other pertinent facts, which can be helpful to the director. If at all possible, both the director and the producer should attend these conferences and then hold their own preproduction briefing with the production team prior to broadcast.

Sports Coverage   The popularity of football, baseball, basketball, hockey, and other sports events has made sports coverage a programming standard for local stations and cable systems, as well as for regional and national networks. In Chapter 22 we will discuss the specific details of preparing and setting up sports broadcasts. For now, we will cover in a more general way the director's planning and preparation for directing sports programming.

As with any production, the director of a sports event must be thoroughly familiar with the rules and play of the game, as well as with the style of play of the particular teams or participants, what they tend to do in various situations, who the outstanding players are, and the possible color stories that surround the main event. Unless you know these things, you cannot do an effective job of covering a fast-moving game, regardless of the sport.

If you have been assigned to direct a game with which you are not completely familiar, the first thing to do is to watch as many events as possible prior to production. Also, do some reading about the sport and the strategies and tactics employed. Generally, the publicity offices of the teams will be able to provide you with team rosters, background information, and, sometimes, useful tips on what may happen during the game. Not only is this information helpful to the director, but it also should be passed along to the play-by-play commentator.

The director relies more on the production crew during a sports event than in any other directing situation. There simply is not time for the director to call for every shot, graphic, replay, or audio cue. The entire team—not just the camera operators—must be completely involved in the production, all doing their jobs with a minimum of directorial commands.

To illustrate, say you are directing a football game and have just covered a successfully completed pass from the quarterback to a receiver. As soon as the live play is over, the videotape replay operator immediately recues to the start of the play. Simultaneously, the character generator operator punches in the receiver's jersey number to retrieve the appropriate lower-third graphic. The switcher has the lower-third graphic keyed over the freeze-frame and ready on preview. As soon as the director asks for the effect on the air, the VTR operator begins the playback, varying the speed to emphasize the crucial elements of the play in slow motion and replaying less critical parts at normal speed. Except for the director's command to punch up the freeze-frame key and to start the replay playback, everything else was done automatically by a crew working closely together.

Ted Nathanson, a sports director for NBC, tells a story that illustrates how alert a crew should be. "One day we were covering a game when all of a sudden a dog ran out on the field, temporarily halting play. Before I said a word all five cameras had the same close-up shot of the dog. Unfortunately, at that very moment the dog was responding to nature's call in front of millions of viewers. Since all my cameras had the same shot there wasn't anything I could cut to. It was a little embarrassing, but I had to give my guys credit for getting the important shot before I ever had a chance to call for it."

Ted Nathanson's preprogram routine is a good example of how a director approaches any sports show. Nathanson spends the week prior to the game studying both teams, their players, and their tactics. He also speaks with the production's play-by-play announcer and the "color" analyst to coordinate isolated shots and possible *color* coverage from the bench, sidelines, or dugout. Just prior to the game he meets with the production team for a program briefing. He outlines the two teams, explains their overall strategies—what might be expected of each team in various situations and which players to watch carefully—and any other relevant details. Each camera operator is assigned a particular area of responsibility, depending on the game situation. The camera operators will be expected to get their shots with a minimum of direction, since not every shot can be called and set during the game. Nathanson gives similar instructions to the VTR operators, the audio technician, and the character-generator and still-frame-unit operators. The AD is used primarily for timing and to coordinate communications between the remote unit and the home studio. The producer calls all isolated and replay instructions and helps to alert the director to important events during the game. You will note that Nathanson tries to prepare the crew to react properly under different circumstances and situations. After the orientation, he expects them to use their own skills and judgments, since it would be impossible for him to call out every cue for every production operation during the frenetic activity of any live sports broadcast.

Finally, the director should remember that many viewers expect more than just the game coverage itself. Although the game is the center of attention, stories from the sidelines, the crowd in the stands, cheerleaders, and other "color" events enhance the audience's enjoyment of the entire sports scene. However, do not become so engrossed in using your cameras for "color" stories that you neglect the main action on the playing field.

Remote Production

Any production shot outside the studio is considered to be a *remote* production. Of course, all the usual directorial considerations for a studio production apply to remotes as well, but the nature of location shooting adds a number of additional complexities for the director to deal with during the various production stages.

ENG Production   Electronic news gathering (ENG) is generally accomplished on a regular basis without a program director per se. Usually, the reporter serves as a producer-director and works closely with the camera crew in setting up shots and camera angles. The fast-breaking nature of news events generally does not lend itself to much preproduction planning, and most day-to-day news situations are covered "on the run."

EFP Production   Electronic field production (EFP) generally means single-camera shooting/video-

taping at a remote location. EFP differs from ENG because the former is usually planned thoroughly, requires much higher overall production values, and generally includes a director who supervises the production.

EFP productions vary in size and complexity from a relatively simple shoot with only a camera operator and another crew member serving as producer-director to an elaborate production involving a large production crew and a full-fledged director. Common EFP situations are entertainment programs, magazine-type feature shows, commercials, and training/industrial productions. Since the EFP technique uses only one camera, the director can concentrate on each camera setup without having to cut between cameras as in a control room situation. However, the EFP production must be carefully preplanned so that all camera angles necessary for postproduction editing are shot and to make certain that continuity requirements are kept in mind. Another crucial consideration for the director working on an EFP production is to determine the crew members and equipment which must be brought to the location. Remember that you will not have the luxury of a fully equipped studio, so lighting, electric power, props, and even such minor items as gaffer tape and extension cords either must be brought along or provision must be made to have them available at the location site.

Multiple-Camera Remotes   A multiple-camera remote involves the use of multiple cameras and a portable control room which is usually contained inside a van or truck. In the large-scale remote (LSR) situation, the director works from a control room setting and functions exactly as he or she would in a studio control room by cutting between cameras during production. Although the LSR situation functions much like the conventional studio operation, it is still a remote, and cameras, microphones, lighting equipment, and so on must be set up specifically for the production.

In Chapter 22 we will cover each of these production situations in much greater detail. The important point for you to remember is that remote shooting requires all the director's usual skills and abilities but makes added demands on the director's capability to work with people and equipment efficiently and effectively and often under conditions that are less than ideal. Careful preproduction planning—while important to the success of any production—is an absolute necessity when you are directing a remote.

SUMMARY

The director's primary responsibility is to supervise the production team in order to transform an idea, concept, or script into the program's actual sounds and pictures. In order to work effectively with the production team, the director must establish a feeling of cooperation, teamwork, and mutual respect among the crew and production staff.

During production, the director must communicate with the entire crew, but especially with the camera operators, switcher, and floor manager. A series of operational commands has been established, and these commands should be used consistently. Commands must be precise, accurate, and economical to be most effective.

The many crucial operations performed by the program's director during rehearsal and production can be shared by an assistant director. The AD generally assumes three functions: (1) timing the show and individual segments, (2) readying upcoming cues, and (3) presetting camera shots on fully scripted shows.

During the preproduction stage, the director should meet as early as possible with the producer to agree on the interpretation, point of view, and approach to the show. Once this has been accomplished, the director can meet with key production personnel to assign specific areas of responsibility. Working with the program script and floorplan, the director (1) blocks camera and talent movements, (2) sets up individual camera shots, and (3) develops the overall shooting sequence.

While the director is not usually needed on stage during studio setup, all sets, lighting, and equipment should be checked and approved prior to rehearsal so that changes and corrections can be made in time. The director's approach in rehearsal varies depending on the show's production mode. Programs which are taped in small segments are usually rehearsed differently from live shows or programs taped in longer sections. Most rehearsal periods are divided into two parts: dry rehearsals, which are held outside the studio, and studio rehearsals, which are held in-studio with full production facilities. During dry rehearsals, the director and cast read through the script and work out talent blocking. Studio rehearsals generally consist of three operations: (1) camera blocking, in which shots are established; (2) run-throughs, when the director begins to integrate the various production elements into a unified show; and (3) dress rehearsal, which should be a replica of the final air show.

One of the director's most demanding jobs is to provide leadership and direction to the production team. In addition, the director must always be in control of the program—as the director, not the directed. As soon as events occur which are not determined by the program's director, the show can run out of control, and it may become impossible to meet the program objective determined in preproduction. A good director must remain flexible and have presence of mind to deal with unexpected emergencies or mistakes, which can happen at any time.

Postproduction consists of viewing taped footage and editing the show. Regardless of how simple or complex the editing job, the director must maintain an objective perspective, even while dealing with relatively small elements of a much larger show.

Although there is a great variation among program formats, from the director's viewpoint, all productions can be divided into four categories: (1) fully scripted programs, (2) semiscripted programs, (3) unscripted programs, and (4) remote production.

PERFORMING FOR TELEVISION

When watching a television program, the audience sees the combined efforts of the producer, director, and writer. However, the audience doesn't think about these team members—or even know who they are. After all, producing, directing, and writing are done out of sight, back-stage. Instead, the audience focuses on who they see right there on the television screen—the actors, singers, comedians, hosts, reporters, and other performers who entertain and inform them. Even if the producers, directors, and writers do their work exceptionally well, the on-camera performers are the ones who must say the lines, sing the songs, tell the jokes, ask the questions, read the reports, and ultimately attract the audience. Therefore, the *talent* is another key member of the television production team.

In television, the term *talent* is used to refer to anyone who appears on camera. The enormous variety of program formats naturally demands a diversity of talent to fit each production requirement. The weathercaster on the local news, the actor in a daytime serial, the emcee of a game show, and the business executive appearing in a corporate training tape are all very different members of the same group. For convenience, we can divide talent into two categories: (1) performers and (2) actors.

Performers appear as themselves, usually in a nonfictional situation, and often speak directly to the audience. Newscasters, announcers, interviewers, and hosts of variety shows are all familiar examples of performers. In corporate and instructional television programs, *nonprofessional talent* such as business employees, researchers, and teachers may become on-camera performers.

Actors, on the other hand, portray fictional roles and attempt to create the illusion of a character. Naturally, actors work in dramatic and comedy productions, but they also appear in such varied productions as musical-variety sketches, commercials, and children's shows. Often in nonfictional programs, such as business training tapes, actors may be cast as "real people," such as employees and technicians. Sometimes professional actors can appear more "real" on television than the "real people" they portray.

Whether in fiction or nonfiction programs, the basic performance fundamentals for all television talent—actor and performer alike—are essentially similar, and all talent have the same objective: to communicate a message, idea, or emotion to the viewer. However, there are some significant differences between the performer and the actor.

The performer often works with only a partial script and with a minimum of rehearsal. The ability to ad-lib, to think and act quickly, and to remain conscious of the program's timing and the director's cues as well as the on-camera performance are all important abilities necessary for a performer. To a great extent, the performer is often as much in control of a semiscripted or unscripted program as the director.

Because the actor usually works on a fully scripted show that has been rehearsed in advance, the television actor requires a slightly different set of skills. Rather than deal with unpredictable events, the actor has as his or her primary job developing and sustaining a believable character, often with very little advance time to prepare, and to deliver an effective performance in the midst of the controlled chaos that usually accompanies any television production.

To perform well in any medium—the stage, film, radio, or television—talent should know something about how the medium operates and how the actor or performer must interact with it. The characteristics of the medium and talent's responsibilities in the production process must be understood.

CHARACTERISTICS OF THE MEDIUM

Because television often seems so lifelike and such a part of our daily experience, we forget that it is an electronic medium with a number of characteristics that influence how we perceive the programming and its talent. In Chapter 2 we described the formal visual structure of videospace. This structure has several important features that actors and performers need to keep in mind. These features include the medium's intimacy and how television's close-up look demands that talent appear natural. Somewhat paradoxically, a performer or actor must move, dress, and apply makeup differently on camera to appear "normal" onscreen.

Intimacy

Television is the most intimate of the visual media, far more than either film or the stage. The reasons for this intimacy have to do with both the viewing environment and the videospace.

Viewing Environment   Although the total audience for a broadcast program may be thirty million people, most television viewing occurs alone or in the presence of the family or a small group of friends. This, coupled with the fact that most viewers watch television in their home and not in a public arena such as a theater, leads viewers to develop a more personal contact with television talent. And, because they often enter the home on a nightly or weekly basis, talent become familiar. These frequent appearances in the privacy of the home tend to develop a special relationship between television talent and the individual viewer.

The Videospace   The influence of the home viewing environment is reinforced by the videospace, which, as we have seen, is the environment created by the television screen. The talent must always be concerned with the impact of the videospace and how the cameras and microphones translate their image and voice to the audience.

(a)

(b)

FIGURE 6-1 **Videospace Proxemics.**
To appear natural in the videospace, performers or actors must work physically close
to one another on-camera. (*a*) This is a comfortable face-to-face distance which
looks too far apart in the videospace. (*b*) Performers at the correct working distance
for television.

SCREEN SIZE AND RESOLUTION The small screen and limited resolution of the television set has led directors to concentrate on close-ups, literally bringing talent closer to the audience. The small screen size and tight composition of most camera shots result in "head shots" that approximate life size. Close miking that parallels tight visual composition moves the audience into close conversational distance. As a result, television mimics interpersonal experience more than other mediums and requires that performances appear and feel *real.* The slightest gesture, expression, or vocal inflection that seems *staged* flaws the television performance. The close scrutiny of the camera as it brings the audience into close interpersonal distance uncovers the slightest phoniness in a performer or actor and demands great skill on his or her part to appear natural.

SCREEN SPACE Actors and performers who are new to television frequently complain that they are uncomfortable working so physically close to each other on camera. However, what feels awkwardly close to talent in front of the camera appears normal onscreen, and when actors and performers stand at a comfortable interpersonal distance, the space between them appears unnaturally large in the television program. This is just one more example of the fact that it is the ap-

pearance in the videospace which ultimately counts because that is where the audience will see and evaluate the performance. (See Figure 6-1.)

In addition to working close, talent must work "slow" and "small." Many studio sets are compact in actual physical dimensions and "stretched" by a wide-angle lens to exaggerate or extend depth. As a result, when an actor or performer moves toward or away from the camera, the speed and size of his or her movements are increased. Approaching another actor or performer at a slow, measured pace will appear perfectly natural on-camera. On the other hand, two steps at normal speed may propel talent halfway through an apparently spacious set when photographed through a wide-angle lens.

IMAGE SIZE Lens characteristics also give *upstaging* a different meaning in television than in the theater. In theater, the term implies "stealing" a scene by moving to the front of the stage in front of another actor. In television, another meaning for the term is mismatching the size of your gestures or expressions with your location in the scene.

For example, the foreground actor fills much of the screen space in a shot. As a result, even small facial twitches or eyebrow raises communicate very powerfully to the audience. However, ges-

146

tures are constrained because large arm movements are quickly thrown outside the screen's borders. On the other hand, the actor working in the background is relatively small on the screen but is surrounded by relatively more space on the set. For this individual, small nuances of expression are lost because of the small size and limited resolution of their image. The loss of these tools is somewhat compensated by being able to use more dramatic and complete body movements and still have their effect captured by the camera lens. The most accomplished actors and performers benefit from knowing the lens focal length setting and by taking their location on the set into account as they prepare their mannerisms and movements for the television camera within each different shot. (See Figure 6-2.)

ASPECT RATIO The screen's aspect ratio also requires talent to gesture and move differently than might feel natural. An example that occurs thousands of times every week on television involves an attractive actor presenting a small product in a commercial. The camera, set to a medium close-up to accentuate the sparkling teeth or shiny hair of the actor, can only see the tooth paste or shampoo if it is held almost parallel with the actor's chin. Without the demands of the camera, most people would hold up a small object for demonstration purposes at around chest level. As an-

FIGURE 6-2 **The Importance of Image Size.**
To act effectively, talent should know how large they appear in the camera shot. Here, foreground talent's raised eye brow communicates, but a background performer would need a larger gesture to reach the audience.

other example, actors trying to demonstrate their passions with "talking" hands find their motion limited to in front of the body rather than in far-flung histrionics.

DEPTH OF FIELD Besides image size and aspect ratio, the television image's depth of field influences how talent behaves for the camera. When depth of field is limited, more of the talent's movements must occur at the same distance from the camera or they will go out of focus and not communicate. For example, many people express interest by leaning into a conversation. In close-up, such an act would throw the talent outside the depth of field. Instead, talent might have to cock his or her head to one side to register interest and to avoid becoming blurred on the screen.

Audiospace The medium's characteristics extend to audio as well as video. On stage or in person, talent must project to the most distant member of the audience. In film, the superior audio systems with which most theaters are equipped allow actors to greatly vary the loudness of their performance. Television is somewhere between the stage and film. In TV, each audience member has a front-row, rather than a last-row, seat. Yet the dynamic range of the television audio system, constrained by the noisy home viewing environment, limits the television talent's use of subtlety. Overall, television talent must speak at a relatively consistent level, relying on pace, word choice, and inflection more than loudness to convey emotions.

Overall, the combination of the medium's audiospace and videospace characteristics and the intimate home viewing environment tend to involve the audience members with talent in a one-to-one relationship. For those performers who communicate directly with the audience—a newscaster or program host, for example—this relationship becomes almost "friend to friend." For actors who portray a role, the intensity of the identification can result in viewers confusing fantasy with reality. The actor is perceived by the audience as the character he or she plays. A number of soap opera actors, particularly those who play "heavies" or villains, have reported being accosted on the street by an outraged fan who mistakenly believes the actor is the character they see regularly onscreen.

Clothing and Wardrobe

Performers generally wear normal street clothing for work, but your on-camera wardrobe should be selected carefully. Your understanding of videospace should tell you that there are some clothing styles, colors, and fabrics which may look fine in person but can appear unflattering onscreen. A performer's clothing must be selected as much for the effects of the videospace as for style and appearance.

Color   The choice of color depends a great deal on your own taste and style, but stay away from colors that are too bold, bright, or deeply saturated. These colors tend to reproduce poorly, do not enhance your looks onscreen, and can actually impair your communication effectiveness. Most performers look best on television in muted, lightly saturated colors.

The set in which you will appear is naturally an important consideration when selecting your clothing. You will want to achieve a good color balance between the set and your clothing and the proper amount of contrast for color reproduction. Clothing colors with too much contrast—a white shirt worn against a black limbo background, for example—can interfere with the camera's operation and affect your appearance. On the other hand, insufficient contrast will not separate you from the background and will create an uninteresting and ineffective impression. One of the costliest clothing mistakes in television history occurred during the 1960 presidential debates. Richard Nixon showed up for the broadcast wearing a light-gray suit which was almost identical in color and brightness value to the light-gray set. The insufficient contrast between Nixon in the foreground and the gray background on the black and white television screen contributed to his overall poor appearance, which, in turn, adversely

affected viewer perceptions and was one of the factors that cost him the debate.

The proper contrast between a performer's own articles of clothing—shirt and pants, for example—and the contrast between clothing and skin tone are equally important. Avoid wearing pure white or deep blacks. A white shirt with a black suit, for instance, may upset the picture's normal contrast ratio and cause camera shading problems, which will hurt your appearance. Reds and oranges also pose problems for television cameras. Shirts and blouses in pastel blues, yellows, and grays are preferable to white and usually photograph better. Dark-colored clothing tends to make a pale subject appear even lighter. On the other hand, light-colored clothing will make dark-skinned or heavily tanned performers look even darker on screen.

An extremely important color consideration concerns the use of chroma key. In chroma key, a selected *key color* in the foreground shot is replaced by a background image. That is how a weather forecaster actually standing in front of a blue wall appears to be standing in front of a map. The map is chroma keyed into the blue part of the foreground shot. If the color of your clothing too closely matches the chroma key color, you may find yourself doing an unintentional imitation of the invisible man as your clothing disappears into the background. If there is any question in your mind about a particular color or article of clothing, check it out on the set to make certain it will not interfere with the chroma key. Remember that the most frequent key color used is blue, and performers wearing blue jeans will make chroma keying difficult. (See Figure 6-3.)

Patterns and Fabrics   The correct choice of clothing patterns and fabrics is an additional wardrobe consideration. Avoid closely lined patterns such as herringbones, checks, and small plaids, which may produce a *moire effect*. This is the annoying flash of multicolored light produced when the clothing's pattern interferes with the camera's scanning operation.

Avoid patterns or fabrics with very small or highly intricate detail. The resolution limitations of the camera may completely wash out the detail on screen. Stay away from very busy patterns which

(a)   (b)

FIGURE 6-3 Chroma Keying.
(a) The color of clothing worn by the talent is different from the chroma key color.
(b) The color of clothing worn by the talent is the same as the chroma key color.

will distract the viewer's attention from the most important part of the show: you and your message. Simple patterns and solids tend to look best, and variation can be added through such accessories as scarfs, ties, and jewelry.

Material that is highly reflective, such as a starched shirt, or material which absorbs a great deal of light, such as velvet or velour, should not be worn on camera. The highly reflective fabric may glare or wash out completely, while velour and velvet are so light-absorbent that all detail is lost as the various dark tones merge together.

Fabrics or patterns with vertical lines tend to give a thinner and taller appearance. Horizontal lines usually exaggerate size and weight. Since television tends to add a few pounds to most people, avoid fabrics or patterns which emphasize your size and weight in an unflattering way.

Line The way clothing is cut often has an impact on talent's appearance. Baggy or loose-fitting clothing will always make you look worse, especially because television gives the impression of added weight to most talent. Clothing that is tailored and shaped is generally best because it produces a clean and tapered line onscreen. Of course, you should not try to wear tight-fitting, tapered clothes if you are not built for it. In general, clothing should fit you well without appearing overly tight or form-fitting. Since most productions use multiple cameras which shoot from a variety of angles, select clothing that will flatter your appearance from all sides.

Accessories Ties, scarfs, and jewelry can help to vary your wardrobe and enhance your on-camera appearance, but they should never distract or overwhelm the viewer. A three-carat diamond hanging from your neck may look elegant, but it is also taking the viewer's eyes away from you. Dangling earrings that move and bracelets that clank together also compete for viewer attention. Unless you have a good reason for doing so, stay away from overly shiny, flashy, or garish jewelry, which can cause glare and specular reflections. Sequins, rhinestones, and glitter also should be worn sparingly, and only for effect. (See Figure 6-4.)

Image Overall, the clothing you wear says a great deal about you even before you have said a single word. We tend to associate types of clothing with certain roles and images, and we become uncomfortable when clothing does not match the role. You would probably be suspicious if a doctor wore overalls while examining you or if you spoke with a banker who wore a suit with leather fringes. If you want to be taken seriously on television, do not show up wearing a tennis shirt and jeans.

Your clothing selection will depend on your program, your audience, and the image you want to convey. Always evaluate the recommendations we have made concerning clothing with respect to the image you wish to create on-camera. Clothing you select should complement the program and your communication objectives. A performer wearing a tie and jacket to conduct an interview on Malibu Beach would look as ridiculous as Dan Rather delivering the network news in a floral print body shirt.

Makeup

More than anything else, television looks at the face of talent, and all the attention paid to clothing is lost if similar attention is not paid to talent's face.

FIGURE 6-4   Wardrobe Accessories.
Some distinctive clothing accessories may appear too showy in the videospace even though they appear appropriate in-person.

Lights "flash" off bright gold

Have you ever noticed how a person's forehead, cheeks, or nose looked bright and shiny in a home video, even though they didn't look that way to your eye when the video was shot? One reason is because natural oils on the skin reflect light into the camera and make some people's faces look unnaturally shiny.

Makeup is the solution. It can help make all talent look natural on television. Makeup is one of the easiest and most effective ways of improving virtually anyone's appearance on camera. Yet at many production facilities makeup is rarely, if ever, used. There is a mistaken notion that makeup belongs in "show business" and has no place outside major entertainment studios. There is also the inaccurate impression that today's modern color cameras are so sensitive that people can look acceptable onscreen without any makeup at all. While performers may look "acceptable," they certainly will not look their best, because the television camera plays tricks on many people's facial features and skin tones. Cameras have a tendency to exaggerate minor skin blemishes which may go unnoticed by the naked eye. Men's beards are usually much more prominent onscreen, and some men appear with a "five o'clock shadow" even though they may have shaved minutes before air time. Color cameras also emphasize the natural red, yellow, and green tones found in skin pigmentation and can produce unflattering and unnatural results onscreen.

When we talk about makeup, we refer to *straight makeup,* which is a basic application of makeup designed to make talent look natural in the videospace. We are not referring to either "corrective" or "character" makeup, two far more elaborate techniques which are used to alter talent's appearance and which requires the skills of a trained makeup artist. Straight television makeup is easily learned, can be applied quickly with a minimum of supplies, and makes an enormous difference on-camera. The idea behind straight makeup is not to transform a plain person into a ravishing beauty, but simply to make performers appear natural and look their best. If you have any doubt about the difference makeup can provide in a performer's appearance, try a simple before-and-after test in your own studio. The results are certain to convince you that makeup should be considered a standard and important part of television talent preparation for all on-camera work.

Makeup Supplies   Television makeup is available from a number of manufacturers, each with their own color and shade classification system. As a general rule, it is not a good idea to use commercial street makeup for television use. This is so because one important reason for using makeup on color television is to counteract the tendency of the camera to exaggerate reds, yellows, and greens. Most commercially available makeup emphasizes yellows and oranges, the very hues we try to tone down on-camera. However, if a subject is allergic to conventional makeup, the hypoallergenic brands can be used as long as they do not contain much yellow-reddish tones and if they register naturally on camera.

Makeup designed specifically for television is available from a number of manufacturers, including Max Factor and Bob Kelly. All the makeup and supplies you will need can be ordered by mail at a reasonable cost.

BASE MAKEUP   *Base,* or *foundation, makeup* is used to completely cover the face and to create the desired skin tone and color. Most base makeup is supplied in either pancake or stick form. *Stick makeup* is grease-based and must be applied with a sponge and then powdered to reduce shine. *Pancake makeup* is a powder and dries with a matte finish. Grease-based makeup covers more easily and is most commonly used. A makeup kit should include a number of different color shades, so the base makeup can be closely matched to the subject's natural skin tone.

ROUGE   Rouge is available in both liquid and brush-on formats for men and women. It is used to accentuate the cheekbones in women and to break up the flatness of the base makeup in both men and women.

POWDER   Translucent powder is a light, colorless powder that is applied over base makeup to set the makeup and reduce shine.

EYE MAKEUP   Eyeliner, mascara, and eyeshadow are used for both male and female subjects. These can be purchased from any cosmetic store,

but as a general rule, avoid blue, green, and purple shades. While these colors may look fine for street makeup, they reproduce poorly in color. Instead, emphasize soft brown tones, which register much more naturally onscreen.

PENCILS   Makeup pencils are used for eyebrows, eyeliners, and to provide detail and definition. Pencils are available from any cosmetic store and should include black and a variety of brown shades.

APPLICATORS   A foam rubber sponge is recommended for applying grease-based foundation makeup. A sable-hair brush is useful for applying rouge. Velour powderpuffs work well for applying translucent powder.

MISCELLANEOUS ITEMS   Cleansers—including a mild soap, cold cream, and baby oil—are necessary for makeup removal. A well-supplied makeup kit also should have tissues, cotton balls and swabs, combs and brushes, hair spray, razor blades, scissors, and an apron to protect the subject's clothing during makeup application.

Usually makeup is applied outside the studio in a room or an area set aside for makeup. You need at least a table, a mirror, a chair, and light. To see how the makeup will look in the studio, the lighting should be the same color temperature as the studio lighting. That is, both should have the same relative reddish or bluish tint. Also, the walls should be painted a neutral color so the makeup doesn't reflect the room color, which will not be present in the studio. Remember, the final proof is how the makeup looks *on-camera*, not to your eyes.

Makeup Steps for Men   CLEAN THE FACE   Have the subject wash his face thoroughly with soap and water to remove all dirt, oil, and perspiration. If the subject has an exceptionally heavy beard, he may have to shave prior to makeup. Tuck in tissues around the talent's shirt collar to protect it from smudges, and drape a towel or a makeup apron around his neck and shoulders.

APPLY THE BASE MAKEUP   Select a shade of creamstick closest to the subject's natural skin tone. If you cannot find the particular shade you need, use two or more creamsticks and blend the different colors to achieve the proper shade. The grease makeup is applied with a dry foam rubber sponge. Lee Baygan, director of makeup for NBC, suggests applying the creamstick with one side of the sponge and then using the other side to wipe off the excess. The makeup that remains is all that is usually necessary. A natural sponge may be used to apply water-based pancake makeup.

Apply the base makeup over the face, neck, and ears. Spread it evenly, leaving no clumps or smears. Bald men or those with receding hairlines should have their heads covered with foundation as well.

If there are discolorations under the eyes, extend the base color to cover the discoloration or cover it with a touch of highlight. A *highlight* is a base shade two or three shades lighter than the base color. Be sure to blend the highlight smoothly with the base makeup until there is no obvious demarcation between the two shades.

APPLY POWDER   Powder the entire face, neck, and ears with translucent powder. The powder is applied with a puff and is lightly pressed onto the skin, not rubbed or "powdered."

APPLY MALE ROUGE   Apply a touch of male rouge over the cheekbones and over the forehead, nose, and chin. This is to break the smooth, flat look of the base makeup and to bring out the natural coloring in the subject's face. Do not overdo it. Using the rouge brush, add enough to make a slight difference, but not enough to call attention to the makeup.

EYES AND HAIR   Use mascara on lashes and makeup pencil on eyebrows only if they are so light that they will wash out under the studio lights. If you do apply mascara, eyeliner, and pencil, never add so much that the makeup looks obvious.

If the subject has a receding hairline, makeup pencil will bring out the definition. Also around the temples, pencil or mascara can provide a slight darkening to prevent blonde or white hair from completely washing out. Do not use pencil or mascara to the point that it appears obvious on camera.

EVALUATE THE MAKEUP   The overall result should be a healthy, normal face without the appearance of makeup or obvious corrections. (See Figure 6-5.)

Makeup Steps for Women   CLEAN THE FACE   All street makeup should be removed with soap and water. Protect the talent's blouse with tissues which are tucked in around the neck and a makeup apron which covers the shoulders.

APPLY BASE MAKEUP   Select a shade of base makeup nearest to the subject's normal skin tone. If necessary, use two or three different shades and blend them together to produce the shade you need. As with male makeup, the base should be applied with a foam rubber sponge and spread evenly across the entire face and neck as far down as will appear on camera. Remember that only a very light application is necessary, and this will avoid the unnatural, caked-on look which too much makeup can produce.

Discolorations under the eyes should be covered with a highlight two or three shades lighter than the base and smoothly blended to the base color.

Subjects with a very broad nose may benefit from the application of shadow along both sides of the nose. *Shadow* is a base makeup two or three shades darker than the overall base. The shadow should be applied sparingly, and it should be smoothly blended with the basic base shade.

APPLY EYE MAKEUP   The eyes are an especially important feature for women, and the makeup is usually more extensive than we use for male subjects. However, eye makeup should still be applied sparingly, so it will appear natural on-camera.

A brown eyeshadow should be applied to the brow bone to shape the eye. Always apply eyeshadow with the subject's eyes open so you can see the effect of the makeup as it will appear on-

(a)

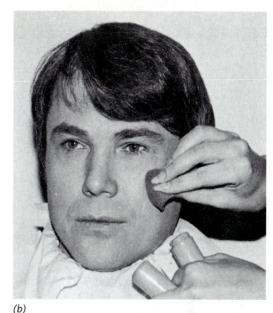

(b)

(c)

FIGURE 6-5 Television Makeup.
Television makeup improves everyone's appearance:
(a) the subject without makeup; (b) makeup applied
with a foam rubber sponge (the creamstick is chosen to
closely match the subject's natural skin color); and
(c) the completed makeup job enhances the subject's
appearance by covering the beard and slightly
accentuating the eyes.

camera. Avoid using eyeshadows of green, blue,
or purple, which do not register well onscreen.

Apply a thin line of eyeliner in a medium brown
shade. The liner can be applied with a pencil, or
a liquid eyeliner and brush can be used. For
women with thin or narrow eyes, a very thin white
line drawn on the bottom ledge of the eye can
make the eyes appear larger and wider.

Mascara in a brown shade is applied to both
upper and lower lashes. If you will use artificial
eyelashes, work them in a bit to eliminate the stiff-
ness. The lashes should be cut so they are no
longer than normal lashes.

Using an eyebrow pencil, shape the eyebrows
and fill in the outer ends, which may wash out
under the lights. Use discretion in penciling the

eyebrows, since too much will look unnatural onscreen.

APPLY POWDER   Using the powderpuff, gently press on translucent powder to set the makeup and reduce shine. You want to achieve a "finished look" that does not appear artificial.

APPLY ROUGE   The application of rouge under the cheekbones helps to contour the face and provides a three-dimensional look. The rouge is applied with a brush directly under the cheekbone and is lightly brushed up and over the bone. Use the same brush and rouge to add a slight touch of color to the forehead and chin and under the eyebrows. This will break up the flatness of the base makeup and add color to the face.

APPLY LIPSTICK   A woman's lips are an important and prominent feature and under normal circumstances should have makeup applied. Avoid bright reds or oranges which do not reproduce well and can upset the color balance of the face. Select lip colors in brown tones with a subtle touch of pink or orange. Lip gloss can be applied last if you want to give the lips a moist look.

EVALUATE THE MAKEUP   The end result should be a healthy, natural-looking subject without an obviously "made up," or artificial, appearance. When you have it right, be sure to complement the performer on her appearance.

Makeup for People of Color   The very same techniques just described apply to all subjects regardless of basic skin color—brown, fair, pink, or olive. There is a large range of skin colors among ethnic groups. It is not recommended to attempt to change a subject's natural skin color by choosing lighter or darker base colors. There are a number of makeup shades produced specifically for people of color, and the makeup artist should select the shade which appears closest to the natural skin tone or should use two or three different shades and blend them to produce the shade closest to natural.

Hand and Body Makeup   Unless the hands or body appear prominently in the show and look too pale, too dark, or otherwise do not reproduce well, no additional makeup is necessary. However, sometimes a talent's hands can look pale in comparison to his or her face, especially if he or she will be holding something in a close-up. In this case, make up the hands using the same base tone as the face. This also will reduce the prominence of any blemishes or undesirable color variations on the hands.

Nonprofessional Talent   Often nonprofessional talent who are not used to appearing on the stage, in film, or on television may hesitate to wear makeup. Business executives may say they don't have the time. Women may say they don't want to change the appearance of their own makeup. Others may not believe it really makes a difference. The best way to convince them that makeup is worth the time, change, and effort is to put a before-and-after example on tape. You also can remind them of the famous Nixon-Kennedy debates, when Nixon refused to wear television makeup. He didn't make the same mistake eight years later. Stress that makeup improves the appearance of everyone on television. Then use the techniques described above. After the shoot, talent not used to wearing makeup may forget about it, so be sure to remind them that it needs to be removed before they hurry back to their jobs.

Evaluating the Makeup   Makeup, like lighting, can be properly evaluated only on-camera. If at all possible, check the performer's makeup while he or she is on the production set. If the performer will be working under hot lights for an extended period of time, the makeup may become blotchy as sweat begins to shine through. A light application of colorless powder will repair minor problems; powder should always be kept handy on the studio floor.

Removing Makeup   Performers who use makeup regularly must be sure to take exceptionally good care of their skin. All makeup should be removed as soon as the production is over. Use cold cream and tissues to remove facial makeup; avoid harsh rubbing, which will only irritate the skin. Eye makeup can be removed using baby oil on a tissue or cotton ball. Once all makeup has been removed, wash the skin with mild soap and water. If you wish, a mild alcohol astringent can be applied last to close the pores.

TALENT'S RESPONSIBILITIES IN PRODUCTION

Understanding television's intimacy and the demands of the videospace helps performers and actors deliver their best performance. And proper selection of clothing and makeup enhance their onscreen appeal. Performers and actors also must realize that the roles they play fit into an entire production team effort. Professionals are aware that the crew can make or break their appearance onscreen. Even the best performance is meaningless unless it is produced onscreen with precision and imagination. By cooperating with the crew, talent ensures looking as good as possible on-camera. Performers and actors must understand their responsibilities within the context of teamwork, for there is no place in a busy production schedule for an egotistical "star." We will first look at the responsibilities of the television performer and then examine some of the additional expectations placed on the actor.

The Television Performer

Developing a relaxed and comfortable on-camera style is absolutely essential in television, and a good performer must be sufficiently flexible to deal with the frenetic pace and complexities of production. Television is often a high-pressure operation with close deadlines, limited budgets, rushed rehearsals, and short production periods. An unexpected technical problem can force sudden changes in the script, revisions in the blocking, even a reshuffling of rehearsal and shooting schedules. Actors used to the leisurely rehearsal pace of theatrical productions are often shocked to discover how much must be accomplished in so little time in television. Experienced television performers are able to cope with these inevitable pressures while still delivering an effective and seemingly effortless performance. The best possible advice for the performer is *be prepared*.

Preparation involves thorough knowledge of the

script, understanding the functions of the production equipment, and developing a special relationship with the floor manager, who serves as the link between director and talent during the actual production.

Working with the Script   There is simply no excuse for an interviewer who has not done his or her background homework, a lecturer or demonstrator who has not prepared and rehearsed the presentation, or an actor who has not memorized lines. Forcing full studio crew to stand idly by while talent learns in the studio what should have been prepared earlier is expensive, wasteful, and infuriating to all concerned.

The best advice is to try to work without a full script whenever possible. Reading from a script, even with occasional look-ups into the lens, interferes with eye contact and can reduce the performer's communication impact. However, for a production situation where it is important to say just the right lines or when there is too much material to memorize, a full script may be the only alternative.

Here are some tips for using a script on-camera:

1   *Type it on colored paper.* A script should always be typed, never handwritten. Some studios have typewriters with oversized characters, but even a normal typeface can be made more legible by double- or triple-spacing. White paper should not be used because it reflects too much light, can be difficult to read under studio illumination, and may interfere with the proper camera contrast range. Yellow, pink, or blue paper is far less distracting, photographs well, and is usually easier to read under television lights.

2   *Use notes whenever possible.* It is hard to follow a script word-for-word and still maintain eye contact and some degree of spontaneity. If at all possible, use the script as an outline and ad-lib within your typed notes. However, it is a good idea to write out the open, close, and transition cues completely, since these must be performed flawlessly and with less time

flexibility than most material within the body of the show.

3 *Mark your script.* Write important cues, blocking moves, and other information clearly on your script. Some performers also like to mark certain words for emphasis and to make additional notes on delivery in the script. Be careful, however, not to overmark the script to the point that it becomes illegible.

4 *Do not staple the pages.* Never clip or staple the script pages together. Instead, clearly number each page in one corner. During the show you can slip each top page underneath as you finish it.

5 *Above all, practice.* Go over the script repeatedly. Even if you do not fully memorize it, the greater your familiarity with the script, the more believable you will appear on camera.

Working with Production Equipment No matter how flawlessly you use the script, your performance must be captured and reproduced properly by the production equipment in order for the audience to see it. A good performer knows enough about production operations to help the director and crew during rehearsal and production. This means understanding sets and lighting, audio requirements, camera positions and shots, and prompting devices. It also involves maintaining an overall sensitivity to production activities and problems.

SETS AND LIGHTING The set and lighting together establish the environment in which the performer appears. Usually set preparation and lighting are completed before the performer enters the studio, but there are times when a performer is asked to stand on-set for final lighting touch-ups. A person's physical size, hair and skin color, and other individual characteristics sometimes require slight lighting adjustments. For example, blondes will use less back light than dark-haired persons, and scrims may be used to soften the light for bald individuals. When you are asked to stand in for lighting, understand that at the final stage, you and you alone can serve this purpose.

Your first time on the set, familiarize yourself by taking a brief walk around. Make a note of steps, risers, furniture, and props so you will know where all necessary items are located and can move with assurance.

The director may show you a series of "marks," usually masking tape on the studio floor, which indicate where you are expected to stand for camera shots, lighting, and audio. It is talent's responsibility to hit all the marks accurately without making it look obvious to the audience. On some sets lit for low key, a performer must be in just the right position to be lit properly. Experienced performers develop a sixth sense in finding their light. You can usually feel the location where the lights are strongest on you and when the light's focus becomes off center. Sometimes only a step or two can make the difference between a poorly lit subject and a properly illuminated one.

TECH TIP One of the most distracting and annoying set-related mannerisms is the performer who insists on swiveling, rocking, or tilting a movable chair. Not only does this make it difficult to frame a shot, but the constant movement makes watching him or her enormously irritating. Many studios use swivel chairs, however, so train yourself to sit still and warn others to avoid such movements on camera.

AUDIO Top-quality sound is as important to a production as a good picture. Talent can help the audio technician achieve this by handling and using microphones properly, giving correct sound levels, and assisting the audio crew whenever possible.

Microphone Handling We will discuss the proper microphone-handling techniques in the audio chapters, so we will just mention the important points which concern talent here. Most performers use on-camera mikes, usually a lavalier, hand-held, or desk mike. Lavaliers should be clipped or hung so that they do not rub against clothing or jewelry, creating annoying extraneous sounds during the show. Performers should never play with the mike or mike cable, should avoid absentmindedly tapping on tabletops equipped with desk mikes, and should be warned against moving outside the pickup range of a stationary desk or stand mike.

Performers who must use a lavalier or hand-held mike and move about the set should tuck some slack cable behind them in their pants, waistband, or belt. This gives you an added safety pad in case you snag the cable while moving across the set. As you move, lead the cable in front of you so you can be certain that the cable is free of obstructions.

Performers should know the microphone pickup pattern of the equipment they use. There is nothing worse for sound than someone speaking into the dead side of a directional microphone or moving outside the pickup range of a stationary mike. If you think the microphone on the set does not permit the flexibility you need, speak with the audio technician and director during rehearsal to resolve the problem.

There are times when a performer must use an off-camera microphone such as the boom. Although the boom microphone relieves talent of any mike-handling chores, in some ways the boom can be the most difficult microphone for a performer to work properly. Booms, like cameras, take time to move large distances, and sudden, unexpected moves about the set should be avoided. Telegraph your intention to move before actually getting up, so you do not wind up with a boom in the shot. If you see that the boom operator is having difficulty positioning the boom, just a step or two in the right direction may be all it takes to improve the sound quality.

Audio Levels Levels are usually obtained by the audio technician prior to rehearsal. When you are asked for a level, speak as you will when on camera. There is no point in setting levels only to have the performer drastically change volume or delivery once the show begins. The most accurate level is achieved when the performer says something from the program's script. This not only eliminates the sudden speechlessness that often accompanies a request for a voice level, but it gives the technician a better sample of your voice than a "Testing 1, 2, 3." If you are hosting a show with nonprofessional talent, you can help the audio technician by asking the guest a question or two so the technician can set levels as the guest replies.

TECH TIP Avoid blowing into a microphone. It does not help set levels; it may damage the mike; and it may leave undesirable deposits on the wind screen.

VOICE-OVERS A picture may be worth a thousand words, but sometimes words are needed to provide information that pictures can't. That is the main purpose of a *voice-over* (V.O.)—an announcement or narration over visual material with the speaker not shown.

In some programs, the choice of talent for a voice-over will be obvious. For example, the thoughts of a character should be spoken by the on-camera actor playing that role. An on-camera host of a documentary usually should narrate the visual sequences. A scientist shown conducting an experiment might do his or her own voice-over.

Sometimes for programs in which the speaker will not be shown, a director will choose an actor who specializes in voice-overs. This always is the case in cartoons and often is true for commercials. The director should choose an actor with a quality of voice and delivery technique that best matches the picture. The best match may be a straight voice, a regional accent, a "real person" sound, or character voice.

A voice-over may be recorded either before or after the video material is produced, and may be recorded on location or in a studio. Reporters may even record their voice-overs right in the editing room. Sometimes the narration is recorded to match edited video, and sometimes video is edited to match a prerecorded narration.

Digital audio recording makes it easier to match up voice-overs with visual material. Narration can be compressed or expanded without changing the speed and pitch of the voices. One special voice-over technique borrowed from film is *automatic dialogue replacement* (ADR), which involves replacing dialogue recorded in the field with new dialogue while keeping lip-movements synchronized.

In Chapter 3 we described writing for television as *storytelling*. In a program with voice-over narration, the voice-over talent is the final storyteller. In that role, he or she becomes a lead player in the production, and is responsible for bringing the writer's script to life.

CAMERAS   In most circumstances, the performer works with two or more cameras which shoot from a variety of angles. In order to work with the cameras, the performer must consider three things: (1) Where are the cameras positioned? (2) What is each camera shooting? (3) Which camera is on the air?

Camera Positions   You will need to know where the cameras are and their basic area of operation. Keeping this information in mind will enable you to help the director get the best shots and to avoid creating camera problems.

Camera Shots   You ought to know basic camera shots for each camera. This does not mean you must know the shots as well as the director, but you should know the general sequence. Say you are recording a commercial with two cameras. Which camera will shoot you head-on and which camera will shoot the product demonstration close-up? Knowing the close-up camera enables you to set up the demonstration at the most advantageous shooting angle. Knowing which is your camera will ensure that you work to the right camera at all times.

Air Camera   Working with two or more cameras means that you will usually need to know which camera is on the air at any particular time. The tally lights are, of course, one way to tell, but there are times when you will need to know which camera the director will punch up next. Working with three cameras, unless the floor manager tells you in advance which camera will start the show, you will have a one-in-three chance of guessing right.

On some shows where the performer must speak directly to the camera, the program director may wish to change camera shots during the presentation. To do this smoothly and unobtrusively takes coordination between talent, floor

manager, and director. First, the director cues the floor manager to ready talent to switch cameras. The floor manager prepares talent for the switch and, on the director's cue, waves talent to the proper camera. It is talent's job to look down momentarily on the switch cue and then look up into the other camera. The director will cut from one shot to the other during the look up, and when the operation is performed correctly, the switch looks perfectly natural on screen.

For performers who must communicate directly to the audience, eye contact is a vital factor in successfully delivering the message to the viewer. Most performers pretend that the camera is simply a person and speak to it as though speaking normally to anyone seated a few feet away in a living room. Should you find yourself talking to the wrong camera at some time during the show, simply look down, find the tally lights out of the corner of your eye, and look up at the air camera's lens. The floor manager will usually help wave you over if he or she can get there before you realize the error. Avoid making comments like "Where are you?" or "Thought you'd gone away for a while!" They not only sound unprofessional, but they also call attention to a mistake which many viewers may not have even noticed.

Movement On-Camera   Before you move on-camera, remember that it takes the camera operator a lot longer to move a camera across the studio than it takes the performer to get up and cross the set. Especially on unrehearsed shows, try to telegraph your moves before actually making them. Saying something like "Why don't we get up and take a look over here" before rising will help alert the director, camera operator, and other crew members that a move is about to occur. Also, try to rise or sit a bit more slowly than normal. It will make it easier on the crew and yet will appear natural onscreen.

Close-ups On-Camera   Since television is a close-up medium, there may be times when you must show an object or graphic in close-up. A close-up shot magnifies both the size of the object and any extraneous movement, so hold all objects as steady as possible by resting them on a tabletop or by bracing your hand. You can reduce flaring on the shiny side of an object or graphic by

FIGURE 6-6 Cue Cards. Cue cards should be clearly written and held close to the camera lens if talent is to appear natural on-camera.

tilting it slightly downward. Your natural movement is also greatly magnified in close-up. If you know you are being shot very close, avoid sudden moves which are difficult for the camera operator to follow. Only a matter of inches in where you stand or move can make the difference between being in or out of a close-up shot.

PROMPTING DEVICES There are times when a performer cannot use an on-camera script and yet cannot memorize the entire script. In this case, either cue cards or a prompter can be used to prompt the performer while still keeping the copy off-camera.

Cue Cards A *cue card* is a large piece of stiff oaktag or poster board with script copy written in large lettering. Cue cards are usually used by talent when speaking directly to the camera. In this case, the copy should be prepared on long, narrow cards. Cutting a standard piece of poster board or oaktag that is 22 × 28 inches in half lengthwise will produce a 14- × 22-inch strip, which is just the right size. The narrow card allows talent to read the copy while minimizing obvious eye movement. The copy must be written in large, legible print with a broad felt-tip pen. Never use a

pencil, ballpoint, or narrow felt-tip pen because the words will be illegible. Cue cards are always used from a distance, although the exact space between talent and the cards will vary depending on the studio and production circumstances. Usually cue cards must be read from about 8 to 12 feet, so your cards should be legible from at least that distance. Remember, too, that the glare and reflection created by studio lights will make it more difficult for talent to read the cards on the set. The card is held by the floor manager or an assistant with the line of copy you are speaking right next to the take lens. As you talk, the floor manager must move the card upward, always keeping the spoken line next to the lens. Since a new card must immediately follow a card that has just been finished, never print the second part of the script on the back of a card. The floor manager would have to flip the card over in order to continue, and this would disrupt the performer's delivery. Most floor managers prefer to hold the stack of cards next to the lens and to move only the top card upward as talent speaks. Once the first card has been used, the floor manager hands it to an assistant while the next card is already in position for talent to read. (See Figure 6-6.)

Even on fully scripted shows, where the talent

159

holds the script on-camera, the use of cue cards for the opening, closing, and transitions in and out of taped material is recommended. The cards enable talent to maintain eye contact with the audience while delivering lines exactly as written and with highly accurate timing.

Another way to use cue cards is to outline the sequence of events as a reminder to talent. Jay Leno's opening monologue, for instance, is outlined on a series of cue cards positioned just off-camera. Leno delivers the jokes from memory but uses the cue cards to remind him of the proper sequence. The same idea is useful in demonstration or instructional shows, where the talent knows what to do and what to say but may not always remember the proper order or sequence of events. Cue cards used as outlines need not be written on narrow strips or held next to the camera lens, since talent does not read them line-by-line. In fact, the cards can be positioned anywhere off-camera as long as talent can easily glance at them from time to time.

Prompter The *prompter* is a device that enables talent to read continuous copy while maintaining maximum eye contact with the audience. A closed-circuit camera or computer is used to scan the written copy, and a television monitor and mirror system mounted on the studio camera are used to display the copy to talent. The script appears on the face of a one-way mirror which is positioned directly in front of the camera lens. Although the copy is invisible to the viewer and does not interfere with camera operation, the performer can read the lines and still look directly into the camera lens. The speed of the moving copy is variable and controlled by the prompter operator. A single computer/copy stand can feed any number of individual prompters, each mounted on a separate studio camera. (See Figure 6-7.)

While the prompter is much more expensive than cue cards, it offers some obvious advantages. Cue cards must be hand lettered from the original script. It would take literally hundreds of cards and hours of full-time work to prepare cue cards for a half-hour show. You can imagine the

FIGURE 6-7 **Television Prompter.**
A prompter superimposes copy in front of the camera lens, maximizing the talent's eye contact with the audience.

time and expense involved if this were to be done every day. Since the prompter needs no special type of script preparation, any script page that has been normally typed can be run immediately on the prompter. On most daily newscasts, for example, a script written at a word processor may feed several printers. One printout can be given to the talent, another to the director, and a third can be used for the prompter. Some processing systems can send a script directly to the prompter, eliminating the need for any printed copies of the script. In either case, last-minute script changes present no problem, since any page can be easily replaced by a new one. For production situations involving a great deal of copy, where the performer needs to maintain maximum eye contact and still follow a script—such as on newscasts, commercials, lectures, and speeches—the prompter is a valuable production tool.

The Television Actor

A good television actor must be, before anything else, a good actor. No amount of technical expertise can compensate for the ability to develop and sustain a believable performance, whether on film, on the stage, or on television. With this not insignificant talent taken for granted, the next requirement is that the actor have some familiarity with the techniques of television production. With only a few exceptions, all the points we have made concerning the television performer apply equally well to the television actor. In this section we will briefly discuss some of the major differences.

Actor and Director   Television can be a very difficult medium for the actor because just as the character begins to develop and full rehearsals start, the director is up in the control booth inaccessible to the actors. To make matters worse, during early studio rehearsals, the actor is often asked to play what is essentially a prop or stand-in, while camera shots are learned and other production elements are rehearsed. It is not that the director is uninterested in the actor at the moment, only that camera shots and other technical problems must take precedence once studio rehearsals begin.

This means that actors must have a firm idea about character and performance before the studio rehearsals begin. During dry rehearsal outside the studio, the director can give you his or her undivided attention, and this is when problems or questions concerning a role should be raised. Once you enter the studio, stopping rehearsal to discuss a line or a character is expensive because a studio crew and full facilities must wait. Television actors in all performance situations—commercials, situation comedies, daytime serials, and

so on—must be able to produce an effective and believable performance with a minimum of actor-director introspection.

There is a story about a young actress fresh out of school who was hired for a minor part on a long-running daytime serial. As the actors and director assembled for the first read-through, the actress kept interrupting the rehearsal by asking the director a continual stream of questions about her character. At one point she said to the director, "I don't really understand my motivation for the cross to the couch in this part." By this time the director had had enough. "Your motivation," he replied, his voice dripping with sarcasm, "is the paycheck you'll receive on Friday."

Of course, the director must be sensitive to an actor's problems and questions, but actors also must realize that time pressure on the director makes rehearsal time a precious commodity. The better prepared you are, the easier it will be for everyone to accomplish the most during rehearsals. A successful television actor can develop a character or role quickly and still deliver a real, believable, and multidimensional performance on screen.

TECH TIP   Some actors develop complete biographies for their characters. By creating a family, friends, occupation, and history for the character, performers find it easier to behave naturally while interacting with others onscreen.

Costumes and Props   Most costumes are rented especially for a production, since few facilities use them often enough to justify the expense of making and storing them. The only problem with renting costumes is that most are designed for use onstage, where the distance between the actor and the audience is far enough to mask imperfections or a lack of realistic detail. The same holds true for props. A wooden gun may look fine from the balcony of a theater, but on television, in close-up, it looks absurd. In consultation with the set designer and costume designer, check all props and costumes far enough in advance for realism *within* the videospace, so changes or additions can be made to correct their appearance for the camera.

Character Makeup   Character makeup is designed to alter an actor's appearance to suit the role or character being portrayed. Although modern makeup artists can create almost any illusion given the time and money, few production studios can afford to keep a full-time makeup artist on staff. Doing your own character makeup is risky because the close-up camera will reveal the makeup unless it has been expertly applied. If your production will require extensive character makeup, it is a good idea to hire an outside professional to design and apply the makeup on a consultant basis.

Actor and Floor Manager   The floor manager is the actor's communication link with the control room. However, since actors usually work on fully scripted shows with some prior rehearsal, the floor manager's role is slightly different when working with actors than when working with performers. Actors rarely need the continual stream of time and directional cues which are necessary on unscripted and unrehearsed programs. In fact, the floor manager should avoid all eye contact with an actor unless a cue is being delivered. That is so because establishing eye contact can break an actor's concentration and spoil the performance. Of course, when an actor must receive a cue, it is the floor manager's responsibility to move to a position where the actor can see the cue while still remaining in character.

Working with Production Equipment   The ability to deliver a believable and apparently spontaneous performance while still paying close attention to the many technical aspects of a production is among the most difficult skills for a beginning television actor to learn. Unlike the stage, where minor improvisations will not upset anyone, the television actor who misses his or her mark or who intentionally or unintentionally changes a blocking move can seriously upset the camera operator's shots and the director's entire shooting pattern. Of

course, a good director and crew will try to make the actor feel as comfortable as possible, but this does not relieve the actor of his or her own responsibilities during the performance. If you see that an over-the-shoulder shot is being blocked, for example, a step to one side will help the camera operator get the shot faster. If you know you are being photographed in a tight close-up, keep your movements slow and to a minimum. If you are involved in a boom split where the mike is farther away from you, a bit more projection may help the audio technician with the sound.

During rehearsals, the actor should keep the camera positions in mind and make all movements as consistent as possible. It does make a difference which hand you use to open a door, how you face in a two-shot, how far you cross when you walk over the set. Marks are especially important in complex foreground-background shots where talent and camera must be precisely aligned for the shot to work. (See Figure 6-8.)

WORKING WITH PROMPTERS   There is no arguing the fact that the best performances are delivered by actors who have completely memorized their lines. An actor who is not confident with his or her part may give an insecure and hesitant performance that is made even more obvious by the cameras and microphones. There are times, however, when the rapid production pace of television makes the use of some prompting device necessary.

The prompter is usually the most effective way to prompt a play, but the monitor device mounted on cameras does not work well because the actor rarely looks directly into the camera lens. Instead, some productions use the prompter mounted on a floorstand out of camera range, where the talent can refer to it if necessary.

Cue cards are difficult to use for plays because of the enormous number of cards necessary to cover the show's script. However, if you do use cards, remember to position them in the direction the performer will naturally look toward. This is not necessarily next to the air camera. If more than one performer will be using cards, color coding each actor's lines can help to reduce potential confusion.

If you need a line which you have forgotten during a performance, the worst thing you can do is

(a)

(b)

FIGURE 6-8 **Hitting the Mark.**
Missing the mark, a specific spot predetermined for the camera or lighting, can destroy the effect in the videospace: (*a*) talent hits the mark (in key light); and (*b*) talent 12 inches off the mark (out of key light).

to jerk your head around abruptly to read the cue card or prompter. Instead, take a pause, look down, and glance at the prompter; then look back and deliver your line. If you have done the move properly, the pause often seems natural in the context of the play, and your grasping for the next line of dialogue may go completely unnoticed by the viewer.

Regardless of how good an actor is at reading prompters or cue cards, sooner or later the television medium usually reveals the use of these devices. Except in extremely rare circumstances, such as when very extensive last-minute changes to your script have been made, memorize your lines and come to rehearsal and production fully prepared.

TALENT IN PRODUCTION STAGES

In this section we will review the responsibilities and functions of talent during each of the four production stages.

Preproduction

Talent's role in preproduction depends, in large part, on the program format. Actors usually are not very busy during the earliest stage of preproduction, except to read through their scripts and begin forming the character. Performers, on the other hand, may need to do some background research or writing in preparation for their work. Often, interviewers, reporters, and other similar types of

163

performers must write their own material and help develop the program's outline and rundown in conjunction with the director and the producer.

Interviews are a common production format which requires considerable preproduction work on the part of the interviewer. Unless you are familiar with the people you will interview, know and understand the issues involved, and have prepared your line of questioning, the interview will not be effective. On those programs with a full staff, some guests may be preinterviewed, and a list of possible questions is then supplied to talent. These questions should be used only as a guideline, however, since an interview can move in any direction once it begins, and the host must be able to guide the interview as it progresses on the air.

Performers who must work on a demonstration, presentation, or speech should practice it thoroughly until it can be delivered flawlessly and without hesitation. Once you get into the studio, you are apt to be somewhat nervous, so the more familiar you are with the script, demonstration, or presentation, the better the performance you will give.

Setup and Rehearsal

Talent is rarely involved during the studio setup unless special props, set pieces, or other production elements are used which require talent's supervision. Instead, talent is usually involved with dry rehearsals or preproduction meetings at this time. For actors, the first stage of rehearsal is the dry rehearsal, where the actors and director meet to read through the script, develop the characters and the approach, and work out actor movements and blocking. Dry rehearsal is the time for the actor to raise any problems, suggestions, or modifications. Once the production moves into the studio for facilities rehearsals, performer variables should be fairly well settled, so the director can begin work with the cameras and technical crew.

Camera Blocking The first part of the studio rehearsal involves the director and camera operators working out individual camera shots. Camera

blocking can be a tedious time for talent, since you are asked to repeat a move or deliver a line over and over until the director is satisfied with the camera shots. The performer or actor should simply understand the reason for this (it is not your fault; it is for the cameras), expend a minimum of energy by walking through the blocking, and stay as relaxed and patient as possible. Unless the director specifically asks you to perform during camera blocking, do not go all-out in your performance only to find that you have exhausted your energy before the actual production. However, it is very important for you to walk through your blocking and movements as consistently as possible, since this is when the camera operators and director are planning their shots and camera moves. Their work depends on talent's ability to repeat actions without significant variation.

Run-Throughs As soon as the director has completed the camera blocking, he or she will begin a series of run-throughs, in which all the various production elements are integrated into a unified show. Early run-throughs are often a series of stops and starts as problems arise and must be resolved before the production moves on to the next part of the show. Most of the problems at this point are technical, but talent may be asked to change some aspect of performance in order to improve camera shots, audio, or other elements of the production. As the run-throughs progress, the stops and starts become less frequent, and the show should begin to run at its normal pacing and speed. This is when the director can start to evaluate your performance and how well it plays when combined with the camera shots, sound, lighting, and other production elements.

Dress Rehearsal The last rehearsal before production is a *dress,* when all the elements are rehearsed as though it were the final "air" show. By this time you should be in wardrobe and makeup so that the director, lighting director, and video technicians can see how everything looks together and can make changes where necessary. Since the dress is the final performance before air, the performer's full energy should be directed toward producing a believable character. Some directors will videotape the dress rehearsal and edit together the best performances of the dress and air versions into the final production the audience sees.

NOTES   After each rehearsal the director will give out notes to performers. Notes are important because they pertain not only to your own performance, but to problems which relate to camera shots, audio, lighting, and other production operations.

Production

Talent's role in production varies depending on the type of program and how it is produced. A show that has been fully scripted and rehearsed should present few surprises, since all major problems ought to have been ironed out during rehearsals. On taped programs, major mistakes can usually be corrected through retakes and subsequent editing. However, talent should never stop performing until the director or floor manager calls out, "Cut." What may seem like a major error to you may not be considered by the director serious enough to stop tape. It is even possible that the mistake did not appear on the air. In any event, performers and actors should never stop unless told by the director or floor manager. The same goes for ending a show or segment. Always remain in character until you receive the "All clear." You may think a mike is closed or a camera off only to learn they were not. If you treat all mikes as "live" and all cameras as "hot," you will avoid potential embarrassment and costly mistakes during production.

Performers who work on shows with a minimum of rehearsal naturally have to deal with both their performance and the many elements of production, such as timing and pacing. You are controlling the show as much as the director, and you must stay alert and flexible at all times.

One of the hardest lessons for some performers and actors to learn is to listen as well as to speak. Actors who actually "listen" while others deliver their lines are considered by their peers to be among the best in the trade. Not only do they tend to react more naturally, but they also help other actors to motivate their performance and delivery. Careful listening is especially important for such ad-lib performers as interviewers, hosts, and emcees. You may be thinking ahead to the next question or cue, but do not neglect what is being said at the time.

To illustrate the consequences of not listening carefully, consider this story of an unfortunate game-show host who was introducing a new contestant:

"What do you do?" the emcee asked a contestant.

"I'm a housewife," she replied.

"Wonderful!" said the host. "How many children do you have?"

"Three," she answered.

"Wonderful!" exclaimed the emcee. "And what does your husband do?"

"My husband is dead," she said. "I'm a widow."

"Wonderful!" said the host without a moment's pause. "Now let's play our game."

Live Production   No other production situation rivals a live broadcast for the excitement and tension it produces in even the most experienced television talent. A live show demands precision, flexibility, and the ability to do it right the first time, since there is no chance for retakes. Talent must be able to react to cues quickly and still make the performance appear natural and effortless onscreen.

On most live shows where the event itself is unplanned—such as a sports event or special news coverage, for instance—the director may wish to talk directly with talent from time to time. To do this, talent wears an unobtrusive earpiece connected to an interruptible foldback (IFB) system. By pushing a button in the control booth, the director can talk to talent even while he or she is on-camera. It is not easy to listen to one voice while trying to speak coherently, but most performers develop the knack after some practice. A good director will keep IFB commands to a minimum and will try not to interrupt while talent is in the middle of a sentence. (See Figure 6-9.)

Taped Production   Videotape recording and editing offer obvious production advantages, which we have discussed in earlier chapters, but they can present some difficulties for talent as

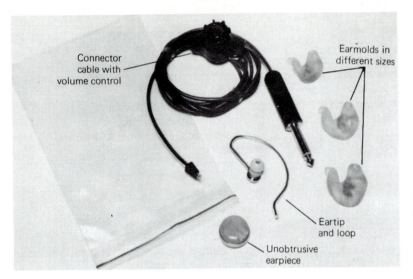

Connector
cable with
volume control

Earmolds in
different sizes

Eartip
and loop

Unobtrusive
earpiece

FIGURE 6-9 IFB Earpiece. An interruptible foldback (IFB) system is a small earpiece through which the director can communicate with talent on the air.

well. A common problem is shooting out of sequence. For convenience and production efficiency, it may be necessary for an actor to tape the opening scene of a play and then immediately afterward tape the dramatic closing scene, which occurs in the same set or location. Although the two scenes will appear in their proper context and sequence on the final, edited version, the performer is expected to reach the right level of intensity and delivery in production without benefit of the intervening parts. Out-of-sequence production requires actors to match themselves perfectly without the natural momentum possible with sequential shooting.

Another problem associated with videotape is the tendency to lose some spontaneity and the natural "edge" which comes from a live or one-time-only production. Performers (and crew) may adopt the attitude that mistakes can always be reshot, and this can result in a dull and lackluster performance. After a long day in the studio, you will be tired, maybe even exhausted, but the audience who watches your show neither knows or cares how much effort went into the production. All that matters to them is your performance as it appears in the videospace, so be sure to discipline yourself to give the best performance you can on each and every take.

Postproduction

Talent's primary job is usually finished when the production is completed. Obviously, on a live show there is no postproduction at all. On some taped programs, however, the director may ask you to remain for *pickups,* which are small sections of action, dialogue, or both which are taped for later use in editing. A pickup can be a close-up shot which was not possible during the actual production, a reaction shot, a move, or the delivery of some dialogue. The most important part in doing pickups is to match yourself as closely as possible. If you are unsure of the right movements or your delivery, ask the director to play back the part of the show which occurs just prior to the pickup point.

On some interview shows the director may ask the host to reread the questions for reverse-angle shots. This is most common with single-camera shoots, but it also may be required when multiple cameras are used. It is important for you to repeat the question exactly as it was first asked and with a natural inflection. Replaying either the videotape or an audiocassette recording of the interview can help you with the precise wording and the proper delivery.

SUMMARY

In television, talent refers to anyone who appears on-camera. There are two talent categories: performers and actors. Performers appear as themselves, usually in a nonfictional situation, while actors portray a character different from themselves in real life.

All television performers and actors must consider the characteristics of the medium in developing their performances. Television is an intimate, close-up medium which often involves the viewer in a one-to-one relationship with the performer or actor. Performers and actors must always recognize the impact of the videospace on their appearance and their actions because this is how they will be judged by the audience.

The relatively small screen space and limited resolution of television result in directors concentrating on tight shots of talent, accentuating the smallest changes in expression and gestures. The aspect ratio requires care in positioning objects for demonstration and in limiting the range of movement. Lens effects and depth-of-field concerns influence how performers and actors move on the set. Similarly, audiospace concerns favor use of inflection, pacing, and word choice over changing volume to express feelings and emotion.

Clothing and wardrobe must always be selected with their on-camera appearance as the most important consideration. The clothing's color, fabric, contrast, and line should be determined by the type of program and the image talent wishes to convey, the set and lighting, and how well the clothing complements talent's appearance onscreen.

Makeup is necessary to make talent appear normal and look their best onscreen. Variations in skin color or imperfections in complexion can be corrected for the camera using simple straight makeup and minor corrective makeup. Character makeup is used to alter an actor's appearance for a role and is more complex, usually requiring a skilled makeup artist for best results.

Performers and actors must always recognize their responsibilities as members of the production team. Aside from being thoroughly prepared for their own performance, actors and performers are expected to understand the basics of television production operations and to cooperate with the director and crew during rehearsals and performance.

Performers need to consider demands of the set and lighting, audio, and camera operations. The performer may work with either an on-camera script or with such off-camera prompting devices as cue cards or the prompter. Actors should memorize their lines for the best performance and rely on cue cards or prompters only in an emergency.

The floor manager is the talent's primary communication link with the director in the control room. During rehearsal and production, the floor manager relays time and directional cues from the booth to talent on the studio floor, usually with silent hand signals. In addition, the floor manager is responsible for cue cards and most floor activities during production.

The television actor must follow the same basic guidelines used by the performer, but with some major variations. The performer on a semiscripted or unscripted show is often controlling the program's pacing and flow as it progresses. The actor works on a fully scripted and rehearsed production but must develop a believable character in a short period of rehearsal time and is expected to deliver an effective performance amidst the distractions of a television production set.

During dry rehearsal, the actor and director work on characterization, dialogue, and blocking outside the studio. These elements should be settled once the production begins in-studio rehearsals, since camera shots and other technical factors revolve around the actor's delivery and movement. Consistency in performance is a crucial element for any television actor.

Videotaped productions require talent to maintain the appearance of spontaneity even after multiple retakes. In addition, actors may be asked to perform out of sequence and are expected to build a character in bits and pieces, all of which must flow naturally together once the program is edited. Live productions create their own natural spontaneity and a one-chance-only pressure. They require talent to think quickly, remain flexible, and still deliver a top-quality performance in what can be a stressful production situation.

PART THREE

PART THREE

During television's early years, the ability to just reproduce a picture was considered so remarkable that both viewers and production people gave little attention to the quality of the accompanying television sound. With everyone focused on the picture, television set manufacturers produced receivers with cheap audio components and tinny speakers. Although television audio had the technical potential to rival the higher quality of FM sound, producers concluded that there was little incentive to take the effort and expense necessary to improve audio since audiences—given the poor quality of their sets—would be unable to hear the difference. Poor production techniques and inferior television sets perpetuated a vicious cycle which relegated audio to second class status.

It wasn't until the mid-1980s that a number of developments gradually broke the cycle. A generation grew up listening to FM-stereo radio and high-fidelity audio equipment. Both audio CDs and home VCRs produced high quality sound and established a higher standard for audio reproduction. Simultaneously, cable television introduced stereo channels and over-the-air television stations began to broadcast in stereo sound. Today virtually every new television set/receiver is equipped to receive and reproduce stereo sound. Together, these developments have created a new environment in which high-quality television audio has become the norm. Television audiences have come to demand the same audio quality from television that they do from their home audio systems.

Although television is a visual medium, the sound accompanying a picture determines much about what the picture conveys and cues the audience's reaction to the visual image. In other words, the *audiospace* complements and enhances the *videospace*. Effective television production requires the creative use of sound that works with the video to create a complete audio/visual message.

The chapters in Part Three describe the equipment and production techniques used to produce audio for television. We've organized the material to follow the audio flow path through the audio system. We begin by reviewing the properties of sound and audio signals. Next, we describe how to pick up live sound sources with microphones and conclude with a rundown of other sound sources. Finally, we describe how audio signals are processed, mixed, recorded, and edited during production and postproduction.

CHAPTER 7

AUDIO PROPERTIES AND SOURCES

In Chapter 2 we described some of the aesthetic considerations in creating audiospace. Applying those principles under actual production conditions requires a practical knowledge of the capabilities of audio equipment and good audio production techniques. However, before we can

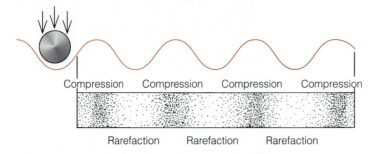

Compression   Compression   Compression   Compression

Rarefaction   Rarefaction   Rarefaction

FIGURE 7-1 **Waves in a Pond.**
Sound waves can be compared to ripples made by tossing a stone into a pond. The waves rising above the water level represent compression of vibrating molecules, and those dropping below the water level represent expansion, or "rarefaction," of vibrating molecules.

begin to discuss either, we must briefly examine the properties of sound and review the kinds of sound signals which are used in the production process.

SOUND WAVES

A sound is a vibration of molecules produced by a moving object. The object could be a guitar string, a vocal chord, a bell, or any object that rapidly vibrates, or *oscillates*, back and forth. As the sound source vibrates, the oscillating molecules are pushed away from the vibrating object in waves, radiating from the source like ripples on a pond when a stone is tossed into the water. (See Figure 7-1.)

It is important to understand that when a sound is produced, the first oscillating molecules don't move the entire distance that the sound travels, just as the water hit by a tossed stone doesn't travel on the ripples all the way to the edge of a pond. Instead, the oscillating molecules bump into nearby molecules, making them move. In this way, pressure variations are passed along like a row of billiard balls where the first strikes the next and so on until the last ball in the row moves.

Because sound waves are cyclical, they can be graphically illustrated by the repeating *sine wave* in Figure 7-2. The sine wave shows two important qualities of sound: its *frequency* and its *intensity*.

Sound Frequency

Sound frequency refers to the number of times each second an oscillating molecule moves back and forth in a complete cycle. Frequency is illustrated in Figure 7-2 by the number of times during each second that the sine wave is completed. In recording studios you often will hear a frequency called *reference tone*, which is 1,000 sine waves per second at 0dB.

One *cycle per second* (CPS) is called one *hertz*, written 1 Hz.

....

TECH TIP Occasionally you may hear someone refer to a frequency in terms of "cycles per second" (CPS), or simply "cycles," but it is more common today to use the synonym "hertz," written "Hz." In addition, to simplify large numbers, the prefixes "kilo," "mega," and "giga" also are used. For example, one thousand CPS is one thousand hertz (1,000 Hz), or one *kilohertz* (1 KHz). One million CPS is one *megahertz* (1 MHz). One billion CPS is one *gigahertz* (1 GHz).

....

The faster an object vibrates, the greater the number of hertz, and the higher the sound's frequency. For example, 1,000 Hz is a higher frequency than 100 Hz. Because we perceive sound frequency as *pitch*, the higher the frequency, the higher the pitch. A 1,000 Hz tone sounds higher-pitched than a 100 Hz tone. A piccolo produces many sound waves per second and a high-

174

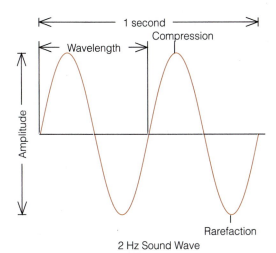

FIGURE 7-2 **Sound Waves.**
A sound wave can be diagramed as a sine wave. The height of the wave is its *amplitude,* which we perceive as loudness. From the start of one wave to the beginning of the next represents one complete cycle, and is its *wavelength.* The number of complete cycles per second is expressed in hertz (Hz) and determines the *frequency* of the sound. The higher the frequency, the shorter the wavelength.

pitched sound. An instrument such as a bass or tuba produces far fewer sound waves per second, and we hear a much lower-pitched sound.

What are the lowest and highest pitches that we can hear? The answer varies because hearing is subjective and we all have different sets of ears that may be affected by heredity, age, health, exposure to loud sounds, damage, and even ear wax. In general, people are capable of hearing frequencies between about 20 Hz and 16,000 Hz (16 KHz). This is called the *frequency range* of hearing.

In the case of audio equipment, frequency range may be called *frequency response*, and usually is shown as a graph on the literature that comes with the equipment. (See Figure 7-3.) While frequency response varies depending on the type and quality of equipment, you should expect it to meet or exceed the frequency range of human hearing. It's common for home stereo components to have frequency responses from 20 Hz to 20,000 Hz, and most professional equipment will exceed that range.

When we talk about the frequency range, we often divide it into three portions:

PORTION OF FREQUENCY RANGE	FREQUENCIES
Low-end (or bass)	Below 300 Hz
Midrange	About 300 Hz to 3,500 Hz
High-end (or treble)	Above 3,500 Hz

Our ears are most sensitive in the upper midrange, from about 1,000 Hz to 3,500 Hz, which is the primary range for speech. Therefore, if we hear three sounds—a low-end, midrange, and high-end frequency—that are at exactly the same volume, subjectively we hear the midrange frequencies as louder than either the low-end or high-end frequencies.

A related perception is *masking*, when one sound seems to cover up another, even though

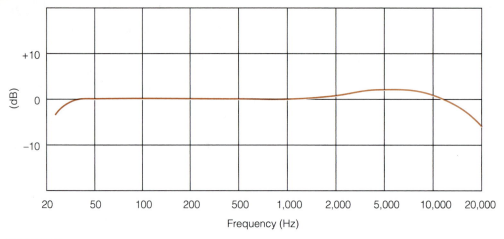

FIGURE 7-3 Frequency Response.
Equally loud frequencies are fed into a microphone and the output levels are measured and plotted on a graph as above. The solid line shows that the mike has a *flat response*—all output levels are equal—except below 40 Hz and above 10 KHz, where the response drops off.

technically they are at the same volume. For example, when we hear a midrange frequency and a low-end frequency at exactly the same volume, the low-end frequency will seem to disappear; it will be masked.

Understanding these subjective responses to frequencies is important in processing, recording, and mixing sound, which we will discuss later in this part.

Sound Timbre   A single frequency is called a *tone*. For example, a common reference frequency used in audio recording and measurement is *1,000 Hz tone*. The only pure single frequencies that exist are those generated electrically by *oscillators*. All other sounds are combinations of frequencies that include the *fundamental* tone, harmonics, and overtones. *Harmonics* are exact multiples of the fundamental tone. In music, exact multiples of a tone are called *octaves*. For example, 1,760 Hz and 880 Hz are harmonics, exact multiples, of 440 Hz (A above middle C on the piano), and each A note is separated by a full octave. *Overtones* are frequencies that resonate with the fundamental tone, but are not exact multiples of it.

Variations in frequencies give each sound a quality called its tone color, or *timbre*. It is one characteristic that makes it possible to tell one sound source from another. For example, whether the note A above middle C is played on the piano or on the guitar, it vibrates 440 times each second (440 Hz). But both notes sound richer and fuller than the pure 440 Hz tone, and most people have little difficulty telling which note is from the piano and which is from the guitar. That is because along with the *fundamental* tone of the A note, we also hear the harmonics and overtones, in a complex variety of frequencies that gives each instrument its distinctive sound quality.

We can illustrate the difference between a pure fundamental tone of a sound and its timbre by comparing a sine wave and a *waveform* of the complex sound, as in Figure 7-4.

Sound Intensity

The intensity of a sound depends on the amount of energy used to produce the pressure variations in the medium that carries the sound. The greater the energy, the greater the pressure variations and the more intense the sound. We perceive sound intensity as "loudness," or volume, and our perception of loudness is dependent upon three important factors: *amplitude, phasing,* and *power.*

176

Amplitude The intensity of sound can be visually represented by the height of a sine wave, as shown in Figure 7-5. The height of the wave is called its *amplitude*. A wave with a higher curve represents a louder sound. A flatter curve represents a softer sound.

Phasing When two or more sounds are produced at the same time, a phenomenon known as *phasing* occurs. Notice what happens to the amplitude of a sound wave if a second wave of equal amplitude is placed on top of it, as illustrated in Figure 7-5. If the waves begin at exactly the same time, the curve representing their combined amplitude is higher. But if the waves begin at slightly different times, the combined curve is lower and we perceive the two sounds as softer than either single sound. In fact, at some point, the two waves cancel each other out completely and the combined curve of the two sound sources actually has no amplitude.

Frequencies that begin at the same time and which result in a combined amplitude or volume which is greater than the individual frequencies are called *in phase*. Frequencies which cancel each other out are called *out of phase*. Phasing is a very important consideration when we attempt to record and reproduce audio—especially stereo—and we will discuss its application to production in the following chapters.

Power We sense variations in sound intensity by comparing one sound's loudness, or volume, to another. This sense of loudness is more a relative measure than an absolute scale, and so we have

come to use a "ratio" of loudness to describe and measure audio volume. This "intensity ratio" is measured in *decibels*, abbreviated as "dB." We generally say that a particular sound is so many "decibels" or "dB" greater or less than another. Since these ratios can get quite large, decibels are measured on a logarithmic scale which enables us to express very large physical values with a conveniently smaller scale of numbers.

The decibel scale is designed so that a doubling of the sound intensity is expressed as a change of 3 dB. In other words, if we double or halve the intensity of a sound, we increase or decrease the sound by 3 dB. Therefore, a change from 3 dB to 6 dB is a doubling of the sound intensity, as is a change from 9 dB to 12 dB. To illustrate the incredible range of sensitivity of the human ear, a whisper can be understood at 30 dB, whereas the pain threshold for healthy ears is not reached until about 120 dB—an intensity ratio of more than 10 million to 1!

TECH TIP The softest intensity at which we first begin to hear sound is called the *threshold of hearing*, at 0 dB. The *threshold of pain* is the intensity at which the sound becomes physically painful, usually about 120 dB (a loudness level exceeded at many heavy metal concerts!). This range from 0 dB to 120 dB is called the *dynamic range* of human hearing and has an intensity ratio of more than 10 million to 1.

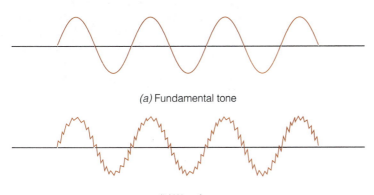

(a) Fundamental tone

(b) Waveform

FIGURE 7-4 Fundamental Tone and Timbre.
(*a*) The sound wave of one pure fundamental *tone*, or frequency, is represented by a sine wave. (*b*) A combination of frequencies giving the sound *timbre* is represented by a waveform.

sound-producing devices as samplers and synthesizers permit you to shape the quality of a sound by manipulating its envelope. We'll deal with envelopes and their use in shaping sound quality in later chapters.

TYPES OF AUDIO SIGNALS

The acoustic sound produced by a vibrating object—whether it's a musical instrument, a human voice, or any other sound-producing source—must be changed into an electrical signal before it can be processed by the audio equipment chain and become part of a television program's soundtrack. In other words, acoustic energy must be converted into electrical energy for the sound to become an audio signal. Converting one form of energy into another form of energy is called *transduction*. The most common "transducer" is the microphone and we will discuss microphone equipment and operation later in this chapter.

When we use a microphone to pick up a sound,

we are creating a series of waveforms that represent the original sound's frequency and intensity in electronic terms. Once the electrical waveform is produced, the electronic signal flows through the audio system where it is processed, mixed, and recorded. The audio signal can be processed and recorded in one of two ways: *analog* processing or *digital* processing. The differences between the two are very significant but in reality you've already become familiar with both: the vinyl LP record is an example of an analog recording process while the audio compact disc (CD) is a common example of digital recording.

Analog

In analog audio systems, the electrical signal represents or creates an "analogy" of the actual sound. (See Figure 7-8.) Making an analog recording can be compared with tracing the shape of a country on a map. Imagine you are given a map and asked to trace a country's shape on another piece of paper. It's highly unlikely that your copy will identically match the original. The copy will look very much like the original but it won't be exactly the same. The same process occurs in analog sound recording. The electrical signals that

FIGURE 7-8   Analog and Digital Signals.
The waveform of the analog signal recorded on tape looks similar to the waveform of the original sound, but the digitally sampled and encoded signal recorded on tape is a series of pulses containing binary digits, or bits, that digitally represent components of the original sound.

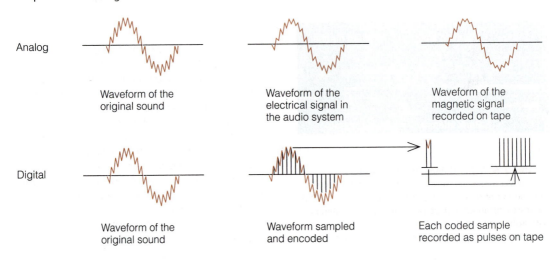

Analog

Waveform of the original sound

Waveform of the electrical signal in the audio system

Waveform of the magnetic signal recorded on tape

Digital

Waveform of the original sound

Waveform sampled and encoded

Each coded sample recorded as pulses on tape

are created by the microphone and passed through the audio system will not match the original sound signals exactly; there are inevitable imperfections which are not part of the original sound. The two most noticeable imperfections in analog systems are *distortion* and *noise*. Another very significant disadvantage of analog systems is that as the signal is processed or copied from one generation to another, these imperfections grow and result in a deterioration of the sound quality.

As we mentioned earlier, the LP record is an analog recording because the grooves of the record are created as analogies of the electronic waveform of the original audio signal. The turntable's stylus follows the variations in the groove and as it vibrates, it re-creates the waveform which is reproduced through your stereo system.

Digital

In digital audio systems, the electrical signals from the microphone are converted into numbers, or digits, that represent components of the original sound signal. This is done by a process called *sampling* in which the original sound waveform—its frequency, intensity, and other attributes—is measured thousands of times each second. The result is a series of computer-type "binary digits," or "bits," which represents the original waveform. The more bits that are used to sample and record the sound, the more accurate the representation, or "resolution," of the sample. For example, 8 digital bits can represent 256 different frequency intensities; 16 bits can represent 65,536! Obviously, a 16-bit recording contains much more information about the original sound, and 16-bit processing is the resolution standard of compact discs and digital audio tape.

Unlike the analog LP record, which is produced with grooves, the digital CD is encoded with millions of microscopic "pits" which represent the digital bits. A laser beam scans the pitted surface and decodes the information into the digital signal which is sent through the audio system for processing, mixing, and recording.

The advantages of digital audio compared with analog are: (1) Far less noise, hiss, and distortion; (2) an increased dynamic range; (3) the ability to manipulate and process the signal and produce

special effects easily with no loss of audio quality; (4) the ability to more accurately edit audio; and (5) the ability to reproduce many generations without audio degradation. However, digital has its disadvantages, too. (1) Loud sounds are more susceptible to distortion; (2) the equipment tends to be more expensive than analog; and (3) digital processing can sometimes sound "colder" and somewhat unnatural compared to the "warmth" of analog recording. Despite these disadvantages, digital processing and recording offers so much power and flexibility that its use as a production standard is inevitable. In fact, as we will see later in our discussion of audio processing and audio recording, digital already plays a significant role in audio production and is likely to completely replace analog systems in the near future.

MICROPHONES

Earlier we mentioned that sound must be converted from acoustic energy to electrical energy in order to be used as source of sound in the audio chain. While there are many possible audio sources for a program's soundtrack, the microphone is the primary transducer which enables you to pick up sound. We'll discuss the various types of microphones which are used in audio production and then deal with the various storage media which enable you to both record live sound as well as play back previously recorded material as sources in building the program's soundtrack.

All microphones contain two basic components: a diaphragm and a generating element. The *diaphragm* is a flexible device that is sensitive to the air pressure variations of a sound wave. The diaphragm vibrates according to the pressure variations of the sound. Attached to the diaphragm is the *generating element,* which converts the diaphragm's vibrations into electrical energy. The current that is produced is routed to the audio-control console, where it is amplified and regulated by the audio technician.

One way to classify microphones is by the generating element used in their construction. Three types of microphones are used in television production: (1) dynamic microphones, (2) ribbon microphones, and (3) condenser (sometimes known as "capacitor") microphones.

Dynamic Microphones

In a *dynamic microphone,* the diaphragm is attached to a coil of wire located close to a permanent magnet. As the diaphragm vibrates according to the sound waves that reach it, the "voice coil" moves back and forth inside the magnetic field. This creates an electric current that is directly proportional to the movement of the diaphragm. The louder the sound, the greater is the diaphragm's movement and the greater is the electrical energy produced. Since dynamic microphones use an internal coil, they are sometimes called "moving coil" microphones.

Dynamic mikes are capable of producing excellent sound fidelity, and their rugged construction makes them durable and relatively insensitive to the harsh handling production mikes are subjected to in daily operation. (See Figure 7-9.)

FIGURE 7-9   Microphone Generating Elements. The most common microphone generating elements used in television are (*a*) dynamic, (*b*) ribbon, and (*c*) condenser.

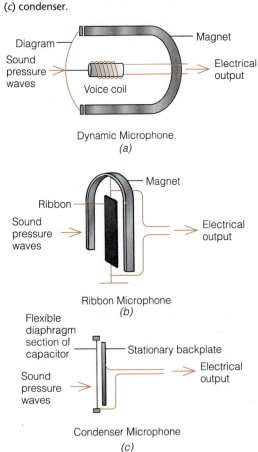

Dynamic Microphone
(a)

Ribbon Microphone
(b)

Condenser Microphone
(c)

Ribbon Microphones

The construction of a *ribbon microphone,* sometimes called a "velocity" microphone, is in many ways similar to that of the dynamic, or moving coil, microphone. Again, a permanent magnet is used to provide a magnetic field, but instead of a voice coil, the ribbon mike uses a thin metal strip, or ribbon, that serves as both the diaphragm, to receive the sound waves, and as the generating element, to produce the electric current. (See Figure 7-9.)

Ribbon mikes tend to be more fragile than most dynamic mikes. They are sensitive to sudden loud sounds. This limits their use outdoors or whenever the microphone is subject to much movement or handling. They produce a very warm, rich, and mellow sound, which is often desirable for miking announcers, singers, and musical instruments.

Condenser Microphones

Condenser microphones use a capacitor as the generating element. A *capacitor* consists of two closely spaced plates that can store an electric charge. Each plate is connected to opposite sides of a dc power supply. When one of the plates moves, the capacitance value changes and creates a corresponding change in the voltage applied across the two plates. The capacitance depends on the physical distance between the two plates and varies as the space between them changes. (See Figure 7-9.)

The diaphragm of a condenser microphone is actually one of the capacitor plates, which moves relative to the other, stationary plate. Air pressure variations from the sound source move the diaphragm and vary the space between the two capacitor plates. This produces an electric output voltage.

Condenser microphones offer excellent audio response characteristics, but they require a power supply to charge the capacitor and a preamplifier to boost the tiny output current. Older condenser mikes used bulky power supplies which limited their use in television. Some condenser mikes receive their power from what is called a "phantom" powering system built into the audio console that supplies a small voltage to the mike through the cable.

TECH TIP Phantom power usually can be controlled at each input of an audio console. When ribbon mikes are used, the phantom power should be turned off at that input or damage to the fragile ribbon can result.

Electret Condenser Electret microphones are capable of the same excellent performance characteristics of normal condenser mikes, but they do not require large power supplies. An *electret* is a special capacitor element that is charged during manufacture and is designed to hold the charge indefinitely. This means that it does not require external power to charge the element for use. The microphone's preamplification is supplied by a tiny battery and associated electronics built into

the microphone or housed in the cable connector jack. (See Figure 7-10.)

Electret condenser mikes can be made very small and unobtrusive and yet deliver excellent audio fidelity. The internal battery supply will last over 1,000 hours, but it is a good idea to have spare batteries always on hand, since the microphone cannot function without battery power.

MICROPHONE PICKUP PATTERNS

Another way of classifying microphones is by their pickup patterns. *Audio pickup* refers to how the microphone responds to sounds coming from different directions. While no microphone can be designed to accept sounds from one direction and totally reject sounds emanating from another direction, the pickup pattern of a microphone indicates its area of maximum audio sensitivity.

A *polar diagram* is a convenient way to illustrate a microphone's pickup pattern. The diagram is interpreted by assuming that the microphone is in the center of the graph facing the 0° axis. The two 90° axes are at the sides of the microphone, and the 180° axis is at the rear of the mike. There are three types of pickup patterns: (1) nondirectional (sometimes called omnidirectional), (2) bidirec-

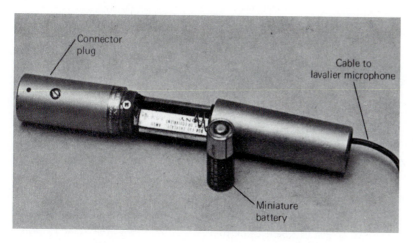

FIGURE 7-10 Electret Condenser Power Supply. Electret condenser microphones require electric power supplied by a battery for operation. When changing batteries, position the battery with the positive (+) end facing the proper direction or microphone damage can result.

tional, and (3) directional (sometimes called uni-directional). (See Figure 7-11.)

Nondirectional Pattern

A microphone with a *nondirectional* (sometimes called *omnidirectional*) pickup pattern is designed to receive sound from all sides equally without discriminating against sound from any particular angle. As shown in Figure 7-11, an omnidirectional microphone has a 360° sensitivity range. Sounds emanating from any direction will be picked up equally well using a microphone with this type of pickup pattern.

Bidirectional Pattern

As its name suggests, the *bidirectional* mike has two "live" sides of equal size. Bidirectional pickups are valuable when two performers wish to work a mike simultaneously and must see each other. These mikes often were used in radio drama, so that the actors could watch each other as they worked the mike. The problem with their use in television is that the side opposite the performer naturally faces the cameras and crew, and the mike has a tendency to pick up extraneous production noise in the studio. For this reason, bidirectional mike pickups seldom are used in monophonic television production. However, they are enjoying a resurgence because of their application in stereo, particularly for the reproduction of music. (See Chapter 10.)

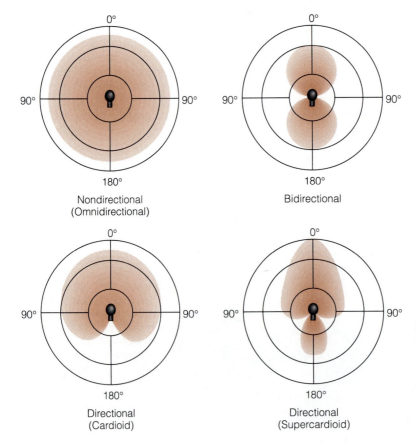

Nondirectional
(Omnidirectional)

Bidirectional

Directional
(Cardioid)

Directional
(Supercardioid)

FIGURE 7-11
Polar Diagram.
A polar diagram is used to represent a microphone's pickup pattern. The microphone's area of audio sensitivity is enclosed in the shaded area.

Directional Patterns

Directional microphones (sometimes called *unidirectional*) are designed to be most sensitive to sound emanating from a particular direction and to suppress or reject sounds coming from other sides of the mike. Directional mikes are also called cardioid (pronounced CAR-DEE-OID) microphones. (See Figure 7-11.)

Cardioid Pickup   The pattern of a *cardioid* microphone, as its name suggests, is shaped like a heart. Although the "live" area pattern varies, most cardioid mikes are highly sensitive within a 120° area facing the microphone. The cardioid pattern is very commonly used because it offers some directional isolation yet has a wide audio pickup range on the "live" side of the microphone. Another advantage of the cardioid pickup is that the performer or subject can work farther from the microphone and still produce better quality sound than is possible using an omnidirectional microphone. (See Figure 7-11.)

Supercardioid Pickup   These highly directional microphones are designed to pick up sound within a very limited angle of acceptance. Since their polar diagram resembles an extreme cardioid pickup, they are called *supercardioids*. (See Figure 7-11.) One misconception about supercardioid microphones (sometimes referred to as "shotguns" because they use a long tube to gather the desired sound and to suppress sounds from the side and rear of the microphone) is that they are constructed in a special way. Actually, the microphone itself is quite similar to cardioid or omnidirectional mikes; it is the design of the tube that funnels sound to the supercardioid microphone that produces the highly directional pickup pattern. "Zoom" shotguns can vary the directionality of their pickup pattern.

Because of their pickup characteristics, highly directional microphones can be used at greater distances from the subject than other mikes and still provide good sound quality. They are frequently used mounted on a boom or hand-held for special pickup applications.

The main problem with a highly directional mike is its *extreme* directionality. Unless the microphone is pointed directly at the sound source,

weak, muffled audio quality can result. At the same time, the narrow pickup pattern of the shotgun cannot reject all spurious noise outside its very narrow-angled cone. While the microphone's pickup sensitivity is great at larger distances, it also is highly susceptible to ambient noise, noise caused by handling it, and echo, which can ruin the overall sound quality. Even with a supercardioid microphone, the closer you can position the microphone to the sound source, the better the sound quality will be.

TECH TIP   The general rule in television audio is that close mike placements are preferable to distant mike placements. Shotguns should be used only when a different mike cannot be placed within a distance equal to four times the length of the shotgun mike's body.

The use of a parabolic reflector permits an ordinary cardioid mike to assume highly directional pickup characteristics. A *parabolic reflector* is a metal or fiberglass dish about 3 to 4 feet in diameter. It is equipped with a microphone mounted in the center of the dish. The microphone does not face outward, but instead is pointed toward the center of the reflector and picks up concentrated sounds as they are reflected off the parabolic dish. Many remote productions use parabolic reflectors to provide an additional dimension to the program audio. For example, parabolic reflectors often are used on football remotes to pick up the quarterback's signals. A technician standing on the sidelines points the reflector toward the quarterback while the signals are called out. (The audio technician in the control room must be careful to turn on the parabolic mike only when necessary, since it can pick up a considerable amount of unintended audio.) On most games, the audio technician will use the reflector mike to pick up the quarterback's signals and the sounds of the two lines colliding after the ball is snapped. The mike is then immediately cut off to avoid the possibility of a player's on-field "remarks" from inadvertently being transmitted. As with any highly directional mike, much of the sound quality depends on how accurately the technician who is operating the mike points it toward the sound source. (See Figure 7-12.)

The 3- to 4-foot diameter of the parabolic reflector makes its size impractical for in-studio use. Since it is rare that the audio technician will have to pick up sounds from as great a distance inside the studio (where conditions can be controlled), the use of parabolic reflectors usually is limited to outside the studio unless very special circumstances require its use indoors.

TECH TIP   Parabolic mikes used at great distances can cause lip synch problems. Since sound travels so much slower than light, the movement of the lips precedes the sound if the mike is very far away. Unless the mike is being used to "overhear" a conversation, wireless mikes or concealed microphones used close to the speakers produce higher-quality, better-synchronized audio.

Using Microphone Pickup Patterns in Production

There is no such thing as a "better" microphone pickup pattern. Each is designed to be applied to a particular audio situation. In recognition of this fact, many microphones have switchable patterns under the control of the user. The idea is to let the pickup pattern work for you by maximizing the microphone's sensitivity to sound that you want to cover and minimizing extraneous sound that would interfere with the audio quality.

For example, if you were recording a musical group with a number of microphones, you would probably choose cardioid pickups, since each microphone should be positioned to pick up only a part of the total sound. Using multiple "omnis" would make balancing sound sources difficult in a studio. Cardioid microphones are also helpful when you wish to minimize reverberation, extraneous noise, and other ambient sounds. An omnidirectional microphone is perfect to use when extraneous noise is not a problem and when one microphone must cover a wide area.

FIGURE 7-12   Parabolic Reflector.
The bowl-shaped reflector concentrates sound waves on the live side of the microphone. This microphone is used to pick up sound at long distances.

MICROPHONE FREQUENCY RESPONSE

The frequency response of a microphone is an important characteristic which determines how sensitive the microphone is to the various audio frequencies it must pick up and reproduce. *Frequency response* is usually provided as a range (for example, 45 Hz to 18,000 Hz) that indicates the lower and upper frequency extremes a mike is capable of reproducing accurately.

A microphone with a "flat" response theoretically would be equally sensitive to all audio frequencies within its response range without unduly emphasizing or suppressing certain frequencies. (See Figure 7-3.) A mike with a flat response is ideal for recording musical instruments where the audio technician wants to reproduce all the frequencies of the instruments with maximum accuracy.

TECH TIP   Frequency response usually is advertised for sound produced directly on-axis. The mike's frequency response for sounds not at the most sensitive part of the pickup pattern will differ. Good microphone construction reduces this off-axis "coloring" to a minimum.

Some microphones are designed with special frequency response characteristics that enhance the mike's usefulness in certain situations. For example, many lavalier microphones are designed to be particularly sensitive to the frequencies that make up the human voice. At the same time, they suppress low frequencies which cause unwanted noise and the "barrel" effect of being located close to the performer's chest cavity. Some mikes contain a switch that permits the audio technician to adjust the microphone's frequency response characteristics to best match the production's audio requirements.

A common feature on many mikes is a "low frequency roll-off" control, which reduces the microphone's bass response and is helpful in eliminating wind noise or the artificially increased bass range, called the *proximity effect*, when a performer works very close to the mike. Roll-off can occur at 50, 100, or 200 Hz, depending on the microphone construction. Be careful not to cut into the range of a man with a low voice. *Tip-up* refers to accentuating part of the frequency response of a microphone and often is built-in at around 3,000 Hz.

MICROPHONE IMPEDANCE

Another important microphone characteristic is its *impedance,* which refers to the amount of electrical resistance in a circuit and is expressed in *ohms* (often abbreviated with the symbol Ω). *Low impedance* means there is relatively little signal resistance and, therefore, a relatively large current flow. *High impedance* means there is a greater resistance and a correspondingly smaller current flow. Professional microphones, such as those used in television production, are always of low impedance (referred to as "low Z"). This is so because low-impedance microphones permit the use of very long cables without any loss of high-frequency signals. Since most professional production applications require mikes to be used with cables longer than 15 or 20 feet, only low-impedance microphones can be used without degrading the sound quality. Low-impedance mikes also are much less susceptible to the hum of fluorescent lights and electric motors than are high-Z microphones.

Low-Z microphones have impedances between 30 and 250 ohms; high impedance mikes run from 10,000 ohms and above. A microphone's impedance should match the input connector impedance on a tape recorder or audio mixer. This usually isn't a problem in professional studios because most microphone inputs are designed for low-Z operation. If the impedance of your microphone does not match the impedance of your inputs, all is not lost. Low impedance microphones can be successfully fed into high-Z inputs. However, doing the opposite will not work because high-Z microphones do not provide enough signal for low-Z inputs. One option is to use a *matching transformer* but it could introduce unwanted noise and distortion.

USES OF MICROPHONES

Another way to distinguish among different microphones is to describe them by how they are used in production. *On-camera microphones* are those which are seen in the camera shot and are used when their presence on screen will not distract the viewer or interfere with the picture. *Off-camera microphones* are those which must be used when the microphone must remain out of the camera's view because inclusion in a shot would destroy an illusion or interfere with the action.

On-Camera Microphones

There are six types of on-camera microphones: (1) lavalier, (2) hand, (3) desk, (4) PZM, (5) stand, and (6) headset.

Lavalier Microphones The lavalier is probably the most commonly used microphone in television production. The lavalier, as its name suggests, can be clipped to the lapel of a coat or jacket; pinned to a tie, dress, or blouse; or hung around the neck like a pendant. Most lavalier microphones are designed with an omnidirectional pickup, but since they are positioned relatively close to the speaker's mouth, extraneous noise is rarely a problem. (See Figure 7-13.)

Unobtrusive "tie-tack" lavalier microphones are electret condensers that can be made so small because the battery (or phantom power interface) and miniature electronics are contained in the cable connector jack out of camera range. Because of the small size and appearance of the lavalier, some audio technicians use two in a *dual-redundancy system*. This simply means that the performer wears two mikes on the same clip. Only one microphone is actually on at any time, but should the mike fail during the production, the audio technician can switch immediately to the back-up mike without audio interruption. (See Figure 7-14.)

USING THE LAVALIER IN PRODUCTION   The lavalier provides excellent audio quality when used for general speech pickup and eliminates many audio-associated production problems. Booms re-

quire additional personnel and a great deal of care in lighting and staging. Hand mikes require the talent to hold the mike at all times. Stand or desk mikes restrict talent movements. In contrast, a lavalier microphone requires no additional production personnel, eliminates lighting problems, and provides hands-free operation and freedom of movement.

However, there are also a number of disadvantages to using the lavalier. First, its small size makes it easily damaged or misplaced unless care is taken to safeguard it. Because of its omnidirectional pattern, it will pick up extraneous sound unless positioned correctly. It is a good idea for the audio technician or a crew member to actually place the lavalier on each performer—especially on nonprofessional talent—before production begins to ensure proper handling and correct placement of the microphone. If the performer will face in one direction during the show, position the microphone on the side where he or she will normally look during conversation. Take care in positioning a lavalier on any performer wearing a

FIGURE 7-13   **Lavalier Microphones.**
Lavalier microphones are small and unobtrusive. They are usually clipped to a tie or the front of a blouse.

FIGURE 7-14   **Dual-Redundancy Miking.**
Dual-redundancy Lavaliers share a microphone clip. Only one is actually live, but if it fails, the second can be quickly activated to continue uninterrupted sound pickup.

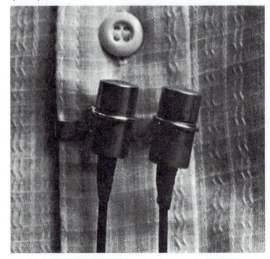

FIGURE 7-15 Desk Microphone.
Some desk microphones can double as hand microphones in the field.

necklace or pin that might jostle the microphone and create annoying sounds during the show. Some directors ask the audio technician to hide the lavalier under a tie or blouse. While this is possible, the audio technician should make a test before production to ensure that the hidden lavalier is not rubbing against the talent's clothing or undergarments and that the sound pickup is clear and unmuffled.

With all its obvious advantages, there are still some production situations where a lavalier is not the best microphone choice. A show with a number of on-camera participants is one example where too many individual lavaliers would be necessary. An audio technician who is assigned to a children's show where the host must interview twenty children would be better off choosing a hand microphone or even a boom rather than attempting to provide each child with a separate lavalier. Also, lavalier microphones are not recommended for production situations where the best-quality audio is necessary. While the reproduction is excellent for general speech, a lavalier is not the ideal microphone to use for covering a singer or musical instruments.

Desk Microphones A desk microphone is appropriate when talent will be seated behind a table or desk or does not have to move and the microphone can appear in the shot. News programs, panel discussions, and news coverage of speakers from a podium or stand are common production situations for a desk mike.

Dynamic, electret condenser, and even ribbon mikes with a cardioid pattern are all used for desk microphones. Dynamic mikes are very popular because of their durability, especially when the desk mike doubles as a hand microphone for field use. (See Figure 7-15.)

USING DESK MICROPHONES IN PRODUCTION As with a lavalier, the audio technician should position the desk mike in the direction talent will normally face during the show. Sometimes one desk mike, properly positioned, can cover two people. Since the desk mike is positioned on the desk or tabletop, it is highly sensitive to noise around the table area. Remind talent to avoid tapping their hands or feet, and make certain that no physical actions are planned on the same surface where the desk mike is located.

PZMs A *PZM* (*pressure-zone microphone*) microphone, known also as a *boundary* microphone, is designed to pick up the audio of a number of sources with equal fidelity, sound presence, and volume. This makes the PZM ideal for group talk shows and for some music applications.

A PZM uses a very small pickup pointed directly down at a hard, metallic plate. Sound from anywhere in the room is "heard" by the PZM as sound reflected from the hard, reflective surface. Since all the sound travels a very short distance between the plate and the pickup, it reaches the pickup at the same time and the possibly disruptive effect of indirect sound (echo) is reduced. The location

189

FIGURE 7-16 PZM, or Boundary, Microphone.
A PZM (pressure-zone microphone) picks up audio from a number of sources with equal fidelity, sound presence, and volume. (*Courtesy: AKG Acoustics.*)

and polar pattern of the pickup also are the reasons why sound presence is equalized. (See Figure 7-16.)

USING PZMs IN PRODUCTION   One characteristic of PZMs is their equal sensitivity to sound produced anywhere in the room. The pickup pattern of the PZM can be reduced by using "blocks" or plates that interfere with sound coming from one side of the microphone. Most professional-quality PZMs offer this block as an accessory so the mike can pick up sounds coming from only one direction and reject camera and crew noise. PZMs may be used to pick up audience questions in an audience-response show where a shotgun mike is not available. However, the microphone's tendency to equalize the volume of all sounds within its range can pose a problem. If a performer taps a pencil, shuffles papers, or makes other unintended noises, the PZM reproduces them nearly as well as the performer's voice. When PZMs are used, talent must be instructed to keep nervous mannerisms to a minimum.

Hand Microphones   The hand mike is commonly used by emcees and singers in the studio and by reporters and interviewers in the field. The advantages of the hand mike are no special lighting or staging requirements, complete talent control over mike position, and good pickup characteristics. The disadvantages are that the performer

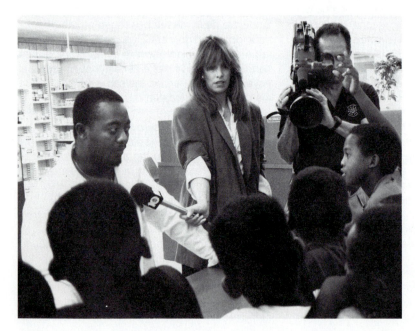

FIGURE 7-17
Hand Microphone.
Hand microphones offer talent control of the audio pickup and provide good audio fidelity. The reporter holds the microphone properly so the pharmacist is heard clearly.
(*Courtesy: WPLG-TV.*)

must hold the microphone and is partially responsible for how well or how poorly the sound is covered on mike. (See Figure 7-17.)

Hand microphones are available with either omnidirectional or cardioid pickup patterns. Although most hand-held mikes take advantage of the rugged durability of dynamic construction, electret condenser hand-held microphones also are available.

Stand Microphones A stand microphone is simply a desk or hand-held mike that is mounted on a mike stand. Stand microphones frequently are used by singers, for miking musical instruments, and for announcer microphones both on-camera and off. The stands come in many different shapes and sizes, from the usual straight mike stand to flexible-neck stands and stationary boom-arm

FIGURE 7-18 **Stand Microphone.**
Stand microphones leave performers' hands free for expressive movement, for playing musical instruments, or for demonstration purposes. *(Courtesy: Capital Cities/ABC-TV, Inc.)*

stands. The latter two are frequently used for miking musical instruments or to position the microphone where a singer-musician can work the mike and simultaneously play an instrument. (See Figure 7-18.)

The major disadvantage with a stand microphone is that the performer's movement is severely limited to an area around the mike stand. The advantages are hands-free operation, no staging or lighting problems, and the ability to position the microphone exactly where it is needed and to keep it at a constant distance from the subject.

Headset Microphones There are certain production situations in which it is important to keep a performer's hands free while at the same time positioning the microphone very close to his or her mouth. This is especially true for remote situations such as sporting events where crowd noise is so loud that it can drown out the announcer's voice unless the mike is very close. The headset microphone is a dual headset with a high-quality mike attached. The performer can hear the program audio in one ear, the director's commands in the other ear, and keep his or her hands free to handle various papers during the production. With the microphone positioned so close to the performer's mouth, crowd noise is kept to a minimum. In addition, the padding in the headset permits the performer to hear the production commands which might otherwise be drowned out. (See Figure 7-19.)

Off-Camera Microphones

Off-camera microphones are used whenever the microphone cannot appear in the camera shot. There are two types of off-camera microphones: (1) boom mountings and (2) hidden microphones.

Boom The term *boom* refers to a family of microphone mounting devices used to position a microphone just out of camera range, but where it can still pick up the sound. Although almost any directional microphone can be used as a boom mike,

FIGURE 7-19
Headset Microphone.
Headset microphones position the microphone close to the announcer's mouth for use in noisy environments. The biaural headset allows the announcer to hear program audio in one earpiece and the director's instructions and cues in the other earpiece. *(Courtesy: Capital Cities/ABC-TV, Inc.)*

specially designed dynamic and electret condenser, cardioid, and supercardioid microphones are manufactured especially for use on booms. These microphones produce excellent audio response, while their highly directional pickup characteristics enable the mike to work at a greater distance from the subject and to reject extraneous noise. (See Figure 7-20.)

There are three types of boom mounting devices: (1) the hand-held fishpole boom, (2) the medium-sized tripod, or "giraffe," boom, and (3) the large perambulator boom.

HAND-HELD FISHPOLE The simplest kind of boom is the *hand-held fishpole boom.* This is a long aluminum tube with a microphone mounted on one

FIGURE 7-20
Boom Microphone.
The boom microphone is highly directional and can be positioned out of camera range and still pick up program audio. *(Courtesy: Capital Cities/ABC, Inc. and Ann Limongello)*

end. The telescoping tube can be extended or re- tracted depending on how much reach is neces- sary to cover the designated playing area. Fish- poles frequently are used on remote locations because of their portability and in the studio when a larger boom cannot be used for lack of space. The problems associated with using the fishpole boom are (1) the boom becomes heavy for the operator to hold after awhile and (2) the boom op- erator does not have maximum control over mi- crophone placement. Once the fishpole length has been set, the operator can extend or retract the boom only by moving his or her body toward or away from the subject. (See Figure 7-21.)

TRIPOD ("GIRAFFE" BOOM)   The *tripod* (or "gi- raffe") *boom* is basically a fishpole attached to a pedestal and mounted on a tripod with wheels so the unit can be moved easily around the studio. In addition, most medium-sized booms are equipped with a rotating device so that the mike can swivel without moving the boom itself. The major problems associated with a giraffe boom are (1) once the length of the boom has been set, it cannot be extended or retracted–instead the entire tripod must be rolled in or out; and (2) the boom's reach is rather short and has a limited op- erating range when compared with a large per- ambulator boom. In a small studio, this can be an advantage, since space is at a premium and a

large boom might cause more problems than it solves in terms of space and camera movement. (See Figure 7-22.)

PERAMBULATOR BOOM   The large *perambulator boom* is a sophisticated and expensive device that uses a series of belts and pulleys to control movement of the boom and the microphone. The two most commonly used booms in television are the Mole-Richardson boom and the Fisher boom. The Mole-Richardson has a disadvantage in that the boom arm can be swiveled only about 180° before the operator is forced off the platform. The Fisher boom has a circular platform which permits operating the boom in a 360° circle. The Fisher boom is also equipped with a seat which can make long production periods easier for the boom operator. (See Figure 7-23.)

Boom Operation   The entire platform and boom are mounted on wheels. A steering device at the rear enables a crew member to position the boom and to move it about the studio during production. The boom arm can be panned horizontally left or right or tilted up or down. The retraction and ex- tension controls permit fast and silent extension or

FIGURE 7-21
Fishpole Boom.
The fishpole boom allows a crew member to position the microphone on the pole's end for best audio pickup.
(Courtesy: Capital Cities/ ABC, Inc.)

retraction of the boom and microphone either out toward talent or in toward the boom operator. It is important for the audio technician and the director to know the maximum extension range of the boom (it varies from model to model) in order to plan performer blocking and audio coverage. The microphone can be rotated almost 360° without moving the boom arm itself. This enables the boom operator to cover a wide area without having to pan the entire boom arm back and forth physically.

All large booms use a counterweight to balance the weight of the microphone and to compensate for the boom arm's extension or retraction. The proper balance can vary depending on the type and weight of the microphone and mount you are using. Always check the boom's balance before a production. If you do not, the boom operator must physically bear the weight of the boom rather than sharing it with the counterweight system. This can tire the operator quickly and lead to inferior audio pickup on the show.

Probably the most difficult boom operation to master is judging accurately the distance between microphone and performer. The microphone must be positioned above and *in front* of talent, or you will not achieve the best audio pickup. A good way to locate this position is to have the performer raise his or her hand upward in a 45° angle. The boom mike should almost touch talent's outstretched fingertips. A good rule of thumb for the boom operator to follow is to keep the microphone as close as possible to the performer without dipping the mike into the camera shot. This means that in close-ups the microphone can be lowered and positioned relatively close to the talent. This will provide not only good sound pickup but also an accurate "sound perspective." In other words, we see the performer in close on the shot, and his or her voice sounds close to us. On the wide shot, the boom must necessarily go up to avoid being included in the shot. At the same time, the sound presence will change, and as we see the actor from a greater distance, we will also perceive the sound as coming from farther away. (See Figure 7-24.)

Many studios have added a small television monitor to the boom platform. This permits the boom operator to see the "air" shot and to position the boom accordingly. In addition, the boom operator usually wears a private-line (PL) headset, which keeps him or her in contact with either the audio technician, the director, or both. Some studios have dual headsets so that the boom operator can hear the director or audio technician in one ear while listening to the program audio in the other ear.

Because the boom operator must position the microphone correctly for proper sound reproduction, the boom operator, audio technician, and di-

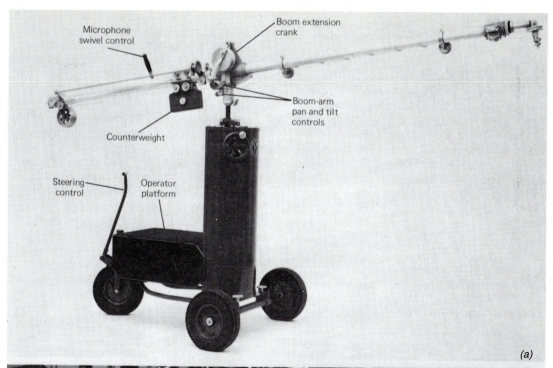

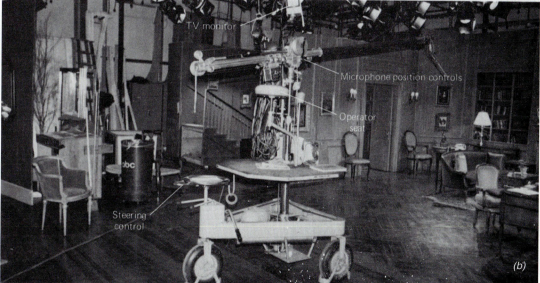

FIGURE 7-23 Perambulator Boom.
(*a*) The Mole-Richardson boom is restricted to a 180° arm swivel, so its use must be carefully pre-planned; (*b*) the Fisher boom offers a much wider arm swivel and has a seat that allows the operator to work in greater comfort. *(Courtesy: Mole-Richardson Co. and Capital Cities/ABC-TV, Inc.)*

rector must carefully coordinate boom moves, shot changes, and talent blocking before production. Of course, in an unrehearsed program, the boom operator must be doubly alert to any sudden moves talent might make. In this case, it is important to impress on the performer the necessity of "telegraphing" any moves before actually making them. Talent should say something like, "Let's get up and go over here," to alert the director, audio technician, and boom operator to the

FIGURE 7-24   Positioning the Boom Microphone.
The boom microphone must be placed in front of talent's mouth for best sound reproduction. The microphone is correctly positioned if talent can almost touch the microphone with a finger stretched at a 45° angle in front of his or her head.

unplanned move. There is nothing more embarrassing than to have a performer rise unexpectedly and hit his or her head on the boom microphone; getting the boom into the camera shot is only slightly less embarrassing.

As with most production equipment, the boom offers its share of advantages and disadvantages. The advantages of the boom are (1) the microphone is out of the picture, (2) talent need not worry about holding a microphone or having to contend with the trailing mike cables, (3) talent has more mobility within the pickup range of the boom, and (4) one boom can cover a large number of performers, although not all at the same time. The disadvantages of the boom are (1) the size of the boom itself—in many small studios, the size of the boom may severely curtail camera movement, since the boom platform takes up so much space, (2) the boom requires additional crew members, which can be costly, (3) the boom necessitates careful lighting to reduce the appearance of boom shadow (while boom shadow can never be completely eliminated, it is possible to light a set so as to throw the boom shadow out of camera range; this requires more planning and setup time to adjust the lights properly for boom shadow); and (4) the boom cannot cover performers who are widely dispersed. Unless you can use more than one boom (a very expensive proposition), it is best to attempt to cover this audio problem in a different way.

The choice of whether to use a boom mike and the specific type of boom mounting depends on the nature of the program, the size of the program's budget, and the equipment available. Because use of a boom requires coordination with other units of the production team, it is an audio decision that should be made relatively early in the preproduction stage.

Hidden Microphones

There are times when it is either impossible or impractical to use a boom and yet the microphone must be kept out of the camera shot. In this case, an alternative would be to hide the microphone either on the set or, in some cases, on the performer. The hidden set mike can be positioned almost anywhere as long as it can cover the necessary audio during the production. Some common hiding places are inside special props, behind flowers or books, or on mike stands just outside camera range.

There are a number of advantages to using a hidden mike. Unlike booms, you need no additional crew members and there is no problem in lighting for boom shadow. The biggest problem with the hidden mike is that you must position your actors very close to the microphone and make certain that their movement is limited to the area in which the microphone can acceptably pick up the sound. For this reason, it is difficult to use only hidden mikes for an entire dramatic program, since the positioning of the hidden mike severely restricts actor blocking. However, the hidden mike can be a valuable addition to a boom microphone if used on a particular set where the boom cannot reach and where actor movement is not essential.

There are a number of considerations to take into account when planning to use hidden microphones:

1 Position the microphone in a location where it will pick up the audio with acceptable quality.
2 Do not place the microphone inside a prop or piece of furniture that might be jostled by performers during the program. This would result in the microphone rubbing against the furniture and producing extraneous noise that would mar the audio.
3 Dress the mike cord out of camera sight, and secure it with gaffer tape so that the performers will not trip over it during the production.
4 During the program, the audio technician should keep the fader pot on the hidden mike closed until it is actually going to be used. This will eliminate extraneous noise from entering the sound track and prevent the "echo" effect that occurs when indirect sound reaches a second mike an instant after the primary microphone picks up the direct sound.

Hidden Hand Mikes   Sometimes the simplest solution to a problem is the best one. If you have a situation in which you need to cover a performer's audio, but a boom microphone is impractical and hiding the mike presents other problems, an alternative is to have a floor assistant simply hold a hand mike near the talent and out of camera range. As long as the floor assistant holds the

mike steady and avoids mike noise, the sound pickup will be acceptable. The director can help the situation by bringing the cameras in close to permit the hand mike to be held as near the talent as possible. Although a highly directional shotgun mike is ideal for this purpose, a cardioid hand mike can serve as an inexpensive and generally adequate substitute. Be sure that the floor assistant holds the mike steady, avoids creating mike noise, and does not place the mike down before the audio technician has closed the mike's fader on the audio console.

Hidden Lavalier Microphones   Lavalier mikes are now made so small and unobtrusive that it is not difficult to hide one on a performer's body under his or her clothing. Of course, you will have to make certain that the microphone cable is out of the camera shot and that the performer will not have to move around much while trailing the mike cable.

The cable problem is eliminated if you use a wireless lavalier microphone that does not require any trailing cable. In this case, the mike's transmitter unit also must be hidden on the performer's body, but these are small enough to hide easily under a jacket or behind the performer's back and out of camera range.

Hanging Microphones   Hanging a microphone from a lighting batten should be the last alternative considered by the audio technician. Except in rare situations, a hanging mike often will produce more problems than it solves. With the mike overhead, there is always the possibility of picking up extraneous production noise. Since the mike's position cannot be varied during the show, unless talent is located in the exact position, the audio may be off-mike. The microphone's height also remains constant throughout the show. If the mike is hung too low, it may appear in a wide camera shot; if too high, poor sound quality will result. Finally, the lighting director may have to contend with shadows created by the hanging mike.

The only time a hanging microphone is useful is when you must cover a large group of performers who remain stationary throughout their perform-ance. For example, a musical group, a choir, or an orchestra can sometimes be miked success-fully with one or more hanging microphones.

OTHER MICROPHONES

There are three other types of microphones you should know about: *stereo, modular,* and *wireless* mikes.

Stereo Microphones

The microphones we have discussed so far are monophonic. In fact, technically, *all* microphones are monophonic. But stereo miking has become the norm in many television productions. Most of-ten, two or more monophonic microphones are positioned and controlled for the maximum stereo effect. We will describe stereo miking techniques in Chapter 10. There also are *stereo microphone systems.* Actually, a stereo mike consists of two monophonic elements inside a casing that pick up sound from two directions. The pickup patterns overlap, but still differ sufficiently to provide depth and dimension to the audiospace. (See Figure 7-25.) By rotating one of the two elements, the au-dio technician can create a number of stereo effects, and may pick up sound in an arc as wide as 170 degrees.

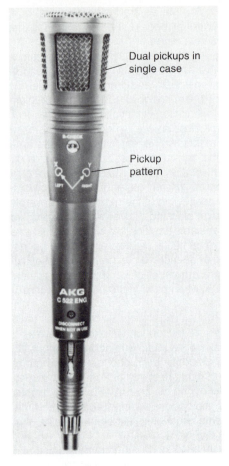

Dual pickups in single case

Pickup pattern

FIGURE 7-25 **Stereo Microphone.**
Stereo microphones enclose two monaural pickups within a single case. *(Courtesy: AKG Acoustics.)*

FIGURE 7-26
Modular Microphone.
Modular microphones allow a single microphone to be adapted to several different situations. *(Courtesy: Beyer-dynamic.)*

(a)

(b)

FIGURE 7-27 Wireless Microphones.
When standard mikes are plugged into external
transmitters, they can be used as wireless mikes.
(*a*) A hand mike with a plug-on transmitter.
(*Courtesy: Lectrosonics, Inc.*) (*b*) A lavalier plugged
into a transmitter that can be concealed under
clothing. (*Courtesy: Sennheiser.*)

shotgun capsules can be attached to the preamplifier housing. These mikes are especially valuable on remote productions where the most ideal
pickup may not be known prior to production. (See
Figure 7-26.)

Wireless Microphones

Wireless microphones operate without any connection cables between the microphone and the
control room. The performer and the audio technician gain all the advantages of a lavalier or hand
microphone without the disadvantages of trailing
mike cables, which can limit a performer's
mobility.

Each wireless microphone uses a small battery-
powered radio transmitter to send its audio signal
via an FM radio frequency to a receiver connected
to the audio-control console. From this point, the
output of the receiver is fed to the audio-control
console and controlled by the audio technician,
as would be the case with any conventional cable
microphone.

Modular Microphones

To increase their flexibility, some microphones are
being packaged as modular systems that permit
a single microphone to be adapted for several different situations. The system consists of a modular
capsule and the microphone's preamplifier circuits. Depending on the job, stand, hand-held, or

The microphones in wireless systems come as either one-part or two-part units. One-part wireless mikes include the transmitter and battery inside the mike case itself. Two-part wireless mikes actually use standard microphones that are "converted" into wireless mikes by plugging them directly into small radiating transmitters, as shown in Figure 7-27, or plugged into pocket-sized units containing the transmitter and battery. (See Figure 7-28.) These units can be hidden easily under performers' clothing.

TECH TIP   To avoid interference with each other, users of mobile radio frequencies must register with the FCC. Obtain a list of the frequencies in use locally and purchase a wireless system that can use a receive-send set of frequencies that does not compete with mobile radio operators in your community. Since future competition can occur, good systems should have a range of three to seven different frequencies on which they can operate.

The transmission range from the wireless microphone to the receiver is anywhere from 50 to 1,000 feet depending on operating conditions. As a rule of thumb, try to position the receiver as close to the microphone as possible. This will ensure even better and more reliable quality. Depending on the microphone and battery system, the transmitter can operate from four to sixteen hours before a new battery is needed.

The advantages of the wireless mike are obvious: freedom from cables both inside the studio and outdoors on remote location. This increases freedom of movement and can make microphone concealment much easier. The biggest disadvantage is the cost, particularly the fact that for each separate microphone you need, you must provide a separate transmitter and receiver.

OTHER LIVE AUDIO INPUTS

In addition to microphones, other devices are used to feed live sounds into the audio system. Three examples are the *direct box*, *samplers*, and *synthesizers*.

Direct Box

Electric guitars and other amplified instruments can be connected to the audio console directly, bypassing the need for a microphone pickup. This is accomplished through the use of a *direct box*. (See Figure 7-30.) The line-level input coming into the direct box is converted to mike level and passed through an XLR plug to the console. The benefits of using a direct box are that it totally isolates the instrument and makes sound bleed from other mikes impossible. This can be important in postproduction mixing. The disadvantage is that the direct feed can sometimes sound sterile and lifeless as compared with miking the speaker of an electric amp, which subtly colors the sound with the acoustics of the studio. Also, direct feeds make a live performance impossible unless all musicians are provided with headsets or separate monitor speakers.

Samplers and Synthesizers

A digital sampler is a device used to record, or "sample," live or prerecorded sounds and then enable you to manipulate, process, and reproduce them. (See Figure 7-31.) A "sample" is a digital recording of a short segment of sound on

FIGURE 7-28   **Wireless Microphone Transmitter and Receiver.**
A microphone is plugged into the transmitter, which sends the audio signal to the receiver, usually located on the perimeter of the set. The receiver is connected by cable to an input on the audio-control console. *(Courtesy: Telex Communications, Inc.)*

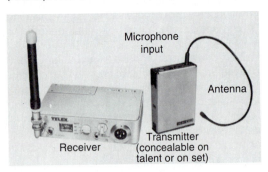

Microphone input

Antenna

Receiver

Transmitter (concealable on talent or on set)

FIGURE 7-29 Microphone Summary Chart.
(*Courtesy: Electro-Voice, AKG Acoustics, Telex Communications, Inc., Shure Brothers, Lectrosonics, Inc.*)

	EXAMPLE	GENERATING ELEMENT	PICKUP PATTERN	IMPEDANCE	APPLICATIONS
Lavalier 	AKG Acoustics C407	Electret Condenser	Omnidirectional	Low-Z	Miniature tie-clasp microphone ideal for news shows, talk shows, interviews, and other situations where unobtrusive microphones should be used.
	AKG Acoustics C414 B/TL	Condenser	Multipattern	Low-Z	Live in-studio vocal performances with wide dynamic ranges.
	AKG Acoustics D3500	Dynamic	Cardioid	Low-Z	Designed to mike instrument amps, percussion, and piano.

FIGURE 7-29 Microphone Summary Chart *(continued).*
(Courtesy: Electro-Voice, AKG Acoustics, Telex Communications, Inc., Shure Brothers, Lectrosonics, Inc.)

	EXAMPLE	GENERATING ELEMENT	PICKUP PATTERN	IMPEDANCE	APPLICATIONS
Hand/Desk/Stand 	Electro-Voice BK-1	Condenser	Cardioid	Low-Z	Live entertainment and other environments where control of feedback is important; both instrumental and vocal performances.
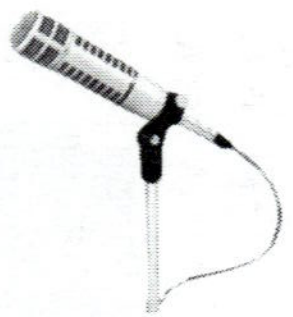	Electro-Voice RE20	Dynamic	Cardioid	Low-Z	Emphasizes flat frequency response and well-controlled off-axis colorization. Useful for recording sessions and on stage. Designed for extremely close use without producing bass "tip-up."
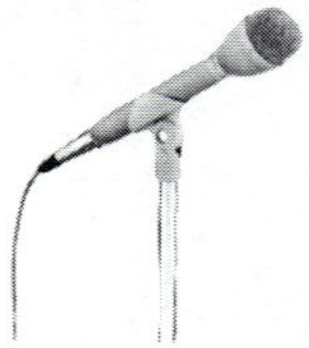	Electro-Voice RE50	Dynamic	Omnidirectional	Low-Z	Shock-isolated design ideal for hand-held use. Ruggedness, tolerance to wide range of temperature and humidity, and resistence to wind noise recommend it for remote location work.
Boom/Shotgun 	Electro-Voice RE45N/D	Dynamic	Super cardioid	Low-Z	Pick-up of voice at relatively long distances. Hand-held or stand mounted.

EXAMPLE	GENERATING ELEMENT	PICKUP PATTERN	IMPEDANCE	APPLICATIONS
AKG Acoustics C568 EB	Electret Condenser	Hypercardioid	Low-Z	Short shotgun with good distant pickup. May be mounted on a boom or camera, or hand-held.
Telex CS-90 Headset	Dynamic	Omnidirectional	Low-Z	Hands-free announcing in noisy environment. Dual headset permits monitoring program audio in one ear and director's production cues in the other.
AKG Acoustics C410	Condenser	Hypercardioid	Low-Z	Ideal for singing performers such as keyboardists, drummers, or dancers.

FIGURE 7-29 Microphone Summary Chart *(continued)*.
(Courtesy: Electro-Voice, AKG Acoustics, Telex Communications, Inc., Shure Brothers, Lectrosonics, Inc.)

	EXAMPLE	GENERATING ELEMENT	PICKUP PATTERN	IMPEDANCE	APPLICATIONS
Wireless Microphone Systems 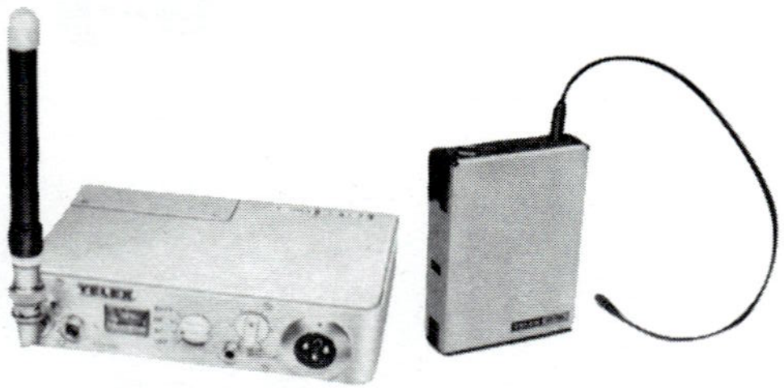	Telex Multichannel System (ENG-4 receiver/WT-400 transmitter)	Depends on microphone plugged into transmitter unit	Depends on microphone plugged into transmitter unit	Low-Z but adaptable to High-Z	ENG and remote production where inconspicuous and wire-free use is required.
	Lectrosonics H185 "plug-on" transmitter (shown with 3 mikes, receiver, and 2 antenna)	Depends on microphone plugged into transmitter	Depends on microphone plugged into transmitter	Low-Z	Permits use of standard mikes in wireless applications.
Boundary (PZM) Microphone 	AKG Acoustics C562	Electret Condenser	Variable depending on placement and use of boundary plates. Typically hemispherical pickup pattern.	Low-Z	Conference tables and podiums. Audience response shows. Off-camera studio (hidden mikes). Instrument miking.

	EXAMPLE	GENERATING ELEMENT	PICKUP PATTERN	IMPEDANCE	APPLICATIONS
Stereo	AKG Acoustics 522	Electret Condenser	Dual cardioid	Low-Z	Live recording and news reporting for stereo soundtracks.
	Shure VP88	Condenser	Switchable between cardioid & triple cardioid	Low-Z	Live recordings in stereo or mono. May be mounted on a boom or camera, or hand-held.

FIGURE 7-30   Direct Box.

An electronic instrument, such as a bass or guitar, may be fed directly into a sound system by plugging it into a *direct box* made for that purpose.

a computer memory chip. Once sampled, the sound can be almost endlessly manipulated and processed. You can lengthen the sound, shorten it, filter it, play it backwards, change its pitch and frequency, and so on. Although technically a sample is a prerecorded sound, we have included samplers with live audio inputs because they are often used to record and reproduce sounds simultaneously, as with a microphone.

A sampler can record either live or prerecorded sounds. Many contemporary soundtracks are made by sampling older recordings and integrating them with new material. Most samplers are controlled with piano-style keyboards, making it possible to play the sample and vary its pitch. Ob-

viously, this is most useful when sampling and reproducing musical instruments, but it can also be used for sampling other sounds as well. In addition, samplers can be used to create entirely new sounds which don't actually exist in the real world. For example, the sounds of the dinosaurs in Steven Spielberg's movie *Jurassic Park* were a combination of various animal sounds which were sampled, processed, and mixed to create an audio effect which has no real-life counterpart.

TYPES OF AUDIO STORAGE MEDIA

The term "storage media" refers to the devices on which recordings are made and saved. There are two basic types of storage media: (1) *tape* and (2) *disc*.

Tape

Both analog and digital audio signals can be recorded on magnetic tape. Magnetic audio tape consists of thin strips of plastic-like material with a magnetic coating, and comes in various widths, lengths, compositions, and formats. The formats vary, depending on the equipment used and the types of recordings being made.

There are four types of audiotape recordings: analog reel-to-reel, cartridge, cassettes, and digital. Digital recordings are classified as: DAT (digital audio tape), DCC (digital compact cassette), and MDM (modular digital multitracks). DAT and DCC use differently sized audiocassettes, whereas MDM formats use videocassettes as their storage media. We will examine tape formats when we discuss audio recording in Chapter 9.

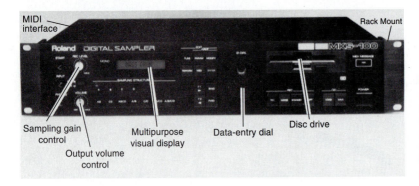

MIDI interface

Rack Mount

Sampling gain control

Output volume control

Multipurpose visual display

Data-entry dial

Disc drive

FIGURE 7-31   Sampler.
A sampler records an audio source which can then be manipulated to produce new sounds electronically. This sampler visually displays information about the sound sample.

Prerecorded digital sound is available on three types of discs: magnetic, optical, and magneto-optical (MO).

TECH TIP   Which way should it be spelled—disc or disk? The convention we will follow is to use *disc* when referring to *optical* storage media, such as compact discs, and *disk* when referring to *magnetic* storage media, such as computer disks.

Magnetic disks are used on devices that employ computer memory media and audio software to store, manipulate, and reproduce audio data. It is possible to use standard 3½-inch computer "floppy" disks, but most professional applications need the greater storage capacity of special high-density floppies or hard disks. Because magnetic disks use a base similar to audiotape, both recording and rerecording are possible, in addition to reproducing prerecorded audio material. Recording direct-to-disk is often called "tapeless recording," which we will examine in Chapter 9.

Optical discs are available in several formats. The most popular is the familiar compact disc (CD). There are two standard sizes of CDs, commonly given as 5-inch and 3-inch, even though those measurements are not the exact dimensions.

TECH TIP   Technically, the official designation for an audio-only compact disc is CD-DA (compact disc-digital audio), which sometimes is shortened to CD-A (compact disc-audio), but usually called simply a *CD*.

Another optical disc format is CD-ROM (compact disc-read only memory). A variation of CD-ROM is CD-I (compact disc-interactive). Both may include graphics along with audio.

When optical discs are played, laser light reflects off "pits" pressed into the disc's bottom surface. These pits contain the audio data, which appears in the laser light beam as varying intensities that are decoded into binary numbers. At first all optical discs were "read only," which meant you could play only what was prerecorded on them at a manufacturing plant; you could not record on

them yourself. A CD is an example of a read-only optical disc.

For recording and sound production, you need a disc that allows you to record, or "write," on it as well as play back audio material. Today recordable optical disc technology is available, called WORM (write once, read many). With WORM technology, it's possible to make one recording on an optical disc, but not rerecord over it. One type of WORM media is CD-R (compact disc-record). (See Figure 7-32.) The way CD-R records is that the laser beam actually melts pits into a special layer on the blank CD-R disc. As the light moves across the layer, the pits "freeze" into place.

Read-only discs are useful for libraries of instruments and sound effects, but CD-R discs permit

FIGURE 7-32   Recordable Compact Disk (CD-R). A "write once" disc means it can be recorded on only one time. *(Courtesy: Studer Revox America, Inc.)*

you to create and store "custom" collections of announcements, musical bridges, and so on.

Magneto-optical (MO) discs combine the capabilities of magnetic and optical technology, and sometimes are called "floptical discs." They can play, record, and even rerecord by using a process that merges magnetic and optical recording. One advantage of the MO format over CD-R is that MO discs have an optical layer that can be reheated so that you can record on them more than once.

One example of the MO format is the *mini disc* (MD), which is about half the diameter of a 5-inch CD but can hold about the same amount of digital audio information. There are two types of MDs: prerecorded and recordable. The difference is in the optical layer. Prerecorded MDs have the same kind of pitted surfaces as CDs, but recordable MDs have an MO layer that can be reheated and rerecorded.

From this overview, it should be evident that there are many type and disc formats that may be used in audio production for television. The formats of the equipment in your production facility will determine to a great extent how you go about producing soundtracks. In the discussion which follows we will emphasize techniques that are widely practiced today, and will suggest future directions for both audio equipment and production techniques.

PRERECORDED AUDIO INPUTS

Records and Turntables

There are few television productions which do not use material from phonograph records at one time or another. In addition to commercially available music and dramatic records, a number of companies produce sound and musical effects on records specifically for use in television production. These services provide an almost unlimited variety of music and sound effects at a very reasonable price.

The operation of the record turntable is essentially the same as for a home player. Most professional turntables are built to meet very exacting technical specifications and are designed to operate for long periods of time. Turntables for professional use are typically designed for two-speed play: 33⅓ and 45 revolutions per minute (rpm), and are equipped with a clutch that enables the operator to engage the motor and start the turntable revolving at the proper speed immediately.

Cuing Records   A record must be *cued* so that the sound will be available the instant the director calls for it during a show. The most common technique for cuing records in television is the *slip cue*, which is done as follows:

1   Place the turntable clutch or speed selector in the "neutral" position.
2   Place the turntable stylus just before the appropriate cut or band on the disc.
3   Turn the turntable fader on the audio console to the "cue" position. This will engage the cue amplifier system and permit you to monitor the record without sending its signal to the program channel.
4   Slowly turn the turntable clockwise by hand until you hear the first bit of desired sound or modulation. This is the *cue point.*
5   Once you have found the cue point, back up the record counterclockwise until you just pass the modulation. The stylus should now be in a silent groove immediately before the start of the record cut.
6   Just before the director needs the record, gently hold the outer lip of the record and start the turntable by engaging the clutch. Professional turntables are designed with a felt surface which allows the turntable to spin while the record is held in position by the audio technician. Hold the record lightly enough so that you do not disturb the turntable's motion, yet firmly enough to prevent the record from revolving with the turntable.
7   At the director's command, release the record and simultaneously bring up the turntable's fader on the control console. The sound will begin immediately. The fade up avoids the possibility of a record beginning when not yet

up to speed. This is called "wow in" and should be avoided. Even if the record wows in or has skipped a groove in the cuing process, fading in the pot can disguise the error. With a little care and practice, you should be able to slip cue records exactly when needed, without any wowing or miscues. (See Figure 7-33.)

There is another method available for cuing records. You cue the record as you do with a slip cue, but instead of holding the disc while the turntable spins, back the record counterclockwise about half a turn. Then, on the director's command, engage the turntable and simultaneously turn up the fader on the audio board. The sound will come in without a wow because most professional turntables are designed to reach a steady speed within a half-turn. The problem with this cuing technique is that a brief period of time elapses before the sound begins. While this is acceptable in some radio productions, most television audio is coordinated with the video, and the audio technician is expected to provide audio precisely on the director's command. For this reason, slip cuing is the preferred method of record cuing.

Compact Discs

As valuable and flexible as vinyl records are, they do have drawbacks. In the television setting, one

of their greatest weaknesses is their susceptibility to wear caused by repeated handling and cuing. After a relatively short time, the clicks and pops created through continual playing make records unusable for serious productions.

The compact disc (CD), a plastic platter that is read by a laser beam, does not develop surface noise from continual contact with a stylus. With reasonable care in handling, the CD will sound as good on its one-thousandth playing as it did on the first. This is especially important for sound effects libraries which are available on CD. The fidelity of the digitally recorded CD also is vastly superior to that of vinyl records.

Playing Compact Discs Playing a CD is much easier than playing a record on a turntable. While different manufacturers provide different features on their CD players, here are typical basic steps in playing a CD:

1 Press the power switch to turn on the CD player.
2 Press the open/close button to open the disc drawer.
3 Insert the disc in the drawer with the label facing up.

FIGURE 7-33
Slip Cuing a Record.
In a slip cue, the record is back-cued about an inch and held so that it does not move when the platter is brought up to speed. When the record is released, the sound will be produced instantly.

4 Press and open/close button to close the disc drawer. Do NOT press the front of the drawer to close it.

5 Press the play button. The disc will play beginning with the first track.

Before the disc begins to play, the number of tracks and total length of the CD will be displayed.

Cuing Compact Discs Cuing a CD also is much easier than cuing a record on a turntable. The reason is that any cut you want to play can be accessed directly with a numeric code, or *index*, rather than by physically moving a stylus to the proper location and holding it there. Here are three standard methods for cuing up a CD:

1 **Direct** Before pressing play, press pause. Next press the number of the cut you want to cue up. When you press play, the selected cut will begin.

2 **Auto cue** Press the auto cue button. Next press the number of the cut you want to cue up. When you press play, the selected cut will begin.

3 **Window search** Press the pause button while playing the cut you want to cue up. Press the window search button. Rotate the search dial until you reach the place where you want to cue the cut. If you have stopped where there is sound, you will hear a brief interval of the sound repeating continuously. Press the play button to play the cut from the repeating interval.

Some CD players have capabilities that are impossible on turntables. They include repeating cuts continuously, repeating a portion of a cut continuously, programming a sequence of cuts, and skipping selected cuts in a sequence. These features are especially valuable during productions when several cuts on a CD are used. For example, a sequence of sound effects may be programmed to play continuously, or using the program and auto cue controls, a sequence may be programmed to cue up another cut automatically after each cut is played.

Some CD players also feature time displays that show the elapsed time and the remaining time on a cut that is playing. They make cuing and back-timing accurate and convenient.

Although a large number of sound effects and background music cuts are available on records, CDs are quickly replacing them as the standards in television production, just as CDs are replacing records in the consumer market.

In fact, compact disc technology is an example of a professional tool that originally was developed as a consumer product. Like home units, studio CDs can accurately locate positions within a musical cut as well as cue up to the beginning of a track. Some studio CD units are enhanced by offering an interface to a video editor which allows the CD to be accessed directly during the editing of the videotape. In addition, it's possible to record directly onto "writable" compact discs with professional CD-R recorders. (See Figure 7-34.)

TECH TIP If a compact disc ever develops skipping or reduced fidelity, polishing it with low abrasion car wax will return it to its original playing condition. This emergency procedure (which is frowned on by CD manufacturers) will work except in the case of very deep surface damage.

Audiotape Recordings

At their most basic level, *audiotape recordings* are analog or digital signals that have been stored on tape for replay later. We will focus on the playback function now, and take you through the complete recording process in Chapter 9.

There are four types of audiotape recordings used in television production: (1) analog reel-to-reel, (2) cartridge, (3) cassettes, and (4) digital.

Reel-to-Reel Reel-to-reel, or open-reel, machines use magnetic tape, which is supplied on spools. Conventional audiotape is ¼-inch wide and comes in a variety of reel sizes and tape lengths. The tape must be threaded onto the machine, where it runs past the heads at a speed of either 7½, 15, or 30 inches per second (ips). The faster tape speeds deliver much higher quality recordings but use two or four times the amount of tape consumed at 7½ ips. In general, 7½ ips is the standard speed for most television recording requirements; 15 ips is used only when the situa-

FIGURE 7-34
Compact Disc Recorder.
With this compact disc recorder it's possible to record directly onto a CD "write once" disc from analog and digital sources. *(Courtesy: Studer Revox America, Inc.)*

tion demands higher fidelity. The 30-ips speed is used for many original audio productions later transferred to video and offers the highest fidelity. (See Figure 7-35.)

TAPE TRACKS The tape recorder organizes the recording information in a specific area of the tape called a *track*. A professional stereophonic tape recorder records in one direction and uses two tracks, one for the left channel and another for the right channel. (You may be familiar with home stereo recorders which divide the tape into four tracks: two tracks for tape running in one direction and two tracks for the tape running in the opposite direction when you turn it over.) Most monaural reel-to-reel professional machines are full-track recorders, which means that the entire ¼-inch width of the tape is being used for recording and playing back a single track. Many professional tape recorders reserve part of the audiotape to record a synchronization track useful for editing. Figure 7-36 shows the arrangement of audio record and playback heads and various tape track configurations.

Because a full-track machine uses the full width of the tape and records in only one direction, you cannot take a tape that was recorded on a two-direction, two-track or four-track home machine and play it back on a full-track machine. If you do, the full-width playback head will pick up the track or tracks going in the right direction as well as those recorded in the opposite direction.

It is always best to try to record your program

material on the same type of tape machine you will use for playback. If this is impossible and you must use a multiple-track machine, erase your

FIGURE 7-35 **Reel-to-Reel Audiotape Recorder.**
Audio reel-to-reel decks provide high-quality sound and offer easy audiotape editing. *(Courtesy: TEAC Corporation.)*

Supply reel Audio heads Take-up reel

VU meter   Input/output levels Transport controls

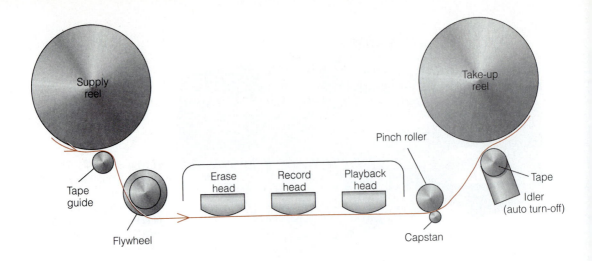

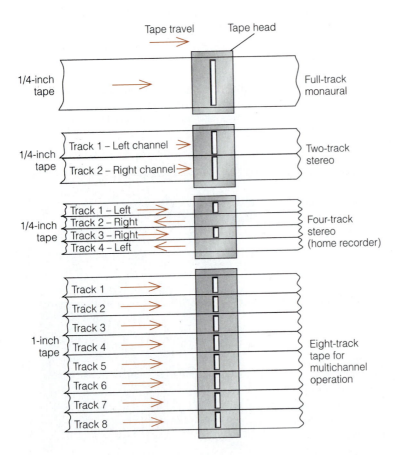

FIGURE 7-36 Reel-to-Reel Tape Recorder Head and Track Configurations. For proper sound reproduction, the record and playback machines must have the tracks laid down in identical configurations.

tape with a "bulk eraser" before recording. (We will describe bulk erasing in the next chapter.) Then record on either one or two tracks in only one direction. Remember, too, that while home tape recorders often record at 3¾ ips, most professional machines will not play back any tape recorded at a speed slower than 7½ ips.

TECH TIP In an emergency, tape originally recorded at 3¾ ips should be mounted on a machine playing at 7½ ips and dubbed onto a machine recording at 15 ips. The tape recorded at 15 ips can then be played back at 7½ ips, resulting in correct-sounding audio.

MULTITRACK RECORDERS Multitrack recorders were first introduced for use in the commercial recording industry. Professional multitrack recorders permit the audio technician to lay down individual parallel tracks which may be controlled independently of each other. In professional music recordings, the artists can record the rhythm on one track, the lead instruments on another track, and the vocal on a third track. The multitrack recorder permits the audio technician and talent to listen to some tracks while recording another. The advantage of multitrack recording is that one track can be recorded while not disturbing the recordings on other tracks. After the initial multitrack recording session is completed, the audio technician can then balance and mix-down the tracks into either a monaural or stereo version. This process permits both performers and audio technicians great flexibility. Instead of having to worry about the final audio mix at the time of initial performance, the engineer can concentrate on recording each track and, after the session is complete, then mix-down the many separate tracks into the final version. As many as thirty-two separate audio tracks are used for some recording sessions. (See Figure 7-37.)

In order to accommodate such a large number of tracks on one tape, multitrack machines usually use wider tape than the conventional ¼-inch tape used on monaural machines. Tape widths from ½ to 2 inches are used, depending on the number of tracks desired.

The use of multitrack recorders has become commonplace on very complex productions. Television audio technicians use a number of individ-

ual tracks for recording the sound portion of an elaborate program. They accomplish this by synchronizing the audiotape recorder with the videotape recorder in a process known as *double-system recording.* The two machines are electronically interlocked and travel at exactly the same speed. Instead of the audio console's sending its output directly to the television videotape recorder, a number of separate, or *discrete*, tracks are fed to the multitrack recorder, where they are recorded on individual audio tracks. The audiotape recorder is synchronized, or *slaved,* to the videotape machine. When the videotaped picture is played back, the audiotape recorder also plays back in perfect sync with the video. In a mix-down session after the initial production has been recorded, the audio technician combines all the audio tracks into either a single monaural track,

FIGURE 7-37 **Multitrack Audiotape Recorder.** Multitrack ATRs place individual audio signals on separate tracks. The tracks are later "mixed down" to a single (monaural) or paired (stereo) configuration. *(Courtesy: TEAC Corporation.)*

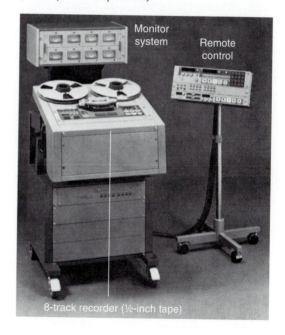

Monitor system

Remote control

8-track recorder (½-inch tape)

which can be laid onto the videotape for later broadcast, or into a two-track stereophonic tape, which can be used as the program's stereo audio. (For a more complete discussion of this synchronizing process, see Chapters 9 and 10.)

Multitracking provides the audio technician with flexibility. During the actual taping, a number of audio sources such as performer dialogue, orchestra, sound effects, and audience applause each can be recorded on a separate track. Multitracking allows the complicated aesthetic judgments of audio balance and stereo effects to be experimented with in the postproduction studio rather than relying on a "one time only" mix through the audio console during the videotaping. After the production, music or sound can be added or altered without holding up the entire production cast and crew. The multitrack technique is becoming a realistic option for many moderate-sized production facilities as the cost of the equipment decreases.

CUING REEL-TO-REEL TAPE   Reel-to-reel tape can be tightly cued so that the program material will begin on the director's command. As with cuing a record, the audio technician must use the cue system on the audio console to prevent the audition system from being sent over the air. To cue a reel-to-reel tape,

1   Place the tape fader on the audio console in the cue position.
2   Play the tape until you hear the first sound. This is the *cue point*. Stop the machine. Hold both the supply and take-up reels and rock the tape back and forth manually, being careful not to stretch or break it.
3   Once you have found the cue point, manually back up the tape about 1 inch. The tape is now cued.
4   If you need a particularly tight cue, you can spin the flywheel, which is located to the left of the tape heads, counterclockwise with your thumb just before starting the machine. If you spin the flywheel immediately before pressing the start button, you will achieve the necessary

momentum to start the tape at the correct speed and avoid the possibility of wow in.

Tape can be visually cued by using the white or colored leader that is commercially available. By splicing several feet of the leader directly before the cue point, you can cue the tape visually without having to use the cue amplifier system. If your tape reel has a number of different cuts, the leader also can visually indicate the number of each cut. Use a felt-tipped pen to write the name and number of each cut directly on the leader. Each tape used in production should have "header leader" spliced to the front of the tape detailing the name of the production, program length, and record speed.

Cartridge   Although it is possible to cue reel-to-reel tape tightly for television production, audio cartridge machines are designed to make this task even easier and more accurate. Audio cartridge machines use ¼-inch magnetic tape similar to that used in reel-to-reel machines. However, this tape is loaded into a continuous loop and inserted into a plastic cartridge. (See Figure 7-38.) When the "cart" is recorded, a cue pulse is recorded on a separate cue track just before the

FIGURE 7-38   Audio Cartridge.
An audio cart is a continuous tape loop that is automatically cued and which provides sound instantly when played.

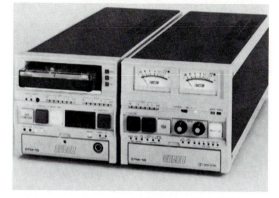

FIGURE 7-39 **Analog Audio Cartridge Machine.**
Analog audio cart machines are available in both stereo and mono. They have been the workhorses of broadcast audio playback.

start of the program material. The audio technician simply inserts the recorded cart into a machine and presses the play button on the director's cue. (See Figure 7-39.) Provided the appropriate fader is open, the cart will begin immediately without wowing in. The cart is designed to play through the program material and to keep running until it reaches the cue pulse, at which time it stops and waits for another play command.

Analog carts are available in a variety of play lengths from ten seconds to five and one-half minutes. The cart you select for recording should be only slightly longer than the program material it contains. This is so because the tape must play through until it reaches the cue pulse before it will stop and recue itself. If you need to record the sound track for a one-minute commercial, do not use a five-minute cartridge. Although some cart machines do have a fast forward operation, it will still take time for the cart to recycle completely. It is also a dangerous practice to remove a cart that has not yet recued, since another operator may insert the cart into a machine and expect it to have been correctly recued. Whenever you have time, preview all carts before air time to ensure they are correctly cued and to preset a cart's audio input level on the audio-control console.

Because of their ease-of-use and reliability, cart machines have been heavily used in television production. However, there has been a trend away from analog carts because of the popularity of new digital tape and disc formats. In response,

manufacturers have developed new cart formats that operate like traditional cart machines, but use floppy disks or recordable CD-Rs as the storage media. (See Figure 7-40.) These hybrids provide the ease-of-operation of analog cart machines with the advantages of digital audio.

Cassettes   Audiocassettes have become very popular for home recording because of their small size and automatic threading. Unlike a cartridge, which employs an endless loop of tape, a cassette consists of tape about ⅛-inch wide on two reels enclosed inside a plastic case. Although the technical level of some cassette recorders achieves broadcast quality, their use in production tends to be limited to the recording of audio in the field. For precision editing, the cassette field audio is dubbed to reel-to-reel. (See Figure 7-41.)

TECH TIP   Program material located in the middle of a prerecorded cassette may be difficult to cue during a production. To make cuing more convenient and accurate, record a countdown at the beginning of another cassette, then dub the program material immediately after the countdown.

Digital   There are three digital audio recording formats: *DAT, DCC*, and *MDM*.

FIGURE 7-40   **Digital Audio Cartridge Machine.**
This digital audio cart operates like an analog cart machine, but uses 3½-inch floppy disks and records from both analog and digital audio sources. Up to sixteen cuts may be stored on an individual disk and played back in any order. *(Courtesy: Fidelipac Corporation.)*

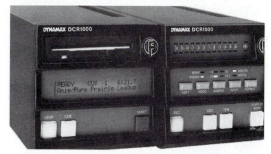

FIGURE 7-41 Audiocassette.
Audiocassettes are popular for recording field audio because of their light weight and excellent sound reproduction. *(Courtesy: TASCAM TEAC, Professional Division.)*

DAT   There are two DAT (digital audiotape) formats: DASH and R-DAT. Unfortunately, the two systems are incompatible, so recordings made on one system cannot be replayed on the other.

DASH stands for Digital Audio Stationary Head recorder. This format looks very similar to conventional analog machines. It has a stationary head, and records digital audio tracks as well as an analog reference track. This allows you to handle the tape like a regular analog tape when editing.

R-DAT stands for Rotating-Digital Audio Tape recorder. (See Figure 7-42.) This format employs a rotating record/playback head, using an approach similar to that in videotape recording. (See Chapter 20.)

All R-DAT systems use a standardized DAT cassette with metal tape. Audio signals are digi-

FIGURE 7-42 Digital Audio Tape (DAT) Recorder.
Digital audio recorders offer excellent audio fidelity, and the master recording can be dubbed through multiple generations without deteriorating the audio signal. *(Courtesy: Studer Revox America, Inc.)*

tized and recorded, along with three types of subcodes: (1) start IDs, (2) program numbers, and (3) skip IDs. These subcodes can be used to locate and play program material quickly and easily, much like compact discs. For example, pressing pause, a track number, and the start button will cue up the selected track in pause until the play button is pressed. Another way to cue up a track is to press pause while playing the track, then to press the backward skip button. The track will be cued up at the beginning in pause until the play button is pressed. This method is handy if you are listening to a track and want to cue it up quickly.

Another feature on DAT players is "intro play," which plays the first few seconds of each track that has a start ID. This makes it easy to search through a cassette for a specific song when you don't remember the track number.

With these and other controls, digital audio recorders can be operated much more quickly and precisely than records, carts, cassettes, and analog audio tape decks. In addition, there is no question that digitally recorded audiotape provides the highest sound quality possible, with an extremely wide dynamic range and the virtual elimination of tape noise and hiss. This is especially valuable when the audio tracks will be processed through multiple generations in postproduction.

DCC   Digital compact cassette (DCC) machines use standard-sized, high-quality audiocassettes as the storage medium. DCC machines can play both conventional analog cassettes and DCCs, but can record only in the DCC format. The fidelity of DCC recordings is better than that of analog cassettes and is near CD quality. Like CDs and DATs, DCC machines also visually display information such as track number and time remaining, but DCC also shows track titles. This permits you to search for and play a track by selecting its title, not just its number.

MDM   Modular digital multitrack (MDM) systems are becoming the standard in multitrack recording and postproduction. MDM systems consist of 8-track machines that can be interconnected for recording and reproducing up to 128 tracks. The tracks may be synched with videotapes, processed, and edited with no deterioration of the sound quality.

The two most popular MDM formats are the Alesis ADAT and the Tascam DA-88. Both employ existing videocassette systems modified to record digital audio. The Alesis ADAT uses S-VHS videocassettes and the Tascam DA-88 uses 8-mm videocassettes. Unfortunately, like the videocassette systems they have adapted, the two formats are incompatible, which means that recordings

made on one system cannot be played on the other. We will describe the digital audio editing process in Chapter 9.

SUMMARY

Sound originates as vibrations produced by a rapidly moving object. Sound moves away from the vibrating object in waves that can be graphically represented by a sine wave. The sine wave shows two important characteristics of sound: frequency and intensity. Sound frequency is perceived as pitch and is measured in hertz (Hz), or cycles per second. The frequency range is divided into low-end, midrange, and high-end frequencies. Timbre is the variation in frequencies that gives a sound its tone color. A waveform of a sound shows the various frequencies making up the sound. Sound intensity is perceived as loudness, or volume, and is measured in decibels (dB). Intensity is represented on the sine wave as the amplitude of the wave. Sound waves in phase reinforce each other, and sound waves out-of-phase cancel each other out. Each sound has an envelope that consists of three stages: attack, sustain, and decay.

Sound must be converted from acoustic energy to electrical energy so it can be fed into production equipment. This process is called transduction. Sound may be converted into analog or digital signals. The waveform of an analog electrical signal represents the waveform of the original sound. A digital signal represents the original sound by computer-type binary numbers. Analog audio signals are susceptible to distortion, noise, and deterioration of sound quality when copied. Compared to analog, digital audio is relatively immune to noise, distortion, and quality degradation; has an increased dynamic range; may be processed, edited, and duplicated with virtually no loss of signal quality; and may be edited more accurately. Three disadvantages of digital audio are its susceptibility to distortion; greater expense; and apparent "colder" sound.

The primary transducer is the microphone. When selecting microphones for television production, there are five characteristics to consider: (1) type, (2) pickup pattern, (3) frequency response, (4) impedance, and (5) use. The types of microphones are classified by their transducer, or element. There are three types of professional microphones: dynamic, ribbon, and condenser (capacitor). Microphones will have nondirectional (omnidirectional), bidirectional, or directional (unidirectional, or cardioid) pickup patterns. Frequency response refers to the range of frequencies that a microphone can pick up. Impedance refers to the electrical resistance to the signal coming from the microphone into the audio system.

Microphones can have either high or low impedance. Professional mikes have low impedances. In television production, microphones may be used on-camera or off-camera. On-camera mikes include lavalier, desk, PZM, hand, stand, and headset microphones. Off-camera mikes are on booms or hidden. Three specialized mikes are stereo, modular, and wireless microphones. In addition to microphones, three devices that pick up live sounds are the direct box, samplers, and synthesizers.

Audio signals may be recorded and saved on two types of storage media: tape and disc. The four types of audiotape recordings are analog reel-to-reel, cartridge, cassettes, and digital. Digital formats include DAT (digital audio tape), DCC (digital compact cassette), and MDM (modular digital multitrack). The three types of discs are magnetic, optical, and magneto-optical. Magnetic floppies and hard disks are used in computer memory media. Read-only optical disc formats include the CD, CD-ROM, and CD-I. With WORM technology it is possible to "write once" on CD-R discs. Magneto-optical (MO) discs have magnetic and optical layers that permit rerecording. One example of MO technology is the MD (mini disc).

Phonograph records carry a diverse assortment of background music and sound effects. They must be cued before use so that program material can be introduced instantly on the director's command. Compact discs, because of their ease of operation, superior fidelity, and greater durability, are replacing vinyl records in studio operations.

There are four types of audiotape recordings used in television production: (1) analog reel-to-reel, (2) cartridge, (3) cassettes, and (4) digital. Reel-to-reel recorders may have different tape widths, speeds, and track configurations. Analog audio carts are continuous loops of audiotape encased in plastic shells. Carts cue automatically and accurately. Gradually replacing analog cart machines are digital versions that use floppy disks or CD-Rs. Audiocassettes, because of limited cuing features and lower fidelity, usually serve only to record audio in the field.

Digital audio recorders enable sound to be recorded, processed, and reproduced without any noticeable degradation in the quality of the original sound. There are three formats of digital audio recording: DAT, DCC, and MDM. The two incompatible DAT (digital audio tape) formats are DASH (Digital Audio Stationary Head) and R-DAT (Rotating-Digital Audio Tape) recorders. DCC (digital compact cassette) looks like a standard cassette machine, but records digital audio signals. The two most popular MDM (modular digital multitracks)—the Alesis ADAT and the Tascam DA-88—are incompatible multitrack recording and postproduction systems that use videocassettes as their storage media.

AUDIO PROCESSING

In the previous chapter we described sources of live and prerecorded sounds that are used in television productions. In this chapter we will discuss *audio signal flow*—how audio signals travel through the equipment that comprises the *audio system*.

INPUTS AND OUTPUTS

The electrical signals produced by microphones, compact discs, audiotapes and other sound sources are fed into the audio system. The physical location where a signal leaves a source is called the *output*, and the location at which it enters the audio system is the *input*. (See Figure 8-1.) "Output" and "input" may also refer to the

FIGURE 8-1   Output and Input.
The output receptacle of an audio source is labeled "out" and an input receptacle of an audio system is labeled "in." Equipment such as audiotape recorders have both outputs and inputs because they serve two functions. At times they output signals as players, and at other times they input signals as recorders.

signals themselves. In addition, "to output" a signal means to take it from a source, and "to input" a signal means to feed it into equipment. Audio systems also have outputs, which we will discuss later in this chapter.

The signals produced by a sound source physically are fed into an audio system by using special audio cables and plugs to connect the output of the source to the input of the system. For example, when one end of a cable is plugged into a microphone and the other end is plugged into an input on an audio mixer, the output signals from the microphone travel through the cable into the mixer. (See Figure 8-2.)

CABLES

Audio cables consist of conducting wires surrounded by a protective insulating sheath. On small lavalier microphones, a thin wire is permanently connected to the mike and terminates in a connector plug. On most other hand, desk, stand, and boom microphones, there is no permanently attached cable. Instead, there is a receptacle in the mike itself that accepts one end of an audio extension cable. The other end is designed to be connected to an input box to feed the signal into the audio control system.

Audio cable is either balanced or unbalanced. All professional television systems use balanced audio. *Balanced* audio uses three-wire cable, in which two wires encased in the protective sheath carry the audio signal and the third serves as a ground. Balanced cables also carry the phantom power from the audio console used to operate phantom-powered mikes. *Unbalanced* cables contain only two wires, of which one is dedicated to the signal and the other to ground. Balanced cables are better shielded and less susceptible to noise and interference than unbalanced cables. (See Figure 8-3.)

When you are running audio cable, be sure you have provided a sufficient length for movements by performers and for the crew member to operate the microphone or boom. Audio cable should be dressed out of camera sight and away from the path of cameras, other equipment, and technical crew members. Gaffer tape is useful in securing the cable underneath tabletops, along the edges of the set, and even to the studio floor to prevent someone from tripping over it.

TECH TIP   Audio cable has a natural coil or curve that you should follow when winding it up. It is never a good idea to wrap the cable around your elbow or tie it together by its ends. This can damage the internal wires and create audio problems. Instead, follow the natural coil and use a plastic twist-holder or even a pipe cleaner to secure the coiled cable together.

FIGURE 8-2   Audio Signals Input to an Audio Mixer.
The microphone converts sounds into audio signal, which are input to the audio-control console.

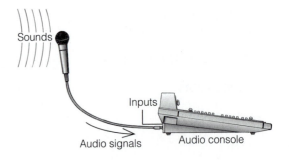

Sounds

Inputs

Audio signals   Audio console

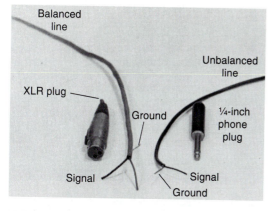

FIGURE 8-3 **Balanced versus Unbalanced Cables.** Balanced cables are less susceptible to noise and interference than unbalanced cables.

CONNECTORS

The four common *connectors* are the XLR, phone, mini, and phono (also called "RCA") plugs. (See Figure 8-4.) Professional microphones and mike cables have XLR connectors, which are balanced and low-Z. Some mikes and audio equipment may have cables with phone, mini, or phono plugs. That usually indicates unbalanced cables and high-Z systems, so they are less common in professional studio settings than XLR connectors. Remember, the microphone, cable, and audio input

FIGURE 8-4 **Microphone Connector Plugs.** The XLR plug is the low-impedance professional standard. The mini, phone, and phono plugs are incompatible and usually are used with high-impedance audio equipment.

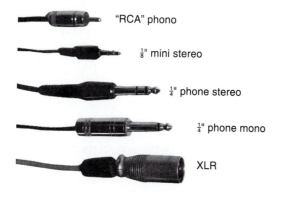

"RCA" phono

$\frac{1}{8}$" mini stereo

$\frac{1}{4}$" phone stereo

$\frac{1}{4}$" phone mono

XLR

must all be the same *impedance* to operate properly as a system.

TECH TIP Cables outfitted with XLR plugs are balanced and low-Z. The balanced lines are more resistant to buzz and hum than the unbalanced, two-wire lines that serve much portable audio. If a balanced low-Z line must be matched to a high-Z audio input, use a *transformer*, not an inexpensive adapter, to maintain the quality of the balanced line.

The *XLR* connector is a three-pronged plug that fits into a receptacle called a *jack*. The plug on the microphone usually is a male and the receptacle is a female. XLR connectors lock together when they are mated, which is a safety procedure to prevent the connection from accidentally coming loose during a production. To disconnect a male plug from a female receptacle, you must first push the little tab button before attempting to pull out the plug. (See Figure 8-5.)

Connector Boxes In most studios, audio connector boxes are located at regular intervals around the wall of the studio. The boxes look like electrical outlets, but they contain female XLR receptacles. Each jack receptacle is labeled with a number or letter which corresponds to its input on the audio-control console inside the control room. This permits the audio technician to route each microphone signal into the proper channel on the audio-control console in the control room. (See Figure 8-5.)

Hard Wiring The cables and connectors described above may be unplugged and the microphones easily removed from the inputs. But mikes (and other audio equipment) may be permanently connected, or *hard wired*, to the system. This usually is done by soldering the wires in cables directly to the leads inside the equipment casing. (See Figure 8-6.)

FIGURE 8-5 Audio Connector Boxes.
Audio connector boxes are positioned along the studio walls so that microphones can be conveniently connected to the audio system. The female connector in the wall requires a male connector on the end of the microphone cable. The release button ensures a positive fit and tight connection but must be pressed before removing a microphone or the cable will be damaged.

FIGURE 8-6 Hard Wired Connection.
An output cable is hard wired to an input of the audio system by soldering the wires in the cable to leads inside the equipment casing.

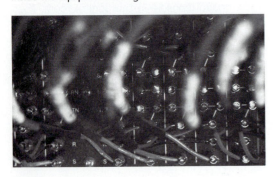

FIGURE 8-7 Audio-Patch Panel.
The audio-patch panel is used to route various audio signals in and out of the audio-control console and through auxiliary audio equipment.

PATCH PANEL

Most pieces of audio equipment in the system are not hard wired to each other. Instead, they are connected to a *patch panel*, or *patch bay*, which gives you flexibility in the interconnection of equipment. The patch panel looks like an old-fashioned telephone switchboard with a large number of connector holes, or jacks, that can be interconnected by means of a special cable called a *patch cord*. Outputs of microphones and other audio equipment are hard wired to jacks on the patch panel, and they are labeled. The inputs to the equipment in the system also are hard wired to jacks on the patch panel, and they are labeled. (See Figure 8-7.) The audio technician can connect a specific output to a specific input by plugging a patch cord into the appropriate jacks. This procedure is called *patching*.

There are three common types of audio-patch panels: open, normalled, and half-normalled.

On an *open* patch panel no outputs are connected to inputs until you patch them. Therefore, each time you use the audio system, you must plug in the appropriate patch cords.

When specific outputs are almost always connected to certain inputs, a *normalled* patch panel is used. (See Figure 8-8.) It automatically connects outputs and inputs, and no patch cords are required as long as the normal connections are desired. For example, if you always want the out-

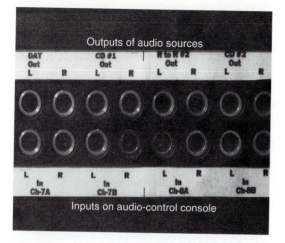

FIGURE 8-8 **Normalled Audio-Patch Panel.**
On a normalled patch panel each output on the top
row is fed automatically to the input directly beneath it
unless a patch cord is plugged into either receptacle.

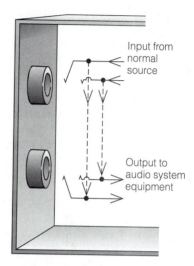

(a) Normal signal flow

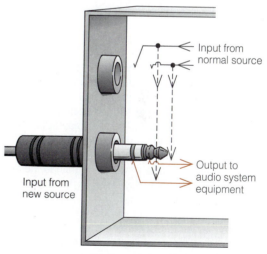

(b) Normal signal is interrupted
by the input patch.

FIGURE 8-9 **Patching Into a Normalled Patch Panel.**
When a patch cord is plugged into a receptacle, the
normalled connection is broken and audio signals are
fed from the new input into the output.

put of a cart machine to be fed to a certain input
on the audio-control console, they should be hard
wired to jacks that normally are connected. You
can disconnect the normal wiring simply by plugging a patch cord into either jack, as illustrated in
Figure 8-9. This breaks the normal connection.

On a *half-normalled* patch panel, you can interrupt the internal connection only when you plug a
patch cord into the bottom (input) jack. If you plug
into the top (output) jack, the signal still goes to
the normal input. This is useful if you want the output fed to the normal input and a second input.
For example, you may want to make an audiocassette recording of a sound source while it also
is fed to its normal input on the audio-control
console.

Sometimes the patch panel is used to simplify
audio operations during a production. For example, if you are the audio technician for a talk show
with five participants, you could patch each mike
into the control console so the positions of the
mikes on the audio console correspond to the way
the participants are seated on-camera. In other
words, the person at the far left would be patched
into fader #1, the next person would be patched
into fader #2, and so on. This will make riding gain
during the production much less confusing.

Because every possible output from a studio

and input to the console must appear on the patch panel, patch fields can appear very intimidating. They are not really as complicated as they seem if you keep in mind the fact that the patch field is usually organized by sound source and function. All mike outputs are located in one area, all tape and record turntable outputs are in another area, and all remote lines are in another area. By properly using the patch panel, the audio technician has far more flexibility and control over sound sources than would be possible otherwise.

CHANNEL ASSIGNMENT MATRICES

Not only can a patch panel be confusing, but it also can be a source of degradation or total breakdown of the audio signal. This is especially true if the patch panel is frequently reconfigured, since plugging and unplugging the patch cables can damage the connectors.

A *channel assignment matrix* can serve as a substitute for the patch panel and is a common feature on newer audio consoles. If there are enough audio inputs on the back of the production console to accommodate all available studio outputs, each audio source (output) can be plugged directly into the console. (If not, then a standard patch panel can feed it.) The studio output is then electronically routed to various channels on the audio-control console by pressing buttons displayed on the console's front panel. Since the audio console's output may need to be sent to a record device (either videotape or audiotape) as well as over the air, production consoles also may feature *master output modules*, which "patch," or route, the audio console's output to the desired record or playback device. (See Figure 8-10.)

AUDIO-CONTROL CONSOLE

The *audio-control console*, or "board," is the central coordination point for all audio signals in a television program. All sound sources, including microphones, tapes, records, compact discs, sound tracks from film and videotape, and remote audio

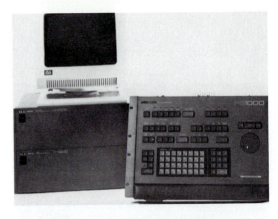

FIGURE 8-10   Channel-Assignment Matrix.
The channel-assignment matrix electronically routes various signals to different audio channels on the production console. It can take the place of a patch panel, saving wear and tear on cables and offering greater convenience. *(Courtesy: Full Compass Systems, Ltd.)*

feed into the audio console are *inputs*. At the console, the various inputs are regulated, mixed, processed, and then *output* to the station's transmitter or to a videotape and/or audio recorder. Later in this chapter we will discuss various audio sources, but first we need to cover the operation of the audio-control console, or "board."

Audio consoles vary in size, configuration, and sophistication, but there are four features common to all audio-control consoles: (1) individual volume controls for all sound inputs, called *faders* or *potentiometers*, (2) a VU meter that visually displays the signal strength of the sound as it passes through the audio console, (3) master level con-

FIGURE 8-11   Audio-Control Console.
The audio-control console accepts various audio inputs, processes the audio signals, and then assigns them to various output channels. *(Courtesy: Yamaha Corporation of America.)*

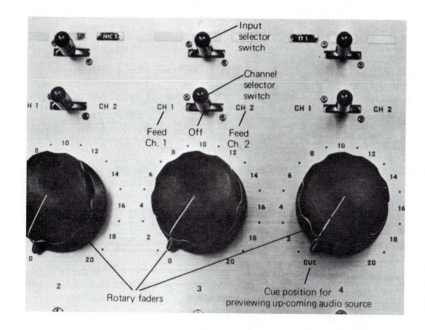

Input selector switch

Channel selector switch

CH 1 — Off — CH 2
Feed Ch. 1 — Feed Ch. 2

Rotary faders

Cue position for previewing up-coming audio source

FIGURE 8-12
Rotary Faders.
Turning the fader clockwise increases the sound level. The switches above each fader are for assigning the fader output to one of two separate channels. The uppermost switches are input selectors, which increase the board's operating flexibility by permitting one fader to serve multiple functions.

trols that regulate the sound level of the entire output of the audio console, and (4) a monitoring system that is used to cue upcoming sources and to listen to the mixed program sound via loudspeakers or headsets in the control room. (See Figure 8-11.)

Faders

The volume of every individual sound source must be set by the audio technician to the proper input level. Consequently, the signal strength of each sound source that enters the audio board must be regulated by its own separate control. These controls are called *faders* or *potentiometers* ("pots" for short). Faders can be either linear slide faders or circular knobs. Slide faders are pushed up to increase the sound and down to reduce, or "attenuate," the volume. Potentiometer knobs are turned clockwise to increase the volume and counterclockwise to attenuate the sound. Every fader regulates its individual sound source independently of the other audio inputs. (See Figures 8-12 and 8-13.)

Low-Level and High-Level Inputs

The terms *low-level* and *high-level* refer to the signal voltage that enters the audio console. A mi-

crophone produces a low-level signal of less than a thousandth of a volt (a millivolt). The output of audiotape or cartridge machines, soundtracks from film or videotape, or remote audio feeds from outside the studio measure 1 V or more, which is a high-level signal. Often, low-level signals are called "microphone level," and high-level signals are called "line level." These input levels are boosted varying degrees to reach the audio console's standard operating level. Microphone levels are fed into *preamplifiers*, which boost them to line levels. This increase in voltage is called *gain*. If a

FIGURE 8-13 **Slide Faders.**
Pushing the fader upward increases the sound level. When the fader is in its lowest position, the input is off.

MODE AUD/PGM OFF CUE — CHANNEL 2
MODE AUD/PGM OFF CUE — CHANNEL 3 — Key Switch
MODE AUD/PGM OFF CUE — CHANNEL 4
MODE AUD/PGM OFF CUE — CHANNEL 5

Slide fader

microphone output is plugged into a high, or line level input, it will not be preamplified and its volume will be extremely low no matter how high you increase the volume on the audio console. On the other hand, if high-level outputs are plugged into microphone-level inputs, they will be amplified beyond the capacity of the system and the audio will become noisy and distorted. On some modular audio consoles, it is possible to switch an input channel electronically to accept either a microphone-level or a line-level input, depending on which is needed for a particular production situation. As stereo grows in importance, phase control of the input signal is showing up on audio boards, since out-of-phase signals can attenuate the overall signal output.

Microphone Padding   There are times, especially when recording live music, when the output signal from a microphone is too high and may overload the audio preamplifier in the control console. To prevent this, the microphone output can be padded by adding electrical resistance to the line to decrease the output voltage and to provide greater control with the audio fader. Otherwise, the slightest fader opening would result in a large and uncontrollable burst of audio which is difficult to mix with other sources and can produce a distorted sound. (See Figure 8-14.)

VU Meters

All audio consoles have at least one VU (volume-unit) meter, which visually displays the intensity of the sound level leaving the audio console. VU meters are calibrated in two scales: *volume units* in decibels and *percentage of modulation.* Figure 8-15 shows a typical VU meter with both scales. The numbers on the bottom scale—which run from −20 to +3—are volume units measured in decibels. The design on the scale on a VU meter takes into account the logarithmic progression of sound intensity and human perception of loudness. The numbers above the scale—which run 0 to 100—refer to percentage of modulation. When the needle reads 100 or 0 dB, we are send-

FIGURE 8-14   Microphone Pad.
The microphone pad is an electrical resister that reduces the mike's output level. It is useful when miking loud sounds that might be distorted when input to the audio system. The reduced signal gives the audio technician more control over the signal's level.

ing 100 percent signal strength through the audio board and into the sound system. When the needle reads over 100 percent, we are "overmodulating" the signal, and we risk transmitting too strong a level, which can overload the circuits and result in distorted audio.

VU meters average sound intensity over a short period of time. Many boards also are fitted with *peak-level meters*, which measure the highest sound amplitude at an instant in time. Peak meters are valuable in identifying some forms of audio distortion. Partly because it is demanded by the function of the peak-level meter, many use LED (light-emitting diode) displays that respond more quickly to signal strength than can a display that uses a needle. (See Figure 8-16.) Some meters

FIGURE 8-15   VU Meter.
The VU meter measures audio power in the system. When the intensity exceeds 100 percent of the VU meter, distortion may occur.

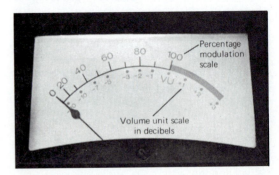

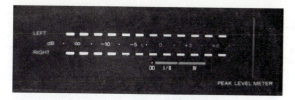

FIGURE 8-16 **Light-Emitting Diode Display.**
You will find light-emitting diode (LED) displays on
most audio equipment today because they respond
very quickly to changes in audio intensity.

use LEDs to present a switchable VU/peak readout. (See Figure 8-17.)

Before we consider the aesthetics of sound mixing, we must be certain that our sound level is
technically acceptable. A sound level that is too
low, or "in the mud," will result in technically poor
recording. Similarly, a level that is too high, or "in
the red," will produce a distorted sound because
we are sending out a larger electric signal than
the system can handle. Keeping the sound at an
acceptable level is known as "riding gain," or "riding levels." In general, the VU meter should register somewhere between 80 and 100 percent
modulation (or −2 to 0 dB) with occasional peaks
into the red (+1 to +3 dB). Consoles have some
headroom above 0 dB so small peaks in the red
will not distort. But great peaks will "pin the needle" above +3 dB and the audio will be distorted.
Peak meters may register slightly "hotter" but also
should be used to monitor output at around 0 dB.
It is important to remember that the VU meter will
display only the intensity of the console board's
output. It does *not* display the proper audio *bal-*

FIGURE 8-17 **VU/Peak Meter.**
This LED VU/peak meter may be switched between
average and instantaneous readings of sound intensity.
Peak meters offer more guidance in avoiding distortion
than do standard VU meters.

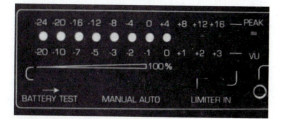

ance between various sound inputs. It is entirely
possible to send out a technically acceptable
sound level that is totally wrong aesthetically. For
example, if an announcer is mixed with a musical
track so that the announcer's voice is so low he or
she hardly can be heard over the music, the
sound level of the board's output might be technically perfect according to the VU meter but balanced incorrectly according to the aesthetic requirements of the program. The audio technician
should use the VU meter as a guide for technical
levels, but the meter can never substitute for an
audio technician's sensitivity in achieving the
proper balance among the various sound
sources.

Master and Submaster Controls

All audio control consoles have at least one *master control fader*, which controls the final mixed
output of the entire audio console. The master
gain control usually is preset in reference to an
internally generated tone before the production by
the audio technician. Master gain should seldom
be touched during a production, since it controls
the entire output level of the board and not individual sound sources. It can be used as a convenience, though, when you must completely fade
in or out a number of sound sources simultaneously. For example, if you are ending a program
with the simultaneous fade of a number of sound
inputs, you can simply fade down the master fader
and all the sources will fade out at the same time
and in the same relative proportion to each other.

Many consoles provide for subgrouping of inputs. These controls are called *group masters*, or
submasters. With these controls, you can assign
a number of separate inputs to one submaster
fader and control the entire group with a single
fader rather than with many. For example, you
might need four separate microphones to cover
an orchestra. It can be very difficult to ride all the
faders accurately and simultaneously and also to
mix in a singer's mike. If you work with submasters, you can simply preset all four audio mikes for
the proper orchestral audio balance and assign

them to one submaster. Then you need ride only two controls; the submaster for the orchestra level and the singer's mike.

Monitoring System

The audio-control console's monitoring system is designed to allow the technician, director, and sometimes performers to listen to the program audio that is being mixed through the board. The monitoring system also allows the audio technician to cue or preview upcoming audio sources. These two tasks are performed with the program monitor and the cue and audition sections of the audio-control console.

Program Monitor   The program monitor control works like the volume control on a radio or television set. It permits the audio technician to adjust the volume of the sound going to the control room and studio loudspeakers independently of the sound level being transmitted from the audio console to videotape or the station's transmitter.

The monitor level should be preset before a production at a volume that provides for comfortable, yet clear listening. Some consoles permit you to adjust the volume in the studio, audio-control area, and production-control area separately so that you can provide the proper monitoring loudness where needed. Once the monitor level is set, leave it alone, because it provides your benchmark for evaluating the overall sound mix.

Unless you are careful, the monitor volume may give you a distorted impression of the actual sound level leaving the board as the signal output to tape or the transmitter. For example, it is possible to have a microphone fader set so low that the VU level is in the mud, but by boosting the setting on the monitor control, you can achieve the aural illusion of a technically acceptable audio level. The VU meter and the monitoring system are partners that must be used simultaneously. First, make certain the meter is peaking correctly; then listen to make sure the audio mix between sources sounds right.

Most studios have an automatic program monitor cutoff circuit that is engaged whenever a mi-

crophone is opened inside the studio. This kills, or *mutes*, the monitor speaker as long as the mike is live and prevents sound emanating inside the studio from looping back via the speaker and reentering the microphone, which creates annoying feedback. *Feedback* is the loud, distorted whistle you sometimes hear when a microphone is held too close to a public address speaker in an auditorium.

Audio Foldback   The monitor cutoff circuit is a great convenience, but it can also be a hindrance when talent in the studio must hear portions of the audio while working with a live microphone. For example, a singer may be accompanied by a prerecorded music track. With the cutoff circuit in operation, there would be no way for the singer to hear the music while singing into the microphone. The solution to this is audio foldback, which enables the engineer to feed the studio monitor selected portions of the audio while deleting the output of the open studio microphones. By *folding back*, or returning only certain parts of the audio, the performer can sing to the prerecorded track and not produce the feedback loop.

Cue or Audition Controls   All broadcast audio consoles are equipped with a separate cue or audition system of amplifiers and speakers. This permits the audio technician to monitor a source before actually mixing it into the program sound. On most boards, certain faders (usually those controlling turntable, CD, tape, cartridge, or remote inputs) have a click-stop switch at the "off" position of the fader or pot that engages the fader into the "cue mode." (See Figure 8-18.) This allows the technician to hear the output on a tiny speaker or over a headset to permit accurate cuing or to check that the source is ready for air.

Audition is a separate channel in a *split-function* board. (See Figure 8-18.) Usually the program channel feeds the transmitter or videotape recorder, but the audition channel can be set to do that. Audition also can be fed to the studio and control room speakers and used for monitoring a source before it is put on program.

Modular Control Consoles

As television audio requirements have become increasingly complex, many production facilities

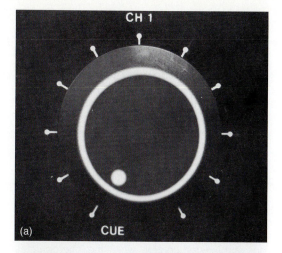

FIGURE 8-18 Cue and Audition.
(*a*) A cue click-stop on the fader or pot makes it possible to feed the audio signal into a small cue speaker or headset. This is useful for cuing up records, tapes, and CDs, but the program levels cannot be preset. (*b*) An audition/program switch on an input module makes it possible to feed the signal to either output of the audio-control console. Audition can be used to monitor audio signals on the larger control room speakers. The signals also will appear on the audition meters and can help to preset levels before feeding them to the program output.

have installed modular audio consoles which are similar in design and operation to the kind used in recording studios. Each module on the console contains a variety of studio controls which enable the audio technician not only to control the sound level, but also to manipulate the quality of any audio source independently from other inputs. For example, echo can be added to a singer's microphone without affecting any other mikes. The

value of the modular console is the enormous flexibility it offers the audio technician to control and shape each of the various inputs which, when combined and mixed together, make up the program's audio. Modular consoles also provide valuable insurance against the console breaking down, since the modules usually are interchangeable. (See Figure 8-19.)

Although specific features vary from manufacturer to manufacturer, each modular strip usually contains the following controls: (1) slide fader, (2) equalizers, (3) echo/reverberation controls, and (4) pan-pot control.

Slide Fader   Each module receives an individual audio input, which can be a microphone, the audio track from a videorecorder, or a phonograph turntable, and so on. The *slide fader* is the device used to control the level of the incoming sound source. Each of the other controls along the module are used to alter the quality of the sound which its corresponding fader is controlling.

Equalizer   An *equalizer* is a device that alters the frequency responses of a sound signal. Using the equalizer controls, the audio technician can modify very specific portions of the audio signal while leaving other portions intact to produce a precise change in the original frequency response and color the texture and sound quality of the original audio signal.

Equalizers permit the audio technician to "cut" or "boost" bass, midrange, and treble responses of a sound source independently of one another. This capability can be used to modify the original sound during production to correct for acoustical problems, to enhance an aural effect, or to provide for special sound effects. Equalizers also are used during postproduction mixing to produce the exact quality of sound desired. Equalizers will be discussed in detail later in this chapter.

Echo/Reverberation Controls   The echo/reverberation controls on the module enable the audio technician to add as much or as little of the echo effect to the original sound source as desired. Again, the degree and quality of the echo can be

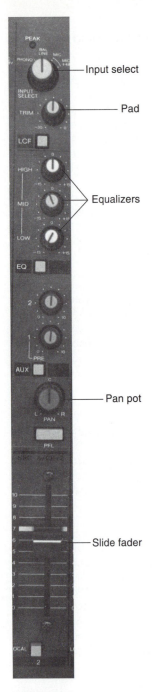

Input select

Pad

Equalizers

Pan pot

Slide fader

FIGURE 8-19 **Modular Audio-Control Console.**
Each module includes a slide fader, equalizer, echo/reverb controls, and a pan-pot control to be used when recording stereo sound.

determined precisely by the audio technician and will affect only the sound source that is being controlled by the specific module. Thus, echo can be added to certain microphones in varying degree without adding echo to other sound sources during a recording. Echo/reverb units will be discussed in detail later in this chapter.

Bus Assignment Controls   The output of each individual module is routed to a particular submaster or master output control using the bus assignment controls. This permits the audio technician to have tremendous flexibility in routing the output of any number of modules to a particular output source. For example, all the microphones used to cover a musical band can be assigned to one submaster control, while the microphones that pick up the singers are assigned to another submaster. Similarly, when we wish to produce a stereophonic mix-down, certain modules are assigned to the right channel and others to the left channel.

Pan Pots   Pan pots are used to position the audio "image" in aural space. This is possible, of course, only when a production is being recorded for stereophonic sound. However, with the use of stereo becoming increasingly common, the pan pot is becoming an indispensable audio tool. With the pan pot in its center position, the sound appears to come from the middle, directly between the left and the right speakers. Rotating the pan pot clockwise or counterclockwise will move the "image" of the sound a corresponding amount to position the sound in dimensional space. The further the pan pot is turned in either direction, the more pronounced the directional effect until the sound emanates only from either the left- or the right-hand side. Of course, it is possible to employ the pan pot during a recording literally to move a sound from one side to another. We will discuss ways in which the pan pot is used in audio production in Chapter 10.

Portable Mixers

With remote production becoming increasingly commonplace, a variety of portable audio mixers have been designed specifically for use in the field. The modern generation of portable audio

FIGURE 8-20   **Portable Audio Mixer.**
Portable audio mixers are available in both mono-phonic and stereo configurations. Most contain at least four inputs and can be operated on both ac and battery power.

mixers combines extremely lightweight portability with a powerful audio production capability. This allows the audio technician to control the input of a number of microphones and to feed one or more outputs to videotape recorders, videocassette recorders, and audiotape recorders in the field.

Most portable mixers can be run either off conventional ac current or with a battery pack to provide complete mobility at the remote location. Monitoring is done through a headset worn by the audio technician and is usually switchable to permit monitoring of the signal at various stages of the mix. For example, it is possible to monitor the sound being picked up by microphones or to switch to monitor the output signal of the mixer unit as it feeds an audiotape or videotape recorder. (See Figure 8-20.)

Auto-Mixing

An audio board characterized by as many as thirty-two inputs, each of which can be processed independently or grouped with other inputs in various configurations and then output to one or several channels, can be a very complex tool to use. This complexity is compounded by the fact that an adjustment of any input or routing instruction influences other modules and could require a new round of adjustments to other modules. To help the audio technician manage this complexity, microprocessors have been introduced to remember the patterns of board settings and the sequences of steps in an audio production.

These "smart boards" contain computer memory circuits that are linked to a number of *voltage-control amplifiers* (VCAs). As the audio technician changes a sound level or any other board setting, the computer automatically records the new setting in its memory. In this way, every change that is made over time is recorded in memory as a spe-

cific audio event and can be duplicated precisely when called up by the audio technician. What once required the board operator to simultaneously move dozens of controls can now be accomplished by simply pushing a single button in order to step through the sequence of mix events.

Another valuable benefit of the "smart boards" is their ability to preset the audio board for a particular production and retain the settings permanently in memory. Then it is merely a matter of recalling the board's memory to completely reset the configuration of mixers, equalizers, reverb controls, and so on. This saves considerable time when a single audio board is used for various productions during the day, such as the early morning news, a local talk show, and an evening news program, each of which requires a different audio board setup on a day-to-day basis.

STEREOPHONIC AUDIO

In order to produce a stereo sound track, you must use an audio-control console that has at least two outputs, one for the right channel and one for the left channel. Typically, a multichannel audio console is used combined with a multitrack audiotape recorder. During postproduction, the various tracks are mixed down to provide a single monaural track and a two-channel stereo track. Of course, on a live broadcast, the stereo and combined mono tracks are simply transmitted directly from the audio console without being recorded on tape. In Chapter 10 we will discuss production techniques for working with stereo sound.

Transmitting Stereo Sound

In television, stereo is broadcast using a system called *MTS*. MTS stands for *multichannel television sound*. MTS sound can be processed as regular, monophonic sound by older television receivers and as stereo sound by stereo television receivers.

MTS sound actually consists of three distinct audio channels. Two of the channels are DBX encoded for noise suppression and carry the high-quality stereophonic sound. The third audio channel is called *SAP*, which stands for *separate audio program*. The SAP channel is used for private communications of audio and data between stations or to carry a separate monophonic sound track to accompany a program. For example, news programs can transmit a Spanish language version of the news on the SAP channel for viewers who prefer listening to their news in Spanish rather than English.

Many cable systems offer stereophonic sound through the use of a vacant frequency on the FM spectrum. The cable operator feeds the high-fidelity stereo signal along the cable, and subscribers tune into the FM stereo channel to receive the stereo sound along with the video. Some cable systems have not upgraded their transmission systems to handle MTS sound and rely on this alternate approach to serve their subscribers.

Before the introduction of MTS, the only method of delivering stereo sound was through *simulcasting*. This is the simultaneous broadcast of the television video signal with a synchronized stereo sound track broadcast over an FM station in the same local market as the television station. Viewers who wished to enjoy the program in stereo simply turned off their television audio and listened to the sound track over their FM receiver. The availability of MTS sound has greatly reduced the use of simulcasting since the quality of MTS sound is exceptionally high.

Another enhancement of broadcast audio is *surround-sound*, which digitally expands the stereo signal during postproduction and redirects it to five channels so the sound seems to come from a full 360 degrees. To hear the full effects of the expanded sound, you must have a surround-sound receiver or decoder and five or six speakers. We will examine surround-sound technology in Chapter 10.

NOISE-REDUCTION SYSTEMS

One of the most noticeable imperfections in analog recording is *noise*. Noise is the hiss you hear along with the sound. All analog recording systems inevitably create noise in the audio signal. The level of noise is measured in decibels.

The *signal-to-noise* (S/N) ratio compares the level of audio signal against the level of noise. The higher the ratio of audio signal to noise, the more the sound will mask the underlying noise, making it essentially inaudible. As a rule of thumb, the higher the S/N figure, the better the audio quality and the less noticeable the noise. For example, analog tape recorders have an S/N ratio of about 50 dB. Digital recorders have an S/N ratio around 110 dB, which means their recordings are far less noisy because the strength of the signal is much louder than the accompanying noise.

An inevitable consequence of manipulating an analog signal is the generation of even more noise. The increase in signal processing and postproduction editing and mixing can result in a final audio track in which the noise has built up to an objectionable level. To improve the S/N ratio, various noise-reduction systems have been developed. You are probably familiar with the consumer-oriented Dolby B and Dolby C reduction systems which are used on many audiocassette and videocassette machines. The use of Dolby B will improve the S/N ratio about 10 dB and Dolby C will improve it about 20 dB.

There are professional versions of the Dolby noise-reduction systems which are commonly employed in production facilities. In addition to built-in noise reduction, several types of freestanding noise-reduction systems are available.

A *compander*, or noise-reduction unit, is designed to keep the noise to an acceptable level. During recording, a compander compresses the audio signal to a restricted dynamic range. It then separates the compressed, relatively high amplitude signal from the low-level noise. During playback, only the audio signal is expanded, which "reopens" the dynamic range of the compressed recording. In contrast, the noise level is not expanded, so it is reduced during playback.

The *Dolby A* and the *dbx* noise-reduction systems are commonly found in broadcast studios. Dolby SR (spectral recording) recently has been introduced as a noise-reduction system, and it rivals digital techniques in signal-to-noise performance. These systems can be placed anywhere along the audio processing chain, but they most frequently are used at the output of the audio console before the signal is fed into either the audi-otape or videotape recorder.

Gates   *Gates* are noise reducers that are particularly useful for suppressing noise during momentary pauses such as between spoken words of dialogue or during momentary silent passages in music. It would take an audio board operator with impossibly fast reflexes to pot the audio down during the silent portions of an audio track (to reduce the noise) and then quickly pot the level back up when the audio signal gets loud enough to drown out the background noise. In effect, the electronic gate does this rapid potting up and down automatically at speeds measured in microseconds.

To use a gate as a noise reducer, the audio technician plays back a track of the audio, and while listening to the output of the gate unit, adjusts three basic variables:

1   *Threshold level:* The sound amplitude level at which the open gate closes down, suppressing noise.
2   *Attack rate:* The speed with which the open gate shuts down, suppressing the audio level.
3   *Release rate:* The speed with which the closed gate opens, allowing the full audio level to pass through.

Because all the audio input sources for a production will not be silent simultaneously, and since the gate works by sensing low audio levels, it is impractical to use a gate at the output of the audio console. Instead, gates are used to process individual audio inputs, either various tracks on a multitrack ATR or specific mikes or auxiliary inputs that enter the board. This way, the final mix blends nearly noise-free individual audio sources.

FIGURE 8-21   Audio Compressor.

For example, the tight, punchy sound of snare drums that is pervasive in popular music is created by combining gating with reverberation.

COMPRESSORS

Dynamic range, expressed in decibels, is the ratio of the loudest to the softest sound contained in an audio passage. Live music has a dynamic range of about 120 dB, and the human ear can respond to a 120-dB dynamic range. Unfortunately, stereo television can only reproduce a dynamic range of about 60 dB. Rather than cut off either the very loudest or the softest sounds of the original source, the dynamic range of the audio signal is *compressed* in the recording and playback process.

You can see the dynamic range of an audio source by watching the fluctuation of a VU meter needle as you record an announcer speaking into a microphone or play back a premixed tape. The audio technician establishes a level so that the needle will not peak too high into the red or remain too low at the bottom end of the scale. If we apply electronic *compression* to the audio source, what we are doing is essentially limiting the dynamic range by pushing the highest peaks downward and bringing the lowest parts upward in level. You can see the effects of compression by watching the VU meter. A compressed signal will show much narrower fluctuations as we force the peaks and valleys of the signal toward a midpoint.

Although some modular consoles contain built-in compression circuits, most compressors are "outboard" devices, which means they must be patched into the audio-control system for the input signal you wish to process. (See Figure 8-21.) Any signal—microphone, record, sound track from film or videotape, and so on—can be compressed. Controls on the compressor enable you to preset the amount of compression—in other words, how severely you wish to constrict the natural dynamic range of the sound source—and

233

when the compression starts and ends. Usually, the audio technician will employ only a slight amount of compression, which smooths out the overall signal imperceptibly to the listener. The engineer's goal is to retain the variations in loudness which are a key element of natural-sounding audio. Overly compressed audio sounds flat and lacking in dynamic range when played back at moderate volumes over a good audio system. Also, overly compressed audio raises and lowers the background sounds along with the primary audio, which can be very distracting.

Compression is used in television audio because if viewers listen to a television program at low volume in their homes, soft audio passages can become completely inaudible. Also, audio compression allows the studio to transmit an audio signal at a higher signal strength so that the noise generated during transmission is less noticeable (in other words, the signal-to-noise ratio is increased).

TECH TIP   The audio in television commercials often is compressed to a very restricted range and then played back at a high level (near 0 dB). This technique, designed to draw the viewer's attention, explains why some commercials sound abnormally loud when compared to regular programming, in which compression has been applied much more sparingly.

EQUALIZERS

The use of equalizers offers the audio technician an added dimension in sound control. *Equalization (EQ)* enables you to shape and texture sound by boosting or cutting input signals at specified frequencies through the use of special electronic filters. The most common equalizers are the bass and treble controls found on a home stereo unit, which boost the low end and high end of the audio spectrum, respectively.

Control consoles without built-in equalizers can use an outboard (not built into the console) *graphic equalizer*, which is patched into the audio-control system. (See Figure 8-22.) The graphic

FIGURE 8-22   Graphic Equalizer.
The positions of the faders give a visual representation of the frequencies that are cut and the ones that are boosted.

equalizer divides the audio spectrum into many different frequency bands and allows the audio technician to cut or boost the signal output in each band. When the graphic equalizer is set up, the positions of the faders give a visual representation of their effects on the audio signal. Although the graphic equalizer works in the same way as a built-in equalizer, it can only equalize one channel at a time, making it somewhat less flexible than modular equalizers, which can equalize multiple sound sources independent of each other.

Modular consoles with built-in equalizers for each channel enable the engineer to apply different equalizations to each sound source. This makes the use of equalization especially flexible, since it is applied specifically to individual sound sources, leaving others unaffected. *Parametric equalizers* are most commonly found on modular consoles. The parametric equalizer actually is a more refined version of the graphic equalizer in which the engineer can select the center point of each frequency band prior to applying EQ. Rather than applying cut or boost in discrete steps as with the graphic equalizer, the cut or boost is continuously variable within each band. (See Figure 8-23.)

A *notch filter* is an equalizer that "removes" a small wedge of the audio spectrum. The filter is tuned to a very narrow frequency range, such as the hum from 60-Hz power, and is designed to severely suppress audio within that specific range. All these types of equalization can be used on any sound source, including microphones, film and tape tracks, prerecorded audiotapes, records, and so on. (See Figure 8-24.) We will discuss using equalizers in production in Chapter 10.

FILTERS

A *filter* is a special EQ circuit designed to pass only selected frequencies while eliminating all oth-

Inside boosts/cuts

Outside selects frequency

FIGURE 8-23 **Parametric Equalizer.** Instead of a limited number of fixed frequencies that can be cut or boosted, frequencies that can be equalized are continuously variable within bandwidths.

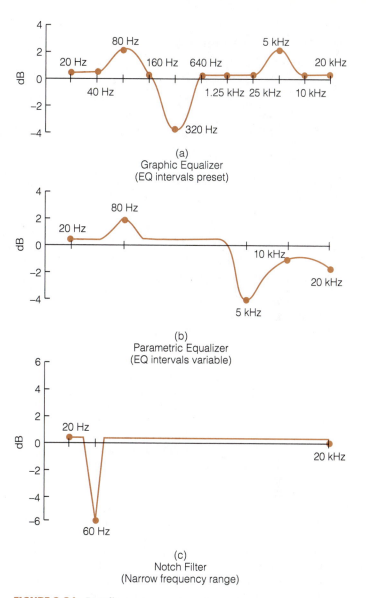

(a)
Graphic Equalizer
(EQ intervals preset)

(b)
Parametric Equalizer
(EQ intervals variable)

(c)
Notch Filter
(Narrow frequency range)

FIGURE 8-24 **Equalizers.** All equalizers change the overall sound by boosting or cutting certain portions of the sound spectrum. (*a*) In graphic equalizers, the audio spectrum is divided into separate bands of a predetermined size; (*b*) parametric equalizers allow the audio technician to set the width and location of the frequency band to be equalized; (*c*) notch filters "cut out" a very narrow frequency range, such as the 60-Hz hum of electric power.

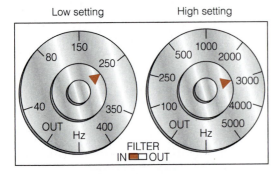

FIGURE 8-25   Band-Pass Frequency Filter.
The band-pass frequency filter allows the audio technician to cut off high and low frequencies to create desired audio effects. In this illustration, a telephone conversation is simulated by passing audio frequencies only between 250 Hz and 3,000 Hz.

ers. Filters are frequency-adjustable, so you can vary the high- and low-frequency cutoff range, and switchable, so that the audio technician can insert or remove the filter effect whenever necessary. A *high-pass filter* cuts off low frequencies, and a *low-pass filter* cuts off high frequencies. A band-pass filter passes frequencies between two cutoff points. (See Figure 8-25.) The most common use of a frequency filter is to produce the illusion of someone speaking over a telephone, through a radio or television speaker, or over a public address system. The effect is achieved by cutting off all low frequencies around 250 to 300 Hz and all high frequencies above 3,000 Hz. These are only approximate guidelines, however. The filter effect should always be set by the audio technician while listening to the sound and varying both the high and low cutoff controls until the correct effect is produced. Any audio source can be run through a filter, although microphones are the most common sources.

REVERB UNITS

The terms *reverberation* and *echo* are often used interchangeably, although, strictly speaking, they refer to two very distinct sound characteristics. *Echo* is the repetition of a sound. *Reverberation* is the persistence of a sound until it totally "decays" or fades away. When we talk about adding echo or "reverb" to a recording, we are really referring to the addition of artificial reverberation to add a controllable amount of reverberation to the sound. This may be done to compensate for a very "dry" and "reverbless" recording environment or to modify the sound quality for creative purposes. A reverberated sound is called a "wet" sound.

Artificial reverberation is produced electronically. Controls on the reverb unit enable the audio technician to vary the amount and duration of the reverb effect. On modular multichannel audio consoles, built-in reverb circuits enable the engineer to assign the output of any audio channel through the reverb unit and to control the type and amount of reverb effect individually for each sound source. The range of reverb effects runs from a subtle coloration, as though the sound were recorded in a warm, reverberant room, to a canyon-like echo effect.

Digital reverb units enable an audio technician to manipulate many characteristics of the original signal, including level, decay rate and shape, and variable EQ. These settings can be aggregated as a preset, and stored in memory. By pushing the preset, an entirely different reverb environment can be recalled. A signal can be given to create the reverb feeling of a great cathedral or of an intimate cabaret. (See Figure 8-26.)

TIME COMPRESSION/ EXPANSION UNITS

Every television producer has known the problem of their program's length not matching the allotted time slot. Rather than re-editing the program, the quick fix would be to simply run the videotape at

FIGURE 8-26   Artificial Reverberation/Delay Unit.
With this digital unit you can add echo, reverb, and delay to any audio signal passed through it. *(Courtesy: Lexicon, Inc.)*

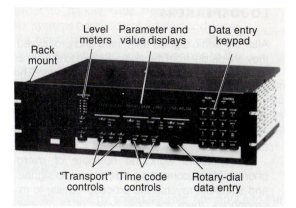

Rack mount · Level meters · Parameter and value displays · Data entry keypad · "Transport" controls · Time code controls · Rotary-dial data entry

FIGURE 8-27 **Time Compression/Expansion Units.**
These allow audio tracks to be shortened or lengthened to match the length of the video. *(Courtesy: Lexicon, Inc.)*

a faster or slower speed. While this technique might fool the viewer's eye, the viewer's ear would detect an error in the soundtrack's pitch. Slow playback perceptibly distorts and slows music and speech, while fast playback makes actors sound like chipmunks.

Mainly to deal with the precise timing of commercials, *pitch correction*, or *time compression/ expansion*, *units* were developed. These machines electronically reprocess sound so that the pitch is lowered when the video is played at fast speeds and is raised when the video is slowed down. The system allows productions to be retimed by as much as 15 percent without disconcerting results. If the speed change was not noticeable visually, especially in close-ups, the time compression/expansion systems could operate over even greater ranges. (See Figure 8-27.)

Harmonizer In addition to shifting pitch to vary a program's length, a special-effects processor called a *harmonizer* allows the audio technician to manipulate the pitch of an audio signal for creative purposes. For example, the harmonizer can change the musical key of a previously recorded track to any key requested by a performer. In addition, the harmonizer can alter the sound characteristics of an audio signal through pitch change, flanging, chorusing, and other effects that enable a performer to "double" himself or herself in either the same pitch or at a different pitch to create instant harmonies.

DIGITAL SIGNAL PROCESSING (DSP)

The audio processing functions that we have described—mixing, panning, noise reduction, compression, equalization, filtering, echo/reverb, time compression and expansion—all can be performed today on a single computer using *digital signal processing (DSP)* software. (See Figure 8-28.) After the original live sounds or prerecorded tapes are stored on the computer's hard disk, they can be edited, processed, and mixed—all on the computer, using a mouse and keyboard.

Depending on the DSP software you use, you usually see the waveform of the sound you are hearing and menus of processing options. Some DSP software screen displays look like the conventional audio hardware, so, for example, when you're mixing sounds, you see the familiar audio-control console slide faders and meters, which you control with the mouse.

The finished master mixdown can be recorded right on the computer's hard disk. Later the soundtrack can be synchronized with video by using a MIDI sequencer locked to SMPTE (Society of Motion Picture and Television Engineers) time code. This process is complex, and we will examine it more closely when we discuss video editing in Chapter 23.

FIGURE 8-28 **Digital Audio Production System.**
This multitrack audio workstation, along with a Macintosh computer, can perform all the digital recording, processing, and postproduction functions in one program. The computer screen graphically displays all the functions being used. *(Courtesy: Studer Revox America.)*

Supply reel

Take-up reel

Transport controls

(a)

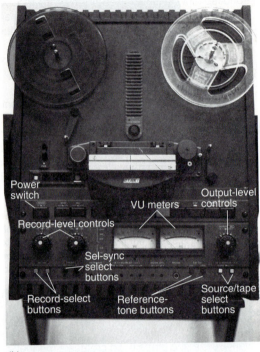

Power switch

Record-level controls

VU meters

Output-level controls

Sel-sync select buttons

Record-select buttons

Reference-tone buttons

Source/tape select buttons

(b)

FIGURE 9-7 **Audiotape Recorder (ATR) Transport and Electronic Controls.**
(a) The audiotape must be threaded properly in order for the ATR transport controls to operate. Improper threading can cause damage to the tape. (b) Electronic switches on ATRs control the input and output signals, and recording and playback levels.

After threading the tape, the tape speed must be selected by setting the speed switch to the desired speed. Professional ATRs may run at 7½ ips (inches per second), 15 ips, or 30 ips. The higher the speed, the better the quality of the recording. The speed used most frequently in broadcasting is 7½ ips. Some ATRs also will have a variable speed control, or *pitch control*, which permits speeding up or slowing down the tape slightly, thereby shifting the pitch of the audio material. Be sure the pitch control is set at "zero" or "off" for normal recording.

TECH TIP   Open reel audiotape comes on reels of different diameters. The most common sizes are

5-inch, 7-inch, and 10½-inch. The same-sized supply and take-up reels should be used. Some ATRs have a switch that you must set to indicate the reel size.

Tapes are played, fast forwarded, rewound, and stopped by pressing the appropriate transport controls, usually clearly labeled on the front of the machine. (See Figure 9-7.)

All professional ATRs will have a counter, usually showing minutes and seconds. (See Figure 9-7.) It's a good idea to set the counter immediately after threading the tape.

244

TECH TIP   One of the most annoying things that can happen when using an open reel ATR is rewinding the tape off the take-up reel and having to rethread the tape. This can be avoided by using the counter and the "Memory" switch. Immediately after you thread the tape the first time, play or fast forward it about ten seconds, reset the counter to "zero," and press "Memory." Now each time you rewind the tape, it will stop at "zero" instead of coming off the take-up reel. A good practice when rewinding a tape is to slow it down when it nears "zero" by pressing the "Fast Forward" switch. This will avoid a sudden stop and prevent possibly stretching or even breaking the tape.

ATR Electronics   The audio signals flow through the *electronics* of the recorder. You will find several controls for the electronics. (See Figure 9-7.) The first is a switch usually labeled *Tape/Source*. It should be set in "Tape" when you want to play a prerecorded tape, and in "Source" when you want to record. In "Tape" the deck's VU meters show the output levels of the playback, and in "Source" the VU meters show the input levels.

When you are ready to record, in addition to se-lecting "Source" on the Tape/Source switch, you also must press the "Record" selector switch. This will enable you to adjust the record levels. However, even if the "Source" and "Record" selector switches are pressed, that does NOT mean the machine will record. To record, both the "Record" and "Play" transport controls must be pressed simultaneously. If only "Play" is pressed, no recording will be made. This is a safety feature designed to prevent the accidental recording over prerecorded material.

Professional ATRs have a "Record" selector switch and "Record Level" control for each track, which makes multitrack recording possible. (See Chapter 7.) For example, on a basic two-track stereo recorder, you could record music on one track, then rewind the tape to the beginning of the music and record sound effects on the other track. Multitrack recorders usually have another control called *selective synchronization*, or *sel sync*. This makes it possible to play one track and record on another with both in sync. This procedure is called *overdubbing* and is common in music production.

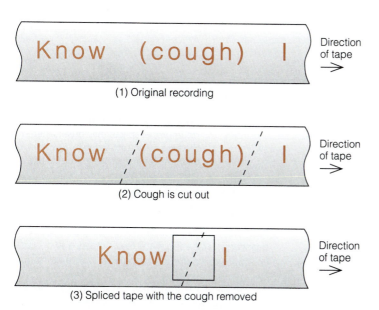

(1) Original recording

(2) Cough is cut out

(3) Spliced tape with the cough removed

(a) Splicing-out mistakes

FIGURE 9-8   Audiotape Splicing. (*a*) Mistakes and pauses may be physically removed from recordings on open reel audiotape. (*continued*)

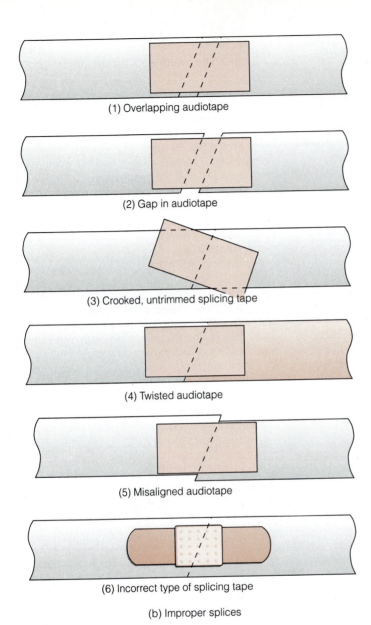

(1) Overlapping audiotape

(2) Gap in audiotape

(3) Crooked, untrimmed splicing tape

(4) Twisted audiotape

(5) Misaligned audiotape

(6) Incorrect type of splicing tape

(b) Improper splices

FIGURE 9-8 (*continued*)
(*b*) Improper splices may break when the tape is fast-forwarded or rewound, and may leave a sticky residue on the tape heads.

We will describe sel sync in more detail in the next chapter.

Editing on Reel-to-Reel Audiotape

One of the advantages of reel-to-reel audiotape is the ability to edit the program material. Editing permits the audio technician to splice in leader tape, to remove mistakes, or "fluffs," without retaping

the entire sequence, to add or delete program elements, and to shorten or lengthen a particular taped cut. (See Figure 9-8.) There are two types of audiotape editing: mechanical and electronic.

Mechanical Tape Editing *Mechanical tape editing* refers to a process in which the tape is actually cut and reconnected with a physical splice. (See Figure 9-9.) To perform a mechanical edit,

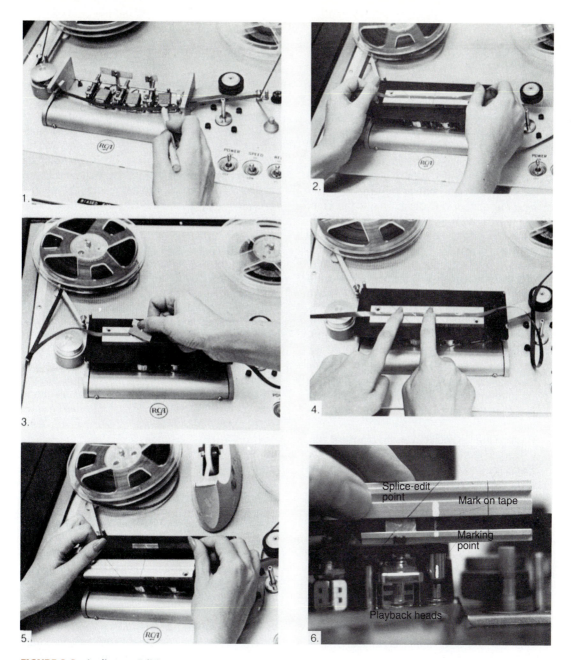

Splice-edit
point

Mark on tape

Marking
point

Playback heads

FIGURE 9-9 **Audiotape Editing.**
To edit audiotape: (1) mark the edit point with a grease pencil directly over the playback head, (2)
place the tape in the editing block, (3) position the edit point over the diagonal slot and cut cleanly
with a razor blade, (4) place the tape ends together and join them with splicing tape, and (5) gently
lift the tape from the editing block, being careful not to damage the edges. (6) Instead of marking
the edit point at the playback head, some editors will mark the tape at a point to the right of the
head, then line it up with a point on the editing block the same distance to the right of the diagonal
slot. This technique prevents "gumming up" the playback head with grease pencil marks.

necessary, you can then dub your final work back to 7½ ips for standardizing your playback speed.

1   Find the correct "out" point. This is the point at which you wish to make an edit. To find this point, gently rock the tape back and forth by hand, listening to the output until you hear where the particular sound ends.

2   Lightly mark this point, which is directly over the playback head, with a colored grease pencil on the base side of the tape.

3   Find the correct "in" point. This is the point where you wish to rejoin the tape pieces. Mark this point, which is directly over the playback head.

4   Gently remove the tape from the machine, and place it in an editing block with the oxide side facing down. The editing block has a ridged slot that will hold the tape in place.

5   Position the "out" point over the diagonal slot, and cut the tape with a razor blade. The perpendicular slot should be used only for extremely tight edits (and for editing digital tape), since the splice may "pop" and will not be as strong as a diagonal splice. Be sure you slice the tape; do not "chop" or "guillotine" it.

6   Position the "in" point over the diagonal slot. Cut again at this mark.

7   Place the "out" side into the edit block, and slide the two pieces of tape together. They should just touch but should *not* overlap.

8   With a piece of $^7/_{32}$-inch splicing tape, join the two ends and press down firmly to get a secure splice. You should never use ordinary cellophane tape because the adhesive will ooze out and leave a deposit on the tape heads.

9   Gently remove the audiotape from the editing block. Use both hands to avoid tearing the tape.

10 Rethread the tape, and listen to your edit.

TECH TIP   If you will need to do a great deal of very close editing, record the material at 15 ips instead of the conventional 7½ ips. The increased speed will doubly space out the magnetically encoded sound on the tape and give you more blank tape in the pauses between words for cutting. If

Electronic Tape Editing   Studio-quality tape recorders are equipped with solenoid switches to enable you to rapidly move among play, fast forward, and fast reverse without tearing or stretching the tape. Machines that are equipped with total transport logic (TTL) permit you to go from fast forward to fast reverse or to stop without damaging the tape. In addition to safeguarding the tape, TTL offers highly accurate tape counters which "measure" the tape in hours, minutes, and seconds. This permits an editor to electronically "mark" specific passages on the playback tape, enabling the autolocator on the tape machine to automatically cue up to the marked passages for editing. In fact, editing electronically means that you never physically cut the tape as you do with mechanical editing. Rather, the editing is a dubbing process in which a playback sequence is precisely cued to specific "in" and "out" edit points and then copied, or dubbed, to a record machine. By proceeding from section to section on the record machine, the engineer electronically builds the edited material into the finished product.

TIME CODE   Even more precise edits can be accomplished if the audiotape has *time code* stripped on the tape. As discussed more fully in Chapter 20, accurate editing of video and audio sources relies on use of the Society of Motion Picture and Television Engineers (SMPTE) time code. A time code address is an eight-digit number in which the first two digits specify the number of hours, the third and fourth digits specify the number of minutes, the fifth and sixth digits specify the number of seconds, and the seventh and eight digits specify the number of frames. This time code is recorded on the audiotape or videotape on a separate track where it is read by a separate playback head. Since each frame of video occurs in one-thirtieth of a second, by knowing a time code address you can find a piece of audio or video accurate to one-thirtieth of a second.

As the master tape is played back, the editor selects "cut-in" and "cut-out" points, which are actually SMPTE time-code addresses. The set of

```
                CUSTOMERNAME                          MIX: READ
    EDIT # 5 EDL: FIRST CUT                  DURATION/
    MACHINE TRACK        IN-TIME      OUT-TIME    OFFSET         MODE: MAN
     M  A  1*        01;00;19;08   01;00;24;21              STP 01;00;07;00 D
     SR B  2         22;00;19;13   22;00;24;26  00;00;05;13  STP 10;04;37;10 T
        C  3         17;59;39;26   17;59;35;22              STP 17;59;35;18 N


    SYSTEM COMMANDS....


    MESSAGES....


    EDIT      --RECORD--      --SOURCE--       SOURCE        MASTER          MASTER
    NUM      REEL  TRACK     REEL  TRACK       IN-TIME       IN-TIME         OUT-TIME
      2       5     2,3      219   1,2     18:00:15:25   22:00:00:00     22:00:30:00
             MUSIC TAG
      3       5     2,3      219   1,2     17:58:53:11   22:00:00:00     22:00:30:00
             NOTE:
      4       5      5       301    1      17:58:24:19   22:00:16:27     22:00:31:22
             DIA: HEY YOU...PUT YOUR HANDS UP
   >  5       5     7,8      219   1,2     17:59:39:26   22:00:19:13     22:00:24:26
   >         SFX: CHIVE
      6       5     7,8      219   1,2     17:59:49:01   22:00:21:26     22:00:30:00
      7       5     7,8      219   1,2     17:59:49:01   22:59:58:05     22:00:41:02

        OFF/DUR     RECORD       SORT        GPI       IN/OUT      SCROLL       EDL
    1:  DUR     2:  ON   3:  EDIT NUM  4:  OFF   5:  RECORD  6:  MANUAL  7:  EXT
```

FIGURE 9-10 Time Code Edit Sheet.
Electronic editing uses SMPTE time code to select cut-in and cut-out points. These
edit decisions are compiled sequentially in an edit decision list.

selections made is called the *edit decision list.* The edit decisions can be recorded on paper and, often with the help of an autolocator, executed one after the other by the audio technician. When the editor marks an edit, the record deck electronically switches into record at the cut-in point and then out of record at the cut-out point. The material from the playback deck is electronically inserted cleanly, without the need for cutting the tape. (See Figure 9-10.)

A much more efficient approach puts the entire editing process under the control of a computer that shuttles both the master tape and the slave tape (or edited master), performs the edit, and then reviews the edit for the aesthetic judgment of the audio technician. The computer sequentially performs all the edits detailed in the edit decision list displayed on the computer's monitor. Many computer-aided editing systems can handle multiple audio inputs from both audiotape and videotape recorder sources. As part of the material in the edit decision list, the audio technician simply indicates which source deck should be accessed. (See Figure 9-11.)

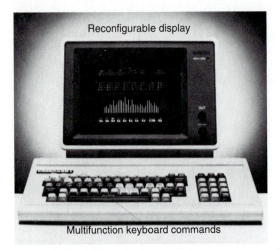

Reconfigurable display

Multifunction keyboard commands

FIGURE 9-11 Computer-Assisted Editor.
Computer-assisted editors offer accurate and fast audio editing capabilities. *(Courtesy: CMX Corporation.)*

Recording Cart Material

Recording material on cartridge is relatively simple. You can record material from any sound source, but reel-to-reel tape is the preferred method because you can edit the program material first before transferring it to the cart for air use. The operation for cart recording is as follows:

1 Select a cartridge that is slightly longer than the length of the program material. They come in lengths from ten seconds to five and one-half minutes.

2 Bulk erase the cartridge. This is especially important because, unlike open-reel recorders, cart machines do not automatically erase previously recorded material and record cues.

3 Place the cart into the machine, and press record. The built-in VU meter will now register any audio input.

4 Play the program material and set the proper input level on the cart machine according to its VU meter.

5 Cue the program material. If it is on reel-to-reel

tape, rotate the reels backward—or clockwise—exactly one quarter turn.

6 With a finger on the cart play button, use your other hand to start the program material.

7 Push the cart play button and start the program material. The cue should be tight but not upcut.

8 When the recording is completed, close the input source fader and let the cart run until it stops itself at the cue point. Check the cart by playing it back to ensure proper cue start and audio level.

Sometimes you may wish to record a number of very short music selections or sound effects on cart. You can record each on a separate cart, but this can become burdensome if you have ten or fifteen different carts to be used on a show. There is an alternative. Select a cart with a relatively long play time, say two and a half minutes. Let us assume you wish to record a series of doorbells for use in a program. Follow the procedure for recording, but at the end of each cut, stop the cart machine instead of permitting it to recycle. Next, press the record button again. This will ready the cart for another recording. Again, follow the recording procedure, and after each cut is finished, press stop and activate the record button. What you are doing is placing a number of stop-cue pulses on the cart after each cut. Thus, when you play back the cart, it will stop immediately after each cut and will ready itself for the next cut. The only problem with this method is that you must completely recycle the cart if you need to go back to a cut you have just played. This sort of multiple-cue cartridge recording method is best suited for identical cuts, such as a series of telephone rings, doorbells, voice-over announcements, or program themes.

Because carts are so easy to cue, many television audio technicians prefer to prerecord all music and sound effects from records, cassettes, and reel-to-reel tape onto carts for use during the production. There are a number of good reasons for this practice: (1) Since the sound quality of carts is equal to that of records or reel-to-reel tape, a properly recorded cart will exhibit no noticeable audio deterioration. (2) There is always the danger of playing the wrong cut on a record, particularly sound-effects records, which can have as many as twenty-five or thirty separate cuts on one side (ever try to count eighteen cuts in?). (3) Records or tapes can be played inadvertently at the wrong speed, but carts cannot. (4) Records or tapes can wow in, and discs can skip a groove; carts will always start on cue and will never wow in if properly inserted into the cart machine. (5) Each sound effect or musical selection can be on a separate cart. If these are labeled and stored in order of play, there is little chance for confusion, and the audio technician can easily repeat a sound selection or delete a cut during rehearsal or production.

In Chapter 7 we noted that there has been a trend away from analog carts because of new digital tape and disc formats. In response, manufacturers have developed new digital cart formats that operate like traditional cart machines, but use floppy disks or recordable CD-Rs instead of audiotape as the storage media. (See Figure 7-40.) Therefore, with digital carts it is possible to record a number of cuts and play them in any order, eliminating the "recycling" disadvantage of traditional carts. The procedure for recording and playing digital carts combines the steps in recording on analog carts and digital audio tape (described below).

Recording on Audiocassette

Unlike the tape in a cart, which is in an endless loop, the tape in a cassette is in the reel-to-reel format. Therefore, the transport and recording controls on cassettes are similar to reel-to-reel machines. There are two standard types of audio-only cassettes commonly used in audio production for television: analog and digital. (See Figure 9-3.)

Analog Audiocassettes In addition to the transport and recording controls, analog cassettes also have settings for the type of tape being used. The Type I, or *normal*, setting is for tape with iron (ferric) oxide; the Type II *high* setting is for chromium dioxide; the Type III *high* setting is for ferrichrome; and the Type IV *high* setting is for tape with a *metal* surface. (See Figure 9-12.) Both the quality and the cost increase as you go from Type I to Type IV tape.

The lengths of cassettes vary, depending on the amount of tape in the cassette and how thick the

tape is. The total length of a cassette will be written on its case. Common total lengths are 30, 60, 90, and 120 minutes long, using both "sides" of the cassette. To determine how much you can record on one "side," simply divide the total length by two. For example, a 30-minute cassette can hold 15 minutes on each "side."

Shorter cassettes (up to 60 minutes) are more desirable because they use thicker tape (½-mil). The longer cassettes (90 minutes and above) use

FIGURE 9-12 Cassette Tape Type Settings. Most cassette machines will have three tape type settings: normal (Type I), high (Type II), and high (Type IV). Type III tape is rarely used.

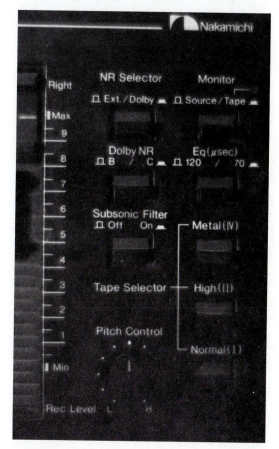

¼-mil tape and the thinner tape is far more susceptible to stretching or jamming in the machine. If a cassette tape breaks, it is very difficult to splice back together, no matter how thick the tape is.

Because audiocassette recorders are portable and convenient to operate, they often are used for location recordings, such as interviews. We will describe location recording in Chapter 10.

Rarely is the analog cassette the medium of choice for studio recording. There are three good reasons: (1) The quality of the recording will be limited. (2) Cassette tapes are difficult to edit and have to be dubbed for editing. (3) Cassettes are difficult to cue.

If you do prerecord audio material on a cassette to use during a production, cuing can be made easier by placing a countdown on the tape before the program material. Although professional cassette recorders may have some features not usually found on consumer machines, the cassette recording process is the same as you would use to record a cassette on your home stereo system.

1   Turn on the power and insert the cassette.
2   Set the tape type switch.
3   Set the noise reduction (NR) switch, if NR is desired.
4   Press the Record and Pause buttons simultaneously. Some recorders will automatically go into pause when Record is pressed. This puts the machine in standby to record.
5   Adjust the recording levels by watching the VU or peak meter. The signal should peak at 0 VU, but high quality tapes may be recorded at higher levels.
6   Press the Play button to begin recording. Remember that there is leader at the beginning and the end of the tape, so fast forward into the tape a little before recording.
7   Break off the "record tabs" to prevent accidental erasure.

One option with none of the disadvantages of analog cassettes, and better quality, is digital audio recording.

Digital Audio Recording

Digital recordings may be made either on reel-to-reel tape or on cassettes. Reel-to-reel tape is used with digital ATRs that have *stationary* heads, and cassettes are used with recorders that have *rotary* heads.

Reel-to-Reel Digital Tape   Open reel digital audiotape is similar to conventional audiotape. Analog and digital ATRs have tape heads, but their arrangements are very different. One digital format, called DASH, does operate much like conventional analog recording. That's because it records both digital audio tracks and a reference analog track with stationary heads. The digital track is what is used for recording and reproduction and the analog track allows you to edit digital tape as you would regular analog tape. Although it is not possible to reproduce digitally recorded sound at slow speeds, you can slowly rock or jog the tape back and forth to locate an edit point by listening to the analog reference track. Then the tape can be marked and spliced just like analog tape.

Even though you can manually edit DASH format tapes, electronic editing in which a time code is used to specify exact edit points is more accurate. In addition, the original digitally recorded tape is never cut or handled excessively.

Digital Cassettes   The second digital audiotape format is the *R-DAT* cassette. (See Figure 9-3.) R-DATs are used with digital recorders that have rotating heads. (See Figure 9-13.) Basically, the rotating heads make it possible to record a lot of data on very small amounts of tape. Digital cassettes are about half the size of standard analog cassettes, but the tape can hold up to two hours of stereo audio with very high fidelity.

Preparing the R-DAT to record is similar to what is done to prepare for analog recording.

1   Turn on the power.
2   Open the cassette drawer, insert the cassette, and close the drawer.
3   When recording with a new DAT tape, fast forward it several minutes and rewind it back to the beginning before recording.

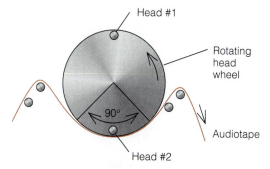

Head #1

Rotating
head
wheel

90°

Audiotape

Head #2

FIGURE 9-13 **R-DAT Rotating Head Format.**
R-DAT machines have two heads opposite each other on a rotating wheel. The audiotape is wrapped around 90 degrees of the wheel. This system permits much more information to be recorded on the tape than stationary heads would.

4 To set the recording level: Press Pause, hold down Record and press Play. Adjust the record level, which should peak between −6 dB and −3 dB (not 0 dB) to avoid distortion.
5 When you are ready to record, simply press Pause.

In addition to recording audio program material, you also can record *subcodes* on the tape that will help you find cuts and cue them when you play back the recording. Common subcodes include Start IDs, Program Numbers (PNOs), and Skip IDs. *Start IDs* mark the beginnings of program elements so they can be located quickly. *Program Numbers (PNOs)* indicate program numbers. *Skip IDs* mark programs to skip during playback.

1 To automatically record *Start IDs*: While in the Record/Pause mode, press the Start ID Auto button. IDs will be registered automatically during recording when the level drops for three seconds then rises again. To record Start IDs anywhere during recording, press the Start ID Manual button while recording.
2 To register *PNOs* automatically and in succession from the beginning of the tape: While in the Record/Pause mode, press the Start ID Auto button and numerical button #1. When Start IDs are recorded, so will program numbers. As long as the R-DAT stays in record

mode, the PNO numbers will increase in succession from #1 to #2 to #3 and so on.
3 To *skip* a program on successive playbacks, press Mark while recording or playing back the program.

Subcodes also can be registered during recording or playback, and can be edited or erased. Here is how subcodes work during playback:

1 When Start is pressed, the first eight seconds of each program element (with a Start ID) play.
2 When PNO and Start are pressed, the selected program will begin playing automatically from the beginning.
3 When Pause, PNO, and Start are pressed, the PNO is cued. The selected program will remain cued in Pause at the beginning until Play is pressed.

Additional subcodes may be included, depending on the R-DAT model and manufacturer. There is no question that digitally recorded audiotape provides better sound quality than is possible with analog recording. The addition of subcodes also makes digital recordings quicker, more accurate, and more convenient to use during productions. However, recordings made with rotating-head R-DAT recorders can only be edited on electronic systems and not manually.

AUDIO-ONLY RECORDING ON VIDEOCASSETTES

The concept of rotating heads used for R-DAT recording was first applied as a method of recording on videotape called *helical scan*. We will describe this format in Chapter 20. Two methods of audio-only recording employ existing helical scan video recording systems, modified to record digital audio. They are ADAT (which uses S-VHS tape) and Hi8 (which uses 8mm videocassettes). Unfortunately, the two systems are incompatible; tapes recorded on one cannot be played on the other.

However, the recording and editing procedures are similar in both formats. Therefore, for the purposes of illustration, we will describe recording and editing only in the ADAT format.

ADAT is a multitrack digital audio recorder that can record from both analog and digital inputs. (See Figure 9-14.) Its transport system is based on the S-VHS format, and uses standard transport function controls such as play, fast forward, rewind, and stop. About forty minutes of audio material can be recorded on eight tracks on one T-120 S-VHS cassette. As you record, a time code is automatically placed on the tape. This time code makes it possible to connect and synchronize up to sixteen ADAT machines for recording and editing on as many as 128 tracks. Usually that number of machines would be used for editing in postproduction.

Since the S-VHS system uses rotating heads, all editing must be electronic. The ADAT editing controls are similar to those on analog reel-to-reel machines. It's possible to overdub from one track to another with no loss in signal. It's also possible to perform real-time insert edits. *Insert editing* is electronic editing in which new audio can be placed in a previous recording, without disturbing material before or after the insert. This practice is called "punching in" by musicians or "read-modify-write editing" by computer people. Insert editing usually is performed automatically by marking the in and out time code points. ADAT editing is extremely precise. Edit points may be marked with "single sample accuracy," or accurate within $1/_{48,000}$ of a second.

FIGURE 9-14   **ADAT Recorder.**
ADAT is a multitrack audio-only recording format that uses Super-VHS cassettes. *(Courtesy: Alesis Corporation.)*

In addition to recording and editing, ADATs also can perform the signal processing functions we described in Chapter 8. For example, echo or delay may be added or the pitch may be shifted. ADAT also may control MIDI instruments and sequencers.

Finally, when it's time to transfer the audio tracks to a videotape, the ADAT may be connected to a video recorder and synchronized to the video.

"TAPELESS" AUDIO RECORDING

Although most audio recording is currently done using some sort of linear audiotape, as we have described, the application of computer technology to audio production has introduced a new and very different approach to recording that is having a rapidly growing impact. As its name suggests, "tapeless" recording does not use conventional audiotape, but employs computer memory media to store and manipulate audio data. What makes tapeless technology so significant is that by using the unique characteristics of digital computer data storage techniques, not only can we record and reproduce sound with extremely high fidelity, but we also can handle the audio in very efficient, flexible, and powerful ways. As a result, tapeless recording offers both tremendous technical quality and significant advances in the techniques of audio production.

There are two basic tapeless processes which apply to television audio production. The first is known as *MIDI*, which stands for *musical instrument digital interface*. The second uses computer disks as the recording/storage/reproduction medium. We will look at each individually, because while they have certain similarities, they take very different approaches to the recording process.

MIDI

The MIDI system is a computer-based hardware and software system that enables various pieces of electronic musical equipment to share information with one another and to operate as a fully integrated system. MIDI came about when various musical instrument manufacturers combined to develop an industrywide communication standard to ensure compatibility, much as the SMPTE time code ensures compatibility among equipment manufacturers of synchronizing systems.

At its most basic, MIDI is used to connect two or more electronic instruments so that they can share information such as tempo, when to start and stop the audio, the location of a particular part of a song, and how to synchronize recording and playback. MIDI allows a single performer using a single instrument—usually a keyboard—to control many different instruments at the same time and to control such audio processing effects as reverb and sound levels.

MIDI would remain of only passing interest to television production if it dealt exclusively with musical instruments and musical performance. However, MIDI offers the television production world a powerful array of new audio tools for a host of nonmusical postproduction techniques in addition to its role in creating original audio. The postproduction applications of MIDI derive from the fact that MIDI can be synchronized to SMPTE time code. This enables a computer to create a musical sound track using a complement of electronic instruments and then to lay the completed piece down in perfect synch with the video picture. (See Figure 9-15.)

Using electronic instruments called *samplers* (which are used to record either live sound or prerecorded sounds that can be played back using a musical keyboard), audio technicians can cre-

ate a precision sound-effects track to accompany the video. (See Figure 9-16.) Live or prerecorded sound effects output from a microphone or other source can be input to the sampler, recorded on disk, and assigned to one of the keyboard keys. When a specific sound effect is needed, the audio technician simply pushes the appropriate key to produce the sound.

This approach makes it simple for a sound-effects engineer to literally "play" a sequence of sounds. For example, the sound effects of a man walking to his car, opening the door, starting the engine, and driving away can be produced as follows. First, the four necessary sounds—footsteps, a car door opening, an engine starting, and a car driving away—are recorded on (loaded into) the sampler using either a microphone or sound-effects library as a source. The engineer can then preview the video and lengthen, soften, equalize, or otherwise modify the sound effect to add realism to the audiovisual match. Then, during the final take, the audio technician simply watches the line monitor and punches the appropriate sampler key to cue each sound at the proper moment.

This process can be done during production, but it is more likely to be done in postproduction with the engineer watching a time-coded video-

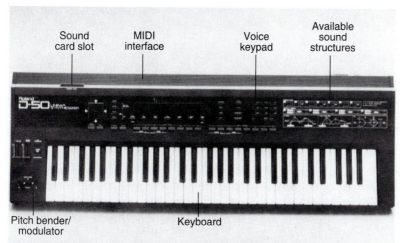

Sound card slot   MIDI interface   Voice keypad   Available sound structures

Pitch bender/modulator   Keyboard

FIGURE 9-15 Synthesizer. Audio synthesizers can create multiple sounds and combine them into a single musical score. An individual synthesizer operator can reproduce the sound of an entire orchestra by recording a group of individual sound tracks and playing them back in synchronization. *(Courtesy: Roland Corporation.)*

Rhythm programmer   Computer displays   Multitrack cassette recorder

Digital synthesizer

Digital sampling keyboard

Computer keyboard

FIGURE 9-16 **Sampler.**
A sampler can be used to digitally record either live or prerecorded sound effects and then play them back at the precise time desired. The sounds can be stretched, compressed, or modified in other ways to meet the program's audio requirements.

tape and "playing" the sound effects in real time or, if necessary, indicating the precise cues using SMPTE time code.

The MIDI process actually does not record musical sounds as a conventional tape recorder does. Instead, MIDI consists of *information commands* which control playing of the various MIDI devices. In some ways, MIDI is the digital equivalent of an old-time player piano, which used a continuous paper roll with hole punches to control the operation of the keys. The paper roll did not record the actual song; it recorded the instructions for notes to be played. In turn, these instructions created the song. In much the same way, MIDI does not record the music; rather, it tells the instrument which notes to play so that the instrument creates the song anew each time. A significant point is that the quality of MIDI-produced music or sound effects is always first-generation, since it is being produced by the instrument every time and not played back from tape.

MIDI offers much more than merely a modern version of a player piano. MIDI data can be edited and manipulated just as if you were editing actual audio information. As a result, the sound track can be manipulated in very rapid and powerful ways. This is so because the MIDI system is actually a computer-supported program that harnesses the speed and power of computers to control various audio functions.

Operations such as inserting new material, deleting parts of a sound track, copying tracks, or merging tracks are virtually instantaneous with MIDI. Consider a situation where you must locate a specific phrase in the middle of a recorded song, eliminate a few notes, and add a few new ones. With linear audiotape—even using "smart machines" which can automatically locate a predetermined point—the tape recorder must physically fast forward to the location, stop, jog back and forth, and finally cue itself. This takes time. Using MIDI and computer memory systems, location of a specific point is instantaneous. Further, editing audiotape, whether mechanical or electronic, is time-consuming and can be complicated. The computer software that supports MIDI does most of the work for you, so audio operations require no more than pushing a few buttons.

Finally, MIDI offers the audio technician certain operations unobtainable with linear tape. For example, using MIDI and associated computer software, you can "slide" a sound track forward or backward in time without disturbing the location of any of the other multiple sound tracks. Thus, if a sound effect or musical solo comes in too early, tapeless technology makes it simple to adjust the specific track to start or stop at the desired time.

You may be wondering why we are spending so much time dealing with a system that sounds terrific but probably is so expensive it's merely of theoretical interest to most of you. In fact, for once an incredible production tool is actually inexpensive. Since MIDI was originally designed for consumer use, it had to be sufficiently inexpensive that musicians could afford it. This marketing necessity, coupled with reliance on mass-produced microcomputer technology, has produced one of the most significant developments in audio/video production in the past decade. In the next chapter we will discuss some of the musical and nonmusical applications of this remarkable tool.

Disc Recording

The second tapeless recording approach uses computer disk devices to store digitally recorded data. (We discussed disc storage media in Chapter 7.) With digital audio data stored on a hard disk, it is possible to perform the complete tapeless recording process on one device, called a *digital audio workstation (DAW)*. (See Figure 8-28.) It combines computer and audio technologies, enabling you to record, process, edit, and sync-up with MIDI and video systems. These functions are performed on a computer, using DAW software. As you work, the software displays *icons*, or pictures, on the monitor that look like traditional analog controls, such as transport controls, slide faders, meters, and equalizers. (See Figure 9-17.) The icons move like analog controls as you control them with the keyboard or a mouse. Some DAW software even has a "scrubbing" function, which simulates the sound made when you rock an analog tape back and forth against the tape head. These features are attempts to preserve the familiar look, sound, and feel of the audio-control console, and to make it easier to adapt to the new technology.

The screen also includes other data such as time code windows and your "edit decision list." In addition, you see the waveforms of the audio tracks. This permits *waveform editing*, visually changing the waveform of the audio signal to change the audio signal itself. For example, the amplitude of the waveform may be changed to alter the volume of the sound.

The DAW also facilitates extremely precise editing. Waveforms may be "trimmed" and "slipped" within a track, or "bounced" to another track. Selections also may be "cut and pasted" with a precision not possible with a razor blade and splicing tape. Also, the original recording is preserved, so if you make a mistake, you still have your untouched original.

Disc Production Techniques   The use of disc technology as opposed to audiotape for recording/playback and sound production offers a number of advantages over tape. These advantages include sound quality and production flexibility.

SOUND QUALITY   Disc recording converts all recorded sound into digital data and consequently offers all the sound-quality advantages inherent in the digital process. Further, discs are superior storage media and the signal does not deteriorate over time, as with audiotape.

PRODUCTION FLEXIBILITY   The special characteristics of disc technology offer a number of production techniques that are either difficult or impossible to do with conventional audiotape, even digital tape. We have already mentioned track "slipping" or "sliding," which is impossible to do on a tape recorder, but is easy to achieve when the material is recorded on disc. Another benefit of disc technology is the ability to "loop" a track so that it will continuously repeat or to "chain" a number of tracks together to play as a unit. These techniques are especially useful in developing both music and sound-effects tracks to fit to a picture. Disc recording also offers instantaneous location of specific points on a sound track. This allows you to store hundreds of different sounds, musical instruments, and dialogue cues on one disc and access each one instantly. The ability to quickly find the needed audio saves time and soothes everyone's nerves.

Once a sound has been located, using the software associated with the system allows you to shape and color the sound in many different ways. While this can be accomplished with conventional

The Display Scale arrows allow you to adjust waveform display.

The Zoomer lets you view audio waveforms at any resolution, down to the individual sample

The Trimmer allows you to "fine tune" your selection.

Quick, high-quality varispeed scrubbing (similar to rocking a reel of tape against tape heads) is available in forward and reverse. Allows for locating edit and other points with pinpoint accuracy.

The Selector is used to define regions of audio and MIDI.

The Grabber moves regions and tracks. Moves can be quantized with Grid mode.

Selection and Position indicators show you exactly where you are in your session.

Nudge/Grid selector indicates value selected for Grid quantization. Regions may also be "nudged" by this amount using the + / − keys.

Current Time indicator.

Time stamping allows regions to retain original location information, which allows for quick return to position and easy identification.

Audio (top) and MIDI (bottom) Regions Lists. Regions can be dragged from these lists and placed in any respective audio or MIDI track.

In addition to transport controls, the Transport window gives you 10 instant and nameable autolocation points, Punch In/Out indicators, and an Online command.

Slip/Shuffle/Spot/Grid Indicator. Use Slip mode to move regions freely within a track, even overlap other regions. Shuffle mode lines up regions end to end for rapid assembly. Use Spot mode to spot audio to picture. Grid mode automatically quantizes your edits to the nearest beat, second, or frame.

The Time Scale indicator lets you view a session in Minutes, Seconds, Bar & Beats, SMPTE, or Feet & Frames.

Track volume and mute changes can be automated quickly and accurately with click-and-drag "breakpoint" editing. Faders and other automatable controls move on-screen to match changes.

Track panning changes can also be automated graphically with click-and-drag "breakpoint" editing.

Each Audio Track is a graphic playlist with controls for volume, panning, solo/mute, and voice priority, giving you visual feedback for rapid, accurate editing.

The Edit window allows each audio track to be viewed individually in waveform, or block format.

Select across multiple tracks of audio and MIDI.

Multiple MIDI Tracks can be edited in blocks along with audio.

Each audio track offers high-quality equalizer options, including high-shelf, low-shelf, peak/notch, high-pass, and low-pass. Two separate EQs are available per track.

Four- and 8-channel systems offer four auxiliary sends per track (not shown).

Each module in the Mixer window gives you total control over EQ panning, solo/mute/record enable/automation record enable status, output channel assignment and level, and voice priority (for virtual tracks). Most of the Mix window controls (except for the track fader and VU meter) may also be viewed and controlled from the Edit window.

Pro Tools' post-fader VU meters are fast and extremely accurate. Meters indicate signal present, level before clipping, and clipping status.

Pro Tools 2.0

Audio Regions List:
44 magnum
AMBIENCE-T1
Background #2
Background #2+
FOOTSTEP1-T1
HATCH CLOSE 2 44.1
Heyday Demo 02 Audio
Heyday Demo 02 Audio 3
MACHINE HUM
METAL DOOR SLAM
Prod.Audio
Prod.Audio●
Prod.Audio●+
PUMP ROOM
SLOSH
Take 2 Audio
WIND LOOP

MIDI Regions List:
B. Clar
B. Bone/Tuba 8va
BD hit C#1 , roll D1
Bones
bass bone /tuba dbl.
bass trem
Castnets hit G3, roll G#
Celesta
Cello Arco
Cello Pizz
Chimes

Transport window:
play start 00:00:53:22
record start 00:00:53:22
record length 00:00:13:12
play end 00:01:07:03

Autolocation:
1 Door Slam   6 Orch. Cue
2 Music HH   7 AOR In
3 Fly By   8
4 Amb. Loop   9
5 Billy, Close   10

digidesign

FIGURE 9-17   Digital Audio Workstation
Software Display.

Windows in this computer display include graphics that
look like the controls on traditional audio-control
consoles, as well as the waveforms of the different
soundtracks. (Courtesy: Degidesign.)

tape and equalizers, the time savings offered by
disc are substantial. Digital disc recording allows
you to manipulate sound, compare it to the original, modify it further if needed, and finally save it
in the desired form.

Since disc recording hardware is a component
of a computer-based system, all the features available with SMPTE and MIDI codes are available in
disc recording. These include the ability to preset
recording and playback by time code number so
that the end result is absolute frame synch with

the picture. Digital disc recording also allows you
to vary the speed of a previously recorded track
without perceptibly affecting its pitch. This allows
you to shorten or lengthen a section of audio so
that it precisely fits the time available on video. For
example, if a musical bed had been recorded in
twenty-five seconds but there were only twenty-
two seconds of video, you could increase the
tempo of the audio track, compressing the audio
by three seconds. Perhaps the nicest feature of
disc technology is that since you are working with
a copy of original audio, you can experiment without damaging the "master tape." The increased
freedom to experiment often allows for especially
creative outcomes.

SUMMARY

Audio recording may refer to either audio-only recording or to the recording
of a sound track to accompany the video on a videotape. The audio signal
that enters an audiotape recorder (ATR) can be stored as either an analog
signal or a digital signal. Analog recorders reproduce the waveforms of the
original audio signals as closely as possible. The incoming signal activates
the analog tape recorder's recording head, which functions like a an electromagnet. The recording head produces a magnetic field (flux) which aligns
magnetic particles on the audiotape into patterns corresponding to the
original waveform.

Audiotape has a plastic-like base, usually a type of polyester, and other
physical and magnetic properties such as width, thickness, and type of
oxide. The most frequently-used width of reel-to-reel tape is ¼-inch width.
The thickness of tape is measured in mils. A mil is one one-thousandth (.001)
of an inch. Professionals prefer the thicker 1½-mil tape for three reasons:
(1) It is less likely to stretch or break. (2) It is easier to splice. (3) It is less
vulnerable to print-through. Oxide refers to the coating of magnetic particles
on the tape. There are four common types of oxide: (1) iron, or ferric, oxide;
(2) chromium dioxide; (3) ferrichrome; and (4) metal.

The erase head on an ATR erases old signals on a tape as new signals
are being recorded on it. It's also possible to erase an audiotape by using
a bulk eraser, or degausser.

When recording on a reel-to-reel ATR, you will be operating the ATR's
transport system and its electronics. The transport system is what controls
the movement of the tape. The electronics involve the audio signal flow
through the ATR. Multitrack recorders usually have another control called
selective synchronization, or sel sync. This makes it possible to play one

track and record on another with both in sync. This procedure is called overdubbing.

One of the advantages of reel-to-reel audiotape is the ability to edit the program material, either mechanically or electronically. Mechanical tape editing refers to a process in which the tape is actually cut and reconnected with a physical splice. Editing electronically means that you never physically cut the tape as you do with mechanical editing. Rather, the editing is a dubbing process in which a playback sequence is precisely cued to specific "in" and "out" edit points and then copied, or dubbed, to a record machine. Even more precise edits can be accomplished if the audiotape has time code striped on the tape, and the entire editing process is put under the control of a computer.

Analog cart recordings are used during productions because they afford good quality, are easy to record and play, and cue themselves automatically. The main disadvantage is that cart tape is a continuous loop that must be "recycled" to the beginning each time it is used. With digital carts, it is possible to record a number of cuts and play them in any order, eliminating the "recycling" disadvantage of traditional carts.

Unlike the tape in a cart, which is in a loop, the tape in an analog cassette is in the reel-to-reel format. Therefore, the transport and recording controls on cassettes are similar to reel-to-reel machines. Analog cassettes also have settings for the type of tape being used. The Type I, or normal, setting is for tape with iron (ferric) oxide; the Type II high setting is for chromium dioxide; the Type III high setting is for ferrichrome; and the Type IV setting is for tape with a metal surface. Both the quality and the cost increase as you go from Type I to Type IV tape. Shorter cassettes (up to 60 minutes) are more desirable because they use thicker tape ($\frac{1}{2}$-mil). The longer cassettes (90 minutes and above) use $\frac{1}{4}$-mil tape. This thinner tape usually does not have as good quality and is more susceptible to stretching and getting "eaten" by the machine. Although cassettes often are used for location recording, rarely is the analog cassette the medium of choice for audio-only studio recording, for three reasons: (1) The quality of the recording will be limited. (2) Cassette tapes are difficult to edit and have to be dubbed for editing. (3) Cassettes are difficult to cue.

Digital recordings may be made either on reel-to-reel tape or on cassettes. Open reel digital audiotape is similar to conventional audiotape. Both analog and digital ATRs have stationary tape heads. The digital format called DASH operates much like conventional analog recording, and records both digital audio tracks and a reference analog track. Therefore, DASH tapes can be edited mechanically. Digital cassettes are used with recorders that have rotary heads and are called R-DATs.

When recording digitally, you can store the audio program material and subcodes that will help you find cuts and cue them when you play back the recording. Common subcodes include Start IDs, Program Numbers (PNOs), and Skip IDs. The addition of subcodes makes digital recordings quicker, more accurate, and more convenient to use than analog tapes. However, recordings made with rotating-head R-DAT recorders cannot be edited manually. Two existing helical scan video recording systems have been modified to record digital audio: ADAT (which uses S-VHS tape) and Hi8 (which uses 8 mm videocassettes).

"Tapeless" audio recording uses computer memory media to store and manipulate audio data. MIDI (musical instrument digital interface) is a computer based hardware and software system that enables various pieces of electronic musical equipment to share information with one another and to operate as a fully integrated system. MIDI does not record musical sounds as a conventional tape recorder does. Instead, it consists of information commands which control the playing of the various MIDI devices. MIDI offers a host of new tools for nonmusical production techniques, including synthesizers, samplers, and sequencers. Digital audio workstations (DAWs) combine computer and audio technologies, enabling you to record, process, edit audio signals, and coordinate them with MIDI and video systems.

Disc production techniques as opposed to audiotape have a number of advantages: Disc has better sound quality than tape. Discs have greater production flexibility. The features of SMPTE time code and MIDI are readily available. Disc is a better storage medium than tape.

CREATING AUDIOSPACE

MIXING AND PRODUCTION

Producing good television audio is a difficult job. The problems of sound recording and reproduction that face the television audio technician are similar to those faced by recording or radio engineers. However, these challenges are compounded by the fact that the television audio technician is expected to produce high-quality audio while minimally interfering with the program's visual elements. The radio engineer can select a microphone and position it without regard to the mike's appearance or whether its position obscures the performer from an audience's view. Yet these and other similar considerations are of paramount importance to the TV audio technician in addition to the basic requirement of producing good sound.

To make matters worse, the recording or radio engineer has the advantage of a studio that was acoustically designed for sound production. Even the best designed television studio is an acoustical nightmare with high ceilings, hard floors, and personnel and equipment constantly moving about during the production. These facts are not cited to excuse audio technicians, but to represent the reality they face. To produce consistently good audio under these difficult conditions requires skill, imagination, and talent.

In this chapter we will discuss audio production techniques, special audio effects, and audio operation in the four production stages.

PRERECORDING PROGRAM MATERIAL

There are times when the television director or the audio engineer may decide to prerecord certain audio segments for use during an actual production. The four most common types of prerecorded program material are (1) *voice-overs*, (2) *prerecorded musical tracks*, (3) *lip syncs*, and (4) *sound effects*.

Prerecorded Voice-Overs

Prerecorded voice-over refers to playing a previously recorded voice track over the visual portion of a program. A common example of the voice-over is the use of narration over a segment of silent film. The narration is recorded prior to the program, sometimes with the talent watching a playback of the film, and permits greater control over the synchronization of audio track and video.

On some dramatic shows, the director might use a voice-over segment to give the viewing audience the impression that it is hearing the actor's "thoughts." This effect is accomplished by prerecording the audio segment and inserting it into the program over a close-up of the actor deep in thought. The actor hears the voice-over track through the studio monitor speakers and can act and react accordingly.

Sound perspective should always be considered when recording a voice-over. Because the voice-over is often mixed with live audio, it is a good idea to record the voice-over in the same studio that will be used for the actual production. This will keep the sound quality of the voice-over similar to the quality of the live audio. Of course, if audio matching is not important, because the sound will be altered through filtering or reverberation, then the voice-over can be recorded in any convenient studio. Voice-overs can be played back from reel-to-reel tape recorders or dubbed to an audio cartridge for ease in cuing during production.

Prerecorded Music Tracks

Sometimes it is impractical or impossible to provide a singer with a live musical accompaniment. There are many possible reasons. The limited size of the studio may prevent setting up a full orchestra or band, or the program's budget may not be able to afford the expense of a full orchestra. Other times a singer may wish to re-create his or her unique "sound" and may want to use the musical track from the original commercial recording.

Whatever the reason, it is not uncommon to have to mix a live performer with a prerecorded musical track. The singer sings into a microphone, and the mike input is then mixed with the track through the audio board. The tricky part is that the singer must be able to hear the musical track, but the studio monitor system cannot be used because it is designed to turn off, or *mute*, when the singer's mike is turned on to avoid feedback. The solution is to play the musical track through the audio console and simultaneously feed the output of the prerecorded musical track into the studio on a separate *foldback speaker* that can be heard by the singer. Since many singers must hear the music at high volume levels to sing on key, it is important to rehearse the foldback volume level prior to production.

Another complication occurs if there is more than one singer and they need to hear each other as well as hear the musical track over the foldback system. In this case, outputs from the mikes are fed into foldback speakers along with the musical track. The speakers must be positioned carefully, and directional mikes used with their "dead sides" facing the speakers to avoid producing feedback. In this case, why not simply use the studio monitor system? The reason is that it usually will have wall-mounted speakers that are too far away from the singers to be helpful, and will increase the chances of creating a feedback loop. Floor speakers that can be positioned precisely relative to the microphone, singer, and cameras are a much better choice for use with live microphones.

Aside from the obvious advantages in terms of studio space and budgetary savings, prerecording the music track eliminates the task of balancing each instrumental mike and then mixing the entire orchestra or band with the singer. Since the music is already premixed, the audio engineer needs only to balance the singer with the single orchestral track.

Lip Sync

Lip sync, short for *lip synchronization,* is accomplished by having a singer pantomime to a previously recorded composite vocal and musical sound track. Alternately, a performer may rerecord his or her audio after completing the video portion of the work. As an example of prerecording audio for lip sync, there are times when it is impossible for a vocalist to sing during a live television production. The singer may be involved in an elaborate dance or production number and the boom might not be able to cover the area adequately. Also, it is difficult for a performer to dance and sing at the same time or to sing while recovering from an energetic dance routine. The program director might ask the singer to prerecord the entire song in advance and then to fake singing while the mixed track is played back on the studio monitor speakers.

A remote production, where good-quality audio is very difficult to achieve, is an example where a postproduction lip sync may be required. To establish an accurate lip sync in postproduction requires that the performer be able to see his or her actions and replicate the actual words and their inflection for the tape recorder. Since this is a matter of split-second timing, which requires practice and guidance, a technique known as *looping* has evolved. Looping begins by separating the original audio and video while retaining their synchronous time code. These audio and video "loops" are joined with a time-coded blank piece of audiotape. While watching the original video and monitoring the original audio through headsets, the performer sings or speaks and his or her voice is recorded to the clean audiotape. Since an accurate lip sync usually requires many takes, an edit controller is set up with in and out cues and automatic recue. After the performer has successfully matched the video and attained the proper inflection, the audio technician still may have to work with the signal to match sound perspective or the ambient noise surrounding the dialogue.

An alternate approach to lip sync is to use an *automatic dialogue replacement* (*ADR*) *device.* An ADR digitizes sound and breaks the original words into a bit stream. The replacement dialogue is also recorded digitally and then stretched, compressed, and otherwise altered to match the original dialogue. If the replacement dialogue sounds unnatural, the replacement sound is modified until a perfect match has been accomplished.

TECH TIP   It is a good idea to record lip synced audio to alternating tracks. Then you can compare the second take to the first. The third take is recorded over the poorer of the original two. Eventually, a successful lip sync emerges from this competition.

Sound Effects

Sound effects, like music, often can be among the subtle but effective elements which make an ordinary production better than average. Sound effects contribute to creating the overall mood or atmosphere of a program and help convey a special illusion to the audience. Often sound effects are combined with special effects to manipulate both the videospace and the audiospace simultaneously. For example, a number of special lighting effects can provide the visual illusion of a fire, but the sound of crackling wood is needed to complete the overall effect.

Sound effects must be planned and coordinated carefully, however, because nothing is worse than producing a sound effect at the wrong time in a show. A classic case of mistiming occurred during one of the early live television dramas in which an actor playing a detective was supposed to shoot another actor on-camera. The sound of the gun was on a record which the audio technician was to play from the control booth. For one reason or another, the record was miscued, and when the actor fired his gun, no sound accompanied the action. The actor tried again and again, but there was no gunshot sound. Finally, in desperation, the actor pointed the gun at his adversary for a final time, cocked the hammer, and as he fired the gun, he yelled out "Bang!" A split second later the audio technician finally got the record cued properly and sent out the sound effect of the gunshot.

During the heyday of radio and in the early days of television, many sound effects were created live through mechanical means. A technician was positioned in a corner of the studio surrounded by odd-looking equipment which, in skilled hands, produced an array of sound effects. Unfortunately, mechanical sound effects have a number of significant disadvantages: they take up valuable studio space, they need an isolated area so the sounds are not picked up by the performers' mikes, and they require at least one additional sound technician.

The availability of almost every conceivable sound on disc or tape, combined with the use of CDs and audio cartridges that provide accurate cuing and timing, has virtually eliminated the use of most mechanical effects. At many production studios, a sound-effects library is indexed on cards or as a computer file and cross-referenced to specific records, tapes, or compact discs. This permits the audio technician, director, or production assistant to locate quickly whatever sounds are needed. You often will find a number of different versions of the same sound so you can select the particular one that best fits your particular needs.

Sound-effects sources may have over a thousand individual effects and effect variations. To eliminate any possible confusion during production, most audio technicians prefer to dub the effects to open-reel tape or to an audio cartridge. Compact discs avoid this problem because the cut can be selected by punching in a cut number rather than relying on a visual cue. CDs also can be programmed to replay a sound effect multiple times. Still, at many studios the CD is used only as a storage medium and the audio technician will dub the needed effect to tape for editing and for use during production.

A very useful property of prerecorded sound effects is the ability to produce variations on the original sound by playing the tape faster or slower than normal speed. Never forget the concept of audiospace; the only consideration is how the sound will be perceived by the audience. Viewers will never know that the roar of a building explosion, which sounds so convincing, was really produced by playing a recording of a cannon blast at half speed. This can be done easily with a *sampler*, which we described in Chapter 7. Different sound effects can be assigned to individual keys on the sampler's piano-like keyboard and "played" by the audio technician. A similar ap-

proach is to use *MIDI files*, which are databases of sound "clips" that can be located using a computer program. Like prerecorded samples, MIDI clips can be digitally processed, stored, and used during production or postproduction.

SOUND MIXING

Sound mixing is an art that combines an audio technician's creativity with the technical skills and abilities necessary to produce a sound track that complements the visual elements of a production. In the preceding audio chapters we discussed the use of the audio-control console to regulate the level of incoming sound sources in order to produce technically acceptable sound quality. This, of course, is only the barest minimum required for a television production. The audio technician also must mix together the various sound sources so that the relative loudness of each is in direct proportion to their importance in the overall audio message. For example, a singer and a backup band must be mixed properly to produce the correct audio balance between the two sound sources. But *mixing* does not refer exclusively to music. Virtually every television production has a variety of sound elements that must be mixed and balanced to produce a sound track which is both aesthetically pleasing and communicates effectively to the audience. For example, in a newscast, the audio technician may have to mix the sound levels from reporters in the studio, sound tracks from various videotape and film sources, a live feed from a remote news location, and music and sound effects that occur throughout the production. (See Figure 10-1.)

Sound Levels

Before beginning any television production, the audio technician must set the basic sound levels for each audio input. This requires listening to each sound source individually and adjusting its corresponding pot or fader for an approximate operating level. We can divide sound sources into

A window separates the audio-control area from the video control room

Video monitors

Audio-control console

VU meters

Input modules

Slide faders

FIGURE 10-1

The Audio-Control Area.
The audio-control area should be compact, so that all equipment is within easy reach of the audio technician. Ideally, the audio-control area is in a separate room which allows the audio technician to mix sounds and to preview the upcoming audio without interfering with the director or other studio control-room operators. (*Courtesy: Capital Cities/ABC, Inc.*)

two large categories: (1) *microphone sources,* which pick up live sound and are low-level inputs, and (2) *premixed sources,* high-level inputs that include the previously mixed sound from records, CDs, audiotapes, and the tracks of video recorders and film chains. Premixed sources also include the feed from another audio console, such as the output from a live news unit at the scene of an event.

Microphone Levels   Here is the procedure for setting microphone levels:

1   Close all studio microphone faders.
2   Open one mike, and have the talent who will use the microphone speak a few lines of dialogue or read from the script. Professional actors and announcers usually will provide a stable sound level throughout the entire production. Nonprofessionals have a tendency to project differently (usually more loudly) during the sound level check than they will during the actual production. In this case, have the performer read a few lines from the program script or talk to the host of the program in order to give you a more accurate representation of how he or she will speak once on the air. Under no circumstances should you permit talent to give you a simple "Testing, one-two-three" for a level check because this sort of sentence fragment is unrepresentative of how the per-

former will actually speak during the program.
3   While the talent speaks, adjust the fader until the VU meter indicates the proper audio level. The meter should read between 80 and 100 percent modulation with very occasional peaks into the red. As you check for sound level, listen carefully for sound presence and adjust the position of the subject or the mike if necessary. If one microphone must cover a number of different performers, be sure to check each performer's level individually. You also should check any ensemble levels that might be necessary if one microphone must pick up multiple sounds simultaneously.
4   After setting one input level, close its fader on the audio console and repeat the procedure with all other microphones, one at a time.

This level check will provide you with only an approximate setting for each microphone. During the rehearsal, you will have to readjust the levels for the proper balance once you hear how all the sound sources interact with each other.

Setting levels on a boom microphone is a little trickier, since both the boom and the talent will be moving during the course of the production. In this case, obtain a basic level with the boom in a fairly normal position and be prepared to ride gain continually during production. You also should check levels for those times in the script where the performer must speak very loudly or must whisper softly. During rehearsals it is especially important to listen for sound presence and to correct both fader levels and boom positioning.

Premixed Sound Levels   Since prerecorded material should have been properly recorded when it was originally produced, establishing levels for such a source usually is easy. Simply preview each sound source to establish the proper fader position on the audio-control board. Premixed feeds from remote locations already are balanced, but you must establish the proper fader position at the master audio console before the production.

Although premixed sound sources generally remain constant in their level because they have already been mixed, you often will use them in combination with other sound sources, so you will have to vary the levels of both the premixed source and the source from the studio to achieve the correct overall sound mix during production.

In addition to the voltage control amplifier (VCA) circuits (see Chapter 8) used for complicated postproduction mix-downs, audio *compressors* can be helpful for balancing premixed and live inputs. In a process known as *ducking,* two sound sources, say, a voice track and background music, are passed through an audio compressor. The compressor is designed such that the level of one source will fall a preset level when the other sound source is part of the mix. So, for example, when the announcer speaks, the background music automatically "ducks under" his or her voice. The degree to which the volume of the secondary source is softened can be varied.

Marking Faders   On most audio boards there is room for the audio technician to attach a strip of plain masking tape across a row of faders. This allows the engineer to identify each control's function by name. As you run through microphone level checks, be sure the name or identification on the masking tape strip corresponds to the proper microphone. This makes it easy to identify each microphone's fader quickly and accurately. Once the production is over, pull off the masking tape to leave a clean board for the next production. Never write directly on a board with any kind of pen or pencil.

If you know you will have to combine a live microphone with another sound source—a musical

theme and an announcer, for example—it is a good idea to rehearse this mix and to set preliminary levels. You can mark the fader setting for each control with a tiny piece of masking tape so you can quickly return both faders to the predetermined (preset) positions.

TECH TIP   If you are working with a large number of microphones, as in a panel discussion with five lavaliers, it can be difficult to identify which subject is using which microphone. To make certain you have properly identified each pot, have a floor assistant *gently* scratch each microphone as you open its fader. Since the light scratch will be picked up only on the open mike, you can accurately locate the microphone positions.

MUSIC IN TELEVISION

Music plays an important part in virtually every television production. Whether it is the opening theme which identifies the program and sets up the audience's expectations and mood or a musical program where the music is the primary program content, anyone working in television production needs to be familiar with some of the fundamental aspects of music. Although there are many different ways to use music, we can organize them into the following broad categories: (1) theme music, (2) background music, (3) live music, and (4) music videos.

Theme Music

A program's opening theme is usually the first audio element the audience hears. The music should be selected to catch the audience's attention, stimulate its curiosity, and set the mood or tone for the show. A program's theme often becomes its trademark, so it is worth whatever time and effort it takes to find the particular selection that works best.

You can find theme music from a number of sources. The commercially available production music libraries are a quick and easy way to find specific instrumental tunes that convey a particular mood because they are specially composed and recorded for production purposes. If an index is used, it is easy to locate possible selections under such categories as "action," "documentary," "industrial," "religious," or "weird, eerie, and space." Unfortunately, these selections tend to sound trite and canned, and you may be better off spending more time with contemporary or classical selections which are harder to find but usually sound better.

As a general rule, avoid overly familiar tunes— both popular and classical—which have been used time and time again. The opening theme for the movie *Star Wars* was a brilliant use of music to establish a mood and to set up the audience for the story to come. However, it has become so overworked since then that its use sounds clichéd. It is best if your show's theme is identified only with your program and does not carry along dozens of other impressions for the viewer. Of course, there are circumstances in which you may want this familiarity to work to your advantage, but these are generally special situations. A number of theme songs, such as Jan Hammer's *Miami Vice* theme, proved so successful that they be-

came hit records independent of the television show.

Sometimes a piece of a larger work can be excerpted and modified for use through tape editing. A short section can be extended in play length by recording it a few times and editing the pieces together. Similarly, an overly long selection can be edited down to a shorter segment.

Background Music

Background music is designed to enhance a production subtly without upstaging the primary program content. Often we are unaware that music is present on a program unless we listen especially for it. Yet it has been shown repeatedly that, properly used, background music can contribute a great deal to setting the overall tone or mood of a scene or program segment. Since background music is designed more to establish a mood than to be an identifiable piece of music, the easily accessible selections from production music libraries are usually very useful for this purpose. Looking under the various categories in the catalogue should lead you to some appropriate selections of varying lengths. (See Figure 10-2.)

Sometimes music is used as a thematic element itself by associating a certain piece or even a few notes with a particular action. The idea works

Catalogue No.	Title	Composer	Timing
5249 A2.	**FOLLIES NUMBER** In the manner of a chorus line, with a kick routine before the footlights, but lighter in texture without bawdiness.	George Chase BMI	1:27
5249 B1.	**METEOR'S TRIP** Fast motion into the unknown. Speed in outer space. Modernistic laboratory of bubbling retorts and flashing lights.	Roger Roger BMI	2:01
2.	**DREAMING AWAKE** Awakening into strange surroundings. Lost memory.		:41
5250 A	**ROLLING MILL** Suggesting activities in an industrial plant or logging operations in the big woods. Melodic treatment.	George Chase BMI	2:32
5250 B1.	**MARTIAN'S PATROL** Weird march, with a definite drum beat, suggesting approach of strange or unearthly creatures.	Roger Roger BMI	1:53
2.	**STRATOSPHERIC DREAM** Strange and bewildering sights. An unknown fairyland of fantastic beauty. Sights never seen before.		1:56
5251 A1.	**SPELL OF THE UNKNOWN** Awesome approach to new worlds. A new planet looms into view.	Roger Roger BMI	1:27

FIGURE 10-2 Production Music Library Catalogue. A production music catalogue contains a list of musical selections described in terms of mood, tempo, and running times. (*Courtesy: Thomas J. Valentino Co.*)

something like Pavlov's dog experiments. By playing the music a few times and associating it in the viewer's mind with a particular mood or action, you need only play the theme later on to trigger the same reaction in the audience. In the famous movie *Jaws,* the signature low notes of cellos and bass are immediately associated with the killer shark. Once this is established in the audience's mind, merely playing the theme can result in the audience anticipating danger without having to see the shark on screen. Many suspense and mystery films are able to keep the audience guessing through the clever use of music.

Musical Approach   There are a number of factors you must consider when selecting background music. These include the musical style, the atmosphere or mood, the instrumentation, and the tempo. *Style* refers loosely to the genre, such as rock or jazz. *Instrumentation* refers to the number and type of instruments used. Not every production situation lends itself to a full orchestral treatment. Perhaps a simple guitar, flute, or piano would be more appropriate. *Tempo* is the speed of the beat or rhythm, whether the music is fast or slow. *Mood,* of course, is the overall atmosphere which the piece conveys.

Music selection for any production is never an easy task. It takes time, patience, and perseverance. However, music is one of the most effective ways to build the audiospace, and the right music selection used at the right time can be the little touch that enhances a production and takes it above the ordinary.

Producing Original Music   Sometimes no available prerecorded music can meet the needs of a television program, and you will have to produce an original sound track. Until recently, the time, equipment, and unique talents involved in composing, scoring, and performing original music were so expensive that it was not feasible for most production facilities to afford the considerable costs. The introduction of synthesizers, samplers, and MIDI systems has changed all that. (See chapters 7 and 9.) While talent is still the needed, unique resource, it is now possible, and very affordable, for a single individual to write, score, and actually perform original music using synthesizers and samplers.

In general, the composer should meet with the program's producer and director as early as possible to discuss the program's objectives and the music requirements. Is the theme music all that is needed? Should "bumpers" (musical transitions in and out of commercial breaks) be created? Or does the program require both these and original background music as well?

Once the composer has met with the producer and director, she or he can begin working on some basic thematic ideas and perhaps the transitions. If the composer is commissioned to produce background music that must be synchronized perfectly with the video, she or he will have to receive a rough cut of all the video segments that must be scored.

Music must be performed to synchronize exactly with the video portion of the program. To do this, the composer/conductor receives a videocassette of the rough cut with a *click track* laid down to accompany the video. As its name suggests, the click track is a series of metronomic clicks that helps to guide the tempo of the music as it is performed. While it was traditional for music tracks to be performed by a number of musicians playing together, the synthesizers and samplers now available allow a single composer/performer to duplicate the sound of virtually any musical instrument and "build" a complete orchestra track by track. This approach saves both time and money and gives complete creative control to a single individual.

Once a composer has selected the desired instruments to be produced with the synthesizer and sampler, a computer software program is used to link the MIDI-controlled musical system with the SMPTE time code on the videotape. Since the MIDI is "slaved" to the time code, the music is laid down in perfect synchronization with the video.

The foregoing exactly describes how the trendsetting music for *Miami Vice* was produced. Composer-performer Jan Hammer worked out of his home studio in New York, 1,500 miles from Miami where the program is shot and 3,000 miles from Hollywood where the film is edited. Each week

Hammer received a rough cut of the episode on cassette and scored it using synthesizers, samplers, and a variety of acoustic instruments. Hammer shipped his completed mix-down back to Hollywood, where it was combined with dialogue and effects track in the program's final audio mix.

The Hammer–*Miami Vice* partnership is being duplicated on many smaller productions because the necessary musical equipment and associated video synchronization gear have become very inexpensive. With a synthesizer, sampler, and sequencer combination available for less than $3,000 (although sophisticated equipment like Hammer's may cost $50,000 to $75,000), original music is showing up in the once unheard of domains of university productions and industrial videotapes.

In spite of their revolutionary potential, the new technologies are not without their share of problems. For example, digital audio is generating many issues with respect to copyright or the ownership of creative property. For example, if a Phil Collins drum sound is recorded off a record or CD and onto a sampler and then modified ever so slightly by the sampler operator, should Phil Collins receive a royalty for the use of his work? The copyright issue revolves around the concept of *substantiality*, or whether the derivative work is "substantially similar to" the original. How to define *substantiality* remains a topic of intense debate.

Mixing Live Music

Live music presents one of the most difficult challenges to the audio technician. The objective in balancing music is to blend all the individual microphones together to produce a good-sounding mix. This is usually a matter of trial and error, since studio acoustics, the position of the band, and the "sound" of the music will vary for each production. Remember that the VU meter will reflect only the amplitude level of the audio. It is up to the audio technician to listen to the music carefully and to adjust each microphone until the desired balance is achieved. Figure 10-3 illustrates some common

musical situations and suggested methods for positioning the microphones.

If you are using an audio console with a submaster system, you can balance the individual musician mikes and leave them in their preset positions. Then assign all the preset microphones to one or two submaster faders. You then could divide the band, assigning the rhythm section to one submaster, brass and horns to another, and everything else to an additional submaster. This allows you to preset individual mike levels and ride gain on the entire band with a minimum number of fader controls.

When mixing a vocalist with a back-up group, listen carefully for the proper balance between the singer and music. If necessary, the audio technician can alter the sound quality of either the instruments or the singer by adding reverberation and equalization.

There are a number of excellent books which deal with music mixing and recording in far more detail than we can cover here. The Bibliography

FIGURE 10-3

Microphone Placement for Music Pickup.
(*a*) Drum set: (1) dynamic mike for kick drum, (2) condenser or dynamic mike mounted on boom for toms and cymbals, and (3) dynamic mike mounted on boom to pick up snare and hi-hat. Position microphones to achieve the balance and overall sound quality desired. (*b*) Piano: condenser, ribbon, or dynamic mike mounted on boom and positioned over second or third hole in soundboard. (*c*) Electric amplifier for guitar, bass, and piano: dynamic mike mounted on stand in front of amplifier speaker. Aim at the center for bright sound; off center for a fuller, more mellow sound. (*d*) Electric organ Leslie speaker: mount dynamic or condenser mike on stand or boom. Placing mike at top, bottom, or in the middle of the sound louvers will vary the sound quality. (*e*) Acoustic guitar and vocalist: (1) dynamic or condenser mike for vocalist (use microphone with windscreen to prevent popping and to permit vocalist to work close to mike; proximity effect of microphone also should be considered when selecting a particular mike for vocalist), and (2) dynamic or condenser mike mounted on stand to pick up guitar. (*f*) Brass: dynamic or condenser mike mounted on stand or boom and positioned slightly off center of instrument's bell to reduce high frequencies, wind noise, and excessive brilliance.

(a) Drum Set

2

3

Cymbal

Hi-hat

Snare

Floor toms

Shell tom

Kick

1

(b) Piano

Cover open

Mike positioned over 2d or 3d hole in soundboard

(c) Electric Guitar/Bass Amplifier

(d) Electric Organ Leslie Speaker

(e) Acoustic Guitar and Vocalist

Vocal mike 1

Guitar mike 2

(f) Brass

271

in the back of this book indicates a number of suggested sources for more detailed information.

Music Videos

The importance of music videos, in which songs are visualized for an audience, is that they provide a creative outlet for much experimentation in television. A music video segment averages about three minutes in length, but it is still a complete program. Because each music video spot is a three-minute commercial for a performing group and their music, the budget can be higher than for most other program formats on a per-minute cost basis. These economics, the audience's appetite for music videos, and the demands of musically trained performers for excellent sound have advanced the role of audio production in television.

Music videos usually are produced in one of three genres: (1) the artist presenting an onstage performance of the music, (2) a narrative in which a story line suggested by the music is scripted and shot, and (3) fantasy, in which the music provides some unity for dreamlike, perhaps disjointed video segments. Of the three, the fantasy provides the most artistic license, and the production switcher and digital video-effects generator are prominent tools. The onstage performance offers considerable challenge to the audio technician because the music is showcased but still must be produced to conform to the video demands of the program. The narrative format has its timing dictated by the rhythm and pace of the music.

STEREOPHONIC SOUND

One of the most exciting and significant audio developments in recent years has been the emergence of stereophonic sound for television. Stereo not only provides the illusion of depth to the audiospace, but the superior technical components used in its production and playback also significantly improve the quality of the entire audio track. But the effective use of stereo requires additional planning and more care in production and post-production.

Creating Stereo Sound

The audio technician's prime responsibility is to build the audiospace paying special attention to the depth made possible by stereo sound. For example, using stereo, you can build the sound stage on which a group is performing. With the proper miking techniques and console operation, you could "place" the drum kit dead center and behind, with the bass just to the drummer's left. The guitars could be up front, with the rhythm guitar on the right and the lead guitar to the left. On solos, the lead could be brought "center stage," while throughout the singer is centered and made to stand out prominently.

Stereo requires that a sound source be represented by two inputs. In both monophonic and stereo, different miking techniques offer different sound presences. In general, audio is reproduced by (1) a single microphone placement at a distance from the sound sources or (2) by using multiple microphones, with one placement dedicated to each sound source.

Distant Miking   Distant miking is common for recording audio in an acoustically "correct" theater or concert hall. The overall assumption of distant miking is that the environment is an integral part of the musical experience and an effort should be made to capture the resonance, or "life," of the room. The best of distant-miking techniques are represented by a full orchestra playing classical music in Carnegie Hall. In the distant-miking procedure, no more than three microphones placed in front and slightly above the musicians would be used to capture the direct sounds of the instruments and the reverberations of the hall. (See Figure 10-4.)

Close Miking   Since TV studios tend to be acoustically poor and because there often is a high level of ambient noise, a close-miking technique is much more common in studio production. In close miking, each sound source will have a dedicated mike placement. The closer the placement, the greater is the isolation of each sound source and

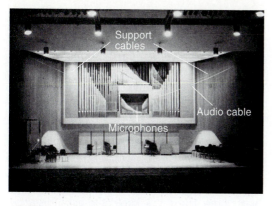

FIGURE 10-4 **Distant Miking.**
In distant miking, two or three microphones are placed in front and slightly above the performers, where the hall's acoustics will provide a balanced mix of direct sound from the performers and the reverberations of the hall.

the easier it is for the engineer to create an effective mix at the audio console. However, each situation is somewhat unique, and you cannot solve your miking problems simply by placing one mike as close to each sound source as possible. The "throat," or quality, of a sound source depends greatly on precise placement. Close miking is always a compromise between a desire to maintain isolation and a desire to fully capture the timbre of sound. (See Figure 10-5.)

The closer the mike is to the subject, the greater is the sound presence, which we perceive as sounding full, rich, close, and intimate. This is so because the ratio of direct to indirect sound waves which reach the microphone is high. When a performer works farther from the microphone, more and more indirect sound waves are picked up and the sound presence lessens. As a result, the sound quality is perceived as distant, thin, and lacking intimacy.

FIGURE 10-5 **Close Miking.**
In acoustically poor locations, close miking isolates the sound sources from the ambient noise, and makes it easier to produce an effective mix at the audio-control console.

A room that is acoustically "dead" absorbs indirect sound waves, preventing them from bouncing off walls and ceilings back into the microphone. Dead rooms, such as heavily carpeted bedrooms, produce close-up audio. An acoustically "live" room, such as a kitchen or bathroom, generally has many smooth wall, floor, and ceiling areas where sound bounces off, indirectly reaching the microphone and affecting the sound presence. In general, television studios tend to be live rooms.

Stereo Miking Techniques   Not only is distance from the sound source important in producing stereo, but the overlap of the the two pickup patterns also influences the overall sound. Stereo recording employs a stereo microphone, which has the two microphone pickups in a single housing, or two separate monophonic mikes. The use of two separate mikes offers the audio technician the most control. There are three general approaches to stereo mike orientation: (1) the spaced technique, (2) the X/Y technique, and (3) the M/S technique. (See Figure 10-6.)

SPACED TECHNIQUE   In the *spaced technique,* two microphones are placed equally far away and perpendicular to the emanating surface of the sound source. The distance between the mikes and the source, the distance separating the mikes, and the pickup patterns of the microphones all will influence the stereo imaging.

If two microphones are positioned incorrectly relative to each other, their signals can be out of *phase.* (See Figure 7-5.) Out-of-phase signals cancel each other out, muting or eliminating some frequencies of the audio signal. This is called *phase cancellation.* You can avoid phase cancellation by following the *3 : 1 rule,* which states that the distance between the two mikes should be at least three times the subject-to-mike distance. (See Figure 10-7.) As stereo grows in popularity, test equipment that shows proper phasing is appearing. One example is the Lissajous scope, which shows an easily interpreted readout of microphone phasing.

X/Y TECHNIQUE   In the *X/Y technique,* two microphones are placed with their heads together but not touching. The angle at which the two mikes come together influences the width of the stereo image.

M/S TECHNIQUE   The *M/S (mid/side) technique* places a cardioid microphone and a bipolar microphone very close together. The cardioid mike will point toward the sound source and provide the direct sound (the M channel). The bipolar

FIGURE 10-6   Stereo Mike Placement.
The three general approaches to microphone placement for stereo recording are (*a*) the spaced technique, (*b*) the X/Y technique, and (*c*) the M/S (mid/side) technique. These are starting points only; microphone placement always involves experimentation to record the "right" sound.

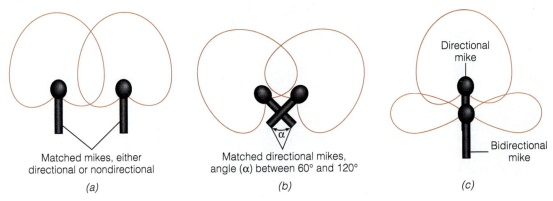

Matched mikes, either
directional or nondirectional

(a)

Matched directional mikes,
angle (α) between 60° and 120°

(b)

Directional
mike

Bidirectional
mike

(c)

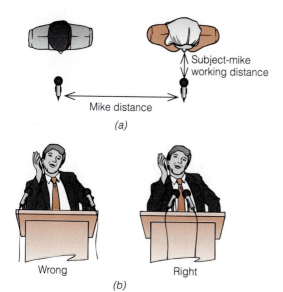

(a)

Wrong   Right

(b)

FIGURE 10-7 **Microphone Phasing.**
Microphone phasing problems occur when two different mikes record the same sound. If the mikes are out of phase, portions of the audio spectrum are recorded at very low levels. By following the 3:1 rule, phase cancellation is avoided. (*a*) The distance between microphones should be at least three times the subject-to-mike distance to avoid phasing problems. (*b*) How to mike a podium speaker to ensure proper audio phasing.

mike receives the reverberant sound (the S channel). The outputs of the two mikes are then combined into a sum and difference matrix, or M + S and M − S.

There are two benefits to the M/S technique. First, the stereo signal can be processed to cancel the side information, doubling the direct sound. This is advantageous for monophonic reproduction. Second, as a stereo source, the engineer has great control, since the relative contribution of the M and S channels can be modified at the board.

The spatial perspective that stereo offers is sometimes a temptation to create artificial positioning, which is called *Ping-Ponging*. As the name suggests, Ping-Ponging occurs when we move various elements across the audiospace or have one character's voice emanate from the left speaker and the other character's voice emanate from the right speaker. When used to excess, this effect can sound like some of the stereo demon-

stration records produced during the early days of high fidelity when bongos would be heard first from the left speaker and then from the right. Most audio technicians who are experienced in working with stereo for television advise against such obvious techniques. They recommend that stereo be used extensively for music and sound effects, but that dialogue be positioned toward the center of the audiospace. Some separation in space improves intelligibility of speech, but drastic separation sounds as if individuals are speaking to each other across a room. Of course, each situation demands an individual approach, but, in general, stereo should be used naturally and not in such a way that it calls undue attention to the panorama effect.

It is crucial for the audio technician who is mixing in stereo to monitor the mix both in monaural and in stereo. Remember that a substantial portion of the audience still receives the sound track monaurally, and there are times when an excellent stereo mix produces a very poor mono track. The secret is to produce an effective stereo track, but not at the expense of the mono version.

TECH TIP *Center-channel pull* describes the tendency of the left and right stereo speakers to create a centered "phantom" speaker. When stereo TV is viewed from the side of the screen, the phantom speaker disappears and the illusion that the voices are coming from the actors on screen disappears. To retain this illusion, most audio technicians recommend recording dialogue in mono, reserving stereo for the ambient background sounds and the music track.

Surround-Sound and Ambience Audio Although stereo offers much more spatial perspective than monaural sound, it still fails to re-create the full perspective you would hear at the location where the sound was originally made. For example, the same song performance will sound different in an intimate nightclub, a concert hall, a movie theater, or your living room. One reason is that each location has its own acoustics, which alters the sound perspective. Two technologies that simulate acoustic differences and produce a fuller sound than stereo are *surround-sound* and *ambience audio*. Used together, they create the most "realistic" television sound available, even if it is just an illusion.

Basically, *surround-sound systems* expand the two-channel stereo signal to five channels. This is done in postproduction with a digital *surround processor* that adds a code called "Dolby Surround" to the original stereo signal. Put very simply, the operating principle is that room acoustics are revealed in the differences between the left and right stereo signals, which are coded and sent out of phase to a pair of rear speakers. This process is based on the concept of *phase cancellation* that we described in Chapter 7. The result is that the sounds coming out of the rear speakers simulate the sound reflections produced at the original location. This process is too complex to describe in detail here, but it is examined in references suggested at the end of this book.

To hear full surround sound, you need a surround-sound receiver or a decoder with Dolby Pro-Logic circuitry, and at least five speakers: three front (left, center, and right) and two rear (left and right). The two front speakers carry the standard left and right stereo sound. The two rear speakers are low power and carry the simulated reflected sound. The center speaker is needed to place sounds such as dialogue onscreen, and is either mono or a sum of the front left and right channels. Usually the center speaker is placed on or under the television screen. Also, a subwoofer may be placed somewhere in the room to enhance the low-end signals.

Another method to simulate spatial perspectives in television sound is *ambience processing*. Basically, it involves digitally processing a signal to create artificial reverberation and sound reflections, which simulate different spatial perspectives. For example, you can choose "stadium" ambience for a football game, or "cathedral" ambience for Mozart's *Requiem*. You can even simulate surround-sound effects from mono by sending ambience signals to the five speakers.

Surround-sound and ambience are controlled

at the receiver. At that point, of course, audio quality control is out of the hands of the audio technician and into the hands of the audience. Surround-sound and ambience processing can be overdone and can seem unnatural, or, if they are controlled properly, can enhance the video image with audiospace that has three dimensions— width, depth, *and* height.

SIGNAL PROCESSING

In Chapter 8 we described several devices that are used to shape and color sound during recording and reproduction. In this chapter we will examine the creative uses of *equalization, artificial reverberation, compression*, and *noise reduction* in audio production.

Equalization

Equalization is used for two basic reasons: (1) to correct for existing acoustical problems and (2) as a creative means of sound modification.

EQ for Acoustical Problems   Despite the audio technician's best attempts, there are times when inferior room acoustics or poor recording situations on location result in sound quality that is less than ideal. For example, on location shooting there is sometimes no way to eliminate the annoying buzz produced when audio lines are run too close to electrical power cable. In this case, a notch filter can be used to cut the 60-Hz portion of the original sound signal to eliminate the hum without unduly affecting the other frequencies of the sound signal. Similarly, a very "boomy" room can sometimes produce a sound quality that is muffled and irritating to the listener. Adjusting the EQ of the sound source by boosting the midrange while attenuating the bass may help to produce a more pleasing sound quality.

Equalization also is useful in matching separate sound recordings produced at different locations or under varying conditions. Acoustic engineers can record a standard reference signal in each room and apply equalization to one or both signals until they match. This EQ setting can then be transferred to the audio tracks recorded in the two locations. For example, re-recording an actor's lines inside the audio studio may have to match dialogue recorded earlier on the set. Equalizing one or both of the sound tracks can disguise this re-recording from the audience.

Although equalization can do some wonderful things in correcting poor-quality audio, it should never be viewed as an all-purpose cure for audio problems. The most important rule of audio is exactly the same as for video: Begin with a high-quality original that exhibits clarity and a high signal-to-noise ratio. Then work from there. Despite the seemingly magical tricks we can play with sound using EQ, there is no way to produce a high-quality sound track from an inferior original through equalization. If equalization is overused, it can produce a thin, unnatural sound that lacks richness and presence. You are far better off changing microphones or experimenting with the subject-to-mike positioning than attempting to improve mediocre sound quality solely through the use of equalization.

Equalization As Creative Sound Modification

The creative application of EQ as a means of modifying original sound to produce a particular sound quality has become a standard procedure for all music recording sessions, and the technique is easily applied to television audio production too. Boosting or cutting certain frequencies can improve the sound of an instrument or vocalist, help to shade or color sound quality and texture, or make a particular instrument or performer stand out more prominently without actually increasing the microphone sound level within the overall audio mix.

As an example, we can add sound presence to thin- or transparent-sounding musical instruments such as the acoustic guitar by boosting frequencies in the 100- to 300-Hz region. We can make a voice-over narrator stand out more prominently from a track that combines music and live "natural" sound by boosting the lower-midrange frequencies between 800 and 2,500 Hz.

It is difficult to provide any hard-and-fast rules concerning the creative use of equalization, since the ultimate sound quality depends not only on the particular sound source you are working with, but also on the interaction of all the sound sources that are mixed together to produce the overall sound track. Most audio technicians begin by broadly

applying some equalization to an individual sound source. Then they refine the EQ by gradually adding more or less at various frequencies until they achieve the desired effect. It is crucial to check the equalized sound source along with all other sources that will be added into the mix to make certain that the combined effect achieves the exact quality of sound desired.

Although creative use of equalization offers tremendous flexibility to the audio technician, as is true with any good thing, too much can cause problems. Not every sound should be equalized, and not every sound source will benefit from equalization. The use of EQ is only one of many techniques the audio technician should use in producing television sound. The proper selection of individual microphones and the positioning of the subject and the microphone can often produce the exact quality of sound desired without the need for additional sound modification. As a general rule of thumb, use equalization sparingly, and when in doubt, use less rather than more.

Equalization in Postproduction   The use of equalization during postproduction multitrack mixing offers the audio technician increased control and creative flexibility in producing the optimum final sound track in which all sound sources are combined to produce the most pleasing and effective final mix. During a postproduction mixdown, individual sound tracks can be further modified both to improve the quality of the original audio and to integrate it better into the final program sound track. The advantage of multitrack postproduction mixing is that various sound problems can be corrected and eliminated and the overall track can be shaped and balanced through equalization and the application of other special audio processing techniques without the entire studio production crew waiting until the audio is perfected.

Artificial Reverberation

Artificial reverberation is frequently used to modify a program's sound for a psychological or emo-

FIGURE 10-8 Digital Reverb/Delay Processor.
(*a*) "Mix" controls the balance between the original "dry" sound and the reverberated "wet" sound. (*b*) The "Program Selector" lets you choose between various room, hall, and other reverb/delay effects. (*c*) The "delay" and "decay" control these variables. (*Courtesy: Lexicon, Inc.*)

tional effect. An announcement enhanced with slight reverberation (a "wet" sound) will be "thicker" and have more impact than a "dry" sound. Unreal settings, fantasies, or dream sequences can be suggested by adding reverb to a narration or voice-over. Reverb also may be used to distinguish between a character's "thoughts" and spoken dialogue. In addition, reverb may be employed to produce a logical sound perspective. If the director shows a performer inside a large, cavernous hall, the sound should reverberate in order to produce the proper sound perspective and to improve the overall illusion. All of these effects can be artificially created with a digital reverb/delay processor. (See Figure 10-8.)

There is a tendency when using a digital reverb/delay processor for the first time to "thicken" the sound too much and make it "spacey" and "dense." The result is that the spoken words may become unintelligible and the music may become muddy. This can be avoided by mixing the "wet" sound with the original "dry" sound until a proper balance is achieved, using the "mix" control on the processor.

Digital reverb/delay processors also may be used with MIDI. Instructions for many different effects can be stored and recalled using a MIDI controller, sequencer, or synthesizer. For example, reverberation settings for different locations can be stored, and as characters change location, new sound perspectives can be created with the push of a button.

Reverberation is commonly used in music recording to enhance the sounds of vocalists and instruments. A popular technique in music record-

ing is known as *automatic double tracking*. A music track is fed through a *digital delay line* and returned to a multitrack unit a fraction of a second later as a second track. Both singers and instruments sound richer, fuller, and more dominant with the right application of this technique. Unfortunately, there are no simple "recipes" to follow in using reverb. The amount and type of reverberation is a matter of the audio technician's taste and judgment. Especially during live recording, reverb should be used sparingly, since you cannot remove or decrease reverb once added. This is one instance where multitrack recording techniques offer a significant advantage. All the individual tracks can be recorded "dry," or without reverb. The reverberation is added later in the mixdown, so the audio technician can experiment until he or she finds the right amount for each channel and not worry about ruining a recorded track by adding too much or too little.

Compression

Compression is very useful in two common situations: (1) when we are faced with a sound source that varies considerably in level and requires constant attention to regulate the signal, and (2) when we wish to make a particular sound source more prominent by raising its level in the overall mix without risking overloading the signal during occasional peaks or bursts of high intensity which would produce a distorted sound.

In the first case, imagine a vocalist who tends to move toward and away from the microphone continually during a performance. The audio tech-

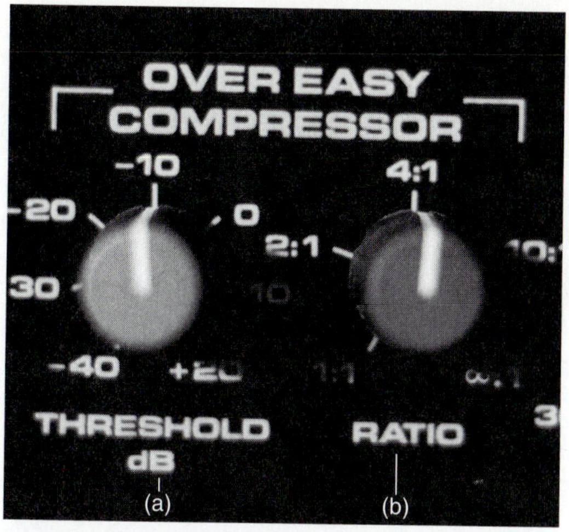

FIGURE 10-9 Compressor Controls.
A compressor limits the dynamic range of sound intensity. (*a*) The "threshold" is the level at which the compressor begins to compress the dynamic range of the signal. (*b*) The "ratio" knob controls how much the signal is compressed above the threshold. For example, if the ratio is set at 4:1, for every 4 dB increase in the input level, there will be only a 1 dB increase in the output level.

nician must constantly ride gain on the performer's mike in order to smooth out these variations and produce a quality sound track. This is possible, of course, but the audio technician is usually so busy with many faders at one time that it is difficult to focus his or her attention completely on the singer's mike. In this case, by feeding the singer's mike through a compressor, it is possible to smooth out these variations automatically and produce a better-sounding track without constantly riding the singer's microphone fader. (See Figure 10-9.)

In the second case, we can use compression to take a sound that is relatively low in level and boost its gain without risking distortion. For example, say we are producing an industrial training tape and we wish to mix in the natural sounds of a factory with narration and music. The factory sounds are generally low in level, but there are occasional peaks which must be smoothed out or we risk distorting the signal. By compressing the track, we can raise its gain, resulting in a more prominent sound, and yet eliminate any sudden

intensity peaks which might result in a distorted signal.

Noise Reduction

A *noise gate* is used to eliminate unwanted background sounds between foreground sounds. For example, distracting traffic sounds in the background of a location interview may be removed, or *attenuated*. To do this a *threshold* level is set on the noise gate, below which all sound is cut off. The threshold level setting must be between the level of the background and the foreground sounds. All sounds below the threshold level will disappear, but any sounds above it will remain. Therefore, if the sound levels of the traffic and the interview are the same, no traffic sounds can be removed. Two additional controls on the noise gate determine how quickly the background sound is removed, and how fast it is returned to normal. (See Figure 10-10.)

FIGURE 10-10 Noise Gate Controls.
A noise gate cuts off unwanted background sounds. (*a*) The "threshold" control sets the level below which signals are eliminated. (*b*) The "change rate" may be set at "fast" or "slow."

Common uses of noise gates are with musical instruments and vocal recording. For example, if you are recording several instruments with a separate mike on each instrument, the sounds of other instruments can be reduced by using a noise gate with each mike. This technique is effective with loud instruments such as drums and cymbals. A noise gate also can be used with a vocalist's mike to eliminate unwanted off-mike sounds that may intrude.

The controls on a noise gate must be set carefully, otherwise the foreground sound will cut out and return unnaturally. The best approach is to start with a low threshold level that lets almost all the sound through, then gradually increase the level until you obtain the desired response. The gating is less noticeable when the foreground sound is eventually mixed with a music bed or sound effects.

AUDIO IN PRODUCTION STAGES

Audio is one of the key elements in any show, and the audio technician is a primary member of the production team. The audio technician's involvement in a production spans all four production stages from preproduction planning through postproduction operation.

Preproduction Planning

As in all phases of television production, the proper care and attention given to preproduction planning will pay off in a smoother technical and creative operation during production. Before the actual production, the audio technician must meet with the program director to determine the audio requirements for the production:

1   *How complex will the audio be?* Interview programs, instructional presentations, and talk shows are usually of low audio complexity and require less crew and setup time. Musical or dramatic programs are usually highly complex and require a larger audio crew, more setup time, and considerable rehearsal.

2   *What kinds of microphones and mounting equipment are necessary?* Can the mikes be seen on-camera, or must they be kept out of camera range? Knowing this will help determine the kinds of microphones you will use and the type of microphone mounting.

3   *Are there any special audio pickup problems?* For example, how much talent movement can be expected? Will some performers have to share a mike with other performers? Will additional mikes be needed to cover other studio areas? If a great deal of talent movement is expected, a boom or wireless lavalier microphone might be the best choice.

4   *Are there any music requirements?* If you will be covering live music, what is the composition of the band or orchestra, and where does the director intend to place them, on-camera or off-camera? Do you need to use prerecorded sound tracks? If so, will special monitoring requirements, such as audio foldback, be necessary?

5   *Are there any special audio effects?* Will you need to use sound effects? If so, will they be live or prerecorded? If they will be live, where will you place the sound-effects technician, and how will you mike the live sounds? Will you need any special electronic effects such as frequency filters, compressors, equalizers, or echo? Which mikes must be used with the special effects? How are the effects to be used during the production? For example, will the effects have to be synchronized with on-camera talent moves, or will they be used in the background?

6   *Miscellaneous audio requirements?* Will the program require an opening musical or sound-effects track and a closing track for credits? Who will select theme music? How long must the theme music run to cover the open and close of the production? Will you have to patch in audio from the film chain, videotape recorder, or remote feeds? How will these audio sources be used during the production? Will you require any special communication system, such as a headset PL to the floor crew, sound-effects technician, or boom operator? Will there be a studio audience? If so, how will it be arranged? Will the audience interfere with audio operations such as boom microphones or cable runs? Will you have to provide micro-

phones to cover audience responses or to pick up audience participants who may speak during the show?

It is extremely important for the audio technician to be thoroughly familiar with the studio and all the audio requirements. If the program is scripted, the audio technician should receive a copy of the script to use to indicate specific audio cues. (See Figures 10-11 and 10-12.) After meeting with the program director, the audio technician usually will meet with the audio production crew to go over specific job assignments, crew responsibilities, and possible problem areas. (The director of the

program does not usually supervise the audio team.)

The Creative Use of Sound   Once the audio technician learns of the specific audio requirements, he or she can begin to plan the sound production. Audio planning involves two related considerations: technical and creative. On the technical level, we would expect, at a minimum, the quality of the audio reproduction to be tech-

---

```
ADIRONDACK MOUNTAIN CLUB

Christine Martin

Page 1 of 1


SFX: CHAIN SAWS & HAMMERS (FULL, THEN UNDER)

HEATHER:     Today more than ever the private lands of the

             Adirondack and Catskill parks face development

             pressures.                                        :10

SFX CROSSFADES TO UPTEMPO MUSIC (FULL, THEN UNDER)

STEVE:       The Adirondack Mountain Club is a

             non-profit organization with goals of

             land acquisition, conservation, recreation, and

             education for New York State.                     :18

HEATHER:     Members of the club work to protect the forest

             preserve for the park users of today and for

             the enjoyment of future generations.             :26

SFX: OUTDOOR SOUNDS (UNDER WITH MUSIC)

STEVE:       As publicly-owned lands, the wilderness beauty

             of the Catskills and Adirondacks can be enjoyed

             through hiking, skiing, canoeing, and

             mountaineering.                                   :35

MUSIC & SFX FADES OUT

PAMELA:      For more information about the Adirondack

             Mountain Club...and how you can help save

             unique and valuable parcels of land from

             development...please write...

             the Adirondack Mountain Club

             P-O Box 8-6-7

             Lake Placid, New York 1-2-9-4-6.

HEATHER:     Your membership pledge and caring are needed.    :57

MUSIC STINGER FULL, THEN OUT                                  1:00
```

FIGURE 10-11
Audio-Only Script.
This is a standard format for an audio-only script. The names of the readers appear in UPPER CASE and **BOLD**; sound effects and music are in UPPER CASE and underlined; and spoken lines are double-spaced in UPPER and lower cases. The spoken lines also are indented one inch from the margin. In this format, the names, music, and sound effects stand out clearly on the page.

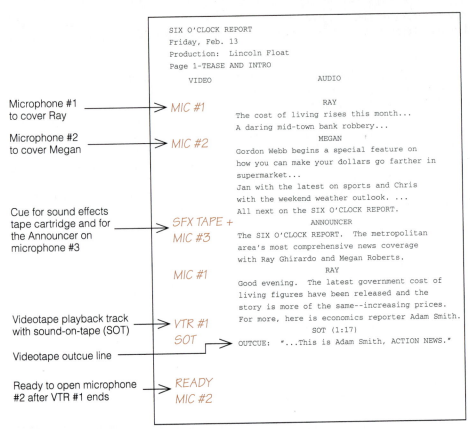

```
                    SIX O'CLOCK REPORT
                    Friday, Feb. 13
                    Production:  Lincoln Float
                    Page 1-TEASE AND INTRO
                       VIDEO                    AUDIO
```

Microphone #1 to cover Ray ——→ MIC #1

RAY
The cost of living rises this month...
A daring mid-town bank robbery...

Microphone #2 to cover Megan ——→ MIC #2

MEGAN
Gordon Webb begins a special feature on
how you can make your dollars go farther in
supermarket...
Jan with the latest on sports and Chris
with the weekend weather outlook. ...
All next on the SIX O'CLOCK REPORT.

Cue for sound effects tape cartridge and for the Announcer on microphone #3 ——→ SFX TAPE + MIC #3

ANNOUNCER
The SIX O'CLOCK REPORT. The metropolitan
area's most comprehensive news coverage
with Ray Ghirardo and Megan Roberts.

MIC #1

RAY
Good evening. The latest government cost of
living figures have been released and the
story is more of the same--increasing prices.
For more, here is economics reporter Adam Smith.

Videotape playback track with sound-on-tape (SOT) ——→ VTR #1 SOT

SOT (1:17)
OUTCUE: "...This is Adam Smith, ACTION NEWS."

Videotape outcue line ———

Ready to open microphone #2 after VTR #1 ends ——→ READY MIC #2

FIGURE 10-12 Marking the Television Script for Audio.
In television production it is common to use a "split-page" detailed script. (See Figure 4-2.) The audio technician can use a copy of the script in this format with a blank "video" column, then mark the audio cues as shown.

nically acceptable. But the audio also must be planned creatively to provide the maximum contribution that sound can make to the show. For example, in the film *The Commitments,* the early music produced by the band is made to sound amateurish, which matches the visuals of its early performances at local social events. Later, as The Commitments develop a tight rhythm 'n' blues sound and play in more upscale pubs, the audio technician records the same songs performed earlier so they sound more professional to match the new surroundings.

As you select equipment and plan its use, you must keep both the technical and the creative considerations in mind. For example, will you need very precise cuing for sound effects or music? If so, cartridges are the best choice. Are the microphones you selected appropriate for the coverage pattern and the material that must be picked up? If you have a choice of equally good frequency responses and pickup patterns, you might consider how the microphones will look on-camera to determine which one you ultimately choose. Are the types of microphone stands you have selected the ones that will give talent the most flexibility during the performance? Are there any ways in which sound can be used to complement the director's visual concept, such as special sound effects, music, or audiospace manipulation?

The point is that with the director preoccupied

with so many production details, the audio technician must serve as both artist and technician. While almost anyone can spot a glaring audio problem, it is only a creative and skilled audio technician who can provide the many subtle audio elements which do so much to help the program's sound fulfill its indispensable role in the production.

Setup and Rehearsal

Television is a team operation, and each crew member should know his or her specific job responsibilities. In an efficient production operation, each production area—audio, lighting, cameras, and so on—should be working simultaneously so that the setup can be completed in a minimum of time. It is vital for the audio technician and crew to most efficiently use the available time to position microphones, check cable connections, set audio levels, and balance audio sources. Division of responsibility and closely coordinated teamwork are the keys to a smooth setup.

During the setup period, the audio technician not only must supervise the activity of the audio crew on the studio set, but also must patch in the correct feeds; identify each fader on the audio-control console; audition all tapes, compact discs, and cartridges; and check all incoming remote feeds, including videotape and film sound track levels.

On the studio floor, all microphone cables should be run neatly around the set, taped to the floor or behind set pieces if necessary, and connected to the proper mike outlet boxes along the studio wall. The audio technician should run through each microphone individually to make certain it has been patched into the correct fader on the console and is working properly. Audio crew members should secure hand and lavalier microphones in a place where they will not be damaged. Booms must be positioned and checked not only for audio but also for compatibility with the needs of the program director and the lighting director. Live sound effects should be checked, and audio levels should be obtained. The audio technician also must test all communications systems with the production crew on the studio floor and, if necessary, with the control-room crew. Finally, the monitor levels in the control

room and studio should be set, checked, and approved by the director or the assistant director. This is particularly important for unscripted programs where there is little, if any, rehearsal time available for a complete run-through before air time.

If there will be a camera rehearsal before the actual production, make a final check on all sound levels, balance, and sound perspective. If multiple microphones are being used, pay special attention that all are operating in-phase.

Production

During the production phase, the audio technician works from inside the control booth, riding levels, cuing discs and tapes, and coordinating the activities of the audio crew on the studio floor. The audio technician has a television monitor which displays the video portion of the program as it leaves the control room. Some studios also provide the audio technician with an additional "preview" monitor, which shows the next video source to be put on the air. The preview monitor is the video counterpart to the audio "audition" system in that it displays the next video source before it is actually placed on the air. This is particularly advantageous if the director will be rolling in a film or videotape segment with an audio track or if the program will use a remote video/audio feed originating from outside the production studio.

Operational Cues   Once the program is underway, the audio technician receives instructions from the director. The following are commonly used operational cues and their meaning:

Open mike: Audio technician should open the microphone fader.

Fade in audio: Audio technician should open the fader and then smoothly pot it up to the proper level. The speed of the fade-in is variable and should be established during rehearsal.

Fade out audio: The opposite of a fade-in. Audio

technician gradually closes a fader. The speed is variable.

Hit music: Usually refers to music on a prerecorded tape, CD, or cartridge. At this command, the director expects the music to come immediately and at full level.

Cut sound (Kill sound): Abruptly cut off a sound. This can refer to a microphone, prerecorded material, a remote feed, or the entire show.

Sneak sound in (or out): Slowly fade in (or out) a sound under existing sound. For example, "Sneak music in under announcer" would mean to fade in music slowly under the announcer's voice.

Sound up and under: Sound should come in at full level and then be faded under for mixing with another sound source which will be dominant. This is often used in conjunction with an announcer.

Segue (pronounced SEG-WAY). Follow one sound immediately with another. This usually refers to prerecorded material, although it also can apply to microphones on different studio sets. A segue means nothing is in the transition between two sound sources.

Cross-fade: Simultaneously fade in one sound source while fading out another. This refers either to prerecorded material or to live sound. The speed of the cross-fade can vary depending on the director's command. This is the audio equivalent of the video "Dissolve."

Dead-roll time (Backtime): Prepare a prerecorded music or sound track so that it will end at a predetermined time. If the director wanted the musical theme of a program to end exactly as the program ended, the audio technician would have to dead-roll the record or tape. This is accomplished by first timing the prerecorded material. Once you know how long the material runs, simply subtract the running time from the clock time when the tape or record should end. The result is the *dead-roll time* when the material

should be started but with the fader closed. At the appropriate time in the program, the audio technician fades in the sound and it will end exactly when the program ends.

For example, a show is scheduled to go off the air at twenty-eight minutes and fifty seconds after the hour. The audio technician has timed the theme, and it runs two minutes and fifty seconds. Subtract the running time from the program's end time:

28:50	(program's end time)
− 2:50	(record's playing time)
26:00	(dead-roll time when record should be started)

At exactly twenty-six minutes after the hour, the audio technician must start the record with the fader closed. When the director calls for the music, fade it in. The record will end just as the director fades out the video.

The only major problem with dead-roll timing is that the audio technician must remember to start the sound source at exactly the right moment. The assistant director should cue you, but it is a good idea to mark the dead-roll time in your script as a reminder.

Postproduction

For a live broadcast, the only postproduction operation is to strike all microphones and audio cables, clear the patch panel, and return the audio-control console to normal. Records and CDs must be returned to the sound library, and tapes and audiocassettes should be erased so they can be reused.

The ATR and Postproduction Sweetening   For productions that are video-recorded for editing during postproduction, audio can play a very important role in the postproduction process. This is especially true when the audio is recorded on a multitrack recorder and *mixed down* and "sweetened" to improve audio quality, adjust the mix of audio levels, and add additional voice, music, and effects tracks to the final stereo or monaural sound tracks.

The use of a separate multitrack audiotape recorder (ATR) combined with a video recorder requires use of the SMPTE time code to synchronize the VTR and audiotape machines precisely. On an elaborate musical program, the program's sound may have been recorded directly onto a multitrack ATR, which was run in sync with the VTR that recorded the program's video. In this case, the existing tracks are mixed together; and EQ, reverb, and other audio processing techniques are applied as necessary to each track until the final mix is achieved.

If the program's audio was not recorded on a multitrack machine, the first step is to strip the original program audio which was recorded on videotape onto a multitrack machine that is run in sync with the VTR using SMPTE time code. After the audio is "laid down" to the multitrack ATR, additional music, narration, and sound effects can be added, or *overdubbed,* to individual tracks. Also, errors on individual tracks can be corrected using a technique called *punch-in/punch-out.* The time code of the audio flub is noted and a cue-in and cue-out point is marked. At the cue-in point, the single erroneous track goes into the record mode and a musician or actor who has been monitoring the track with headphones lays down new audio. At the cue-out point, the track switches back to play. Using punch-in/punch-out, expensive audio tracks with occasional flaws can be saved rather than rerecorded. After overdubbing and error correction, the final set of program tracks exists on the ATR awaiting the final mix.

TECH TIP Occasionally, there are too few available tracks on an ATR to complete a lay-down in a single pass. In a process known as *track bouncing,* the output of a group of the tracks, say, the first six, is rerouted to the console and fed as input onto tracks seven and eight. In the process, tracks one through six again become available for recording.

Once all the individual tracks are laid down on the multitrack ATR, the audio technician and program director work through the mixdown, balancing each track to achieve the final monaural and/or stereo sound track. On very complex mixdowns, a computer-assisted system can remember many of the engineer's decisions and execute them automatically in the final take. (See Chapter 8 for a discussion of automated mixdowns.)

Finally, the mixed multichannel audio track is rerecorded, or *laid back,* in perfect synchronization onto the original videotape.

Digital Audio Postproduction   Much postproduction sweetening and multitrack mixing are being done today in *digital audio postproduction,* using digital audio workstations (DAWs) and digital signal processing (DSP) software. (We briefly described DSP in Chapter 8 and the DAW in Chapter 9.) The DAW converts analog sounds to digital signals and records them either on a hard disk or in a computer's random access memory (RAM). The recordings immediately can be played, or *read,* on the computer and overdubbed, mixed, or processed while preserving all the original sounds on the hard disk. Since the original recording remains unchanged throughout the process, this method is called *nondestructive editing.*

The workstation also may be interfaced with videotape recorders by using a MIDI machine controller (MMC) and SMPTE time code. The video may be seen on its own monitor or in a window on the computer screen along with the audio and MIDI data. (See Figure 10-13.) With this system you can work with very short segments of audio that would be difficult to manipulate as precisely using a multitrack ATR and a video recorder. For example, a sound track on a videotape that you want to equalize (EQ) can be transferred to the DAW and seen as a waveform in a window on the computer monitor. Then you can select portions of the waveform and EQ them graphically. The portions may be any length and have completely different EQ settings. The entire EQed sound track can then be transferred back to the videotape in sync. The final sound track will sound clean and the EQing smooth. It would be difficult and time-consuming to achieve the same results with a multitrack ATR synched to a videotape.

Another common task for the audio technician in postproduction is to add a series of sound effects, music clips, voice-overs, or other short segments to the track. As in production, often this is done with cart machines. Most DAW software can operate like a cart machine, but with several ad-

Video monitor

Mixer

Machine controller

Tablet

Keyboard

FIGURE 10-13
Digital Postproduction Mixing System.
This system, called *Scenaria*, includes a 38-channel mixer, 24-track random access recorder, multitrack audio editor, multiple machine controller, automated routing system, and random access video system. (*Courtesy: Solid State Logic.*)

vantages. Once the segments are stored on the hard disk or in RAM, you can access and play them in any order; you don't have to wait for them to cue up; and their quality will exceed analog cart recordings.

REMOTE AUDIO PRODUCTION

All the equipment and techniques we have discussed in this and the previous chapters on audio apply equally to productions which are produced on location as well as those produced inside a studio. The only difference is that the audio technician's normally difficult job is complicated further by working on a remote location where there are few available controls over the acoustical environment and where there is extraneous noise

and the lack of elaborate built-in equipment normally found inside a production studio. Nonetheless, producing a high-quality sound track that is technically clean and aesthetically effective is just as important when working in the field as it is inside the studio.

Sometimes an audio technician will need to make audio-only remote recordings. For example, natural sound may be needed to enhance a silent film, or interviews may be needed for voice-overs. Usually, audio-only remote recordings will be made on cassette recorders because they are small and convenient to operate. Here are some pointers for remote recording on cassette:

1 Before you leave, make a test recording. It's better to discover equipment problems before you're on the road.
2 Take a pen to label your cassettes and paper to make field notes.
3 Use new batteries, and take extra batteries and an ac adapter or power cord. Use ac whenever possible.
4 Use an external microphone, not the mike built into the recorder. The difference in quality will be noticeable.
5 Take a headset, or at least an earpiece, to monitor your recording in the field.
6 Use the best quality cassette, and take one more than you think you could possibly need.
7 Remember that there is leader at the beginning and the end of the tape, so fast forward into the tape a little, and avoid recording to the very end of the cassette.
8 Break off the "record tabs" after recording to prevent accidental erasure. Don't leave the tabs in the recesses on the cassette.

In general, location production will be remixed during a postproduction session, so the primary goal is to produce a quality audio track that can be processed, manipulated, and ultimately mixed later on. With postproduction in mind, it is always a good idea to record SMPTE time code during the original shoot. Also, a separate ambient noise track should be recorded at high signal strength for future use. Finally, when possible, work with close mike placements for the foreground audio. No amount of postproduction can salvage an inferior original recording.

In Chapter 22 we will discuss the specifics of audio remote production for the three common location production situations: electronic news gathering, electronic field production, and multiple-camera remote production.

SUMMARY

Prerecording audio material is common in television production. Prerecording voice-overs, music tracks for backgrounds and lip syncs, and sound effects are three common techniques.

Sound from multiple audio sources is mixed by adjusting the individual fader controls on the audio-control console until the proper sound balance has been achieved. First the audio technician establishes basic audio levels for each audio input. Once this is accomplished, the engineer varies the signal strength for each source until the mix sounds correct and reflects the proper relationships among the various audio sources.

Prerecording audio material is common in television production. Voice-over, prerecording music tracks, and lip sync are three commonly used techniques. Care should always be taken when recording material for use within a show to make certain the sound perspective and sound presence between the live audio and the prerecorded material match properly.

Music is an important aspect of television sound, and music videos deserve a lot of credit for improving television sound. Aside from its role as a primary element in entertainment programming, music is used for opening and closing themes as well as for background to help establish a mood or atmosphere. Sound effects also are useful in shaping the audiospace and enhancing the visual image. Effects can be produced mechanically inside the studio, but most are obtained from compact discs or tapes that are available commercially. The recorded sound effect can be modified or altered by editing it on tape or by varying the playback speed to achieve a specific effect. MIDI-based audio systems are becoming prominent in the production of sound and sound effects.

A number of special electronic effects are used to manipulate the original sound for dramatic or creative purposes. Equalizers enable the engineer to "color" the sound quality by boosting or attenuating certain frequencies within a sound signal. This manipulation can be used to correct for acoustical problems or to modify the sound for creative purposes. Artificial reverberation enables the audio technician to add "echo" to the original sound to compensate for a "dry" recording studio or to enhance the sound for aesthetic reasons.

Compression permits the audio technician to limit a sound source's dynamic range to smooth out variations in level or to permit the engineer to raise a particular sound source so that it achieves greater prominence in the overall mix without distorting during occasional high peaks in intensity. Noise gates are employed to eliminate or reduce extraneous noise.

The audio technician is a key member of the production team and should attend all major preproduction meetings. Once the audio technician learns about a show's sound requirements, he or she can begin to plan the audio approach from both a technical and an aesthetic standpoint. During setup, the audio technician supervises the activities of the audio crew. During rehearsal and production, the audio technician works the audio-control console, mixing the various sound sources to fashion the program's audio. If the program has been videotaped with the sound recorded on a synchronized multitrack audio recorder, during postproduction the audio technician can remix the sound, "sweeten" it to improve its quality, and add additional audio such as narration, music, or sound effects. Regardless of the opportunity for postproduction sweetening, always strive for a superior original recording with a high signal-to-noise ratio.

The highest quality audio can be maintained throughout postproduction by using digital audio workstations (DAWs). Digital signal processing (DSP) has been made possible by the marriage of audio and computer technologies. MIDI machine controllers (MMCs) with SMPTE time code can interface videotape recorders and DAWs to make audio postproduction cleaner, easier, and faster.

Remote audio production is similar to studio recording, but can be complicated by undesirable acoustics, extraneous noise, and the lack of sophisticated audio equipment usually available in the studio. Audio-only recordings often will be made on cassette recorders because they are small and convenient to operate. Most remote audio will be remixed during postproduction, so the primary goal is to produce a quality audio track that can be processed and mixed later on.

PART FOUR

PART FOUR

The first attempts to create video images took place more than 100 years ago, and were based on the optical, mechanical, and electrical technologies available at the time. Experimental video systems employed imaging devices such as light-sensitive cells, spinning disks with holes punched in them, and even light bulbs. The electronic television technologies used today were developed and refined during the 1920s. In the decades that followed, technical standards for the broadcasting systems in different countries were set by engineers and government regulators, but those standards are rapidly changing today.

During the 1980s there were technical breakthroughs as enormous as those made during television's entire 100-year history. The major advance was in the application of digital technologies to audio and video. Digital production equipment made new techniques possible, especially in video imaging, processing, and editing. Computer microprocessors were incorporated into television production equipment, making new transmission and reproduction systems possible. The 1990s have brought High Definition Television (HDTV), the first new broadcast television standard in thirty years. All of these changes have created new challenges for today's television producers: they must be familiar with both the old and the new systems.

In Part Four we will give you a balanced introduction to the current and the emerging video technologies. The first four chapters provide an overview of video equipment and production techniques. In the fifth chapter we describe how to use them to create high-quality visual images, or *videospace*.

V I D E O   I M A G I N G

Because television essentially is a visual medium, your first priority must be to create high-quality visual images, or *videospace*. Creating videospace involves both aesthetic and technical principles. We discussed the aesthetic principles for creating videospace in Chapter 2. In this chapter we describe the technical principles and explain how video works, beginning with the key concepts that we will be using throughout our discussion of video. The chapter concludes with an overview of computers and their increasing importance in television production.

TYPES OF VIDEO IMAGING

Video images begin as either (1) *camera images* or (2) *generated images*. (See Figure 11-1.)

Camera Images

Camera imaging involves converting optical energy into electrical signals by focusing light onto the photosensitive surface of an imaging device

293

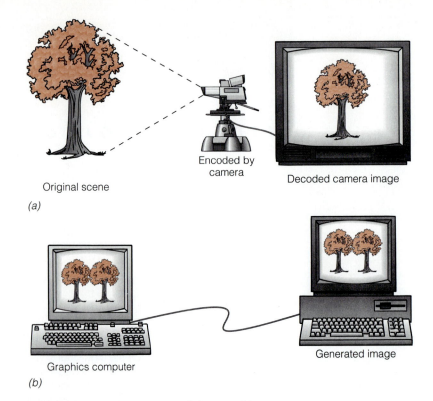

(a)

Original scene

Encoded by camera

Decoded camera image

Graphics computer

(b)

Generated image

FIGURE 11-1 **Camera Images and Generated Images.**
(*a*) Camera imaging: The imaging device in the camera encodes the scene into a stream of electric impulses which become part of the video signal. The monitor decodes the video signal, converting it back to the original image. (*b*) Generated image: The image is generated on the computer with video graphics software. A video card encodes the signal, which is decoded and displayed by the monitor.

in a video camera. The imaging device converts the light into electrical signals. Bright parts of the original image produce a larger charge, and darker parts of the original image produce a lesser charge. These signals are then passed through the video system for processing, routing, and ultimately reproduction into the image we see on one video screen.

Generated Images

The second method of video imaging involves producing electrical signals in the video system itself, using a generating device such as a video synthesizer, a character generator (CG), or a com-

puter system. In this method, the light from an external, "real" image is not converted into electrical signals. Instead, the video images consist entirely of generated electrical signals. However, generated images are not necessarily unrecognizable, abstract shapes. They may look "real," or photorealistic. We will examine this method more closely later in this chapter.

The two video imaging processes can be compared to using microphones and musical synthesizers to create a music sound track. Just as the element in a microphone transduces live music into electrical signals, so the imaging device in a camera transduces light into video signals, and just as a musical synthesizer electronically cre-

294

ates musical tones, so the video generating device creates video signals.

In both imaging methods, the video signals flow into and through the video system; are manipulated, or processed; and finally end up stored on tape or disc, and/or converted back into light, in the form of images on a video monitor or television receiver. (We will explain the difference between a monitor and a receiver later in this chapter.)

During the production process, camera images and generated images may be combined. For example, a newscaster photographed by a video camera may be placed beside a computer-generated graphic on the television screen. In addition, generating devices, or microprocessors, may be built into a video system and used to enhance the shots from video cameras. For example, a digital effects device may be employed to stretch or shrink the subject of a camera shot.

In this chapter we will discuss both camera images and generated images. To understand our discussion, you will need a basic understanding of how video works.

HOW VIDEO WORKS

The way in which video works is a highly complex procedure. Our purpose in explaining this operation is not to make you into a video technician, but to give you a basic understanding of the process, because many production decisions are based on the technical capabilities and limitations of the video system.

Understanding how video works begins with knowing two characteristics about the way you see. The first is an illusion called the *persistence of vision*, which works like this: If a series of photographs separated by black frames is shown to you very rapidly, at a certain point you stop seeing the black frames and you see only the photos. Persistence of vision is a mental process that holds visual information in memory and integrates it with new visual information. It allows us to perceive continuous movement even though we are really watching a series of rapidly changing individual still photographs.

The second characteristic of vision is called the *phi phenomenon*, and is best illustrated by the

"moving lights" on theater marquees or billboard advertisements. The lights are not actually moving, but they create an illusion of motion as they turn off and on in sequence.

The combination of these two illusions results in "motion pictures" like those you may have seen in animated "flip books." These illusions also make possible motion pictures and television.

Although motion picture film and television are two entirely different systems, understanding how film reproduction works is helpful in understanding video. Both motion pictures and television consist of a rapid series of still images with black or blank frames in between the images, during which the images change. If the change is too slow, a flicker, or wavering, in the light results. Early silent films were projected at sixteen or eighteen frames per second, and appeared to flicker. Eventually, when sound was introduced, the motion picture industry standardized the speed of 16-mm film at twenty-four frames per second, which eliminated flicker. Unfortunately, the international television industry did not standardize on one frame rate, and today there are two incompatible systems: twenty-five and thirty frames per second. A third rate—sixty frames per second—will be the standard for some new high definition television (HDTV) formats on the horizon. (We will examine HDTV later in this chapter.)

Scanning and Reproduction

Motion picture film is a chemically-based medium that captures complete photographic frames. If you hold a 16-mm film in your hand, you can see the twenty-four still frames that are projected each second to create the illusion of motion on the screen. Video is different. It consists of a series of photoelectric frames. In this case, light ("photo") is translated into electronic signals ("electric"), which are either recorded as signals on a storage medium—tape or disc—or reproduced on a monitor or receiver. You cannot actually see any video frames on the tape or disc because they are in the form of electronic signals.

Because video can use only one piece of information at a time, its electronic circuitry was designed to break down images into pixel-sized dots.

TECH TIP   *Pixels*, or picture elements, are the smallest possible components of an image. Technically, not all picture elements in video images are pixels. Therefore, we are using the nontechnical word "dot" to refer to these tiny elements in video images.

The image is dissected by an electronic beam that sweeps from side to side, and slices each entire image into a series of horizontal scan lines consisting of the pixel-sized dots. (See Figure 11-2.) It's as though your eye were scanning the lines on this page and picking out the individual letters in every word as you read.

The image could be sliced into any number of lines, but the two most common are 525 and 625. However, it's possible for a video image to consist of more than a thousand scan lines. The number of scan lines gives vertical resolution to the video image, and the number of dots on a scan line gives horizontal resolution to the image.

Resolution   *Resolution* refers to the ability of the

FIGURE 11-2   Scan Lines.
The video image is made up of horizontal scan lines, which you can see if you take a close-up look at the screen.

FIGURE 11-3   Resolution of Magazine Photogaphs and Television Images.
Magazines use more dots to render images (top), and their photographs appear sharper and more detailed than those which appear in television (bottom).

imaging system to reproduce, in clear and sharp detail, all the aspects of the original subject. A high-resolution picture distinguishes fine detail in the subject. A picture with low resolution is incapable of differentiating and reproducing minute detail. The more dots used, the more detailed the image can be, since each individual dot represents less of the total information. Smaller and more numerous dots permit the entire reproduction process to discriminate more subtle differences in the subject. For example, magazines use more dots to render images, and their photographs appear sharper than those which appear in television. (See Figure 11-3.) The more scan lines, the more total dots there will be. Therefore, the overall resolution of the entire video image depends on both the number of scan lines and the number of dots on each line.

Scanning Once the entire image has been dissected into electronic slices, or scan lines, the signals are processed and ultimately sent to a storage medium or a television monitor or receiver. The monitor or receiver's function is to decode the signal and convert it back into the original image.

There are two scanning methods: *interlaced* and *progressive*. (See Figure 11-4.) In both methods the scanning process begins at the upper left-hand corner of the image. From there, the electronic beam moves across the image in scan lines from the top to the bottom, and from the left to the right, turning off between lines. When the beam reaches the lower right-hand corner of the screen, it turns off and returns to the upper left-hand corner, ready to begin again.

INTERLACED SCANNING In *interlaced scanning*, the beam scans every other line as it moves. This pattern is analogous to how a typewriter carriage set for double spacing returns to the left margin, skipping a line each time. The beam scans all the odd lines first, then goes back and scans all the even lines, filling in the rest of the image. Each odd or even set of lines is called a "field," and two fields (one odd and one even) make up one frame. In other words, two fields are "interlaced" to create one frame.

In a "sixty-field system," thirty frames are produced each second. In this case, we say the field rate is one-sixtieth of a second and the frame rate is one-thirtieth of a second (one-sixtieth for the odd lines plus one-sixtieth for the even lines). In a "fifty-field system," twenty-five frames are produced each second. Interlaced scanning is the current type of scanning used to reproduce video images.

PROGRESSIVE SCANNING In *progressive scanning*, the beam does not skip lines; instead, it scans each line in sequence, from the top to the bottom of the screen. (See Figure 11-4.) This is done sixty times each second. Progressive scanning is the type used to reproduce computer images on computer monitors.

Unfortunately, interlaced and progressive scanning are incompatible. That is one reason why normally videotapes cannot be reproduced on computer monitors, and computer images cannot be

reproduced on video monitors or television receivers.

International Standards

Another complicating factor in how video works is that different electronic television systems have been adopted around the world. The three primary international standards are (1) *NTSC*, (2) *PAL*, and (3) *SECAM*. Their main differences are (1) in the number of scan lines, (2) the rate of scanning, and (3) how information, such as picture brightness and color, is encoded.

NTSC Standard *NTSC* stands for National Television System Committee, the industry committee in the United States that devised the system. The NTSC standard has 525 scan lines and thirty frames (sixty fields) per second, and sometimes is called the 525/60 standard. NTSC is the television standard in the United States and Japan.

When television developed in the United States, 525 scan lines was the most practical number that could be used. By the time it was possible to increase the number of scan lines and improve resolution, all the stations in the country, as well as all the home receivers, were already designed for 525-line operation. To change the number of lines would have required extensive retooling of all television studio hardware and home receivers. Since the investment in equipment was too large to consider such extensive modifications, the 525-line system has remained the U.S. standard. Those countries which introduced television later were able to take advantage of the newer technology.

PAL Standard *PAL* stands for "phase alternate line," which refers to the electronic method used to reproduce the image. The PAL standard has 625 scan lines and twenty-five frames (fifty fields) per second. There are modifications of the PAL standard used around the world, including PAL-B, -G, -H, -I, -M, and -N. PAL is the television standard in the United Kingdom, and modified PAL systems have been adopted in parts of Europe, South America, the Middle East, and Africa.

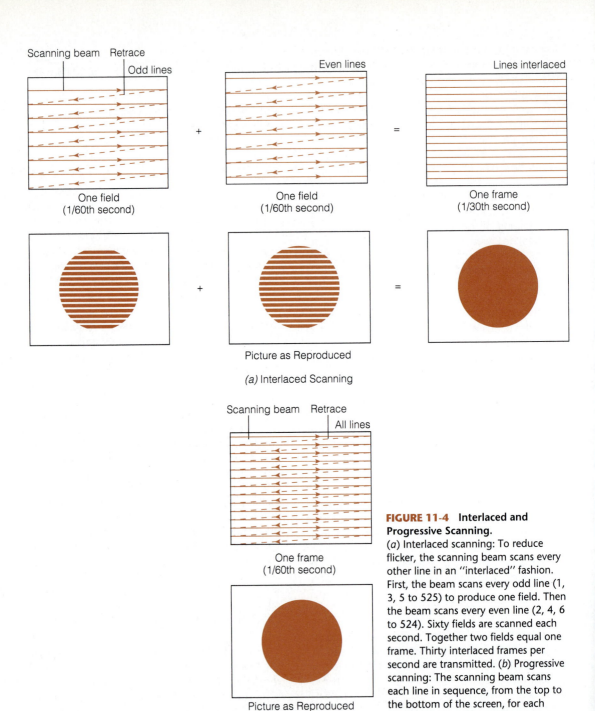

Scanning beam **Retrace**
Odd lines

One field
(1/60th second)

Even lines

One field
(1/60th second)

Lines interlaced

One frame
(1/30th second)

Picture as Reproduced

(a) Interlaced Scanning

Scanning beam **Retrace**
All lines

One frame
(1/60th second)

Picture as Reproduced

(b) Progressive Scanning

FIGURE 11-4 **Interlaced and Progressive Scanning.**
(*a*) Interlaced scanning: To reduce flicker, the scanning beam scans every other line in an "interlaced" fashion. First, the beam scans every odd line (1, 3, 5 to 525) to produce one field. Then the beam scans every even line (2, 4, 6 to 524). Sixty fields are scanned each second. Together two fields equal one frame. Thirty interlaced frames per second are transmitted. (*b*) Progressive scanning: The scanning beam scans each line in sequence, from the top to the bottom of the screen, for each frame. Sixty progressive frames are scanned and transmitted each second.

298

FIGURE 11-5 **Standards Converter.**
This standards converter is capable of sensing and selecting the incoming
international standard automatically, then converts it to a designated standard.
(*Courtesy: CEL Broadcast.*)

SECAM Standard *SECAM* stands for Sequential
Couleur Avec Memoire, which roughly translates
as "sequential color with memory." Like PAL, the
SECAM standard has 625 scan lines and twenty-
five frames (fifty fields) per second, but the SE-
CAM system of encoding color is very different
from PAL. SECAM is the television standard in
France, Eastern Europe, and some countries in
the Middle East and Africa. PAL and SECAM
sometimes are referred to as the 625/50 standards.

Unfortunately, the international standards are
not compatible. This means that videotapes made
in NTSC cannot be played on PAL or SECAM machines. However, this obstacle is being overcome
by (1) standards converters, (2) multistandard videocassette players, and (3) digital HDTV systems.

Standards Converters Digital technology has
made it possible to make cross-standard videotape copies with a device called a *standards converter*. (See Figure 11-5.) There is relatively little
loss in quality; however, because of the differences in the scanning rates, some frames are either dropped or repeated. This can affect the
smoothness of motion in the copy. Also, some
color can be lost in the conversion process.

Multistandard Videocassette Players As global
communication channels have opened up, *multistandard videocassette players*, such as the one
shown in Figure 11-6, have become more common worldwide, including in the United States.
Videocassettes recorded in either the NTSC, PAL,
or SECAM standards may be played on a multistandard player by simply selecting the appropriate standard. The video monitor or television receiver also must be switchable between the three
standards.

HDTV Standards One solution that is likely to
further bridge the international standards gap is
digital HDTV. HDTV is the name given to new technical standards that promise superior color and
sharpness in the video image, approaching the
quality of the image obtained from 35-mm motion
picture film. HDTV is not a single standard, but a
combination of six: one interlaced-scanning and
five progressive-scanning standards. All the sig-

FIGURE 11-6 **Multistandard Videocassette Player.**
Videocassettes recorded in either the NTSC, PAL, or
SECAM standards may be played on a multistandard
player by simply selecting the appropriate standard.

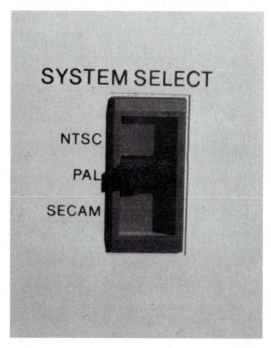

299

nals will be transmitted digitally, which means that present-day home receivers will be unable to decode HDTV signals.

HDTV receivers will have microprocessors built into them that internally and automatically determine the standard of the incoming signal and decode it. For example, on an HDTV receiver you could watch a newscast on one channel with 787.5 interlaced-scanning lines at thirty frames per second (787.5/30), then change the channel to a movie shown at 1,050 progressive scanning lines at sixty frames per second (1,050/60).

The reason for having several scanning formats and frame rates is that it's less expensive to transmit signals with fewer scan lines and frame rates, and some programming may not need the highest quality imaging. Still, the newscast images transmitted at 787.5/30 will look better than those on current 525/60 or 625/50 systems. The much higher-quality 1,050/60 images of the movie would come close to what they would look like in a theater . . . especially if you have a thirty-four-inch or larger receiver with surround-sound audio in your family "home theater."

Since home delivery of HDTV requires the ability to solve a number of complex technological and policy questions, it seems likely that HDTV will be used first as a production medium in the development of top-quality master tapes. These master tapes then will be used to dub copies of the productions onto conventional videotapes. Even though the videotape copies will be limited by the existing number of lines in our current television systems, the ability to produce programs electronically of quality similar to 35-mm motion picture film offers tremendous savings in production costs and greatly expanded flexibility, since all the various electronic methods of processing and manipulating the video signal which we currently employ in television production can be applied in HDTV production as well.

Horizontal and Vertical Blanking Intervals

In our discussion above about scanning and reproduction, we noted that there are two times in the scanning process that the electronic beam turns off completely. Those two periods are called the horizontal and vertical blanking intervals.

Horizontal Blanking Interval (HBI)   During the scanning process the electronic beam turns off each time it reaches the end of a scan line. Then it moves to the beginning of the next line, turns on again, and repeats the process for the next line. The period of time that the beam is turned off is called the *horizontal blanking interval (HBI)*. The reason this happens is so that the beam does not interfere with the picture information on the scan lines as it moves diagonally from the end of one scan line to the beginning of the next line. Normally you wouldn't see any evidence of the HBI in the video image.

TECH TIP   If *horizontal hold* on a video monitor is not adjusted properly, the sweep of the beam will be tilted diagonally on the CRT and the picture will be scrambled.

Vertical Blanking Interval (VBI)   During the scanning process the electronic beam turns off each time it reaches the lower right-hand corner of the image. Then it returns to the top left-hand corner of the image, turns on again, and repeats the process. The period of time that the beam is turned off is called the *vertical blanking interval (VBI)*, or simply *blanking*, and is the period of time between fields in interlaced scanning and between frames in progressive scanning. In the NTSC standard the vertical blanking interval lasts for a period equal to the time it takes to scan twenty-one lines. This means that twenty-one of the 525 scanning lines are blank and are not seen on television receivers. Therefore, no visual information is transmitted during the VBI. However, the video system does use it to carry information essential for the overall operation of the television system. (We will examine some of that information later in this chapter.)

In addition, other data may be carried in the VBI. For example, the signals that provide closed-captioning for the deaf are carried there. Also, when you switch or edit images, these changes occur during the VBI, which is between frames. Normally you should not see any evidence of the VBI in the video image.

TECH TIP   If the *vertical hold* on a video monitor is not adjusted properly, the frames will roll up or down on the CRT with black bars between them. These black bars contain the VBI.

As you could infer from our discussion about scan lines and blanking intervals, the *timing* of the components of video signals is critical to the quality of the video image. For example, if the horizontal blanking interval (HBI) is too wide, portions of the video may be lost. If it is too narrow, there may be unwanted signals in the video. If the timing of the vertical blanking interval (VBI) is too wide, a black bar may appear at the bottom of the picture. If it is too narrow, the entire picture may jump or roll. Therefore, the components of each signal must occur at exactly the right times and at constant rates. This precise timing is accomplished by inserting electrical signals called "synchronization pulses" into the horizontal blanking interval.

Synchronization Pulses

You can think of *synchronization pulses*, or *sync pulses*, as the electronic equivalent of the sprocket holes in motion picture film. (See Figure 11-7.) Without sprocket holes, the film could not move through a projector, even if the individual frames were perfect. Likewise, without sync pulses, television pictures would not be possible, even if all the other electrical information were perfect. Sync pulses keep the electronic beam, scanning lines, fields, and frames moving at constant, proper speeds. There are two types of sync pulses: internal and external.

Internal Sync   Each piece of video equipment generates its own sync pulses, or *internal sync*, along with its picture information and blanking intervals. (See Figure 11-8.) Internal sync is all you need if you have only one source of video plugged directly into a monitor or recorder, such as with a single camera plugged into a videotape recorder.

However, what if you have more than one video source and you want to switch between them, as you would in multicamera studio production? Unless the internal sync pulses of all the video sources occur at exactly the same time and at exactly the same rate, the video signal will be interrupted each time you change between sources and will result in the picture breaking up. There must be perfect synchronization among the various cameras, videotape recorders, video switchers, television receivers, and other equipment

FIGURE 11-7   Motion Picture Film Sprocket Holes and Video Sync Pulses. Sprocket holes are needed to move motion picture film through the projector at the proper rate. Video sync pulses keep the electronic beam, scanning lines, fields, and frames moving at constant, proper speeds.

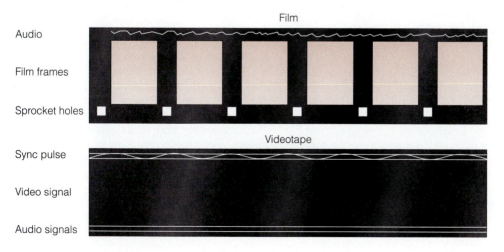

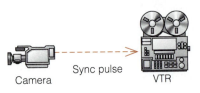

Sync pulse

Camera   VTR

(a) Internal Sync Pulse

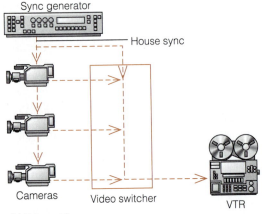

Sync generator

House sync

Cameras   Video switcher

VTR

(b) External Sync

FIGURE 11-8
Internal and External Synchronization Pulses.
(a) Internal sync is generated by each piece of video
equipment, along with its picture information and
blanking intervals. *(b)* To synchronize the entire
scanning and reproduction operation in a video system,
internal sync is stripped and house sync is provided by
an external sync generator. This makes it possible to
change between video sources and maintain a
continuous sync signal and a steady picture.

which relies on sync pulses, for continuous television pictures to be possible. This is achieved by
the second type of synchronization: external sync.

External Sync   *External sync* is a series of electrical timing pulses used to control the entire scanning and reproduction operation in the video system. It is produced by a device known as a sync
generator, short for synchronizing generator, that
provides house sync. The process works like this:
Internal sync is "stripped" from the horizontal

blanking interval of each individual video source.
Then the external sync pulse produced by the
sync generator is "looped" through all the electronic reproduction equipment. (See Figure 11-8.)
Now they all have house sync and operate in uni-
son. Therefore, whenever a change is made
between the video sources, they will be in sync,
and no picture breakup will occur. Ultimately, without the sync information provided by the sync
generator, the monitor or receiver could not re-
constitute the original image produced by the
video sources.

There are three methods to synchronize other
sources to the video system: (1) *genlock*, (2) *frame
synchronization*, and (3) *time-base correction*.

Genlock   An in-house source not normally part of
the video system can be synchronized to it by a
method called *genlock*. To genlock, a reference
composite video signal is needed. This signal has
the video and blanking sync pulses embedded in
one signal. (We will describe other types of video
signals later in this chapter.) The video in the reference composite signal is not used, but the
whole system—including the external source—is
locked to its blanking sync pulses. Any source
with genlock capability can be synchronized with
all the other equipment. For example, a portable
camera may be added to the standard array of
studio cameras. Computers with genlock cards
may be synchronized with composite signals to
feed titles and graphics into the video system.
Once the signals are genlocked, all the sources
will be in perfect sync, and their composite signals
can be fed into the video system through a
switcher.

Frame Synchronization   As television production has ventured farther and farther from the studio, problems in synchronizing various feeds with
in-house video sources have become increasingly
difficult. ENG and EFP feeds are routinely microwaved back to the the station from all over town.
Cameras are run from boats, planes, helicopters,
blimps, and automobiles. Satellite feeds are commonplace as both broadcast stations and cable
systems establish interconnection networks for
news and special events coverage. Until the introduction of the frame synchronizer in 1974, synchronizing these various remote feeds was han-

dled in a variety of ways, none of which was completely satisfactory. The digital frame synchronizer ("frame-sync") unit has eliminated these problems. The frame-sync unit is designed to accept a "wild" (nonsynchronized) feed from any source, convert the signal to digital bits, synchronize the signal with in-house video, and then read out the processed signal in analog form, where it enters the switcher like any other video source. The frame sync unit also has introduced a number of digital production techniques, which we will examine in Chapter 14.

Time-Base Correction *Time-base correction* permits a nonsynchronous signal from a videotape or videocassette recorder to be fed into the video switcher and incorporated into program material. This is performed by a device called a "time-base corrector" (TBC). We will examine time-base correction in more detail when we discuss videotape recording in Chapter 20.

COLOR REPRODUCTION

Up to this point we have discussed scanning and reproduction only as they apply to monochrone, or black and white, television. Although color television uses essentially the same scanning process, the reproduction of color information requires some additional elements in both the scanning and reproduction systems.

The Nature of Color

Before we can talk about the operation of a color system, we must spend a little time discussing the basic properties of color. Visible light is a portion of the electromagnetic spectrum. Our eyes perceive light sources as "white light," although white light actually contains the full spectrum of colors from red to violet. Objects appear colored because they selectively absorb some of the colors of the spectrum and reflect others.

The color of light is described with respect to three characteristics: (1) hue, (2) saturation, and (3) luminance.

Hue *Hue* describes the wavelength of light. In effect, it is the color we see. Red, green, and blue

are known as the primary colors and are examples of different hues.

Saturation *Saturation*, usually referred to in television as *chroma*, is a measure of color purity, or the amount a hue has been diluted through the addition of white light. A 100 percent saturation represents the pure hue with no white light added. For example, 100 percent red is highly saturated and appears very strong and vibrant. Diluting the saturated red with white light produces a weaker, washed-out pink.

Luminance The brightness component of the color is called *luminance* and depends on the amount of light an object reflects. A color with high luminance reflects much light and appears bright. A low-luminance color reflects little light and appears dark.

By presenting combinations of the three primary colors (or hues) in different luminance and saturation levels, we are able to produce any color in the visible spectrum. This is the basic idea behind color television reproduction. (See Color Plate 1.)

In television, color is reproduced using the *additive principle*, which means mixing the three primary colors of red, green, and blue in varying proportions to create every color in the visible spectrum. To illustrate the additive principle, imagine red, green, and blue spotlights which are positioned to overlap slightly along their edges. (See Color Plate 2.) Where the three colors overlap equally, we produce white light. Where two primary colors overlap, a *complementary color* is formed. Red and green produce the complementary color yellow. Green and blue produce cyan. Red and blue produce magenta. An absence of all three primary colors produces no light, or black.

TECH TIP Color can be produced through a subtractive process as well as by the additive process used in television. For example, motion picture film produces color through a subtractive process and relies on magenta, cyan, and yellow as the primary colors.

Color Signals

There are three main forms of color video signals: (1) *RGB*, (2) *composite*, and (3) *component*. They all originate as three signals, one for each of the primary colors—red, green, and blue—and are referred to as RGB signals.

In *RGB* systems the three signals are kept separate all the way from their point of generation to their final display on a monitor that has separate RGB color inputs, referred to as an "RGB monitor." All computers have RGB systems.

In *composite* video systems (VBS), the three color signals are combined, or encoded, and then flow through the system as one signal until they are separated, or decoded, at the color monitor or receiver. This method is the basis for the ways that both NTSC and PAL systems encode color into their signals. Unfortunately, the encoding process loses some information and adds other unwanted noise and distortion to the color. To avoid these problems, component video has been developed.

Put very simply, *component* video keeps the three color signals independent throughout the process, but not in the same way as RGB systems. There are two primary methods of recording component video. One method, sometimes referred to as the "true" component video, keeps the luminance signal (designated by the letter "Y") and two chrominance (C) signals completely separate. The other method, called *Y/C* recording, keeps the luminance (Y) signal separate, but combines the chrominance (C) signals. Although the Y/C system may not be considered "true" component video, it is an improvement over composite video.

Although all broadcast television is composite video, component video has become a popular production format because it has sharper and cleaner color than composite video. Component video also maintains its color quality better than composite video during the editing process.

MONITORING VIDEO IMAGES

During television production, we must make sure that all the components of the composite video

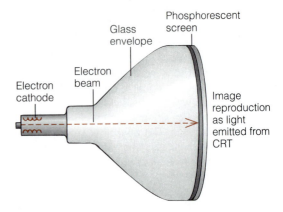

FIGURE 11-9
Operation of the Cathode-Ray Tube (CRT).
The electron grid of the CRT emits an electron beam which is an exact duplicate of the original scanning beam in the camera pickup tube. The beam scans the phosphorescent face of the CRT, which emits light whenever it is struck by the scanning beam. The greater the intensity of the electron beam in the CRT, the brighter the phosphorescent dot glows. Our eyes perceive the rapidly changing dot patterns as complete, moving images.

signal are functioning properly. This is done both visually using *video monitors* and electronically through the use of special equipment, the *waveform monitor* and *vectorscope*.

Monitors and Receivers

The heart of the *video monitor* is the cathode-ray tube (CRT), commonly called the "picture tube." It is a sealed, glass tube, which has a narrow "neck" at one end and a wider, flat "tube face" at the other end. The inside of the tube face is coated with a phosphorescent material that glows when an electronic charge strikes it. (See Figure 11-9.)

Electrons are focused into a beam and accelerated, or "shot," from the neck toward the tube face. The beam is deflected by magnetic fields surrounding the neck so that the beam scans lines across the tube face. Sync pulses in the signal coordinate this scanning process.

Pixel-sized dots in the scan lines on the tube face are struck by the beam, and they glow. The brightness of the glow is directly proportional to the intensity of the signal produced during the reproduction process. A strong signal causes a very bright glow, while a weaker signal causes a dimmer glow or no glow at all. The result is a replica of the original video or computer image. If the original was a moving image, because of the persistence of vision and the phi phenomenon, we perceive the changes in the glowing dots as the motion of the original image.

Color CRTs

Instead of using a single electron beam as in monochrome, the *color CRT* has three, one for each of the primary colors—red, green, and blue (RGB). On the phosphorescent surface of the tube face, each dot is made up of three pixels in the RGB colors. (See Color Plate 5.) When struck by electrons from the beams, the RGB pixels glow in their respective colors. The varying intensities of the three pixels create the hues that you see on the screen. When all three pixels glow simultaneously and with equal strength, the RGB triad appears to be white. When only a single pixel glows, that primary color is generated. If two pixels glow together in combination, a complementary color is formed. For example, when the red and blue pixels glow with equal intensity, yellow is formed.

Approximately one million RGB pixels are arranged in these triad dots across the face of the tube. If you look closely at a color CRT in operation, you can see the many dots which make up the overall picture. However, at normal viewing distances, the closely spaced dots blend together and display a smooth color image.

The RGB color system is "compatible" with monochrome monitors because they simply ignore the color information and use the luminance signal to reproduce the picture in black and white.

The CRT also is at the heart of television receivers and computer monitors, as well as the video monitor. However, all three display devices are incompatible. In other words, you cannot normally show a video image on a television receiver, or a television picture on a computer monitor, or a computer image on a video monitor. The reasons for this incompatibility will become clear as we examine each display device.

Video Monitors

Video monitors have interlaced scanning, as illustrated in Figure 11-4. However, they can accept only video signals fed over a video cable from the output of a video system or

piece of video equipment. They are unable to receive a broadcast or cable television channel.

Television Receivers

Television receivers also have interlaced scanning, but they are unable to display video signals unless they are modulated on a radio frequency (RF) channel, then transmitted to the receiver. The modulated signal also will include FM (frequency modulated) audio signals accompanying the video.

RF modulation may be achieved by a broadcast transmitter, a cable television system, or a device called an "RF modulator." You are able to play back videocassettes on a videocassette recorder (VCR) and see them on a home receiver because the VCR contains an RF modulator that outputs combined video and audio signals on a channel (usually Channel 3 or Channel 4). A tuner, or demodulator, in the receiver then picks up the modulated signals and converts them back into separate video and audio signals that are sent, respectively, to the CRT and to the speakers in the receiver.

Computer Monitors

Normally, neither video signals nor television channels can be displayed on computer monitors. Nor can computer images be reproduced on video monitors or television receivers. We will examine the incompatibility later in this chapter.

Although we can tell a lot about the video signal from a good quality monitor, it's a mistake to use a monitor alone. It is unable to provide any information about the signals we cannot see, such as sync pulses and blanking intervals. The two most common means to observe these signals are with the *waveform monitor* and the *vectorscope*.

The Waveform Monitor

The primary device used to observe video signals, match the signals from different video sources, and provide additional information about the video signal is the *waveform monitor (WFM)*. (See Figure 11-10.) It performs the role in television production that the volume unit (VU) meter performs in audio production. You may think a WFM looks compli-

Video monitor

Vectorscope

Waveform
monitor

Video switcher

FIGURE 11-10   **Monitoring Video Signals.**
The three primary means to observe video signals are
(*a*) the video monitor, (*b*) the waveform monitor,
and (*c*) the vectorscope. All three will commonly be
found in control rooms and editing suites. (*Courtesy:
Tektronix, Inc.*)

cated, but you need no technical training to be
able to "read" one.

The WFM is an oscilloscope, or a screen on
which electronic signals are graphically displayed. There are two scales marked on the
screen. (See Figure 11-11.) The first scale, in IRE
units from −40IRE to 100IRE, appears on the vertical axis. This represents the total composite
video signal.

TECH TIP   IRE stands for the Institute of Radio Engineers, the first broadcast engineering group.
One IRE represents one percent of the difference
between the 0IRE and 100IRE.

A second scale, in microseconds, is shown on
the horizontal axis. It is used to measure the timing
of the components of the electrical signals.

This is how the WFM works in its standard
mode, called the 2H display: A graphic representation, or waveform, of the electronic signal is displayed on the face of the tube behind the scales.
(See Figure 11-11.) Amplitudes, or levels, of components are shown on the vertical axis, two scan
lines at a time. The area of the display from
−40IRE to 0IRE represents the sync signals, and
the area between 0IRE and 100IRE represents
active video, which is what we can see on the
video monitor.

Three key levels on the display are 0IRE, the
blanking level; 7.5IRE, the reference black level;
and 100IRE, the reference white level. Active
video should appear between 7.5IRE and 100IRE.
These levels represent the blackest black and the
whitest white in the video image. If the bottom level
of the video is lower than 7.5IRE, all detail in the
dark areas of the image will be lost. If the bottom
level of the video is too high, there will not be
enough contrast, and the image will look gray and
washed out. If the top level of the video is above
100IRE, the image will "bloom," "glow," or be
"clipped." In addition, if the video level is above
120IRE a buzz can be heard in the audio signal.
If the top level of the video is too low, the image
will look dull.

Each component of the composite video signal
has its own name and location on the waveform.
Figure 11-12 shows and defines the main waveform components: (1) reference black level, (2)
reference white level, (3) horizontal blanking, (4)
the front porch, (5) the sync pulse, (6) the breezeway, (7) the color burst, and (8) the back porch.

Although the WFM is used primarily to observe
monochrome components of the video signal, it
also can tell us some basic information about the
color encoding.

First, we can see whether there is any color at
all. If color is encoded, there will be a color burst
on the waveform of the signal. (See Figure 11-13.)
Next we can tell if the color is weak or strong by
looking at the size and shape of the color burst. It
should rise from −20IRE up to +20IRE and be
fairly rectangular. If not, the color signal will be
weak and the color could be lost or improper.

The WFM also displays information about two
color characteristics: *luminance* and *chroma*. *Luminance* is the brightness component of the color.
Luminance amplitude should not exceed 100IRE.

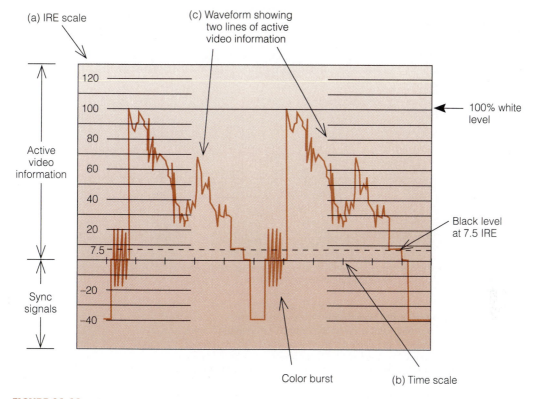

(a) IRE scale

(c) Waveform showing two lines of active video information

100% white level

Black level at 7.5 IRE

Active video information

Sync signals

Color burst

(b) Time scale

FIGURE 11-11 **Waveform Monitor Scales.**
The waveform monitor has two scales: (*a*) The first scale appears on the vertical axis and represents the total video signal in IRE units from −40IRE to 100IRE. (*b*) The second scale appears on the horizontal axis and measures the timing of electrical signal components in microseconds. (*c*) The waveform is a graphic representation of the total video signal displayed on the face of the tube behind the scales. The area of the display from −40IRE to 0IRE represents the sync signals, and the area between 0IRE and 100IRE represents active video, which is what we can see on the video monitor.

To observe the luminance level in a system, a test signal called "NTSC color bars" can be used. (See Figure 11-13.) It includes a white bar on the left. When color bars are input to the WFM, a flat horizontal line representing the luminance level of the white bar appears at 77IRE (or 100IRE on some color bar test signals). There also is a black bar on the right, and a flat horizontal line representing the black level appears at 7.5IRE. (See Figure 11-13.)

Chroma appears in this test signal on the waveform as six vertical stripes coinciding (from left to right) with the yellow, cyan, green, magenta, red, and blue color bars. The tops of the first two stripes, representing yellow and cyan, should peak at 100IRE, and the bottom of the third stripe, for green, should rest at 0IRE. (See Figure 11-13.) If chroma levels are set properly, there will be just the right amount of color saturation in the image. If the stripes are compressed toward 50IRE, it means there is less chroma and the color in the image will look washed out. Unlike luminance, chroma levels may go above 100IRE and below 0IRE. However, if they extend too far, the colors will become oversaturated and look too bright.

While the WFM is adequate for observing these

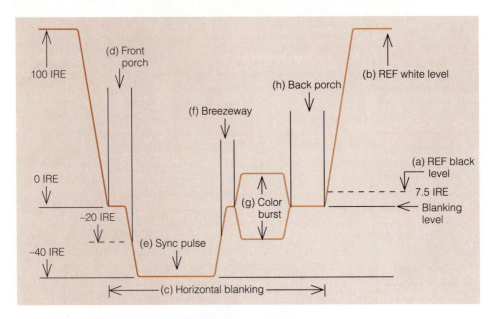

FIGURE 11-12 Components of the Waveform.
(*a*) **Reference black level** is 7.5IRE, and is called the "setup" or "pedestal" level. This should be the bottom level of the darkest part of your image. (*b*) **Reference white level** is 100IRE. This should be the top *luminance* level, or the brightest part of the image. (*c*) The **horizontal blanking** period is the time from the start of the front porch to the end of the back porch, or the period between fields. Both the synchronization pulse and the color burst also are within the horizontal blanking width. (*d*) The **front porch** is the slight distance within horizontal blanking between the end of the active video signal and the beginning of the synchronization pulse. (*e*) The **synchronization pulse** level should be at −40IRE. If it is not, the video system will not operate properly. Correcting a sync problem is a job for the video technician. (*f*) The **breezeway** is the slight distance between the synchronization signal and the color burst. (*g*) The **color burst** should be from −20IRE to +20IRE and fairly rectangular. If not, the color could be lost or improper. (*h*) The **back porch** is the slight distance within horizontal blanking between the end of the color burst and the beginning of the active video signal.

basic characteristics of color signals, a more detailed view requires another monitoring device called a *vectorscope*.

The Vectorscope

The *vectorscope* is the primary device used to observe the color in a video signal and match the signals from different video sources. (See Figure 11-14.) It is round like a clock, with a circular scale in degrees. Six boxes are marked inside the scale, with a smaller "window" inside each box. The

boxes are labeled for the six colors on the NTSC color bars test signal.

The vectorscope displays a graphic representation of the color in a video signal. (See Figure 11-14.) There are six interconnected lines of light, called "vectors," which represent the six colors. A separate short vector line extending from the center represents the color burst.

When color bars are input to the vectorscope, and the color burst vector is positioned at nine o'clock, a dot at the tip of each interconnected vector should fall inside the window in each ap-

(a)

Color
burst

(b)

FIGURE 11-13   NTSC Color Bars Test Signal on the Waveform Monitor.
(a) The test signal. (b) The test signal as it appears on the waveform monitor.

FIGURE 11-14 Vectorscope Scales and NTSC Color Bars Test Signal.
The vectorscope displays a graphic representation of the color in a video signal
inside a circular scale in degrees. Six boxes are marked inside the scale, with a
smaller "window" inside each box. The boxes are labeled for the six colors on the
NTSC color bars test signal. Six interconnected vectors represent the six colors on
the test signal. A separate short vector line extending from the center represents the
color burst.

propriate box. This represents a color image with
the proper chroma levels and proper hue. If the
chroma level, or chominance, is too high, the dots
will extend beyond the boxes. If it is too low, the
dots will fall toward the center, inside the boxes.
(We pointed out the results of improper chroma
levels when we discussed the waveform monitor.)
If the hue is improper, the dots will rotate clockwise or counterclockwise outside of the boxes.
This means that colors will be shifted in the image.
For example, faces might have a green tinge to
them or trees might look bluish.

The vectorscope also is used to synchronize the
color burst phasing between multiple video

sources. This must be done so that the colors and
the timing are consistent between sources.

COMPUTERS AND VIDEO

We are focusing our discussion about generating
video images on the computer because it is at the
heart of noncamera image generation today. Without computers it would not be possible to create
most of the exciting graphics and special effects
we see every day in motion pictures and on television.

During the 1980s computer graphics and computer-assisted editing began to change the visual style of television productions. Today computer generated imaging is used widely in a variety of applications such as computer graphics, titles, paint systems, digital video manipulation, three-dimensional animation, and nonlinear editing. We will examine all of these applications in the chapters which follow.

One reason for the growth of computers in television production is that high-quality computer imaging for video no longer requires large, expensive computers. Instead, relatively inexpensive but powerful personal computers (PCs) can be used.

Computer-to-Video

The five primary considerations when using a computer in video production are its: (1) *platform*, (2) *power*, (3) *speed*, (4) *capacity*, and (5) *interface*.

Platform   Sometimes the word *platform* is used simply as a synonym for "computer." For example, you will hear references to the "Amiga platform" or the "Mac (Macintosh) platform." Technically, "platform" refers to the combination of a computer's central processing unit (CPU) and its operating system software, which together determine how the computer processes data and performs its operations.

Each computer manufacturer uses a different operating system. For example, Commodore uses AmigaDOS in the Amiga computer and Apple uses System 7 in the Macintosh. Both of these operating systems are proprietary and neither company will permit other computer manufacturers to install them. In contrast, IBM has licensed its operating systems to other companies, and it has two platforms—MS-DOS and OS/2—for IBM-PCs and IBM-PC-compatibles.

Unfortunately, none of these operating systems are compatible. Normally, data and graphics created on one platform cannot be reproduced on any of the others. For example, if you want to use Avid's "Media Suite Pro," for computer-controlled video editing, you must have the Mac platform. The editor "Lightworks" runs on the IBM-PC MS-DOS platform, and the "Video Toaster" uses the Amiga platform.

Power   When someone refers to how "powerful" a computer is, they usually mean how many bits of information its CPU can handle at one time. The more bits, the more powerful, and the larger the amount of information the computer can handle. For example, a 32-bit CPU is more "powerful" than a 16-bit CPU.

Speed   Although a number of factors are involved, the *speed* of a computer is determined by a "clock" that synchronizes all its operations. Instead of minutes and seconds, the computer clock is measured in megahertz (MHz), or millions of cycles, per second. Most PCs operate between 15 MHz and 50 MHz. The higher the number, the "faster" the clock, and the "faster" the computer.

Capacity   The overall *capacity* of a computer is a combination of the capacities of its hard disk and its random access memory (RAM). The hard disk is the storage medium and usually is mounted permanently in a "drive" inside the computer casing. The disk capacity is given in *bytes*, with each byte consisting of eight bits of information. It is common today for hard drives to have capacities of more than 100 megabytes (Mb). RAM is temporary memory where programs and information are stored while you are using the computer. Like disk capacity, the amount of information you can store in RAM is given in bytes. It's common today for PCs to have from 4 Mb to 8 Mb of RAM. In both cases, the more bytes, the better, because you can run more complex programs, work with larger amounts of data, and store more information.

Interface   There are a number of technical obstacles to overcome when you use a computer to produce graphic images for video. Figure 11-15 lists the major differences between NTSC composite video images and computer images.

The mere fact that video images are reproduced by interlaced scanning and computer images by progressive scanning is enough of a barrier between the two signals. However, the other differences listed in Figure 11-15 also create prob-

FIGURE 11-15   Major Technical Differences between NTSC Composite Video Images and Computer Images.

	NTSC COMPOSITE VIDEO IMAGE	COMPUTER IMAGE
Type of Scan Lines	Interlaced	Progressive
Horizontal Scan Rate	15.734 kHz	No standard rate
Frame Scan Rate	29.97 per second	No standard rate
Field Scan Rate	59.94 per second	No standard rate
Pixel Shape	Rectangular*	Square
Resolution	640 × 480*	Up to 1,280 × 1,024
Screen Scan	Overscanned	Underscanned
Color Encoding	In 1 signal	In 3 signals

*Assumes a digital video signal and 4:3 image aspect ratio.

lems that show up on the screen in five areas: (1) resolution, (2) screen scan, (3) flicker, (4) signals, and (5) color.

RESOLUTION   Generally, the *resolution*, or sharpness, of computer images is better than that of video images. At their best, computer images have almost twice the resolution of video images. The reason is that, in general, computers have more scan lines, more pixels, and faster scanning rates than video.

Resolution for computer images is given as the number of horizontal and vertical pixels. For example, 1,280 × 1,024 refers to a computer image 1,280 pixels wide and 1,024 pixels high. However, computers have no single standard for the number of pixels, or for scan lines or scanning rates for that matter. Instead, display cards are inserted to give a computer a level of resolution. Figure 11-16 lists some computer display cards and their resolutions. For comparison, the resolution of video generally is considered to be 640 × 480 pixels, or the equivalent of the maximum Video Graphics Adapter (VGA) resolution.

Another difference that can affect resolution is the fact that computers have square pixels and video does not. Some video pixels may be rectangular, but they cannot be manipulated as easily or cleanly as square pixels. Therefore, the digital signals of computers would be distorted if input directly to digital video systems.

SCREEN SCAN   Usually, computer images are underscanned and video images are overscanned. (See Figure 11-17.) That is why you see black borders on a computer monitor, but not on a video monitor, unless intended.

FLICKER   Narrow horizontal lines in computer graphics would appear to "flicker," when used in video images. This is because computer images are progressively scanned and video images have interlaced scanning. Progressive scanning fills in each line in sequence, and nothing is missing, but interlaced scanning skips every other line, then fills them in. Therefore, narrow horizontal lines

FIGURE 11-16   Selected Computer Display Cards and their Maximum Resolution.

	Maximum Number of Pixels	
DISPLAY CARD	HORIZONTAL	VERTICAL
Colorgraphics Adapter (CGA)	640	200
Extended Graphics Adapter (EGA)	640	350
Video Graphics Adapter (VGA)	640	480
Super VGA	1,024	768
Graphics Workstation	1,280	1,024

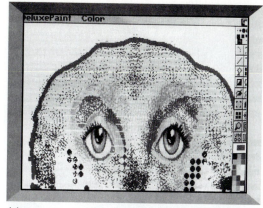

(a)

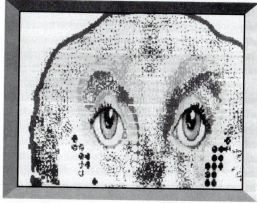

(b)

FIGURE 11-17 **Underscanned and Overscanned Computer Images.**
(a) Usually the computer image is underscanned and the borders are visible. *(b)* To eliminate the borders when a computer image is converted to video, the image must be overscanned.

could disappear and return rapidly, creating a flickering effect. To eliminate this problem, deflicker devices are available.

SIGNALS The composite video system combines all color information into one signal. However, computers keep all RGB signals separate. Therefore, the computer RGB signals can be controlled more precisely.

COLOR This is the one place video may win out. Video offers a wide range of colors, but most PCs will have narrower ranges to offer than video.

The technical barriers between computer and video imaging can be overcome by a number of devices: (1) video display and genlock cards, (2) scan converters, (3) video input/output cards, (4) the Amiga and Video Toaster, (5) video workstations, and (6) digital HDTV.

Video Display/Genlock Cards *Video display cards* are devices that can be installed inside computers to convert their output to interlaced-scanning images. All display platforms now have video display cards.

In addition, for computers to be incorporated into video systems, they must be able to genlock to the system. Genlock cards are available, and many video input/output cards include the genlock function.

Scan Converters External *scan converters* can be connected between a computer and a video system and used for the same purpose as video display cards. (See Figure 11-18.)

Video Input/Output Cards *Video input/output cards* are designed to provide a two-way interface between the computer and video. The forerunner of the video input/output card was the frame buffer. Essentially a *frame buffer* is a device that digitizes video signals in real time and stores them in its own memory. This information can then be transferred to the computer's hard disk or converted back to analog signals and recorded on videotape. At a certain point, frame buffers were put on cards that could be installed inside the computer. One of the first was AT&T's *TARGA* series. Today there are a number of commercial video input/output cards that act as frame buffers and more.

FIGURE 11-18 **Scanning Converter.**
A scanning converter transfers signals between video systems with different numbers of scan lines.

The Amiga and Video Toaster An exception to
the difficulties of transferring images between
computers and video systems is Commodore's
Amiga, which was specifically designed to interface with video systems. For example, the Amiga
normally outputs images that have interlaced
scanning, overscanning, and analog rather than
digital outputs. A card for the Amiga called the
Video Toaster is capable of performing many
functions of traditional video production, in addition to generating computer graphics. (See
Figure 11-19.)

FIGURE 11-19 Video Toaster.
The *Video Toaster* is a card for the Amiga computer. It is
capable of performing many functions of traditional
video production, in addition to generating computer
graphics.

FIGURE 11-20 Video Workstation.
A video workstation is able to generate digital video
effects (DVE), operate paint systems, and create three-
dimensional animation. (*Courtesy: KGTV-TV.*)

Video Workstations A *video workstation* is a
huge frame buffer controlled by a PC that does
the work of a video editing suite. It can record,
process, edit, and reproduce television programs
using a computer instead of the traditional video
switcher and editing controller. A high-end video
workstation also will be able to generate digital
video effects (DVE), operate paint systems, and
create three-dimensional animation. (See Figure 11-20.)

Digital HDTV The *digital HDTV* standards
agreed to by the television industry include both
scanning techniques. Decoders in HDTV receivers will read the incoming signals to determine
whether they have interlaced or progressing scanning. This means that HDTV receivers can be
used for both television and computer images.

Video-to-Computer

In addition to all the differences already noted,
there are two more hurdles in converting video to
computers. The first is that video is made up of
analog signals and everything in computers is digital. However, that obstacle was overcome with the
analog-to-digital converters that have made digi-

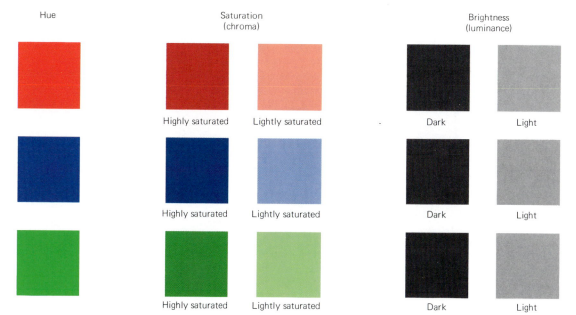

Hue	Saturation (chroma)		Brightness (luminance)	
	Highly saturated	Lightly saturated	Dark	Light
	Highly saturated	Lightly saturated	Dark	Light
	Highly saturated	Lightly saturated	Dark	Light

COLOR PLATE 1 **Hue, Saturation, and Brightness.**

Hue refers to the tint of the color. *Saturation* (sometimes called "chroma") refers to how much or how little white light is mixed in. The square on the left is highly saturated with the pure hue and no white. The lightly saturated square shows how the same hue would appear when mixed with white. *Brightness* (or *luminance)* values show how the colors in the second column will reproduce on a black and white receiver.

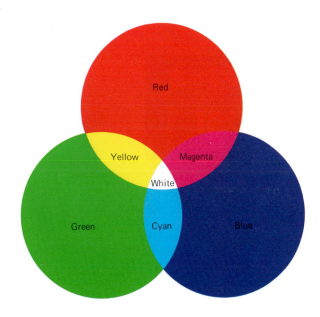

COLOR PLATE 2 **Additive Property of Color Light.**

When two of the three primary colors of light are combined, they produce a complementary color. Equal amounts of the three primary colors produce white. Any color in the spectrum can be created by combining the primary colors in varying degrees of hue, saturation, and brightness.

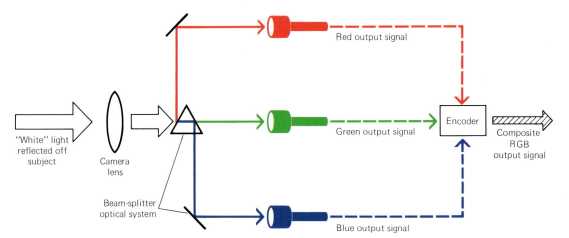

COLOR PLATE 3 **The Color Camera.**
The light reflected from a subject contains many colors in varying combinations of hue, saturation, and brightness. The light is collected by the camera lens and focused onto a beam-splitter optical system, which dissects the "white" light into the three primary colors and sends each color to the respective pickup tube. The electronic output of each tube is fed into an encoder, which combines the three color (chrominance) signals with a brightness (luminance) signal to produce a composite video signal.

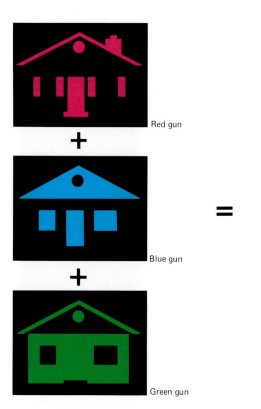

Composite color image

COLOR PLATE 4 **Operation of Three-Gun Color Camera.**
Each of the three primary color pickup tubes reproduces only that part of the actual picture which contains its color. In this illustration, the images from the red gun, blue gun, and green gun are combined to produce the composite, full-color image.

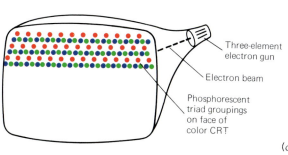

Three-element electron gun

Electron beam

Phosphorescent triad groupings on face of color CRT

Color CRT operation

(a)

CRT electron gun

Electron beam

Close-up of single phosphorescent color triad group

(b)

COLOR PLATE 5 Color Cathode-Ray Tube.
The top illustration shows how a single triad group of red, blue, and green phosphors is made to glow when struck by the CRT electron beam. The lower diagram shows the configuration of triad groups as they appear on the face of the CRT.

COLOR PLATE 6 High-Definition Television.
(a) Photograph shot off a 525-line monitor showing limited resolution and discernible scanning lines; *(b)* photograph of the same subject shot off a high-definition monitor using 1,125 scanning lines showing much higher resolution and improved color.

(a)   *(b)*

Color reproduction   Monochrome reproduction   Color reproduction   Monochrome reproduction

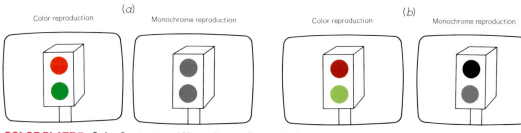

COLOR PLATE 7 Color Contrast and Monochrome Reproduction.
(a) The reproduction of the traffic light in color appears normal, but the same picture on a monochrome receiver shows two lights of identical shades of gray because the brightness of the red and green lights is equal. *(b)* The green light is brighter than the red light, so it appears lighter on the black and white TV set.

COLOR PLATE 8 Paintbox in Freehand Mode.
Paintboxes can reproduce images drawn freehand. The artist can use a "brush" of varying thickness for drawing. *(Courtesy: Ampex Corp.)*

COLOR PLATE 9 Paintbox in Geometric Mode.
Paintboxes also have a geometric mode, which uses geometric shapes as building blocks for constructing images. These shapes are easily colored, moved, and resized as needed by the artist. *(Courtesy: Ampex Corp.)*

tal video possible. The second hurdle is that re-cording digital video images requires enormous amounts of computer memory. That obstacle was overcome by a technique called *compression*, which reduces the memory capacity needed.

Today computers with video input/output cards, and sufficient memory, are able to digitize live video images, record them on a computer disk or recordable optical videodisc, and reproduce them on a computer monitor. There are a number of production applications for this process. For ex-ample, images from videotapes, still video cam-eras, or copystand video cameras can be "grabbed" and saved as still images, then used later during productions. Videotapes can be put into computer "windows" in nonlinear editing sys-tems. For example, Apple's QuickTime "movies" can be used on Macintosh computers for this pur-pose. Also, digital video interactive (DVI) technol-ogy makes it possible to view video clips from CD-ROMs in Microsoft's Video for Windows on IBM-PCs. (We will discuss still image systems in Chapter 16 and nonlinear editing in Chapter 23.)

Tapeless Video Systems

The final step in "computerized video" is the broadcast quality all-digital *tapeless video sys-tem*. It consists of three parts: (1) a *digital camera*, (2) *digital storage media*, and (3) a *computer workstation*.

Digital Camera   Unlike traditional video cameras that output analog signals, a *digital camera* trans-duces images directly into digital video signals.

Digital Storage Media   The digital video signals may be recorded on either a hard disk or a re-cordable videodisc storage medium. Recording on disk requires a fast computer with enough RAM and disk capacity to record the enormous amount of information contained in the video signals. A rewritable optical videodisc can record about

FIGURE 11-21   "Tapeless" Video Production. Producer Scott Billups has been a pioneer in modifying video equipment and computers in order to record digital video without using films or tape. (*Courtesy: Scott Billups.*)

thirty minutes of motion video or 54,000 individual still frames.

Video Workstation   As we described above, a *video workstation* consists of high-end computer hardware and the software needed to process and edit digital video signals. (See Figure 11-20.)

The edit master is "played" on the computer or videodisc and the digital signals converted to an-alog signals for broadcast or display on a monitor. The first broadcast documentary produced digi-tally and completely on the computer was aired in 1993. (See Figure 11-21.)

The marriage of television production tech-niques and computer technologies has opened up new creative possibilities for television pro-ducers.

SUMMARY

Video images begin as either (1) camera images or (2) generated images. In camera imaging, optical energy is converted into electrical signals by focusing light onto the photosensitive surface of a photoelectric transducer in a video camera. The second method involves producing electrical signals in the video system itself, using a generating device. During the production process, camera images and generated images may be combined.

Two characteristics of sight, the persistence of vision and the phi phenomenon, make motion picture and television images possible. Video consists of a series of photoelectric frames shown at the frame rates of twenty-five, thirty, or sixty frames per second. Each frame consists of horizontal scan lines made up of the pixel-sized dots that are illuminated on the CRT face by an electronic beam sweeping from side to side. The overall resolution of the entire video image depends on both the number of scan lines and the number of dots on each line. There are two scanning methods. In interlaced scanning all the odd lines are scanned and then all the even lines. Each set of lines is called a field, and two fields are "interlaced" to create each frame. In progressive scanning each line is scanned in sequence, from the top to the bottom of the screen.

There are three primary international standards. The NTSC standard has 525 scan lines and thirty frames (sixty fields) per second. The other two standards, PAL and SECAM, have 625 scan lines and twenty-five frames (fifty fields) per second. The standards are incompatible, but this obstacle is being overcome by (1) standards converters, (2) multistandard videocassette players, and (3) digital HDTV systems.

During the scanning process the electronic beam turns off each time it reaches the end of a scan line for the period called the horizontal blanking interval. The beam also turns off each time it reaches the lower right-hand corner of the image for the period called the vertical blanking interval. No information is transmitted during vertical blanking, but it is used to carry information essential for the overall operation of the television system and other data.

Sync pulses keep the electronic beam, scanning lines, fields, and frames moving at constant, proper speeds. There are two types of sync pulses. Each piece of video equipment generates its own internal sync, along with its picture information and blanking intervals. External sync is a series of electrical timing pulses used to control the entire scanning and reproduction operation in the video system by a device known as a sync generator. The combination of the visual information produced through scanning, the vertical and horizontal blanking intervals, and the synchronization information is called the composite video signal, as opposed to outside noncomposite signals. To incorporate them into the video system, noncomposite signals must be genlocked to the house sync.

The color of light is described with respect to three characteristics: (1) hue, (2) saturation, and (3) luminance. Color in video images is reproduced by adding the three primary colors: red, green, and blue. The equal presence of all three colors creates white light; their complete absence is black. There are three main forms of color video signals: (1) RGB, (2) composite, and (3) component.

The monochrome CRT has a single electronic beam. The color CRT has three beams, one for each of the primary colors. Each dot on the phosphorescent surface of the tube face is made up of three pixels in the RGB colors. Color signals are combined, or encoded, and then flow through the system until they are decoded at the color monitor or receiver. Video monitors, television receivers, and computer monitors are incompatible. Video monitors can accept only video signals fed over a video cable from the output of a video system. Television receivers can reproduce only signals modulated on a radio frequency (RF) channel, then transmitted to the receiver by a broadcast transmitter, a cable television system, or an RF modulator. Normally, video signals and television channels cannot be displayed on computer monitors, and computer images cannot be reproduced on video monitors or television receivers.

The most common means to observe sync pulses and blanking intervals is the waveform monitor, an oscilloscope on which a graphic waveform of the electronic signal is displayed. The main waveform components are: (1) reference black level, (2) reference white level, (3) horizontal blanking, (4) the front porch, (5) the sync pulse, (6) the breezeway, (7) the color burst, and (8) the back porch. The waveform monitor also displays information about two color characteristics: luminance and chroma. A more detailed view of the components of color signals is shown on the vectorscope, which displays a graphic representation of chroma levels and proper hue.

Today computers are being used widely in a variety of applications in television production. The five primary considerations when using a computer in video production are its: (1) platform, (2) power, (3) speed, (4) capacity, and (5) interface. There are technical obstacles to overcome when interfacing a computer with a video system because they differ in (1) the type of scan lines, (2) scanning rates, (3) pixel shape, (4) screen scan, and (5) color encoding. These differences show up on the screen in five areas: (1) resolution, (2) screen scan, (3) flicker, (4) signals, and (5) color. The technical barriers between computer and video imaging can be overcome by a number of devices: (1) video display and genlock cards, (2) scan converters, (3) video input/output cards, (4) the Amiga and Video Toaster, (5) video workstations, and (6) digital HDTV.

In addition to all the differences already noted, there are two more hurdles in converting video to computers: (1) Video is made up of analog signals and everything in computers is digital. This obstacle is overcome with the analog-to-digital converters. (2) Recording digital video images requires enormous amounts of computer memory. This obstacle is overcome by a technique called compression, which reduces the memory capacity needed.

The final step in "computerized video" is the broadcast quality all-digital tapeless video system, consisting of three parts: (1) a "digital" camera, (2) digital storage media, and (3) a computer workstation.

CHAPTER 12

TELEVISION CAMERAS, LENSES, AND MOUNTING EQUIPMENT

The video camera is the primary instrument of television production. Because it is the basic tool, the camera's capabilities and limitations greatly influence most production decisions and techniques. To use the camera effectively, you must understand what it can and cannot do. In this chapter we will cover the basic characteristics of the camera: how it works and its operation in production.

We also will cover camera lenses and mounting equipment because they are closely related to camera operation. The lens is what focuses the image on the camera's imaging device. Your choice of a lens and the way you use it will determine many characteristics of the camera image. The type of mounting equipment you use will limit camera movement and determine the types of camera shots you can obtain.

TYPES OF TELEVISION CAMERAS

Only a few years ago comparatively few camera models were manufactured, and those were either top-quality broadcast models or "industrial" cameras which were developed for nonbroadcast, closed-circuit use. The industrial cameras were much less expensive, but the quality of their pictures was clearly inferior. Today there is a wide variety of cameras for every price and performance range, and of most importance, each produces an excellent picture within its respective price level. Although there is little question that more expensive cameras produce technically superior pictures, the remarkable fact is that even the most inexpensive professional television camera available today delivers a picture quality that is equal and, in some cases, superior to images produced by the most expensive broadcast cameras a decade ago.

The basic differences among the cameras of various price ranges are the additional features which offer you greater production flexibility and, of course, better picture quality. You will quickly discover that all cameras, regardless of model or manufacturer, operate pretty much the same way. Once you have learned how to use one camera, learning to operate another is easy. It usually takes only a brief orientation to a new camera before you feel comfortable operating it.

With so many cameras available, we have divided them into two broad categories: (1) *studio cameras*, and (2) *portable cameras.*

Studio Cameras

The studio camera is the workhorse of the television industry. Although it is most commonly found inside the studio, it is also used outside in the field, where it is mounted in a relatively fixed position.

All studio cameras use a camera-control unit in which the video levels are regulated by a video technician during production. Studio cameras also require conventional ac power for operation and generally are mounted atop pedestal devices which enable the operator to wheel them around the studio floor to set up various shots during a show.

The imaging device, or *photoelectric transducer*, in a studio camera may be either a *CCD* (charge-coupled device) or a pickup tube. The number of CCDs or tubes used to produce color signals will vary, and there are different sizes of tubes. One factor that determines the type and number of transducers in a camera is the camera's price. Studio cameras vary tremendously in price, from less than $5,000 to more than $100,000. The least expensive studio cameras use single-CCDs or single-gun pickup tubes to produce their images. These systems require optimum production conditions and lighting to deliver consistently good images. Cameras in the middle price range ($5,000 to $40,000) have a much broader operational capability than low-end cameras and can tolerate much lower light levels and more extreme production conditions without sacrificing picture quality. These cameras generally employ either three-CCD systems or three-gun pickup tubes, and their overall picture quality is close to that provided by the most expensive camera models. High-end three-CCD and three-tube studio cameras cost $50,000 and up. The advanced electronic and optical systems contained in these cameras produce exceptionally beautiful pictures across a very wide range of production conditions. (See Figure 12-1.) The finest cameras available are high-definition television (HDTV) cameras that produce wide-screen (16×9) images with extremely high resolution and clarity. HDTV cameras use three multilayer CCD imaging devices, and cost well over $100,000. (See Figure 12-2.) In each price level, CCD cameras tend to be less expensive than tube cameras with similar quality.

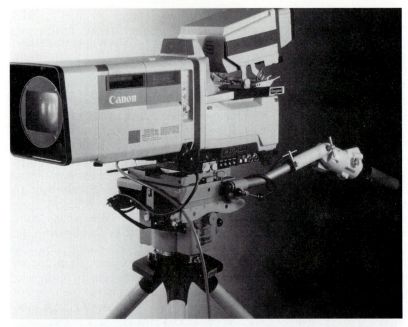

FIGURE 12-1 Studio/Field CCD Camera System. This camera can be mounted on either a pedestal or a tripod and used in the studio or in the field. It operates off of ac power and is regulated with a camera control unit (CCU). It is equipped with a large viewfinder. *(Courtesy: Ikegami Electronics, U.S.A.)*

FIGURE 12-2 Portable High Definition Television (HDTV) Camera. *(Courtesy: Thomson Broadcast, Inc.)*

Portable Cameras

The development of a lightweight portable television camera has literally revolutionized television production. Portable cameras are used so often today that it is hard to realize that only a few years ago most television productions were confined inside the walls of a studio because it was too expensive and time-consuming to haul tons of heavy studio cameras and support equipment into the field for a location shoot. Not only have portable cameras completely changed the way we cover news, but they also have affected almost every kind of television production by providing the producer and director with the ability to leave the studio and shoot in the field when the production warrants it.

Although a variety of portable cameras are currently available, they all have certain operational characteristics in common. They are powered by a battery pack for complete mobility, they do not require a camera control unit but feed the video signal directly to a videocassette or videotape recorder, and most have automatic gain controls which enable the camera operator to cover the action without riding video levels and still produce a technically acceptable picture. Since they are commonly used with a videotape or videocassette recorder, most portable cameras have controls for stopping and starting the tape machine and the ability to view previously recorded material through the camera's electronic viewfinder.

We will discuss portable cameras by dividing them into four categories: (1) ENG and EFP cameras, (2) convertible cameras, (3) camera/recorders, and (4) camcorders.

ENG and EFP Cameras

The primary reason for the development of the portable camera was to replace 16-mm motion picture film for television news production. Electronic news gathering (ENG) employs a battery-powered camera and videocassette recorder to record both sound and picture in the field. There are dozens of ENG cameras available, with the CCD as the most commonly used technology. Most ENG cameras offer automatic operation to enable the camera operator to maintain his or her attention on covering the story without having to worry about the camera's video level.

Electronic field production (EFP) is really an extension of ENG operation, but EFP work usually is considered to be any remote production with a single camera which does not include straight news. For example, producing training tapes, commercials, segments which will be inserted within a studio produced production, and documentaries or magazine-type feature programs are all examples of EFP. Although EFP often uses the same cameras as ENG, some production facilities use higher-quality cameras for EFP in order to produce a better-quality image, which may be combined with footage shot by top-quality studio cameras. Some EFP cameras are capable of being connected to a camera-control unit which offers manual shading of the video level and can produce a better-quality image than is possible with automatic gain controls.

ENG and EFP cameras generally weigh between 6 and 15 pounds, depending on the number of pickup tubes. CCD-equipped cameras can weigh less than 5 pounds. Although they are commonly powered by a battery belt, portable cameras can be run from an ac power source by using an adapter. (See Figure 12-3.)

Convertible Cameras

A number of high-end ENG/EFP cameras are capable of being converted from a portable configuration into a studio-type camera head complete with a large viewfinder and sophisticated zoom lens system. The advantage of the convertible camera is that you get two cameras for the price of one. On a remote production, the camera can be used in its portable configuration, and back in the studio it can be hooked up to its camera-control unit and operated like any studio camera. Many production facilities which do a great many remotes requiring multiple cameras, such as covering sports events or special entertainment events, use the convertible camera in its studio configuration. The convertible camera is much lighter in weight than a studio camera, which makes setting up and striking a number of cameras much easier. (See Figure 12-4.)

FIGURE 12-3
ENG and EFP Cameras.
These cameras are designed
for field use and can be
"mounted" on the shoulder
of the camera operator. The
cameras can operate from
both ac and battery power.
*(Courtesy: Ikegami Electronics,
U.S.A.)*

FIGURE 12-4 **Convertible Camera.**
Convertible cameras can be converted from a portable
ENG/EFP camera to a full-size studio camera complete
with large viewfinder. *(Courtesy: Schwem/Tinsley
Laboratories.)*

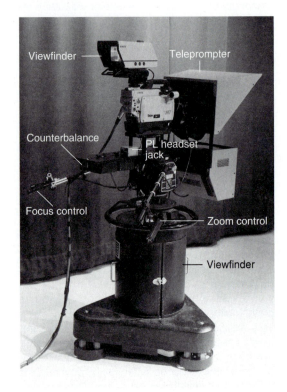

Viewfinder

Teleprompter

Counterbalance

PL headset jack

Focus control

Zoom control

Viewfinder

Camera/Recorders The *camera/recorder* consists of a camera and a recorder designed to fit together and operate as a single unit. The camera is referred to as being "dockable" with the recorder. An ENG/EFP camera that must be connected to the videocassette recorder by a cable limits the camera operator's mobility and can break when subjected to the stress of a camera operator's pulling against the VCR cable connection. With an integrated camera/recorder, there are no external cables, and a single operator can control both camera and video-recording operations.

Dockable cameras operate like conventional ENG/EFP cameras and most utilize CCD image pickups to reduce the size and weight of the unit. Today most broadcast quality camera/recorders use the Betacam SP and MII videocassette formats, although the S-VHS and Hi-8mm formats are increasingly popular for ENG production. (See Chapter 20 for a discussion of videotape formats.)

Camcorders The *camcorder* is a portable camera with a built-in videocassette recorder. (See Figure 12-5.) The camcorder has the operating

advantages of the camera/recorder and is lighter and more compact. Camera/recorders commonly weigh about 15 pounds, while camcorders weigh about half as much. The only drawback to professional-level camcorders is that the tape has a maximum record time of twenty minutes. If greater record time is needed, the camcorder can be attached to an external videocassette recorder.

CCD and Tube Cameras

The camera's imaging device is its most important component. The imaging device is to the camera what the element is to the microphone. Both are *transducers* and convert one form of energy into another. The microphone element converts sound into audio signals, and the imaging device converts light into video signals. Another name for the camera imaging device is the *photoelectric transducer*.

There are two types of photoelectric transduc-

FIGURE 12-5 **Camcorder.** Camcorders combine videocassette recorder and camera in a single package. Camcorders are lightweight and can be carried and operated by a single person. *(Courtesy: Minolta Corporation.)*

ers: the *charge-coupled device (CCD)* and the *pickup tube*. Both are widely-used in television production; however, the physical structures of CCDs and pickup tubes are radically different.

CCD   CCD stands for *charge-coupled device*. The CCD basically is an integrated circuit, or computer chip, with a target "window" of photosensitive picture elements, or *pixels*, on its surface. (See Figure 12-6.)

TECH TIP   Because CCDs are computer chips, CCD cameras are also called "chip" cameras.

The pixels are shaped like rectangles and arranged in horizontal rows on the CCD. Each pixel emits an electric signal when struck by light. There are three families of CCD chips: the *frame transfer (FT)* CCD, the *interline transfer (IT)* CCD, and a combination called the *frame interline transfer (FIT)* CCD. The differences between them are in their internal designs and the methods they use to transfer their signals. The FIT CCD delivers the best quality, but also is more complex and more expensive than the other formats.

TECH TIP   The FT CCD relies on a photosensitive grid which transfers information to a second grid for storage and output. A shutter-like filter wheel blocks the light during the transfer process. The IT approach interleaves the photosensitive and stor-

FIGURE 12-6   CCD and Pickup Tube.
(*a*) The CCD is a computer chip with a target of photosensitive pixels on its surface. When struck by light, the surface grid of pixels sends an electric charge to a second grid for storage and output to the video system. (*b*) The pickup tube has an electronic beam that scans a light-sensitive surface and "reads" the light intensity of every dot along the scanning lines. The signal from the beam is amplified and enters the video system.

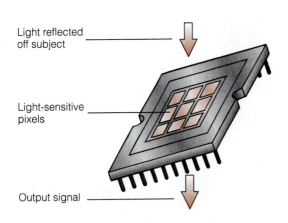

Light reflected off subject

Light-sensitive pixels

Output signal

(a) CCD

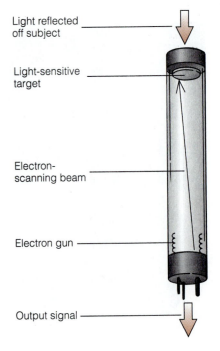

Light reflected off subject

Light-sensitive target

Electron-scanning beam

Electron gun

Output signal

(b) Pickup Tube

age areas on a single register rather than using two separate grids. Although it eliminates the need for a shutter mechanism, the IT CCD is susceptible to producing vertical streaks of light called "smear" on highlights. The FIT CCD combines the best of FT and IT approaches. It has two grids, but no mechanical shutter. Instead, the transfer process occurs electronically during the vertical blanking interval.

The two common CCD sizes today are ⅔-inch (18-mm) and ½-inch (12.5-mm) in diameter. A good ⅔-inch CCD can have nearly 1,000 pixels on each row, giving it almost 500,000 pixels overall. In general, the larger the chip and the greater the number of pixels, the better the image quality.

Pickup Tube   The *pickup tube* was the first video imaging device. It is a round cylinder with a photoconductive face at one end. (See Figure 12-6.) Modern tubes have different trade names—such as *Plumbicon*, *Staticon*, and *Harpicon*—but they all work basically the same. When the tube is struck by light, an electronic beam scans the image on the photoconductive surface, which emits electrical signals. (This is the reverse function of the scanning beam in the monitor, which we discussed in Chapter 11.) The photoconductive surface has a continuous coating, instead of being made up of discrete picture elements like the CCD. Therefore, it is common to refer to the picture elements of the tube as pixel-sized *dots* rather than pixels. The three common tube sizes today are 1-inch (25-mm), ⅔-inch (18-mm), and ⅓-inch (9-mm). All things being equal, the larger the tube face, the better the image quality. The smaller tubes enable manufacturers to make lighter, more compact cameras, particularly useful for electronic field production (EFP) and electronic news gathering (ENG). However, CCD chips allow miniaturization to the point that some CCD cameras are so light and compact that they are difficult to hold steady. (See Figure 12-7.)

Because of the differences in their physical structures and the methods they use to transduce signals, CCDs use less power than tubes. Therefore, CCD cameras are more desirable in EFP and ENG when batteries have to be used. In addition, CCD cameras are more rugged and, as integrated

circuits, have much longer lives. Another difference between CCD cameras and tube cameras is that the *shutter speed* of CCDs can be changed from its normal rate of ⅟₆₀ second. This feature can be useful for grabbing sharp and clear still images of rapid action, such as a baseball pitcher throwing a fast ball. However, at shutter speeds above and below ⅟₆₀ second, there will be discontinuous motion and a strobing effect. Figure 12-8 compares CCD and pickup tube technologies.

The Color Camera

The color camera contains four basic components: (1) the *beam splitter*, which divides the light entering through the lens into the three primary colors; (2) *photoelectric transducers*, which transform the light into electrical signals; (3) the *chrominance* and *luminance signals*, which provide the color and brightness information; and (4) the *encoder*, which processes the color and brightness information for transmission through the video system. (See Color Plate 3.)

The Beam Splitter   After the light reflected from the subject passes through the lens, the next thing it does is to pass through a *beam splitter*. Today there are two main types of beam splitters: the prism block and the striped filter. In three-CCD or three-tube cameras, the *prism block* contains prisms and filters that split the light and aim it at the three photoelectric transducers, one for each of the primary colors. *Striped filters* are used in a camera with a single imaging device. All together the beam-splitter, filters, and related devices that dissect and aim the light are considered the internal optical system of the camera.

The Photoelectric Transducer   The highest-quality color cameras use three separate CCD chips or three pickup tubes. When the light reflected from the subject is dissected by the beam splitter, each of the three CCDs or tubes receives part of the light in direct proportion to the amount of the primary color present in the subject. For example, if the camera were focused on a pure red

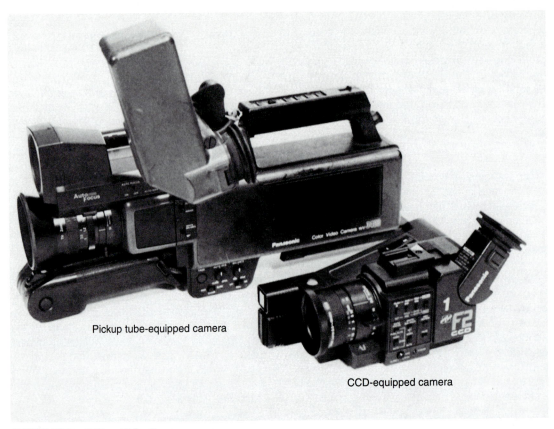

Pickup tube-equipped camera

CCD-equipped camera

FIGURE 12-7 CCD vs. Tube Cameras.
The tiny CCD transducers have allowed cameras to shrink in size. Smaller cameras
are very light in weight, but they may be difficult to hold steady.

card, red light would enter the red chip or tube, but since there is no blue or green light present, no light would pass through to the other two. If the camera were focused on a yellow card (which actually is a mixture of red and green light), about half the light would reach the red CCD or tube, and about half would reach the green CCD or tube. Since there is no blue light present, no light would enter the blue tube. A pure white card (which reflects a combination of red, blue, and green light) would activate each CCD or tube, since the beam splitter would permit each primary color to pass through to its respective CCD or tube.

Once the light reaches each CCD or tube, it converts it into an electrical signal called the chrominance signal.

The Chrominance and Luminance Signals The *chrominance (chroma) signal* comprises the red, blue, and green signals transferred by the photoelectric transducers. They flow in one channel called the *chrominance channel*. The percentages of the three signals in the channel determine the colors in the image. In addition, from the total of the three percentages, the *luminance*, or brightness, can be calculated. In the majority of cameras, the green primary color signal does double duty and also provides the luminance information.

Luminance information is used in three ways: (1) to provide brightness information for the color reproduction; (2) to outline and separate colors in the picture, and provide more sharpness and detail; and (3) to produce a monochrome signal for black and white receivers.

The Encoder Once the chrominance and luminance signals have been provided, we need some means of processing and transmitting the signals simultaneously while keeping their information separate. This is the function of the *encoder*, a device designed to combine the color signals (chrominance) with the brightness information (luminance) into a camera output signal. As we discussed in Chapter 11, the video signal may be encoded in two main ways. One method is *composite video*, in which chrominance and luminance are combined into one signal. Another method is *component* video, which keeps the chrominance and luminance signals independent.

Alternative Color Systems The three-CCD and three-tube method of color reproduction produces the highest-quality pictures in terms of both color and resolution. (See Color Plate 4.) This is why it is the method used in all top-level studio production cameras. However, given all their electronic circuitry, three-CCD and three-tube cameras are expensive, complex systems.

Alternative color systems have been developed which are used on less complex and less expen-

sive color cameras. Although these systems cannot compete with the picture quality available from the three-CCD and three-tube methods, they do offer advantages in terms of decreased cost, lighter weight, increased portability, and less technical maintenance.

SINGLE-TUBE SYSTEMS The single-tube system uses only one pickup tube to provide both chrominance and luminance information. In the single-tube design, a special color filter made of fine, crisscrossed color stripes is positioned over the face of the pickup tube. The tube views the subject through the mosaic of color stripes. Usually the striped filter contains only two primary colors, since the third color can be derived mathematically by subtracting the known colors from white. Special electronic circuits separate the color information into three discrete color signals, which are encoded and sent through the system.

Besides being much less expensive, single-

FIGURE 12-8 Comparison of CCD and Pickup Tube Technologies.

FEATURE	CCD	PICKUP TUBE
Camera size and weight	More compact and lightweight	
Ruggedness	Solid state device resists shock and vibration problems	Glass envelope fragile
Power consumption	About 30 percent less power needed	
Start-up	Immediately ready for shooting	Tube must heat up for stable performance
Registration	Factory preset	Auto or manual
Signal-to-noise ratio	High end about 62 dB	High end about 57 dB
Resolution	Excellent	Superior, especially in three-tube design
Lag and comet-tailing	None	A problem with highly reflective surfaces
Burn-in	Except for direct sun shots, no problem	Potential for destroying the pickup tube
Image distortion	Corner-to-corner resolution is equal	Geometric distortion at edges of tube
Smear	Shows vertical banding around bright objects	None
Aliasing	Some jaggedness of curves and diagonals	None
Maintenance	CCD semiconductor long-lived	Tubes need regular replacement and care

tube cameras require no registration. Also, fewer pickup tubes require less electric power, which is a significant advantage when using battery-powered cameras on location in the field.

However, the pictures produced with single-tube cameras offer somewhat less resolution and color quality than do images produced with three-tube cameras. Nevertheless, many of the better single-tube cameras can produce remarkably good pictures, particularly when they are used in less-demanding production situations such as for news gathering or for nonbroadcast closed-circuit application.

CCD CAMERAS   Single-chip CCD cameras use one chip to reproduce all colors just as single-tube cameras do. Three-chip CCD cameras work in two different ways. One three-chip approach allocates one chip per primary color similar to the three-tube color system. A second approach uses two chips to record the green information, while the third chip is sensitive to both red and blue light. The double green system offers improved resolution, addressing one of the major criticisms of the CCD camera.

CAMERA CHAIN

Although we have been concentrating on the photoelectric transducer, it is only one small part of the overall television camera system. The overall imaging system is called the *camera chain*, and it consists of (1) the *camera head*, which contains the optical and electronic systems required to convert light energy into electrical signals, and (2) the *camera-control unit* (CCU), which contains the power supply and controls necessary for regulating the technical quality of the camera's picture.

Camera Head

The camera head consists of five basic systems: (1) the *lens system*, (2) the *internal optical system*, (3) the *photoelectric transducer* and associated electronic equipment, (4) the *viewfinder*, and

(5) the *camera communication system*. (See Figure 12-1.)

Lens System   All television cameras are equipped with a lens system which gathers the reflected light from a subject and focuses the light rays onto the camera's pickup tubes. All modern cameras use a zoom lens with a continuously variable field of view. The zoom lens is operated by a control situated at the rear of the camera.

To fit different production situations and budgets, the lens usually is sold separately from the camera head. Since the lens can be removed, special lenses for very low light, long distance, or wide vista work can be attached to the camera head. We will examine camera lenses later in this chapter.

Internal Optical System   All color cameras use an internal optical system, which dissects the light focused by the lens into the three primary colors. This is done by the *prism beam-splitter*, which provides maximum light output with a minimum of light loss or optical distortion. The camera may also have a *filter wheel* that must be adjusted to different lighting conditions. We will discuss lighting in chapters 18 and 19.

Photoelectric Transducer   As described previously, the photoelectric transducer, either the CCD(s) or pickup tube(s), converts the optical image into an electronic signal, defines the camera's operating characteristics, and determines its picture-reproduction capability.

Viewfinder System   All television cameras are equipped with an electronic viewfinder, which continuously shows whatever the camera photographs. The viewfinder is simply a tiny television CRT ranging in size from about 3 to 9 inches in diameter. Many viewfinders can be tilted, to give the camera operator a better viewing angle. Others can be rotated, making it convenient for the camera operator to see the viewfinder while shooting from the most favorable angle.

The camera operator uses the viewfinder to frame, compose, and focus the camera shot. Some camera viewfinders also display an indication of the focal-length setting of the zoom lens.

On most cameras, the viewfinder can be switched from displaying the camera's picture to showing an external feed from the video switcher in the control room. This valuable feature enables the camera operator to see how his or her camera shot will combine with the shot from another camera for certain composite special effects. For example, if you had to follow a baseball runner on first base in the upper right-hand corner of the shot, the external viewfinder feed would help you frame the subject accurately within the small corner square.

Camera Communication Systems The camera operator is always in direct contact with the program's director and other members of the production team through a headphone intercom system, sometimes called a "private line" or "PL." Throughout the production, the camera operator sets up each shot according to the director's commands over the PL. The technical director, video technicians, and assistant director also can talk to the camera operator over the PL. The camera operator can talk back through a small mouthpiece on the headset. Some camera communication systems use a dual headset in which one earpiece transmits the production commands and the other transmits program audio. This is particularly valuable on such unscripted productions as a sports remote, where the camera operator may have to follow the commentator's words quickly in order to cover the event.

Because television production uses a number of cameras operating simultaneously to pick up different shots from a variety of angles, we need some means of notifying the camera operator and performers which camera has been selected by the director and punched up on the air at any particular time. This is accomplished silently with *tally lights*, the large red light or lights atop the studio cameras which turn on to signal the crew and performers that the camera's shot is on the air. The camera operator has another, smaller tally light located next to the viewfinder, where it can be seen as the operator watches the viewfinder picture. The tally lights operate automatically when the camera's picture is switched on the air.

Camera-Control Unit

The second half of the camera chain is the *camera-control unit (CCU)*, which is located outside

the studio, in the control room or a remote location. The CCU includes all the controls necessary to register and regulate the picture's exposure during camera operation. (See Figure 12-9.)

All color cameras with more than one imaging device must be *registered*. The light focused on all the CCDs or pickup tubes must be aimed at exact locations on each device so the individual images will overlay each other perfectly in the encoded signal. If they don't, multiple images and blurred colors will result. The separate CCDs or tubes must be precisely registered with each other to produce a clear, sharp, and color-true image. All tube cameras must be registered prior to use. Usually the video technician will register the camera before the talent and crew enter the studio for rehearsal or production. Once a tube camera has been set up and registered, it should never be removed from its pedestal or tripod, since that would tend to upset the registration and deteriorate the picture quality. Unlike tube cameras, CCD cameras do not need to be registered because they are permanently aligned at the factory and have no field controls for this purpose.

While a production or rehearsal is under way, the video technicians must adjust certain controls to compensate for variations in scene brightness and to keep the exposure of each camera within the proper technical limits. On color cameras, the shading is accomplished with two controls: iris and master black.

The *iris control* operates the diaphragm, or f-stop, of the camera lens through a remotely controlled electric motor system. Opening the iris allows more light to enter the camera and is particularly noticeable in the whites of the picture. The *master black* level *controls* the black reference, or "pedestal," and mostly affects the dark portions of the picture. Together, iris and master black controls determine how the camera will reproduce the various light and dark objects in a scene. The video technician manipulates both controls while watching the picture monitor and a *waveform monitor*. As the camera focuses on a new shot or scene, the shader "rides levels" to keep exposure

Studio monitor

Waveform monitor

Camera montiors

Camera controls

FIGURE 12-9 Camera-Control Unit (CCU). The CCU is used to set up and align cameras and to shade them during operation. The entire CCU consists of a video monitor, waveform monitors, and operational controls.

constant and within the necessary technical limits for proper video reproduction.

Many color cameras have automatic *white* and *black balance-control circuits*, which enable the camera operator or shader to balance the camera for optimal color reproduction under different lighting conditions quickly and accurately. The white balance compensates for changes in the color temperature of the light, which makes objects appear too red or blue if the camera has not been white balanced. Automatic white balancing occurs by focusing the camera on a white card and depressing the white balance button. For black balance, you simply press the black balance button and hold it three seconds. The black level (also called *setup* level or *pedestal*) should be at 7.5 IRE on the waveform. Black level is adjusted at the CCU. Balancing the white and black levels ensures good color reproduction, just as taking a preliminary audio level before making an audio recording ensures accurate sound.

Another feature commonly found on many cameras is a *gain control*, which enables the video operator to increase the output of the camera by electronically amplifying the video signals. This permits you to operate the camera under less than ideal low-light conditions and is quite valuable on remote productions where lighting cannot always be controlled. Since the amplification results in an increase in picture noise and a slight deterioration in overall quality, gain should be used only when necessary. (See Figure 12-10.)

DIGITALLY CONTROLLED CAMERAS

The newer-generation video cameras are controlled digitally. Unlike older cameras, which required large, multiconductor cables to send and receive picture information and operating commands between the camera head and the CCU, digital camera systems transform all analog signals into computerlike digital impulses or code signals. These digital signals are not only more precise than conventional analog signals, but they also are impervious to electrical interference over long cable distances. This provides the digital cameras with a number of significant advantages over conventional cameras:

1 Digitizing the electronic signals permits a number of different commands and operations to be "multiplexed," or combined, to travel together along a single conductor cable. Digital cameras use triaxial cable, which is lighter and narrower than the multiconductor cable which conventional cameras use. Since the triaxial

FIGURE 12-10 **Video Gain.**
Gain amplifies the video signal under low-light conditions. While the picture is brightened, it is also slightly "noisier." A 12 db gain represents four times more gain than 6 db gain.

cable is one-fifth the size and weight of multi-conductor cable, more cable can be carried on remote trucks and run to cameras in much shorter time by fewer crew members. In the studio, the smaller cable results in easier camera operation and fewer cable problems than with the heavier, more rigid multicore cable.

2 Digital signals are extremely flexible, and because they are not affected by long transmission distances, they permit a much greater operating distance between the camera head and the control unit. Digital cameras are capable of operating distances of up to 1 mile from the CCU, and the signals can even be transmitted via public telephone lines, radiotelephone systems, or radio-frequency (RF) links.

3 Since digital techniques utilize the same operating principles as computers, the camera head includes an internal memory which automatically retains the correct technical camera settings. Once the memory is programmed and the proper technical values are established, the camera automatically checks to ensure that it is always operating within its proper technical limits. Any deviations from these values are sensed by the camera and immediately corrected. This ensures accurate timing and synchronization between the camera and the base station, or CCU, at all times. The cameras also contain rechargeable batteries which automatically switch on after all ac (alternating current) power is shut off, providing a small current to keep the memory system operative. This means that a digital camera can be shut off, turned on the next day, and will still "remember" its proper technical values and settings, automatically correcting the camera to match them if necessary.

4 Registering and aligning the three separate pickup tubes to produce a sharp and color-perfect image is done automatically with a digital camera by using a microprocessor. Registration and alignment operations can be accomplished in literally seconds, and the results are consistent for each camera because

of the ability of the computer to perform highly complex functions with great accuracy.

In digital systems, the complex camera-control unit is called a *base station*. The base station's primary function is to transform all electric signals—camera controls, synchronizing pulses, audio channels, program intercom channels, and remote viewfinder feeds—into digital pulses which the camera can understand and process. The base station also continuously sends the camera information concerning the camera's technical operation and automatically corrects any deviations from the memory's preset values.

Of course, all manual operations such as shading iris and black level still are performed by the video technician. These signals also are digitized and sent to the camera head over the triaxial cable.

The advantages of the digital cameras are obvious: maximum control and operational flexibility, the ability to operate the camera head at long distances from the base station without interference of the camera signals or command data, the choice of using lightweight triaxial cable or alternative transmission systems, and the camera's internal memory system, which simplifies setups and ensures precision operation of all technical functions.

The disadvantages of the digital camera systems are primarily its cost and its extremely sophisticated construction and design. The highly advanced electronics which control the camera's operation are borrowed from computer and integrated circuit technology. This makes the digital camera more expensive to purchase and requires sophisticated technical maintenance to keep it working properly. However, the camera's inherent advantages outweigh its disadvantages, and digital cameras are quickly replacing conventional cameras.

OPERATING CHARACTERISTICS OF THE TELEVISION CAMERA

If a television camera were capable of reproducing an image exactly as our eyes see it, many pro-

duction problems would be made much simpler. We would know immediately that whatever we see with our eyes is what will appear on the television screen. Unfortunately, this is not the case, and no television camera yet devised is as sensitive and discriminating as the human eye. Since the camera is not nearly as responsive as our eyes, we must continually take into account its operating abilities—what it can and cannot do. The most important of these characteristics are (1) the operating light level, (2) the contrast range, and (3) the picture's resolution. Taken together, these characteristics outline the television camera's operating capabilities and limitations.

Operating Light Level

All cameras require a minimum light level to function properly. The primary determinant of the minimum operating light level for any camera is its *signal-to-noise (S/N) ratio*, which is the ratio of video signal strength to electrical "noise," or interference. S/N ratio is measured in decibels (dB). All electronic devices generate a certain amount of noise during normal operation. However, the strength of the signal or, in this case, picture information is usually strong enough to overcome the interfering noise. To illustrate this, imagine a television receiver which is unhooked from its antenna. The screen is covered with grainy snow, which is "noise." Because the signals in the air are too weak to overcome the noise and mask it, the picture is very ill-defined. Once the antenna is connected to the receiver, the signal strength increases sufficiently to overpower the noise, making the noise unnoticeable in the picture.

Television cameras work in much the same way. High-quality cameras are able to overpower noise and deliver crisp, high-quality pictures even under low light levels. For example, today it is common to find inexpensive portable camcorders with better than 48-dB S/N ratios and expensive high-quality studio cameras with better than 60-dB S/N ratios. Since decibels are on a logarithmic scale, it means that the video signals from both these cameras are far stronger than the background noise level in their signals; however, the less expensive camera is somewhat "noisier" and less sharply defined than the more expensive model. In comparison to tube cameras, CCD cameras have better S/N ratios. The signal-to-noise ratio and the minimum number of footcandles necessary to overcome the inherent noise in the system determine the camera's basic operating light level.

Modern pickup tubes have a high signal-to-noise ratio and the ability to reproduce pictures even under low light conditions. In the studio, most of the standard pickup tubes can operate quite comfortably at light levels between 75 and 250 fc. CCD cameras may operate at even lower light levels, literally down to 1 fc! A more comfortable range is 75 and 175 fc. On remote locations, however, where lighting cannot be controlled as easily, the camera still is capable of producing quality color pictures with light as low as 5 or 10 fc. For low-light conditions, most cameras are equipped with a gain switch that can be used to boost the signal. Most gain switches have two settings, one of 9 dB and the other of 18 dB. While the use of gain increases the signal strength, it also introduces more noise into the picture.

Additional Light-Level Characteristics

There are a number of additional operating characteristics which are directly related to the camera's operating light level and to lighting conditions. They are lag, burn-in, blooming, and comet-tailing. These characteristics are influenced by whether the camera is CCD- or tube-equipped as well as by the prevailing lighting conditions.

Lag Under low-light conditions, pickup tubes are susceptible to image smearing, or *lag*, either as the subject moves across the camera's range of view or as the camera pans or tilts across the scene. As the pickup tube ages, the appearance of lag tends to increase, but the problem is compounded by decreased light levels. In an attempt to reduce lag, many color cameras are equipped with a *bias light* inside the camera head. The bias light is a tiny bulb which floods the faceplate of the pickup tube with a soft, uniform illumination. This keeps a small, constant current flowing through the tube and decreases its tendency to lag or smear. The bias light can be switched on when the camera must operate under low-light conditions and switched off for normal operation. The bias light is a valuable accessory, particularly for those cameras which must operate on remote locations. CCD cameras exhibit almost no lag under all light conditions.

Burn-in When a tube-based television camera is trained on a scene with high contrast, if it has been focused on a static picture for an extended period of time or has been accidentally pointed into a light, the pickup tube tends to retain an "after-ghost" of the original image, which "burns" into the tube. Usually the burn disappears quickly by itself, but some severe burns must be removed by panning the camera across a neutral area such as the studio floor or a lit cyclorama. Burn-in tends to increase as the tube ages and can be an annoying problem if it appears too frequently.

Most modern-generation pickup tubes are quite insensitive to burn-ins and, in fact, can be focused directly into studio lights or onto highly reflective surfaces without damaging the tube. This ability to reject burn-ins offers the director some dramatic production possibilities. Two exceptions to the rule, however, are direct sunlight and an electronic flash from a still camera: either can damage the camera tube beyond repair. Even inexpensive CCD cameras are less susceptible to burn-in than expensive tube cameras and are an excellent choice for shooting night scenes with severe contrast ratios. On the other hand, inexpensive single-tube cameras can be damaged severely by pointing them directly into bright light sources.

FIGURE 12-11 Aliasing.
Aliasing refers to the slightly jagged edges that appear in diagonal or curved lines when imaged by a CCD-equipped camera.

Blooming and Comet-Tailing Expensively bright lights or highly specular reflections from metal or jewelry can cause a portion of the picture to "bloom." On color Plumbicon and other vidicon tubes, blooming appears as a multicolored highlight or smearing. If the subject or camera moves, this blooming is sometimes called "comet-tailing," since the resulting image looks like a comet with a reddish tail. This is quite common in coverage of football games when the sunlight reflecting from a player's helmet produces the comet-tail effect. Although blooming and comet-tailing can be induced purposely for a special effect—when shooting a musical group, for instance, or for a fantasy effect—it is usually a distracting annoyance, and there are a number of ways to reduce its appearance in a shot.

Some cameras include an anticomet-tailing tube and circuitry, which enable the camera to handle a highly exposed portion of a scene without washing out detail or blooming. Another solution is to coat the offending surface with a dulling spray which will minimize its reflection and the resulting comet-tailing.

CCD cameras are insensitive to blooming, flare, and comet-tailing and can be exposed to very bright lights without being destroyed. However, under very bright conditions, the CCD is somewhat susceptible to vertical "smearing," the appearance of a band of bright alterimages above and below the actual image.

Aliasing

Since the pixels on a CCD chip are arranged in horizontal rows and perfectly aligned vertical columns, diagonal or curved lines are produced as stairsteps rather than as smooth lines. This effect is called *aliasing*, and it can be observed as somewhat jagged diagonals and curves on low-resolution CCDs, which have relatively few pixels per row. Aliasing, or the "jaggies," is not a problem with tube cameras, since the pickup tube uses a continuous sweep rather than sampling discrete blocks. (See Figure 12-11.)

Contrast Range

The *contrast range* refers to the ability of the television camera to pick up and faithfully reproduce the variations in brightness within a scene. The contrast range is usually expressed in terms of a *contrast ratio*, which generally should not exceed 30:1. In other words, the brightest portion of any scene should not be more than thirty times lighter in footcandles than the darkest area included in the shot. If you exceed this contrast range, the camera has difficulty reproducing both the light and dark elements of the picture, and you must sacrifice brightness detail at one end or the other. (See Figure 12-12.) The video technician can shade for the excessive white values in the picture by compressing the dark grays and shadows completely to black. If you want to capture the de-

FIGURE 12-12 Exceeding the Contrast Range.
If the contrast range is exceeded, the camera has difficulty reproducing the light and dark elements of the picture and detail in the image is lost.

tail in the dark end, the video technician must "stretch" the blacks, merging the light grays and highlights completely into white.

It is important to understand that the contrast range is a *relative* concept and is a separate consideration from the basic operating light level. Regardless of how much light is present on the scene—50 or 500 fc—if the difference between the brightest and darkest portions of the picture is greater than a 30:1 ratio, the picture quality may suffer because you have exceeded the contrast range. However, this does not mean that you should design your setting without any contrast. Including some contrast is important—both technically and aesthetically. A picture that consists only of medium brightness values will look tired and washed out, without the punch and snap of a contrasty scene. Generally, CCD cameras handle contrast variations better than tube cameras. The camera's contrast range is one of those operating characteristics which always must be approached from an aesthetic, as well as a technical, standpoint. The most important consideration is to be certain that the principal portion of the picture—which generally is the subject's face—falls well within the contrast range. Also, avoid having excessively bright and dark areas overlap, which may create camera shading problems.

Sometimes, particularly on out-of-studio productions, it is impossible to control for excessively wide contrast ratios. For example, many outdoor athletic stadiums develop a deep shadow over a portion of the playing field during late afternoon. Often a player will start in bright sunlight and run into the shadow area. As the camera follows the player, the extremely wide difference in contrast becomes too much for the camera to handle and either the picture blooms, overexposing the lighter portions, or completely darkens into the blacks, losing all definition and detail. To avoid this, many top-level cameras are equipped with a special *contrast-compression device*, which electronically increases the camera's contrast-handling capability and permits the camera to capture picture detail in the shadow and dark areas without overexposing the white highlights.

TECH TIP *Gamma* refers to the relationship between the brightness in a scene and the strength of the resultant video signal. In high-contrast sit-

uations, compressing the camera's internally controlled gamma will permit you to reproduce the brightest parts of a scene while still retaining some detail in the shadows. Some CCD cameras offer excellent control of gamma.

The contrast range is of particular concern to the lighting designer and the scenic designer, since they must plan the lighting and sets around the contrast capabilities of the television camera. We will consider contrast range and its effects on lighting and set design in later chapters.

Resolution

As we noted in Chapter 11, *resolution* refers to the ability of the video system to reproduce, in clear and sharp detail, all aspects of the original subject. Resolution in video depends on the number of scan lines and pixel-sized dots used to reproduce the image. Resolution will be affected by other interacting factors, such as contrast range, the lens system, and the camera's imaging device. Most medium- and top-level cameras employ an *image enhancer*, which is attached to the output of the camera to improve picture sharpness and reduce noise. Even with modern CCDs and image enhancers, a conventional, 525-line television picture cannot compare in sharpness and detail to 35-mm motion picture film. However, HDTV offers superior resolution and color to the video image that bring it closer to film.

Because of the relatively small size of receivers and the resolution limitations of the broadcast picture, television has had to resort to using very tight shots to overcome resolution problems. This is why television is often called a "close-up medium." You should always keep the resolution limitations of the television medium in mind, particularly when approaching such production decisions as the shot size and the design and use of graphics, lighting, and sets.

TECH TIP Since the number of scan lines is fixed, the resolving power of cameras and monitors mainly is a function of the number of dots per line (measured in vertical lines) that the camera or monitor can resolve. High-end studio cameras can resolve 750 vertical lines, or 750 dots on each of the 525 horizontal scan lines. In comparison, home video cameras typically reproduce 300 to 350 vertical lines.

TELEVISION LENSES

Before the television camera can begin to scan and reproduce a scene, a lens must focus an image on the camera's photoelectric transducer. While the primary function of the lens is to produce a sharp image of the subject, the lens actually does much more. The type of lens selected and the way it is used determine the magnification and size of the subject and the field of view that is photographed. The lens also establishes the viewer's visual perspective of the scene. Since the lens is a primary production tool, you should understand its physical properties and its optical characteristics.

PHYSICAL PROPERTIES OF LENSES

A lens is made up of three basic parts: (1) the optical elements, (2) a variable iris, and (3) the mounting system used to attach the lens to the camera head.

Optical Elements

A lens contains a number of optical elements which are housed inside a metal cylinder. The elements are ground glass with special coatings to reduce internal reflections. The optical elements collect the light rays reflected from the subject and focus them through the rear of the lens into the camera. The internal elements not only magnify and focus the image, they also correct for optical and color aberrations which occur whenever light rays are bent, or refracted. Whenever we speak about a single "lens," we really are referring to a complex optical system consisting of a number of elements designed and constructed to operate together as a unit. (See Figure 12-13.)

As light travels through the various glass components, some of the rays are absorbed by the interior elements of the lens before they can reach the camera. For this reason, no lens made can transmit 100 percent of the light that enters it. Top-quality lenses used in television production are capable of transmitting about 75 to 80 percent of the original light, which means about 20 percent of the light that enters the lens is lost before it reaches the camera. Generally, the more complex the lens, the more internal optical elements there are resulting in less overall light which reaches the photoelectric transducer. This is why some very sophisticated zoom lenses or high-powered telephoto lenses require somewhat higher light levels, since they tend to absorb more of the original light from the scene than less complex lenses.

FIGURE 12-13 Cross Section of a Zoom Lens.
Each of the individual glass elements is designed to help magnify and focus the image which enters the lens and to correct for optical distortion. Zooming in or out moves certain of the elements, which varies the optical focal length and changes the picture size and field of view.

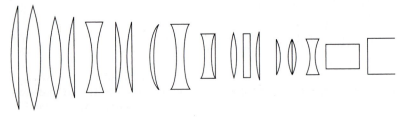

As f-stop number gets larger
the aperture opening gets smaller

f/2   f/16

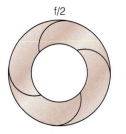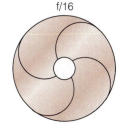

FIGURE 12-14 **Lens Iris.**
The iris, or aperture, on the left is "opened up,"
permitting more light to enter the camera. The iris on
the right is "stopped down," reducing the amount of
light reaching the camera's pickup tube or CCD.

Iris (Aperture)

As we walk from a bright outdoors area into a dark
indoor area, the pupils in our eyes enlarge to increase the amount of light that reaches the retina.
The opening and closing of the pupil enable our
eyes to function effectively across a variety of
light-level conditions. Lenses also have the ability
to vary the amount of light that enters a camera.
Inside a lens's body is a variable *aperture*, or *iris*.
The iris is a series of thin metal leaves which can
be positioned to control the quantity of light passing through the lens. When the circular iris opening is wide open, the lens transmits the maximum
amount of light into the camera. If we close or
"stop down" the iris, reducing the size of the aperture, we permit less light to enter the camera.
(See Figure 12-14.)

The size of the iris opening has been calibrated
as a series of numerical *f-stops*, which run from
about f/1.4 to f/22. As the numerical f-stop *increases*, the amount of light that enters the camera *decreases* because we are closing the opening of the iris. Therefore, a lens set at f/2 would
permit much more light to enter a camera than a
lens set at f/16.

TECH TIP The f-stop is the ratio of the aperture
size divided by the lens focal length. As the aperture size (the denominator term) increases, the ratio naturally gets smaller. This is the reason that
smaller f-stop numbers indicate larger aperture

sizes. For example, an f/2 suggests a 12.5-mm aperture size (25 mm/12.5 mm = f/2), whereas an
f-stop of 11 indicates an aperture slightly larger
than 2 mm (25 mm/2.27 mm = f/11).

Lens Mounting Devices

Most cameras use a zoom lens that has been specifically matched to the camera's internal optical/
pickup tube system, and it usually is purchased
along with the camera head. However, most cameras also can be fitted with a variety of different
lenses, increasing their flexibility in production.
Two frequently used mounting systems are (1) the
C-mount, which is a screw-type mounting system
used on most 16-mm film camera lenses and
adapted for television use, and (2) the *bayonet
lock mount*, which permits lenses to be quickly
mounted and dismounted by fitting the rear of the
lens into a keyway slot in the camera head, securing the lens in place with a half-twist. The bayonet lock generally is preferable because it resists
wear better and is easier to use than the C-mount.
(See Figure 12-15.)

Camera Mount Adapters   Although most production situations can be adequately covered
with the usual complement of television camera
lenses, there are times when certain visual effects
call for the use of special lenses which are produced primarily for motion picture work. To attach
these special lenses to the television camera,
camera mount adapters that fit between the lens
and the camera body must be used. The adapters
are most commonly needed with extremely long
and short focal length lenses.

Lens Formats

Photoelectric transducers in video cameras are
different sizes. For example, the most common
CCDs measure about ½-inch and ⅔-inch diagonally, and common face sizes of pickup tubes are
1-inch, ⅔-inch, or ½-inch in diameter. The image

is too small, there will be a dark border around the image. Figure 12-16 lists the target sizes for the common CCDs and pickup tubes. For comparison, the target areas for 35-mm still film and 16-mm motion picture film are given. Lenses designed for 35-mm cameras cannot be used on video cameras because the images they create would be too large for any of the CCD/tube targets. However, cameras equipped with 1-inch pickup tubes often use 16-mm film format lenses. CCD and tube cameras with ⅔-inch and ½-inch targets must use shorter lenses.

OPTICAL CHARACTERISTICS OF LENSES

All lenses have two important optical characteristics that determine the size and magnification of the image, produce the horizontal view of the scene photographed, and establish the visual perspective of the shot. These characteristics are (1) focal length and (2) f-stop.

Focal Length

The *focal length* is a basic lens quality that determines the amount of image magnification and the horizontal field of view the lens photographs. The focal length is determined by measuring the distance from the "optical center" of the lens (which is not always its physical center) to the point at which the light rays converge at the rear of the lens to produce a perfectly focused image, which, in a video camera, is the face of the pickup tube or

FIGURE 12-15 Lens Mounts.
The C-mount, or screw mount, on the top has been adapted from 16-mm film cameras for television use. The bayonet mount on the bottom is sturdier and easier to use than the C-mount.

size produced by the camera lens must match the corresponding target size of the transducer. Otherwise, the image formed by the lens will be either too large or too small for the target area. If it is too large, some of the image will be lost; if it

FIGURE 12-16 Target Sizes for Selected Video and Film Formats.

IMAGE DEVICE	Target Size (in mm)	
	HORIZONTAL	VERTICAL
1/2-inch CCD/Tube	4.8	6.4
2/3-inch CCD/Tube	6.6	8.8
1-inch Tube	9.6	12.8
16-mm Motion Picture Film	7.9	10.3
35-mm Still Film	24.0	36.0

CCD chip. The distance is measured in millimeters (25 mm = 1 inch), so if a particular lens requires a distance of 2 inches to focus the image, it is a 50-mm lens.

Lenses are frequently described in terms of their focal length. A "normal-angle" or "medium" lens reproduces a scene much as our eyes do. Its horizontal field of view and image magnification are comparable to what you would see if you were standing where the camera is. In the 16-mm lens format size, a normal or medium lens is about 25 mm. Lenses with a focal length shorter than 25 mm are called "wide-angle" or "short" lenses because the lens produces a wide horizontal field of view and decreases subject magnification. Lenses with focal lengths greater than 25 mm are called "narrow-angle" or "long" lenses because they provide a narrow horizontal field of view but magnify and enlarge the subject. Lenses with focal lengths of l00 mm and beyond are frequently called "telephoto" lenses. They are used to shoot subjects from great distances and provide images that appear similar to those produced by a telescope. (See Figure 12-17.)

TECH TIP Do not be confused by the fact that the normal lens in 35-mm photography is 50 mm in focal length, while in television the normal lens is 25 mm in focal length. The reason for the difference is that the image area of 35-mm film is roughly double the image area of a 1-inch pickup tube.

Horizontal Field of View The *horizontal field of view* of a lens tells you how wide a shot the lens will deliver. Knowing the horizontal field of view for any particular lens in advance helps the director preplan shots and camera locations. For example, some smaller studios require cameras equipped with relatively wide angle lenses. You can determine the horizontal angle that any lens will produce by using the following formula:

$$\frac{676}{\text{Focal length (in mm)}} = \begin{array}{l}\text{horizontal angle of}\\ \text{the lens (in 16 mm)}\end{array}$$

If we were using a 25-mm lens, then 676/25 = 27°. This means that the horizontal angle of the lens is 27° or that the lens will include all objects

FIGURE 12-17 **Focal Length and Image Size.** Short, normal, and long focal length lenses offer different degrees of image magnification and angles of view.

within a 27° angle. Later on, we will discuss how to use this information in planning shots and camera angles with a studio floorplan.

Fixed Focal Length Lenses

A *fixed focal length lens* is designed to operate at a predetermined focal length, producing a fixed amount of image magnification and horizontal field of view. These lenses are available in a wide variety of focal lengths from extreme wide-angle lenses with focal lengths as low as 6 mm to extreme telephoto lenses with focal lengths as long as l,000 mm and beyond. In most studio and remote situations, fixed focal length lenses have been replaced by the more flexible variable focal length, or "zoom," lens. However, some special purpose fixed focal length lenses—such as the extreme wide-angle "fisheye" lens or the extreme telephoto lens—are still used on studio or portable cameras to achieve a unique visual perspective. Fixed focal length lenses also have some applications in low-light conditions because they transmit more light than the zoom lens does.

Zoom Lenses

The most popular lens used in television production is the *variable focal length*, or *zoom*, *lens*. The zoom lens can be continuously varied throughout its entire focal length range from its widest horizontal angle to its narrowest, or longest focal length. You can start at any desired focal length and zoom in or out, varying the magnification of the subject and the size of the horizontal field of view at any desired speed. The large number of focal lengths which are instantly available with the zoom lens makes it easy for the camera operator to frame a shot precisely without moving the camera. (See Figure 12-18.)

A location/remote production may require the camera to be placed on an unstable surface, such as a bouncing platform at a sporting event or rock concert. The result can be a bouncing picture, especially in close-up shots. To provide steady video, a *stabilizing zoom lens* may be used instead of a normal zoom lens. (See Figure 12-19.)

Zoom Range   A zoom lens is commonly described with a two-number figure such as "10 × 12" (pronounced "ten by twelve"). The first number, 10, is the *zoom range* and is the ratio of the shortest focal length of the lens to the longest focal length. Here it is a 10:1 ratio. The second number, 12, is the shortest focal length in millimeters which produces the zoom lens's widest angle of view. Knowing this information makes it easy to see that

FIGURE 12-18 **Zoom Lens.** The television zoom lens combines multiple focal lengths within a single lens barrel. Many zooms have electroservosystems that control focal range, focus, and iris opening.

FIGURE 12-19 **Stabilizing Zoom Lens.**
Shooting from a shaky platform, a boat at sea, a news chopper, a motor vehicle, or any unsteady location will result in bouncing pictures. A stabilizing lens will help to steady image vibration. *(Courtesy: Tinsley Laboratories, Inc.)*

our 10 × 12 lens is capable of zooming from 12 mm (the shortest possible focal length) to 120 mm (the longest possible focal length).

Most studio cameras are equipped with lenses with a zoom range of about 10:1 or 15:1. These lenses combine the necessary wide angle for studio work with a sufficiently long focal length for tight close-ups. Since in-studio cameras most often require the widest possible angle at the short end of the range, studio zooms usually are made with the maximum wide angle as an important consideration. However, if you will be shooting many remote productions where it is necessary to magnify subjects from great distances and bring the action closer, you may wish to sacrifice the extreme wide angle for more magnification power at the longer end of the zoom range. A number of manufacturers have produced a "universal" zoom lens, which provides the camera operator with the best of both worlds—the shortest focal length setting of the lens offers a sufficiently wide angle for in-studio use, and the same lens has a very powerful long range for telephoto field work. Some of these universal zooms have ratios as large as 42:1, with a wide-angle capability of a 12.5-mm focal length lens and a maximum image magnification provided by a focal length of 525 mm.

As you probably have realized by now, a zoom lens is capable of producing a virtually unlimited number of focal lengths within the extremes of its zoom range. Whenever we use a zoom at the short focal length end of its range, we will produce pictures with all the characteristics of a wide-angle lens. Similarly, if we use the zoom at long focal length settings, we produce pictures with the characteristics of long lenses. Throughout the remainder of this chapter, whenever we refer to a "short," "medium," or "long" lens, we are referring to the characteristics of the image that are produced by a zoom lens which is positioned at a particular focal point along its zoom range.

Range Extenders   *Range extenders*, or "multipliers," are supplementary optical devices used to extend the range or focal length of a zoom lens. *Fixed extenders* have a predetermined power, which is rated in terms of the amount of additional magnification provided. For example, a "2×" (pronounced "two times") extender on a normal 12- to 120-mm lens will double the focal length across the entire zoom range, producing, in effect, a 24- to 240-mm lens. Some range extenders are *variable* rather than fixed and permit the camera operator to change their multiplying power continuously. These "double zooms" give the camera operator the flexibility to select the exact multiplier magnification power for every shot.

Using a range extender is always a compromise, since the extender increases focal length at the expense of the lens's operating light level. A 2× range extender will reduce by four times the amount of light that would have entered the camera without the extender. This can be a serious problem on remote telecasts when light levels, which cannot be controlled easily, get critically low.

Zoom Lens Operation   Zoom lenses come in two varieties: (1) *manual zooms*, in which the camera operator controls the angle and speed of the zoom by turning a handle-crank, and (2) *servozooms*, in which the angle and speed of the zoom shot are controlled by operating a switch that activates a small electronic motor inside the lens.

Zoom speed control

(a)

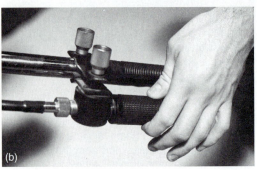

(b)

FIGURE 12-20 **Manual Zoom and Focus Controls.**
(*a*) On a manually controlled zoom lens, the camera operator turns the zoom "crank" on the right pan handle to change the focal length of the lens. (*b*) Focus is controlled by turning the handle grip on the left pan handle.

MANUAL ZOOM OPERATION Most manual zooms are controlled with a crank attached to the right-hand pan handle at the rear of the camera. Turning the crank varies the focal length of the lens. Many controls also have a two-gear switch that permits either "slow" or "fast" zooms by changing the number of turns necessary to cover the entire zoom range. Focus is controlled by rotating a handle-grip located on the left-hand pan bar. (See Figure 12-20.)

SERVOZOOM OPERATION Lenses equipped with a servosystem use a tiny electric motor inside the lens to control both the focal length and the focus. The zoom range is controlled with a thumb switch located on one pan bar, which is pushed either right to zoom in or left to zoom out. The farther from the central position you push the switch, the faster is the zoom's rate of speed. Focusing also is ac-

complished electronically with a control on the other pan handle. Because the servosystem is electronic, the zooming speed need not depend on the operator's manual touch, and servozooms produce exceptionally smooth and precise zooms. (See Figure 12-21.)

Servozooms generally are used with a *shot box*, which enables the camera operator to preset a number of specific focal lengths, much as you preset your car radio for a number of different station frequencies. During the production, the camera operator simply presses the appropriate button on the shot box and the lens automatically moves to the preset focal length. (See Figure 12-22.)

TECH TIP Unless the servozoom motor is very quiet, an on-camera microphone will pick up the whir of the servomotor as it zooms the lens. Check for this objectionable noise using earphones if an on-camera microphone will be used on a camera equipped with a servo-driven lens.

CALIBRATING THE ZOOM   A zoom lens can maintain perfect focus throughout its entire range only if you have "calibrated," or "prefocused," the lens before each series of shots. The calibration, or prefocus, operation is relatively simple:

1   Zoom the lens all the way in to the longest possible focal length (even though the shot may

be too tight to use), and use the focus control to make the principal subject perfectly sharp. If a person is the subject, focus on the eyes.

2   After focusing, frame the shot by setting the zoom at the desired focal length. The picture will remain in perfect focus throughout the entire zoom range as long as neither the camera nor the subject moves from its original position.

3   If the camera-to-subject distance changes a

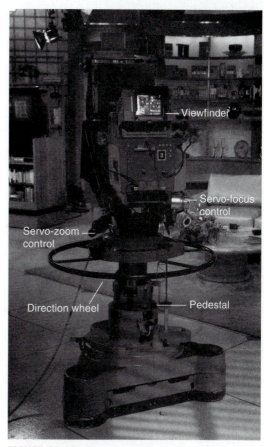

FIGURE 12-21   **Servozoom Controls.**
(*a*) The servozoom is controlled with a thumb switch located on the left pan handle. (*b*) Focusing is accomplished electronically with a focus control on the right pan handle. (*Courtesy: Capital Cities/ABC, Inc.*)

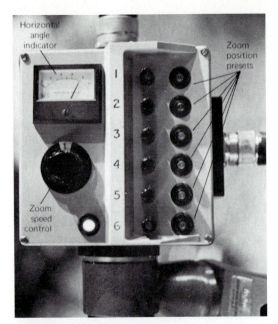

FIGURE 12-22 Shot Box Controls.
The shot box at left allows the studio camera operator to preset six specific lens focal lengths.

substantial amount, or if you must set up for a shot on another subject at a different position, you must recalibrate your focus to create a sharp image. As soon as the director switches to another camera shot and your camera is "off air," zoom in tight, refocus, and back off to the proper framing. Good camera operators automatically calibrate their zoom focus each time they set up a new shot to ensure accurate focus across the entire zoom range.

BACK FOCUS The method described above to calibrate the zoom assumes that *back focus* on the lens is set properly. *Back focus* involves phys-

ically changing the distance between the back of the lens and the CCD or tube face so that the image is in sharp focus when the lens is zoomed all the way out to the widest possible focal length. Once back focus has been set on a studio camera, adjustment is rarely needed, but if it is, a video technician usually makes it inside the camera. However, some lenses, particularly on portable cameras, may have an external back focus control to correct slight changes that may occur while transporting the camera. Another name for this control is *flange focus*.

F-Stop

We mentioned earlier that all lenses are equipped with a variable iris which permits us to control the amount of light that enters the camera. The exact iris opening has been calibrated as a series of numerical f-stops. As the numerical f-stop *increases*, we close down the opening of the iris and *decrease* the amount of light that enters the camera.

F-stop numbers for television lenses run from about f/1.4 to f/22, and the aperture is designed in such a way that changing from one f-stop to the next doubles or halves the amount of light entering the camera. For example, if we go from f/4 to the next highest f-stop, f/5.6, we decrease by one-half the amount of light that enters the camera. Similarly, opening the iris one full f-stop, from f/4 to the next largest f-stop, f/2.8, doubles the amount of light that enters the camera. (See Figure 12-23.)

Lenses are commonly rated in terms of their widest possible f-stop, since this determines the maximum light-gathering capability of the lens. A lens with a maximum iris aperture of f/1.4 or f/1.8 would be considered a "fast" lens because the lens is capable of gathering more light under low-light conditions.

You might wonder why all lenses are not simply

FIGURE 12-23 Lens F-Stops and Iris Openings.
As the numerical f-stop increases, the diameter of the iris opening decreases and less light enters the camera.

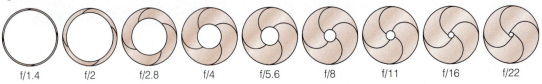

| f/1.4 | f/2 | f/2.8 | f/4 | f/5.6 | f/8 | f/11 | f/16 | f/22 |

designed to operate with the largest possible f-stop. The problem is that it requires a great deal of sophistication and complexity in the design and construction of a lens to increase the aperture size and still produce a sharp, distortion-free image. As the speed of a lens increases, its flexibility increases, but its cost rises dramatically. A fast lens is not crucial if it will be used exclusively inside the studio, where more light can be added to a scene without much difficulty. However, if you expect to use your lens on remote locations where extra light cannot always be added easily, a faster lens will provide you with greater shooting capability under varying light conditions.

TECH TIP While most lenses are advertised with respect to their maximum aperture (widest f-stop), the more important specification is the lens's *t-stop*, a scale of numbers that accurately describes how much light is *transmitted through* the lens. The t-stop takes into account light absorbed by the optical elements of the lens, whereas the f-stop does not.

Remote Iris Contol Virtually all studio cameras are equipped with a remote iris control which permits the video technician to control the f-stop from the CCU. In fact, once a color camera has been properly aligned, varying the f-stop from the CCU is one of the primary methods used to shade the camera to compensate for exposure variations during production.

Many cameras, particularly remote cameras, also are equipped with an *auto-iris*, which automatically changes the size of the iris as the exposure varies on the scene being photographed. The problem with the auto-iris is similar to that found with many home still and video cameras that also use an automatic exposure control. The auto-iris reads the average amount of illumination in the scene but cannot discriminate between the various elements within a camera shot. Therefore, it simply shades for the best average exposure without any regard for the most crucial elements within the shot. For instance, if the principal subject is standing in front of a bright background, the background area, which contributes the most illumination to the scene, will be exposed perfectly by the auto-iris, but the important foreground subject probably will appear too dark. This is why the auto-

iris really cannot substitute for the human touch of a video technician, who can take both aesthetic and technical considerations into account when shading the picture. (See Figure 12-24.)

Manual Iris Control Cameras without a remote or automatic iris require the aperture on each camera lens to be preset manually by adjusting the f-stop ring on the barrel of the lens prior to production. The video technician generally will set the f-stop for the average illumination level on the set and then shade the camera electronically while the f-stop remains fixed. Of course, if the light levels change too drastically during the production, the lenses may be reset manually to

FIGURE 12-24 Auto-Iris.
The lens auto-iris control has set the exposure for the background, rather than the foreground subject.

provide the shader with more range of control at the CCU.

Focus

A camera shot is in *focus* when the light rays leaving the lens converge precisely on the face of the camera's pickup tube or CCD chip. Since this distance varies depending on the focal length of the lens and the camera-to-subject distance, we must continually adjust the distance between the lens's optical center and the pickup tube in order to maintain accurate focus. This is accomplished by turning the focus control, which usually is located on the left-hand pan handle.

Focus and Focal Length   The closer an object is to the camera lens, the greater is the distance necessary between the lens and the pickup tube in order to focus the image. All lenses—both zoom and fixed focal length—have a minimum object-focusing distance, which is the shortest possible distance between the object and the lens where the picture still can be focused. In general, shorter focal length lenses can operate with objects closer to the lens than longer focal length lenses. As the focal length increases, you need greater distance between the lens and the object.

TECH TIP   If you are asked to obtain an extremely tight shot of a very small object or graphic, zoom out to a short focal length and move the camera closer to the subject. This will allow you to fill the screen with a tight shot of the small object and still maintain focus, since the short focal length does not require a large lens-to-pickup tube distance to appear in focus. However, you will usually have to get the camera within inches of the subject, which may cause lighting problems or increase the possibility of including the close-up camera in another camera's shot. (See Figure 12-25.)

Close-up and Macro Lenses   If your production requires shooting a great many small objects extremely close, you might consider using an auxiliary close-up lens attached to the camera lens.

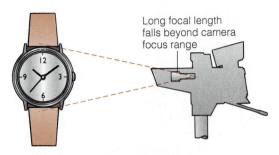

Long focal length falls beyond camera focus range

Watch is out of focus

Viewfinder

Long Focal-Length Lens Shooting from a Distance

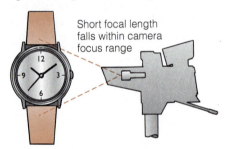

Short focal length falls within camera focus range

Watch is in focus

Viewfinder

Short Focal-Length Lens Shooting Close

FIGURE 12-25   Lens Focal Length and Focusing. It may be impossible to obtain sharp focus when attempting to shoot extremely tight close-ups with a long focal length lens. If so, use a short focal length setting and move in close to the object to obtain proper focus.

This increases the camera lens's magnification and permits a zoom lens to vary its focal length within predetermined limits. A close-up lens usually will allow you to shoot small objects from

FIGURE 12-26 Macro Setting.
Many zoom lenses have a macro setting which enables focusing on small objects very close to the front of the lens.

greater distances than the wide-angle, short focal length technique we have just mentioned and may solve some lighting and camera problems. However, when you are using a close-up lens, your normal lens capability is extremely limited and the lens can focus only on objects located within a fairly small range.

Another approach to photographing small objects at close distances is to use the *macro* setting available on the focus ring of some zoom lenses. On the macro setting, the lens can focus on objects within inches of the front of the lens. However, to then focus on objects far from the camera, the lens must be taken off the macro setting. (See Figure 12-26.)

Depth of Field

Whenever a lens is focused on a subject, there will be an area in front of the subject and behind the subject in which all objects *appear* to be in focus. This area of acceptable image sharpness is called the *depth of field*, and it is an important variable influenced by lens choice that we can use as a creative tool. When there is a very large space surrounding the principal subject in which objects are still seen as in focus, the lens is said to have a "wide" or "deep" depth of field. If the area surrounding the subject is not very large, the

lens is said to have a "shallow" or "narrow" depth of field. (See Figure 12-27.)

TECH TIP   It is important to remember that there is only one plane of perfect focus. *Depth of field* refers to the area in which images are "close enough" to being in focus that our eyes accept them as in focus. Remember to recalibrate your zoom for new shots; do not be misled by a large depth of field.

Depth of field is important for both technical and aesthetic reasons. Technically, a shot with a wide depth of field makes it relatively easy to follow the action. A shallow depth of field requires you to continually change the focus—in effect, shifting the depth of field—as either the camera or the subject moves. Aesthetically, the depth of field plays an important role in creating the shot's overall visual perspective.

Three factors determine the depth of field in a scene: (1) the lens's focal length, (2) the f-stop, and (3) the camera-to-subject distance. (See Figure 12-28.)

FOCAL LENGTH   The shorter the focal length or the wider the zoom lens position, the deeper is the depth of field. As the focal length increases, the depth of field decreases.

F-STOP   The smaller the lens opening (the larger the f-stop number), the deeper is the depth of field. As we open the iris (decrease the numerical f-stop), we decrease the depth of field.

CAMERA-TO-SUBJECT DISTANCE   The greater the distance between the subject and the camera, the greater is the depth of field. The shorter the camera-to-subject distance, the shallower is the depth of field. Also, depth of field is always greater *behind* the principal subject than in front of the subject, which means that you have more range of focus with those objects positioned behind the principal subject than in front of it. In fact, depth of field extends twice as far behind a subject as in front of a subject.

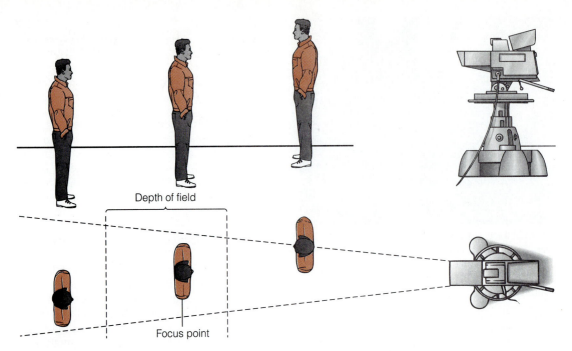

Depth of field

Focus point

FIGURE 12-27 **Depth of Field.**
The *depth of field* is the area of acceptably sharp focus in front of and behind the
object on which the camera is focused. Depth of field extends approximately twice
as far behind the point of critical focus as in front of it.

Although each of the three factors will influence depth of field, the most practical means of varying depth of field is to change either the focal length of the lens or the camera-to-subject distance. You can certainly light at high illumination levels, which will permit the lens to be stopped down and increase the depth of field, but lighting levels often are dictated by such other considerations as the camera's minimum operating light level. Varying the overall light level is usually the least versatile approach to controlling depth of field.

TECH TIP We have described focal length as affecting depth of field because it is a commonly cited and useful rule of thumb. However, image magnification is the real cause of different depths of field. Long focal length lenses create large image sizes and our eyes can discriminate more easily what is not in focus. The image sizes produced by short focal length lenses often are so small that our eyes lack the acuity to notice.

SPECIAL-PURPOSE LENSES

Although most studio/field cameras use a zoom lens, some production requirements call for special-purpose lenses that provide unique effects impossible to obtain with conventional lenses. These are usually fixed focal length lenses and are conveniently used on portable cameras, where the flexibility of movement combined with the special effect produced can result in some very striking visuals.

Fisheye Lens The fisheye lens is an ultrawide-angle lens that provides a 180° panorama view. Of course, the lens radically exaggerates the depth perspective, but this distortion is usually the very effect the director wants to achieve. Although the fisheye lens can deliver some very dramatic subjective or surrealistic effects, its distortion is so obvious that it must be used sparingly and with an obvious motivation. (See Figure 12-29.)

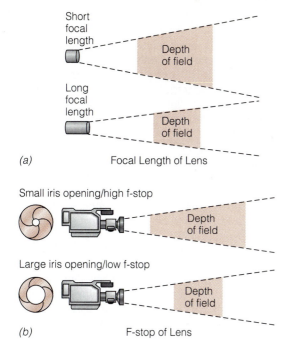

(a)   Focal Length of Lens

(b)   F-stop of Lens

(c)   Camera-to-Subject Distance

FIGURE 12-28 **Factors Influencing Depth of Field.**
(a) The shorter the focal length, the greater is the depth of field. *(b)* The higher the numerical f-stop, the greater is the depth of field. *(c)* The greater the camera-to-subject distance, the greater is the depth of field.

Diopters and Lens Splitters These lenses, adapted from motion picture production, give you the ability to focus clearly on subjects at two different distance planes within the same shot. The lenses work like bifocal eyeglasses in which one-half is a wide-angle lens and the other is a telephoto lens. Using the split lens and carefully positioning the subjects enable you to frame and

focus two widely separated subjects. (See Figure 12-30.)

Starburst Filters The starburst filter produces a multipointed star effect whenever the camera shoots a highly specular, reflective subject. This can be a visually beautiful effect and frequently is used on musical programs or for some dramatic fantasy scenes. Although called a "filter," the starburst is really a lens because it is specially designed to refract light in multiple directions, creating the starlight effect. (See Figure 12-31.)

FILTERS

Filters are devices that change or modify the nature of light before it enters the camera. Some tele-

FIGURE 12-29 **Fisheye Lens.**
A fisheye lens is an extremely wide-angle lens that creates unusual visual effects.

FIGURE 12-30 Split-Field Lens.
The split-field lens is like a bifocal lens. This allows the foreground and background to both be in acceptable focus. It is important to position the demarcation line between near and far objects so that it will not show on screen. *(Courtesy: Tiffen Mfg. Co.)*

shoot under light conditions where the level of illumination is too high for the camera to handle. The neutral-density filter reduces the light intensity by a predetermined factor, giving the shader a greater range of control at the camera's CCU. They are most frequently used on remote telecasts where high light levels from a bright, sunny sky must be reduced to permit accurate camera shading.

Another use of the neutral-density filter is to force the camera to operate at a wider f-stop than normal—in effect, decreasing the depth of field. This is helpful in achieving selective focus or rack focus effects, which would be impossible if the camera lens had to be stopped down to reduce the amount of light.

Color Correction Filters   If you do any still or motion picture photography, you know that in order to use ''indoor'' film outdoors or vice versa, you must use a *color-correction filter*. This is so because the film is designed for the color quality of indoor light, which is different from that of outdoor light. Indoor lamps and bulbs produce a ''white'' light that actually has a reddish tinge. Outdoors, the light from the sun and sky has a bluish tinge. The filter you use on your film camera changes the color quality of the light so that indoor film can faithfully reproduce colors outdoors.

The television camera works along the same basic principles. It is usually adjusted for indoor lighting instruments, which produce light with a slightly reddish tone. Outdoors, on a remote, the camera must either be electronically rebalanced for the bluish light or a color-correction filter must be used to modify the color quality, or ''color temperature,'' of the light.

The filter that changes the color temperature of outdoor light to match the camera's indoor adjustment is an orange ''85'' filter. You can get this filter alone or combined with a neutral density filter to both correct for color temperature and reduce the amount of light that enters the camera. These combination filters are called ''85N3,'' ''85N6,'' and ''85N9.'' The higher the figure following the ''N'' (for neutral density), the greater is the light-reduction capability of the filter and the less light that is transmitted into the camera. Another useful color-correcting filter removes the excessive greenish tinge common to fluorescent lighting. Color-

vision cameras are equipped with a filter wheel that is positioned between the lens and the pickup tube. The filter wheel holds a number of different filters, each of which can be quickly moved into position when needed. On cameras without a filter wheel, you must attach a filter directly to the camera lens.

Neutral-Density Filters   A *neutral-density filter* is a gray filter that reduces the light level without affecting the color quality of the light. Neutral-density filters are used when the camera must

(a)

(b)

FIGURE 12-31 **Starburst Filter.**
Starburst filters are available with a variety of points and with different spacing between the starburst patterns. (*a*) the scene shot without a filter; (*b*) the scene shot with a four-point starburst filter; (*c*) an eight-point star filter is used. *(Courtesy: Tiffen Mfg. Co.)*

(c)

correction filters are becoming less common on television cameras because the color correction is being handled electronically through a process called *white balancing*.

Diffusion Filter   The *diffusion filter* softens hard lines in a shot, producing a soft, vaguely blurry image which is ideal for dreamy, fantasy, or romantic visual effects. (See Figure 12-32.) Different filters produce varying amounts of diffusion, and some are available with a clear center, with the diffusion increasing gradually toward the outer edges of the filter. Slightly diffused filters sometimes are used to eliminate facial blemishes or wrinkles on a performer's face in a close-up.

TECH TIP Nylon stockings stretched across the front of a lens create an effect that mimics the effect of a diffusion filter. Another approach is to smear a clear glass filter with petroleum jelly and then attach it to the camera lens. At no time should you apply the jelly, or any other substance, directly to the front of the camera lens. You can remove and clean a clear glass filter, but applying a substance on the camera lens itself can damage the expensive lens permanently.

CAMERA MOUNTING EQUIPMENT

During a production, the camera operator must be able to move the camera with relative ease and maximal flexibility. Even though a large studio camera may weigh well over 100 pounds, it must be moved, panned, and tilted quickly and smoothly without jerking or shaking. This is made possible by attaching the camera to a special camera head and mounting device that permits smooth and flexible operation.

Camera Mounting Heads

The camera itself rests on a mounting head, which is attached to a tripod or pedestal. The mounting

FIGURE 12-32
Diffusion Filter.
The top scene is shot without a diffusion filter in place. Below, the blurry, dreamlike feel is created with the use of a diffusion filter. *(Courtesy: Tiffen Mfg. Co.)*

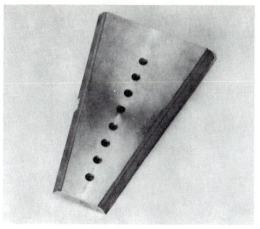

FIGURE 12-33 **Camera Wedge Mount.**
The camera wedge (*left*) is attached to the camera. The wedge mount receptable (*right*) is attached to the tripod or pedestal. The wedge-mounted camera can quickly and easily be affixed to pedestals and tripods when necessary. *(Courtesy: Innovative Television Equipment Corp.)*

head's function is to hold the camera securely in place while permitting smooth rotation horizontally (panning) and vertically (tilting).

Some heads use a quick-release *wedge mount*, which simplifies the mounting operation of the camera to the head. A plate with the "male" wedge is attached permanently to the underside of the camera. The camera and wedge are then inserted into the "female" slot, which is bolted to the top of the pedestal or tripod. This is a particularly convenient system if your cameras will often be used on remote productions where frequent mounting and dismounting must be done quickly and safely. (See Figure 12-33.)

Friction and Fluid Heads   The simplest and most basic mounting is the *friction head*, which uses a heavy spring to control the camera's movement. Friction heads are not recommended for most studio cameras because they offer little control over such heavy equipment and have a tendency to overbalance when the camera is tilted at extreme angles. *Fluid-head* tripods use a thick fluid in which the head moves to offer more control and result in smoother camera movements. Fluid heads also are subject to overbalancing when used with heavy cameras. Friction and fluid heads

both have two controls which enable the camera operator to set the amount of friction, or resistance, on the pan and tilt for the smoothest movement. (See Figure 12-34.)

Cradle Head   The *cradle head* is designed to balance a heavy studio camera automatically even when it is tilted at the most extreme vertical angle. Two controls on the side of the cradle head permit the camera operator to adjust the amount of "drag" or friction over the pan and tilt. A separate control locks the cradle into any preset position. (See Figure 12-35.)

Cam Head   The *cam head* uses a number of cams, or cylinders, to control the camera's pan and tilt movements. These heads are designed especially for heavy studio/field cameras and offer extremely smooth, effortless pan and tilt control. The cam head is equipped with both pan and tilt drag controls to adjust the friction, and with brake controls to lock the camera securely into any position. (See Figure 12-36.)

On any type of head, the pan and tilt locks should be loosened *before* the camera is tilted or panned. Otherwise, the locks will be stripped and useless. A good comparison is driving an auto-

353

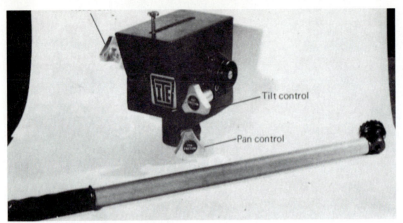

(a)

(b)

FIGURE 12-34 **Friction and Fluid Heads.**
(a) The friction-head camera mount uses a strong spring to control camera movement; (b) the fluid-head mount uses a chamber filled with a viscous fluid to smooth camera movement. *(Courtesy: Innovative Television Equipment Corp. and Miller Fluid Heads (U.S.A.) Inc.)*

mobile with the emergency brake on. In a short time, the emergency brake would be damaged. That's the same thing that would happen from panning and tilting a camera with the pan and tilt locks tightened. In addition, the pan and tilt friction controls should be tightened until there is only a slight amount of drag. They should never be fully tightened or used as locks.

Camera Tripod

The simplest camera mounting device is the *tripod*. Tripods generally are lightweight and collapsible, which makes them ideal for use on remote productions. (See Figure 12-37.) However, the operating height of the camera cannot be varied during the production, which may be a serious limitation. Tripods with wheels attached to the legs are more flexible than simple tripods since the camera can be moved around the floor. If stationary operation is desired, the wheels can be removed.

Camera Pedestals

Camera pedestals are the most commonly used camera mounting devices and are found in almost all production studios. The pedestals are designed to move smoothly across the studio floor and to permit the camera operator to easily change the camera's height, even while on the air.

Studio/Field Pedestal The *studio/field pedestal* is a combination tripod and pedestal. It is suffi-

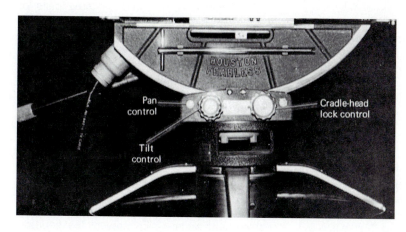

FIGURE 12-35
Cradle Head.
The cradle head can balance
heavy cameras.

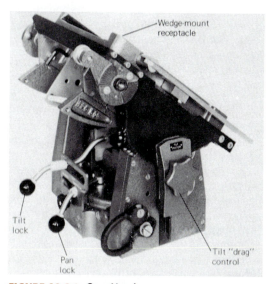

FIGURE 12-36   Cam Head.
The cam head offers very smooth pan and tilt controls.
(Courtesy: Listec Television Equipment Corp.)

FIGURE 12-37   Camera Tripod.
The tripod is ideal for field work where light weight and
portability are important. *(Courtesy: Miller Fluid Heads
(U.S.A.) Inc.)*

ciently lightweight to be carried easily to remote locations, yet its oversized wheels permit the camera operator to move the camera and pedestal smoothly across a studio floor. The camera's height can be varied by pumping air or turning a crank to raise the vertical column, but the operation is jerky, and the camera's height cannot be changed while its shot is on the air. (See Figure 12-38.)

Counterweight Pedestal   The *counterweight pedestal* is one of the most commonly used and most flexible mounting devices. The camera is mounted atop the pedestal's center column, which can be raised or lowered effortlessly by a slight pressure from the camera operator on the large center lifting ring. The pedestal is counterbalanced with weights and springs and is

FIGURE 12-38   **Studio/Field Pedestal.**
A combination tripod and pedestal that is light enough to transport on location, but heavy enough for moving smoothly across a studio floor. *(Courtesy: Innovative Television Equipment, Inc.)*

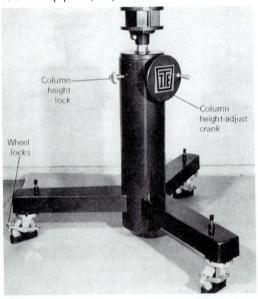

adjustable for each individual camera weight, enabling one to vary the camera height even while on the air.

The pedestal is mounted on three pairs of wheels, which can be adjusted to steer in two different modes. The most common method is to lock all three pairs so they steer in parallel. This is called *crabbing*, and it permits the pedestal to move smoothly in any direction. However, if you must rotate the pedestal itself, then you have to change the steering to the *tracking* mode, in which the first wheel steers while the rear wheels remain locked in parallel, much like a child's tricycle. The selection of steering modes is accomplished by a foot switch located at the base of the pedestal. The camera operator steers the pedestal by turning the large center ring in the appropriate direction. The wheels of the pedestal are covered with cable-guard skirts, which prevent the pedestal from running over cables on the studio floor. (See Figure 12-39.)

The pedestal's major advantages are its ease of operation and its even movement across the studio floor, resulting in smooth dollies and trucks. However, because the pedestal is large and heavy, coordinating camera movement and pedestal operation takes some practice. Also, its large size and extremely heavy weight make it impractical to use on remote locations.

Pneumatic Pedestal   A more sophisticated version of the counterweight pedestal is the *pneumatic pedestal*, which uses compressed air to operate the action of the telescoping center column to change the camera's height. Operation of the pedestal is very flexible. Some pneumatic pedestals permit the camera to vary over 3 feet, from as low as 21 inches off the studio floor to a maximum height of 58 inches.

Operation of the pneumatic pedestal is identical to operation of the counterweight pedestal except that center-column height is controlled through the use of compressed air, which is carried in an air tank. Since the pedestal uses air and not heavy counterweights, the pneumatic pedestal is much lighter than the counterweight pedestal. This makes it easier for the camera operator to move and guide the camera and pedestal across the studio floor. (See Figure 12-40.)

Cradle head

Column lift/steering ring

Column lock ring

Weight system travels up and down

Counterweights

Steering mode controls for "tracking" or "crabbing" operation

Cable connector

Cable guard skirts

FIGURE 12-39
Counterweight Pedestal.
The counterweight pedestal uses counterweights to balance cameras of different weights. They include wheels which allow the camera to be moved around the studio floor.

SPECIAL-PURPOSE MOUNTING EQUIPMENT

Although the camera pedestal provides sufficient flexibility for most in-studio requirements, some productions require the camera to operate from angles that are inaccessible with the studio pedestal. For these special purpose applications, cranes and dollies can be used. However, their increased cost, whether purchased or rented, and the additional personnel needed for their operation are serious disadvantages.

Crab Dolly The *crab dolly* had been borrowed from the motion picture industry, where it is the mainstay of film camera mounting devices. The camera is mounted atop a small arm, which is raised or lowered electrically and provides a wider range of operating height than with conventional pedestals. Most crab dollies permit the camera to operate from a minimum height of 14 inches to a maximum height of 61 inches.

The camera operator sits on a small seat next to the camera and rides with the arm as it travels up and down. A second operator pushes and

FIGURE 12-41 Dolly and Track.
The camera operator sits on the seat and is pushed by a
production assistant. The track smooths out the ride
and results in steadier tracking shots. *(Courtesy: Band
Pro Film/Video.)*

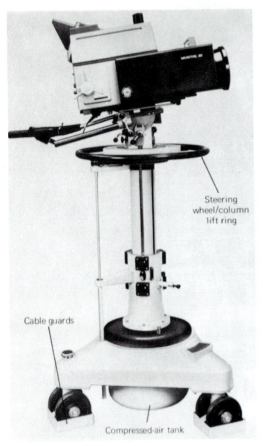

Steering
wheel/column
lift ring

Cable guards

Compressed-air tank

FIGURE 12-40 Pneumatic Pedestal.
The pneumatic pedestal uses compressed air for
adjusting the center column height. Its light weight
makes movement easier than with cameras mounted
on the heavier counterweight pedestal. *(Courtesy: Listec
Television Equipment Corp.)*

steers the crab dolly across the studio floor. The
dolly's four wheels move in a parallel, or "crabbing," fashion, hence its name. For location/re-
mote production, the dolly wheels ride on portable
tracks for the smoothest "crabbing," or "tracking,"
movement. (See Figure 12-41.)

The advantage of the crab dolly is increased
camera flexibility and very smooth dolly move-

ment, but the additional cost in personnel and the
size of the equipment are major disadvantages.

Camera Crane The *camera crane* is a huge
mounting device with four pairs of wheels on a
base and a large arm extending outward. The arm
is hydraulically controlled and may raise the camera more than 20 feet above the floor. (See
Figure 12-42.)

Mini-cranes may be used in smaller spaces,
and even smaller camera mounts, called *jibs*, may
be used. Only the camera is mounted on the end
of the jib; the camera operator works it from floor
level. Using a television monitor, she or he operates the pan, tilt, zoom, and jib operations with a
series of servocontrols. This jib provides cranelike
moves and perspectives, but it is much smaller
and is far less expensive to operate than a crane.

Body Mounts Occasionally, a director will require extreme camera angles or rapid, fluid moves
that cannot be achieved with fixed mounts. In this
case, the camera operator will need a more flexible body mounting device to position the camera

for the shot. When used by a skillful operator, hand-held cameras offer enormous versatility in shooting angles. Imaginatively used, the portable camera can even substitute for the studio crane.

The *body mount* attaches around the operator's waist, distributing the camera's weight and keeping it balanced. Even though a camera may be "portable," it is still heavy and gets heavier after only short periods of use. The body mount helps the operator keep the entire weight of the camera off his or her arms and shoulders and results in much smoother camera movement. (See Figure 12-43.)

Stabilizers Some special body mounts are equipped with a series of servostabilizers which absorb shake and jitter, maintaining a rock-steady picture even when the operator is in motion. The body stabilizer allows the camera operator to replace pedestals, dollies, and cranes while delivering dolly-smooth, jitter-free, hand-held moving shots. An added advantage is that the body stabilizer can be used to shoot from moving cars, trucks, trains, or helicopters, turning almost any vehicle on location into an instant camera platform. (See Figure 12-44.)

FIGURE 12-43   Camera Body Mount.
The weight of the camera is distributed to the operator's waist from the arms and shoulders, reducing fatigue on long and difficult remote productions.

FIGURE 12-42   Camera Crane.
The camera crane is used to lift a camera to high angles. It permits very fluid movements in both horizontal and vertical directions. *(Courtesy: PBS.)*

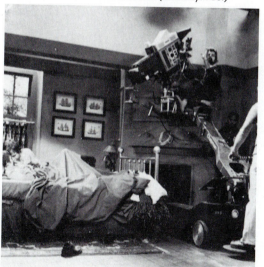

TECH TIP   Because of the relatively high cost and infrequent need for these special camera mounts, many production houses rent them on an "as needed" basis rather than owning them outright.

Robotic Camera System   A *robotic camera system* consists of camera and pedestal hardware that permit remote control of studio camera movements such as panning, tilting, zooming, and focusing. Mounting the camera on an *XYZ pedestal* makes it possible, in addition, to remotely command the camera to move left, right, forward, backward, up, and down. (See Figure 12-45.) The commands are given by the camera operator from a computer workstation in the control room. The most sophisticated robotic camera systems have

(a)

the capability to store camera shots that can be recalled simply by touching a replica on the work-station monitor screen. (See Figure 12-45.) Robotic camera systems are used primarily for newscasts and other studio programs where the talent is stationary and the shots are predictable.

FIGURE 12-44 Steadicam™.
The Steadicam™ enables the camera operator (*a*) to achieve rock-steady pictures, even while moving or (*b*) shooting from difficult positions. *(Courtesy: Cinema Products Corp.)*

FIGURE 12-45 Robotic Camera System. (*facing page*)
(*a*) Studio cameras mounted on XYZ pedestals can be remotely controlled. During the rehearsal, camera shots can be stored in the controller. (*b*) To recall a shot during production, the operator touches it on the screen and the proper camera gets it automatically. Afterward, a storyboard may be printed from the computer display. *(Courtesy: A. F. Associates, Inc.)*

(b)

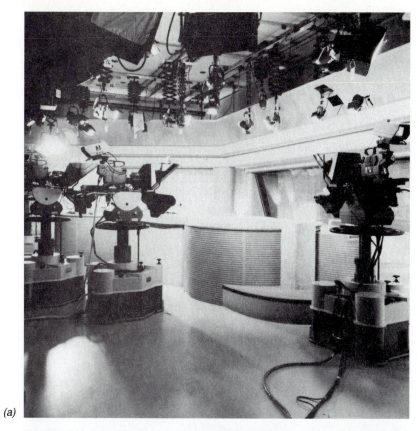

(a)

(b)

**PART 4   VIDEO SYSTEMS: EQUIPMENT AND
OPERATION**

SUMMARY

The camera is the basic instrument of television production. Because of its central role, almost every production decision must revolve around the camera's capabilities and limitations.

Cameras are grouped into two major designs: (1) studio cameras, which operate on a tripod or pedestal, and (2) portable cameras, which are lighter in weight than studio cameras and are operated hand-held, shoulder mounted, or in a convertible design as either mounted studio/field cameras or portable shoulder-mounted cameras. Most portable cameras operate on battery power.

The camera's imaging device, or photoelectric transducer, is the most important component. Production cameras use either the charge-coupled device (CCD) or the pickup tube.

The color camera contains four basic components: (1) the beam splitter, which divides the light entering through the lens into the three primary colors; (2) photoelectric transducers, which transform the light into electrical signals; (3) the chrominance and luminance signals, which provide the color and brightness information; and (4) the encoder, which processes the color and brightness information for transmission through the video system. High-end color cameras have either three-CCD or three-tube photoelectric transducers. Alternative, less expensive single-CCD and single-tube color cameras offer several advantages, although their picture quality is not as good.

The camera chain consists of two major systems: (1) the camera head, including the lens, internal optics, photoelectric transducer and amplifiers, viewfinder, and camera communications systems, and (2) the camera-control unit, or CCU, containing all the necessary equipment to set up and control the camera's operation.

Three important operating characteristics define the camera's capabilities and limitations: (1) the operating light level, (2) the contrast range, and (3) the camera's picture resolution. Most modern cameras are capable of operating under widely varying light levels, some with light levels as low as 5 or 10 fc. For optimum picture reproduction, the contrast range—the difference between the brightest and darkest areas of the picture—should not exceed a 30:1 ratio. The camera's resolution—its ability to distinguish detail in the picture—is limited, even with electronic picture enhancement. Camera shots, angles, and design considerations must be planned to take this restriction into account.

The function of the camera lens is to collect reflected light rays from the subject and form the subject's image on the camera's electronic pickup tube or CCD. The type of lens that is selected and the way it is used determine the image magnification, the size of the subject, and the field of view that is photographed. In short, lens choice establishes the viewer's visual perspective of the scene.

A lens is made up of three parts: (1) the optical elements, which form and shape the image, (2) a variable iris, which is opened or closed to control the amount of light that enters the camera, and (3) the mounting system, which attaches the lens to the camera.

The optical characteristics of lenses which determine the size, view, and perspective of an image are (1) focal length and (2) f-stop.

Focal length determines the image magnification and field of view. The shorter the focal length, the wider is the field of view of the shot and the smaller is the size of the subject. The longer the focal length, the narrower is the field of view and the larger is the size of the subject. Lenses are described in terms of millimeters. Short lenses run from about 12 to 25 mm; normal or medium focal length lenses, from about 25 to 75 mm; and long focal length lenses, from about 75 to 250 mm. Extremely wide and telephoto lenses are also available for special-purpose applications.

A zoom lens is a variable focal length lens that can bring a subject closer or move it farther away in the videospace without actually moving the camera. A fixed focal length lens produces the same degree of image magnification and field of view at all times. Fixed focal length lenses usually are extremely long or short and are used for special purposes.

The f-stop is a numerical term used to describe the size of the iris opening of a lens. Changing the f-stop permits more or less light to enter the camera, compensating for variations in light level. The higher the f-stop number, the smaller is the aperture opening. Smaller apertures reduce the amount of light which enters the camera.

A lens is in focus when the light rays from the rear of the lens converge precisely on the face of the camera's pickup tube. Depth of field refers to the area of acceptable focus in front of and behind the principal object on which the lens is focused. A large area of acceptable focus is a "deep" depth of field; a narrow area of acceptable focus is a "shallow" depth of field. Depth of field is controlled by three factors: (1) focal length—as focal length increases, depth of field decreases; (2) f-stop—as the f-stop number increases, depth of field increases; and (3) camera-to-subject distance— as camera-to-subject distance increases, the depth of field increases.

Filters are used to modify or transform light before it enters a camera. A neutral-density filter reduces light intensity without affecting its color quality. Color-correction filters modify the color temperature of light. Starburst filters refract light from specular objects into star-shaped patterns. Diffusion filters are used to soften hard lines, producing a romantic, dreamlike visual effect.

The most common camera mounting equipment is the pedestal, which operates with either counterweights or air pressure, and it enables the operator to vary the camera's operating height smoothly even while on the air. For portability on remote productions, tripods or studio/field pedestals are used. Such special mounting devices as camera cranes and dollies offer dramatic camera angles and flexible movement. For portable cameras, various body braces are available, some with built-in stabilizers which eliminate shake and jitter and produce extremely steady hand-held or shoulder-mounted shots.

O P E R A T I N G   T E L E V I S I O N   C A M E R A S   A N D   L E N S E S

In Chapter 2 we introduced the principles of media aesthetics and discussed what image elements mean in the *videospace*. Now that we have presented the primary tools of video imaging, the camera and the lens, we will show how the camera operator uses them to build the videospace. We will begin by describing methods to frame and compose still and moving images. Next we will examine the use of lenses to create perspective and depth in video images. Then we will conclude with practical guidelines for camera work in studio and field productions. Our goal in this chapter is to provide the camera operator with practical techniques for achieving aesthetically pleasing video.

A good camera operator combines a strong visual sense for form and composition, an aesthetic sensitivity for the program's overall concept and approach, and the physical skills and coordination necessary to operate the camera smoothly and with precision. Effective camera work comes only through practice and the experience you gain after working in a variety of different production situations.

BUILDING THE VIDEOSPACE: FRAMING AND COMPOSITION

Unlike the theatrical stage, where the audience can direct its attention to any part of the stage (as well as to any part of the theater), the television audience must rely totally on the director and the camera operators to organize and compose the sequence of shots that convey the action taking place in front of the cameras. Although the director ultimately is responsible for selecting the different shots and angles to cover the program, the camera operator must find and frame the shots. To do this well, you must develop a feel for pictorial composition, which is, to a great extent, learned through a combination of intuition, practice, and experience. Fortunately, a number of excellent guidelines have been developed over many years through the work of painters, sculptors, photographers, and motion picture cinematographers. You can use these guidelines to help you start thinking visually.

One way to think of framing and composition is in terms of building the videospace for the viewer. Since the audience's only measure of what is taking place before the camera is what it sees on the television screen, how you represent this reality in terms of the videospace is of crucial importance. During the course of a production, the director and the camera operators are faced with an almost unlimited number of pictorial choices. Exactly what you decide to include within the television frame, what you decide *not* to include, and how you show this information determines to a large extent how the audience perceives the visual portion of the program.

As an example, take a simple three-person interview. If we shoot all three participants in a wide shot, there is no visual cue for the viewer as to which speaker is the most important. Assuming that lighting and other production considerations are equal, the audience most likely will focus on whomever is talking at any particular time. Now, if we isolate one of the participants in close-up, we automatically exclude from the audience's sight any potentially distracting elements, forcing the viewer to watch the one person who is filling the videospace at that time.

Naturally, many things must be taken into account when deciding exactly how to shoot a subject. However, we can include all these considerations in two important points: (1) show the viewers what they *need* to see and (2) show the viewers what they *want* to see. Needless to say, you should make every attempt to show both what the viewer needs and wants to see in as interesting and imaginative a way as possible.

Let us take the case of a program demonstrating how to play the guitar. When the host begins to talk about finger positions on the guitar's neck, the audience *needs* to see a close-up of the host's fingers in order to understand and appreciate what is being communicated. If, later on in the show, the host plays a tune to show how a practice exercise ought to sound, the audience *wants* to see a good close-up of the guitarist's fingers in order to enhance their enjoyment and appreciation of the show.

While these two "rules" may seem overly general, if you keep them in mind during a production, you will not go wrong. However, there are times when you may want to violate the rules for special effect. At the start of a murder mystery, for instance, the viewers might want to see the face of the killer, but they are willing to suspend—for a time—seeing the villain in order to enjoy the who-dunit. However, if you frustrate the viewers too often or in the wrong places, you run the risk of confusing or annoying them to the point where they no longer understand or enjoy the show.

As we determine what the audience needs and wants to see, we are building the videospace. It is convenient to look at this building process from the camera operator's point of view as a combination of two different, but related functions: (1) *framing* the shot and (2) *composing* the shot. Although these terms often are used interchangeably, for now it would be a good idea to differentiate between them.

Framing refers to the inclusion (and exclusion) of various pictorial elements within the videospace and how these elements are shown to the viewer. For example, in the interview program we just mentioned, the framing decisions include who among the participants we show in a particular shot, the kind of shot we use (a wide shot, close-up, etc.), and the particular camera angle (normal, low-angle, high-angle) that we select.

Composition refers to the organization of these pictorial elements in such a way as to present a picture to the audience that is unified, shows the relationship between the elements within the frame, and provides an aesthetically pleasing visual image. Of course, the two concepts of framing and composition are very closely related to each other. While we will discuss them independently for now, once you get to the point where you are selecting shots and angles and composing a shot, you must automatically combine the two as you build the videospace.

FRAMING THE SHOT

As you stand behind a camera and frame a shot, there are a number of technical decisions as well as aesthetic judgments to make. The technical matters include such obvious points as which subjects to include and which to exclude, how to present the subject with maximum visual clarity, and how to frame the scene to include the most important elements within the essential area of the picture frame. The aesthetic decisions include the particular field of view that the shot will encom-

pass, the camera angle you will use, and how to frame and follow subject movement. Together these factors play an important role in building the videospace.

Visual Clarity

A primary consideration when framing any shot is its *visual clarity*. Obviously, a shot that does not show the important action clearly to the viewer cannot be an effective shot. Undoubtedly, at one time or another, you have watched a television program in utter frustration because the shots the director selected or the camera operator framed simply did not deliver the visual information you wanted and needed to see to enjoy the show. For example, a profile shot usually is weaker and conveys less information than a full-face shot. This is particularly important when the subject is speaking directly to a viewing audience, as in a commercial or an instructional program. In this case, the better shot would be a head-on shot.

In almost every production situation, regardless of content, there usually are some shots and compositions that are more effective than others. Needless to say, it is impossible to give you any rules or guidelines, since each situation is different. Your intuition and experience must determine the framing which will provide the best communication to the viewing audience by making optimum use of the videospace.

Essential Area

The picture you see in the camera's viewfinder is not the same picture the television audience ultimately sees. This is so because as the signal from the camera passes through the television system, the outer portions of the picture are "cropped" or lost, reducing the size of the picture and eliminating the subject material along the outer borders. The central portion of the camera's picture which is transmitted to the viewer is called the *essential area,* and every camera shot should be framed to include the most important visual information within this space.

A good rule of thumb to use in framing a shot is

Image on camera
viewfinder

Essential area on
typical TV receiver

(a)

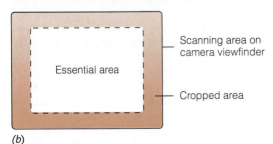

Scanning area on
camera viewfinder

Essential area

Cropped area

(b)

FIGURE 13-1 **Essential Area.**
(a) The camera viewfinder overscans the image,
showing more information than what the viewer will
ultimately see. The camera operator must compensate
for this cropping by composing shots in the viewfinder
so that the most important visual material is kept within
the essential area. *(b)* The essential area is sometimes
referred to as the "safe" area. The cropped area can't
be measured exactly, because the amount of
overscanning of TV receivers varies. However, it's
usually about 10 to 15 percent of the scanning area.

to assume that the outer 10 to 15 percent of the
camera viewfinder's shot will be lost to the viewer.
Some camera operators like to draw a square on
their viewfinders with a grease pencil to remind
them to keep all important shot elements—the performers, the sponsor's product, graphic titles, and
pictures—within the essential area. Of course, the
program director must ultimately determine the
framing and composition, but it is a lot easier on
everyone if you automatically frame each shot with
the essential area in mind. (See Figure 13-1.)

Field of View

One of the most important choices facing the director and the camera operator is exactly how
large to show the principal subject and how much
of his or her surroundings: the *field of view* of the
shot. You might think of the field of view as the
balance between the principal subject and her or
his surrounding background area. A very wide
field of view will take in a great deal of background
but makes the size of the subject rather small in
the shot. On the other hand, a tight close-up gives
dominance to the subject, who fills the screen, ex-
cluding any distracting background elements
from the shot.

In the early days of motion pictures, many directors followed a basic shot progression sequence. The convention was to begin each scene
with a wide, establishing shot to help orient the
viewer to the spatial relationships among the elements in the scene. Once the audience was sufficiently comfortable, the shots would become
progressively tighter, isolating the principal subjects and eliminating more and more background.
Although a strict adherence to this formula is no
longer necessary, since audiences can follow the
action without such an obvious orientation, the
various shots within the progression make a convenient way to break down and organize the component parts of the videospace. (See Figure 13-2.)

Extreme Long Shots (ELS) These produce a
very wide field of view in which the camera takes

FIGURE 13-2 Field of View.
This sequence of shots shows the progression from an extreme long shot to a close-up.

in the entire playing area. The principal subject or subjects are small in relation to the background and tend to compete with the surroundings for the viewer's attention.

Long Shots (LS)   These produce a slightly closer field of view than extreme long shots, but the subject remains dominated by the much larger background area. Establishing shots are either extreme long shots or long shots.

Medium Shots (MS)   Here the subject becomes much larger and more dominant. The background is still important but now shares the videospace with the subject.

Medium Close-up (MCU)   This is the most prevalent shot used in television. The subject's head and shoulders make up the MCU. Although different directors may see it slightly differently, a good

starting point for framing the MCU is to include the first button of talent's open-collar shirt.

Close-up (CU)   The subject becomes the primary focus of interest within the shot. Only a small portion of the background is visible.

Extreme Close-up (ECU)   The subject virtually fills the screen and is clearly the central focus of the shot. Some directors call an extreme close-up on a subject's face a "slice shot" because the shot is so close it literally shows only a portion, or a slice, of the subject's face.

Needless to say, these descriptions of the camera's field of view are relative and can vary depending on the other shots in the sequence, the individual director, or the program's subject matter. For example, in an intimate dramatic show, the director may tighten all the shots so that a normal medium shot is the widest shot in the show. The notion of what constitutes a "long," "medium," or "close-up" shot also can vary. One director's close-up may be another's medium shot. A good camera operator learns to adapt quickly to each director's personal style in framing the field of view. Finally, a shot can be long, medium, or close in relation to the size of the subject. A close-up of Mount Everest would probably be considered an establishing long shot for most other subjects. Similarly, an establishing long shot of an ant farm would be, under most other circumstances, an extreme close-up.

Cutoff Lines   There is another way to designate the field of view of a shot when the subject is a person. This approach uses the body's natural *cutoff lines* as references. They fall at the top of the head, the neck, the bust, the waist, the knee, and the toes. If the top of the frame is at the top of the subject's head and the bottom falls at one of the natural cutoff lines, the following shots result: the *head shot* (HS), the *bust shot* (BS), the *waist shot* (WS), the *knee shot* (KS), and the *full shot* (FS). (See Figure 13-3.) The advantage of this system is that the framing desired is clear. For example, the line at which a waist shot should cut off

Head

Head
shot

Neck

Chest

Chest
shot

Waist

Waist shot

Knee shot

Knee

Head-to-toe
shot

Toe

FIGURE 13-3 Cutoff Lines.
A convenient way to organize
framing and to refer to shots
is by using natural cutoff lines.
This can help eliminate
confusion, because a
"medium shot" may be
framed differently by different
people, but a "waist shot"
specifically describes the
desired shot.

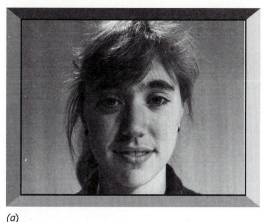

(a)

(b)

FIGURE 13-4 Closure.

(a) This framing, exactly at two natural cutoff lines—the top of the head and the neck—illustrates the effects of closure. The head is cut off at the neck, leaving it disembodied and "floating" within the frame. (b) In this case, by framing below the natural cut-off line, the shoulders provide a solid foundation for the head and suggest a body outside of the frame.

is more well defined than that of a medium close-up. However, framing by natural cutoff lines can lead to a displeasing psychological effect called *closure*, or completion, in the frame. This may create the feeling of a "bobbing" head or "legless" body. Cutting the shots off slightly below the natural cutoff lines will avoid closure and suggest an extension of the subject beyond the frame. (See Figure 13-4.)

Multiple Subjects   When you must frame more than one person in a shot, most directors call the shot by the number of subjects to be included. For example, there is a *two-shot* and a *three-shot*. Anything wider than a three-shot is generally called a "wide" or "long" shot. Another grouping that is commonly used is the *over-the-shoulder shot* (OS). This is an effective shot because it establishes a relationship between characters and, at the same time, enhances the depth of the shot. (See Figure 13-5.)

Camera Angles

The angle from which the camera photographs a subject or a scene is another important factor in building the videospace. Not only can a variety of camera angles provide the viewer with the most

advantageous or interesting viewpoint, but certain camera angles produce a unique perspective that can affect the audience's perception of what is happening on the television screen.

Normal Angle   The *normal angle* positions the camera at approximately the subject's eye level,

FIGURE 13-5   **Over-the-Shoulder (OS) Shot.**
The over-the-shoulder shot of Patrick Buchanan emphasizes his confrontation with Michael Kinsley on CNN's *Crossfire* program. *(Courtesy: Turner Broadcasting Systems and Videssence, Inc.)*

371

shooting the scene as we would normally view the world. Of course, the "normal" angle depends to a large extent on the subject being photographed. If we were shooting a group of small children at play, our "normal" adult angle would be too high. In this case, the camera should be lowered to shoot at the child's eye level.

As you operate your camera, remember that the normal angle refers to the subject's position, not to the camera height that will be most convenient and comfortable for you. If a subject is seated, the camera must be pedestaled down to eye level. If the subject gets up, the camera should pedestal up to maintain a normal angle. This is why most interview shows build their sets and chairs on risers to raise the seated height of the participants so that the camera operators can shoot at a normal angle without stooping or bending during the production.

High Camera Angle

A *high camera angle* positions the camera above eye level, with the camera shooting down on the subject. A high camera angle is very useful when trying to show the audience an overview of the set or playing area. In addition, a high camera angle tends to make the subject appear to be smaller in size and stature. Looking down from a high camera angle invests the subject with a feeling of loneliness, lack of power, and loss of dominance.

Low Camera Angle

A *low camera angle* positions the camera below eye level so that the camera shoots up toward the subject. Shooting up from a low angle tends to increase the audience's perception of the subject's size and suggests a feeling of power, dominance, and dynamism. This is why so many political candidates prefer to have their commercials shot from a slightly lower camera angle to give the audience the impression that they are physically taller and psychologically powerful and dominant. The same psychological effect can be used in product advertising. For example, many new car commercials are shot with the camera at a low angle position, making the car seem larger, sleeker, and more powerful to the viewer. Figure 13-6 presents several examples of camera angles.

Canted Angle

A *canted angle* is produced by tilting the camera on its horizontal plane. The picture that is produced is dynamic, exciting, and unstable. It suggests a feeling of fantasy, suspense, or unreality to the viewer. A canted angle is very easy to achieve with a portable camera by simply asking the camera operator to tilt the camera to the desired angle. On studio pedestal cameras, which are not easily tilted horizontally, you can achieve the same effect by using a special prism device fitted over the lens. Turning the prism will tilt the image at any desired angle producing the canted effect.

The canted angle is clearly dynamic and exciting and shows us the world in a way we do not ordinarily see it. For this very reason, however, the shot calls attention to itself and should be used sparingly to be most effective. (See Figure 13-7.)

Subjective Camera Angle

A *subjective camera angle* puts the camera in the place of a character and shows us the scene from the character's point of view. This is called a *point-of-view (POV) shot*. When used effectively in a dramatic production, the POV shot can have a great impact on the viewer. For example, let us consider a scene in which a man is running away from an attacker. Shooting with a hand-held portable camera that travels along the same route as the man will involve the viewers in the action, making them feel a part of the play. The same technique can be used in instructional programs or in documentaries. Shooting a racing car speeding around a track from an objective angle might be exciting, but it cannot compare with placing a camera inside the driver's cockpit, showing the audience what the driver actually sees as the car races around the course. (See Figure 13-8.)

Framing Movement

The camera operator must frequently deal with a moving subject. Since both the subject and the camera itself can move, framing movement is an important dimension in building the videospace.

Generally, movement toward or away from the camera is more forceful, dynamic, and interest-

FIGURE 13-6 Camera Angles.
Low angles suggest dominance, normal angles invite equality, and high angles are sometimes used to indicate weakness. Eye-level shots are neutral.

FIGURE 13-7 Canted Angle.
A canted camera angle suggests action, excitement, or instability.

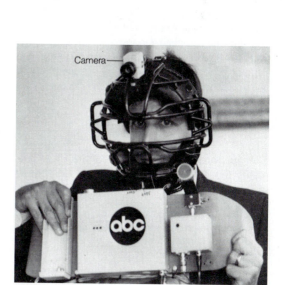

FIGURE 13-8 Subjective/Objective Camera Angle.
A subjective camera angle places the viewer into the action. Here, the camera mounted on the umpire's mask can capture the sensation of a fast ball. (*Courtesy: Capital Cities/ABC, Inc.*)

ing than movement perpendicular to the camera-subject axis. This is so because movement toward or away from the camera tends to increase or decrease the subject's size in the videospace. This, in turn, enhances the depth perspective of the shot, producing a visually interesting and exciting picture. Lateral movement does not change the subject's size and, consequently, is not as dynamic or exciting.

When you follow a moving subject, particularly one moving across the screen perpendicular to the camera-subject axis, try to lead the subject by giving him or her more space in front than behind. This will prevent the illusion of a moving subject's being forced against the leading edge of the picture frame.

Framing and following movement are not easy, and they get even harder when shooting a tight shot. Unless you can rehearse the move carefully, you may have to shoot slightly wider to keep the subject properly framed and to reduce camera shake during the move. (See Figure 13-9.)

COMPOSING THE SHOT

Composition is the organization of the visual elements within the videospace. A well-composed

FIGURE 13-9   Framing Movement.
When photographing a moving object, provide lead space in the direction of movement rather than centering the moving object.

shot (1) is unified, (2) establishes the spatial and psychological relationships between the various components, (3) directs the audience's attention to the most important elements within the scene, and (4) produces a picture that is aesthetically pleasing and interesting to watch.

Composing in Depth

A television picture occupies a two-dimensional screen. A sense of depth in the shot is achieved through the careful use of camera angles, performer blocking and such production variables as set design, lighting, and makeup, as well as picture composition.

When you compose a picture, try to enhance the depth of the videospace as much as possible. You might think of the scene as consisting of a number of different depth planes: the foreground, the middle ground, and the background. If a shot contains information from more than one depth plane, its depth perception is enhanced and the shot looks more interesting and alive to the viewer.

One way to do this is to shoot subjects from an angle rather than straight-on. Just as moving subjects appear more dynamic when seen moving toward or away from the camera, so too is the depth increased when a scene is shot from a slight angle. Another way to enhance depth is to make good use of the background area. A neutral background, which has little or no depth itself, will not convey to the viewer a feeling of space and distance between the principal subject and the background. Using the foreground plane by including foreground interest in the shot is another excellent way to increase depth. The degree to which depth planes overlap one another influences the suggestion of depth. (See Figure 13-10.)

Organizing the Videospace into Groupings

Whenever we view a scene in our everyday lives, we unconsciously attempt to organize the various elements into some sort of cohesive, unified whole. This makes it easier for us to comprehend and follow the action as it takes place. The great masters of painting, sculpture, and photography have capitalized on this to help focus and direct our attention to the most important elements within their works.

(a)

(a)

FIGURE 13-10 Composing in Depth.
(a) The camera is positioned perpendicular to the action axis, creating no depth in the scene; *(b)* the camera is positioned to introduce depth and interest in the scene.

ment or dynamism, and the feeling of equilibrium.

If the major pictorial elements are not equidistant from the center, the image is *asymmetrical*. Asymmetrical images may be either balanced or unbalanced. In *asymmetrical balance*, a subject is positioned to one side of the frame with a counterbalancing element on the opposite side to equalize the "weight" of the subject. Examples of both symmetrical and asymmetrical balance appear in newscasts. A shot in which a reporter is shown alone and centered on the screen has symmetrical balance. If the reporter is placed on one side and a background location, such as a government building, appears on the other side, the image has asymmetrical balance. Besides containing more visual information, the shot with asymmetrical balance will look more interesting and pleasing aesthetically. Employing the principles of the *Golden Mean* and the *rule of thirds*, which we illustrated in Chapter 2, will lead to asymmetrically-balanced composition.

An asymmetrical image that does not have counterbalancing pictorial elements is *unbalanced*. An unbalanced composition conveys the impression of instability and the potential for dynamic movement. It focuses the audience's attention on that particular element or portion of the shot which has the greatest visual weight. Many music videos use unbalanced images to intensify their imagery and focus attention on the performers. (See Figure 13-11.)

Although the number of possible groupings is virtually limitless, we can organize them into three major categories: (1) balanced and unbalanced groupings, (2) triangular groupings, and (3) foreground-background groupings.

Balanced and Unbalanced Groupings   *Balance* refers to the overall apparent steadiness or stability of an image. If a pictorial element is centered or two similar elements are equidistant from the center, the image is said to have *symmetrical* balance, and all the major pictorial elements are equal in visual attraction or dominance. Symmetrical balance suggests stability, the lack of move-

Triangular Groupings   The triangular grouping, as its name suggests, organizes elements within a frame into a triangular fashion, the visual dominance usually occurring at one of the apex points of the triangle. Although a triangle has three sides, this does not mean that the grouping can be used only with three subjects. Fewer or more than three subjects can be grouped into a pyramid design. The number of subjects organized is unimportant; it is the overall shape and grouping within the videospace that matters. The triangular grouping imparts a feeling of strength and stability within the videospace.

The triangular approach is a very effective

(a)

(b)

(c)

FIGURE 13-11 **Balanced and Unbalanced Composition.**
(*a*) Symmetrical balance is stable but uninteresting.
(*b*) Asymmetrical balance also creates a sense of stability, but is more dynamic and interesting.
(*c*) Unbalanced composition creates feelings of instability and insecurity.

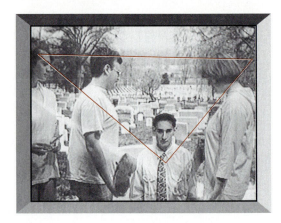

FIGURE 13-12 **Triangular Grouping.**
Triangular grouping of subjects adds depth and visual interest to a scene.

grouping for a number of reasons. First, it enables you to include more subjects within a tighter shot than would be possible with a less compact grouping. Second, dominance can be easily achieved through effective positioning of the subjects and using the natural apex points to direct the viewer's attention. Finally, the triangular grouping can position subjects on different depth planes and enhance the depth dimension of the shot. (See Figure 13-12.)

Foreground-Background Groupings A foreground-background grouping arranges subjects on two or more depth planes within the videospace. Needless to say, this grouping is very effective in enhancing depth perspective because the composition naturally uses foreground and background planes. It is also an effective way of conveying visual dominance. Although the foreground element is usually the stronger in the shot, because of its enlarged size and prominence within the frame, this dominance can be modified through the use of selective focus and the effective use of depth of field. The composition also produces a very interesting and dynamic shot, which is one of its advantages. (See Figure 13-13.)

OVER-THE-SHOULDER SHOT The over-the-shoulder shot frames a scene from over a subject's shoulder. This is usually used when two or more characters are speaking, since it helps to estab-

FIGURE 13-13 Foreground-Background Grouping.
The group in the foreground is dominant because of its size in comparison to the group in the background.

lish the relationship between them. It is also frequently used on interview shows for the same reason. The over-the-shoulder shot is effective because it introduces depth in the shot, establishes a relationship between subjects on different depth planes, and offers a great deal of versatility in framing different shots from the same basic camera and subject positions. (See Figure 13-14.)

FOREGROUND TREATMENT Positioning an object or subject in the foreground of a shot to help frame background elements is an effective, interesting, and visually strong compositional technique. Sometimes the foreground element is an important thematic device—for example, the whiskey

bottle that tempts the reformed alcoholic seated in the background. Used a different way, the foreground element might simply be a set piece, prop, doorway, or window that helps to create depth and provide a visually interesting shot. (See Figure 13-15.)

Birdseye Shot When a camera is placed at an extreme high angle so that it is looking down from the top of a set, it is called a *birdseye angle*, or *aerial perspective*. Birdseye angles provide al-

FIGURE 13-15 Foreground Treatment.
A well-positioned foreground object can create depth and establish meaning in a scene.

Bell suggests a wedding in the chapel in background

FIGURE 13-14 Over-the-Shoulder Shot.
Different framings of the over-the-shoulder shot create different senses of intimacy or involvement.

FIGURE 13-16 Birdseye View.
A birdseye view is highly stylized and offers the audience a unique perspective on a scene. (*Courtesy: Capital Cities/ABC, Inc.*)

most no depth information but offer a unique perspective for showing spatial relationships. Even everyday events can take on geometric regularity or show chaotic movement. Busby Berkley's signature in his 1930 film musical was the geometric pattern created by dancers photographed from above. The aerial perspective also is a signature of Alfred Hitchcock, as the bathroom scene in *Psycho* attests. Today, some sports events such as football are covered from a birdseye angle to provide an informative viewpoint of the on-field action. When used at the appropriate moment, a birdseye angle can provide the audience with an attractive and unusual visual element. (See Figure 13-16.)

Compositions to Avoid

Any shot that does not show the subject clearly, that is visually disagreeable, or that unintentionally confuses the viewer is poor composition. Some of the most common pitfalls to avoid are the following:

Profile Shots   In general, a full-face shot is far more effective and much more flattering than a profile shot of a subject. Whenever possible, avoid stark profiles or "ear shots" that do not show the viewer much of a subject's face. Naturally, there may be special circumstances which call for a profile shot, but in most cases, cross-shooting or arcing the camera around slightly will provide you with a much more effective three-quarters or full-face shot instead of the weaker profile. (See Figure 13-17.)

Lack of Headroom   Remember to consider the essential area, particularly when framing close-ups. A head shot that is tightly framed in the camera's viewfinder will usually mean insufficient headroom on the home receiver. Since all four sides of a frame are cropped by the TV system, insufficient headroom is a common problem. (See Figure 13-18.)

Lack of Lead Room   When shooting a subject at

378

(a)

(b)

(c)

(a)

(b)

FIGURE 13-18   **Headroom.**
(a) Sufficient headroom; (b) too little headroom can leave the viewer feeling cramped.

FIGURE 13-17   **Camera Angles.**
(a) The profile shot leaves the viewer wishing to see more of the subject's face; (b) the three-quarters shot is a large improvement; (c) the full-face shot involves the audience with the subject.

an angle, or in profile, give the subject some *lead room*, also often called "lead space" or "nose room." You do this by placing the eyes of the subject on the side of the frame from which he or she is looking. There should be more space in front of the subject than behind. The amount depends on the angle at which the subject is looking across the frame. (See Figure 13-19.) If the subject's nose is next to the frame, we can't see what's immediately in front of the subject's face. It could be empty space or it could be a boxer's glove about to deliver a punch. We don't know so we have no way of inferring the psychological state of the sub-

(a)

FIGURE 13-19 Lead Room.
(*a*) Nose Room: When a subject looks off screen, frame the subject with more room in the direction of the look.
(*b*) Lead Space: When a subject is in motion, frame the subject with more space in the direction he or she is moving.

(b)

ject and the motivation for his or her expression. Also, if there is no lead room for a subject shot in profile, the composition most likely will be unbalanced and unstable. In addition, if the shot is in a sequence of close-ups during an interview or discussion, the framing will not lend itself to the sequence. Instead of appearing to be looking at the other participants, the subject will appear to look away from them, out of the frame.

If the subject is in motion from left to right or right to left, the subject should not appear to be moving out of the frame. The subject should be in the side of the frame from which he or she is coming. There should be more space in front of the subject than

behind. (See Figure 13-19.) The subject should have lead room so the audience knows what's ahead. For example, does the halfback have a clear field ahead or is a huge defensive back about to crush him? A shot framed with proper lead room will inform the audience and present a better visual impression.

Too Much Screen Space If you frame a shot with too much space in the center of the screen, you may draw the viewer's attention away from the principal subject over to the background area. This can be a problem in two-person interviews where each participant frames the edges of the

380

FIGURE 13-20 Too Much Screen Space.
Subjects should be placed close together on a set to avoid too much screen space in which the visually important central screen area is empty.

show coming down to the child's height—or a riser should be used to raise the shorter subject higher in the frame. (See Figure 13-21.)

Unsuitable Camera Angle   Be certain that the camera angle you are using to photograph a subject complements the visual impression you want the viewer to receive. For example, inadvertently shooting down on seated subjects may give the audience the erroneous impression that they lack dominance, authority, and power.

Distracting Movement   All things being equal, a moving subject will invariably draw the audience's attention more than a static subject. Veteran performers know this only too well and sometimes use little movements to steal a scene from another actor. When you compose a shot, keep this factor in mind so that the audience's focus is not inadvertently drawn away from what should be the dominant portion of the videospace.

screen, directing the audience's attention to the center of the videospace. Either move the subjects closer, shoot from an angle, or modify the set, lighting, or both to avoid having the central area compete for the viewer's attention. (See Figure 13-20.)

Differences in Subject Height   Unless you are shooting an extremely wide shot, be careful to compensate for obvious differences in subject sizes. Either the taller subject should come down to the lower level—as in the host of a children's

Poor Juxtaposition of Subjects   The flower pot growing out of a person's head and the set piece extending from a subject's ear are unintentional compositions that you should avoid. Repositioning either the camera, the subject, or the back-

FIGURE 13-21 Mismatched Heights.
Placing performers so their heads are at approximately the same height improves picture composition.

(a)

(b)

FIGURE 13-22 Poor Juxtaposition of Elements in Shot.
(*a*) Here the background object appears to be growing out of the performer's head;
(*b*) slight camera repositioning eliminates the problem.

ground element should correct the problem. (See Figure 13-22.)

MOVING THE CAMERA

There are two types of motion of concern to the camera operator: primary and secondary motion. (There also is *tertiary* motion, but since it mainly concerns the editor, we will save it for Chapter 15.) *Primary motion* refers to the movement of the subject, and *secondary motion* refers to the movement of the camera. A shot may be designed for the subject to move within the frame or to move out of the frame. That is primary motion. It requires the operator merely to hold a steady, well-framed shot as the subject moves. However, the director may call for a *follow shot* in which the camera operator must follow the subject. This combination of primary and secondary motion presents several challenges. The camera operator must follow at a smooth, even pace that matches the speed of the subject. That takes good anticipation, physical coordination, and practice. Another form of secondary motion takes place when a camera moves to *reframe* a shot. For example, as two people seated in a crowded room begin a conversation, the camera may move from a group shot to a two-shot of the couple.

There are two ways for a camera to move: (1) the camera head can move atop its stationary pedestal, and (2) the entire camera and pedestal can move together as a unit. When a director wants either type of movement, he or she will issue a direction or command. As with any specialized field, television production has developed a language all its own to communicate directions and commands quickly and accurately. In the case of the camera, there are a number of special terms to describe its operation. Figure 13-23 summarizes the key commands, and we will explain them throughout our discussion. You should try to learn them as quickly as possible, and get into the habit of using them as you work in production situations. While reading the descriptions of the various camera movements, refer to Figure 13-24 for visual clarification.

Pan

The camera head revolves horizontally on a stationary pedestal or tripod.

Command: "Pan right" or "Pan left." Sometimes the director may give you more specific instructions, such as "Pan right with the host as he walks to the table." As with other camera commands, the *direction* is from the perspective of the camera operator, not the talent, so a pan to the right will follow talent moving to their left.

Beginning camera operators often become confused by the seemingly simple directions "Pan left" and "Pan right." The confusion arises because two "opposites" are at work in panning a television camera: First, the operator must move

COMMAND	MEANING
Pan (left/right)	Move the camera lens horizontally left/right. The pedestal does not move.
Tilt (up/down)	Move the camera lens vertically up/down. The pedestal does not move.
Pedestal (up/down)	Move the pedestal vertically up/down.
Dolly (in/out)	Move the pedestal toward/ away from the subject.
Truck (right/left)	Move the pedestal horizontally right/left.
Arc (right/left)	Move the pedestal in a half circle, combining a dolly and a truck.
Crane (up/down)	Move the crane vertically up/down.
Zoom (in/out)	Using the zoom control, reduce/increase the field of view.
Loosen	Zoom out or dolly out slightly.
Tighten	Zoom in or dolly in slightly.
Hold	Stop any camera movement.
Single shot	Frame one person in a shot (usually medium).
Close-up	Frame one person from the shoulders up.
Head and Shoulders	Frame a close-up that includes the shoulders.
Medium shot	Frame a person from about the waist up.
Head-to-toe	Frame a person from the toes up.
Two-shot	Frame two people in a shot.
Three-shot	Frame three people in a shot.
Cover shot	Frame a wide shot that covers the whole scene of action.
Frame up	Reframe slightly. (Must be obvious.)
Focus up	Get the shot as sharp as possible.
Rack focus	Shift the focus from one subject to another.

the pan handles in the *opposite* direction from the director's pan command; and, second, the subject on the screen moves on the screen in the *opposite* direction from the director's pan command. For example, when you are directed to "Pan right," you must move the pan handles to the left, and the subject will appear to move to the left on the screen. An easy way to always know the proper direction you should pan is to remember that "Pan right" means to pan the *lens* to the right. "Pan left" means to pan the *lens* to the left.

Sometimes beginning directors also will get "Pan left" and "Pan right" confused. If a director wants a subject positioned more to the right in the frame, the director must say "Pan *left*" to the camera operator. Occasionally you will hear a director say "Frame the subject right." In this case, the camera operator would pan *left*. In any case, the camera operator must be awake, think quickly, and react almost instinctively. This terminology may seem confusing at first, but it takes only a short time to get used to it. You should make the effort because it is the standard practice in television production. Camera operators are judged by how quickly they get the needed shot, as well as how the shot looks when they get it.

Panning is done differently on air and off air. The essence of the off-air pan is *speed*. If your camera is off air and the director tells you to pan to a subject, the off-air pan should be done as quickly as possible no matter how it looks. However, when your camera is on air, your pan should be steady, smooth, at an even pace, and should stop with the subject well framed. However, there is one kind of on-air pan that breaks this rule. A special kind of pan is the *swish pan* or *whip pan*. This is a very rapid move that looks like a blur of light on the television monitor. It is sometimes used for transitions or for other special effects.

A pan across a scene never should wander aimlessly but should have a definite starting point and a definite ending point. Whenever possible, the pan should be "motivated." Sometimes you can have a subject look in the direction of the pan and then execute the camera move to reveal to the viewer what the subject sees. If this is neither pos-

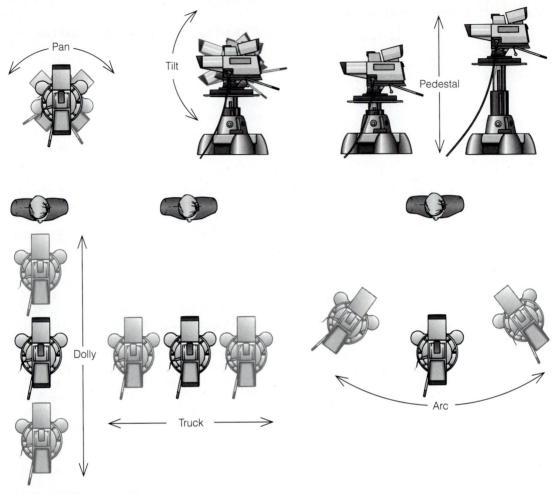

FIGURE 13-24 **Camera Movements.**

sible nor desirable, be sure to have definite starting and stopping points fixed in your own mind so the pan movement will be decisive and direct.

Tilt

The camera head pivots vertically on a stationary pedestal or tripod.

Command: "Tilt up" or "Tilt down." The term *tilt* always refers to a vertical movement, and the term *pan* always refers to a horizontal move. This distinction helps eliminate confusion on the part of the camera operator. As with the pan, the "oppo-

sites" are at work. Remember that "Tilt up" means to tilt the *lens* up, and "Tilt down" means to tilt the *lens* down. As with the pan, establish definite start and stop points to guide your tilt from subject to subject.

Pedestal

The camera head moves up or down as the center telescoping column of the pedestal is raised or lowered.

Command: "Pedestal up" or "Pedestal down." The pedestal control on a camera changes its point of view just as though you viewed a scene sitting down and then stood up to look around. Because it actually raises or lowers the camera's height, the pedestal results in a much different visual perspective of the scene and can be used to great advantage by the director.

It is important to realize that pedestaling up or down is not the same as tilting up or down. Tilting the camera simply changes its angle of view from a fixed operating height; pedestaling actually varies the camera's height.

While it is usually most comfortable for the camera operator to set the pedestal at a convenient operating height, this may not coincide with the best pedestal height for the shot. Good camera operators adjust the height of the pedestal for the best view of the subject, not for their working comfort. This also avoids unintentional high or low camera angles on subjects. Often the director may ask you to set the pedestal height to keep the camera at approximately eye level with the subject, even if this puts you in an awkward working position.

Since you may be asked to change pedestal height frequently during a program, it is best never to lock the pedestal into position. If the pedestal has been properly adjusted, the camera's weight should be perfectly balanced and the pedestal will remain at any height until changed by the camera operator. Working with the pedestal lock off allows you to move the pedestal quickly and smoothly, both on air and off air.

TECH TIP Most cameras have a tiltable viewfinder on the camera to allow the camera operator to work comfortably at high or low pedestal settings. Be sure to adjust the viewfinder and not the pedestal for your comfort.

Dolly

Movement of the pedestal with its camera either toward or away from the subject or scene.

Command: "Dolly in" or "Dolly out." The director usually will tell you how fast or slow the speed of the dolly should be.

Truck

The lateral movement of the pedestal with its camera.

Command: "Truck right" or "Truck left." The truck can be used to adjust the camera's position to compose and frame a shot better, as well as to follow a moving subject as it crosses the set. If you are following a moving subject, the camera move is sometimes called a "tracking" shot.

Just as there is a difference between a tilt and a pedestal, there also is a big difference between a truck and a pan. The pan changes the camera's horizontal field of view from a stationary position. The truck actually moves the camera, establishing a new shooting angle, which results in a much different view of the subject or scene photographed.

Arc

A combination of a dolly and a truck, the arc is a semicircular movement of the pedestal and its camera.

Command: "Arc right" or "Arc left." The arc is frequently used to show circular movement or to reveal a view from behind the principal subject.

Crane

A crane is movement of the camera atop the long arm of a crane.

Command: "Crane up" or "Crane down." Sometimes the command "Boom up" or "Boom down" is used. A horizontal movement of the crane arm is called *tonguing,* and the command is "Tongue right" or "Tongue left."

Combination Movements

Of course, it is very common to combine one or more of these camera movements during normal operation. For example, as you dolly in, the director may ask you to pedestal down. At the same time you will probably have to pan and tilt slightly to keep the subject framed properly. This interplay of movements will not be called by the director, but as the camera operator, it is your responsibility to maintain correct shot composition as you execute the required move.

If you expect to undertake a number of highly

complex camera movements during a production—as is common in musical, dance, or dramatic programs—you may wish to have the floor manager or a camera assistant work with you to pull cable and help move the pedestal while you operate the camera and the lens controls. Whenever you work with a camera assistant, it is important to establish a carefully coordinated working relationship so that you do not work at cross-purposes. It is usually best if the camera operator takes care of pan, tilt, and lens operations, leaving the camera assistant to steer and help move the pedestal.

TECH TIP   Moving a heavy studio pedestal is safer and smoother when the pedestal is pushed rather than pulled. The only exception to this rule should occur when a camera assistant must perform a dolly-in by pulling the camera.

USING LENSES IN PRODUCTION

The particular focal length chosen for any shot depends on a number of production considerations as well as on the visual perspective you wish to provide for the viewer. We will discuss the uses of lenses in production by dividing them into three broad focal length groups: normal-angle lenses, wide-angle lenses, and narrow-angle lenses. Figure 13-25 summarizes important information about lenses of different focal lengths.

TECH TIP   The focal lengths given in Figure 13-25 and our discussion are for 16-mm film. Whether a certain focal-length lens produces a "natural," or "normal," field of view (considered an angle of view between 25° and 35°) depends on the area of the imaging device. For example, a 25-mm lens produces a normal field of view for 16-mm film but not for 35-mm film, which needs a 50-mm lens for a normal field of view. Since the image area of 16-mm film is comparable to the face size of the 2/3-inch CCD or pickup tube, the same focal-length lenses could be used for each with similar results. However, a smaller imaging device would need a shorter focal-length lens to produce a normal field of view. For example a 1/2-inch CCD or tube cam-

era requires a lens with a focal length of about 18.5-mm to produce a normal field of view. A 25-mm on a 1/2-inch CCD or tube camera would produce a field of view of about 15°, close to being a narrow-angle field of view. Today video cameras are equipped with zoom lenses that can produce narrow, normal, and wide angles of view for that camera's CCD or pickup tube.

Normal-Angle Lenses

Field of View   A normal-angle lens provides approximately the same field of view as our eyes do. In 16-mm format, a normal-angle lens is approximately 25 to 35 mm.

Perspective   A normal- or medium-angle lens produces natural depth perspective with no exaggeration of foreground-to-background subject size, depth, or speed of movement.

Depth of Field   Normal-angle lenses generally provide a medium depth of field with objects at the extreme foreground and background areas of the picture thrown slightly out of focus, but with a fairly wide area of acceptable focus around the principal subject.

Movement   The movement of subjects toward or away from the camera appears at normal speed. Similarly, camera movement is not exaggerated but appears natural to the viewer. It is rather easy for the camera to follow a moving subject on a normal- or medium-angle lens because the magnification is not very great. Camera movement can be accomplished smoothly on a normal-angle lens, although extremely mobile camera moves should not be attempted on this lens because the jitter and shake of a moving camera can appear obvious.

Distortion   Normal-angle lenses produce little apparent picture distortion. The very slight flattening effect they produce can be quite flattering for many subjects, since it tends to de-emphasize some prominent facial features.

Wide-Angle (Short) Lenses

Field of View   The wide-angle lens provides a broad horizontal field of view with reduced image magnification. Principal subjects appear relatively

FIGURE 13-25 The Effect of Lens Choice on Visual Aspects of the Scene.

LENS	FOCAL LENGTH	HORIZONTAL ANGLE	PERSPECTIVE	DEPTH OF FIELD	DISTORTION CHARACTERISTICS	PRODUCTION USES
Wide angle (short)	(16-mm format) 12–25 mm	57°–19°	Forces Perspective. 1. Foreground subject appears larger than background subject. 2. Increases perception of depth; set looks larger than it is. 3. Exaggerates subject/camera movement, making it appear faster than reality.	Very deep. Almost all elements within picture are in acceptable focus.	Barrel distortion. Subjects working too close to lens appear distorted, prominent features are emphasized and can look grotesque and unnatural.	Excellent lens for camera movement, tends to minimize camera shake. Excellent for use with portable cameras which are hand- or shoulder-mounted. Use for wide establishing shots and where cramped quarters require its wide angle. Its short focusing distance makes it a good lens for extreme close-up work on graphics or demonstration material. Deep depth-of-field makes it excellent for moving camera shots.
Normal angle (medium)	(16-mm format) 25–75 mm	20°–9°	Normal Perspective. Relationship between objects appears as it would to our eyes, no exaggeration of depth, subject size, or speed of movement.	Medium. Fairly large area of acceptable focus around principal subject. Objects in extreme foreground and background are out of focus.	No apparent distortion. Slight flattening of facial features tends to flatter most subjects.	Good lens for camera movement and for following subject movement from closer angle than wide lens provides. Usually produces most flattering effects on subject's face and features with minimum of distortion. Excellent all-purpose lens.
Narrow angle (long)	(16-mm format) 75–250 mm	9°–3°	Compresses Perspective 1. Squeezes objects together in frame, reduces perception of distance. 2. All subjects appear equal in size. 3. Makes subject movement appear slower than in reality.	Very shallow. Small area of focus around principal subject. Rest of foreground and background are thrown out of focus.	Severe flattening of features on some subjects may be unflattering. Compression of depth can distort audience's sense of space. Heat wave effect on extreme long lens can produce blurry, annoying effect on scene.	Magnification makes it ideal for location shooting, or in-studio for close-ups of subjects at large camera-to-subject distances. Compression of perspective can be used for special effects when warranted. Poor lens for camera movement or portable cameras as it magnifies camera shake and its critical depth-of-field makes it difficult to follow action.

small in relation to the overall background, and it is somewhat difficult to discern much detail in a very wide shot. In 16-mm format, most wide-angle lenses have focal lengths from about 12 to 25 mm. However, there are some extremely wide angle lenses with focal lengths as low as 6 mm, and these are used for special-purpose applications.

Perspective Wide-angle lenses used close to subjects force perspective and exaggerate the impression of depth and distance. The forced perspective makes foreground subjects appear much larger than background elements.

Depth of Field Wide-angle lenses produce a very deep depth of field in which virtually all elements within the frame appear to be in focus.

Movement The wide-angle lens exaggerates the speed of subject or camera movement. Objects tend to grow in size and recede very rapidly. Subject movement is very easy to follow on the wide-angle lens, since the wide horizontal view, minimal magnification, and deep depth of field eliminate camera jitter and focus problems. The wide-angle lens is an excellent choice when you must move your camera on air, particularly for complex movements or for hand-held cameras, since the low magnification will cover up slight camera shake and the great depth of field masks imprecise focusing.

Distortion The forced perspective of the wide-angle lens can result in a distorted image if the subject works too close to the lens. Wide-angle lenses also tend toward "barrel distortion," in which vertical lines appear to bulge outward in the middle of the picture and to converge at the top and bottom.

Limitations The very wide vista on some establishing shots makes picture definition and detail less sharp and may make it difficult for viewers to see all objects clearly, particularly in the "close-up medium" of television. Also, since the great depth of field offers little selective focus, fore-

ground, middle, and background objects may compete for the viewers' attention. Finally, the wide-angle lens is highly susceptible to lens "flare" because its wide vista may inadvertently include some studio lights which can produce a distracting, multicolored effect. Flares usually are eliminated by changing the camera's position, by repositioning the lighting instrument, or by attaching a lens hood to the front of the lens to block the light.

Narrow-Angle (Long) Lenses

Field of View A narrow-angle lens produces a narrow field of view and increases subject magnification. In 16-mm format, long lenses are generally those with focal lengths running from 75 to about 250 mm. Lenses with focal lengths greater than 250 mm rarely are used, except for wildlife and some sports programming because their minimum focusing distances are too great for use in the studio.

Perspective The long lens used far away from a subject compresses perspective, reduces the perception of space, and makes subjects on different depth planes within the videospace appear about equal in size.

Depth of Field Long lenses produce a very shallow depth of field with a small area of acceptable focus around the principal subject. The depth of field can be so narrow, in fact, that at close operating distances, objects only a few inches from the principal subject may appear out of focus.

Movement The extreme magnification and narrow horizontal field of view make the long lens difficult to use for most movement situations. Following a rapidly moving subject is very hard because the depth of field is so shallow and the field of view is so narrow. The magnification power of the lens also makes on-air camera movement virtually impossible, since the magnification of the lens will emphasize the slightest camera shake or jitter. For this reason, long lenses should never be used on a portable camera unless the camera is used on a tripod or on a sturdy camera brace.

Distortion The long lens's perspective flattens a

subject's features as well as the three dimensionality of the shot. The lens may magnify heat waves from the ground when used for extremely long distances on remotes, which can make the image appear wavy and distorted.

Limitations
On-air camera movement is virtually impossible, and following moving subjects must be planned carefully in advance.

The Zoom versus the Dolly

There is an important difference between the visual perspective achieved with a camera dolly—in which the camera physically moves toward or away from a subject—and a zoom in or out on a scene. Unfortunately, the wide use of the zoom lens and its obvious ease of operation have resulted in some camera operators and show directors automatically substituting a zoom for any camera dolly even though there is a distinct visual difference between the two.

A zoom lens simply *magnifies* (zooms in) or *de-magnifies* (zooms out) an image, whereas a camera dolly conveys the more dynamic impression of *actually moving* in or out of the scene. In a zoom, the camera-to-subject distance remains constant, even though the subject is magnified. In the camera dolly, the movement of the camera results in continually changing the set of spatial relationships between objects in the shot as the camera physically moves nearer or pulls farther away from the scene. This visual impression is particularly important when the camera dollies past doorways, arches, or furniture or attempts to convey a subjective view of the action.

The change in spatial relationships and the more active viewer involvement which the dolly provides as compared with a zoom are important aesthetic considerations that both the camera operator and the program's director should keep in mind when approaching such a shot.

Of course, if there is no depth to the subject—such as with a photograph or a camera title card—there is no apparent difference between the zoom and the dolly. Since these two-dimensional subjects have no depth, it generally is preferable to use a zoom lens rather than a camera dolly to shoot a card or picture because the zoom will look smoother on air.

Lens Operation

A number of commands refer specifically to the operation of a camera's lens system.

Zoom
Use of the zoom control to continuously vary the camera lens's field of view.

Command: "Zoom in" or "Zoom out." Some directors refer to zooming as "Push in" or "Pull out." For example, "Start with a close-up of the host, and pull out to reveal the guest." Other directors will refer to the zoom's effect on shot length and use "tighten up" to refer to zooming in and "loosen up" to mean zoom out.

A special-effect zoom is the *snap zoom,* which is an extremely rapid zoom in or zoom out used to emphasize a dramatic point or to punctuate an important moment in the program. The effect obviously calls attention to itself and should be used sparingly for maximum impact.

Focus
Adjusting the camera lens to achieve the sharpest possible picture.

Command: "Focus up."

Rack Focus
Shifting the camera's focus from a background object to a foreground object, or vice versa.

Command: "Rack focus." The rack focus is employed to shift the viewer's attention in a scene. Rack focus usually is most effective when the zoom is set at a relatively long focal length.

Zoom Calibration
A zoom lens always must be calibrated or prefocused each time the subject or camera moves to a new position. This should be done automatically as soon as your camera shot goes off the air and before setting up your next shot.

USING DEPTH OF FIELD IN PRODUCTION

Depth of field refers to the area in which objects appear to be in focus, as we discussed in the last chapter. It can be increased or decreased, depending on the focal length of the lens, the lens f-stop setting, and the distance of the subject from the lens. By controlling these factors, depth of field can be used as an element of production.

Camera Movement

If a camera must move around a set and still keep the picture in sharp focus while on the air, the widest possible depth of field will make camera operation easier and ensure a sharply focused picture. As the depth of field narrows, relatively short movements of either the camera or the subject will require you to refocus the picture constantly. A deep depth of field also is helpful when using a portable camera, because you will not have to worry about frequently refocusing the picture as you move about.

Isolating Important Picture Elements

Most camera shots are composed to isolate a principal subject or subjects which are of central importance to the viewer. In order to help make this distinction and to avoid distracting the viewer by other elements within the shot, use a slightly shallow depth of field—partially or completely blurring foreground and background elements—to direct audience attention to the most important subjects within the frame.

Fortunately, this often is accomplished automatically with the particular lens you would normally select to frame a shot. In a wide-angle shot, you want to show the audience an establishing view of the entire scene. The short focal length that produces a wide horizontal field of view also provides a very deep depth of field in which almost all elements appear sharp. As we zoom in to a tighter shot , the depth of field becomes shallower, blurring background and foreground objects slightly and increasing the visual dominance of the principal subject. An extremely tight close-up, in which the subject is prominent in the shot, will produce a very shallow depth of field, since the long focal length lens and/or the close subject-to-camera distance necessary to frame the shot also conveniently produces a shallow depth of field.

Using Deep Depth of Field

A very wide or deep depth of field can be effective when we wish to show viewers a number of different actions that occur on different depth planes within the same shot. One of the most effective uses of maximum depth of field can be seen in Orson Welles's classic film *Citizen Kane*. Welles frequently used a very deep depth of field to show one character in the foreground of a shot while showing the actions of another character in the background. In general, a deep depth of field can establish a strong visual relationship between various elements within a shot and often eliminates the need to cut between different cameras. Deep depth of field often is associated with realism, since the viewer can look anywhere within the image and see objects clearly. (See Figure 13-26.)

FIGURE 13-26   Deep Depth of Field.
A deep depth of field, in which all objects are in focus, enables the viewer to see all elements within the shot clearly.

FIGURE 13-27 **Shallow Depth of Field.**
A shallow depth of field forces the viewer to focus attention on a single element or object within the scene.

Using a Shallow Depth of Field

In general, a shallow depth of field is desirable when we wish to isolate the principal subject against a nondistracting background. This approach commonly is used to shoot a sponsor's product: the product is seen against a blurred background which does not compete for the viewer's attention. (See Figure 13-27.)

Shallow depth of field also can work to your advantage when you must shoot through foreground

FIGURE 13-28 **Selective Focus.**
Foreground objects outside the depth of field tend to disappear, allowing the viewer to concentrate on the intended event.

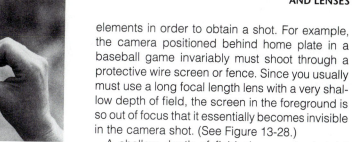

elements in order to obtain a shot. For example, the camera positioned behind home plate in a baseball game invariably must shoot through a protective wire screen or fence. Since you usually must use a long focal length lens with a very shallow depth of field, the screen in the foreground is so out of focus that it essentially becomes invisible in the camera shot. (See Figure 13-28.)

A shallow depth of field also can be helpful when you lack an effective background set. For example, a director needed to show a character seated inside a car during a rain storm. The production was being shot on location with a portable camera and videotape recorder, but it was inconvenient and too expensive to wait for a rainy day to shoot the scene. Instead, the director used a long telephoto lens on the camera to shoot a close-up of the subject seated inside the car while a stagehand sprayed the car with a garden hose to simulate rain. Since the long lens produced an extremely shallow depth of field, the character was seen in perfect focus while the background area through the rain-streaked windows was blurry and out of focus. Through the effective use of a shallow depth of field, the director was able to maintain the illusion of a rainy day with a convincing background. Shallow depth of field often is associated with subjective productions in which the director wants to focus viewers' attention rather than allowing them to look anywhere they choose within the scene.

Rack Focus

A variation on the use of a shallow depth of field is to vary the focus within a shot. This technique selectively draws viewers' attention to a number of different objects which lie on various depth planes within the frame. *Rack focus* is accomplished by using a lens with a narrow depth of field and instructing the camera operator to "rack," or "throw," the focus to different subjects in the shot. For example, you might have a character who is waiting for an important telephone call. The director could set up the shot with the telephone in the foreground and the character seated in the background. Using a long focal length lens, the camera operator would first focus on the telephone in the foreground, throwing the background slightly out of focus. As the phone rings, the camera operator racks focus to the background, showing the character's reaction to the ringing phone and directing the audience's attention from the telephone to the performer.

The rack focus may also be used subtly. An excellent example is in the movie *Jurassic Park* when the computer whiz Dennis (Wayne Knight) is stealing dinosaur embryos. The shot starts on a storage cylinder in the background. Then, the lens racks focus to close-up of a fake shaving cream can in the foreground. After an embryo is stuffed inside, the camera tilts up to the swindler's sweaty face. The viewer's attention is focused so intently on what Dennis is doing that the splendid camera works goes by almost unnoticed.

Another use of rack focus is to draw graphic material on a clear plastic or Plexiglas plate positioned close to the camera in front of the set. When the focus is trained on the graphic, the background appears blurry and out of focus. As the focus is slowly racked to the background, the foreground graphic visually "disappears" as it is thrown far out of focus and the audience's atten-

tion is now directed to the background area of the shot. (See Figure 13-29.)

PERSPECTIVE IN PRODUCTION

A long focal length lens and a short focal length lens produce two very different views of the same scene. The long lens has a greater magnification and, as a result, works farther from a subject than does the short lens to produce the same size image. This difference in working distance is one more crucial difference between long and short focal length lenses, since the distance between the camera and subject greatly influences the physical relationship between various foreground and background elements within a shot. This characteristic is called *perspective,* and it plays an important role in the audience's perception of the visual information contained in the videospace.

"Normal" and "Forced" Perspectives

"Normal" perspective shows us the natural depth and juxtaposition of elements as though our eyes were viewing a scene from the camera's position.

A wide-angle, short focal length lens (used close to the subject) "forces" perspective, exaggerating the depth dimension of a shot and increasing the size of foreground objects relative to those in the background. Forced perspective also

FIGURE 13-29 Rack Focus.
Rack focus is used to shift the attention of the viewer from a foreground to a background object.

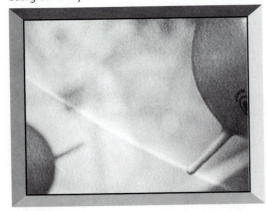
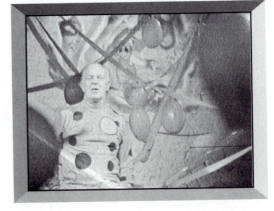

makes subject movement toward or away from the camera appear faster than it really is. Oncoming subjects appear to grow larger much more quickly, and subjects moving away from the camera recede at increased speed.

A narrow-angle, long focal length lens (used far from the subject) "compresses" depth perspective, squeezing foreground and background elements together visually and apparently reducing the space between the foreground and background in a shot. This compression gives the illusion that subjects moving toward or away from the camera travel much more slowly than they really do. In some extreme cases, the subject can appear to be moving on a treadmill, seeming to cover no distance.

To show you how the difference in perspective affects your perception of a shot, take a look at the three frames in Figure 13-30, which contain the same material in each frame. The first picture was shot with a medium focal length lens, and the depth and perspective appear normal, as though we were standing in place of the camera. The next frame was taken with a short focal length lens used closer to the subject. Notice how the per-

spective exaggerates the size of the foreground subject relative to the background and how the amount of space between the subjects appears to be quite large. Now look at the third frame, which contains the same subjects, but which conveys a much different visual impression. The long telephoto lens, used from far away, has compressed space, flattening foreground and background subjects, and suggests little apparent distance between them. In addition, the perspective created from the camera position used with the long focal length lens makes the foreground subject and the background subject appear to be about the same size.

Effects of Perspective on the Videospace

Filmmakers and television directors long have used perspective to enhance the visual meaning of their shots. Most television studios look larger than they really are because the director uses

FIGURE 13-30 **Lens Effect on Perspective.**
(*a*) A normal lens presents natural perspective and distance relationships; (*b*) a short focal length lens increases the size of foreground objects and "opens up" space; (*c*) a long focal length lens compresses space and makes distant objects appear to be the same size.

(a)   (b)   (c)

a wide-angle lens to force perspective and exaggerate depth. Automobile manufacturers frequently shoot their car commercials and advertisements with a short focal length lens to increase the apparent size of their car's interior. In general, wide-angle lenses that force perspective tend to make space appear larger than in reality and make subjects appear more powerful and dominant. (See Figure 13-31.)

The opposite effect is provided by the compressed perspective of the long lens. In this case, the lens flattens out subjects, compressing depth and equalizing the size of foreground and background objects in the picture. (See Figure 13-32.) This perspective can be quite effective when used with script material that calls for such a visual impression. A good example is in the movie *Scent*

of a Woman when Lt. Col. Frank Slade (Al Pacino) coerces Charlie Simms (Chris O'Donnell) to take an expensive new car for a test ride. We see them enter a New York City street from the compressed perspective of a telephoto lens, which reduces the space between vehicles to nothing. This intensifies the congestion and conveys Charlie's fear of driving the expensive new car in busy city traffic.

Of course, there are some production situations in which we might wish to avoid the particular effects of forced or compressed perspective. In many sports situations, for instance, the long telephoto lenses required to bring distant players close also distort the viewer's spatial perspective. This is why the center field camera which shows the pitcher, batter, catcher, and umpire in a baseball game makes it appear as though the pitcher is directly in front of the batter when, in reality, they are about 60 feet apart. A similar situation occurs during a football telecast when shooting a play from a camera located at field level. The long lens

FIGURE 13-31 Wide-Angle Perspective.
Short focal length lenses are popular for creating the appearance of spaciousness.
(*Courtesy: Capital Cities/ABC, Inc.*)

FIGURE 13-32 Long-Lens Depth Compression. Long focal length lenses create an impression of compressed space.

will pick up the runner, but the flattened depth perspective may give the viewer a distorted impression of the distance between the players.

A wide lens's forced perspective also can produce unintended distortion, particularly when a subject works too close to the lens and his or her facial features are distorted into the familiar "banana nose" or "elastic arm" effect. (See Figure 13-33.)

CAMERA WORK DURING THE FOUR STAGES OF PRODUCTION

As with all members of the television team, the camera operator's job can be divided into particular responsibilities during each of the four production stages.

Preproduction

Camera operators are rarely included in early preproduction conferences because their presence is not required when early production decisions are being made. Usually, the camera operator will learn about production details on the first day of studio rehearsal. However, on extremely complicated productions or in some unscripted situations—such as sports coverage—the director may wish to have a brief conference with the camera operators prior to rehearsal to explain the overall production approach and to assign each camera its general area of responsibility.

Setup and Rehearsal

Just prior to the rehearsal, the video technician will register tube cameras for the best possible picture reproduction. However, camera registration is not necessary for CCD cameras. Once the cameras are released for use, here are the things you should do during *setup*:

1   You will find the camera turned on. Do not turn it off at any time.
2   You should find the camera in its storage position on the perimeter of the studio. It should remain there until the set and lighting are ready.
3   When the set and lighting are ready, pull out enough cable to move the camera across the floor without snagging it on other equipment.

FIGURE 13-33   Wide-Angle Lens Distortion. Wide-angle lenses can overemphasize foreground objects, creating distortion. In this case the torso looks unnaturally large in comparison to the size of the head.

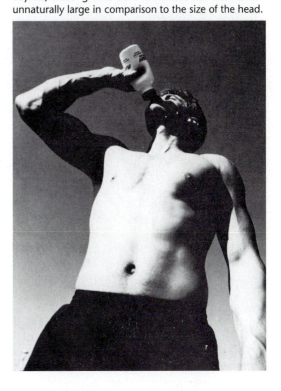

4   Unlock the pedestal column brake, or the tripod wheel locks, and move the camera into
position. Use the pedestal steering ring to
move the camera. Do not push or pull the
camera with the pan handles. When in position the camera cable should lie flat on the
floor so no one trips over it. Avoid stepping
on the camera cable (or any cable, for that
matter).

5   *Before* you pan or tilt the camera head, make
sure the locks are loosened and the friction
controls are adjusted so the head operates
smoothly. If you must leave the camera,
tighten the locks firmly, but not overly tight.
Never leave a camera without tightening the
pan and tilt locks.

6   Put on your headset and check the intercom (PL) system. Keep your headset on from
now on.

7   If there is a filter wheel on your camera, make
sure it is set properly for the lighting conditions. For example, most studio lighting is at
3,200° Kelvin and usually a #1 filter. Once the
proper filter is selected, do not change it.

8   If there is a cap over the camera lens, remove
it and place it where it will not get lost during
the show. Then, call the video technician and
request that your camera be electronically
uncapped.

9   Once the lens is uncapped, set the camera's
black and white balance, unless it is done automatically. Then, zoom out to a medium-
wide shot of the lighted set, and hold the
camera stationary while the video technician
shades the picture.

10 Once the camera has been shaded, check
the lens controls to make certain that the
zoom and focus controls work smoothly and
without sticking or pulling. Make sure you
know which way is a zoom *in* and which way
is a zoom *out*.

Prior to the rehearsal, the director should give
you shot sheets. Before the director begins the
rehearsal, there are several things you should do
to prepare further:

1   Memorize your camera number because the
director will address you by your number, not
by your name.

2   Adjust the pedestal or tripod height according
to the needs of the show, not to your height or
comfort.

3   Preset your lens for zooming in focus.

4   Practice getting the shots on your shot sheets
as quickly as possible.

5   Practice zooming, panning, and tilting, truck-
ing, dollying, and any other camera moves that
will be required.

During the first part of the rehearsal period,
the director's primary concern will be "camera
blocking."

Camera Blocking   This is when the camera
shots, angles, and movements are determined
and coordinated. Camera blocking is the time to
make sure that you can deliver whatever the director asks of you. If you find a shot, an angle, or
a movement is causing problems—it may come
too soon, the subject may be obscured, or other
production equipment may be in the way of your
camera pedestal—be sure to tell the director so
that whatever changes are necessary can be
made before the rehearsal time is over. Once the
director has indicated your various working positions, mark them with tape so you can find them
easily during production.

Consistency is important in how you frame and
compose your shots and in the speed of your
zooms and dollies. It is no help to the director
when your two-shot or your dolly-in keeps changing in screen size or speed each time you rehearse the program. The more consistent you are,
the fewer shot corrections the director will have
to make during later rehearsals and the actual
production.

You will soon find that every director has a personal style in approaching the rehearsal and production and in selecting and setting up camera
shots. It is a good idea to find out exactly what
your director means for each basic camera shot.
For instance, a "medium close-up" for one director might be a "tight close-up" for another. After a
short time, however, you should begin to get a feel
for the director's ideas and start framing up the
shots as he or she visualizes them. Some directors

are also extremely precise about the kind of shot and angle they want to see; others are "shot shoppers" who like to give the camera operator a chance to suggest different shots for them. Regardless of how your director approaches the show, it is important never to try to "outdirect the director." You may have a beautiful shot lined up, but only the director, sitting in the control room and watching all the camera shots, has a complete picture of what is going on. A program can have only one director, whose judgment must always take precedence and whose decision is final.

Unscripted Shows You probably will work on many productions that are either partially scripted—such as an interview or demonstration show—or completely unscripted—such as news events or sports coverage. On such unscripted shows, the director usually will assign each camera operator a particular area to cover. For example, on a home cooking demonstration program, the director may assign Camera 1 to follow the talent, Camera 2 to follow the cooking demonstration in close-up, and Camera 3 to follow talent and the demonstration wide, ready to zoom in or out as necessary. On sports events, the director usually will assign one camera to follow the ball, another to stay fairly wide on the action, another to "isolate" on a particular player, and so on.

Even shows that are completely unscripted often will follow some sort of basic format. For example, interview or game shows generally follow a regular format which can help you and the director in setting up shots. Of course, an unscripted show means that the director must rely on the camera operator's initiative and judgment to stay alert, follow the action, and quickly set up shots with a minimum of directions. Successful sports directors will tell you that their most important asset is a good camera crew that is able to get the shots and angles which make the director look good.

Scripted Shows If the program is completely scripted—such as a dramatic, musical, instructional, or educational show—the director should have preplanned all the shots and camera angles before the camera blocking session begins. Many directors like to hand out *shot sheets* to each camera operator. These sheets indicate every cam-

era's shot by number. The camera operator follows along the shot sheet as the director or assistant director readies each upcoming shot by camera and shot number. (See Figure 13-34.)

If the director does not hand out prepared shot sheets, you should make up your own as the director leads you through the camera blocking session. The only real difficulty with using shot sheets is that the director is locked into a preset sequence; if a variation should occur, it may lead to confusion among the camera operators on the studio floor. (See Figure 13-35.)

Production

Once you have gone past the dress rehearsal, the camera operator's most important job is to deliver

FIGURE 13-34 Camera from Camera Operator's Point of View.
Note the viewfinder, shot sheet, and zoom and focus controls. (*Courtesy: Capital Cities/ABC, Inc.*)

CAMERA 2

• • •

2. WIDE SHOT-DEMONSTRATION AREA

• • •

4. WIDE SHOT-DEMONSTRATION AREA

• • •

7. CU HOST-PULL OUT AS SHE WALKS TO TABLE

• • •

9. 2-SHT HOST AND GUEST

• • •

14. ECU DEMONSTRATION ON TABLE

• • •

16. MCU HOST

• • •

19. 2-SHT HOST AND GUEST

FIGURE 13-35   Camera Shot Sheet.
On a fully scripted show, the director can provide each camera operator with a detailed list of shots. The shot numbers missing on this sheet refer to camera shots assigned to other cameras during the production.

the shots and camera moves planned and rehearsed earlier. This is no time to try to discover new shots and angles. The performers, director, and other crew members expect to see what has been rehearsed and have planned their jobs accordingly. At this point in the production process, no one appreciates surprises. Changing a previously rehearsed shot or camera sequence without rehearsing the new one is an invitation to disaster.

Here are objectives for your working the camera during production:

1   Frame and focus all shots properly.
2   Hold all shots steady.
3   Zoom, pan, tilt, truck, dolly, and pedestal smoothly and in the proper direction.
4   Make all off-air moves quickly.
5   Make all moves exactly when called by the director.

During the production, you must listen attentively to the director in order to respond to commands immediately. You should remain quiet and avoid talking on the PL unless absolutely necessary. In addition, you should avoid the tendency to "help" the director by suggesting shots or blurting out criticism, even though you may be absolutely right.

If Something Goes Wrong   Television is always subject to Murphy's law, which states with brilliant conciseness: "If something can go wrong, it will." No matter how much you have planned and rehearsed, something can always go awry, particularly on live broadcasts where there is no chance for a retake. As the camera operator, you should be alert to possible problems, such as the director's calling for the wrong shot, an actor's blowing a rehearsed line, or a piece of equipment or another performer moving in the way of your previously planned shot. The first, and most important, thing to remember is, "Do not panic." Often, after what may have seemed like the biggest blowup since the H-bomb, you will find that the viewers never even noticed the problem. Remember the good advice of John Litvack, who directed CBS-TV's *Guiding Light:* "No one out there has your script or knows the shots you were supposed to get." If you and the director keep a clear head, you may be able to get out of a tight spot without viewers realizing that there was a problem at all.

Postproduction

Once the production has been completed, the camera operator's job is basically over. You are responsible, though, for seeing that the camera head is safely locked, the lens is capped, and the camera and pedestal are stored away properly.

Here is a checklist for postproduction camera operation in the studio:

1   Wait until the director gives the all clear before you lock and cap up.
2   Lock the pan and tilt controls firmly, but not overly tight. Return the pedestal to its lowest height position, and apply the pedestal column lock.
3   If your camera has a lens cap, place it securely over the lens, defocus the camera lens completely (so random reflections or lights will

not damage the pickup tubes), and request the video operator to electronically cap the camera.

4 Return the camera and pedestal to its storage position. Coil the camera cable in a neat, wide figure eight.

5 Remove scripts or shot sheets from the camera, and pull up any masking tape you may have used to mark camera positions on the studio floor.

6 Remove your headset, and store it away.

TECH TIP Always remove your headset at the very end of postproduction. This allows the director to remind the operator if something was forgotten.

CAMERA WORK IN THE FIELD

The guidelines we have outlined for operating a camera during the four stages of production apply to both studio and field productions. However, operating a portable camera in the field has additional responsibilities. The portable camera operator often is called on to fill the additional roles of video technician and program director in the field. Not only does this increase the camera operator's technical and aesthetic responsibilities, it also removes the safety net of having other crew members around to catch inadvertent errors. Because you are on your own, you have far more responsibility in the preproduction phase of a program than does a studio camera operator.

Field Equipment

Since the studio might be many miles away, the field camera operator must be sure to carry all needed equipment and to be certain it is operating properly before taking it into the field. In addition to the camera and VCR, audio, power, and lighting must be considered. And of course, the camera operator should have an adequate supply of videocassettes for the expected assignment as well as enough spare tape to cover unanticipated developments. (See Figure 13-36.)

Camera and the VCR
Before taking the camera/VCR into the field, be sure that it is recording properly. By recording a short segment in the studio

before leaving, you will know that all the connecting cables are in good working order and the record head of the VCR is not clogged or dirty. Check that the record monitor (usually a small red light in the viewfinder) is operating and that the white balance indicator appears to be working. Play back the segment you recorded, and watch it carefully in the viewfinder. If there is any "snow" or picture noise, the record head should be cleaned. If the signal shows breakup and picture loss, you may be faced with an intermittent cable or a bad connector. Finally, if the camera fails to go into the record mode at all, you will want to check that the videocassette has not been protected against accidental erasure. If you are using ¾-inch tape, the red button on the back of the cassette must be in place. In the ½-inch format, if the small rectangular tabs on the back of the tape are broken off, the VCR will not engage in the record mode. (See Figure 13-37.)

TECH TIP In an emergency, apply gaffer tape across the space where the record-prevent tab on ½-inch tape or the button on ¾-inch tape is supposed to be. This will "fool" the VCR into allowing you to record onto the protected videotape.

Audio Equipment In the field, the camera operator usually is responsible for audio recording, especially if you are using a camcorder or portable VCR unit. The following are some basic audio considerations, and these are covered in greater detail in later chapters on audio, ENG, and remote operations.

You will want to start by recording a short test using all the microphones included in your portable gear. Probably, this will include a hand-held microphone and the microphone built into the camera body. ENG work often includes a shotgun microphone that mounts onto the camera body. Use of an external microphone usually disables the built-in camera microphone. However, knowing that the built-in mike will work in an emergency can be very comforting. Be sure to carry spare microphone batteries and adequate microphone cable. Some camera operators prefer to carry two cables, each about 15 feet in length. This provides

FIGURE 13-36 **Remote-Camera Gear.**
A field camera operator is responsible for more than just the camera. Be sure to carry needed audio, power, and lighting equipment as well as spare videotape.

FIGURE 13-37 **Record-Safety Tabs.**
When the record button is removed from ¾-inch tape or the tabs are broken off a ½-inch cassette, the VCR cannot record on the cassette.

a spare for the most common working distances of 5 to 15 feet and the option of hooking the two cables together for greater working distances. Other camera operators prefer to use a single, long cable because it removes the possibility of a bad connection between the two shorter cables. The trade-off is the greater likelihood of tangling or tripping over the longer length of cable.

Power   Too often field camera operators are stingy with the tape they shoot for fear of draining their power supplies. Typically, the camera operates off of a battery housed in the VCR unit. The VCR usually has a gauge that displays the level at which the internal battery is charged. Always leave the studio with the internal battery registering full and at least one, and preferably two, fully charged spares.

FIGURE 13-38 Nicad Battery.
The batteries that power portable cameras are called *nicads* (nickel-cadmium) and should be fully charged before being taken into the field.

The batteries that power remote gear usually are nickel-cadmium, or "nicad" batteries. The nicads can be recharged many times before they must be replaced. Unfortunately, nicads have a "memory" that influences how long they deliver adequate power for operation. (See Figure 13-38.)

Batteries that are only partly discharged before recharging become conditioned to need more frequent recharging. If a battery with a stated sixty-minute life is constantly used only twenty minutes before recharging, it will soon become a twenty-minute, rather than a sixty-minute, battery.

Since you want to go into the field with fully charged, long-lived batteries, you must occasionally fully discharge a nicad battery. This will restore its useful life beyond its memory. To effectively use nicad batteries, you must always maintain a spare so you can fully discharge one of the batteries to restore it to full life.

Besides batteries, carry extension cords rated at 20 amps for use on interior locations. Also, carry adapters that allow your three-prong cables (hot, neutral, and auxiliary ground) to plug into the two-prong sockets that exist in older homes. When available, ac power is preferable to battery power because the power is very stable and will not run out.

TECH TIP Rather than conserve on the amount of tape shot, to save power a camera operator should remember to put the camera on standby when it is not in use and to switch off the VCR during long breaks in shooting.

Lighting The same precautions refer to the battery belts that power portable lights. You want to carry a spare battery belt and be sure not to use the lights except while actually taping. Remember to carry spare lamps and fuses as well, since fully charged batteries are useless if the fuse has been melted or the lamp has burned out.

Field Operation While having the needed equipment and spares is a big part of successful field operation, you still must use the equipment properly to achieve good results. First, remember to white balance the camera. With every lighting change, aim the camera at a white object such as a sheet of typing paper and press the camera's white balance button. This will allow the camera to properly reproduce colors in the scene. Whenever possible, position your subject so that adequate light is falling on his or her face. Avoid backlighting because it can result in the face of your subject appearing too dark if the camera's automatic aperture adjusts to reduce the bright backlight. If you have a choice, do not use the gain button for low-light conditions; the amplified signal also includes more noise. Of course, if the illumination is very weak, using gain will be necessary to form an acceptable image.

Although very weak light presents problems, so does very strong light. Never point your camera directly into the sun or any other source of illumination because it could burn out the pickup tube. CCD cameras are less susceptible to this problem, but bright lights will still degrade the camera's image. Establish the habit of avoiding extremely bright lights; you will not make a fatal error if you end up with a camera that uses a pickup tube and your CCD work will look that much better.

Aesthetic Judgments Since you often must act

very quickly without the benefit of a script, it is better to overshoot than to record too little footage. Anticipate how the scenes are likely to be edited into sequences. In addition to covering the main event, shoot some additional scenes that an editor can use to manage the running time of a story. Often this will mean including some reaction shots from onlookers or a cutaway to a reporter listening to an answer to a question. While working with close-ups often adds drama to a story, slightly looser framing allows you to respond to unpredictable events and helps you follow the action while avoiding a shaky picture caused by a moving camera.

Portable Cameras in Studio Sometimes a director will use a portable camera in the studio by connecting its cable directly into the video switcher so that he or she can intercut the portable camera with the studio pedestal cameras. The portable camera enables the director to take advantage of its fluid movements and ability to operate from unique vantage points. While the operation of a portable camera is essentially the same as that of a pedestal-mounted camera, there are a few important differences that you should keep in mind when using one.

1 Be sure to check all your cable connections before you begin shooting. When you begin moving, a loose connector could break up the video signal created by the camera.

2 Check your camera mounting equipment to make certain that the camera head is securely attached and that all straps and buckles are tightened to give you optimum camera control along with maximum operating comfort.

3 Coordinate your moves with your camera assistant. Be sure your assistant always has sufficient cable slack and will clear a path for you if you must make some major moves during production.

4 Remember the wider the lens angle, the less obvious camera movement will appear in the

picture. If you must use your lens at a long focal length, try to brace yourself against a sturdy wall or set piece. If a sturdy area is not available, position your body firmly on the ground.

5 Make on-air moves with the zoom lens set to the widest possible angle.

6 During camera rehearsal, have your camera assistant mark important positions on the studio floor with masking tape. This will help you to find the exact point for a particular shot and angle with a minimum of readjustment.

7 Even when your camera is off-air, try to stay as ready as possible, since you never know when the director might need your shot.

8 Keep in mind the operating limits of your cable length. Never make a major move without first ensuring that you will have sufficient cable slack and that the cable will not get tangled with other equipment.

9 Know the limits of your operating area so that you do not walk into another camera's shot or in the way of other equipment.

10 During a break in the production, place your camera where it will not be damaged or kicked over. Never leave the camera in the middle of the studio floor or the production location. If you must leave the camera for a period of time, be sure to cap the lens to prevent the tube from being inadvertently damaged by dirt or spurious light reflections.

Portable Camera Movement and Operation

The same commands are used for portable camera operation as for pedestal- or tripod-mounted cameras. Of course, the difference is that the camera operator's body performs the dolly or truck instead of a pedestal or movable tripod. The major advantage of a portable camera is the flexibility of movement that a good operator can lend to a production.

If you are going to use a portable camera, have a camera assistant assigned to pull cable, to help steady the camera operator if he or she must change position, and to help clear the way, since the operator's vision may be restricted to the camera's viewfinder. To minimize picture shake, move your camera on the air at the widest angle lens setting possible. Unnecessary camera movement that results in the appearance of shaky picture movement is one of the most distracting problems associated with portable cameras. To minimize this, good camera operators try to make the camera an extension of their bodies. This offers maximum control, cushions the camera against their movement, and reduces camera jitter.

TECH TIP The most often overlooked, but best, advice for reducing picture shake with portable cameras is: Use a tripod!

SUMMARY

The camera operator's most important job is to build the videospace through framing and composition. Framing is the inclusion of various elements within the videospace and how they are shown to the viewer. One of the most important framing considerations is the essential area—the part of the camera's picture that will not be cropped or cut off during transmission. The field of view determines the subject size and varies from the extreme long shot (ELS) through the long shot (LS), medium shot (MS), medium close-up (MCU), and close-up (CU) to the extreme close-up (ECU). The camera angle is another important factor in framing a shot. A normal angle shows the scene as we would usually see it. A high angle positions the camera above the action, shooting down on the subject. A high angle tends to make the subject appear small, isolated, and psychologically weak. A low angle positions the camera below the action, shooting up at the subject. A low angle tends to make a subject appear large, strong, and psychologically more dominant. A canted angle tilts the camera on the horizon and produces a disorienting, dynamic, and tension-filled shot. A birdseye angle offers a unique establishing shot or a way to emphasize the spatial relationships among picture elements.

Composition is the second major element in building the videospace. Composition refers to how the various pictorial elements are arranged within the videospace. A well-composed shot is unified, shows the relationship between the elements in the picture, concentrates the viewer's attention on the most important aspects of the shot, and produces a picture that is aesthetically pleasing and interesting to watch.

Elements within the videospace can be organized into any one of three major groupings: (1) balanced-unbalanced groupings, (2) triangular groupings, and (3) foreground-background groupings. Since television is a two-dimensional medium, shots which are composed to enhance the viewer's perception of depth are generally more interesting and more dynamic.

Camera operation commands are designed to convey information quickly and accurately between the program's director and the camera operator. Commands for camera movement on a stationary pedestal are pan, tilt, and pedestal. Commands that refer to the movement of both the camera and its base are dolly, truck, and arc. A zoom, in which the lens magnification changes, produces a different effect of motion than does a dolly.

Depth of field may be used as a production tool to ensure sharply-focused pictures, to isolate important picture elements, and to vary the center of attention.

Perspective refers to the way a lens portrays depth, dimension, and spatial relationships within the videospace. A normal-angle lens produces a normal perspective; the videospace appears as if our eyes were in place of the camera. A wide-angle (short focal length) lens used close to a subject forces perspective, enhances the perception of depth, and exaggerates the speed of camera and/or subject movement toward and away from the camera. A narrow-angle (long focal length) lens used far from a subject compresses perspective, reduces the perception of space by flattening depth planes together, and slows down the speed of camera and/or subject movement.

Of the four production phases, the camera operator is most concerned with two: rehearsal and production. In rehearsal, the director will set up shots and angles during camera blocking. On scripted shows, the camera operator usually will receive a shot sheet which indicates each camera shot by number. If the show is unscripted, the camera operator will be told the basic shots which are expected, but the director must rely heavily on the operator's initiative and judgment to follow the action. On remote shoots, the camera operator assumes the director's and studio engineer's responsibilities and must give careful consideration to preproduction as well.

VIDEO PROCESSING

The video portion of a television show results from the blending of many different camera images and generated images to create the videospace. The blending, or mixing, is done during production or postproduction and is called *video processing*.

The primary tools of video processing are the *video switcher* and the *special effects generator* *(SEG)*. Using the switcher you can choose among the video sources, select the types of transitions between them, and combine a number of sources to produce composite images. The SEG can shape a picture's size and dimensions, and with the addition of more sophisticated processing equipment, produce a visual reality that exists only in the videospace.

The video switchers used in production and postproduction are somewhat different. The *production switcher* must be able to be used quickly during live productions. That means it should take very few "button punches" to select a video source, set up a transition, and put the source on the air. The *postproduction* switcher can be more complex and require more "button punching" because there is more setup time between each change. Many postproduction switchers today are computer workstations that would be difficult, if not impossible, to operate during live television shows. We will examine these postproduction systems in Chapter 23.

In this chapter we will discuss the functions and operation of the production switcher, including the basic transitions. Then we will cover some of the more sophisticated special electronic effects used in production.

THE PRODUCTION SWITCHER SYSTEM

The production switcher is really a multipart system that includes the program switcher (the array of buttons and lights that controls the program source), special-effects generators (which manipulate and combine video sources), and an array of television monitors (which display the incoming video sources as well as the switcher's video output). The program switcher is mounted at a long desk called the *production console.*

Production Console

The production console is located inside the control room, where the program's director and other key personnel control the production operation. Seated at the production console are the switcher operator, the program's director, the assistant director, and such other production personnel as the producer and the production assistants. (See Figure 14-1.)

The Switcher Operator   The crew member responsible for operating the production switcher is known variously as the *switcher* or the *technical*

FIGURE 14-2   **Production Console.**
It's standard practice for the director to sit between the TD and AD at the production console.

director (*TD*). Although, strictly speaking, the term *technical director* refers to the senior technical crew member responsible not only for operating the switcher, but for all the technical aspects of a show, the terms *TD* and *switcher* are often used interchangeably.

At some studios there is no TD or switcher assigned, and the program's director is expected to do the switching. Since the operational and personnel situations vary so widely from studio to studio, we will follow our usual practice of referring to the crew position in terms of its production role. Whether the person operating the switcher is a technical director, switcher, or the program's director, the functions and responsibilities associated with the job remain the same.

You might think of the position of TD or switcher operator as the video counterpart to the audio technician. Just as the audio technician must control various audio sources, mixing and balancing them to create the final program audio, the switcher operator must control various video sources and, by selecting and manipulating the video inputs, create the videospace. In fact, in England the TD or switcher is aptly referred to as the "vision mixer."

The TD sits in front of the switcher-control panel, where he or she can operate all the controls and see the various monitors that face the control console. (See Figure 14-2.)

The Program's Director   The director sits in the

FIGURE 14-1   **Control Room.**
Although the layout of control rooms may vary slightly, the basic equipment and how it is positioned are intended to allow the director and switcher to easily see and select from among the video sources.

middle of the production console next to the switcher. From that position, the director can see all the video monitors and can communicate directly with the switcher operator.

On the production console, in front of the director, are a number of communication systems. A microphone and switch are a part of the *studio address (SA) system,* which enables the director to speak to the entire studio floor using loudspeakers mounted in the studio. During rehearsal and production, when live mikes in the studio would create feedback if a studio monitor were used, the director's main communication link to camera operators, the floor manager, and other key production personnel is the headset *private line (PL).* Telephone lines usually are installed to allow the director to communicate with remote production sites.

In front of the director are a number of black and white television monitors, which display the picture output of every video source available to the production. There is a separate monitor for each camera, VTR playback machine, character generator, telecine camera, remote feed, and so on. The director composes camera shots and selects video images based on the monitor pictures.

In addition to the smaller black and white monitors, there is a larger, prominently placed color monitor labeled "program" or "line." This monitor shows the final output of the video switcher and indicates which picture is being fed to the station transmitter or recorded on videotape. In some control rooms there are additional larger monitors labeled "preview" or "preset." We will explain how these monitors are used later on.

A *tally light* on each monitor lights up whenever that video source is fed on the air. If two or more sources are combined to produce a composite picture (such as a superimposition), a tally light will show on each of the monitors whose pictures are involved in the effect. The tally lights are important because they remind the director and crew which of the many picture sources is being fed out of the studio at any time.

Production Switcher

The production switcher plays a central role in control room operations. At first glance, some of the more elaborate switchers, such as the one in

FIGURE 14-3   **Video Switcher.**
All video switchers operate on similar principles but offer different levels of flexibility depending on their cost and sophistication. *(Courtesy: The Grass Valley Group, Inc.)*

Figure 14-3, can look terribly intimidating, having literally hundreds of buttons, switches, and controls. Actually, all switchers operate in pretty much the same way, and once you understand the concept of switching, it is easy to learn to use any switcher, regardless of how simple or complex it is.

The many different models of switchers available make it impossible to provide step-by-step operating instructions here. Instead, we will "build" a "typical" switcher component-by-component to illustrate the basic principles of switching and the switcher's production capabilities. First, we will start with the simplest switcher system possible, and then we will add to our basic model.

Program Bus

Every production switcher must have at least one *bus,* which is a row of buttons that represents every video source available for the production. Every video source is represented by its own individual button on the switcher console which lights up when that video source is selected by the operator. If, for example, a studio has three cameras, a character generator, an electronic still store (ESS), and a videotape playback machine assigned to it, the switcher would require a minimum of six input buttons plus another button as-

FIGURE 14-4 Program Bus.
The video source punched up on the program bus is sent to the transmitter or videotape recorder and displayed on the line monitor.

signed to video black. Other common inputs are color bars, color backgrounds, a graphics generator, and a film chain. Many times buses will have several blank buttons to permit the addition of more sources as the studio acquires new equipment. (See Figure 14-4.)

The function of the program bus is to determine which video source leaves the switcher as the television program. The director watches the black and white source monitors and tells the switcher which image to select. The switcher then depresses the button representing that video source. Whatever video source is "punched up" on the program bus is the image that appears on the line, or program, monitor and leaves the control room to be recorded or broadcast.

Cuts

A *cut* is an instantaneous switch from one video source or camera shot to another. The cut is the most direct method of switching between sources and usually the least noticeable transition between shots. With the single bus illustrated in Figure 14-4, the *only way* to change between video sources is with the cut. If you want to see Camera 1 on the air, press the button labeled "CAM 1." If you want to replace the Camera 1 shot with VTR footage, press the button labeled "VTR," and the program cuts from CAM 1 to VTR. With only one bus, we can start our show in black and end it the same way, but with a single program bus, we can only cut between the various video sources. In order to produce more complex transitions, we need to add a mix "bank."

TECH TIP The term *cut* originally was a film term. A synonym for cut common in television is *take*.

Mix Bank

As you can see in Figure 14-5, we have added two more buses with a fader-bar control between them. This is called a *mix bank*. Notice that the

layout of each new bus is identical to the layout of the program bus and that we have added one new button, labeled "MIX," next to the program bus. We will now look at each of these new additions individually.

The Mix Button

In the first example, when we had only a program bus, our switcher contained only *primary sources,* that is, those video inputs which actually produce a picture or image, such as cameras, VTRs, character generators, and so on. The button labeled "MIX," next to the program bus in Figure 14-5, is a *secondary source* because it represents the output selected on the mix bank above. You will remember that unless a video source appears on the program bus, it will not go out over the air. The secondary source button, labeled "MIX," enables us to select (or create) a video image on the mix bank and then send it to the program bus as though it were any other video source. In a moment you will see why secondary sources are important when we wish to do more complex switching and transitions.

Mix Buses

The two buses in Figure 14-5 labeled "MIX A" and "MIX B" consist of the identical primary sources on the program bus. As you can see, "CAM 1" appears in the same position on all three buses, "VTR" appears in the same position, "BLACK" appears in the same position, and so on. This eliminates any possible confusion when working with any of the switcher buses, since the same video source appears in the same location on every primary source bus.

Fader Bar

What makes the mix bank unique is the fader-bar control positioned between MIX A and MIX B. Actually, the fader bar consists of two handle controls, which are *ganged,* or locked together, to travel as one. The fader bar is, as its name suggests, a *potentiometer,* such as those used on audio-control boards or lighting dimmer

408

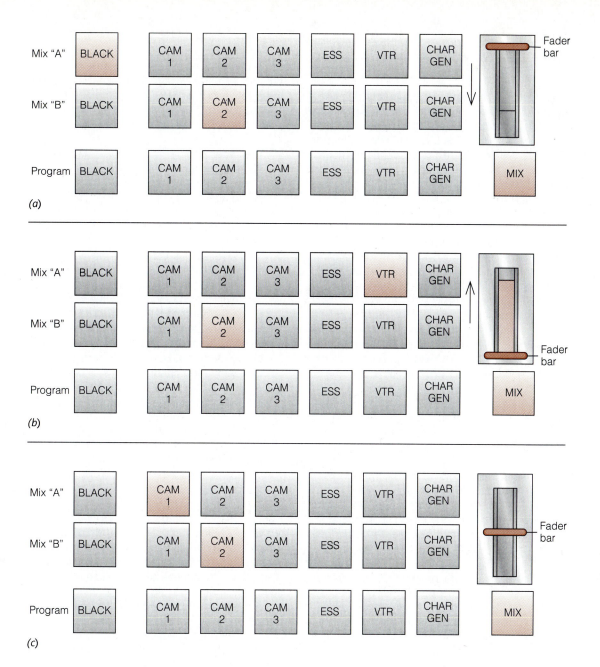

FIGURE 14-5 Program Bus and Mix Bank.
(a) A switcher equipped with a mix bank and program bus allows dissolves, wipes, and fades among video sources. This switcher is set to fade in from black to Camera 2. Notice that the mix bank is punched up on the program bus. (b) This switcher is set to dissolve between Camera 2 and VTR. (c) This switcher is set to produce a super of Camera 2 over Camera 1.

boards. Using the fader, you can vary the video output of either bus over a continuous range from 0 to 100 percent signal strength. As you increase the video output of one bus, the video output of the other bus decreases a corresponding amount.

Whenever the fader bars are 100 percent in the upward position, adjacent to the MIX A bus, that bus is activated and the MIX B bus is completely deactivated. Whichever video source is punched up on MIX A will be "hot" and, assuming "MIX" is also punched up on the program bus, will feed the program bus and go out over the air. On the other hand, if the fader bar is at the bottom, or MIX B, position, the MIX B bus is activated. If, for instance, the fader control is adjacent to MIX B, only sources punched up on MIX B will appear on the line monitor (if the "MIX" button is pushed on the program bus). Regardless of which source is punched up on MIX A, the MIX A source will not appear because the bus is inactive at the time.

The fader bars are the key to producing a new set of transitions between video sources to add to our basic cut. Using the two mix buses and the fader, we can produce three new transition effects: the fade, the dissolve, and the super.

Fade A *fade* is a gradual transition from black into a picture (fade-in) or from a picture into black (fade-out). In order to produce a fade, we require two video sources: (1) the image source, and (2) video black. For example, assume we wish to fade in from black to CAM 2:

1 Be sure "MIX" is punched up on the program bus, so that the mix bus signal will feed the program bus and consequently the line monitor and studio output.
2 Punch up "BLACK" on MIX A.
3 Preset "CAM 2" on MIX B.
4 On the director's command, move the fader handle from MIX A to MIX B. Since the program bus is taking the feed from the mix bus, the program monitor will show the fade-in as you move the fader bar controls toward MIX B. The speed of the fade is variable, depending on how quickly or slowly you move the fader controls. (See Figure 14-5.)

Dissolve A *dissolve* is a simultaneous fading in of one picture while fading out another. The dissolve is produced exactly like a fade-in or fade-out, but instead of using black, our transition occurs between two video sources. For example, say we are on CAM 2 and the director wishes to dissolve to VTR (see Figure 14-5):

1 The fader handle is already on MIX B with "CAM 2" punched up. Since the "MIX" button is still punched up on the program bus, this is the source going out to the program line.
2 Preset the upcoming source—"VTR"—on MIX A. Since the bus is inactive, it will not show on the line monitor.
3 On the director's command, move the fader bar from MIX B to MIX A. As it begins to move, you will see the VTR picture begin to appear faintly on the line monitor. By the midpoint of the fader bar's travel, both CAM 2 and VTR have transparent images which share the videospace equally. As the bar moves closer to MIX A, the VTR source becomes visually prominent and CAM 2 looks progressively weaker. At the end of the fader bar's travel, as it reaches the MIX A position, VTR accounts for 100 percent of the signal strength and the CAM 2 picture on MIX B totally disappears as the MIX B bus becomes inactive. As with the fade, of course, the speed of the dissolve is variable, depending on how quickly you move the fader bar from one position to the other.

In a dissolve or fade, it makes no difference which mix bus you start from and which you end on; just remember to be sure to preset the proper video source *before* you begin to move the fader. Once the fader bar has been moved even slightly, the videospace will include the image of the source punched up on the other mix bus.

Super A *superimposition,* or *super,* is simply a dissolve that has been stopped midway. Usually a super is produced at the midpoint in the fader bar's travel between the two buses, but this can vary depending on the picture brightness of the two sources. A darker picture will require more signal strength than a lighter one. Most supers must be set by watching the effect as it is produced on the video monitor and setting the fader bar at the position that offers the best visual mix.

While you are in the super position, you can *undercut,* or change, either video source on MIX A or MIX B while the super effect is on the air. (See Figure 14-5.)

The command for super is "Super CAM 2." If you want the superimposed image taken out, the command is "Lose super." If you want to keep the superimposed image and lose the previous source, the command is "Super through to CAM 2."

TECH TIP Supers are no longer common in television for titles because they tend to appear transparent and indistinct. Keys and mattes (discussed shortly) are much more prevalent and should be referred to as such when the director communicates with the switcher.

Switching Program on the Mix Bank Using the simple switcher we have illustrated so far enables us to produce four transitions or effects: cuts, fades, dissolves, and supers. Many programs can be switched entirely on the mix bank with the secondary "MIX" button depressed throughout the entire show on the program bus. For cuts, simply cut between sources on whichever bus is active, either MIX A or MIX B. For fades, dissolves, and supers, use the fader controls and preset the upcoming source on the inactive bus.

There are some situations, however, when you will need to use both the mix bank and the program bus. For example, say you are still feeding VTR from the mix bus and the director wants to cut to a super of CAM 1 and CAM 2. Using the switcher we have "built" in the illustration, there is only one way to do this:

1 As soon as possible, punch up "VTR" on the program bus (which frees both buses on the mix bank). Since VTR has been on the air via the mix bank, the audience continues to see the VTR source, but the direct feed of VTR from the program bus allows you to work off-air with the mix bank.
2 Preset your super, using the MIX A and the MIX B buses and the fader handles.
3 On the director's command, punch the "MIX" button on the program bus. On the air, the switch will show a cut from VTR to a super of CAM 1 and CAM 2.

Preview Bus

In the example just mentioned, where the director wished to cut to a preset super, it would certainly be helpful to see what the super looked like before it went on the line. Without a preview ability, we would have to take our chances that the effect which was set up blind would be acceptable. To enable us to look at an effect or, in fact, at any video source before it is punched up, most switchers have a *preview* bus, which feeds a separate video monitor labeled "PREVIEW."

In Figure 14-6, we have added a preview bus to our switcher. Both the primary and secondary buttons on the preview bus are identical to those on the program bus. Now we can examine any single video source or any mix effect by punching it up on the preview bus before taking it on the air. For example, if the director wanted to cut from the electronic still store (ESS) to a super of CAM 1 and CAM 2 that we mentioned earlier, the switcher operator could punch up "MIX" on the preview bus and adjust the fader bar to produce the exact video mix the director wanted. Once the director approves the super, it can be put on the air when needed by punching up the "MIX" button on the program bus. (See Figure 14-6.)

Preset System

Some video switchers employ what is called a *preset system*, or simply *preset*. Instead of a preview bus, a *preset bus* is located directly under the program bus. The function of the preset bus, as its name suggests, is to enable the TD to preset the next shot or effect. For example, assume that the director has CAM 1 on the air and plans to cut next to CAM 3. Using the preset system, the switcher operator punches up "CAM 3" on the preset bus as soon as the director says, "Ready three." As the "CAM 3" button is pressed on the switcher, Camera 3's picture automatically appears on the large preset monitor, which is located next to the line monitor. This enables the director to glance from one monitor to the next to see how the two shots will cut before actually making the switch on the air. (See Figure 14-7.)

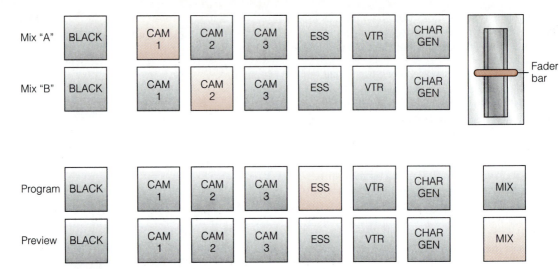

FIGURE 14-6 Switcher with Preview Bus.
This switcher is equipped with a preview bus. The preview bus allows us to examine and preset an effect before taking it on the air.

FIGURE 14-7 Preset Bus.
The preset bus allows the TD to preset the next shot or effect, which helps the director evaluate an effect before punching it up on line. The cut and auto trans buttons and the fader bar operate the flip-flop circuit.

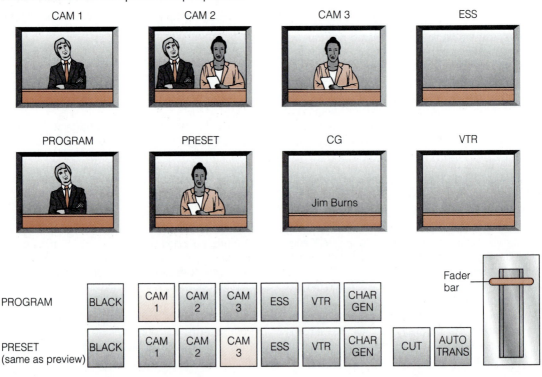

Flip-Flop Controls When the director calls for the TD to "Take 3," the TD could easily punch up "CAM 3" on the program bus. However, if the preset bus system is used, there is a more convenient way to make the switch, and this involves what are called *flip-flop controls*.

A flip-flop circuit is designed automatically to exchange, or flip-flop, the video sources that appear on the program and preset monitors whenever the *cut* button is pressed by the video operator. In the preceding example, the TD has CAM 1 on the program bus and has preset CAM 3 on the preset bus. Now on the director's command to "Take three," the TD presses the *cut* button, which instantly cuts to CAM 3 on the line monitor. At the same time, the video sources flip-flop, so CAM 3 now lights up on the program line and CAM 1 appears on both the preset bus and the preset monitor.

There are two reasons for presetting: First, it enables the director to see what has been preset and prevents the switcher from pressing the wrong button on the air in the excitement of a production. It is harder to make a mistake when you have seen the correct picture on the preset monitor and you have only to press a single take bar rather than to locate one button along a row of identical buttons on a conventional primary-source bus. Second, it has been found that a great deal of cutting within a show often occurs between the same two cameras. Using the flip-flop system, the switcher can cut back and forth between two cameras, or two other video sources, without having to constantly punch each up on the program bus or other primary-source bus. This is especially helpful to a busy switcher who must cut the show while preparing for upcoming effects or transitions.

With a preset system you do not need a mix bank to perform fades and dissolves. If the transition were a fade or dissolve, the flip-flop system would work the same way as the fader-bar handles. However, unlike with the mix bank, it makes no difference in which position the fader bars are located. A movement of the fader in *either* direction automatically fades out the program source and fades in the preset source. At the completion of the fade or of the dissolve, the video sources on program and preset automatically flip-flop.

Another way to fade or dissolve on a preset system is to press the *auto trans* (short for "automatic

transition") button. It disengages the fader bar and performs the transition smoothly at a pre-arranged rate. The speed may not be changed once the transition starts, but a dissolve may be stopped for a super by pushing the auto trans button before the dissolve is completed. Another push of the auto trans button, and the dissolve continues. As with the fader-bar control, at the completion of the fade or of the dissolve, the video sources on program and preset automatically flip-flop.

Switching on a preset system is easier than a mix bank, because there are only two buses to worry about—program and preset. However, in an extremely fast-paced show it may be impossible to preset every shot before punching it up on the air. In this case, the TD would simply do most of the cutting directly on the program bus and use the present system when convenient.

Special Effects Generator (SEG)

The program bus and the mix bank are capable of producing the basic transitions: cut, fade, and dissolve. While they may be sufficient for the simplest of shows, contemporary television production demands far more video flexibility. We need to increase our repertoire to include at least *wipes*. To do so, we must add a special effects generator (SEG) to our switcher.

A *special effects generator* is an electronic circuit board that allows you to electronically combine two or more video signals in a variety of ways, such as wipes, split screens, insert boxes, keys, and mattes. The SEG controls usually appear near the top of the switcher. (See Figure 14-8.) The video output processed by the SEG is controlled and routed to the switcher at various places, depending on the special effect desired.

Wipes A *wipe* is a video transition in which one picture gradually covers another. Swtichers usually offer several basic *wipe patterns*—such as horizontal, vertical, diagonal, rectangular, and circular patterns—and the capability of adding custom wipes. The pattern is selected by pressing the *pattern-selector button* displaying the pattern you

FIGURE 14-8 Basic Mix/Effects (M/E) Switcher.
This switcher has a mix effects (M/E) system which includes a pair of M/E buses, a key source bus, and a special effects generator and controls. This setup allows us to produce sophisticated wipes and other video transitions. *(Courtesy: The Grass Valley Group, Inc.)*

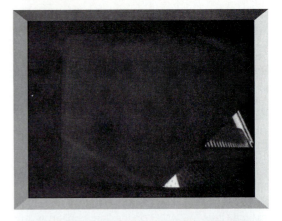

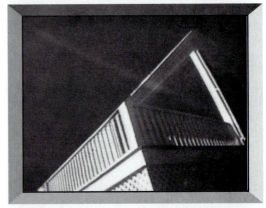

FIGURE 14-9 Diagonal Wipe Pattern.
The diagonal wipe pattern is selected. When the fader bar is moved, the diagonal wipe slides across the screen, revealing a new image.

want. (See Figure 14-9.) Although the actual operation of a wipe may vary from switcher to switcher, it usually is done by first pressing the *wipe* button (Figure 14-8) to change the type of transition from mix to wipe, then moving the fader-bar control or pressing the auto trans button.

You can wipe from and to black by punching up "BLACK" instead of a video source with a picture on one bus. If you have a color background generator in your switcher, you have the option of replacing black with a color and wiping to a color instead of black.

DIRECTION   There are three common *directions* of a wipe: normal, reverse, and normal/reverse. (See Figure 14-10.) The *normal* direction is indicated on the SEG's pattern-selector button. When *normal* is selected, each time the wipe is performed it will move in the direction indicated by the arrow. When *reverse* is selected, the wipe will move *opposite* of the direction indicated on the SEG's pattern button. When *normal/reverse* is selected, the wipe will move in *alternating* directions, first normal, then reverse.

EDGE EFFECTS   If a switcher has the capability, the edge of the wipe can be hard, soft, or a border. (See Figure 14-11.) Normally the edge of a wipe

414

FIGURE 14-10 Wipe Directions.
The normal direction of a wipe is indicated by an arrow on the SEG's pattern-selector button. The wipe may also move in the reverse direction, or in alternating normal/reverse directions, depending on which button is pressed.

is *hard*. In other words, the edge of the pattern provides a distinct separation between the two images. Switchers equipped with a *soft* wipe edge permit you to blend or merge the edge of the wipe pattern. The amount of softness or blending along the edges is variable, and the diffused effect produces a gentle transition between the two images. A *border* wipe edge produces the most obvious and distinct separation between images and is valuable when you want to convey to the viewer that there is a significant difference between the images being wiped across the screen. For example, some directors use the border wipe when going from live action on a sports event to an instant replay. The border makes the distinction clear between what is live and what is being replayed. The width and the color of the border are adjustable from the SEG panel.

Switchers equipped with the capabilities can enable you to rotate a wipe and modulate its edges. The edges of a *rotary* wipe spin as the pattern sweeps across the screen. The rate of speed is variable from a minor turn to a conspicuous whirl. The edges of a *modulated* wipe vibrate. The frequency and amplitude of the vibration are adjusted at the SEG.

Split Screens and Insert Boxes If you stop a wipe before one picture completely replaces another, you create a *split screen* or *insert box*, depending on the wipe pattern. In either case, two (or more) images share the video space. However, part of each image is covered up by the other one. (See Figure 14-12.) Any pattern wipe can be a split screen, although horizontal, vertical,

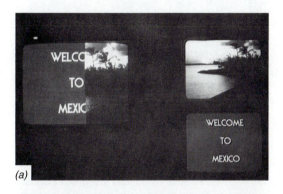

(a)

(b)

(c)

FIGURE 14-11 Wipe Effects.
(*a*) A hard wipe; (*b*) a soft wipe; and (*c*) an edge wipe.

and diagonal splits are the most common. Insert boxes usually are produced from rectangular wipes. Because a split screen or insert box is a "paused" wipe, all the edge effects for wipes are

(a)

(b)

FIGURE 14-12 Split-Screen and Insert-Box Effects.
A wipe may be stopped to create either (a) split-screen or (b) insert-box effects. Since they are wipes, all the wipe edge effects are available.

available for use with split screens and insert boxes.

Split screens are very useful when you wish to show a subject or scene from a variety of different angles or viewpoints at the same time. For example, baseball games frequently use a split screen

FIGURE 14-13 Wipe Shape and Position.
The shape of an insert box may be changed by adjusting the aspect control. The positioner can be used to change the location of a wipe or insert box.

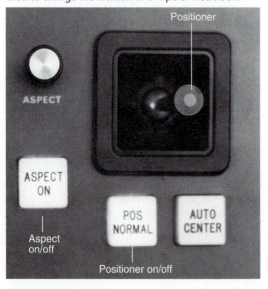

to show the batter and the base runner simultaneously. Insert boxes with border edges are frequently used in newscasts to show graphic materials in a corner next to a reporter.

SHAPE AND POSITION   On most SEGs it's possible to vary the shape and position of a split screen or insert box by using two controls called the aspect control and positioner. (See Figure 14-13.) The *aspect control* is used to change the shape of a split screen or insert box, and, for example, turn a rectangle into a square. The *positioner* can be used to change the location of a wipe on the screen. For example, you can produce an insert box, then position it high, low, to the left, or to the right, where it best suits your purposes.

The positioner often is used in conjunction with a *spotlight effect*, which slightly darkens an entire picture except for an area in the shape of the split screen. Combining the spotlight effect with the positioner control enables you to use the effect like an electronic pointer to accentuate any part of the screen. For example, a country referred to in a report could be highlighted on a world map for clarity.

Key   Another way the SEG combines images is to "key" them. In television production, the term *key* refers to a family of video effects in which one video signal is electronically cut, or *keyed*, into another. Unlike a super, in which two (or more) video

416

sources share the total signal strength, producing a faint and transparent image, keying permits all sources to reproduce at 100 percent intensity, since the key source is literally inserted into a video hole in the background picture.

There are three types of keys: insert keys, matte keys, and chroma keys. All three have become standard in television production and, because of their flexibility, offer almost endless possibilities for every type of program.

INSERT KEY   *Insert keys* are used to display words, lettering, and other graphics on a composite picture which includes the background image and the keyed information. The source of an insert key can be a graphic photographed by a studio camera, a graphics computer, or a character generator.

The insert key operates by using the brightness, or luminance, level of the key source to activate, or "trigger," the effect. The insert key also is known as a *luminance key*, sometimes shortened to *lum key*. As the camera's output is routed through the special-effects generator, an electronic switch senses when the scanning beam strikes a high-luminance portion of the key source picture. At a particular level of brightness, or intensity, the switch changes from the input of the background to the insert-key source. This is why graphics used for keying work best with white lettering against a black or dark background. This provides enough

contrast for the keying system to sense the brighter letters and trigger the key effect. (See Figure 14-14.)

Clip Control   The switcher operator uses a clip control to adjust the level, or "threshold," at which the keying action will occur. The correct clip setting is the point where it produces the cleanest insert onscreen without tearing or bleeding around the edges of the key. Clip adjustments must be made each time a new key is set up, since variations in subject brightness and camera shading will affect the clip level. The output of the mix/effects system you are using to prepare an insert key should always be checked first on a preview monitor to enable you to adjust the clip level before punching up the key effect on air. The video technician can contribute to a good insert by using the camera's shading controls at the CCU to increase the picture contrast between the white lettering and the dark background.

Producing the Insert Key   An insert key requires two video sources: (1) the key source—from a character generator, graphics computer, or camera, for example—and (2) a background source, which can be any video source picture, black, or

FIGURE 14-14 **Insert Key.**
The insert key places lettering or other images within the primary video source.

FIGURE 14-15 Mix Effects (M/E) System with a Key Bus.
This M/E system is set up to perform the insert key illustrated in Figure 14-14. The character generator (CG) is the key source and Camera 2 is the primary background video on the program bus. The VTR has been preset as the next primary source.

color background. The key source must be "punched" on a *key bus*, found above the program bus. (See Figure 14-15.) The "background" will be whatever source is punched on the program bus. When the *key* button is pressed, the key will appear over the background. Depending on your switcher's capabilities, an insert key can be "popped" in or out instantly, faded in or out, or wiped onscreen or off.

Undercutting and Overcutting As with superimposition, you can either *undercut* an insert by selecting different sources on the program bus, or *overcut* the key by changing the key source on the key source bus while keeping the same background picture.

Key Reversal Switchers equipped with a key-reversal feature enable you to produce insert keys with black lettering on white backgrounds as well as the more conventional white lettering on black.

Key Edge Effects If a switcher has the capability, a border, an outline, or a shadow can be added to the edge of the key. (See Figure 14-16.) A *border* feature enables you to outline the insert key to make the lettering or graphic stand out more prominently on the screen. A black border around lettering is especially helpful when you must key letters over a light background. In the *outline* mode, the inserted lettering appears only as an outline, as though punched out of an electronic stencil. The background scene shows through the lettering. A *shadow* on the insert key can help the

lettering stand out and gives it a three-dimensional appearance. On most switchers with these key edge effects, their hue, saturation, and luminance can be adjusted at the SEG panel.

MATTE KEY In an insert key, the hole cut out by the key source signal is filled in with its own video information. In a *matte key*, however, the hole is filled in with a solid color. (See Figure 14-17.) This makes it possible to "colorize" white lettering in a lum key, and to create two-dimensional figures in a chroma key.

Producing the Matte Key A matte key is produced somewhat like an insert key. The matte key source is punched on the key source bus, and the background will be whatever source is on the program bus. In addition to pressing the *key on* button, the *matte* button also must be pressed. Then, the hue, saturation, and luminance are adjusted at the SEG panel. Matte key will work with either the lum key button or the chroma key button pressed. In either case, the key hole will be filled by the matte key.

CHROMA KEY Use of chroma key has become so widespread that what was once considered an exotic special effect is now as commonplace as a dissolve or a fade. Chroma key permits the insertion of any object or subject into a background picture to create a reality that exists only in the videospace. (See Figure 14-18.)

As its name suggests, chroma key utilizes a specific color to trigger the keying operation. Al-

418

(a)

(b)

(c)

FIGURE 14-16 Key Edge Effects.
(a) A key edge border; (b) a key edge outline; and (c) a key edge shadow.

FIGURE 14-17 Matte Key.
The matte key is similar to an insert key, but the hole cut in the primary source can be filled from other sources. When these white letters are insert keyed, they are difficult to read. But when they are matte keyed and filled with a dark hue, they are easier to read.

though most keyers enable you to select virtually any hue as the "key color," blue and green have been found to work best for most production situations. This is so because the two hues are farthest from the colors of normal skin tone and produce cleaner looking keys with a minimum of technical imperfection.

Producing the Chroma Key   The operation of a

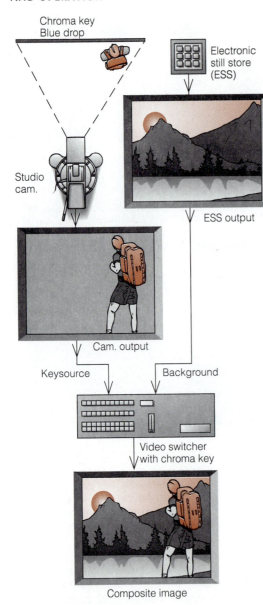

Chroma key
Blue drop

Electronic
still store
(ESS)

Studio
cam.

ESS output

Cam. output

Keysource

Background

Video switcher
with chroma key

Composite image

FIGURE 14-18 Chroma Key.
The chroma key is tremendously useful for inserting
one image into another to create a composite image.
Chroma key works by replacing a specific color (usually
blue or green) in the primary image with video from
another source.

chroma key closely parallels insert and matte key-ing in many ways. However, instead of sensing brightness level variations, the chroma key trig-gers the keying operation whenever it detects the chroma key color in the source picture. As with insert and matte keys, the chroma key source is punched on the key source bus, and the back-ground will be whatever source is on the program bus. Next press the *chroma key* button, and select the key color at the *hue* control. When the *key on* button is pressed, the background will appear in the selected chroma area on the key source. Ad-just the *key clip* and *key gain* controls until the effect is clean.

The most familiar chroma-key production ex-ample is the weather person in front of a chroma-key blue or green set. During the key operation, whenever the scanning system senses the key color of the studio set, it automatically switches the video to the background picture. (See Figure 14-19.)

Needless to say, the chroma-keyer cannot dis-tinguish between "important" and "unimportant" parts of any picture. Anything in the key source picture that approaches the hue and saturation of the key color will disappear and be replaced with the background video source. This is why the color of talent's clothing, the lighting and the colors used in the foreground set, and the color of on-camera graphics must all be carefully consid-ered whenever you intend to use chroma key in production.

Chroma-keyers are available in two different formats with very different production capabil-ities: (1) RGB chroma-keyers, and (2) encoded chroma-keyers. The *RGB chroma-keyer* requires three separate and discrete red, green, and blue video signals from the camera in order to produce the key effect. The advantage of RGB keyers is their superior keying quality. However, since the RGB keyer must use separate signals, its use is limited to cameras which supply RGB video; it cannot be used to produce keys with such com-posite video sources as VTR playbacks or remote feeds.

The *encoded chroma-keyer* uses a composite video signal, enabling it to key from any video source, including VTRs, various remote feeds, and non-RGB cameras. However, we pay for this increased production capability with a key that is

FIGURE 14-19   *Chroma Key Used on the Weather Set.*
The weather person appears to be standing in front of the map, but actually is in front of a blue wall.
(Courtesy: Capital Cities/ABC, Inc.)

neither as clean nor as sharp as the one produced with the RGB format. Most switchers offer encoded keyers as standard, with RGB as an option. In this case, you can select the keying format that will give you the best results for every key situation. When you will key only studio cameras that feed RGB, use the RGB mode. When you must key in composite video, use the encoded keyer.

Hard Keys   Just as a hard wipe preceded more complex patterns, a hard key was the first keying mode available for television. A hard-keyer produces a very distinct, hard edge around the keyed subject, as though the insert were cut out with an electronic cookie cutter. Unfortunately, the hard edge is susceptible to picture imperfections such

as image "tearing" or "crawling" along the edges of the key. That is so because the hard key operates on an all-or-nothing principle. The key system either triggers the foreground key subject or inserts the background video source. The on-or-off operation gives the insert a "keyed in" look, and minute objects such as hair or subjects without a well-defined edge tend to key poorly.

Soft Key   The soft key eliminates many of the problems associated with hard keying because it does not operate on the all-or-nothing principle. Instead, the soft-keyer samples the key source subject and the background video for both color and brightness value. The electronic switching operation is then controlled proportionately, based on both the color and brightness values in the composite shot. This results in a soft outline around the key insert which blends naturally into the background picture. The soft key is adjusted by a "gain" pot in conjunction with the key clip. The degree of softness is variable, so with a little experimentation you can produce the most realistic-looking effect. (See Figure 14-20.)

Soft-keyers not only make conventional chroma keys look better on screen, but they also permit the otherwise impossible keying of such transparent objects as glass, fire, smoke, and water. Since the soft-keyer uses the proportion of color and brightness in the foreground and background images to produce the composite effect, it is sometimes variously referred to as a "linear," "proportional," or "luminance" keyer.

Shadow Key   One of the easiest ways to detect a chroma-key composite is the lack of shadow falling from the keyed subject onto the background. Conventional hard-keyers either could not capture the shadow at all, or if they did, the shadow created bleeding and tearing, which ruined the key. These problems are solved with the shadow-keyer, which captures the shadow detail in the foreground key picture and casts it naturally onto the background scene, producing a very realistic and lifelike composite image in the videospace.

FIGURE 14-20 Soft Key. A soft key creates more realistic composite images. Notice how it is possible to see through the glass vase insert to the background video in this chroma-keyed image. *(Courtesy: The Grass Valley Group, Inc.)*

Using Chroma Key in Production The effects possible with chroma key are limited only by your imagination and ingenuity, especially when using the new soft- and shadow-keyers, which produce exceptionally clean and natural-looking composite pictures. Chroma keying is used routinely on news and informational shows, on sports programs, and on many entertainment shows. With chroma key, the viewer can be shown a reality that exists only in the videospace: a boy and girl flying over a city skyline on a children's show, a dancer whirling across the walls and ceiling of an otherwise normal room, a demonstrator actually walking through a car engine in an instructional program.

By experimenting with chroma key, you can find many more imaginative ways to use it in different types of productions. Transitions are one effective way to employ chroma key. Any object on the set that is painted the chroma-key color can be revealed while the next program scene is inserted in the "window." If the camera on the key source zooms in and increases the amount of chroma-key color in the slot, the background picture becomes increasingly larger until it completely fills the screen. Colored window shades, balls, pages in a book, doors, and other set and prop materials can be easily used in this way.

The most important factor in producing a clean key is to pay careful attention to such production details as lighting, staging, performer wardrobe, and camera angle. Even the best and most expensive keyers cannot deliver high-quality pictures unless the background chroma key set is evenly lit without hot spots or random shadows. The encoded keyers require more illumination on the colored background than RGB keyers to produce a clean key effect. If at all possible, check your lighting, costumes, and other production variables with the keyer before you begin rehearsals.

TECH TIP When setting up a full-frame chroma-key background on a hard-key chroma-keyer, slightly defocus the background image. This increases the naturalness of the hard key and somewhat simulates the effect of a soft key.

Mix/Effects (M/E) System

We started our discussion of the production switcher with the simple program bus (illustrated in Figure 14-4) and the almost-as-simple mix bank (Figure 14-5). As we went along we built more and more capabilities into the switcher, and added an SEG. What we ended up with (in Figure 14-15) is called a *mix/effects (M/E) system*. It consists of (1) a pair of M/E buses and the key source bus, and (2) the special effects generator and controls. Each M/E system will have a fader-bar control or auto transition button between the M/E buses. All the effects we have just discussed—wipes, split screens, keys, and so on—are possible using a single M/E system, although not necessarily at the same time. However, modern television production requires the ability to produce a number of special effects simultaneously or to execute various transitions between composite video effects. For example, if we want to wipe from a chroma-key composite with a graphic insert to another chroma key with another graphic, we will require a number of individual M/E systems in order to create the two effects and the transition between them.

Multiple M/E Systems   The reason large production switchers appear so complex and intimidating is because they contain multiple M/E systems to provide greater operational flexibility. (See Figure 14-21.) You might think of the two, three, or more M/E systems on a switcher as being like having several small switchers all contained in one switching console. The output of any one of these M/E mini-switchers, which, by itself, is capable of producing an elaborate composite video effect, can serve as an input to a second M/E mini-switcher with the same operational capabilities. Thus a composite image produced by one M/E system—let us say it is a split screen produced

by two cameras—can be entered into another M/E system where a performer on a third camera is chroma-keyed over the original split screen. If we have a third M/E system available, we can take the composite split-screen/chroma-key image and by entering it into the third M/E system produce another video effect, say, an insert of a graphic across the lower third of the screen. You can keep on going like this until you have exhausted your supply of M/E systems.

CASCADING   Switchers with multiple M/E systems operate on a "cascading" principle with the video flow starting at the M/E system at the top of the switcher and working its way down through each subsequent M/E system on the board. At any point the output of one M/E system can be reentered into the switcher by using the *secondary-source buttons,* which control the output of each M/E bus. While all this may sound complicated, we really are not doing anything more than we did when we used one M/E system. The only difference is that we can continue to reenter the composite image produced by one system into another, take that newly created video and enter it into a third system, and so on, with each new M/E system adding another layer of video manipulation to the image. (See Figure 14-22.)

Multiple M/E systems allow such complex production effects as a dissolve from a single source to a scene consisting of a chroma-key insert over a multi-image split. It is also possible to wipe a chroma-key background from one source to another while maintaining the keyed subject and a third graphic on screen during the background transition. The more M/E systems available, the more elaborate and sophisticated your switching capabilities become. However, this also increases the complexity of working the switcher and requires an operator who can keep track of the many video sources and transitions and correctly preset them so as not to exhaust the M/E systems before completing a composite or transition switching sequence.

Video *cascades* through multiple M/E systems like water flows from a creek into a branch then

FIGURE 14-21   A Multiple Mix/Effect (M/E) System Switcher.
This is a large-scale video production switcher with digital effects. (*Courtesy: The Grass Valley Group, Inc.*)

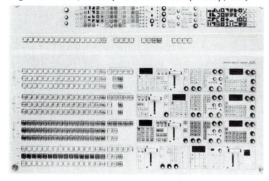

Individual Video Sources

VTR #1

VTR #2

Studio camera

Character generator

Downstream Building of Composite Image

VTR #1

VTR #1 + VTR #2

Wipe to
split screen

VTR #1 + VTR #2
+ Studio camera

Chroma-key talent
over split screen

VTR #1 + VTR #2
+ Studio camera
+ Character generator

Insert matte lower-third
graphic over composite

FIGURE 14-22 **Video Cascading.**
Video cascading is used to "build" a complex composite image.

into a river. An inner tube placed in the branch will float downstream into the river, but never upstream into the creek. The first M/E in the system is said to be *upstream*, and from there the cascade always is in the *downstream* direction.

Downstream Keyer

As its name suggests, the *downstream keyer* enables you to insert or key a video source over the output of the program bus "downstream," at the point just before the video signal leaves the switcher. The advantage of the downstream keyer is added production capability because it can produce an insert key without using any of the switcher's M/E systems. This frees all the M/E systems for the production of more elaborate effects,

such as wipes, or for chroma keys and still enables the switcher to produce a final video insert such as a lower-third graphic over the composite image.

Downstream keyers are used frequently on news programs, where a great deal of M/E work is already done on the video signal, such as a chroma-key insert of a news graphic or live picture with its own caption insert behind the camera shot of the newscaster. Another lower-third graphic insert is easily produced with the downstream keyer without affecting any of the other M/E presets. Downstream keyers are very easy and convenient to use, especially in situations such as news programs, instructional shows, or sports events, where a great deal of graphic material must be quickly inserted over a composite image which is

424

FIGURE 14-23   **Downstream Keyer (DSK).**
A downstream insert key will appear over the video
from all upstream M/E systems. The master black
control will fade all video to black simultaneously,
including a downstream key.

produced with one or more M/E systems. Most
downstream keyers are equipped with a master
fader which enables you to fade the entire output
of the switcher either up or to black. (See Figure
14-23.)

Programmable Switchers

As production switchers become more versatile,
they also become increasingly complex. Although
modern switchers are capable of virtually limitless
effects and transitions, the ability of the switcher
operator to keep track of the various operations
can be the most serious limitation in the switching
system. For example, a thirty-second commercial
may utilize multiple keys, inserts, wipes, and split
screens, all of which must be preset and executed
flawlessly in less than half a minute.

To help the switcher operator produce these effects and transitions, a *computer-assisted programmer* is available that is interfaced with the
switcher. These "smart switchers" are able to
memorize a complex sequence of switching
events and execute them precisely on command.
To program the memory, the switcher operator
simply runs through each sequence of events,
one step at a time, as they are to appear on air.
Once the sequence is in the computer's memory,
a single press of a button will produce the prepro-

grammed series of switches and transitions. (See
Figure 14-24.) Obviously, a number of complicated sequences can be programmed in advance, each being assigned a different cut number. Then the switcher operator can call up any
one of the cues whenever necessary throughout
the production. An added bonus is the ability of
the smart switcher to interface with a computer-
assisted videotape editing system to produce
frame-accurate postproduction switches and
transitions.

DIGITAL VIDEO EFFECTS (DVE)

The use of digital technology has made it possible
to greatly expand our production capabilities. We
have already mentioned digital technology in
terms of digital audio and the digitally controlled
camera, and Chapter 16 will discuss computer-
generated images in detail. Digital video effects
(DVE) incorporated into a switcher introduces the
tremendous flexibility of digital signal manipulation
to all the various video sources available. DVE allows the user to zoom, tumble, rotate, spin, and
crop a video image.

Digital Operation

In order to understand digital equipment and its
use in production, we must remember the basics
of digital operation. Digitizing video is accomplished using a process similar to that described
in Chapter 7 for digitizing audio. You should remember that a conventional television signal is an
analog signal because it uses the variations in
electric current to represent or reproduce an
"analogy" of an image that is photographed. From
our discussion of the scanning and reproduction
process in Chapter 11, you should recall that it is
the variations of the electric current in the CCD or
pickup tube which correspond to the brightness
values of the subject before the camera. The voltage level produced by the CCD or pickup tube
and associated electronic circuitry within the camera varies across a theoretically infinite range of

A "smart" switcher can be programmed to remember complex transitions. They are saved on disk, and called up as needed. This saves valuable setup time between transitions.

values in order to reproduce accurately the subject's image on the television screen. In effect, what we are dealing with is an electronic *waveform* that is a continuously varying electronic signal.

A *digital signal,* on the other hand, does not use current variation or waveforms but instead converts the analog signal into a series of numerical code numbers, one number for each element of the picture.

In order to process video signals digitally, we must first convert the analog waveforms into a digital signal. This is accomplished by "sampling" the analog signal over time as it enters the digital converter and dissecting each sample of the original picture into any one of 256 brightness levels. A code number is assigned to each sample according to its brightness level and its position on the television raster. The higher the brightness value, the higher is the digital code number. In this way, the entire video signal is broken down into a series of computer-type binary-code numbers which represent the original picture. Of course, the sampling and conversion process must be done very rapidly, since a new video field occurs sixty times a second and a complete new video frame is produced thirty times a second. Once the analog video signal has been *digitized,* or converted into digital code numbers, it can be processed, manipulated, and then reconverted back into its original analog waveform at the output of the digital device. Figure 14-25 shows the analog-to-digital conversion process.

Why go through all this trouble? Because using digital signals, as opposed to analog signals, offers us a number of significant advantages. First, digitizing enables us to store, process, and re-

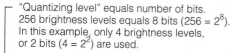

"Quantizing level" equals number of bits.
256 brightness levels equals 8 bits ($256 = 2^8$).
In this example, only 4 brightness levels,
or 2 bits ($4 = 2^2$) are used.

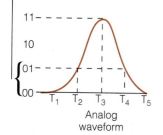

Analog
waveform

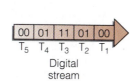

Digital
stream

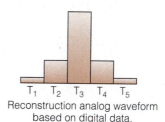

Reconstruction analog waveform
based on digital data.

T = Time sample taken
from time 1 to time 5. Samples
taken at least twice as often as
highest frequency (cycle rate)
in signal.

Higher sampling rates
reduces "stairstepping"
and smooths the digital
reproduction of the analog
signal.

FIGURE 14-25 **Analog to Digital Conversion.**
An analog signal is converted into digital information by sampling the analog signal
and assigning it a number that represents one of 256 brightness levels (an 8-bit
digital word is needed to represent 256 brightness levels). Each location on the
screen is digitized and reassessed for each video field (or sixty times per second).
Digital signals are cleaner and more easily manipulated than analog signals.

trieve an enormous amount of video information within a relatively small memory area. Data processing computers have long used this concept, and now such television production equipment as the digital video effects unit or the still-frame-storage device use digital techniques to hold and manipulate an enormous amount of complex information. The greater the memory capability, the more we can manipulate the digital signal in a variety of highly sophisticated ways. Also, because digital television equipment relies heavily on computer technology, we reap the continuing advantages of increasingly more powerful equipment at lower cost.

Second, once a signal is digitized, the equipment works only with the numerical code numbers and not with the actual electronic signal itself. This means that there is virtually no degradation in picture quality regardless of how much we process and manipulate the digital signal. The ability to manipulate video with "transparent" processing is extremely important and permits us a tremendous amount of production flexibility without the prob-

lem of deteriorating picture quality. In fact, some digital devices, such as the time-base corrector and the video noise reducer, actually produce a better-quality picture leaving the device than the original signal that was entered into it before any processing or manipulation.

Finally, and perhaps most important, digitizing the signal enables us to manipulate the video in ways that are impractical or impossible using analog techniques. DVE units can produce video effects which were possible earlier only by using film and the optical printer, a costly and time-consuming process at best. When we use the DVE unit, it takes only the press of a few buttons and controls to instantly transform an image in countless ways. Digital video effects have become so widespread that it is difficult to think of any area of production where they have not been applied to produce exciting and effective visual techniques.

With this simplified explanation of the digital process in hand, we can now look at a number of digital devices and see how they can be used in production.

FIGURE 14-26   Built-in Time Base Corrector (TBC).
The TBC built into this helical VCR makes it possible to
feed its output into a video switcher so it can be
incorporated into a television production.

Time Base Corrector (TBC)

The *time base corrector (TBC)* is another digital
device we introduced in Chapter 11 that adds important capabilities to the video switcher. Until
TBCs were introduced during the early 1970s,
videotapes that used a recording method called
helical scan recording could not be fed into a
switcher. (We will thoroughly describe helical recording and time base correction in Chapter 20.)
Basically, this meant that no EFP or ENG tapes
(and no *funniest home videos*!) could be used on
air directly out of the camera. When a TBC is used,
any helical machine can produce video signals
that meet the technical requirements for direct on-
air broadcast. It also permits the nonsynchronous
signal from an inexpensive VCR to be fed into a
program switcher and used along with an array of
special electronic effects, such as wipes, dissolves, and keys. Today many professional VCRs
have their own built-in TBCs. (See Figure 14-26.)

Frame Synchronizer

We described the frame synchronizer in Chapter
11. To review: The *frame synchronizer* is a device
that accepts "wild" (nonsynchronized) feeds from
any video source, converts the signal to digital

bits, synchronizes the signal with in-house video,
then reads out the processed signal in analog
form, where it enters the program switcher like any
other video source. (See Figure 14-27.) The result
is a signal that is completely synchronous and can
be keyed, wiped, or dissolved in the switcher.

In addition to synchronizing a remote video
source, the frame synchronizer offers two valuable
production options: (1) freeze-frame and (2) image compression.

Freeze-Frame   The frame synchronizer works by
storing a complete frame of video and then reading it out in step with the in-house sync generator.
The device is also programmed to hold the last
complete video frame and continually repeat it in
case a new signal does not arrive from the remote
source. For example, a signal being microwaved
in from a moving car or helicopter may pass
through a blind spot where transmission is temporarily interrupted. The frame synchronizer simply reads out the last complete frame over and
over until microwave reception is restored. Since
the freeze-frame effect can be produced intentionally with a control switch, this provides a new
way of freeze-framing video without using a slow-
motion disc.

Image Compression   Since the frame synchronizer reads out the processed video signal in synchronization with the in-house sync generator, if
we vary the rate at which the stored signal is read
out, we can reduce the size of the complete picture in the raster. For example, if the unit is told to
read out the stored signal twice as fast as normal,
the result is an image with half the normal vertical
height and half the normal horizontal width. In
other words, an image that is one-quarter normal
size. Using a joystick control, we can position this
compressed image—which is the complete video
picture squeezed down to one-fourth normal
size—anywhere on the screen.

The advantages of image compression are obvious. Camera operators no longer need compose
a split-screen or chroma-key shot in the camera
viewfinder. A normal, full-frame action image can
be electronically shrunk to any size and positioned
precisely on screen. For example, we can compress the image of a field reporter and position it
behind the anchor's shoulder. Since the com-

FIGURE 14-27 Digital Frame Synchronizer (DFS).
The DFS can (1) synchronize remote video to in-house sources, (2) freeze frames, and (3) compress images.

pressed image is always in sync, the newscaster at the studio can have a two-way live talk with a reporter in the field, and the compressed background image can then be faded, wiped, or popped off the screen whenever necessary.

Digital Video Effects (DVE) Unit

The digital video effects (DVE) unit is a remarkable device which greatly expands the operational potential of the video switcher. The DVE unit is integrated with a full-capability production switcher providing the operator with enormous flexibility in manipulating and modifying the video image. What is especially important is that the manipulation of the image takes place instantly, in real time, so you can see exactly how the effect appears in the videospace and modify it until you are satisfied with the result.

Over the past few years, a number of manufacturers have produced DVE units under a variety of trade names. Rather than discuss each one in detail, we have designed the following description to acquaint you with the wide range of potential possibilities which a DVE unit offers. While some of the effects mentioned may not be available on every unit, for the most part DVE systems provide

basically the same type of video manipulation capabilities regardless of the individual manufacturer. (See Figure 14-28.)

Continuous Image Compression The DVE unit goes the frame synchronizer one better by enabling the operator to compress a full-frame picture *continuously,* and in real time, until it literally disappears. The effect appears as if we electronically zoomed out on the picture, which, of course, we have. Naturally, we can stop the compression at any point and then position the compressed image anywhere on the screen by using the joystick positioner control.

Picture compression and positioning also are used to build a graphic electronically by combining the compressed and positioned image along with additional graphic material, which is usually provided by an electronic character generator. You have seen this effect often in news, in sports, and on many instructional programs. (See Figure 14-29.)

Continuous Image Expansion The reverse of the compression technique is continuous picture expansion, which, again, appears as though we are electronically zooming in on a picture. This ef-

FIGURE 14-28 Digital Video Effects (DVE) Unit. This high-end DVE can take a two-dimensional picture, wrap it into a "solid" shape, then whirl it in space. This process is called *3-D modeling. (Courtesy: CEL Broadcast, U.S.A.)*

fect permits the director to enlarge an image much as a photographer might enlarge a negative in the darkroom to eliminate areas along the edges of the frame which are unimportant and emphasize better the relevant parts of the picture in the videospace. Some DVE units permit up to eight times normal image expansion, although extreme image expansion can produce "blocky" images that show the pixel structure to a distracting degree.

The possibilities of image expansion are tremendous and offer the director new production capabilities which were never before available. The director can literally move around inside a normal frame, highlighting a portion of the picture by expanding it and then positioning the newly expanded image anywhere within the videospace. This has been used to great advantage in news and sports coverage, where certain scenes are recorded on videotape, replayed in slow motion, and then expanded to provide the viewer with an even closer and more vivid look at the action. (See Figure 14-30.)

Image-Stretching Effects The DVE unit makes it possible to expand or compress either the horizontal or vertical dimensions of an image independently. This means that you can literally reshape a picture's aspect ratio, although some distortion becomes evident after a certain amount of stretching. (See Figure 14-31.)

Image-Rotation Effects Using a DVE unit, you can take an image and rotate it within the videospace about all three axes. When we rotate an image on the x axis, we create a "tumble" effect similar to viewing an object rolling over from front to back. Rotating about the y axis creates a "spinning top" effect. Rotating along the z axis creates a depth perspective that gives a three-dimensional look to the image. Some sophisticated DVE units enable you to control the depth of the perspective, so that as an object passes from one plane to another, you control the amount of warpage or "keystone" effect.

On most DVE units these sophisticated rotation movements can be preprogrammed and stored in the system's memory so you can re-create the exact movement and number of rotations which you rehearsed precisely on cue. (See Figure 14-32.)

Transition Effects Among the various transitional effects possible with the DVE unit are the *push-off*—in which one image literally pushes another off the screen—and the *video split*—in which the image is literally split apart, providing space for a new image behind it. The *page flip,* as its name suggests, appears as though the new image is flipped across an existing picture as if you were turning the pages of a book. There are also a family of *matrix wipes,* in which small squares of the screen randomly disappear to be replaced by a new image.

All these transitional effects can be varied and modified by using different controls on the DVE unit and the switching console, providing literally dozens of different transitional effects. (See Figure 14-33.)

Additional Effects Since the DVE unit operates

(1) (2)

(3) (4)

FIGURE 14-29 Image Compression.
The full-frame image is digitally compressed until it disappears, in contrast to a wipe,
in which portions of the image are gradually covered by another video source.

FIGURE 14-30 Image Expansion.
The image is electronically expanded much as a photographer would enlarge a
negative.

FIGURE 14-31 Stretching Effect.
The DVE unit can stretch an image on either the horizontal or vertical axis.

FIGURE 14-33 Digital Transition Effects.
The DVE unit is often used to create digital transitions between video sources. Here an image "unfolds" onto the screen. *(Courtesy: Quantel, Ltd.)*

much like a digital computer, manufacturers are continually developing new software programs which enable the operator to produce countless new and interesting effects. For example, the *star-trail* effect leaves a decaying trail of starlike dots as the image moves across the screen. This can be combined with rotated lettering to create a striking graphic image, which can, in turn, be inserted over another picture. The *multifreeze* effect produces an apparently never-ending series of multiple images much like those we see in a hall of mirrors in an amusement park, where the orig-

FIGURE 14-32 Rotating Effect.
The DVE unit can rotate visual images in a variety of different ways, such as these two flat images wrapped into a cone. *(Courtesy: Quantel, Ltd.)*

inal image is repeated to infinity. *Mirror-imaging* reduces the mirror-reversed image of a subject and can be used to create realistic-looking reflections. *Bouncing* moves the image like a Ping-Pong ball across the screen from edge to edge until it is in its predetermined position in the videospace. (See Figure 14-34.)

All of these—and other effects described in detail in Chapter 16—can be modified or combined to create entirely new visual images. The biggest problem in using a DVE unit is in knowing when to stop manipulating the image because it is so effortless to create dozens of entrancing and visually startling effects. The secret, of course, as with any item of production equipment, is to apply the technology to the primary objective, namely, effectively communicating to the viewing audience.

Chroma-Key Tracking Combining a DVE unit with a chroma-key special-effects generator enables the DVE system to compute automatically the size and position of the chroma-key cutout and to fit the compressed picture into the chroma-key window. As the size of the window increases or decreases as a result of the camera panning, tilting, or zooming on the shot, the size of the compressed picture insert varies proportionately so that the proper perspective between the foreground subject and the compressed keyed image in the background is maintained at all times. This eliminates one of the most irritating production problems associated with chroma key and pro-

(a)

(b)

(c)

FIGURE 14-34 **Digital Video Effects (DVE).**
Three DVE effects: (*a*) mosaic; (*b*) posturization; and
(*c*) negative.

duces a key effect that looks extremely natural and realistic.

Postproduction with a DVE Unit The DVE unit is especially useful for postproduction work as well as during actual production. We have already mentioned how a director and a graphic artist can use picture compression and positioning to integrate a camera shot or still-frame picture or slide with graphic material to build an electronic graphic. However, this is only one of the many production capabilities offered by DVE units in postproduction.

The primary advantage of the DVE unit is that the director can use any normally produced full-frame camera shot, film, electronic still store, or videotape and, by modifying its size, shape, and position within the videospace, integrate it perfectly with other production elements. Without the ability of the DVE unit to vary the full-frame image's size and position, these elements would have to be shot with the final matte insert position in mind, and no last-minute changes in picture positioning would be possible, greatly reducing the director's postproduction flexibility.

The image-expansion capability is also useful in correcting minor compositional mistakes such as a boom microphone or some other unwanted element which appears on the edges of a camera shot. By replaying the videotape and slightly expanding the image size, we can completely eliminate the offending item from the edges of the videospace without having either to reshoot the scene or settle for an imperfect shot.

The transitional capabilities of the DVE unit are also a natural for postproduction work. If two or more videotape recorders are played through the switcher and the DVE unit, highly effective transitions (see Chapter 15) can be made and recorded on another VTR machine. The ability to interface the switcher and DVE unit with the VTRs through use of SMPTE time code enables the edit computer to accurately control all DVE operations and ensures perfect transition effects during a coordination session. In combination with a digital paint system, the DVE unit offers many creative options to the graphic artist (see Chapter 16).

SUMMARY

The production switcher is used (1) to select the particular video source which is to appear on the air and (2) to manipulate the picture's size and shape and/or to produce composite images with multiple sources. The switcher is commonly located in the control room facing a bank of video monitors. Each monitor continuously displays the output of a potential video source—cameras, VTR machines, telecine, character generator, and so on.

Each video source is represented by a separate button on the switcher, which has rows of buttons called buses. The video source punched up on the program bus goes over the air or to the record VTR. A mix bank with a fader-bar or auto trans control allows the switcher to produce fades, dissolves, and superimpositions in addition to the cuts that can be accomplished on the program bus. The video output of the mix bank is routed to the program bus with a secondary-source button located next to the program bus. A preview bus enables the TD to see a source before it is on air. A preset system flip-flops the sources on the program and preset buses.

To produce more elaborate effects, a switcher must be equipped with a special effects system, consisting of (1) a pair of mix/effects (M/E) buses with a fader-bar or auto trans control and a key source bus, and (2) a special-effects generator (SEG). The special-effects system enables the switcher to produce such video effects and transitions as wipes, split screens, and keys. Again, an M/E secondary-source button next to the program bus allows the switcher to feed program from mix/effects.

A wipe consists of one video source literally wiping another off the screen in a preselected pattern. A split screen is a wipe stopped part way through the transition, so that two or more pictures share the videospace simultaneously. Wipes and splits can have hard edges, with an obvious distinction between the two pictures, or soft edges, where the edges blur slightly for a less obvious distinction. Borders and color can be added to the edges of the wipes and split screens on some switchers. These transitions, as well as keying operations, are created on M/E banks.

There are three types of keys: insert keys, matte keys, and chroma keys. The first two are used normally to insert graphic material into a background picture. The insert key simply cuts itself into the background; the matte key enables the switcher operator to fill in the cutout space with a color, with special borders, or with a drop shadow.

Chroma key uses a particular color to trigger the insert operation. Any portion of the key source camera shot containing the preselected color will be replaced on-air by the background picture. A hard chroma key produces a sharp, defined edge to the insert. A soft key produces a softer blending between the key and the background, producing a more realistic and natural composite effect. Soft-keyers also permit keying transparent objects, and some enable the switcher operator to include the foreground subject's shadow in the background composite.

More complex switchers simply increase the number of M/E buses so that the output of the buses can be recombined in a process known as cascading. Downstream keyers affect the video signal just before it leaves the switcher output, increasing the flexibility of the switcher. Although switchers often appear intimidating, they all consist of ways to precombine video signals before routing them to a program bus from where they are sent over the air to a VTR or through a final downstream keyer.

Digital technology permits the processing and manipulation of video signals in a variety of unique ways. The digital operation requires a conventional analog video signal to be converted into digital code numbers before being processed, manipulated, and then reconverted to analog at the output. A digital time base corrector is needed to input helical video recorders and nonsynchronous recorders into the switcher. When using remote video feeds, a digital frame synchronizer ensures perfect synchronization and also permits still-framing and image compression.

The digital video effects (DVE) unit enables the operator to manipulate the image by continuously expanding or compressing it and to modify its size, shape, and position in a variety of ways. The various digital effects are under software control and are continually being updated.

CREATING
VIDEOSPACE

CUTTING AND EDITING

- **CREATIVE EDITING DECISIONS**
  Juxtaposition of Shots
  Timing the Shots
  Transitional Devices
  When to Change Shots
  When Not to Cut

- **SUMMARY**

After acquiring a number of video images from live or prerecorded sources, the director decides how to join them to make a program. This process is called "editing," or "cutting." The term *cutting* comes originally from motion picture film, where the film editor physically cut and spliced together individual pieces of film with different shots on them. In television production, *editing* may be accomplished in either (1) real time or (2) post-production.

Real-time editing occurs as the director watches a number of video source monitors simultaneously and swtiches to the desired shots "on the fly." The director must make editing decisions quickly, almost instantaneously. In contrast, *postproduction editing* offers more time to

consider each edit, and more latitude to experiment and find the most effective juxtaposition of shots. The creative decision-making process that we discuss in this chapter is applicable in both situations—real-time switching, covered in Chapter 14, and postproduction editing, covered in Chapter 23.

CREATIVE EDITING DECISIONS

Regardless of the editing approach used, the aesthetic considerations are identical. The television director and the editor both work with three related elements: (1) the juxtaposition of shots, (2) the timing of shots, and (3) the transitional devices used to go from shot to shot.

Juxtaposition of Shots

In the early 1920s, two Russian filmmakers and theorists, V. I. Pudovkin and Lev Kuleshov, ran an interesting experiment. They filmed a close-up shot of a male actor with a blank expression on his face. Next, they shot three different scenes: (1) a stationary bowl of soup, (2) a small child playing, and (3) an old lady lying in a coffin. Each of these three images was edited next to the identical close-up of the man to create the following three segments: (1) close-up—*soup*—close-up, (2) close-up—*child*—close-up, and (3) close-up —*coffin*—close-up.

Different groups of people were asked to watch one of the three scenes and then were questioned about what they had seen. Those watching the first version with the soup thought the actor looked absolutely famished. The audience who saw the second version commented on the obvious love the man had for his daughter. The group that saw the third series of shots remarked how grief-stricken the man appeared. These different interpretations were offered even though the actor's "performance" (blank expression) was identical in each sequence.

What the Russian filmmakers were trying to demonstrate was how the juxtaposition of shots— the order and sequence into which they are assembled—affects an audience's perception of what it sees. In every case, the audience psychologically related the event and the actor's reaction, creating different meanings in the process. This is a fundamental concept in editing, since the shots you select and the sequence, or order, in which you use them has an impact on how the viewers perceive your message.

Juxtaposition of shots is often used to make the audience think they saw something they really did not. The terrifying stabbing sequence in the shower from Hitchcock's classic film *Psycho* is a perfect example. Although audiences swear it is one of the most violent and bloodiest scenes they have ever seen, a careful inspection of the sequence in a film viewer reveals that there is not a single frame showing the knife actually penetrating the murder victim. Hitchcock shot and edited the sequence so cleverly that the audience thought it had seen something absolutely horrible.

Used properly, the juxtaposition of shots plays a major creative role in a show's direction. Given the same raw footage, three different directors or editors will create three different sequences, with variations possible on the emphasis of the scene, the characterization, the dominant elements or events, and even with which actor the audience's sympathy or emotions lie.

Juxtaposition plays an important role in nonfic-

tional programs as well. News and documentary programs are particularly vulnerable to manipulation through the sequencing of shots. Events can be intentionally or unintentionally distorted by the addition or elimination of something as seemingly innocent as a reaction shot at a strategic point in a show.

TECH TIP   Dialogue that precedes a related video sequence adds impact to the visual. For example, a phone conversation that precedes the reuniting of lost lovers adds emotional impact to the visual scene. Conversely, showing something prior to discussing it adds weight to the dialogue.

The juxtaposition of shots in a sequence involves controlling content and time to convey your intended meaning to the audience. If the *content* of the material is the main linkage between the shots in a sequence, the approach is primarily *thematic* editing. This approach is used for the television sports promos with the theme "we love this game" that consist of highlights from many events. Another example of thematic editing is a sequence of shots with conceptual similarities, such as spinning wheels on different types of vehicles to introduce a travel program.

The second factor in juxtaposing shots is your control of time. The three main approaches to controlling time while editing are (1) continuity editing, (2) parallel cutting, and (3) flashforward/flashback techniques.

Continuity Editing   The most common type of editing attempts to convey to the audience that the action they see on the screen is continuous. A major change in continuity—such as a subject seated in one shot and standing in the next—obviously would be a disturbing cut for the audience. Although a discontinuous sequence may be created intentionally to jar the audience, more often your goal in editing will be to preserve the natural flow of movement. This is not hard to achieve with multiple-camera approaches and real-time switching, since all the cameras cover the same action and you are cutting the show in real time.

In that case discontinuity between the live camera shots will not be a problem. However, when you edit a videotape in postproduction, even with multiple-camera/multiple-VTR recordings, the editing must be done carefully to preserve the continuity in a subject's movement. For example, if a subject sets a glass of milk on a table, a cut to a close-up of the table must be timed so that the glass does not appear to "pop" onto it. (See Figure 15-1.) The easiest approach is to duplicate the action in each shot and then cut on the action.

Another approach is to use a cutaway, which we described when we discussed ENG editing. A cutaway, such as a reaction shot, can be used to join two discontinuous shots. For example, in Figure 15-1, the close-up of the subject may be inserted between the wide shot and the close-up to make the action appear continuous to the audience.

COMPRESSING AND EXPANDING SCREEN TIME
Along with cutaways, inserts and reaction shots can be used to alter the screen time of the action so that it is compressed or expanded, but still creates the illusion of continuity in the mind of the audience. For example, in Figure 15-2 the close-up of the actor may be inserted between the empty glass and the full glass to reduce the time on the screen that it takes to fill the glass, without making the action appear discontinuous to the audience.

SCREEN DIRECTION
Because televison subjects move about the videospace, we must always be conscious of their screen direction. Violating some of the basic rules of screen direction can disorient the viewer and create some unintended confusion. The audience is used to having screen direction established through cutting and on-camera movement. The borders of the television frame are constant and provide a reference point for the audience. This is why in a cops and robbers chase we must show both the pursuers and the pursued traveling in the same direction. It would look awfully odd if the robbers were moving left to right while the pursuing cops moved in the opposite direction, from right to left.

(a)

(b)

(c)

FIGURE 15-1 Continuity Editing.
The glass will appear to "pop" onto the table in a cut directly from frame (*a*) to frame (*c*) because the action is not matched in each frame. However, if cutaway (*b*) is inserted between (*a*) and (*c*), continuity will be preserved in the sequence (*a*), (*b*), (*c*).

On the other hand, opposite screen direction implies that two forces are about to meet. Think of the typical running-lover scene where the man runs left to right through city streets, the park, down a bank of stairs while we intercut to show the woman running right to left through hallways, into the street, and finally into her lover's arms. By establishing the basic screen direction for each, we establish a sense of direction in the viewer's mind that should not be violated.

Not all screen-direction problems are as romantic. Take the case of a football player, for instance. We must always see the football players run across the field in the same direction from one shot to the next. The way to maintain consistent screen direction is to use an imaginary line running through every subject that is called the *action axis*. As long as all your camera shots are made from the same side of the action axis, the direction onscreen remains consistent. If you cross the action axis, you will reverse the screen direction.

That is why football games are generally covered with all cameras on the same side of the field. Otherwise, one or more of the shots would cross the action axis and literally flip the runner into the opposite direction onscreen. For this reason, when a camera does cross the action axis to show action that is obstructed from the normal camera angles, it is clearly labeled on the screen as "reverse angle" so that the viewer does not become confused. Naturally, you can change screen direction, but you must clearly establish the change for the audience. The easiest and most direct method is to show a subject change direction in a shot. Another way is to shoot the subject head-on, which is a neutral direction, and then cut to a camera shot from the other side of the action axis. (See Figure 15-3.)

(a)

(b)

(c)

FIGURE 15-2 Compressing Time.
It may take this subject thirty seconds in real time to fill the glass, which would seem much longer on the screen. The screen time could be cut in half by showing the subject (a) beginning to pour for five seconds, (b) looking down for five seconds, and (c) finishing for five seconds. The sequence would seem natural to the audience because the close-up would preserve the continuity and the timing would seem acceptable.

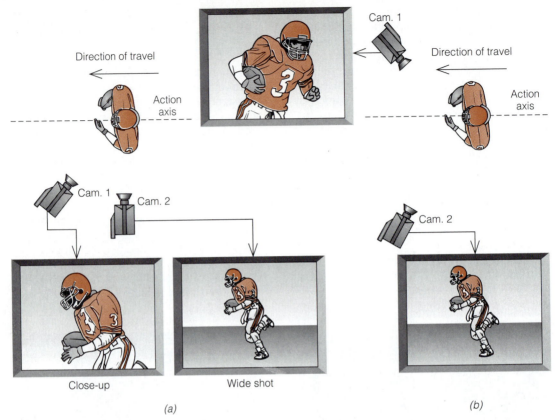

Close-up   Wide shot

(a)   *(b)*

FIGURE 15-3 Action Axis.
Camera placement should be on the same side of the action axis to maintain the proper screen direction. In (*a*) both cameras are on the same side of the action axis, while in (*b*) Camera 2 crosses the action axis and the football player seems to reverse direction on the screen, confusing the viewer.

JUMP CUTS A *jump cut* is a radical, or startling, transition from one camera shot to another. Generally, jump cuts are to be avoided because they call attention to the transition and can easily disorient the viewer. Of course, you can use a jump cut when this dramatic or startling impact is the very reaction you would like the audience to feel. Still, jump cuts must be used carefully because too many in the wrong places will irritate the audience rather than involve them in your show.

Here are some of the classic jump-cut problems that crop up in every director's programs from time to time and some ways to avoid them.

Change in Subject Size Cutting from an ex-

tremely wide shot to a tight close-up, or vice versa, produces an obvious jump cut. Again, you can use this for a dramatic effect—for example, when someone receives startling or unexpected news. To avoid the jump cut, cut to a shot or subject size midway between the two extremes to help smooth the transition.

Change in Camera Angle or Point of View A radical change in the camera angle or the audience's point of view of a scene produces a jump cut. Cutting from a high-angle to a low-angle shot or from a straight-on shot to a stark profile are some examples of a radical change in camera angle. Similarly, changing the audience's point of view without sufficient notice also should be avoided. For instance, avoid cutting from an objective shot to a subjective shot without first preparing the audience for the change.

Change in Screen Direction

As mentioned earlier, a radical change in screen direction without reestablishing the viewer's perspective is a jump cut that can be avoided by keeping all cameras on the same side of the action axis.

Change in Screen Position

Inadvertently changing screen position is a common jump cut that is

usually associated with two different shots containing two or more subjects. For example, say three performers are on the set. Camera 1 may have subjects *A* and *B*; and Camera 2, subjects *B* and *C*. Cutting between these shots will make subject *B* appear to leap across the screen. You can eliminate the jump by cutting to a wider or tighter shot first and then zooming either in or out or simply panning across to the other subject. (See Figure 15-4.)

Cutting from a Moving Camera to a Stationary Camera

Cutting from a moving camera to a stationary camera is the visual counterpart to slam-

FIGURE 15-4 Change in Screen Position.
The director will produce an apparently magical (and disorienting) flip of talent *B* if he or she cuts directly from Camera 2's two-shot to Camera 1's two-shot. To avoid this, zoom in on talent *B* with Camera 2 before taking Camera 1's two-shot.

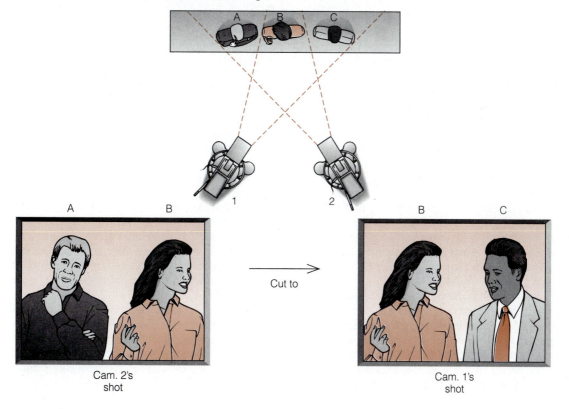

Cut to

Cam. 2's shot

Cam. 1's shot

ming on the brakes of a fast-moving car. The effect can be distracting, although on some live sports or news programs it may be difficult to avoid all the time. Try to get the moving camera to stop—if only for a moment—before you cut to the next shot.

TONAL AND COLOR CONTINUITY   Two technical considerations in continuity editing are the tonal and color values in the shots. We discussed meanings commonly implied by different colors in Chapter 2. For example, differences in the time of day, temperature, feelings, and moods can be suggested by different tones and colors. These effects should be considered when sequencing shots to create a sense of continuity, as in, for example, a sequence of shots that become darker as a character becomes more and more depressed.

CAUSE AND EFFECT   An important consideration in continuity cutting is the impression of cause-and-effect relationships that editing can create. This is illustrated by the Pudovkin/Kuleshov experiment described earlier. It verifies that audiences usually perceive the first action in a sequence to cause the second action. For example, if King Kong growls in the first shot and a soldier fires a weapon at him in the second shot, the impression is that the soldier is responding to Kong's growl. But what if the shots are reversed? In that case, the solider appears to fire first and this time Kong is reacting with the growl. The second sequence implies completely opposite cause-and-effect relationships. Obviously, the capability of editing to suggest a cause and an effect is extremely important when editing news and documentary footage, and any alteration in the chronology of an event can mislead the audience.

Parallel Cutting   Many dramatic shows will have subplots or more than one story line occurring simultaneously. However, more than one story can be told at a time by using *parallel cutting*, which takes the viewer back and forth between two or more events and implies that they are occurring simultaneously. Most television soaps and sixty-minute dramas use this approach.

Flashback and Flashforward   Events that occurred in the past or that will occur in the future can be suggested through editing. The key to using flashbacks and flashforwards is to cue the audience that the time is being shifted. Two techniques that have been used to do this so often that they now amount to visual clichés are to insert the face of a clock with rapidly turning hands or a calendar with the pages turning. Transitions such as slow dissolves and soft-edge wipes also can be used. Often, the dialogue will provide a sufficient cue to the audience. A variation is the *split edit*, where either the picture or the sound, but not both, changes. Split edits, where the new sound is edited in and the video edit follows, may be done in cuts-only documentaries to smooth out the transitions.

Timing the Shots

The director not only must determine what to show and in what sequence, but also must consider the timing of each shot and how quickly or slowly to switch from one shot to the next. The timing, or rhythm, of the shots is an important element in the program's overall pacing. *Pacing* is the audience's perception of the speed of the show, a psychological and emotional impression. Of course, editing alone is only a part of a program's pacing, but the timing of the shots, along with the performer's delivery, determines the audience's perception of screen time.

Naturally, the shooting rhythm ought to reflect the program's content and the director's objectives. Watching a singer perform a moody, romantic number, we would expect the timing of the shots to be fairly slow to match the overall mood established by the song and the performance. On the other hand, a documentary about increasing industrial productivity might call for a rapid cutting tempo to convey the feeling of great activity and progress.

The timing of shots depends on a number of interrelated factors, including the content of each shot, the complexity of the shot's image, and the context of the shot within the overall sequence. A shot containing essential content or a shot including a very complicated image should remain on-screen longer than a simpler shot or one without important content. The audience's familiarity with a shot's content is also significant, since if we are already familiar with what is included in a particular shot because we have seen it before, the director can usually cut more rapidly without disorienting the viewer. A reaction shot of an interviewer listening to a guest's remarks can usually be made quite rapidly because we are familiar with the host and this shot is not terribly important at the time. On the other hand, a close-up of a complex demonstration in an instructional program might well require a much longer time on-screen before the director cuts to the next shot.

The timing of the shots is a highly relative concept, since the rhythm of cutting and the transitions used in prior sequences can play as important a role as the absolute speed of the cuts. A show with relatively little cutting can be speeded up appreciably with a moderately paced cutting rhythm. A fast-action chase sequence, however, which involves many short cuts would require much faster cutting and shorter shots in order to convey a similar increase in cutting tempo. The director should always be concerned with the cutting rhythm and with pacing, even in such programs as an interview or panel show, demonstration program, or instructional presentation. Try to avoid settling into a predictable shot routine, because this can diminish the viewer's interest.

TECH TIP One fundamental rule of pacing is to change shots only when the change is motivated. The new shot should provide new information that contributes to the audience's understanding or enjoyment. Cutting for the sake of cutting jars the viewer and takes her or his attention away from the program's content.

Transitional Devices

The particular device we use to switch from one camera to another depends on the production circumstances and the particular impression the director wishes to convey to the audience. There are four basic transitions: (1) the cut (or take), (2) the fade, (3) the dissolve, and (4) the wipe.

Cut A *cut* is an instantaneous change from one

shot to another. A synonym for *cut* is *take,* and in fact, *take* is the term we use for cutting between two cameras during a studio production. You might think of a cut as the shortest distance between two shots. A cut from one shot to another is similar to what our eyes do as they rapidly shift to various parts of our surroundings. However, the cut can also radically change time and place in the videospace and, if used improperly, can disorient the viewer.

Used correctly, the cut is the least obvious transition because it occurs quickly and appears natural. The speed of a cut is fixed and constant and, unlike other transitional devices, cannot be varied.

MOTIVATING THE CUT   A cut should be motivated by some element in the show. The motivation might be action, the beat of the music, dialogue, or some other apparent reason to change camera shots.

CUTTING ON ACTION   Except in the rarest of circumstances, a cut should be as unobtrusive as possible. Cutting on the action is one way to accomplish this, since the movement will usually cover the transition from one shot to another. If, for instance, you had a wide shot on Camera 1 of someone entering a room and a close-up on Camera 2 of the actor sitting down, the cut from one camera to another should occur during the action as the subject makes the move. Cutting before the action occurs or after the action is completed is not as fluid and usually does not look "right" on-screen. (See Figure 15-5.)

CUTTING ON MUSIC   Music is frequently used to establish the timing of cuts. Cutting on the beat has been found to be an effective and aesthetically pleasing way of timing the cuts from one camera shot to another.

CUTTING ON DIALOGUE   A very common motivation for cutting is to use spoken dialogue as a cue for shot transitions. It is best to cut from one speaker to another at the end of one person's statement or thought and just before another per-

FIGURE 15-5 **Cutting on the Action.**
Cutting on the action shows the audience what it wishes to see and provides a natural transition between shots. In this case, when the cashier looks toward the door, the director cuts to another camera showing the person in the doorway.

son begins speaking. This applies equally to a spontaneous interview show as to a prepared dramatic scene or an on-camera speech. There are exceptions, though, particularly when you want to cut to a reaction shot to show another individual's response to what is being said. In this case, the reaction itself is the major motivation for making the cut. You should try to establish a cutting pattern which complements the on-camera dialogue. Cutting too frequently may create a choppy impression, which inhibits the viewer's ability to follow the discussion. At the other extreme, remaining on one shot for too long can be visually boring.

ADDITIONAL USES FOR CUTTING There are some special situations where cutting is used to achieve a special visual effect. One is a *montage*—a rapid succession of shots in sequence. The dramatic impact of a montage is derived from the total effect of all the shots as a whole and not from any single shot or cut. Because a montage is traditionally a series of short, rapid-fire cuts, it is usually produced on film or videotape so that the many individual shots can be edited together. Using a montage, you can race through the 200 years of our nation's history in a few minutes or quickly establish a setting, emotion, or background for a program. Montages are frequently used for opening and closing program titles and to establish a situation or mood in a very short period of time.

Cutting between two or more shots also can

provide the illusion of movement or *animation.* You can prove this to yourself by setting up two camera shots of the same subject. Have Camera 1 show the subject in a long shot positioned on the left side of the screen and Camera 2 show the same subject on the right side of the screen. By cutting rapidly between the two cameras you create the illusion of movement as the subject jumps back and forth across the screen. This illusion of motion caused by the transition is referred to as tertiary motion.

Fade In a *fade,* the picture either runs from black to an image (a *fade-in*) or from an image to black (a *fade-out*). Unlike the cut, the fade is an obvious transitional device that punctuates a program segment much as a period ends a sentence. The fade is often thought of as being similar to the curtain in the theater that is used to separate each act. The fade also can be used to separate different program elements such as the show material from the commercials. Fades are often used in drama to indicate a major change in time or space.

The speed of the fade is variable—it can be almost as rapid as a cut or as slow and deliberate as you wish. One way to use a slow fade is to give the audience time to reflect on what they have just seen. For example, if you just showed a particularly tragic news story, a slow fade to black gives the audience a chance to think about what has been shown. The same effect can be quite dramatic when used appropriately within a play. In the television version of *Death of a Salesman,* Willie Loman (Dustin Hoffman) selects a tragic end to a tragic life by purposefully crashing his automobile. The impact of the final scene was made even more devastating through the director's painfully slow fade to black.

Dissolve A *dissolve* is a simultaneous fade-in on one shot and fade-out on another. The effect on screen is a gradual blending of one shot into the other. If the dissolve is stopped midway, the effect produced on screen is a *superimposition,* or *super.* Since a dissolve is always a super during part of the transition, it is important to compose both shots so that they will complement each other.

The speed of a dissolve is variable, and dissolves can be produced either rapidly or slowly. The dissolve is frequently used as a less abrupt video transition than a cut. If you were directing a slow ballet, for example, cutting from camera to camera during the fluid movements of a dancer would appear too harsh and disturbing. Dissolves, on the other hand, permit the transitions to flow smoothly, suiting the mood more appropriately than a series of cuts. In a dramatic show, dissolves are sometimes used to suggest a minor change in time or place or simultaneous actions occurring at two different locations.

Because a dissolve can be made effortlessly with the video switcher and because it produces such an interesting visual effect, it is often subject to overuse or abuse. Remember, a dissolve is a much longer route between two shots than a cut, and it should be used sparingly to be effective. If your intention is to show the viewer what is happening onscreen in the most direct way, the director should travel as quickly as possible from camera shot to camera shot. In the case of an interview show, for example, a dissolve between panelists would be totally inappropriate, since the cut is a more direct and straightforward transition that better complements the particular production situation.

MATCHED DISSOLVE An interesting variation on the dissolve is a *matched dissolve.* This is accomplished by matching two different camera shots so that the effect produced is of one shot blending

subtly into another. For example, shooting identical shots of a disheveled Jim Rockford (James Garner) shaving in the morning with a dapper Jim Rockford shaving in preparation for an evening out produces a matched dissolve that conveys the passage of time and mood to the audience. Another example of the matched dissolve is the opening of a rock concert in which the director locked a camera on a wide shot of the empty arena. As the audience began to fill the seats, the director recorded a few minutes of videotape at regular intervals until the seats were completely full. During postproduction, the director set up *A* and *B* VTR rolls for a coord and by dissolving between various taped segments produced the effect of the hall filling up with an audience in only a matter of seconds.

The trick to a matched dissolve is to set up both camera shots properly. Whether you will be producing the dissolve between two or more cameras in real time or will be using videotape and producing the dissolve in postproduction, as with the rock concert example we just mentioned, it is essential for the different shots to match as closely as possible. If your camera viewfinders can show the mix/effects output, it makes it easy for the camera operators to align their shots precisely by using each other as a reference until a perfect match is achieved.

PAN/DISSOLVE A variation on the dissolve is to *pan,* or *tilt,* both cameras simultaneously while dissolving between their shots. The effect produced is a very smooth and fluid movement in the videospace that is often highly effective in musical or dance numbers. The usual way to set up this shot is to have one camera start on the subject while another camera begins by shooting off the subject, usually into a dark or neutral area of the set. On cue, the camera that is shooting the subject pans or tilts so that the subject moves out of the frame while the other camera pans or tilts to include the subject in the frame. At the appropriate time, the director dissolves between cameras, creating the effect onscreen. The transition must be carefully rehearsed, since its success depends on the combination of cameras moving at the right speed and the precise timing of the dissolve. The shot looks best against a limbo or cameo background, which eliminates distractions in the shot and provides the illusion of the subject moving across infinite videospace.

FOCUS/DEFOCUS DISSOLVE   As its name suggests, the third variation on the dissolve involves one camera going out of focus while the second camera comes into focus. As the cameras simultaneously focus/defocus, the director dissolves between the two. The diffused and dreamy quality of the effect can be used to show a change in time or place; to suggest altered perception, hallucinations, or dreams; or simply as an aesthetically pleasing transition in a musical or dance production.

Wipe   In a *wipe* transition, a new picture literally wipes across the screen replacing the existing image with a new shot. The pattern and direction of the wipe are variable, and most modern production switchers offer a large assortment of wipes. A wipe is the most artificial transitional device and, consequently, the most obvious to the viewer. It is useful, however, when you especially want to call attention to the transition. For example, in sports coverage the transition from live action to a videotape replay is frequently made with a wipe to show the viewer clearly the change from live action to replay.

A variation on the conventional hard wipe is a *soft wipe,* which features diffused, graduated borders. This lessens the impact of the transition and makes the soft wipe appear more like a dissolve than a hard wipe.

Switchers and editing systems which are equipped with a digital video effects unit can produce a number of special wipe transitions such as push-offs, flips, image compression, and so forth. Although these effects appear quite artificial and call attention to themselves, they are very effective transactions in nondramatic applications such as news, sports, commercials, or training productions.

SPLIT SCREEN   The speed of a wipe is variable, and when a wipe is stopped midway, it creates a *split-screen effect.* The split screen is very useful when you must show two or more events simultaneously or when you wish to show a single event from various perspectives.

In the first situation, split screens are frequently used in baseball games to show the batter at the plate and the runner leading off first base. In the second case, a director of a cooking show might use a split screen to show both the on-camera talent at the top of the screen and a close-up of her or his food preparation on the bottom half of the screen. Home shopping networks often combine a close-up of a product with a long shot of the product's use being demonstrated.

As many as four split-screen images are possible with many production switchers (even more if you use special-effects equipment and editing), but beware of excess. The size of the television screen is limited, and the viewer can process only so much visual information at one time. The greater the number of split-screen images you use at one time, the smaller is the size of each. In addition, the amount of information the viewer receives may reach the "overload" stage, where it is either ignored or becomes confusing and distracting.

TECH TIP   The number of satellite-linked interview situations has created a new split-screen convention for the director's use. To establish the conversation, the two participants appear in boxes on either side of the screen. As one speaker launches into an extended monologue the screen fills with his or her image. Later, to reestablish the feeling of an interview, the director calls for the split screen again.

When to Change Shots

Knowing when to change a camera shot is one of the many important choices facing the director. To a great extent, the decision you make must be based on the specific situation at the time, but there are a number of guidelines to help you in cutting from shot to shot. Incidently, the term *cutting* is often used to refer to all video transactions, although cuts are the most frequently used transitional devices.

In general, you should cut to another shot when you have exhausted all the information contained within the existing shot, when you want to show the viewer something entirely different, when you want to show the same subject from a different perspective, or when you want to vary the emphasis and direct the audience's attention to other elements in the videospace.

Show Something New The most obvious time to cut is to show the viewer something new. If we start an interview show with a close-up of the host, we will want to see the guest when introduced. Similarly, if a performer in a full shot picks up an object for us to examine more closely, the director will cut to a close-up to show the new object that has come to our attention.

Show a Different Angle Usually a camera is positioned for a particular kind of shot. The same camera position may not show a close-up as well as it shows a long shot. Since the viewer often needs to see the same scene from a different and more advantageous angle, the director should use the opportunity to cut to the better camera shot. This is done constantly in sports and news coverage to give the viewer "the best seat in the house." We also do it on dramatic programs when, for example, we cut from a two-shot to an over-the-shoulder angle or in an interview show when we cut from a wide establishing shot of the panelists to a tighter close-up of the speaker.

When the Shot Is Motivated Onscreen Imagine a medium shot of a man working at a desk when we suddenly hear a loud crash off-camera. The man turns to see what has happened, and this movement, accompanied by the offstage sound, motivates a cut to a new shot to show us what caused the commotion. Motivation for a cut need not be so obvious, though. A glance, a turned head, a pointed finger, or dialogue can all be used as motivating factors to cut to another shot.

Reaction Shots As the name suggests, a *reaction shot* shows the viewer the reaction of a subject or a group to onscreen events. Although the reaction shot may not carry the program's principal message, reactions are useful in establishing character involvement or in showing the audience

a more complete picture of a situation or event. A shot of wildly cheering fans during a ball game is a common example of a reaction shot. Although the ball game is of primary interest, screaming fans and banners waving after a big play help to show another side of the same event and establish the relationship between the game on the field and the fans in the stands.

Interview or talk shows also benefit from the director's use of reaction shots. Of course, frequently in a drama it may be more important to see a character's reaction than to see the performer who is actually speaking.

When Not to Cut

One of the most difficult things for a beginning director to learn is when *not* to cut. Too much of any good thing is bad, and overcutting a show will not necessarily make it more interesting or more effective. In fact, overcutting can actually hurt your program. This is so because every time we cut, we risk pulling the visual rug out from under the viewers, breaking their concentration, and disorienting their perspective of the events onscreen. As the program's director or editor, you have probably seen and heard the show so often during planning and rehearsal that you are apt to become bored with a shot long before the viewer. Remember that the audience is seeing your show—and each shot—for the first time. In fact, you may have to restrain yourself from cutting too often, especially on instructional or demonstration programs, because the viewer who is trying to learn a technique or understand the presentation needs extra time to process all the visual information contained in any particular shot.

As a rule of thumb, ask yourself before changing shots: "Am I showing something new or different by cutting to this shot?" If yes, then make the cut. If you find you are cutting only for visual variety, you may risk overcutting the show. From a purely production point of view, overcutting can tie up some of your cameras with unnecessary shots, making it more difficult for you to use them later for some really important shots.

Alternatives to Cutting   Although cutting from shot to shot is one way to show new information or give the viewer a different perspective, there are a number of alternatives to cutting that you ought to consider. Among these are camera movement, performer movement, use of focus/depth of field, and the use of plastics.

CAMERA MOVEMENT   Simply moving the camera—pan, tilt, dolly, arc—can often sufficiently change the audience's point of view and eliminate the need to cut to another camera shot. Since a zoom often resembles camera movement (although it lacks the depth perspective of a dolly), we can consider it in the same category. While overzooming is definitely to be avoided, combining a zoom with performer movement can disguise the zoom move and still vary the point of view of the shot. For example, say you wish to show an actor enter a room in a medium shot and then show a wide shot as she crosses from the door to the middle of set. You could accomplish this with two cameras: Camera 1 shoots a waist shot at the door, and Camera 2 shoots a wide shot of the set. As the actor leaves the frame on Camera 1, the director would cut—on the action—to the wide shot. An alternative would be to use only one camera to pick the actor up in a waist shot as she enters the door and looks around. As she moves forward, the camera zooms out with her to produce the wide shot.

Remember that cameras are mounted on wheels and can move on the air as well as off. You might want to combine the zoom we mentioned above with a slight arc, so that the camera's wide shot is more centered and provides an even better perspective for the audience.

Moving cameras also enhances depth in the videospace, particularly when the cameras move past foreground objects or through doors or arches. Pedestaling up or down also can eliminate the need to cut. By pedestaling down as an actor walks into a room and sits in a chair, you maintain the proper camera angle without cutting to another camera shot.

Camera movement offers you a number of important advantages. First, it is a more fluid way of changing the viewer's point of view than resorting to cut after cut. Second, economy in cutting means that your cameras have more time to prepare for their next shot, and both you and the camera operators can spend more time on framing and composition. Of course, moving the camera presents its own set of difficulties, but practice and coordination between the camera operator and a floor assistant can make even the most difficult moves possible.

PERFORMER OR ACTOR MOVEMENT   Another way to change a shot onscreen is to move your on-camera performers or actors to frame the shot for you. For example, let us start with two actors photographed in a medium two-shot. As the scene develops, one moves forward a few steps, forming a new shot—a foreground/background shot. If the foreground actor turns around and faces the background actor, we now have a third shot—an over-the-shoulder shot. Finally, if the actor facing the camera walks off and the other actor turns to look at him, we have a fourth shot—a close-up. Notice that we did not move the camera at all except to reframe the picture slightly as the actors moved, yet we produced four different shots for the price of one. (See Figure 15-6.)

Performer or actor movement requires precision blocking of both talent and cameras. You will have to rely on performers or actors to hit their marks consistently, and it is a good idea to have the floor manager put down masking tape to indicate each position. It may take some time and effort, but varying the shot with talent blocking can be especially valuable in maintaining the flow of a scene and increasing the number of different shots you can produce with a limited number of cameras.

USE OF FOCUS/DEPTH OF FIELD   We naturally turn our attention to areas of the videospace which are in sharp focus, and we look away from those areas which are out of focus. Consequently, the director can use focus and depth of field as another alternative to cutting. Using a shallow depth of field and throwing focus from subject to subject permit you to vary the audience's attention within the same shot. (See Figure 15-7.)

PLASTICS   The use of lighting and sets also can change your camera shots without cutting. A commonly used lighting technique is to illuminate a

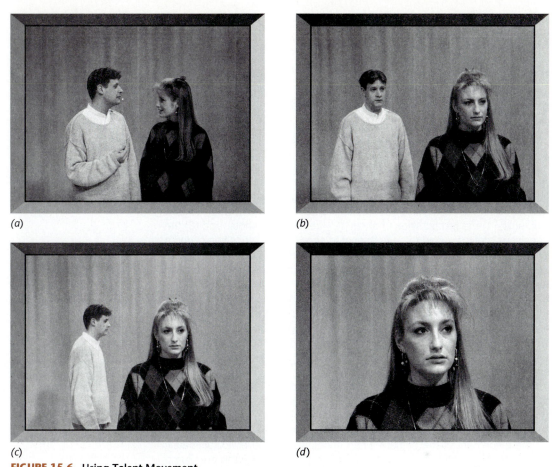

(a)

(b)

(c)

(d)

FIGURE 15-6 **Using Talent Movement.**
By carefully coordinating talent movement and camera shots, the director can
produce a number of visually different shots without cutting to another camera. In
this scene, the director starts off with both subjects in a two-shot (*a*). As the woman
walks toward the camera, a new shot—foreground-background—is created (*b*).
When the man walks out of the frame (*c*), zooming in creates a close-up (*d*).

FIGURE 15-7 **Using Depth-of-Field.**
Using depth-of-field to direct the audience's attention
to the desired object or person in a scene can be an
effective director's tool.

449

foreground subject in cameo, with the background completely dark. By assigning background lights to their own separate dimmers, we can light the background on cue, creating a new "camera shot." Other lighting variations are changing from silhouette to normal lighting or varying the color of a cyclorama.

Sets can be cleverly brought into the shot or removed either on wheels or "flown" above the studio on counterweight battens. The content or composition of the shot changes without cutting to another camera.

SUMMARY

Individual shots must be edited, or joined together, into a meaningful sequence. Both the television director and the editor work with three related elements: (1) the juxtaposition of shots, (2) the timing of shots, and (3) the transitional devices used to go from shot to shot. The juxtaposition of shots in a sequence involves controlling content and time to communicate your intended meaning to the audience. The content is conveyed first through thematic editing.

Three main methods to control time while editing are (1) continuity editing, (2) parallel cutting, and (3) flashforward/flashback techniques. Continuity may be achieved through cutting on action; using cutaways and reaction shots; and tonal and color editing. Screen time may be compressed or expanded by editing. The sequencing will imply cause-and-effect relationships between the subjects in the shots.

Since subjects move within the television frame, the director and editor must be conscious of the rules of screen direction. Using the action axis— an imaginary line that runs in the direction the subject is moving—can help keep track of screen direction. Screen direction largely will be determined by the placement of the camera when shooting, but the editor ultimately sequences the shots. One discontinuous sequence is the jump cut. Jump cuts are abrupt or radical changes from one shot to another and usually startle or disorient the viewer. Among the most common jump cuts are radical change in shot or subject size, severe change in camera angle or point of view, jump in screen direction, discontinuity, and cutting from a moving camera to a stationary shot. In other words, the approach that has become recognized as "MTV style."

The timing of the transition and knowing when or when not to change shots are important directorial decisions. In general, we change shots when we want to show the viewer something new or a different or more effective angle or view of a scene or when there is obvious motivation for the cut. Each of the four basic transitional devices—the cut, the fade, the dissolve, and the wipe—is most appropriate for a different situation.

There are a number of alternatives to changing shots which allow the director to vary the viewer's perspective without actually switching to another camera. These include camera movement, performer movement, use of focus and depth of field, and manipulation of plastics, such as lighting.

Design refers to the various details that give a show its distinctive "look" or style. Design is not neutral. It cues the audience whether a show is formal or serious, informal or humorous. Most important, design can help (or hurt) in communicating your ideas. Good design enhances communication. It makes your meaning clear, easy to understand, interesting, and involving. Poor design impedes communication. It confuses, bores, aggravates, and can alienate your audience.

In television production good visual design is crucial because television is a visual storyteller. The production designer has a number of video design elements to consider. Three key elements are (1) *graphics*, (2) *sets*, and (3) *lighting*. They provide the understructure, or hidden framework, for camera composition and shot sequences. Good video design provides unity, coherence, and continuity to the videospace.

Unfortunately, like good style, good design is difficult to learn. It's more than simply mechanics. Video design involves relating art to technology. There are no hard and fast rules for production design, but there are some fundamental guidelines which can start you on your way to discovering your own style.

TELEVISION GRAPHICS

Prior to the 1980s, the primary means of producing a graphic image for television was to draw, paint, or print the image; cut it out; glue it on a card; then shoot the graphics card with a camera. While this technique is occasionally used today, it has largely been replaced by electronic graphics production. The television graphics artist has become a designer who combines graphic elements from many sources, such as freehand illustrations drawn with an electronic pen on a computer graphics tablet, electronic "still store" frames grabbed from videotapes, and lettering created by a character generator. The primary tools of today's graphics designer are more likely to be computer paint systems than ink pens, scissors, and rubber cement. As low-cost computer graphics systems have become available, even the most modest production facilities now have access to animated three-dimensional logos and graphics. In addition, because television computer graphics are digital, they can be stored on disks, recalled instantaneously, and modified easily.

In this chapter we are going to describe mechanical, photographic, and electronic graphics production for television. Our emphasis will be on the electronic technologies, such as character generators, video digitizers, paint systems, and three-dimensional animation. The chapter will conclude with an overview of graphics in the four stages of television production.

Just as it has changed so many of the work patterns in other parts of the industry, the computer has changed the way television graphics are produced. Yet even with their heritage in high-tech flight simulators and silicon chip design, computer graphics serve a very utilitarian function on television: to convey information to the viewer. Before we can discuss how graphics are produced, we need to consider exactly why they are used.

Graphics show the audience many things. Think about how a program opens. Usually there are program titles, which communicate the show's style as well as its content. The titles that appear before a suspenseful murder mystery look much different from the titles that introduce a situation comedy. The graphics' "look" is the first tool at the producer's disposal to help build expectations and to keep the viewer tuned to the program. To do this, graphics must be aesthetically pleasing and, at the same time, effective in communicating their message to the audience.

You can begin to develop an eye and appreciation for graphic design by watching your local television stations carefully. Stations use their *logos*, or identification symbols, to present the station's "personality." Is the station the traditional "solid citizen" in town? Is its competitor the progressive station for the contemporary audience? Just by watching the station's use of graphics you will have a good idea what image the management is trying to portray.

In educational and corporate programming, graphics frequently play another significant role. Since these productions often deal with complicated ideas and processes, well-designed graphics can clarify program content and focus the audience's attention on the most important elements in the presentation. The graphics over the shoulder of a newscaster are designed for the same purpose: to help the viewer understand.

In short, effective television graphics

1   Establish a show's overall image, mood, and tone.
2   Convey information clearly and directly.
3   Help to simplify complex facts, concepts, or processes by presenting them visually.

GRAPHIC DESIGN

When you start to design a graphic, there are a number of *technical* and *aesthetic* factors to consider. The technical considerations are those necessary to adapt the graphic concept to the capabilities and limitations of television's formal visual structure. We introduced those elements in Chapter 2, and explained the technology behind them when we described how television works in Chapter 11. Now we will examine those technical considerations in terms of graphics production because no matter how imaginative and creative a graphic may be, it must reproduce well over the television system to successfully reach the audience.

Technical Design Considerations

The five technical design considerations are (1) *size*, (2) *shape*, (3) *sharpness*, (4) *contrast*, and (5) *imaging*.

Size   The size of the television screen is relatively small, and the videospace can be easily cluttered with excessive detail. Television graphics should be as simple as possible. For example, compare the two graphs and two maps in Figure 16-1 to see the benefits of eliminating clutter. Here's a rule of thumb: If in doubt, leave it out.

FIGURE 16-1   Cluttered and Simplified Graphics (*facing page*). (*a*) "Chart junk," in which too much detail is included, prevents clear communication. (*b*) Only essential information is conveyed, creating an effective presentation. (*c*) The focus of attention is unclear on this "road" map. (*d*) The viewer immediately knows where to look on this simplified map.

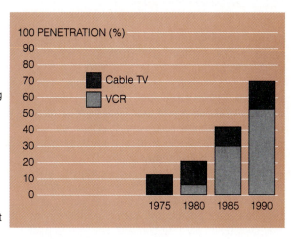

Vertical writing hard to read

Box unneeded

Connect lines redundant

Not in 4:3 aspect ratio

Wasted space

Penetration (%)

Competing stripes too busy

YEAR ——— Redundant

Cable TV

VCR

(a) Cluttered Chart

100 PENETRATION (%)

Cable TV

VCR

(b) Simplified Chart

(c) Cluttered Map

(d) Simplified Map

457

Shape   With the exception of high definition television (HDTV), all television screens, regardless of their size, are designed in 4:3 (pronounced "four-by-three") *television aspect ratio*. (See Figure 16-2.) This means that all pictures must be framed in proportions of four units wide to three units high. Graphics which are designed for television must fit this ratio or must be adapted to it. What if you have a photograph that you must use as a graphic, but it is not in 4:3 TV aspect ratio? For example, suppose you're shooting a documentary on a professional basketball player and he gives you a photograph from his family album that shows him on the court with his high school team. The only problem is that the photo is shot vertically, eight inches wide and ten inches high. You have three options. (See Figure 16-3.) First, you could show the entire photo and accept the fact that the television picture will have borders along the sides of the screen. If the color of the mount card is selected carefully, the audience may not notice that the photo does not fill the screen. Second, you could crop the photo and

show only the basketball player. Third, you could use the photo as a *tilt graphic* and tilt up or down on it, depending on how it fit into your sequence of shots.

A horizontal photograph would present similar problems if it were too wide for television aspect ratio. The solutions are the same, except instead of using the photo as a tilt graphic, in this case you would use it as a *pan graphic*. (See Figure 16-4.)

Some graphic images used in television were originally photographic slides. Fortunately, the 3:2 ratio of a 35-mm slide (which has a 1½- × 1-inch image area) is close to television's 4:3 ratio, and with a little forethought, there are no serious format problems in shooting slides for use in the film chain. When shooting slides for television, two rules to follow are (1) loosen the framing of your image slightly so important elements are not cut off, and (2) compose the image horizontally. If you use a vertically framed slide in the slide projector of the film chain, black edges will show on both sides of the picture. You also risk cropping important visual information at the top and bottom of the television screen.

A photographic image that has been properly framed into the 4:3 aspect ratio enables you to

FIGURE 16-2   **Television Aspect Ratios.**
All television graphics should be designed to fit within television's aspect ratios. The current standard aspect ratio is (*a*) four units wide by three units high. However, the high definition television (HDTV) aspect ratio is (*b*) sixteen units wide by nine units high. It is possible to use a graphic in both formats, if the essential information is within the 4:3 format and the background fills the 16:9 space.

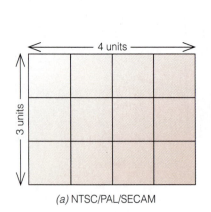

(a) NTSC/PAL/SECAM

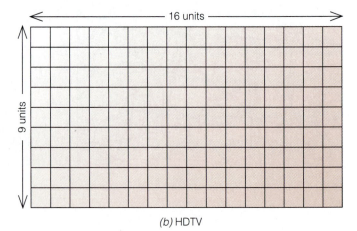

(b) HDTV

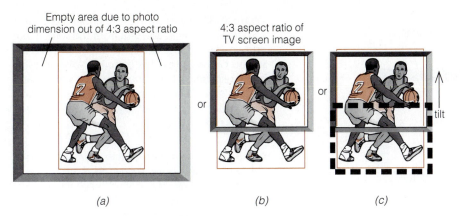

FIGURE 16-3 **Using a Vertical Graphic.**
If an existing vertical graphic is not in 4:3 aspect ratio: (*a*) shoot the entire graphic and accept the border edges, (*b*) crop the graphic and include only a portion, or (*c*) shoot a portion and tilt the camera to reveal the rest of the graphic.

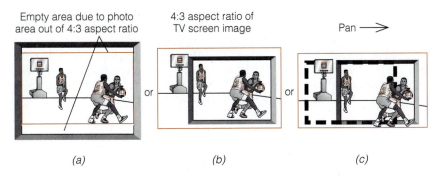

FIGURE 16-4 **Using a Horizontal Graphic.**
If an existing horizontal graphic is not in 4:3 aspect ratio: (*a*) shoot the entire graphic and accept the border edges, (*b*) crop the graphic and include only a portion, (*c*) shoot a portion and pan the camera to reveal the rest of the graphic.

make the most efficient and effective use of the videospace. Many professional still cameras feature a focusing screen that crops the viewfinder image correctly for television. (See Figure 16-5.)

SCANNING AND ESSENTIAL AREAS We mentioned in Chapter 13 that the picture you see in the camera's viewfinder contains much more information than that which ultimately appears on the audience's television screen. That is so because the outer edges of the picture are lost as the video signal travels through the television system. To

make certain that the audience sees the most important visual information, you must be sure it is contained within the *essential area*—the portion of the picture that will definitely appear on all television receivers.

Figure 16-6 shows a graphic card that is divided into two areas: the essential area inside is the "safe" area that will be seen by everyone. The larger area is the *scanning area*, the total area seen by the camera. The edges of the scanning area contain information that is imaged by the television camera but which may not appear on all

459

3:4 Aspect ratio marked
on 2:3 35-mm focus grid

FIGURE 16-5   TV Focus Screen.
Many 35-mm cameras can be equipped with a TV
focus screen so that the photographer can easily crop
the image for television.

audience receivers. This sometimes is called the
cropping area. However, since many members of
the audience will see all or part of the scanning
area, it should contain some visual information but
none of the essential words or illustrations which
must be seen in order to understand the message.

TECH TIP   Home viewers lose approximately 10 to
15 percent of the image sent from the station, but
no two viewers lose the same amount. Since the
station cannot adjust the scanning yoke on every
home television, they compensate by keeping important material in the essential area and sending
complementary, but not critical, material in the
scanning area.

Sharpness   *Sharpness*, or *resolution*, refers to the
ability of the television system to reproduce picture detail clearly. The limited resolution of television is an important factor in the planning and
preparation of graphics. Lettering styles and sizes
should be selected for the best television reproduction. Large type is more legible and encour-
ages the use of fewer words, which helps keep
the graphic clear and uncluttered. With respect to
type style, avoid light, ornate typefaces with fine
lines and delicate serifs. The resolving power of
the television system simply cannot handle the
fine detail, and your lettering on screen may be
unreadable. Most of the sans serif styles with good
visual weight and clarity reproduce well on television. Helvetica and Chicago are popular type
styles for television graphics. (See Figure 16-7.)

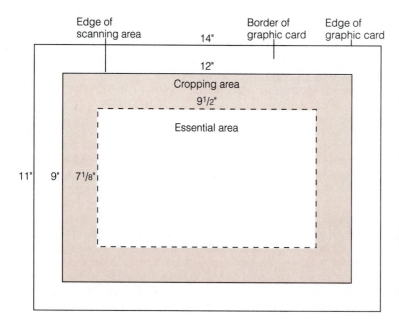

FIGURE 16-6
Essential Area.
The essential area is the center
"safe" area of the image,
where important information
should be placed so the
viewer will surely see it. The
scanning area will be cropped
differently by different home
television sets because of
limitations in the television
reproduction system. Areas
along the edges that may be
cropped should contain parts
of the visual image which are
not essential for conveying
your message.

Figure 16-7

ABCDEFGHIJKLM
NOPQRSTUV

*ABCDEFGHIJKL
MNOPQRSTUV*

**ABCDEFGHIJKLMNOPQRSTUVWXYZ
abcdefghijklmnopqrstuvwxyz 1234567890**

𝕬𝕭𝕮𝕯𝕰𝕱   aopqrstub $5678

*AXYZABCDEFGHIJK
aqrstuvwxyzabc $567*

APQRSTUVWXYZAB
abcdefghijklmnopqrst

AZABCDEFGHIJKLMNO
aijklmnopqrstuv $12345

**AOPQRSTUVWXYZ
apqrstuvwxyz $567**

Not suitable

Good choices for TV graphics

FIGURE 16-7 Typefaces for Television.
There are many different families of typefaces. Use simple, bold typefaces. Avoid light, ornate styles with fine lines, which are difficult to reproduce on screen.

You also must consider resolution limitations in planning the use of photographs or illustrations. Photographs should not contain extremely small details, which will blur or become invisible on the television screen. Very complex illustrations, such as maps or technical diagrams, must be simplified and redesigned for television use.

If in doubt about the legibility of a type style or illustration, preview the graphic on a 13-inch monitor from 12 feet away. This will give you a good idea how the graphic will appear in the average viewer's living room.

TECH TIP A good guideline for selecting legible type is the 16*H* rule. The 16*H* rule states the letters should be readable from 16 times the height of the television image. For example, since the 13-inch monitor (13 inches on the diagonal) is approximately 9 inches in height, a properly sized graphic should be readable from 12 feet (16 inches × 9 inches = 144 inches = 12 feet).

In practice, seven lines of twenty-four point type is very easy to read, and ten lines of thirty-two point type is about the smallest you should use.

Contrast From our earlier chapters on cameras and lighting you already know that the television system works best when it photographs a scene consisting of a contrast ratio that is about 30:1. This is called the *contrast ratio*. Since the television camera cannot reproduce pure white and pure black accurately, we work with television white (about 60 percent reflectance) and television black (about 3 percent reflectance). The 30:1 ratio also applies to color graphics, so the brightest luminance in a graphic image should not exceed the dimmest luminance by more than thirty times. The only exception to this rule is the preparation of "key" graphics, where pure-white lettering or line drawings are prepared against a jet-black background. The key graphic is electronically superimposed on or inserted into another picture.

The television *gray scale* is especially helpful to graphic artists for a number of reasons. First, a well-designed graphic needs good contrast between foreground lettering and background elements. This applies to color graphics as well as black and white. Most graphic artists suggest maintaining at least two gray-scale steps between foreground and background. Good contrast within the proper range will not only make your graphics look and reproduce better, but it also will improve the legibility on screen. (See Figure 16-8.)

Imaging All video images begin as either (1) *camera images* or (2) *generated images*. We dis-

461

(a)

(b)

FIGURE 16-8   Contrast Ratio.
(a) This image exhibits an adequate contrast ratio and reproduces well on television. (b) This image lacks adequate contrast and reproduces poorly on television.

cussed both methods extensively in Chapter 11 and Chapter 12. Now we want to focus on imaging devices as graphic tools.

CAMERA IMAGES   In camera imaging, the light reflected from a graphic is focused on a *photoelectric transducer*, either a pickup tube or a charge-coupled device (CCD) inside the camera.

Camera graphics must "read" faithfully, or look as much like the original as possible, on the camera's imaging device. To accomplish this, the graphic artist must be concerned with the technical principles of size, shape, sharpness, and contrast, and the aesthetic principles which we will cover later in this chapter.

GENERATED IMAGES   *Generated images* are created right from the start as electrical signals within the video system itself. Essentially, the video monitor is the canvas and the electronic beam is the brush. The use of digital technology enables the graphic designer to produce and manipulate both text and images in a variety of powerful ways. The five primary types of digital graphics systems are: (1) *character*, or text, *generators*; (2) *paint systems*; (3) *video digitizers*; (4) *three-dimensional graphic systems*; and (5) *animation systems*. Today a large menu of computer graphics software is available that can run on hardware from conventional personal computers to large-scale networked mainframes. Each hardware and software system has its own capabilities and its own "look."

We will examine the five types of computer graphics systems later in this chapter.

Regardless of the graphic production tools used, the characteristics of television's formal structure will dictate certain design approaches. Technical considerations always come first and foremost because they determine how a graphic will appear in the videospace. After those considerations are met, the aesthetic, or creative, considerations are the elements that will make the graphic both interesting to look at and effective in communicating your message to the audience.

Aesthetic Design Elements

After you have met the various technical requirements of graphic design, you can begin to tackle the aesthetic design elements. Traditional design elements that we described in Chapter 2 are line, angle, shape, mass, space, texture, pattern, balance, and color—and these are all essential ingredients in graphic design. Additional elements that are important in animated graphics are time, motion, and sound. The interaction between various elements also is an important design consideration.

Composition   The arrangement of the aesthetic elements in a graphic is referred to as its *composition*. The same basic rules that apply to picture composition for cameras hold true for graphic design as well. A well-composed graphic organizes the various elements into meaningful and related units, conveys the necessary information to the audience, and presents a visual design that is aesthetically pleasing and interesting to look at.

It is a good idea to organize different graphic elements into a series of distinct groupings. Graphics may contain a number of different kinds of groupings or units; some are pictorial, and some are lettered. By experimenting with various ways of organizing the videospace, you will come up with those combinations which work best. For example, it has been found that written information is read and understood most easily when it is organized into related units. The program-promotional graphic in Figure 16-9 groups the information into three units: the show title, the picture, and the air date and time. Do not forget to consider aspect ratio, essential area, and the other

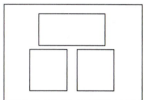

FIGURE 16-9 **Organizing Graphic Elements.**
Graphics should be designed as organized series of elements. The graphic shown
here is organized into three groupings, as indicated in the diagram.

technical factors when you compose your graphic.

Graphics are frequently most effective when they are arranged or composed with an asymmetrical balance. The overall impression which the graphic makes will be one of stability, yet also energy. You might decide to run written copy flush left along one edge of the screen and a picture on the other side of the screen. The result is an asymmetrically-balanced visual that is interesting to look at and still easy to understand. (See Figure 16-10.)

Of course, there are times when unbalanced compositions can be very effective. Graphics are by definition two-dimensional. Inducing a depth dimension by running lettering or pictures along

the diagonal and giving the illusion of depth through perspective are useful techniques. The imbalance and instability will add a feeling of tension and immediacy to the graphic, drawing the viewer's attention more closely to the screen. (See Figure 16-11.)

FIGURE 16-10 **Asymmetrical Balance.**
The graphic masses of the text and picture have
asymmetrical balance, which suggests a neutral
stability. Balanced designs usually are easily understood.

463

FIGURE 16-11   Unbalanced Design.
Unbalanced graphic design imparts a sense of
excitement or tension. Unbalanced design often
attracts attention to the graphic. *(Courtesy:
Ampex Corp.)*

Your layout and composition will depend, in
part, on how the director intends to use the
graphic in production. For example, a graphic that
is to be "keyed" during the show must be positioned so the combination of foreground key and
background picture produce a well-composed
shot. The key also must be composed so that it
does not overlay very light parts of the image.
Otherwise, the lettering will blend into the background and be unreadable.

Color   Color is naturally an important production
element in the design and preparation of graphic
material. You will recall that a color depends on
three factors: (1) *hue*, which is the actual color,
such as red, green, or blue; (2) *saturation*, which
is the intensity of the pure color or how much white
has been mixed in to dilute the pure color; and
(3) *brightness*, how light or dark the color appears.
Brightness is particularly important in designing
graphics because we are concerned with both
black and white reproduction and color reproduction. Colors must vary not only in hue and saturation, which naturally register on a color receiver,
but also in different brightness values—the only
way to indicate color differences in monochrome.
Take two colors such as red and green, for ex-

ample. They may be completely different in hue
and saturation, but because they have nearly
identical brightness values, there is no apparent
difference or contrast between them in a black
and white reproduction. (See Color Plate 7.)

Not all colors reproduce equally well on television. Even the most expensive and sophisticated color camera has difficulty in reproducing
red and orange hues accurately. If possible, avoid
using large areas of deeply saturated reds, which
may reproduce off-color. Also, be careful of pair-
ing certain colors. One of the most annoying color
combinations is red and blue, which represent different ends of the visible light spectrum. As the
eye tries to focus on the different wavelengths, it
quickly fatigues, leaving the viewer with a physi-
ologically based sense of irritation.

Using Color in Graphic Design   Color can be a
vital element in graphic design if used well or
astonishingly ineffective if used poorly. To make
the best use of color, you must understand some
of its basic principles.

One fundamental color principle is the fact that
colors are influenced by their surroundings. For
instance, the greater the light intensity that shines
on a color, the brighter and more saturated the
color appears. Another important point is that a
light color against a dark background looks larger
and even lighter than a light color against a dark
background. Take a look at the two squares in
Figure 16-12. The size of the two letters is identical, but the darker background makes its letter
appear larger than its identical twin. The idea is
easily applied to lettering and layout design, regardless of the television screen's size. Important

FIGURE 16-12   Light Lettering on Dark Background.
Light letter on a dark background *(left)* appears larger
and seems to come toward the audience, while an
identically sized dark letter *(right)* appears smaller and
tends to recede on a light background.

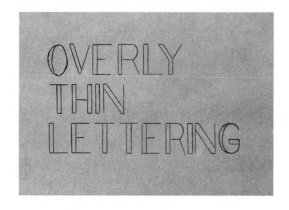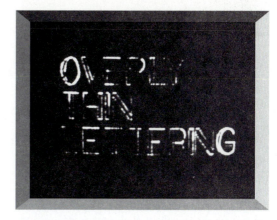

FIGURE 16-13 Blocked-up Lettering.
Overly thin lettering tends to block up on a television monitor and become difficult to read.

foreground elements ought to be lighter in color and brighter than the background so that they will stand out more prominently and attract the viewer's attention. You will notice that nearly all graphics prepared for television use light lettering on a dark background. Because of this design decision, the words come toward the audience, while the background recedes.

TECH TIP Because of the characteristics of television electronics, light-colored lines "bleed" across the screen's scan lines, increasing their apparent size. While this usually contributes to legibility, light-colored lines too close together will blend together and "block up" the image. As always, remember to preview your work on a television monitor. Do not trust your eye examining an art board. (See Figure 16-13.)

When you are working with color, keep in mind the need for good contrast in hue, saturation, and brightness. Viewers watching in monochrome, where only brightness values register, require a distinct change in the gray scale in order to perceive any difference between two colors. Good brightness contrast will make your graphic more interesting and effective in color too.

Colors also play a part in how the audience perceives a subject. Some experts claim that colors influence our judgments of size, weight, and temperature and even affect our psychological state of mind. Introductory art classes make the point

that reddish colors appear "warm" and bluish colors appear "cold." We tend to associate certain colors with different activities. Reds are linked with warmth, fire, and tension. Blues are associated with cold, steel, and ice. According to Herbert Zettl, colors can be viewed as being either high-energy or low-energy colors. *High-energy colors* are reds, oranges, and yellows, particularly when they are deeply saturated. *Low-energy colors* are cooler blues, browns, and purples, especially when they are less saturated. According to the theory, high-energy colors tend to involve the audience more directly and with greater impact than do low-energy colors.

Of course, these color rules are not necessarily true at all times, and they often vary depending, in large part, on a particular color's surroundings and the relative brightness and saturation of adjacent shades. A normally warm red may appear cool in comparison to an even warmer red nearby. Our intuition does tell us, nevertheless, that certain colors just seem to go better with certain subjects or emotions. Lighter colors look happier and give an uptempo feeling. Darker colors suggest a somber, dramatic, moody atmosphere. The graphics for a daily morning show would most likely be designed in bright and cheery reds and yellows rather than in dark browns and purples. Yet the darker colors might be just right for titles for a Shakespearean tragedy, since they match the program's mood and tone.

Style   All the elements that go into a graphic—the lettering, the illustrations, the composition, the color scheme—make up its visual *style*. A program's graphics should be designed to complement the show's style and approach. A contemporary music show might benefit from graphics that are designed in a highly stylized and abstract way. A more straightforward and traditional graphics style might best enhance a public affairs show. The graphic introductions in many contemporary newscasts are excellent examples of how graphics set the tone of programming. (See Figure 16-14.)

A particular graphic style is frequently used by a station or production company in its logo or identification symbol. The CBS "eye" is one of the most effective and enduring logos. While the style has been changed over the years to reflect modern taste, the CBS logo still provides instant identification, recognition, and impact whenever it is used. Graphic style also can unify a series of individual shows. For example, all CBS news programs use the same style lettering to give them a unified and integrated graphic "look." (See Figure 16-15.)

Before work begins on a production's artwork, the graphic artist and the program producer must discuss the concept of the show, the program's overall tone and objectives, and how the graphics are to be used. This will help the artist to design a graphics style that will complement the production. Of course, style also must be functional. You should not necessarily use old English lettering in an instructional program on Chaucer's poetry. The lettering style, while admittedly English, is unsuited for TV reproduction. The result may be words that prove to be unreadable. The idea is to set the mood and tone with a style that is still effective in communicating with the audience.

Designing for Effective Communication   When you come right down to it, a graphic's basic function is to impart information to the viewer. No matter what the particular message is—a program title, the sponsor's product, a station's call letters, a key point in an instructional presentation—the graphic must be designed for the most effective communication possible.

Graphics rarely stay on screen for very long, so they should be designed to make an immediate

FIGURE 16-14   Style.
The style of this promotional graphic for a musical performance show suggests its contemporary approach. The animated graphic was produced on a computer system to give the visual elements a three-dimensional form. *(Courtesy: Microtime, Inc.)*

FIGURE 16-15 Logos.
A logo is an identification symbol which is immediately identifiable in the audience's mind. The CBS eye is one of the most effective and enduring logos, although it has been updated over the years to present a more contemporary look. *(Courtesy: CBS.)*

impression on the viewer. Sometimes images that are frequently associated with a subject can help. A news story about money might use such common symbols as a dollar bill or coins. If it takes a long time to absorb everything of importance in a

graphic, it will not be very meaningful to the audience. Graphics communicate best when they are clear, simple, and direct.

Illustrations are particularly important in many shows, but they must be designed carefully and prepared for maximum communication impact. You will most likely have to adapt existing illustrations to television's demanding specifications or develop new ones completely from scratch. Ironically, the less material contained in a single illustration, the more effectively the information is communicated to the audience. That is so because removing excess detail makes your important points or facts stand out more prominently.

MECHANICAL AND PHOTOGRAPHIC GRAPHICS PRODUCTION TECHNIQUES

Although today electronic graphics production techniques are the most prevalent in the preparation of television graphics, mechanical and photographic technologies are still in use. In this section we will cover some of the most common lettering and illustration techniques used to create camera graphics cards.

Lettering Techniques

Lettering can be produced mechanically with rub-on transfer lettering or photographically with photoset type.

Rub-on Transfer   As its name suggests, rub-on lettering uses special self-adhesive letters which, when rubbed, are transferred from a plastic carrier sheet to the artwork. Transfer lettering is available from a number of manufacturers under such brand names as Letraset, Presstype, and Instantype. (See Figure 16-16.)

Rub-on letters can be applied to almost any dry surface, including illustration or matte cards, photographs, transparent acetate cels, or glass. Acetate cels are particularly convenient when you are lettering information to be used with a photograph

FIGURE 16-16   Transfer Lettering.
Rub-on transfer lettering transfers self-adhesive letters
from a clear acetate sheet to the desired artwork. Rub-
on lettering is an inexpensive but time-consuming
technique for titling.

or illustration. By lettering onto the cel sheet, you
can layer the lettered cel over the illustration and
vary the position of the lettering without permanently marking the background picture.

Rub-on lettering is relatively inexpensive and
convenient to use. Since you need no special
equipment, you can produce graphics almost
anywhere. The technique does take time, patience, and an eye for the proper spacing of letters
and words.

Photographic Techniques

Television is a visual medium, and television
graphics naturally rely heavily on pictures and
photographs. If you have the opportunity to take
the pictures yourself or to assign someone to do
original photography, you can control for all the
usual graphic requirements. The photographs
must be composed in the 4:3 aspect ratio, they
should have sufficient contrast in both color and
monochrome, and they should follow the recommended guidelines for picture detail, resolution,
and essential area. At times, you will not be able
to take your own pictures, and you may have to
rely on a file of existing pictures, on wire-service
photographs, or on cutouts of pictures from
books, magazines, or even newspapers. Remember, if you use copyrighted materials, you must

acquire permission for their use in your show. Bias
your selection toward prominent foreground images framed by blurred, uncomplicated backgrounds.

Slides   *Slides* are 35-mm transparencies in 2- ×
2-inch mounts which are projected from the slide
chain. Slides can be used as both a principal
photographic medium and a production medium.
In the first case, pictures are photographed with
slide film, and the slides are entered in the still
store or used in place of camera cards. Using
slides rather than art cards eliminates the cost of
developing and mounting prints and also ensures
that the graphics will never be out of sequence
during the production. In addition, if a still store is
not available, replacing all camera cards with
slides releases a valuable studio camera from any
graphics responsibilities, giving the director
greater flexibility in shooting the set.

Slides have their share of disadvantages too.
Once a slide is mounted and loaded in the projector, you cannot animate the picture or change
the position of the artwork. This is very critical
when you are keying a slide over another picture
or inserting the slide into a chroma-key window on
the studio set. Since the slide is fixed in space, the
only way to change the relative position of the key
slide against its background is to vary the background camera shot.

TECH TIP   The most commonly used film for
shooting key slides is Kodak's Kodalith film. Kodalith is a negative film, so it reverses black letters on
white paper, creating the desired white-on-black
slide. Special felt-tip markers can be used to color
the stark white lettering if color is preferred. The
negative of regular black-and-white film also may
be used as a key slide.

Slides are either processed at the studio or sent
to a professional laboratory. Professionally processed slides usually return in cardboard holders,
but it is a good idea to remount the slides in a more
permanent plastic holder with glass panels. These
holders completely enclose the slide to prevent it
from getting scratched or dirty, and the glass
keeps the film from buckling or warping under the
heat of the slide projector.

TECH TIP   Kodak's Ektachrome slide film can be developed in about one hour in most local laboratories. Kodachrome slide films are to be avoided because they require several days to be developed and can be processed at only a few plants around the country.

Photographic Prints

If you are producing photographic prints to be used on studio camera cards, make the prints on nonglossy, matte paper which will not glare under studio lights. A good working size for prints is 8 × 10 inches. Prints much smaller than this are difficult to frame in the camera and do not permit steady movement of the camera across the photograph to animate the picture.

TECH TIP   In an emergency, hairspray can be used to dull the finish of glossy prints to reduce glare under studio lights.

MOUNTING PHOTOGRAPHS AND PICTURES

Photographs and cutout pictures can be mounted on illustration boards in a number of ways. The easiest and most convenient method is to use spray adhesive or rubber cement. Rubber cement is inexpensive and has the advantage of being almost "goof-proof." As soon as the rubber cement dries, excess cement is easily removed by rubbing it gently with an eraser. Rubber cement solvent can be used to remove pictures and photographs from an art card, allowing you to recycle the card for future use.

A more elaborate mounting procedure uses the *dry-mount press*. To use this device, the picture and mounting board must be preheated inside the press. Using a hot tacking iron, adhere a sheet of dry-mount tissue to the back of the picture. Trim off the excess mounting tissue into the shape of the original photograph or cutout. Finally, cover the picture with plain paper to protect it, and insert the picture with the mounting tissue into the press for ten to twenty seconds at about 225°F. Remove the mounted graphic and let it cool under a book to avoid curl.

The dry-mount press takes much longer than adhesive spray or rubber cement, but it does a much more neat and permanent mounting job. (See Figure 16-17.)

PHOTO LIBRARY

A photo library is a valuable resource for pictures and illustrations. Some studios and stations make it a practice to save old books and magazines so the graphic artist can cut out different photographs as necessary. You can either cut out pictures to be used individually, paste them up into a collage, or trace the picture for an outline or silhouette which is cut out from colored art paper. Of course, you must be careful not to use copyrighted material without permission. It is also a good idea to file old pictures and photographs from past productions, since you never know when they may come in handy or can be modified for another purpose.

Many broadcast stations keep photo files of subjects, especially for news programs. Stock photographs of commonly used places and subjects such as city hall, the mayor, city officials, and

FIGURE 16-17   **Dry-Mount Press.**
Dry-mount presses bond photographs to art board and are useful for creating permanent studio cards.

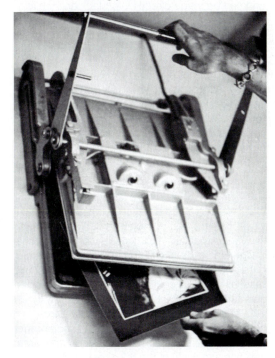

national figures are filed and indexed so they are available quickly when needed.

Copy Stand   The *copy stand* is a device that enables you to photograph original artwork or to reproduce copyright-cleared pictures from books or magazines. You can buy a professionally made stand, or you can design and construct a simple one yourself. You will need a flat surface for the artwork, a long upright column with an adjustable screw mount so you can vary the camera's height, and a light source to illuminate the artwork evenly. A small carpenter's level is valuable in keeping the camera parallel to the artwork so that keystoning is avoided. Some stands are constructed as double-deckers with a top level made of glass and a second level below. This lets you use cels on the top level and helps to induce depth and dimension between foreground and background elements. (See Figure 16-18.)

A 35-mm reflex camera is commonly used because the film is inexpensive, easy to process, and can be made directly into black and white or color slide transparencies for the telecine slide projector. Preferred film choices are Kodalith for black and white and Ektachrome for color.

TECH TIP   Light copystand work with two photofloods mounted about 18 inches from the work on either side. Place a pencil in the middle of the photograph. When the shadows from the pencil are equally dark, your light is evenly distributed. To reduce glare, place polarizing filters over the lights or over the camera lens.

Camera Cards   A *camera card* is a graphic card that is placed on an easel or card stand so a television camera can photograph it. Camera cards are variously called "flip," "studio," or "title" cards.

Camera cards vary in size from studio to studio, but the 11- × 14-inch card is very popular for two reasons. First, since it is exactly one-quarter of a standard 22- × 28-inch illustration board, with two cuts of the artist's knife you have four cards and no waste. Second, by working with a 1-inch border all around, the artist has a 12- × 9-inch work area, which is a multiple of the 4:3 aspect ratio.

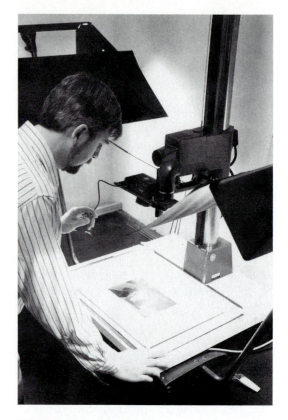

FIGURE 16-18   Copy Stand.
A copy stand holds a camera above artwork to be photographed. By moving the camera up and down, different croppings can be achieved.

Even if you choose not to work with 11- × 14-inch cards, it is important that your cards are all kept the same size. Not only will this keep your aspect ratio and essential and scanning area calculations consistent for all artwork, but a uniform size will prevent a smaller graphic from getting lost in a stack of cards and make it easier for the camera operators to frame successive shots.

Each card should be indexed and numbered with a small piece of masking tape. The numbered tabs, which are staggered to run along one edge of all the cards, help to identify each graphic and to make the job of pulling cards during a show much easier.

One of the major advantages in using camera cards is the opportunity to "animate" the graphic by panning, tilting, and zooming your camera across the card. If you use two or more cameras, each with its own set of camera cards, and move the cameras over the graphics while cutting, wiping, dissolving, and so on between them, you can produce some interesting and effective visual essays. A camera card also makes it easier to recompose a poorly framed graphic and gives the director more flexibility in positioning the graphic within the camera shot. (See Figure 16-19.)

Combining Lettering and Illustration

Most television graphics—whether produced electronically or mechanically—combine both lettering and illustration into a composite graphic. The easiest way to combine lettering and illustration is electronically, although you also can transfer rub-on lettering directly to a camera card and position the lettering where needed on a photo-

graph or drawing. Regardless of how the graphic is prepared, the graphic artist must consider some of the technical and aesthetic aspects of the television medium when preparing a combined graphic.

As a general rule, you must consider the legibility of the letters and numbers against the color and brightness of the background. Also, remember that the limited resolution of the television picture requires uncluttered compositions. When combining lettering and illustration, the rule of thumb that "less is more" always holds. Among the most common types of composites are maps, diagrams and charts, and integrated graphics.

Maps   Maps are one of the most common illustrations used, especially on news and informational programs. Conventional maps are impossible to use on television because they contain far too much fine detail. The map must be redesigned for simplicity, and you may have to eliminate or refine some unessential details such as roadways or rivers to present the most important information to the viewer. (See Figure 16-1.)

All art departments should have a number of atlases and map directories on hand, since you never know what sort of map you may need, especially for news events. Using a camera, flat bed scanner, or clip art software, you can scan the map into a paint box. The paint box is ideal because you can have the system enlarge or reduce its size to give the needed dimensions. The color of the land area can vary, but representing land masses as lighter in color and brightness than water, which is shown in darker shades, is common practice. Once you have produced an outline, fill in important landmarks. Then use a character generator to label cities, countries, and so on. Remember to keep the map simple. The point is to orient the viewer, not to give explicit directions.

Diagrams and Charts   Charts and diagrams, whether produced on artboard or an electronic graphic system, are helpful in explaining ideas, issues, or processes. Once again, clarity and simplicity are essential in producing an effective diagram. Avoid using an illustration taken directly

FIGURE 16-19   **Camera Cards.**
Camera cards equipped with pull tabs are placed on an easel before a studio camera. The tabs keep the camera cards in order and make them easier to pull during production.

Numbered pull-tab

Single camera card with tab

Numbered tabs

Stack of camera cards with tabs staggered along edge

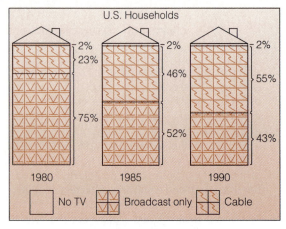

(a) Representational Chart

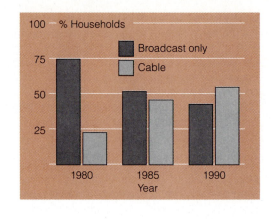

(b) Bar Graph

FIGURE 16-20 Charts and Graphs.
(*a*) This representation chart uses conceptual images to convey information, but the result is too complex for a television graphic. (*b*) Although not as interesting conceptually, this bar graph is simple and clear, and will work better on the television screen.

from a book or other printed material. In addition to copyright problems, these diagrams usually are unsatisfactory because they were not designed for television reproduction. Instead, it is up to the graphic artist to adapt the basic idea of the chart or diagram for television use. The same is true when preparing graphs. Only the barest amount of information should be included in the legend along a graph's horizontal and vertical axes. Remember to run all lettering horizontally and to use the same units across the tick marks on the scale. Many graphs employ representational figures to communicate more quickly. Compare the impact of the two graphs shown in Figure 16-20.

Integrated Graphics An *integrated graphic* is one that combines illustration with lettering. Common examples are the opening credits to a program, "bumpers" which are used before and after commercial breaks, and station IDs. In creating integrated graphics, positioning the lettering is most important. You do not want the lettering to obscure an important part of the illustration, but it must be legible for the viewer. If you are keying white lettering, try to find a dark area in the background for placement. Light illustrations may require dark lettering or at least dark outlines and a

pastel color for the interior of the letters. The objective is to combine the lettering and illustration so that they communicate more effectively together than either could by itself. (See Figure 16-21.)

ONSTAGE GRAPHICS

Some graphics, known as *onstage graphics*, appear directly on the studio set. Since they must integrate into the scene with live talent, they deserve special mention. Onstage graphics include chroma-key windows, hand or desk cards, and various graphic set pieces.

Chroma-Key Window

The chroma-key window is one of the most frequently used onstage graphics. The "window" is an area of the set which is painted a chroma-key color, usually blue or green. Using the program switcher, any video source can be inserted into this window. It is used mostly in news shows, but it has application in countless other production situations. (See Figure 16-22.)

If you do not have a computer graphics system

472

FIGURE 16-21 **Integrated Graphic.**
This station ID graphic combines illustration and lettering to communicate the channel number and its location. *(Courtesy: WIXT-TV.)*

with resizing, or if the capability is not built into your special-effects generator, the most important factor in preparing graphics for the chroma-key window is to preplan the positioning and layout of the material so that it will fit into the limited window area. You have to know in advance on which side of the screen the director plans to use the key. Precise registration of picture material is not overly critical with camera cards. A properly designed

FIGURE 16-22 **Chroma-Key Window.**
Graphic images can be inserted into a chroma-key window on a television set. The chroma-key window is especially popular on news shows.

card with sufficiently wide borders permits the camera operator to vary the graphic's position in the shot to match the window. With slides, the original graphic location is very critical, since the slide cannot be repositioned.

Hand and Easel Cards

Sometimes you may want your performer to handle graphic cards onstage. The *hand card* is a conventional camera card that is usually held by talent. If used on an easel or stand, it is called an *easel card.*

The advantage of a hand card is that talent can completely control the appearance and timing of the graphics and can easily point out specific features. The problem is that some performers find it hard to hold the cards steady, and close-up shots greatly magnify any shaky or unsteady handling. To minimize this, instruct your talent to prop the bottom of the card on a solid object, such as desk, an arm of a chair, or even his or her lap, to help hold it steady. Also, be sure to tell the talent which camera will be used to shoot a close-up of the graphic. To avoid glare, the card should be held vertically or tipped downward slightly.

Graphic Set Pieces

Graphics are frequently used as set pieces, making them an integral part of the setting and its surroundings. The set piece can be as simple as a blackboard or drawing easel or as complex as the mammoth tally boards used for television coverage of national elections. You are undoubtedly familiar with a common graphic set piece—the weather map, a set piece designed so talent can either draw on it or attach words and symbols to it. The same basic graphic idea can be adapted to a variety of production situations.

Blowup Photographs These are photographs or illustrations which are enlarged to poster size and mounted on thin plywood boards. The boards can be hung from the studio lighting grids with heavy-test fishing line or mounted on spring-loaded "polecats" and positioned around the studio floor.

Blowups are useful for adding depth and dimension to the studio set and for integrating graphics with on-camera talent.

Mounting Boards   Although these have been adapted from the classroom, some television programs can benefit from their use. They consist of a mounting device—usually magnetic pieces or a hook and loop—which permits talent to attach graphic material directly to the board.

Other common set-piece graphics are name plates, to identify participants on panel shows, and logos or lettering for desks or set areas.

ELECTRONIC GRAPHICS PRODUCTION TECHNIQUES

Television graphic techniques have undergone an enormous evolution because of the application of computer technology. From the simplest character generator to the most sophisticated digital three-dimensional animation system, television graphics are virtually entirely produced, manipulated, and stored electronically. In fact, for the most part, television graphics do not physically "exist," at least not in a form in which we can readily hold and touch them. Instead, they reside in a digital storage medium, such as a still store, hard drive, or tape, available for instant retrieval whenever necessary.

Computer techniques can save a tremendous amount of time and money, can provide spectacular effects which are difficult or impossible to achieve any other way, and can enable people with little real "artistic ability" to produce respectable graphics. The price of this "technological cornucopia" is that we can become caught up in the technology to the extent that we lose sight of why we are using the graphics in the first place: to effectively communicate information to the viewer. When it takes only the push of a few buttons to have lettering and illustrations change colors, move around the screen, and metamorphose into myriad geometric shapes and patterns, the tendency is to use every technique just

FIGURE 16-23   **Character Generator.**
The character generator is a standard tool of television production for titling. *(Courtesy: Chyron Corp.)*

because it is there. Too much reliance on technical visual effects leads to graphics presentations that look like used-car commercials in a late-night movie instead of an effective enhancement to a production. Keep this in mind as you read the following sections on character generators, paint systems, video digitizers, three-dimensional graphics manipulation, and animated graphics.

Character Generator

The electronic character generator (CG) is the simplest and most widely used piece of computer graphics equipment. With a wide variety of CGs available in all price/performance ranges, the CG has become as standard a production device as a camera or microphone. (See Figure 16-23.)

Creating Lettering   All CGs operate pretty much the same way and require absolutely no artistic skill to produce perfect lettering. The device consists of a computer-type keyboard which is used to create the lettering and to control the positions of the characters on the television screen.

Most CGs offer a choice of type fonts and sizes so you can select the right type for each production situation. Most also offer the capability to add special graphic effects such as boxes, backgrounds, underlines, and edging. (See Figure 16-24.)

There are many different brands of CGs, with different operating procedures. In general, messages are prepared simply by typing out the let-

FIGURE 16-24 Electronic Type Font.
Character generators are capable of producing a wide range of different type fonts, usually in different sizes and in both upper and lower case.

ters and arranging them on the screen. A *cursor*, or position marker, shows the location of each character as it is typed. (See Figure 16-25.) By placing the cursor at specific locations on the screen, it is possible to precisely position characters on the screen. For example, you can key the output of a CG over a map of the United States and position the characters to display the temperature at key cities across the nation. The director simply keys the output of the CG over the camera card or still-store graphic of the map.

TECH TIP   Since a CG's letters appear dot-by-dot on the square grid of pixels that make up a television screen, perfect pixel alignment occurs only in vertical and horizontal lines. As a result, curved parts of letters will exhibit some degree of jaggedness, since the dots are not in a straight line. An "antialiasing" function smooths out some of this jaggedness and is a popular feature for CGs.

Character Manipulation   In addition to typing the message on screen, the operator can manipulate characters in a number of important ways. Most CGs have automatic centering, which enables you to quickly center each line of type with the push of a button. You can also flash individual letters, words, or sentences; color words, letters, or paragraphs for special emphasis; and outline the lettering with edging or drop-shadow to give added prominence to the text once it is keyed against a background image.

Crawl and Roll   CGs also can move lettering across the screen either horizontally (*crawl*) or vertically (*roll*). The horizontal crawl is commonly reserved for news and weather bulletins, although it also has many other production uses. We are all familiar with the end-credit roll at the conclusion of

FIGURE 16-25 Cursor.
The cursor shows the location of each character as it is typed on the CG. It appears only on the CG preview monitor, not the line monitor.

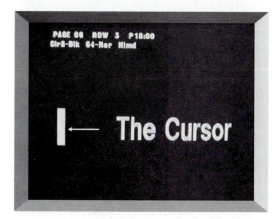

a program, where a list of production and performer personnel is run from the bottom to the top of the screen. Once the roll and crawl were prepared on a long sheet of paper that was physically pulled past a camera by a production assistant to create the moving lettering. The CG makes a crawl and roll easy to create, and the list can crawl or roll up the screen at various speeds.

Memory Storage and Retrieval   As with any computer system, the ability to store and retrieve information quickly is one of the CG's primary features. All character generators include internal memory, which allows the operator to store a number of previously prepared "pages" of type and to recall these instantly when needed. Since internal machine memory is *volatile*, which means that its contents are cleared when the machine is turned off, most CGs use a computer disk system (either floppy or hard) to store pages. External disk drives easily can handle hundreds of pages of text.

The CG operator prepares each graphics page according to a list provided prior to production. The list might include opening credits, lower-third keys, and closing credits. As the CG operator prepares each graphic, or "page," it is assigned a page number as it is entered into the CG's memory. For example, the opening credits might be assigned to page 01, the key title of the program's host to page 02, and so on. The CG operator makes up a list of the page number and the graphic it refers to so that during the production it is possible to recall any graphic instantly as it is needed by merely entering the graphic's number. Some CGs enable the operator to sequence pages in memory so that each graphic can be called up in order simply by pushing one button to move through the set of stored pages.

Key   One of the most common ways to use lettering in television production is to key the letters over a camera's picture. The "key" is created electronically, inserting letters into another video source. Keys are very useful to integrate visual and descriptive information simultaneously. For example, you can see the baseball player at the

FIGURE 16-26   **Lower-Third Key.**
A lower-third key places an identifying caption across the lower third of an image.

plate as he bats and also read his statistics on the lower third of the screen.

Keys are used to identify speakers in news clips or during panel discussions by placing their names and titles or affiliations on the lower third of the screen. In fact, the term *lower-third* is commonly used to describe such a key. Of course, keys can appear anywhere on the screen and are frequently centered, such as in the opening credits of a program or during the ending credits. The key usually is produced by the video switcher, who combines the text output from the CG with another video source (camera shot, film chain, videotape playback, remote feed, etc.) to create the key effect. (See Figure 16-26.)

Image Capture   Most digital graphics systems are capable of capturing images from other video sources, incorporating them with lettering, and storing the combination frame for use later. For example, a company logo may be captured, colorized like the original, and positioned on the screen. Images from videotapes or paint systems can be captured as backgrounds for lettering. This eliminates the need for two video sources for bumpers or similar graphics.

Paint Systems

Although the character generator employs many computer techniques in its design and operation, it takes advantage of only a small part of what computer technology can offer the television graphic artist. Where the computer's enormous capability is realized is in the development of *digital paint systems*, which enable the graphic artist to harness the vast memory of the computer along with its ability to define visual images as a series of numerically defined points and through rapid mathematical calculations, produce the electronic equivalent of a painter's canvas on which the graphic artist works.

Designing on the Paint System Since most graphic artists are not computer scientists, the trick is to make the computer's operation transparent so that the artist can create a graphic in ways as close as possible to the traditional mechanical and photographic methods of cutting, pasting, airbrushing, and composing. With this in mind, three design goals for graphic paint systems are (1) to divide the screen into the smallest possible units to improve resolution, (2) to give the greatest amount of control over each unit or pixel to depict subtle differences in shading, shape, and color, and (3) to make the computer easy to use so that the artist makes only aesthetic decisions and the computer carries out the technical operations. In fact, this is exactly what the digital paint box systems offer because they permit the

artist to intuitively input instructions to the computer and to immediately view the result of his or her work without any need to deal with the computer or its program at a technical level. This is called making the user interface *transparent*. When the graphics artist "paints" with the electronic pen, it feels like painting with a brush.

A paint system uses an electronic stylus as an input device, much as an artist would use a brush and palette to draw on a canvas. The stylus is shaped like a pen, and the artist uses its point to first select some characteristics of the stylus (or "brush") and then to "draw" with the brush directly on a television monitor or on a *bit pad*, which rests on a table like a sketch pad. Every design choice expressed on the bit pad is reproduced on the television monitor. (See Figure 16-27.)

Working in a *freehand mode*, the artist would first select a color from the palette and a width of the brush stroke. For example, the outline of a hand might be drawn with blue "paint" and a brush two pixels wide. After selecting the color and width of the brush, the artist would touch the stylus to the bit pad at the location he or she wanted the hand to appear and draw its outline.

FIGURE 16-27
Paint System.
An artist can draw on a bit pad with a stylus and have his or her work appear on the television monitor. The color, size, and shape of the work can then be modified with the help of the computer.

To draw the fingers, the artist would return the stylus to the palette, point to the color red, and change the width of the brush stroke to ten pixels to quickly color the fingers. If the artist ever needed to "erase" a line, he or she would simply select the background color from the palette and trace over the line created earlier. (See Color Plate 8.)

In addition to a freehand mode, most paint systems offer a *geometric mode*, in which the artist touches points on the screen and has the computer connect them based on some geometric shape. For example, in the circle mode, the artist would first locate the center of the circle by touching a spot on the bit pad. He or she would then locate another dot some distance from the center dot. The distance between the two dots would instruct the computer to draw a circle with that particular radius. Most systems would then give the artist the option of filling the circle in with a color selected from the palette. (See Color Plate 9.)

Once the artist has created an image, all or part of it can be manipulated in many different ways. Some of the most common options are described below.

RESIZING   Once an image has been drawn, it can be expanded or compressed in either or both dimensions. If more compression or expansion is applied to the width or the height of the image, it distorts in a stylized manner.

ROTATION   The image can be rotated along the *x*, *y*, or *z* axis. When it rotates around the *x* axis, the image simply is canted on the screen. If the rotation occurs on the *y* axis, a perspective effect may be introduced in which one side of the screen is made to appear further off through the use of foreshortening. The same effect can occur with a *z*-axis rotation, in which either the top or bottom of the screen appears closer.

POSTERIZATION   In *posterization*, the middle values of the gray scale are dropped out and the image is presented in high contrast, with just the darkest and lightest gray-scale values. The effect,

usually created in one or two colors, is posterlike, hence the name.

AIRBRUSHING   The outlines of shapes can be airbrushed or gone over so that pixels adjacent to the line are produced in complementary colors to the airbrushed object. The effect is to soften or blur the object's boundaries.

WINDOWING   If an artist wants to work on only a portion of an image, he or she *windows* it, which draws an electronic boundary around that section of the image. The material in the window can be copied to another portion of the screen, moved, recolored, inverted, or subjected to a host of other operations. The image outside the window stays as it was originally drawn. Another use of the windowing function is to blow up a small portion of the screen, refine the details while in the magnifying window, and then to reshrink it, resulting in a more finely drawn image than possible if the object were drawn in its original screen space. Don't confuse this paint function with MS-DOS "Windows." (See Figure 16-28.)

Video Titling Systems   *Video titling systems* are either built into or can be incorporated into most paint systems. They operate like CGs, but usually have more fonts and edge effects. In addition to crawls and rolls, titling systems usually are capable of producing transitions such as *fades, dissolves*, and *pushes*—when one image pushes another off the screen. Letters may be stretched and twisted, and positioned different ways on the screen, even in a circle. Also, custom logos may be stored and used as characters. Video titling systems tend to give graphics artists more creative control than most CGs.

Storage Systems   An essential feature of paint systems is that images created on them can be stored. Once an image has been created, the artist saves it, usually on a *hard disk*, which is a computer peripheral that has a large memory. Then the saved image can be recalled and any of the techniques described earlier can be applied to it. For example, if a picture of a building is required for a newscast, the artist can recall the prototype building, perhaps change the coloring, and then add a new title to create a new graphic. By using

(a)

(b)

(c)

Airbrush tool

(d)

(e)

FIGURE 16-28 Image Manipulation on a Paint System.
The computer image may be manipulated many ways.
Here are five examples: (a) resizing, (b) rotation,
(c) posterization, (d) airbrushing, and (e) windowing.

479

a common set of base images, a television station is able to establish a "style" as well as to save a great deal of the artist's time.

TECH TIP   Paint systems are becoming so prevalent that many traditional graphic support services are appearing in electronic form. Electronic clip-art on various subjects is sold by the disc to serve as base images on which the graphic artist can build. Computer-based storyboard systems are becoming popular because of the realism of their images and the ease with which scenes can be "cut and pasted."

Video Digitizers

While there are tremendous advantages to having an artist draw an image in freehand based on his or her imagination or trace a photograph on the bit pad, another less time-consuming approach is to use a television camera to input a live image into the computer's memory. This is precisely the function of a *video digitizer*, sometimes known as a "frame grabber," since it captures a video image in memory and then converts it into a series of digital values. Once the image has been digitized and stored as a bit-mapped display, it can be manipulated in exactly the same ways as an original image created by an artist. (See Figure 16-29.)

TECH TIP   Since digitizers can capture existing images, it is important to have copyright clearance before using previously published artwork or illustrations. New technologies are raising many issues in the ownership of intellectual property (copyright), and abuse of the technology can lead to expensive law suits.

Electronic Still Store (ESS)   When a video digitizer is used as a stand-alone unit during the production process, it is often called an *electronic still-store (ESS) unit*, or simply a *still-store* device. The still-store device enables the operator to "capture" and store a complete video frame in its memory so it can be recalled and punched up on the air whenever necessary during a production.

The still-store unit can store and display a camera shot or a slide, or it can capture and store a composite graphic made up of two or more video sources such as a camera picture and a character-generated key. (See Figure 16-30.)

Use of the still-store device is popular in television graphics because it enables the director to create composite graphics quickly and easily and have them available instantly as needed during a production. For example, on coverage of a football game we can use the still-store unit to produce a number of electronic "slides" combining a photograph or a player with his name, number, and some relevant statistics. First, we shoot the player in close-up with a conventional television camera. If you are using a digital video effect (DVE) unit, you can compress this picture and position it wherever you want on the screen. This is usually done prior to the game using a camera, or you can use slides or photographs if they are available. Then use the character generator to display the player's name, number, and relevant statistics. The CG lettering is inserted over the picture of the player, and the composite image is captured by the still-store device memory. The process is repeated for every player until we wind up with a library of electronic slides available to the director during coverage of the game. (See Figure 16-31.)

The same technique can be used to build a news graphic by combining a photograph or a still frame from a camera or videotape with CG text. Once in the still-store memory, the newly created graphic is instantly available to the director during production. If this approach is used, it is possible to create and store a number of complex graphics combining illustrations and lettering quickly and relatively easily, an important factor on news and sports productions where quick graphics turnaround is essential. (See Figure 16-32.)

Digital Video Still Cameras   *Digital video still cameras* use high-capacity floppy disks instead of film. Up to fifty images may be recorded on one disk, then saved as a standard graphics file on a hard disk or input directly to a still-store device. This eliminates the intermediate steps of developing the film, printing the photograph, then digitizing it.

Weather Graphics   Another type of digital video

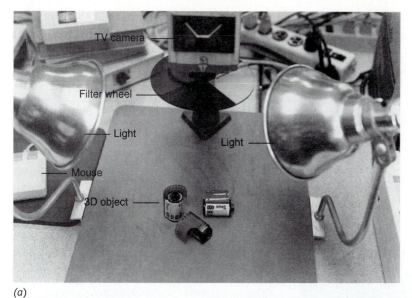

TV camera

Filter wheel

Light

Light

Mouse

3D object

(a)

FIGURE 16-29
Video Digitizer.
(*a*) A video digitizer uses a camera to "capture" an image, even of a three-dimensional object, and then digitize it. (*b*) Once the image has been digitized, it can be modified with respect to color, size, and so on. (*Courtesy: Cubicomp.*)

Display monitor

Disk storage and CPU

Stylus

Keyboard

Bit pad

Objects digitized for graphic manipuation

(b)

(a)

(b)

FIGURE 16-30 Electronic Still Store (ESS).
(*a*) This ESS can dissolve between stored images. The preview monitor is on the left, and the line monitor is on the right. (*b*) The operator selects a stored image by pressing PLAY, the image number, then ENTER.

image seen frequently is the *weather graphic*. Almost twenty years before satellite weather maps appeared on TV, satellites were looking down at the earth and sending information about its surface and atmosphere to researchers on the ground. TV cameras mounted in the satellites imaged the earth, and the digitized signal was sent, bit-by-bit, to earth stations that could decode it and plot the camera's image on paper.

This same process, now much faster and containing color, continues today. It has reached the television screen through the efforts of Weather Service International (WSI) and others, which receive the satellite images at their earth station and distribute them over modems to television stations. The local TV station then overlays the cloud patterns on top of a map of the United States or

their particular surface area. The land map can be any color desired and can contain character-generated information such as the names of cities or graphic images such as a yellow sun to signify pleasant weather. The progress of a weather front can be portrayed by storing a series of cloud formations taken over time and playing them back at thirty frames per second. The result is that the cloud mass seems to move across the country and approach the viewer's local area. Doppler radar, which detects rapid changes in the speed and direction of the atmospheric winds, can identify storm centers and the direction of their move-

FIGURE 16-31 Electronic Graphic.
The various type fonts were all created on a CG and the helmet was digitally "captured." A close-up of the player will be chroma-keyed into the blue window at left. The composite image is then captured and held in an electronic still store. *(Courtesy: Thomson–CSF Laboratories, Inc.)*

"Floating" box inserted into the on-air picture | "Floating" box | Storage device

Keyboard | Controller | Tablet

FIGURE 16-32 Still-Store News Graphics.
Quantel's *Picturebox* can create "floating" graphics and animated/multilayered sequences for use on air during newscasts. *(Courtesy: Quantel, Ltd.)*

ment. These Doppler maps, transmitted live, offer stations very accurate and attention-grabbing visuals to show local weather activity. (See Figure 16-33.)

TECH TIP A *modem* (*mo*dulator-*dem*odulator) allows computers in different locations to share in-

FIGURE 16-33 Weather Display Systems.
Doppler radar portrays the movement of a storm front and is a popular tool for weather graphics. *(Courtesy: Alden Electronics.)*

formation over telephone lines. The modem's job is to take the digital information from one computer, modulate it onto the analog telephone lines, and then convert it back to a digital signal for use by the other computer. High-speed modems convey weather maps and other digital information among service providers and television stations.

Three-Dimensional Graphics

The bit-mapped graphics we have described provide the basic means for dealing with two-dimensional images. However, there is another whole series of digital effects in which the viewer seems to travel around an object, looking first at its front, then at its side, and finally at its back. This is "object-oriented vector graphics." To achieve this effect, the computer must first be able to create a three-dimensional "solid" model and then display it on a two-dimensional screen. This is called *three-dimensional modeling*.

WIRE FRAMES Three-dimensional models are created with a computer by identifying points in three-dimensional space and then connecting them. Each point has three identifiers: (1) an *x*-axis coordinate which locates it on the *horizontal* dimension, (2) a *y*-axis coordinate which locates it on the vertical dimension, and (3) a *z*-axis coordinate which locates it in *depth* with respect to a viewer. Lines, which can be either straight or curved, connect these points. These skinny lines which frame the three-dimensional object give the appearance of being wires when seen on a CRT, so the display of the three-dimensional model is called a *wire frame*. The wire frame is a rendering of a three-dimensional object based on the reduction of that object into its simplest skeletal form.

SURFACE MAPS Once the wire frame has been constructed, a "skin," or *surface map*, can be wrapped around it. This process is referred to as *rendering*. The skin can be smooth or have color, texture, reflectance, and other surface dimensions that make it look "real." (See Figure 16-34.) Various *map programs* add the details to the sur-

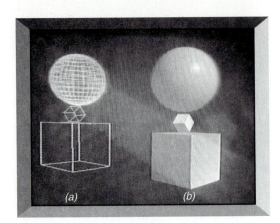

FIGURE 16-34 **Modeling and Rendering.**
To create a three-dimensional object, (*a*) a wire frame model is created and (*b*) a "skin" is rendered by wrapping a surface map around the wire frame.

face. For example, a *texture map* can add patterns to the skin, such as scales on a fish or feathers on a bird. *Opacity maps* determine how transparent or opaque the surface is. For example, a sphere may appear translucent or solid. The surface may be made to look reflective by using a *reflectance map* or rough by using a *bump map*.

Although current computer graphics are quite realistic with respect to color, texture, highlighting, and rendition of shadows, two new approaches, fractal geometry and ray tracing, offer even greater realism. *Fractal geometry* is an approach to making natural objects, such as mountains and plants, look more realistic. Fractal geometry introduces a sense of randomness into the perfectly ordered computer image that enhances its realism. *Ray tracing* models the effect of lighting by calculating how light rays reach the eye as they bounce many times among objects in the scene. Essentially, ray tracing averages direct and indirect light in a scene and in the process more closely approximates natural light. Ray tracing also greatly increases resolution and the time it takes to render or calculate an image, thereby making it more costly to produce. (See Figure 16-35.)

Point of View   Representing a computer-generated three-dimensional object on a two-dimensional screen is just half the battle. The computer

also should be able to present viewpoints of the object from different locations, just as the viewpoints would change if a camera were shooting an object from the left or the right, from the front or the back, from above or below, and so on. For example, stop reading for a moment and take a look at the chair you are sitting in from different viewpoints. If you walk away from the chair, it appears to get smaller, and it grows larger as you approach it. This is known as *foreshortening*. As you circle around the chair, at some point the seat will be hidden by the back. Another way to put it is to say that the back of the chair *occludes*, or *hides*, the seat. Also, as you move around, the light on the chair appears to change as you look at the front in the light, then at the back in darkness. The *shading*, or *shadowing*, changes. Many other things change, including the direction of highlights and texture.

Fortunately, at least from the view of the computer programmer, foreshortening, occlusion, shadowing, and other surface characteristics can be calculated mathematically. Unfortunately, even for the computer, these calculations are very complex and take time, and the results of the calculations, or the new viewing angle created by movement, cannot be displayed on the screen until the calculations are completed.

These kinds of puzzles have long been solved in the computer-aided design (CAD) world. The

FIGURE 16-35   **Ray Tracing.**
Ray tracing is a computer algorithm which produces highly realistic visual images for display by modeling directional light, shade, and specular highlights. Quantel's Starlight is shown here. (*Courtesy: Quantel, Ltd.*)

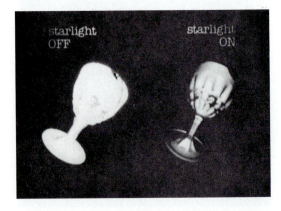

484

designer asks the computer for a rear view of the automobile that he is designing. In early systems, the computer might have taken thirty seconds to do all the needed calculations and then present the new perspective. Compared to the long process of drafting a new perspective on the car, a thirty-second turnaround is absolutely outstanding. This is called *non-real-time modeling*.

Computer Animation

What if you wanted to put together a sequence showing different viewpoints of a three-dimensional object so that it looked as though a camera were circling around it? Or as though the object itself were moving? (Remember, we're talking about a *computer-generated object*, not a real one like your chair.) In other words, what if we wanted to create a computer animation of a three-dimensional object? One approach would be to use non-real-time modeling.

Non-Real-Time Modeling   You could simply accept the fact that creating new perspectives on a three-dimensional object takes time, but that each viewpoint, or frame, once created, can be "linked" or "edited" together for television at thirty frames per second. Thus, in this *off-line* method, the computer does a complicated set of calculations, renders a frame, and places it in storage. Then it selects another viewpoint, reruns the calculations with new *x*, *y*, and *z* coordinates, and places the next frame in storage. This render-store-move process goes on until the desired amount of "travel" takes place. To display complicated scenes, a relatively "slow" microcomputer could take hours of processing time. In fact, if it took the computer thirty seconds to create each frame, it would take a total of *fifteen hours* to create just one minute of animation! Many systems used in television graphics create motion off-line using this render-store method. However, there is a faster way to do it.

Real-Time Animation   Many types of software programs exist today that offer *real-time* computer animation. After modeling and rendering the two- or three-dimensional object, *key frames* in the motion *path* are identified. They occur at major points such as starts, turns, and stops. After indicating

the speed that the object should move, the computer provides the frames between the key frames. The animated sequence usually is stored on a hard disk or optical disc for replay at thirty frames per second. There are many levels of animation software for all the computer platforms, from personal computers to video workstations. Six approaches are: (1) *color cycling*; (2) *squeezes*, *pushes*, and *flips*; (3) *pipeline processing*; (4) *surface pinning*; (5) *morphing*; and (6) *compositing*.

COLOR CYCLING   An easily created animation sequence involves a process called *color cycling*. This refers to the ability of a computer graphic to cycle through a fixed palette of a hue, creating the illusion of motion. For example, assume you want to show water flowing through a pipe. Cycling the color blue inside the pipe through a fixed palette from dark blue to white (commonly called "blue spread") will make the water appear to move. (See Figure 16-36.) Color cycling is often used in weather graphics to add motion to rain falling from clouds.

SQUEEZES, PUSHES, AND FLIPS   Judging from the names assigned them, many of the digital effects come from an acrobatic background. Whether an image is *squeezed* (reduced in one dimension, either width or height), *pushed* (in which one image comes from off the screen and seems to push the onscreen image away), or *flipped* (the image spins relative to the *x* axis), the effect can be

FIGURE 16-36   Color Cycling.
Color cycling rapidly turns a color on and off. The effect can create limited animation.

Water appears to flow in this direction $\longrightarrow$

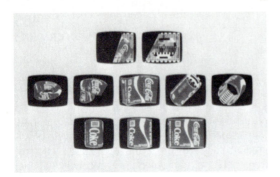

FIGURE 16-37 Manipulating Digital Images.
Once digitized, an image can be squeezed or made to flip or move across the screen in a variety of ways. *(Courtesy: Quantel, Ltd.)*

traced to an underlying mathematical formula that systematically addresses each pixel value and replaces it with another. (See Figure 16-37.)

PIPELINE PROCESSING   More expensive systems use faster computers that are capable of performing *pipeline processing* to achieve real-time animation. Pipeline processing uses a set of co-processors, each working on a small part of the problem at the same time (in parallel) so that every move of a positioner shifts the location of the

three-dimensional object on the screen. Standard processing uses one processor which carries out the list of instructions (calculations) one after the other (sequential processing). (See Figure 16-38.) Pipeline processing uses co-processors to handle assigned functions while the main processor proceeds with other tasks.

SURFACE PINNING   Another approach with a different effect is *surface pinning*. The essence of this system is to take a wire-frame model which was created off-line and then attach a surface to it consisting of a selected video image. In other words, as the wire-frame model turns in space, a video signal from a camera, still-store device, or videotape is mapped onto its spinning image. One of the many benefits of surface pinning is that the computer does not have to calculate all kinds of visual information; it already is contained in the video. All the system has to do is position the video signal, a less demanding process. (See Figure 16-39.)

MORPHING   *Morphing* is the special effect that made it possible for the chrome robot in *Terminator 2: Judgment Day* to melt into different shapes, and for a dozen people from different countries to merge in the Michael Jackson video *Black and White*. In morphing, one subject is

FIGURE 16-38 Pipeline Processing.
Standard processing uses one processor to carry out a list of instructions sequentially. However, pipeline processing uses a set of processors to carry out several instructions simultaneously. The result is real-time animation of very complex images. *(Courtesy: BTS Broadcast Television.)*

FIGURE 16-39 Surface Pinning.
Quantel's Encore attaches moving images to a model's surface during playback in a process called "pinning." *(Courtesy: Quantel, Ltd.)*

subjects may be two- or three-dimensional, and either stationary or in motion. However, the three-dimensional and moving subjects require more complex morphing techniques and high-end workstations. In all cases, the subjects must be *congruent*; that is, the same sizes and orientation, and in similar places in the frame. Another type of morphing is called *warping*, in which the subject becomes distorted, instead of stretching into another shape. Morph programs also can add effects such as those illustrated in Figure 16-42. These effects cannot be created in real time. They must be rendered frame by frame, which can be time consuming.

COMPOSITING   *Compositing* refers to the process of combining layers of images from various sources, such as computer-generated two- or three-dimensional images, text from a character generator, and even live video. Compositing software requires a high-capacity computer system, and especially large amounts of disk storage space. Most animation systems combine appli-

FIGURE 16-40 Morphing.
When animated, the child "morphs" into the owl. *(Courtesy: ASDG, Inc.)*

transformed, or *metamorphosed*, into a dissimilar subject, but the visual effect is nothing like a mere dissolve between two images. Instead, the first subject seems to stretch into the second subject through a third shape. (See Figure 16-40.)

The way a morph works is that you choose two subjects, the one to start with and the one you want it to morph into. Then, you overlay a *control mesh*, or grid of points which are to merge, onto the two subjects. For example, a point may be placed on the nose of a man and the nose of a woman it will become. This is called *geographic mapping*. (See Figure 16-41.) There may be 50 to 100 points in a typical control mesh. You choose the duration of the morph, and press a "render button" on the computer. It does the rest. The computer pulls the points together through a set of intermediate points, and during that brief period the third shape emerges, displaying characteristics of the other two subjects. In morphing, the

FIGURE 16-41 Geographic Mapping.
To morph the woman's face into the man's face, both are mapped with a control mesh containing points that are to merge. The window shows an intermediate stage in the morphing process. *(Courtesy: Side Effects Software, Inc.)*

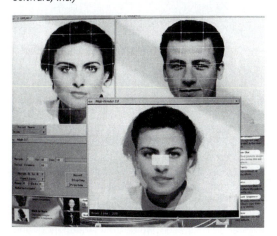

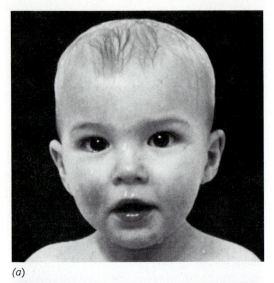

(a)

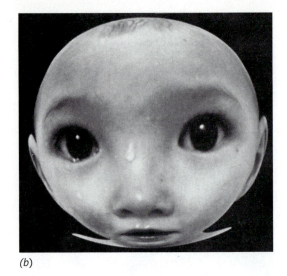

(b)

FIGURE 16-42 **Morphing Effects.**
(a) The original image, (b) stretched, (c) ripples.
(Courtesy: ASDG, Inc.)

usually is more complex to operate, but produces the highest-quality results in less time. For illustration, three popular integrated systems are (1) Autodesk's 3D Studio, (2) NewTek's LightWave 3D, and (3) Silicon Graphic's Wavefront.

3D Studio is software that runs on the IBM-PC platform. (See Figure 16-43.) It can model three-dimensional images; render them with photorealistic textures, automatic reflections, and shadows; then animate the models. 3D Studio comes with

FIGURE 16-43 **3D Studio.**
(Courtesy: Autodesk, Inc.)

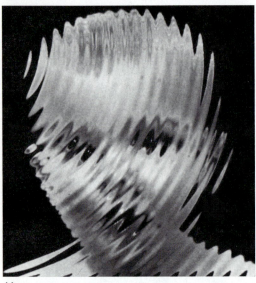

(c)

cations software that work together to perform the steps in the process—modeling, rendering, importing text and video, animating, and compositing. The prices of integrated systems that can do almost everything vary considerably, and as with most computer equipment, the more expensive the hardware, the more powerful its capabilities. While some of these techniques are achievable on high-end personal computers, to really get the most out of the software's capabilities requires a high-end workstation, which costs much more and

488

libraries of 3-D objects, patterns, textures, and animations, and other standard design and text files may be imported.

LightWave 3D is included with NewTek's Video Toaster. (See Figure 16-44.) The *Video Toaster* is a hardware/software package designed originally for the Amiga platform that performs many of the functions of a video switcher and a special effects generator. (We will examine the capabilities of the Toaster when we discuss desktop video in Chapter 23.) LightWave's capabilities include wireframe modeling; photorealistic rendering; ray tracing; morphing; effects such as fog and motion blur; and multilayer image compositing. LightWave can import freeze frames from video through the Toaster's still store/frame grabber, and images from ToasterPaint and ToasterCG. A card called the DPS Personal Animation Recorder can be plugged into the Toaster and used as a single frame controller while rendering the animation and a digital video recorder to store the completed sequence.

The *Indigo* actually is a workstation that is ca-

pable of producing high-resolution paint graphics, playing animations in real time, and even processing digital audio. (See Figure 16-45.) With a video board added, the Indigo can record video direct-to-disk, simultaneously with audio. All editing and layering is done on disk, then recorded on videotape. Animation software for the Indigo platform includes IRIS Indigo, Alias Animator, and others.

USING GRAPHICS IN PRODUCTION

Most graphics planning and preparation are handled during the preproduction stage. During setup and rehearsal, the CG and still-store memory addresses are listed, and the graphics are organized in the studio. During production, graphics are integrated into the show. During postproduction,

FIGURE 16-44
Video Toaster.
(Courtesy: NewTek.)

FIGURE 16-45 IRIS Indigo®.
(Courtesy: Silicon Graphics, Inc.)

graphic images may be added to clarify previously recorded material. In this section we will discuss all graphics-related activities as they occur in each of the four production stages.

Preproduction

At some point in the preproduction stage, the producer and director must meet with the graphic artist to discuss the graphics needs for the program. The producer explains the show's overall mood, tone, and objectives to the artist so he or she can begin to work up a style and approach for the graphics. Artists will usually prepare a few rough sketches to give the producer and director some idea of how the graphic artist conceives the graphics look. Once the style decisions are made and agreed on by the producer, director, and graphic artist, the show's graphics are then developed.

One of the most frequent complaints from graphics artists is that they are never given sufficient advance time to design and prepare a show's graphics properly. Of course, on news

programs it is not always possible to know far in advance which graphics will be necessary, but there is little excuse for a late graphics request on other scripted shows, especially those which will require elaborate or time-consuming graphics preparation.

The graphics artist also needs to know money and equipment availability. Some graphics techniques require outside work, and the budget must have money allocated for such activities.

Here is a quick checklist of some of the graphics considerations which should be discussed during preproduction:

1. *How much time is available for graphics?* What is the due date? This is usually rehearsal day and not necessarily the taping or air date.
2. *How are the graphics to be used in the show?* Is it simply a matter of opening titles and credits? Will the show require elaborate graphics as are often necessary in informational or educational programs?
3. *What types of graphics are necessary?* Titles for the program? Key cards? Any special illus-

trations, such as maps, drawings, or graphs? Should graphics be delivered from a still-store unit? On camera cards? In the case of chroma key or key cards, how will the director use them? Is there a special videospace area where they should be positioned, or can a special-effects generator position them?

4 *What onstage graphics are necessary?* Will you use chroma key? Are any special onstage graphics, such as blowups, required? These may have to be sent to a special laboratory to be produced, and this can take time. Are special set-piece graphics needed? For example, identification panels for speakers, mounting devices such as magnetic panels, or integrated set and graphic pieces? These set plans should be coordinated with the set designer and the lighting director.

5 *Can stock photographs or file graphics be used, or will all graphics have to be specially prepared?*

6 *Does the graphic artist have all necessary names and spellings for lower-third identification keys and for the program credits?* Be sure to double-check the correct spellings of names and places and the proper use of official titles (for example, Dr. John Doe, Senator Robert Smith).

Setup and Rehearsal

Setup By studio setup time, all the graphics—computer-generated, camera cards, and set pieces—should be available to the show's production team. The storage disk addresses are brought to the studio; the tabbed and numbered camera cards are taken by the floor manager or a floor assistant and placed on the proper camera stands.

If you are using a character generator, preprogram as many graphics as possible during the setup period. Each separate "page" or graphic display should be stored in the CG memory, and a sheet should be drawn up listing all memory numbers and their content. This sheet will help you to retrieve any graphic immediately when called for by the director. In the case of a news program, all the show's titles, lower-third ID keys, and sports and weather information should be preprogrammed. All you need to do during the show is

to punch in the correct memory address to retrieve the graphic. Of course, existing messages can still be updated instantly while the show is on the air.

If you intend to build electronic graphics by using a still-store device, you must plan sufficient facilities and crew time during setup to permit you to produce all the graphics necessary. Remember that this will require use of the switcher console, so make certain that engineering is aware of your plans and has cameras, videotape recorders, and the CG available for use. If you will be preparing still-store graphics for use during sports coverage, use the same memory-number system we described earlier so that you can store and recall each player's composite graphic by using his or her jersey number.

The graphic floor stands are lit, along with the rest of the set, by the lighting director. Camera card stands are usually illuminated best with two fresnel spotlights that are flooded out, scrimmed, and positioned at 45° angles to the camera card. (See Figure 16-46.) The angle prevents most reflections and glare from reaching the camera lens. Onstage graphics also must be lit carefully, especially large mounting-board panels or blackboards. The lighting must be arranged so the talent's arm or hand will not throw distracting shadows across the graphic set piece.

The camera shooting the camera card must be positioned at a direct 90° angle from the card stand. If the camera position is not perpendicular, the graphic will *keystone*, producing a distorted image on screen. (See Figure 16-47.)

Rehearsal During the show's rehearsal period, the director will start to integrate the graphics within the production. Even the simplest graphics should always be rehearsed, or the program's overall timing can be thrown off. Programs which rely heavily on visuals may have to spend even more rehearsal time coordinating all the various graphic elements.

If a floor assistant or floor manager will pull camera cards, the director must decide how the floor assistant will receive the cue to pull the next card. Some directors prefer to give a specific graphic

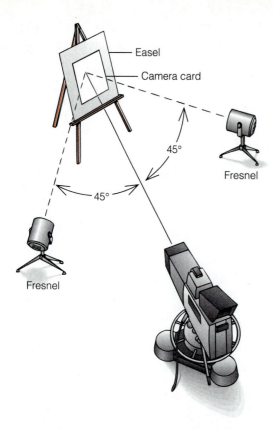

FIGURE 16-46 **Lighting the Camera Card.**
Two fresnel spotlights, flooded out, should be positioned at 45° angles to the camera card. This will provide even light and eliminate glare from the surface of the card.

FIGURE 16-47 **Keystone Distortion.**
If the camera is not directly perpendicular to the card on the graphic stand, the resulting picture will show keystone distortion.

"pull" or "flip" cue. Others have the floor assistant automatically pull the card as soon as the camera's tally lights go off, indicating that the director has cut to another camera. Whichever way you decide, be sure to keep it consistent throughout both rehearsal and production.

The still-store and CG operator should practice calling images and titles from the machine's memory and establishing their timing so that he or she can provide the director with the next image on the preview monitor as soon as possible. If some images will be built live, the coordination between CG operator and camera operators should be practiced.

Camera operators must have an opportunity to rehearse their break from the studio set to the graphic stand and back. If you wish to have the camera animate the graphic, be sure to rehearse each camera's moves just as you would any other sequence of camera shots. Camera operators should be alerted if they will have to shoot close-ups of onstage graphics so they can plan their moves and shots accordingly.

Do not slight graphics during your rehearsal period. Integrating keys, camera cards, and electronic graphics into a show takes practice and coordination among a number of production and crew team members. By the end of the dress rehearsal, every graphic that will be used in the show—including the opening titles and the closing roll—should have been rehearsed at least once.

Production

During the production, electronic graphics usually present the least difficulty. Electronic character generators and still-store units are preprogrammed, and the operator's biggest job is often simply to call up previously prepared graphics from the memory systems. Of course, the operator also should be prepared to change existing copy if necessary. (See Figure 16-48.)

During the production, the director should get

FIGURE 16-48 **Preprogramming the CG.** The CG operator precreates images and stores them in the computer's memory prior to a production. When information changes at the last minute, he or she also may have to create new images on the spot.

into the habit of referring to each studio camera card by its number, not by its description. Describing the card is easy if it is a picture of the president of the United States, but what happens if you are directing a show on an exotic subject which neither you nor the crew knows much about? A picture of one chemical molecule can look a lot like another.

Visual essays can be very effective by using two or more studio cameras and by cutting, dissolving, or wiping between them as the cameras move across the pictures. Remember though, if you are trying to establish a mood or illusion with the graphics, you cannot use poorly composed or formatted graphics that are outside the normal aspect ratio. If your shot reveals the mounting board of the camera card or shows the sides of a vertical slide, you will ruin the illusion of reality which you are trying to create in the videospace.

Some graphics are more effective when you add information step-by-step onscreen. This can enhance the viewer's understanding of the information and increase the graphic's visual impact. This technique, known as a *reveal*, is easily produced by preparing a set of aligned images in a character generator. If you are using camera cards, you can produce a reveal effect by positioning an art card behind a plain card. Information on the art card is revealed in stages by pulling the front card away. Most mechanical animation of this sort is done with key graphics, since the black background will disguise the various animation tricks used to achieve the effect. (See Figure 16-49.)

The roll used to end many shows can be used as a pad to vary the show's overall timing. Slowing down the speed of the roll will stretch out the show's time; speeding up the roll will shorten it. Be careful, though, of either slowing down or speeding up the roll excessively. If your time problems result in a roll moving at a snail's pace or so fast that it is an unreadable blur, you ought to find some other way to adjust the program's timing.

Postproduction

Graphics can be added to a videotaped program during the postproduction editing stage. This is done either by editing the tape or by performing a key or insert of the graphic as the videotape plays through a program switcher.

In the first instance, a graphic is added by per-

REVEALS IMPROVE

REVEALS IMPROVE
• CLARITY

REVEALS IMPROVE
• CLARITY
• RECALL

FIGURE 16-49 **Reveals.** A reveal adds information step-by-step, building the viewer's understanding of a complex idea or story.

493

forming a video edit. Usually this will be a *video-only insert*, since you can keep the original sound track and alter just the video portion of the show. For example, while reviewing a recorded tape, you realize that instead of seeing the talent describe an object, it would be better to show a diagram of the object as the talent continues talking. By executing a video-only edit at the appropriate point, you can insert the new graphic while retaining the original sound track narration. Once you have shown enough of the graphic, punch out of the edit and return to the original video.

Keys or inserts are accomplished by playing back the recorded tape through a program switcher as you produce the composite effect. For example, you may have recorded a panel discussion and realized that the viewer would follow the discussion better if the speakers were identified from time to time. If you are editing the show, you can play segments through a switcher, create the lower-third key, and record the composite video output on another videotape recorder.

SUMMARY

Television graphics include all the lettering, illustrations, photographs, titles, and drawings which are used on a television production. Effective television graphics will (1) convey information clearly, (2) establish a show's mood and tone through the graphics' style, and (3) help to present facts, concepts, or processes visually so the viewers will better understand and appreciate the program content.

There are two major considerations—technical and aesthetic—in the design of graphics. Technical considerations include all the factors necessary to prepare a graphic within the technical specifications and limitations of the television system. These include size, shape, sharpness, contrast, and imaging. Aesthetic considerations are the creative elements which make a visual both interesting to look at and effective in communicating its message to the audience. These factors include composition, use of color, and style.

Graphics are created mechanically, through photographic techniques, and with electronic technologies. Computer-generated graphics offer great flexibility and have become dominant in television graphics. However, mechanically-produced graphics are still useful. They may be designed to be used on-camera or onstage as part of a set.

Electronic graphics production techniques include character generators (CGs), computer paint systems, video digitizers, three-dimensional systems, and animation systems. Computer animation may involve non-real-time modeling or real-time modeling. Six types of computer animation are: (1) color cycling; (2) squeezes, pushes, and flips; (3) pipeline processing; (4) surface pinning; (5) morphing; and (6) compositing.

Graphic design and preparation occur during the preproduction stage. The graphic artist must be told both the program's objectives and how the graphics will be used so that the artwork can be designed to best enhance and complement the show. Good graphics take time to prepare and ought to be requested early enough so that they can be designed and produced properly.

Graphics always must be rehearsed along with all other production elements. By dress rehearsal, every graphic that is to appear in a show should have been rehearsed at least once. Although graphics are most commonly integrated during the actual production, they also can be added to a videotaped program in postproduction editing.

S E T   A N D   S T A G I N G   D E S I G N

Sets and staging are used to create the physical environment in which a show takes place. On most shows, the audience's first impression of the program comes from the set. A set that is well designed and effectively staged instantly communi-

495

cates the show's intentions, tone, and atmosphere to viewers. It literally "sets up" the audience for the production.

By *sets* we mean the scenery, curtains, properties, and furniture that appear on-camera. *Staging* refers to how these various elements are designed, arranged, and integrated within the studio to create the mood or atmosphere for a production and to provide the performers with a working environment. While large budgets and elaborate production facilities make set design easier and more accessible, the most important ingredients are imagination and ingenuity, neither of which is the sole property of the networks or large production facilities. Sets and staging are important visual elements which contribute to building the videospace. They deserve as much care and attention as any other facet of a production.

THE SCENIC DESIGNER

The team member responsible for set and staging design is the *scenic designer,* sometimes called the "art director" or "set designer." At larger production facilities, where a great many sets must be designed for various productions, the scenic designer is occupied solely with the job of set design and construction. At smaller facilities, where there may be less call for the design of new sets on a regular basis, the job of scenic designer is often combined with that of lighting director, since the two roles overlap in many areas. At even smaller facilities, the program director or producer may be the person who is expected to design a set, frequently using stock set pieces which already exist. Even if you do not plan to become a scenic designer, an understanding of the basics involved will make it possible for you to communicate with whomever is designing the sets and to understand better the many possibilities which sets and staging offer to a production.

According to Otis Riggs, a veteran art director at NBC, a good scenic designer is someone who combines a heightened visual and aesthetic sense with the skills of design, interior decoration, and drafting. It is the scenic designer's job to con-

vert the writer's script, the director's approach, and the producer's budget into the physical environment in which a show takes place.

A television scenic designer is bound to work on many, varied productions. A comedy or drama offers obvious design challenges, but so does the set for a nightly news show, a weekly interview program, an instructional series, or a children's show. Every production presents the designer with a unique set of requirements and problems, and the designer must come up with fresh and interesting designs which will "work" for the production. This means the set must (1) establish the proper atmosphere and environment and (2) facilitate the technical production operation so that the director, crew, and performers can work within it comfortably.

The scenic designer is one of the key members of the production team. Not only are sets and staging important elements in building the videospace and the audience's perception of a show, but from a technical standpoint, the sets and staging interact closely with many other production operations such as lighting, camera and performer blocking, and audio.

FUNCTIONS OF SETS AND STAGING

Sets and staging should be designed to serve four basic functions:

1 *To provide the background and physical environment for the action.* At its most fundamental level, set and staging design provides the scenery, furniture, and props with which the performers work.

2 *To set the time and place and to establish the mood.* The set should tell the audience something about the time and place in which a show occurs. In dramatic productions, this means the specific location, the time of day, and the chronologic period. For example, a set might be designed to suggest a bedroom at nighttime in Victorian England. Or a kitchen set might have to establish a kitchen in the daytime in contemporary America.

The mood or atmosphere of the show is suggested by the script, determined by the producer and director, and interpreted into a physical reality by the scenic designer. Set design can suggest happiness, sorrow, loneliness, tragedy, impending doom, fantasy, or any number of different emotional tones. Even sets for nondramatic shows should strive to establish an overall atmosphere. The set for a news program, for instance, might be designed to convey the feeling of sincerity, responsibility, and efficiency to the viewer.

3 *To give the show a unique style which unifies its visual elements.* Style is the visual treatment or the "look" of a production. It is used both to unify the visual elements of the show and to enhance its mood and tone. A set's overall style could be designed to be sleek and contemporary, comfortable and homey, businesslike and efficient, or lavish and extravagant, to mention only a few examples.

4 *To work as an effective production element which complements the overall show.* The set must "work" for the performers, for the director and crew, and for the viewing audience. This is probably the most elusive function to put into precise words, yet it is also the most important. If a set fails to do its multifaceted job for a production, the entire show can suffer. A well-designed set is conceived with the performer's needs in mind, provides sufficient shooting opportunities for the director and cameras, and still establishes the necessary environment to enhance the audience's appreciation of the show. While an elaborate and expensively produced set is rarely enough to overcome a weak script or poor direction, even the best written, performed, and produced show works under a serious handicap when using an unimaginative or inappropriate set and staging design.

ELEMENTS OF DESIGN

The various elements which make up set design consist of (1) style, (2) composition, (3) line and texture, (4) contrast, and (5) color.

Style

It is convenient to divide set design into three stylistic approaches: (1) neutral, (2) realistic/representational, and (3) stylized/abstract.

Neutral   The simplest and most basic style approach is *neutral,* which can consist of as little as empty space. Two television variations on a neutral setting are cameo and limbo. *Cameo* refers to a black void, while *limbo* refers to a light gray or colored background behind the foreground. Both these effects are created in large part through careful lighting.

A neutral set obviously focuses the audience's interest on the foreground subject, since there is little, if anything, in the background to distract its attention. However, since the neutral setting has no real depth perspective, the picture may appear flat and uninteresting. Some designers use hanging pictures, logos, silhouettes, or abstract designs in the background to break up the background monotony. The advantage of a neutral set, aside from giving the foreground subject prominence in the videospace, is its ease of setup and its very low cost. (See Figure 17-1.)

Realistic/Representational   This stylistic approach attempts either to produce a realistic setting or to represent a normal reality on-camera. Most dramatic and comedy programs use a realistic set, which is usually designed as a boxlike, three-walled setting. Many nonfiction productions, such as news shows or instructional presentations, use a representational set in which the overall environment is used to represent the program's content and objectives. (See Figure 17-2.)

Stylized/Abstract   A stylized or abstract setting attempts to suggest a particular reality (or unreality) through the careful selection of sets, scenery, props, and staging. Unlike a realistic/representational set, which is designed to be as accurate in detail as possible, a stylized/abstract approach uses a minimum of detail and often fragments the set by including only certain elements and exaggerating others. Stylized/abstract settings are usually *open sets* without the solid three-walled background found in most realistic approaches. (See Figure 17-3.)

Before we leave the topic of approaches to style, a word of caution. These three categories are used as illustrative examples of basic design

FIGURE 17-1 Neutral Set.
A neutral set focuses attention on the foreground subjects and is relatively simple and inexpensive to construct.

FIGURE 17-2
Representational Set.
A representational set creates a realistic setting and may be integral to the story. Representational sets are more costly and complex than neutral sets to construct. *(Courtesy: Capital Cities/ABC-TV, Inc.)*

FIGURE 17-3 Abstract or Open Set.
An abstract set suggests a particular reality but uses minimum detail for realism as compared to a representational set.

approaches and not as hard-and-fast categories. Obviously, many settings borrow from each approach, and the lines of distinction often overlap. Exactly when to use one approach over another depends on the show's objectives, the director's approach, the production facilities and budget, and the scenic designer's concept of the particular set and staging design that will best serve all these factors.

Composition

Effective visual composition is as much the responsibility of the scenic designer as it is the responsibility of the program's director. As with a theatrical set, the scenic designer must produce a setting that looks balanced and unified in the videospace. Unlike the stage, however, where the full set appears across the entire stage at all times, television dissects the full set into smaller segments as the director combines various camera shots and angles to build the videospace. This means that the television scenic designer should have some idea of the director's overall shooting plan so that background areas will look well composed and framed from any shooting angle and from many shot lengths.

As an example, think of a simple two-person interview show. The opening shot from a center camera will be used to open and close the show and from time to time to provide some visual variety. But the director is more likely to concentrate on medium or close-up shots of the host and guest which are photographed from side camera angles. In this case, the scenic designer should consider three separate set compositions: the overall wide shot, the background on the guest's medium or close-up shot, and the background on the host's medium or close-up shot. (See Figure 17-4.)

Line and Texture

Line refers to the set's overall shape, form, and use of depth and perspective. *Texture* refers to the physical quality of its surface. Naturally, the two are closely related, and both can be used to the designer's advantage in shaping the audience's perception of the videospace.

Line The shape, structure, and form of a set

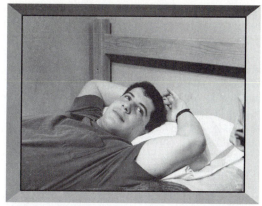

(a)

(b)

(c)

FIGURE 17-4 Set Design and Camera Shot Length. The entire set (*b*) is not the only way the set will appear in the videospace. More often the director will show subjects in close-up as well, as pictured in (*a*) and (*c*). The set should be designed to be equally effective for both shots. *(Courtesy: Adam E. Krantz.)*

should provide a sense of unity and composition while at the same time communicating the show's atmosphere or mood to the viewer. Line is an effective way to do this. A realistic setting will probably use normal lines and perspective, since the set must appear normal. A stylized or abstract set, however, might use distorted lines and exaggerated perspective to produce a fantasy or surreal impression.

Since the television medium is two-dimensional, scenic designers frequently use line to enhance the viewer's perception of depth. We react to larger objects as being physically nearer and to smaller objects as being physically distant, so the scenic designer can use these perceptual processes in adding the impression of depth and dimension to a set. Lamp posts or telegraph poles can be made to appear as though they are receding into the distance by making each one slightly smaller than the one which precedes it. The use of perspective lines, which are painted or drawn on the studio floor, is another common technique to add depth and dimension to a studio. (See Figure 17-5.)

Texture   Texture can be applied physically either

FIGURE 17-5   **Perspective Lines.**
Painting or taping perspective lines on the studio floor can enhance depth and make a set appear larger than it actually is.

by building the set with a three-dimensional surface or through the use of painting and lighting. Needless to say, nothing is as effective as physical depth on a setting to enhance depth and to give the lighting director some texture to work with. The surface quality of scenery also affects the viewer's perception of color and brightness. A smoothly textured surface looks brighter and more colorful than a rough surface, which cuts down reflection and appears darker and less vibrant onscreen.

Contrast

As we have mentioned in earlier chapters, the television camera operates with a contrast range of approximately 30:1. The familiar ten-step gray scale is a useful reference in selecting the proper brightness values for scenery, furniture, and props. Avoid using pure white or pure black, both of which fall outside the acceptable contrast range as represented by the gray scale. Peak whites should reflect no more than 60 percent of the light falling on them; blacks, no less than 3 percent.

Despite the fact that the designer should try to keep brightness values from exceeding the limits of the contrast range, a set without sufficient contrast produces a dull and lifeless image, which is equally bad. A minimum of two steps on the gray scale is necessary to create a recognizable difference in contrast on-camera. Sets should be designed within the full contrast range using appropriate highlights and shadow to add visual variety and interest. Of course, lighting plays an important part in setting the overall contrast. As a general rule, the background set should appear about two-thirds as bright as the foreground subject. Needless to say, the foreground-to-background brightness relationship will vary sometimes because of special circumstances, but generally, as the background brightness increases, it tends to draw the viewer's attention away from the foreground subject.

TECH TIP   Full-contrast ranges in the set counteract the tendency of television electronics to "squash" contrast ratios. Include at least a small visual "anchor" of 60 percent white and 3 percent black among the objects on the set to enhance realism.

Color

Color plays an obviously important role in production because it adds depth, dimension, and realism to the videospace. However, the use of color must be carefully and intelligently planned to be most effective.

Color Reproduction   It is the scenic designer's job to understand how the television camera translates colors, basing the use of color primarily on its rendition in the videospace. The most accurate way to evaluate a particular color is to see it on-camera under the same set and lighting conditions that will be used on the show. Since this is not always possible or practical, you will need some guidelines to follow in selecting and using color for television.

As you already know, color depends on the interaction of hue, saturation, and brightness. Colors that are very light or highly unsaturated reproduce poorly on color television. The colors tend to wash together into a uniform white or light gray. At the other extreme, dark colors, which are very low in brightness value, also tend to merge together into dark gray or black. These extremes should be avoided because the camera simply cannot distinguish between variations in color at either end of the brightness and saturation scales.

Certain hues also tend to reproduce poorly on-screen because of the limitations of the camera picture tubes and the phosphors on the face of a television receiver. Reds, oranges, and magentas can be troublesome, especially when they are highly saturated. This is not to say that you must never use these colors, but that you must apply them carefully and avoid them on large areas of background.

Color Perception   It has been found that most people react to various colors in similar ways. Scenic designers can use this perceptual phenomenon to their advantage in the selection of color schemes for television productions. Here are some basic guidelines in the expressive use of color:

1   Warm colors, such as reds, yellows, oranges, and browns, look larger and physically closer than cool colors, such as blues, cyans, and greens.

2   A bright color against a dark background appears larger and more prominent than it really is.

3   A dark color appears stronger when positioned before a dark background.

4   Strong, highly saturated colors look visually heavier and more solid than light, unsaturated pastels. This can be used to the designer's advantage by balancing a large pastel-colored area with a physically smaller, but psychologically heavier-looking area of saturated color.

5   When identical colors are used, a smoothly textured surface looks brighter and lighter than a rough surface, which makes colors appear to be darker and more saturated.

6   Colors reflect onto different surfaces. If you paint the desktops of your news set orange, they will reflect orange light onto talent's face, producing an unflattering color effect. Avoid unintentional color shifts due to color reflection either by separating the surfaces or by using a neutral shade that will not upset the proper color tones in the shot.

7   A subject's color is influenced by the color quality (color temperature) of the illuminating light source. Always match colors under the same 3,200°K color temperature, which is the standard for all color studio lighting instruments.

Developing a Color Scheme   A designer's color scheme involves the colors used on all the background scenery, furniture, and props. On some elaborately costumed productions, the wardrobe designer also must coordinate color schemes with the scenic designer.

To work out a show's color scheme, you will find it helpful to refer to the color wheel in Figure 17-6. Notice that the three primary colors—red, blue, and green—appear opposite their respective complementary colors. It has been found that those colors which appear opposite each other on the color wheel look best when they are combined in the same shot. All human skin tones are a variation of yellow hues, which is one reason why blue is such a popular background color in television.

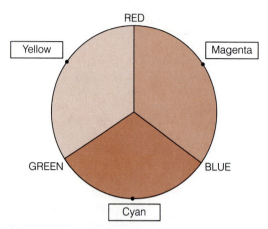

FIGURE 17-6 **Color Wheel.**
The complementary colors opposite their primary colors on this color wheel match well on screen. For example, yellow (the complement) and blue (the primary) go well together on camera.

You need not use the exact opposite color, incidentally. Variations in brightness and saturation within the same basic family of hues will work just as well. For example, browns and some oranges look just as good as yellow against a blue background.

Colors play an important part in creating the atmosphere and mood of a setting. For example, Woody Crocker and Kenneth J. Berg, the production designer and art director of *Northern Exposure*, use various "color palettes" in the town of Cicely's different settings. The interior of Mike's modern dome house is decorated in off-white and desaturated blue and gray tones to convey a sense of the cold, sterile conditions in his isolated environment. In contrast, the deep reds and browns of the natural materials in Holling and Shelly's Brick Restaurant project feelings of warmth and intimacy.

CYCLORAMA

The *cyclorama*, or *cyc*, is a muslin, canvas, or scrim fabric designed to appear as a seamless, continuous backdrop. The cyc runs around the edges of a studio suspended from a curtain track. Most studios curve the cyc in a U shape around at least two or more corners to produce a horizonless vista that suggests greater depth. (See Figure 17-7.)

To produce the smooth, continuous surface, the cyc must be stretched taut from the ceiling to the floor by applying tension on the cloth from below. Most cycs use a series of ties at the bottom edge which are attached to a pipe that runs along the floor of the studio in parallel with the curtain tracks above. To set up the cyc, the studio crew secures each tie to the cyc pipe, constantly stretching out the material to remove all wrinkles until it looks completely flat. Another method of maintaining tension is to run a pipe in a skirt pocket on the bottom of the cyc. The pipe's weight pulls on the cyc and creates enough tension to smooth out its surface. When the cyc is not needed, it can be quickly untied from the bottom pipe, bunched together, and pulled along its track until it is out of the way.

Cyc material is typically a neutral gray, which, if similar in color and brightness to the studio floor, can be used to create a seemingly endless vista on screen. A curved set piece unit called a *ground row* is used to blend the floor and cyc together. The ground row is positioned in front of the cyc, where it hides the pipe and any cyc lights which are positioned on the floor to illuminate the bottom half of the cyclorama. (See Figure 17-8.)

A good cyclorama is an extremely flexible, all-purpose scenery element for a variety of reasons:

1 The cyc produces a spacious, horizonless background that enhances the illusion of depth even in smaller studios.
2 The cyc can be "painted" with colored light to produce an endless series of background effects. The use of projected light patterns offers additional variations.
3 A cyc complements many different types of production situations and design styles. Inexpensive cardboard, wood, or Styrofoam patterns, logos, or lettering can be hung in front of the cyc to break up the flat background and provide visual variety. Silhouette effects as well as many different foreground/background lighting effects are easily produced using the cyc.

FIGURE 17-7 Cyclorama.
The cyclorama is a cloth scrim stretched tightly along the edges of the studio. Cycs offer very flexible staging opportunities and are a standard backdrop in many studios. *(Courtesy: Group W.)*

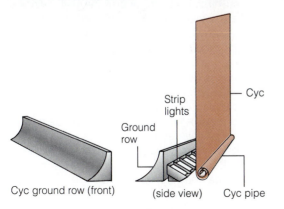

Strip lights

Cyc

Ground row

Cyc ground row (front)

(side view)

Cyc pipe

FIGURE 17-8 Cyclorama Ground Row.
The cyclorama ground row is a curved molding placed in front of the cyclorama curtain. It creates a horizonless vista on the set and conceals the cyc pipe and cyc lights used to illuminate the bottom part of the cyclorama.

503

CURTAINS AND DRAPERIES

Studio curtains are draperies which are hung from traveler tracks running along the edges of the studio. The traveler track enables the curtains to be quickly positioned anywhere along the studio edge or to be bunched together and moved out of the way when necessary. Pleated curtains are a simple and inexpensive background element, but unless they are imaginatively used in combination with other set pieces, they can look dull and uninteresting on screen.

Black Velour Curtains

Although a neutral gray curtain is the most versatile of backdrops, a black velour curtain is valuable for producing a cameo setting. Although the cameo effect is created primarily through the use of lighting, any background reflectance can ruin the cameo effect of infinite darkness. Especially in smaller studios, where it is difficult to provide much separation between the foreground illuminated area and the dark background, a black velour curtain will absorb much of the ambient light and enhance the cameo effect.

TECH TIP Except for the cameo effect, avoid black backdrops. Moody, nighttime, or dramatic sets should be created with lighting, not velour.

Chroma-Key Drops

A *chroma-key drop* is simply a large piece of chroma-key blue or green fabric which is hung behind a subject that is to be inserted into another shot. Because the drop is lightweight and easy to put up and take down, it is a highly flexible scenery item. Chroma-key drops are useful on remote productions too because they are lightweight and can be hung virtually anywhere to enable talent (such as a sports commentator) to be keyed into another picture.

SCENERY AND SET PIECES

In this section we will cover the major scenery and set elements and the techniques used in television staging. These include flats, twofold and threefold units, risers, and some special-purpose staging materials and techniques.

Flats

A studio set is constructed by joining together a number of individual units, or *flats.* Flat sizes will vary depending on the size of the studio and other production considerations. A 4-foot width is a convenient size that allows an individual to carry the flat without assistance. Special flats are also made in larger and smaller widths. The height of the units depends on the grid height of the studio. Smaller studios with lower ceilings use 8- to 10-foot-high flats; studios with higher ceilings or, where the director wishes to shoot up from a low angle, may use 10- to 12-foot-high flats.

A flat consists of four parts: (1) the wooden frame, (2) the face of the unit, (3) the hardware used to join the units together, and (4) a support device. (See Figure 17-9.)

Frame The frame of a flat is made of 1- × 3-inch or 2- × 4-inch lumber cut to size and then joined together with corner blocks or keystones made of ¼-inch-thick plywood.

Face The face of a flat can be made either from such hardwall materials as composition board, paneling, or plywood or from softwall material using a canvas fabric that is stretched over the wooden frames.

Hardwall flats are the most commonly used set pieces in television because they are durable, enable the designer to add three-dimensional texture to the face of the flat, and permit pictures, mirrors, and other set dressings to be nailed or tacked directly to the face of the unit. Hardwall flats are heavier and more expensive than softwall flats, however, which may be a disadvantage at smaller production studios. *Softwall flats* are frequently used for backing pieces; the outdoor scene you see through a set window is a typical example. Softwall flats are susceptible to tearing and sagging and must be handled with care because repair is very difficult. Flats can be painted with spray paint and stencils, with airbrushes, or with brushes and rollers. Also, softwall flats should be treated with fire retardant because painted canvas can be very flammable.

Hardware There are a number of ways to join

Corner
block

Toggle rail

Keystone

Back of
flat wall

Corner
brace

Flat facing

FIGURE 17-9 **Flat Construction.**
A flat consists of a frame and either hard or soft facing.
Flats are painted and used to create studio backdrops
and set walls.

individual flats into a complete set. One of the simplest is the *lashline technique,* which uses hardware cleats attached to the frame of every unit. A rope is tied securely around the cleats joining the two flats together.

Another approach is the use of *metal fasteners,* which consist of a pin and hinge unit. The hinges are attached to the wooden frames, and a pin is used to secure the two flats together. The disadvantage of the metal fastener is that the positioning of the hinges on every unit must be accurate enough so that they will fit together properly when assembling the flats in the studio.

Clamps are probably the most convenient and strongest method of joining the two flats together. The C-clamp is an adjustable device which is tightened on the edges of two frames to secure the units. (See Figure 17-10.)

Flat Supports   Once flats are joined, they must be supported so they can stand solidly in place. This is accomplished with the use of braces, or *jacks,* which are attached behind the flat to the wooden frame. The jack is attached either with hardware, such as a pin and hinge, or simply joined with another C-clamp. The bottom of the brace is secured with a sandbag or stage weight. Bracing each individual flat is not usually necessary, but braces should always be applied at such stress points as doorways or windows, on such heavy flats as fireplaces and archways, and at set corners. (See Figure 17-11.)

Flat Construction   The construction of a simple flat is easy, and the necessary supplies and tools are readily available. More elaborate flats containing doorways, windows, and wall pieces may require more advanced carpentry skills.

1   Establish the dimensions you will use and the number of flats you will need. Order either 1- × 3-inch or 2- × 4-inch lumber for the frames. Also ¼-inch plywood is adequate for the face of the hard flats.

2   Decide on either hardwall or softwall flats. Hardwall flats are preferable for most television settings. Determine what the face of the flat will consist of: wood paneling, composition board,

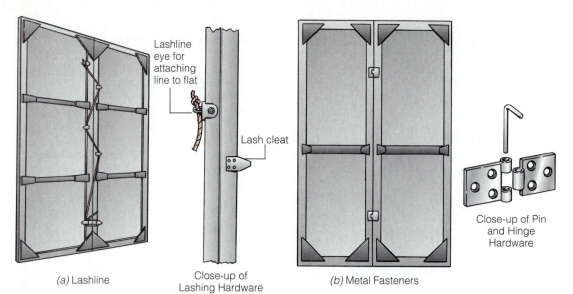

Lashline eye for attaching line to flat

Lash cleat

(a) Lashline

Close-up of Lashing Hardware

(b) Metal Fasteners

Close-up of Pin and Hinge Hardware

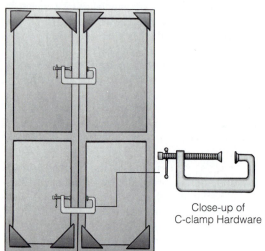

Close-up of C-clamp Hardware

(c) C-clamp

FIGURE 17-10 Fastening Flats Together.
Flats can be fastened in several ways: (*a*) the lashline uses a strong line which is wrapped around hardware cleats to join flats together; (*b*) metal fasteners consist of a pin and hinge combination; and (*c*) C-clamps tighten on the frames of adjoining flats to hold them together.

FIGURE 17-11 Bracing Jack.
A bracing jack attaches to the rear of a flat with hardware or a C-clamp and is secured by using stage weights or sandbags. (*Courtesy: Capital Cities/ABC-TV, Inc.*)

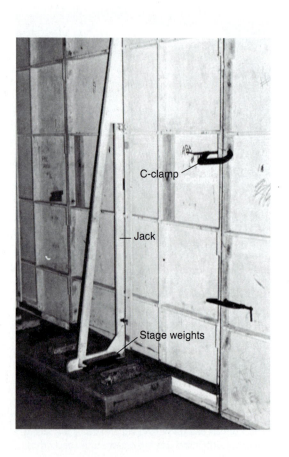

C-clamp

Jack

Stage weights

or plywood. Paneling should be selected for its color, brightness, and appearance on television. Avoid very light or dark colors and overly shiny panel surfaces that may reflect light and create camera or lighting problems. Composition board or plywood is easily painted or wallpapered depending on your needs.

3 Cut the frame lumber to size. Butt the corner joints together using a carpenter's square to ensure a perfect right angle.

4 Position a keystone or corner block piece with the plywood grain running across the joint. This produces the strongest support. Drive the nails partially in and check the shape of the butt joint. If all the corners are tight and square, sink the nails completely. (See Figure 17-12.)

5 Turn the frame over to ensure that no nails are protruding from the face side. Nail the hardwall face material onto the constructed frame.

6 Paint the face or wallpaper as necessary. If wallpaper is too light or reflective, it can be toned down by spraying or spattering a darker tone over the area. Spattering is done by tapping a wet brush against your hand or arm, covering the entire area with tiny droplets. The droplets are invisible on camera, but they reduce the brightness and color saturation of the background.

7 Attach connecting hardware to the rear of the frame.

Twofold and Threefold Units

Twofold and *threefold units* are simply hardwall flats which are permanently joined together with a number of hidden hinges. The advantage of a two-fold or threefold unit is that the unit is completely self-supporting provided the outer wings are not opened too far. A number of neutral twofold and threefold units are convenient to have on hand because they can be used in a wide variety of production situations and can be quickly set up and taken down. Dressing the standard unit with different set trimming will create a unique unit with little cost in money or time. The disadvantage of twofold or threefold units is their large size and heavy weight, which makes them more difficult to maneuver than ordinary flats. Some studios add casters on the bottoms of the units to permit the

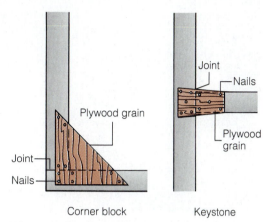

Corner block   Keystone

FIGURE 17-12 Corner Blocks and Keystones.
Corner blocks and keystones add structural strength to flats. They should be positioned with the plywood grain running across the joint.

floor crew to wheel them in and out of the studio more easily.

Risers

Risers are large platform sections made of plywood and 2- × 6-inch lumber which are used to raise a set above the normal studio floor level. Risers are a very convenient and flexible staging element for the following reasons:

1 Risers elevate the height of seated talent to a reasonable camera pedestal operating height. On an interview show, for example, placing the subjects' chairs on risers enables the camera operators to work their cameras at a more comfortable and convenient height while still photographing the subjects at eye level. (See Figure 17-13.)

2 Risers add depth and dimension to a set, especially when the entire set is shot on a wide shot.

3 Risers can be joined together in modular fashion to create a multileveled set for dramatic, dance, and musical productions. (See Figure 17-14.)

Riser

FIGURE 17-13 **Risers.** Risers, which are sturdy, elevated platforms, are used to bring seated talent up to reasonable heights for the camera and to add depth to a set. *(Courtesy: KGTV-TV.)*

FIGURE 17-14
Modular Risers. Modular risers fit together in different patterns to create sets adaptable to different production situations. *(Courtesy: KRON-TV.)*

Risers are easily constructed with a large sheet of ½-inch or ¾-inch plywood and a frame of 2- × 6-inch wood planking. Common riser sizes are 4 × 4 feet and 4 × 8 feet. A few smaller risers about 2 × 4 feet and 2 × 8 feet are useful as steps. Risers are usually painted black, although they should be covered with carpeting to provide a nicer appearance and to eliminate the sound of footsteps as performers walk across the hollow platform.

Miscellaneous Set and Scenery Items

Although drapes, flats, folding units, and risers are the most commonly used staging and scenery items in television, there are a number of additional techniques which are convenient and effective for a variety of special production situations.

Polystyrene   Use of the synthetic plastic material polystyrene, sometimes called Styrofoam, has become increasingly popular for various set pieces and trimming because of its low cost and production flexibility. Polystyrene is available from lumber, art supply, and theatrical supply houses in blocks or boards at a reasonable cost. The blocks can be sawed, cut, sculpted, or embossed using a variety of techniques. The most efficient way to cut polystyrene is with a "hot wire," which is a tool

that passes electric current through a thin wire. The electrical resistance heats the wire and lets it cut very precisely through the foam, usually following lines previously sketched with a felt tip pen. A jigsaw also can be used and avoids the problem of the noxious fumes created by the heat of the cutting wire. The large block lettering in the newsroom set pictured in Figure 17-15 was cut from polystyrene.

FIGURE 17-15   **Polystyrene.** On-set lettering can be created by cutting polystyrene with either a jigsaw or hot wire. If a hot wire is used, the melting plastic produces noxious fumes which should be avoided. *(Courtesy: WXIA-TV.)*

Polystyrene can be painted with a latex-based paint. Never use oil-based paints because they contain a chemical that will dissolve the surface of the foam. To avoid glare, use matte, or "flat," paint rather than glossy paint.

Seamless Paper   Seamless paper is available on large rolls in a variety of colors and surfaces. The paper makes an ideal neutral background for close-up demonstrations and for product shots. The roll can be mounted on a wall and the paper curved onto the floor to create a horizonless background.

Polecats   A *polecat* is a spring-loaded pole designed to be braced between the studio floor and the ceiling or overhead lighting batten. Large posters, pictures, graphics, and sometimes even flats can be attached to upright polecats. A number of polecats with various graphics attached can be strategically placed about a neutral set to add depth and visual variety to a normally flat background area.

Hanging Set Pieces   Hanging pictures, graphics, abstract designs, logos, or lettering is an inexpensive and visually interesting way to dress a set.

Polystyrene, cardboard, and thin plywood are excellent materials for this purpose, and both white and black high-test hanging line is available from theatrical supply houses. For relatively light loads, heavy-test fishing line may serve as a ready substitute for theatrical line.

Modular Set Units   A number of manufacturers produce set units which are molded out of a polystyrenelike base. It is possible to buy bookcases, molded paneling, and even a custom-designed, vacuum-formed background based on a program's logo or a station's call letters. Although these units are not inexpensive, they are lightweight, flexible, and look good on camera.

Floor Treatment   An ideal studio floor is made from poured concrete to reduce building vibration and is painted a neutral gray. Floors can be repainted with a water-soluble paint, which permits floor decoration without interfering with camera and equipment movement. Depending on the production requirements, the floor can be painted a solid color, decorated with abstract designs or patterns, painted with perspective lines to enhance depth, or patterned to suggest parquet, cobblestones, or wooden flooring. (See Figure 17-16.)

Another method of decorating the floor is to use colored tape in various widths for perspective lines, checkerboarding, or abstract patterns. The

FIGURE 17-16
Floor Treatment.
Paint or adhesive-backed patterned material can be applied to the studio floor. Here, a cobblestone street is simulated. *(Courtesy: PBS.)*

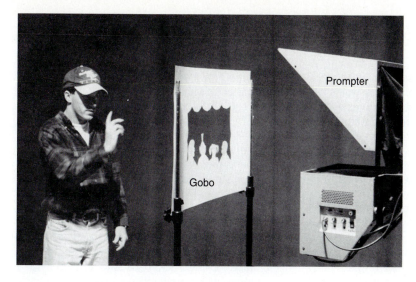

FIGURE 17-17 Gobo.
A gobo is a foreground frame that surrounds talent in the videospace.

tape will not usually interfere with performer or equipment movement, but it may become worn after a few hours of rehearsal.

Carpets and rugs are often used to cover not only risers but the studio floor on some sets. The advantages of carpeting are a lowering of floor reflectance, the ability to treat the color and texture of the floor, and an enhancing of the realistic setting. The biggest problem with carpeting is that it interferes with camera movement. Floor assistants must be assigned to lift the corner or edge of the rug whenever a camera must move in closer to the set or performers.

Gobos   In television, a *gobo* is a foreground frame through which the camera shoots the background. Gobos can be used in a variety of abstract or realistic ways, and they are effective because they naturally enhance the depth in a picture by utilizing distinct foreground and background depth planes. (See Figure 17-17.)

PROPS AND FURNITURE

Properties, or "props," and furniture are the additional items which complete a setting, provide performers with the necessary items they must work with during the show, and add detail to the basic background.

Props

Props are those items which appear on-camera and are neither scenery nor furniture. These include lamps, pictures, curtains on windows, books, dishes, food, and so on. Props are usually classified as either (1) set props or (2) hand props.

Set Props   All the varied items used to set the atmosphere, provide detail, and simply produce a pleasing background setting are *set props*. For example, workshop tools enhance the set of *Tool Time*, Tim and Al's show-within-a-show on *Home Improvement*. They also must be practical; that is, they have to actually work . . . even if Tim doesn't always know how to use them properly!

Hand Props   Whatever properties are needed by the performer in the course of the performance are *hand props*. These include coats, umbrellas, books, guns, knives, telephones, drinks, food, newspapers, and so on. Quite often hand props become part of a recurring theme. For example, in *Seinfeld*, Kramer often drops in to borrow some "Double Crunch," one of the twenty-or-so kinds of cereal on the shelf in Jerry's kitchen.

Acquiring Props   There are a number of standard props which all production studios ought to keep permanently in stock. Pictures, books, lamps, curtains, telephones, dishes, glasses, and

511

eating utensils are required so often that it makes sense to have them on hand. Special props necessary for a particular production are usually acquired from second-hand shops, local stores, and individuals or firms willing to lend the production a property in return for an on-air credit. The latter technique is often used, especially when the needed props are expensive and difficult to obtain. For example, a local sports shop might loan a complete line of skiing equipment and accessories for a skiing series in return for an on-air credit after each program.

Always consider the time, place, and chronological period when working out props. For example, touch-tone phones did not exist in the early 1960s, so they would be inappropriate for a drama based on the life of President Kennedy. Since television is a close-up medium, props that will be shot tight also must look as realistic and detailed as possible.

Furniture

All studios require a minimum amount of stock furniture which is always available and can be used for many different production situations. Sometimes a permanent series, such as a weekly interview show or a nightly news program, will purchase its own furniture expressly for the production. In most other cases, however, the scenic designer will be expected to use the studio's stock furniture, which is why furniture must be purchased carefully so it will offer a great deal of set and staging flexibility.

There are some guidelines to follow in buying or acquiring furniture for production:

1   *The furniture should be durable and well made.* Stock furniture gets constant handling (and abuse) and must be able to stand up to it without obvious damage. Fabrics should be solid midtones and avoid ornate patterns.

2   *Furniture should be easy to handle.* Furniture should not only be durable, but it also should be sufficiently lightweight to be carried back and forth without difficulty. Heavy or bulky furniture pieces are usually more trouble than they are worth unless a production specifically requires them.

3   *The furniture must look good on-camera.* Consider how the furniture will appear on-camera under studio lighting conditions. Very dark or very light furniture may not reproduce well. Polished chrome on modern furniture looks great in-person but may cause flaring problems under studio lights. The furniture also must make performers look their best. An overstuffed chair can virtually swallow up performers. Couches and chairs should not be too soft or too low. Chairs that look or feel uncomfortable also should be avoided.

4   *Avoid chairs which swivel or rock.* Many people—especially nonprofessionals—have a tendency to rock back and forth during a show, and this can drive the director, the camera operators, and the audience crazy. In most cases, you will be better off selecting stationary chairs which are comfortable but do not allow aimless movement.

5   *Select furniture that can be mixed and matched.* While you cannot easily combine starkly modern, contemporary furniture with French provincial, there are a number of styles which lend themselves to many different set arrangements. Of course, there are times when a production requires a very special period setting or furniture style. For most common nondramatic programs, however, a neutral furniture style will prove to be most flexible and will enable you to choose from a wider variety of chairs, desks, tables, and so on.

6   *Have enough identical chairs to accommodate a reasonable number of people.* There is nothing more frustrating for a scenic designer than to have to seat five panel guests in two or three different types of chairs. While extraordinary circumstances requiring more chairs may arise from time to time, every studio should have enough identical chairs for the most common production shows.

SPECIAL MECHANICAL EFFECTS

Special effects are used to create a videospace reality which is either impractical or impossible to actually produce. In Chapter 14 we discussed electronic special effects; here we will cover some basic mechanical special effects which are usually a scenic designer's responsibility.

As a general rule, a special effect is rarely satisfactory by itself. A mechanical effect requires close coordination with talent, the audio engineer, the lighting director, and the program's director to enhance the illusion visually and aurally.

Smoke and Fog

The best approach for producing fog is to use a special smoke-making machine, which can be rented from film and theatrical supply houses. The machine uses a fog oil to produce the smoke vapor, and it produces a continual stream of smoke.

Alternately, dry ice can be dropped into a bucket of hot water to produce a swirling white mist that is often used for fog, smoke, or a dreamlike fantasy effect. Boiling the water increases the smoke, and a small fan can be used to blow the fog over the studio floor. The smoke produced by dry ice and water hangs low over the studio floor and disappears quickly unless it is continuously replenished. A difficult problem with dry ice is the noise of the bubbling water, which may have to be masked with audio sound effects.

Fire

Fire is always a potentially hazardous special effect because the only convincing fire is a real one, and safer substitutes rarely work as well. With the exception of a small, controlled flame, as in a fireplace or campfire scene, avoid attempting special fire effects without the advice of a skilled special-effects technician. You also should consult the local fire codes and have the proper safety equipment on hand whenever you deal with fire in the studio.

For fireplace or campfire effects, most studios use artificial logs made of fireproof asbestos cloth that is molded around a frame of chicken wire. The "logs" will not burn, yet they appear real on-camera. The fire is produced by burning cans of Sterno, which are positioned under the logs out of camera range. The lighting director can augment the effect by producing a flickering light on the subjects illuminated by the fire.

Breakaway Props and Furniture

Some dramatic or comedy productions require the use of breakaway props or furniture designed to shatter harmlessly on contact. Breakaway props such as glasses, bottles, and windows can be purchased ready-made from theatrical supply houses. Breakaway furniture, such as chairs or tabletops, is usually made to order from balsa wood. The joints should be lightly glued together. Never use nails or screws in breakaway furniture because these items can injure a performer during the action.

Snow and Ice

Falling snow—a typical effect on many annual Christmas specials—can be produced in a number of ways. You can purchase granular plastic snow from theatrical supply dealers and use it year after year. The snow is either dropped by stagehands, who are positioned on ladders out of camera range, or held overhead in a large muslin trough with slits in it, which is gently agitated to create the snowfall. A simpler and less expensive method is to use the paper confetti which results from hole punching. Of course, only white paper should be used for this purpose.

Cobwebs

Your setting may be in an old house, a scary attic, or even Dracula's crypt! What spooky set would be complete without cobwebs? There are two ways to add them to your set. First, *cobweb spinners* are available from theatrical supply houses. Fans blow thin streams of quick-drying glue into the air and they "stick" to the objects they touch. Therefore, you should avoid using cobweb spinners near the cameras and lenses. Another approach is to use *angel's hair*, which is sold around Christmas as a holiday decoration. Angel's hair might not look as realistic as spun cobwebs, but it can be used successfully in the background of a set or on a gobo, where it is slightly out of focus.

ELECTRONIC SETS

Sets can be constructed electronically in two different ways: (1) as "sets" constructed layer on top of layer using postproduction editing techniques or (2) as "electronic sketches" produced entirely by computer. Human beings photographed against cameo or chroma-key backgrounds can be integrated into the electronic sets with a high degree of realism. Not only can electronic sets be cheaper than building extravagant physical sets, but also they allow set designers to construct television environments that exist only in the videospace.

Electronically Layered Sets

Using this technique, a "set" is constructed by shooting various objects or by using videotape footage of backgrounds and then combining them through chroma key. In this way, each part of the background is layered onto the next until the complete background video is created. Then the principal foreground objects are added through additional chroma-keying. This process requires extremely precise and elaborate preproduction planning. Also, since electronic sets use many generations of video to create the layered image, the quality of the video can deteriorate rapidly unless very high quality equipment is used and care is taken to ensure the best possible video signal.

Charlex, a New York City-based production house, introduced the general public to layered electronic sets with their music video *You Might Think* produced for The Cars rock group in 1984. In *You Might Think,* all the parts of a car come loose and start moving out of frame at different speeds. Finally, the pieces fall into a can, which turns out to be an open head. Shortly after The Cars video, Charlex won an Emmy for an opening they produced for *Saturday Night Live.* The look was so novel and attention-getting at the time that it set off an entire new "look" for television production.

The *Saturday Night Live* piece, as well as the earlier Cars' work, was created using analog tech-

nology and editing systems. Since then, digital postproduction using Quantel's Harry and other equipment more fully described in Chapter 16 has allowed multilayered digital images to be built without image degradation. In addition, background objects can be "cut in" or "painted out" depending on the objective of the scene designer.

Although electronic sets offer great freedom to set designers, they still operate within limitations. One of the greatest is that lighting becomes quite complicated. For example, if a scene involves human actors that suddenly go spinning out of the scene, realism requires that the scene lighting revolve around the actors rather than stay in a fixed location, as happens if the designer simply revolves the actors using digital techniques. While fully generated computer images can simulate how light changes as an object moves, it is much more difficult when live actors under studio lighting are involved in the electronic set design. (See Figure 17-18.)

Digital Scene Simulation

With this technique, the background is generated entirely by computer. Unlike the previous technique, where the background is built through layering videotaped images which were created from a conventional camera source, this technique creates an image without cameras, using only computer-generated imagery.

An excellent example of this is in the movie *Lawnmower Man*, when characters play a "full-immersion" virtual reality game called "Cyberboogie." In the game, competitors lie on padded "sleds" and race through "cyberspace." This "artificial reality" consists completely of three-dimensional computer-generated graphics and digital-based effects. For other scenes in the movie, videographic compositing combines computer-generated graphics with images shot on film and videotape. While this approach offers tremendous possibilities to create environments in the videospace which cannot be physically constructed, the technique remains costly and time consuming. The twenty minutes of computer graphics used in *Lawnmower Man* took eight months to create, using some of the most sophisticated computer animation hardware and software available.

However, given the rapid pace with which both software and hardware are being developed and the inherent creative and financial incentives of digital scene simulation, it is clear that this approach to set design will become more common in the future. Aspiring set designers would be well-advised to become as familiar with computer software as they are familiar with pencil and tracing paper. (See Figure 17-19.)

SETS AND STAGING IN PRODUCTION

The scenic designer—or whomever is responsible for designing the sets and staging—is a key production team member who should be included in the earliest production meetings. Until a set is developed, designed, and approved, the director cannot begin blocking performers or cameras, the

lighting director cannot plan the lighting design, and other production activities which depend on the set and floorplan cannot be started.

Preproduction

The largest share of the scenic designer's work occurs during the preproduction process as the set is planned and designed, a floorplan is developed, and set construction is started. As with most other areas of production, set and staging design is a combination of aesthetic judgments and technical factors. Compromise between the two is inevitable, and it takes skill and imagination to produce a set that not only complements the production's creative objectives, but facilitates its technical operation as well.

A set and staging design must be developed by the scenic designer working closely with the program's producer and director. If the show is fully scripted, reading and rereading the script will help the designer begin to conceptualize a design approach. If the show is not scripted, or if a full script is unavailable, the designer must rely heavily on the producer and director to establish the production's overall concept, content, and objectives.

As the designer begins to integrate these elements with his or her own creative ideas, two important design areas must be taken into account: aesthetic considerations and technical requirements.

Aesthetic Considerations   Aesthetic considerations are the artistic or creative elements which enter into set design. Among the most important questions the scenic designer needs answered are these:

1   *What are the program's overall concept and objectives?* Is the show designed to inform, entertain, teach, or instruct? What should the set and staging communicate to the audience about the show? How will the set support the production? Will it serve as an integral part of the show or as an unobtrusive background? To a certain extent, the answers to these and similar questions depend on the script and on the producer's and director's concepts of the show. In the final analysis, however, general ideas and notions must be interpreted by the scenic designer into the show's physical environment.

2   *What atmosphere, mood, or environment should the set convey?* This question involves many individual design elements which must be integrated to produce a unified, workable, and meaningful atmosphere that complements the show's objectives.

3   *Which design style or approach will work best?* Should it be realistic, stark and neutral, stylized, or abstract? There is obviously no right or wrong answer, since each production presents its own unique set of aesthetic circumstances and requirements. While the producer and director may have an idea in mind, the scenic designer must present a broad range of design possibilities and translate the producer's and director's initial ideas, along with his or her own, into the final design plan.

Many scenic designers keep a file of different period designs, interior decorations, and clippings from magazines, books on interior design, and other reference sources for ideas and inspiration. Quite often a final design is a conglomeration of ideas and approaches from many different places.

TECH TIP   Although most real-world settings are cluttered with many random objects, set-design aesthetics should be based on "functional minimalism." Each set piece, even if it is intended to suggest the personalized disorder and confusion in which we all live, should have a rationale for its inclusion. If you cannot justify a set piece, it will probably distract from rather than help meet the show's objectives.

Technical Requirements   Technical requirements are the practical considerations concerned primarily with the production process. Among the important technical questions which should be considered are these:

1   *How will the production be produced?* A live

show or one videotaped without editing requires all sets to be standing, since there is no opportunity to strike one set and replace it with another. Productions which are taped in segments to be edited together may permit the scenic designer more flexibility in set design because a set can be struck after shooting is completed and a new one set up overnight for the next day's scenes. Of course, the scenic designer must know the taping schedule, since productions are often videotaped out of normal sequence.

2 *What type of set does the director prefer?* Some directors like to work with a three-walled box set, others prefer a two-walled set, and still others like an open, fragmented setting. Although it is not always possible to accommodate a director's personal preference, the scenic designer should know if a particular type of set makes any difference to the director. Some directors also want foreground elements—such as doorways, windows, archways, props, and furniture—arranged in the set to facilitate foreground composition treatment. The scenic designer also should know the director's basic shooting plan: Are there any special angles planned? Do the cameras need extra room for intricate movements? Will cameras need special access to dolly onto the set for extreme close-ups or other special shots?

3 *How will the performers use the set?* A set must be designed as much for the performers who must work in it as for the crew and the viewing audience. Such practical considerations as ease of movement, placement of furniture, and size and accessibility of steps, stairs, and levels should all be planned with the performers in mind. On some sets performers must use practical graphics such as a chart, picture, or drawing board. These must be positioned at a convenient height and location. In general, the set should be designed to facilitate performer actions and to make performers feel as comfortable as possible within their working environment.

4 *Must the set accommodate special equipment or unusual production techniques?* If the production will use such large equipment as a boom microphone, camera crane, or hand-

held cameras, the scenic designer may have to design the set to accommodate them. The designer also will need to know if the on-camera set must include large special equipment such as a rock band's sound gear or unique devices necessary for instructional or demonstration productions. Similarly, a designer must know whether the director plans to use extraordinary shooting angles. For example, a very low camera angle may require the use of risers for the set and performers and the construction of extra-high scenery flats to prevent the cameras from shooting off the set. A close-up demonstration requires a set which will allow the camera to dolly in close without obstruction.

5 *Will the set be assembled from stock scenery or will it be constructed especially for the production?* Building a custom-designed setting offers the scenic designer great aesthetic flexibility, but it raises budget, personnel, and construction problems. Using stock scenery eliminates these worries, but forces the designer to settle for whatever already exists in storage. It is not always easy to use the limited range of stock scenery, props, and furniture usually available at most studios. Making this stock material work for a show is a real test of a designer's imagination and ingenuity.

The Floorplan A *floorplan* is an overhead view of the set as it is to be positioned on the studio floor. The floorplan includes the size and location of every major item which appears on the set—scenery, curtains, furniture, large props—as well as the general location of major pieces of studio production equipment such as cameras, booms, and video floor monitors. The floorplan is a crucial piece of production paperwork. Not only is it used by the scenic designer, it is also used by the director, the lighting director, the engineers, and other team members during preproduction planning and setup.

To be most useful, a floorplan must be drawn to *scale.* Most floorplans use a scale of ¼ inch equals 1 foot. The floorplan of the production's set

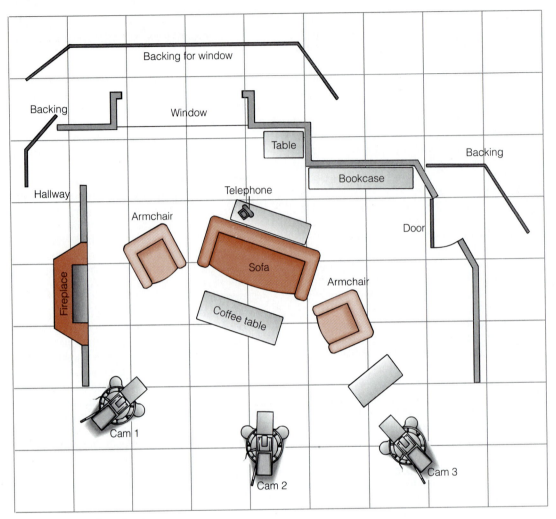

FIGURE 17-20 Floorplan.
The floorplan is used to previsualize a set construction. It should be drawn to scale and indicate the size and position of major set pieces.

is drawn on a *studio plan* or *studio plot,* which is itself a scale drawing of the entire production studio. The studio plan shows the location of real doorways, cable outlets, the control room, and other important studio areas. Most studio plans are imprinted with an overlay of the lighting grid. This is helpful for two reasons: First, it is easy to refer to the printed grids on the floorplan to locate any actual position in the studio. Second, it makes it easier for the set designer to position the set

where the lighting battens are located and for the lighting director to use the location of the actual grids in designing the lighting. (See Figure 17-20.)

Since the floorplan is drawn to scale, the scenic designer must know the actual dimensions of all sets, furniture, and large props that will appear on the floorplan. You should have a complete inventory of all stock scenery, risers, and furniture available with their physical dimensions. You also will need to know the approximate sizes of cameras on pedestals, boom microphones, and video monitors which have to be positioned on the studio floor. If you do not have such an inventory, a day spent backstage with a tape measure will save lots of time and aggravation later on and ensure an accurate floorplan for every production.

Once you know the dimensions of the set and the equipment to be used, you can begin to plot out the floorplan. A drafting ruler, which automatically converts dimensions to scale, eliminates the need for mental calculations and makes scale drawing relatively painless.

A common mistake in working out a floorplan is using studio space which, for any number of reasons, is not actually available for staging. Although a large space may appear on the studio plan, in reality the area may contain a permanent set or may be a portion of the studio that is being used for storage. At facilities with a limited number of lighting instruments, try to position the set where the instruments are already hanging. Another problem is the natural tendency to try to fit large items into small areas. You may be able to fit an 8-foot-wide set into a 6-foot space by cheating on the paper floorplan, but once you arrive in the studio, you will find the actual situation less flexible. The floorplan is indispensable in telling you how sets, equipment, and furniture will actually occupy a predetermined space, but only if you design and use it properly.

TECH TIP In low studios with high flats, lights may need to be hung almost directly over the back flats. The part of the set in which the actors perform must be adequately separated from the background to permit necessary back lighting.

You probably will have to experiment to find the best location for the set, furniture, and studio equipment. It is typical for the scenic designer to spend a considerable amount of time working out the best combination of set, furniture, and equipment positions before coming up with the final production floorplan. Once the plan is approved by the director, it is copied and distributed to other production team members, where it serves as a foundation for many of the interrelated production activities that take place during preproduction and setup.

Sketches and Models   A *sketch* is a perspective drawing produced by the scenic designer to enable the producer, director, and other team members to better visualize the proposed setting for a production. Especially on elaborate productions where a set will be designed and constructed specifically for the show, the sketch will give the producer and the director an accurate indication of the scenic designer's intentions before they authorize the set's construction. (See Figure 17-21.)

Some designers like to build a three-dimensional model of the proposed set using cardboard, toothpicks, and construction paper. Of course, the model is built to scale and ideally should reflect the designer's color scheme as well. Models are very helpful because they show the set's true depth, something even a sketch cannot do, and because lighting, shooting angles, and the overall working environment can be carefully studied and planned before actual construction begins. The problem with using models is the strict time limitations under which most television designers work. There is often little enough time to design a set and rough out a sketch, much less actually to build a scale model with all the trimmings. However, on elaborate productions where the complexity and costs justify the effort, or when the designer has the time, a model can be helpful to everyone in visualizing exactly how the set will appear when constructed. (See Figure 17-22.)

Selecting Colors, Fabrics, and Materials Among the final details which must be determined by the scenic designer are (1) the color of the background, (2) selecting the paint, wallpaper, or paneling for the background, (3) choosing the color and style of furniture, and (4) the set dressing.

The color of the background should be selected on the basis of the various aesthetic and technical considerations mentioned earlier. Of crucial importance is avoiding a color and brightness background which equals or exceeds normal skin tone. For best results, the color and brightness of the background should complement but never dominate the foreground subject. Swatchbooks of var-

FIGURE 17-21 Designer's Sketch.
An artist's sketch is often the first step in constructing a set. It gives the producer and director an accurate impression of the "look" of the set before it actually is constructed. *(Courtesy: Thomas Fichter.)*

ious paint colors are an easy way to select paint, fabric, and paneling color, texture, and finish. Remember to check all swatches under studio lighting so you can match colors under properly balanced light.

As a general rule, the scenic designer tries to emphasize detail, depth, and texture on a normal background. Unless you are purposely stylizing the set, try to keep detail as realistic as possible,

since the close-up camera will reveal substitutes onscreen which might have easily worked on the theatrical stage where the audience is much farther away. At the same time, you should avoid overly ornate or intricate background detail which looks too busy onscreen and can distract the viewer.

Sets should be designed and constructed to appear as solid as possible on camera. Nothing

FIGURE 17-22 Set Model.
Model sets are actual three-dimensional miniatures constructed to scale. They can be used to analyze lighting and other production elements. In some cases, they are photographed to appear as life size in the videospace. This saves considerable expense in constructing some complex sets. *(Courtesy: WBZ-TV, Group W Boston.)*

is more unconvincing than to see a supposedly sturdy brick wall sway precariously back and forth each time a door is slammed.

A list of set dressings and hand props should be drawn up by the scenic designer as the set is designed and the director and designer confer about talents' required hand props. Check the list against the stock property list. Special props will have to be obtained in time for rehearsal and production.

Setup and Rehearsal

The scenic designer must be told when the studio will be available for erecting and dressing the set. The setup phase involves a certain amount of coordination between the staging crew and the lighting crew so that each can do its respective job without getting in the other's way or delaying the production. The set crew usually erects and braces the basic set pieces before the lighting crew begins because it is difficult, if not impossible, to light a set accurately without the major set elements. As soon as the scenery, risers, and large furniture pieces are in place, the lighting crew can hang and focus lights while the stage crew completes the finishing touches on the set.

As soon as the lighting director has lit the set, the scenic designer should make a last-minute check of the entire set and staging on a studio or control room monitor. The color, tonal values, brightness, and overall atmosphere should appear correctly in the videospace. This is also the time to check for any glare from furniture, props, or background. Glare caused by the reflection of studio lights from a highly specular surface can be eliminated or reduced by the application of a dulling spray.

Furniture positions should be marked with a small piece of masking tape, especially if they will be moved during rehearsal and production. During rehearsal, the scenic designer should watch for any floor clutter from props, furniture, or rugs which may interfere with either the production crew or the performers.

TECH TIP Usually, furniture pieces on television should be placed closer together than in a normal room design. Besides making the room appear properly laid out in the videospace, close-spaced

furniture forces inexperienced actors to work at the necessary closer distance to each other to appear natural on-camera.

Production

During the production stage, there is rarely much work for the scenic director if all scenery, backgrounds, furniture, and props were correctly set up during rehearsal. In fact, even if a serious problem arose at this point, there would be little that the designer could realistically do without completely halting the entire production.

Postproduction

Once the production is completed, the scenic designer is generally responsible for supervising the strike, as the set is torn down and stored away. On some regularly scheduled shows, the basic set may remain permanently standing, although smaller props and furniture pieces—which might be stolen, misplaced, or clutter the studio—are stored.

Before you strike a set you will not be using again immediately, it is a good idea to take a snapshot for your files. These photographs, along with your floorplan and sketches, can serve both as a reference should the same set be needed again and as a possible source of future ideas. If the set is to be struck for another production but will be reset the next day or so, mark the location of the set walls and the furniture on the floor with masking tape so you can easily reposition the background and save the lighting.

Set Storage   Flats are usually stored in a large bin outside the studio. The bins should be compartmentalized so that various types of flats can be categorized by their color, type of face, and size. You may find it convenient to label each flat on the outer edge of its frame for ease of identification and access. Risers are stored either stacked on top of each other or standing upright on one end. (See Figure 17-23.)

FIGURE 17-23
Set Storage Area.
A storage area for flats should be provided close to the studio. Each flat is individually numbered and stored in a particular location to make finding specific flats easier when they are needed.

Props Props should be stored in a large closet, bin, or cage depending on the number of properties you have and the amount of space you need. Props should be carefully indexed and stored so they can be easily found without having to sort through mounds of miscellaneous junk and so everyone knows which props are available in stock. A variation of Murphy's law: The prop you carelessly misplace today is usually the very one you will desperately need for next week's production.

SUMMARY

Sets and staging are the responsibility of the television scenic designer. The four functions of set and staging design are (1) to provide the background and physical environment for the action, (2) to set the time and place and to establish the mood, (3) to give the show a unique style which unifies its visual elements, and (4) to work as an effective production element which complements the show's objectives and the production operation.

The various elements which make up set design consist of (1) style, (2) composition, (3) line and texture, (4) contrast, and (5) color. A set's style can be either neutral, realistic/representative, or stylized/abstract depending on the script and the designer's approach. All sets should be designed for effective composition, but the designer also must realize that the various camera shots dissect the entire background into smaller segments which also must appear well composed on screen. Line and texture, contrast, and color are the elements which enhance the overall design approach and help to create the atmosphere and tone for the production.

The most frequently used fabric background in television is the versatile cyclorama, which can be used for a wide variety of production situations. Curtains and drops also are used, usually in combination with other sets and furniture pieces.

Flats are individual units which are joined together to make a complete set. Hardwall flats are most commonly used in television owing to their durability and versatility. Twofold and threefold units are simply individual flats which are permanently hinged together to produce backgrounds which can be set up quickly and struck easily. Risers are modular platforms which enable the designer to vary the floor height for a production. Seated performers look better on risers and permit more comfortable camera operation. Risers are also highly versatile because they can be arranged in numerous combinations of steps, heights, and levels. Among the miscellaneous scenery and staging items and techniques commonly used in television are polystyrene, seamless paper, modular set units, and treating the studio floor with paint, tile, or tape.

Props and furniture are used as functional elements for performers and as set dressing to add detail and realism to a set. Set props are mainly used to enhance the background, although some are "practical," which means they actually operate. Hand props are properties handled by talent during the production.

Special mechanical effects, such as smoke, fog, fire, snow, and the use of breakaway furniture, are usually assigned to the scenic designer. Some can be produced using materials on hand; others require the rental or purchase of special-effects equipment. Electronically created sets are becoming more prevalent as designers become more comfortable with computer software and as digital postproduction techniques improve the image quality of the completed set.

The scenic designer's primary role in production occurs during the preproduction stage, when the set design is conceived and developed. The floorplan is an overhead view of the studio set, drawn to scale, and used by many production team members to indicate the layout of the sets, furniture, and production equipment. During setup and rehearsal, the set designer's stage crew should coordinate their work with the lighting crew, since the two functions are closely related. A final check of the set should be made on the studio monitor once the lighting is completed. Minor changes in sets, furniture, and props can be made once the show begins rehearsal and specific problems arise.

T E L E V I S I O N L I G H T I N G

EQUIPMENT AND OPERATION

Lighting is a fundamental part of any television production. Without proper illumination the television system cannot operate and the camera will not reproduce an image clearly and accurately.

Lighting is also a creative element in television production because the picture itself is made up entirely of light. How a subject is illuminated contributes in large part to how the image looks in the videospace.

Since lighting is a mixture of both science and art, it is sometimes viewed as an almost magical area of production, accessible only to a handful of experts. In this chapter we will discuss some of the science of light and the equipment used in television lighting. In the next chapter we will see how to apply this science in an artistic way. In the process, the "magic" of effective lighting will be demystified.

OBJECTIVES OF TELEVISION LIGHTING

There are six basic objectives of television lighting:

1   *To fulfill the technical requirements of the system.* The lighting must provide a sufficient level of illumination for the camera's CCD or pickup tube to reproduce the photographed image faithfully. This is called *base light.*

2 *To provide a three-dimensional perspective.* The television screen is two-dimensional. Depth must be provided through the use of camera angles, performer blocking, set design, and the careful use of lighting. Our perception of depth can be enhanced by the proper use of light to emphasize texture, shape, and form.

3 *To direct attention to important elements in a scene.* The use of light and shadow can reveal and conceal important elements in a scene. The director uses light to guide the viewer's attention within a scene.

4 *To establish the mood of a scene.* Lighting can provide the viewer with a sense of a scene's emotional mood. Dark, shadowy lighting conveys a feeling of mystery, tension, or drama. Brightly lit scenes impart a sense of happiness, gaiety, or fantasy.

5 *To fix the time of the action.* The angle at which light hits a set and casts shadows, its color, and the overall level of illumination and contrast within a scene all contribute to the feel of morning, noon, evening, or night. The season in which the program occurs also can be represented through lighting.

6 *To contribute to the overall aesthetic composition of a shot and sequence of scenes.* The way actors move into and out of pools of light, the facial features of an actress softened or accentuated through light control, and the way a well-designed set is complemented by the creative use of light all contribute to the television aesthetic.

Of course, not all six objectives are called for in every production situation. The design of the lighting ultimately must serve the program director's concept of the show. Lighting that is inconsistent with the program's overall objectives can confuse the viewer and weaken the production.

THE NATURE OF LIGHT

Light is *electromagnetic radiation,* which is produced by the sun and a number of other natural and artificial sources. Visible light is only a small fraction of the entire electromagnetic spectrum. (See Figure 18-1.) The world we see is made visible through a complex interaction between the

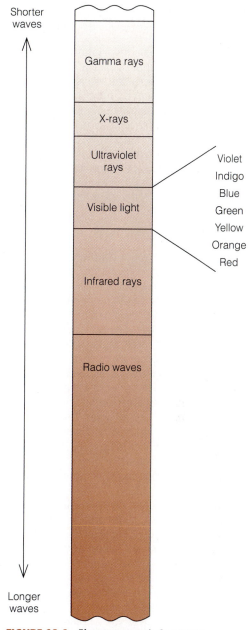

Shorter waves

Gamma rays

X-rays

Ultraviolet rays

Visible light

Infrared rays

Radio waves

Longer waves

Violet
Indigo
Blue
Green
Yellow
Orange
Red

FIGURE 18-1 **Electromagnetic Spectrum.**

light emitted from a source and the properties of the objects that reflect light from the source to the eye.

The shortest wavelengths that we can see appear as violet "spectral hues," or color. The red colors are produced by the longest wavelength visible to the human eye. In between violet and red are all the other familiar colors, including yellows and greens. White light is the presence of all colors, and the "color" black is the absence of any color in the visible spectrum. An apple is "red" because the surface of the fruit absorbs most of the visible light striking it, except for long wavelength red light, which it reflects.

Properties of Color Light

As you know from previous chapters, the three basic attributes of color light are hue, saturation and brightness. *Hue* describes the color of the light. The various hues are seen when white light strikes a prism, producing the familiar "rainbow" of colors. *Saturation* describes the intensity or vividness of a particular color. Highly saturated colors are "pure" and not diluted with white light. Pastels, such as pinks, are weakly saturated colors with a great deal of white light mixed in with the pure hue. *Brightness* is another term for "luminance," or the overall quantity of light reflected from a colored surface. If we look at very bright colors that reflect a lot of light on a monochrome monitor, they all will appear as shades of white or light gray. Low-luminance colors appear dark gray or black in monochrome.

Hue, saturation, and brightness are subjective evaluations and are quite interdependent with each other and surrounding objects. For example, a relatively light subject placed against an even brighter background will appear to be darker than the same object placed against a dark background. Since color is subjective, viewing a scene on a color monitor is the best way to evaluate how color will be seen in a viewer's home.

Color Temperature

When you look at an unfiltered source of light—such as the sun, a living room lamp, a fluorescent light, or a television studio spotlight—it appears to produce uniform white light. In reality, light sources produce mixtures of all the *hues,* or colors, in the spectrum. These mixtures of colors add up to the white light you see. However, different light sources produce different proportions of colors. Even though the results all appear white, there may be a little more red in one, a little more blue in another, or even a little more green in a third. These *spectral mixtures* are described as different "color temperatures" of white light. The *color temperature* of a light refers to its relative reddishness or bluishness, and is expressed in *degrees Kelvin* (written °K).

Before we say any more about color temperature, we want to make sure you understand that there is a major difference between a light's color temperature and its *perceived* temperature. For example, think of walking along a beach during a sunrise. The sky is reddish orange and everything around you appears warm and golden. By noontime, the cloudless sky is bluish white and everything illuminated by the sun and sky appears "cooler," more like its "normal" color. Toward late afternoon, as the sun begins to set, reddish hues again predominate; the sky assumes a rosy glow and objects illuminated by the setting sun reflect a much warmer color tone. In describing this scene, when we said "warm" and "cool" light, we were referring to its *perceptual* effects. They originate in our association of red with "hot" and blue with "cool." We even say "red hot" and "cool blue." But when we refer to "warm" or "cool" light in terms of color temperature, it's just the opposite! The reddish morning and evening light have *lower,* "cooler" color temperatures than the noontime bluish light. In degrees Kelvin, the morning and evening skies would be around 4,500 °K and the noontime daylight could measure more than 10,000 °K. This happens because in the morning and evening when the sun is at a lower angle, more of the short wavelength blue light is absorbed by the atmosphere, so the mixture of visible light that reaches the earth's surface has a greater amount of the longer-wavelength red light and is at a lower color temperature.

Another analogy that explains the concept of color temperature is to imagine a black iron poker placed into a furnace. As the poker's tip heats up, it first turns red. As it grows hotter, the tip changes from red to yellow. If you leave the poker in the fire long enough, the color continues to change from yellow to blue. So the bluer a light source, the hotter the color temperature; and, conversely, the redder a light source, the lower the color temperature.

TECH TIP Color temperature measures spectral distributions, not actual heat. For example, you can hold a firefly in your hand even though it emits a glow that measures 5,000 °K on the color temperature meter. The 10,000 °K noonday sky has an actual thermal temperature well below freezing.

Figure 18-2 lists the color temperatures of selected light sources. The color temperature of a light source is important because it will affect the color of a subject illuminated by that source. You may have had the experience of trying to match two articles of clothing under fluorescent lights in a department store only to find that once you arrived home, the colors no longer matched as well as they had in the store. That is because the color temperature of fluorescent light is around 3,800 °K with a "spike," or large output, of green light. The more yellow tungsten lights at home change the apparent colors of the clothing, and they may no longer match. For that same reason, makeup looks different in different lighting conditions. In Chapter 6 we suggested that performers be made up under the same type of lighting that will be used in the studio.

The two most common lighting situations in tele-

vision production are (1) studio lighting, and (2) daylight. Therefore, the two standard color temperatures in television lighting are 3,200 °K and 5,600 °K. If lighting sources are mixed, the television cameras will reveal the differences in their color temperatures. For example, if you are shooting on location and a subject is illuminated by a portable quartz light, daylight coming through a window, and a fluorescent ceiling light, there will be tinges of red, blue, and green light on the subject in the camera shot. An obvious solution is to turn off the quartz light and the fluorescents, and shoot in only the daylight coming through the window. But what if that's not bright enough and you must use the other lights at the same time? In that case, *color correction filters* can be placed in front of two of the light sources to match them to the third source.

TECH TIP Amber filters reduce Kelvin temperature. Use them on windows to match daylight to quartz lights. Blue filters increase Kelvin temperature. Use them on quartz lights to match them to daylight. Green filters reduce magenta light. Use them on windows or quartz lights to match them to fluorescents.

Once you have set the lighting for one color

FIGURE 18-2 **Color Temperatures of Selected Light Sources.**

SUBJECTIVE FEELING	LIGHT SOURCE	WATTS	COLOR TEMPERATURE IN DEGREES KELVIN
Warmer	Candle Light		1,900
	Table Lamp (tungsten)	60–150	2,600–2,900
	Quartz Studio Light (tungsten halogen)	1–10 kw	3,200
	Reflector Lamp	100–500	3,500
	Fluorescent Lamp	20–40	3,700–3,800
	Morning/Evening Daylight		4,500
	Average Daylight		5,600
	Overcast Daylight		6,800
Cooler	Bright Daylight		10,000+

FIGURE 18-3   **Camera Filter Wheel.**
The filter wheel must be set for the color temperature of the lighting. The standard color temperature for studio lighting is 3,200 °K, and for average daylight is 5,600 °K. The filter wheel usually has a mechanical lens cap that helps protect the imaging device when the camera is being transported.

temperature, you must adjust the camera to operate in that type of light. That is done with (1) a camera "filter wheel" and (2) a camera "white balance" control.

Filter Wheel   *Filter wheels* are located behind the lens on the camera. (See Figure 18-3.) They usually include (1) a 3,200 °K position for studio quartz lighting, (2) a 5,600 °K position for daylight, (3) a neutral density (ND) filter, and (4) a mechanical lens cap. There may be other filters, including a 3,800 °K position for fluorescent lighting. The filter wheel must be set properly before the camera can be "white balanced."

White Balance   The camera is internally color balanced by changing the sensitivity of the pickup tube to different portions of the color spectrum. This process is known as *white balancing*, because the camera is pointed at a white object (such as a piece of typing paper) placed in the same light as that which is falling on the subject

to be videotaped. By pressing a button labeled "white balance," the pickup tube's sensitivity to different parts of the light spectrum is changed, resulting in proper color rendition under the current light source. (See Figure 18-4.) If the lighting is changed (for example, through dimming) or the camera is moved into lighting with a different color temperature, the camera must be re-white-balanced. Some cameras have automated this feature so that the CCD or pickup tube's color sensitivity changes automatically as lighting conditions change.

Hard and Soft Light

In addition to color temperature, the quality of light produced by natural or artificial sources can be classified as either "hard" or "soft." (See Figure 18-5.)

Hard Light   Hard light is directional and creates strong shadows. The light produced by a bright sun in a cloudless sky which casts sharp, distinct shadows is a prime example of hard light. In studio instruments, hard light is produced by shiny, "specular" reflectors which focus rather than diffuse the light source housed in the reflector.

Soft Light   An overcast sky creates very soft light because the light from the sun is diffused and ap-

FIGURE 18-4   **White Balance.**
Pressing the white-balance button while pointing the camera at a white object automatically adjusts the camera's internal circuitry so that it produces colors accurately under different light sources. With each change in light source, the camera must be white-balanced again.

FIGURE 18-5 Hard and Soft Light.
(*a*) Hard light is quite directional and creates hard shadows. It is usually produced by a small-aperture light source using a highly reflective surface. (*b*) Soft light is a more diffused light which produces few, if any, shadows. Soft light is produced with large-aperture light sources using a matte reflective surface.

pears to come from all parts of the very large sky. In a studio, the larger the light source and the more satin the reflector, the softer is the light. Bounce lighting, in which a lamp is directed into a reflector and bounced back at the set, produces very soft light. Screens, scrims, and spun glass are popular for creating nearly shadowless illumination. Skin tones tend to look best under soft light.

TECH TIP Since soft light is more scattered, greater amounts of power must be used to create soft light at any given level of illumination. To save batteries, lower wattage lamps in small, specular reflectors are preferred for ENG work. This is one reason that news lighting tends to be hard and unflattering.

CONTRAST RANGE

No television system yet devised can handle brightness variations as well as the human eye can. Brightness variations are expressed as *contrast ratios* in which the brightest value is compared to the darkest value in a scene or image. By varying pupil size and the sensitivity of its rods and cones to light, the human eye easily can see contrast ranges of 1,000:1 or view scenes in which the brightest object reflects 1,000 times more light than does the darkest object. With the exception of some CCD cameras, television cameras can re-

produce a brightness or "contrast" range somewhat less than 30:1. Practically, this means that the brightest object in a scene should not be more than 30 times brighter than the darkest object. As a result, if a lighting director were to try to record a scene that exceeds this range, either the dark shades would all merge into a single, solid black or the white shades would "block up," rendering no detail in the highlights. (See Figure 18-6.)

To reduce contrast to a manageable range, lighting directors work with *television white* and *television black*. Television white reflects 60 percent of the light illuminating it, and television black reflects 3 percent of the light illuminating it. Television white is creamier than what you would normally consider white, and television black looks like a very dark gray. Using television white and television black as the two ends of the scale, we move through the intermediate shades of gray in ten increments or steps. This is called the *gray scale* and is shown in Figure 18-7.

TECH TIP Since any number of factors degrade the contrast range produced by a television camera, some lighting directors consider the television system as capable of handling only a 20:1 contrast range and work with a gray scale divided into only seven steps. Separating foreground and background values by at least two steps on this more conservative scale ensures good contrast.

529

FIGURE 18-6 Contrast.

Excess contrast in a scene causes the highlights and shadows to lose detail. The details in this performer's blouse and sweater are lost because their contrast ratio is greater than 30:1.

FIGURE 18-7 Television Gray Scales.

By using "television white" (about 60 percent reflectance) and "television black" (about 3 percent reflectance), it is possible to build a stepped brightness scale. Average Caucasian skin tone is about 35 percent reflectance, or 3 on a ten-step gray scale. Average black skin is about 18 percent reflectance, or 5 on a ten-step scale. Many light meters are calibrated to this "18 percent gray" as a way to take average light readings.

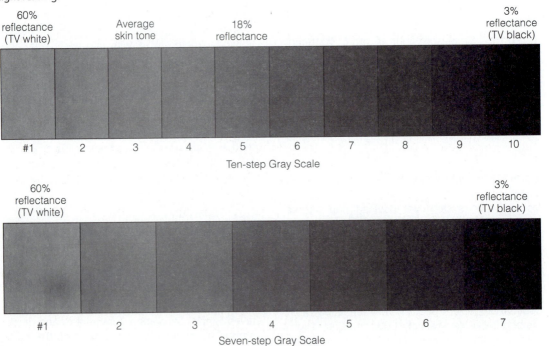

60%
reflectance
(TV white)

Average
skin tone

18%
reflectance

3%
reflectance
(TV black)

#1 2 3 4 5 6 7 8 9 10

Ten-step Gray Scale

60%
reflectance
(TV white)

3%
reflectance
(TV black)

#1 2 3 4 5 6 7

Seven-step Gray Scale

Although it is best that all lighting, costumes, and other production elements adhere to the optimum picture contrast range by using only television white and black, there are times when this is impossible. In these cases, the video technician must compensate for the increased contrast range by "stretching" either the white or black ends of the picture. If the black end of the picture is stretched by lowering the pedestal, the system will merge the lighter tones into solid white. If, on the other hand, the gradations at the white end of the scale are stretched, the blacks and dark grays become indistinguishable from each other. The technician decides where to sacrifice by deciding whether the dark or light parts of the image carry the most information.

Since the performer's face is often the most important part of a picture, this usually means compensating so that skin tones and facial modeling reproduce well at the expense of the highlights or dark tones. Then the background brightness level is set about one-and-one-half or two steps darker than the face so that it does not pull the viewer's eye away from talent. Ideally, every scene will include visual "anchors" at each end of the contrast range. By including even small objects of television black and white, the scene is "opened up" and appears much more natural than a scene that includes only midrange values. However, even a small prop or background area that is too white or too black can upset the carefully planned contrast

range of the lighting director and result in an inferior quality image. (See Figure 18-8.)

TECH TIP   Normal typing paper reflects 90 percent of the light reaching it and ink on the page reflects about 1 percent of the light. If you tried to show an actor reading a typewritten note on television, the contrast range would be excessive and the scene would not reproduce well. Use cream-colored paper, and remember to always examine your program on a monitor. Learn not to evaluate lighting with the unaided eye.

MEASURING LIGHT INTENSITY

To know if there is sufficient illumination for the camera, you must be able to measure lighting intensity. That is done with a *light meter* calibrated in either foot candles or lux. (See Figure 18-9.) One *footcandle* (fc) is the amount of light produced by a candle measured one foot from the flame. One fc equals 10.74 lux.

Using Light Meters

There are two kinds of light meter readings: (1) reflected, and (2) incident.

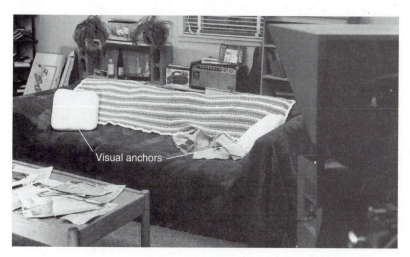

Visual anchors

FIGURE 18-8
Visual Anchors.
A visual anchor is an object that is TV white and/or TV black. Visual anchors "open up" the scene and make the reproduced image appear more natural to the viewer.

FIGURE 18-9   Light Meter.

Reflected   The *reflected* meter reading measures the amount of light reflected from a scene toward the camera. To take a reflected meter reading, stand at the camera and point the meter toward the subject. (See Figure 18-10.)

Incident   The *incident* meter reading measures the amount of light falling on a scene. (See Figure 18-10.) It is the type used most often in television. To take an incident light reading, you stand at the subject's location and point the meter toward the camera or toward the lights directed on the scene.

There are three uses of the incident light reading: (1) to determine that there is adequate illumination for proper operation of the camera; (2) to determine the overall average level of illumination; and (3) to approximate lighting ratios.

Adequate Illumination   All cameras require a minimum level of illumination to properly reproduce an image. Although the particular light-level requirements of cameras vary according to manufacturer, some remote cameras will operate adequately at 20 fc, approximately the light level in a typical kitchen. Inside the studio, most lighting directors prefer to light to a level of 125 to 200 fc. While this exceeds the bare minimum necessary to produce a sharp image of reasonable color, the higher light level enables the camera control operator to stop down the lens, increasing the depth of field and providing greater flexibility in controlling the light and dark areas of the set.

Overall Average Illumination   By changing the lens's aperture, you can adjust a camera to accommodate different levels of illumination. An incident light meter pointed toward the camera will provide a readout of the average illumination level. The lens aperture then is set to properly capture the gray scale exhibited in the scene. Lens apertures in the range of f/4 to f/8 produce sharp im-

FIGURE 18-10   Light Meter Readings.
Incident readings measure illumination falling on a subject and are taken with the meter facing toward the camera. *Reflected readings* measure light reflected from the subject into the camera and are taken by pointing the meter toward the subject.

Measures average light illuminating subject

Measures light reflected off subject

Camera

Camera

Incident-light meter reading

Reflected-light meter reading

ages with adequate depth of field. Studios often are lit to allow cameras to work within this lens aperture range.

Whenever possible, working with lower light levels is preferable to working under higher light levels. Less powerful instruments, less power use, cooler studios, and less glare from the lights are all benefits of working under less light. However, if this rule is taken to its extreme, color rendition and image sharpness suffer. Also, under some conditions, high levels of light are needed to increase depth of field.

TECH TIP Increasing the intensity of the light and closing the lens's aperture size can result in the same amount of light going into the camera while the depth of field is increased. However, shooting for maximum depth of field requires much more light. For example, going from f/4 to f/5.6 requires twice the amount of light and going from f/4 to f/11 takes eight times more light! Besides requiring more powerful lighting instruments, that also takes very tolerant talent.

Approximating Lighting Ratios   By pointing the incident light meter directly at the key and fill lights rather than at the camera, the lighting director can estimate the lighting ratio. For example, if the reading taken with the incident meter pointed at the key light is 300 fc and the measurement taken with the meter pointed at the fill is 75 fc, the lighting ratio is 4:1. While fine-tuning of lighting always requires using a monitor for reference, lighting directors can come quite close to the final lighting plan during set-up using just the light meter for reference.

The average reading obtained with an incident meter is usually sufficient for most television production situations, since activity occurring in many different places on the set makes more precise readings less useful. However, occasionally, very precise control of lighting is needed. Under these conditions, reflected meters are helpful because they take into account how much light is reflected by the object as well as how much light is falling on it. This becomes important when the object being illuminated has light and dark facets. For example, you might take a reflected light reading of a shadow area in a scene and then "place" that reading so the camera would render it as a step five value on the seven-step gray scale. This level

of precision might be important in videotaping a commercial in which the sponsor's logo was a subtle blend of dark tones. A *spot meter,* which is a reflected meter with a pickup angle as narrow as 1°, can be used to make certain the dark values will be separated in the final image. As always, the monitor is the final judge. However, careful use of light meters can save time and money by allowing lighting directors to work without the expense of the camera, crew, and video technician during early setup.

Using the Waveform Monitor (WFM)

As you know from our description in Chapter 11, the waveform monitor (WFM) produces a graphic image of the active video, along with synchronization pulses and other information in the video signal. The overall lighting intensity can be seen in the waveform of the active video. For example, in Figure 18-11 it's easy to tell which scene has too little light on it and which has too much. It's also possible to tell whether a set is lit evenly by looking at the shape of the waveform. It will be fairly flat if the lighting is even across the entire set.

TECH TIP A change of one f-stop on the camera's lens will increase or decrease the waveform about ten IRE units.

LIGHTING AND VIDEOSPACE

Many people are surprised to walk onto a brightly lit set only to discover, once they compare the set to the picture on the television monitor, that it appears as if it were nighttime. This is so because our eyes and the television camera do not perceive the effects of lighting in exactly the same way. The basic difference is that our eyes adjust their sensitivity to lighting in very small areas, "opening up" when they peer into shadows and "stopping down" when they look at bright parts of a scene. In contrast, the TV camera sees the entire scene "all at once" without accommodating for various levels within the scene.

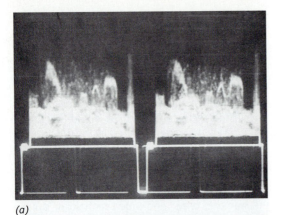

(a)

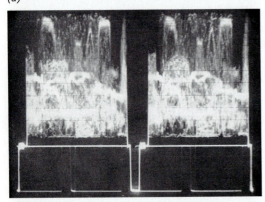

(b)

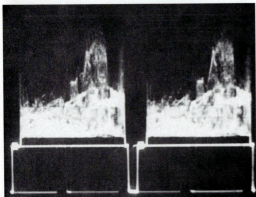

(c)

FIGURE 18-11 Using the Waveform Monitor When Lighting.
The peaks of the waveform represent the brightest elements in the active video. They should rise to 100 IRE. (*a*) Too little light. (*b*) Proper level of light. (*c*) Lighting is uneven, and drops off on the left side of the scene.

534

While we complain about the limits of the TV camera relative to the human eye, these same characteristics are responsible for the camera's ability to create the videospace. Only on television can a 2,000-W instrument produce the illusion of bright sun streaming through a window or enable the same light to serve as a nighttime street lamp. With practice, the lighting director learns that how lights appear in the studio is irrelevant. The final reality is always that which is created in the videospace and sent to the viewers' screens. How the videospace is transformed with lighting equipment is the subject of the next section.

LIGHTING EQUIPMENT

Television studio lighting systems include three components: (1) lighting instruments, or "luminaires," (2) hanging or mounting devices, and (3) lighting control equipment.

Lighting Instruments

Lighting instruments are classified according to the type of light they produce. *Spotlights* concentrate a hard, directional beam of light into a small, circular area, and *floodlights* produce a soft, diffused beam of light that spills over a large area of the set. All lighting instruments consist of (1) a *lamp,* which serves as the actual source of illumination, and (2) the *reflective housing,* which creates the quality of the light.

Lamps For many years, the basic light source was the incandescent tungsten lamp. Although a new tungsten lamp produces its rated output, as the lamp ages, the light output decreases and the color temperature of the lamp changes.

The *quartz-halogen lamp* has emerged as the studio standard because it solves both the tungsten lamp's problems. The quartz-halogen lamp burns at a constant color temperature and light output throughout its life. The lamp itself is smaller than the older tungsten bulbs, so housings can be designed that are smaller, lighter, and less expensive. (See Figure 18-12.)

All professional studio lamps are designed to operate at 3,200 °K. Although, theoretically, almost any color temperature could have been selected

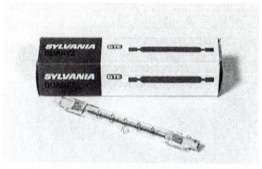

FIGURE 18-12   **Quartz-Halogen Bulb.**
The quartz-halogen bulb is the workhorse of the
television studio. It produces a stable supply of 3,200 °K
light throughout its life.

as the standard, lamps that burn at 3,200 °K offer
a good compromise between light output and
bulb life. Some lamps are designed to produce
5,600 °K light. However, these are designed to
balance daylight and are not found in studios.

TECH TIP   Although rated at about 200 hours of
life, quartz-halogen lamps still must be replaced
periodically. Never use your bare hands to change
a quartz-halogen lamp. The oils from your skin will
cause it to overheat where touched, and the lamp
will burn out quickly. Use a cloth or the bulb's protective packaging to handle a replacement lamp.
(See Figure 18-13.)

Besides color temperature, a lamp is identified
by its *wattage*, a measure of power. Higher-
wattage lamps consume more power. In general,
higher-wattage lamps also produce more light.
However, reflector design is as important in meas-

uring light output as is the wattage of the bulb
used. The most commonly used lamps in television are rated between 500 and 2,000 W (watts)
(2 kW). The "1K," or 1-kW (1,000-W), lamp is the
industry workhorse.

A lamp's wattage is directly related to the
amount of current (measured in amperage)
needed to light the lamp. Watts, amps, and the
voltage of the electrical system are interrelated as
follows: watts ÷ volts = amps. Since voltage is
always a constant of the electrical system (either
120 V for homes and most businesses or 220 V in
TV studios and heavy industry), higher-wattage
lamps use, or "draw," more amps. Most home
electric circuits are designed to carry either 15 or
20 A (amps). If you draw more than the designated amount of current, a circuit breaker trips,
electric power is interrupted, and all the lights go
out. In a television studio, there usually are enough
separate circuits to safely distribute the power required for lighting. However, adequate circuitry
can be a definite concern for remote shooting in
homes or businesses.

TECH TIP   A typical 15-A circuit in an older home
can carry only 1,800 W of power (120 V × 15 A
= 1,800 W). To maintain a 50 percent safety factor, you should not exceed 1,200 W per 15-A circuit for on-location lighting. In studio settings, use
several of the available circuits rather than overloading a single circuit.

Lamp Housings   The reflective lamp housing is

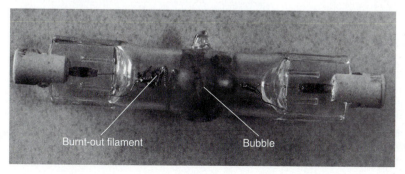

Burnt-out filament   Bubble

FIGURE 18-13   **Improperly
Handled Quartz-Halogen
Lamp.**
A bubble appears where this
quartz lamp was handled with
bare fingers. This caused the
filament to burn out quickly.
Always wear gloves or hold a
quartz lamp with a cloth
when installing it.

Scoop (a)

Fresnel (b)

FIGURE 18-14 Lamp Housings.
(a) The large-aperture, matte-surfaced housing of the scoop produces soft light; (b) the comparatively small, mirror-surfaced housing of this fresnel produces hard light.

as important as the lamp that it contains. The housing affects the quality of the light (hard or soft) reaching the set and determines how the light is emitted and controlled. (See Figure 18-14.)

SPOTLIGHTS   A spotlight is an instrument designed to produce a relatively narrow beam of hard, directional light. The light produces strong shadows on areas not directly illuminated and gives the lighting director considerable control over light and shadow. The types of spots most frequently used in television are (1) fresnels, (2) ellipsoidals, and (3) lensless, or "open-face" spots.

Fresnel Spotlights   The most commonly used spotlight in television lighting is the fresnel spotlight. These instruments are equipped with a thin, heat-resistant fresnel lens that provides a very even and directional beam of light. (See Figure 18-15.)

Inside the fresnel spot, the lamp and reflector ride on a special gear track that moves the lamp closer to or further from the fresnel lens. When the lamp and reflector are positioned close to the lens, the light beam is softened and diffused, or

"flooded out," over a large area. At the back of the housing, the lamp produces its most focused and intense, or "spotted down," beam. This focusing capability is one of the primary advantages of the fresnel spotlight. (See Figure 18-16.)

Fresnels are available in a wide variety of sizes and intensities from minispots of 100 to 150 W through 5,000- and 10,000-W giant spots. The most commonly used fresnels in most small and medium-sized studios are the 750-, 1,000- ("ace"), and 2,000-W ("deuce") sizes. The higher wattage lamps put out more power and are usable at greater distances than the smaller fresnels.

The fresnel spot is the "workhorse" of television spotlights because of its enormous flexibility. The fresnel's flexibility comes from its focusable beam and relative freedom from hotspots. The fresnel is used to illuminate performers, sets, and background areas as well as for special-purpose applications.

Ellipsoidal Spotlights   The ellipsoidal spotlight (sometimes called a "leko") projects a high-intensity beam of hard, directional light with a rapid fall-off in intensity at the edges of the beam. Ellipsoidals are equipped with internal shutters that

536

FIGURE 18-15
Fresnel Spotlight.
The fresnel is the most common studio spotlight.
(Courtesy: Kliegl Bros.)

FIGURE 18-16 **Flood-Spot Focusing of Fresnel Spotlight.**
Moving the lamp and reflector toward the lens spreads out the beam. Moving the lamp and reflector away from the lens concentrates the light rays into a more directional beam. Spotting the beam is sometimes called "pinning the beam."

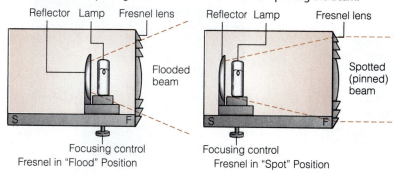

enable you to "trim" the beam's shape and size. The ellipsoidal spot has a relatively limited focusing range and tends to throw a particularly hard light. For these reasons, it is seldom used to light performers. (See Figure 18-17.)

A unique feature of the ellipsoidal spot is the ability of some units to accept patterns for projection. These patterns are called *cucaloruses,* or "cookies," and are available in various designs. The projection of distinctive light patterns to add interest to backgrounds is the principal use of the ellipsoidal spot. (See Figure 18-18.)

Lensless Spotlights   A number of spots are available which do not use a lens to focus the light rays. These lensless spots are not quite as versatile as the fresnel, but they are much lighter and, without

FIGURE 18-18   Cookie Patterns.
Light patterns are created when a cucalorus (called a "cookie) is fitted to an ellipsoidal spotlight.

a fresnel lens to absorb light, make more efficient use of the available lamp wattage. While their primary use in large studios will tend to be as auxiliary instruments, their relatively low cost and high efficiency make them the instrument of choice for remote work and increasingly in smaller studios if less control of light is acceptable. (See Figure 18-19.)

FIGURE 18-17   Ellipsoidal Spotlight.
Ellipsoidal spotlights are often used to project background patterns of light. *(Courtesy: Kliegl Bros.)*

FIGURE 18-19   Lensless Spot.
Lensless spots are lighter and less expensive than fresnel spotlights. They are very efficient but offer somewhat less control than fresnels.

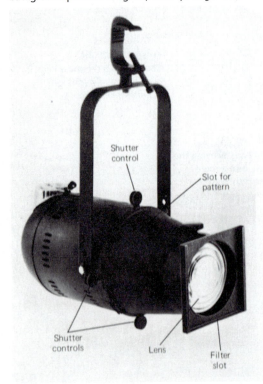

Shutter control

Slot for pattern

Shutter controls

Lens

Filter slot

SPECIAL-PURPOSE SPOTLIGHTS A number of spotlights are used for special-purpose applications. Although they seldom are standard equipment in most small studios, they are ideal for their intended uses.

HMI Instruments An HMI (halogen-metallic iodide) instrument produces 5,600 °K light rather than the standard 3,200 °K light. In other words, the color temperature of an HMI light matches daylight. Since the HMI is balanced for daylight, it is the ideal supplemental light for outdoor work.

If a 3,200 °K lamp is used to fill in the shadows on an outdoor shoot, the filled area will appear too warm or reddish because the color temperatures are not matched. To correct color balance, lighting directors will use an 80A filter over a 3,200 °K lamp, which converts the color temperature to

FIGURE 18-20 **HMI Spotlight.**
The HMI light produces light balanced for daylight (about 5,600 °K) and is useful for producing outdoor fill light. *(Courtesy: DN Labs, Inc.)*

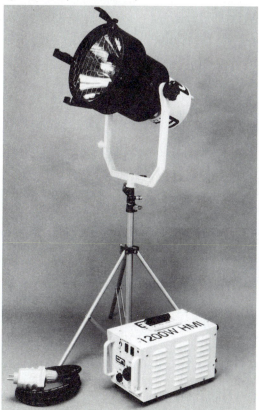

5,500 °K. However, the filter reduces the light's output by about two stops, or 75 percent. For daylight work, a 200-W HMI lamp produces as much usable light as a 1,000-W quartz-halogen lamp. This makes the HMI lamp lighter, less demanding of power, and much cooler during operation. Unfortunately, HMI lights are rather expensive. (See Figure 18-20.)

Follow-Spots The follow-spot is a large, high-intensity spotlight that has been borrowed from the theatrical stage. In the theater, the follow-spot is a quick way of directing the audience's attention toward a particular performer or area on stage. Follow-spots are equipped with controls that enable you to "iris out" or "iris in," enlarging or diminishing the size of the beam through a variable aperture, or iris. The follow-spot can be mounted on a floor stand, and an operator can pan and tilt the instrument to follow the action on the studio floor. (See Figure 18-21.)

PAR Lights The parabolic aluminized reflector (PAR) light is an integrated unit that includes a set of lamps, lenses, and reflectors. Different PAR units are available with beam spreads ranging from "wide" to "medium" to "spot." In addition,

FIGURE 18-21 **Follow Spotlight.**
Follow spotlights are used primarily for live performances in large venues. Because the instrument may be hundreds of feet away from the subject, it must throw a very narrow, bright beam of light.

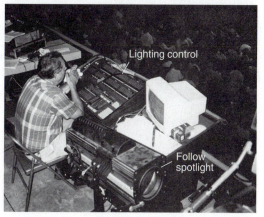

Lighting control

Follow spotlight

Par
unit

Unit
tilt control

Barndoor

Mounting stand

FIGURE 18-22   PAR Light.
PAR lights house multiple
lamps and produce large
amounts of light. *(Courtesy:
Berkey-Colortran.)*

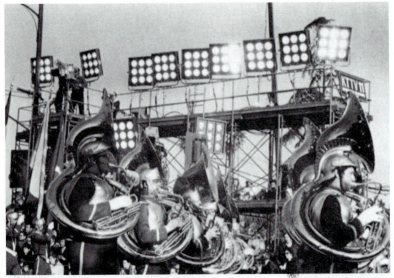

FIGURE 18-23
PAR Lights in Production.
Banks of PAR lights are useful
for filling in shadow areas
when producing outdoors on
location. The instruments
pictured here are balanced for
daylight to match the color
temperature of the natural
illumination. *(Courtesy: Berkey-
Colortran.)*

PAR units are available balanced at either 3,200 °K or for daylight.

Although the multiple PAR lamps are contained on a single mounting, each unit can be positioned individually to distribute light evenly over a large area. The highly efficient PAR units offer high light intensity with a long-range throw capability. They are very useful for lighting large, indoor areas on remote productions. They also frequently are used to provide fill light in daylight situations where large sets are being illuminated. (See Figures 18-22 and 18-23.)

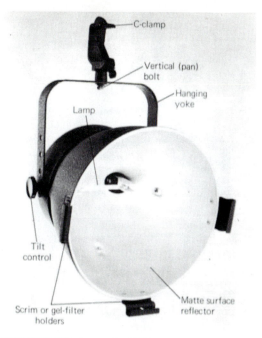

FIGURE 18-24　Scoop Floodlight.
The scoop produces soft, even illumination.

high-angle lighting in small studios where lack of space makes it necessary to light talent from close-up, steep angles. Soft lights are popular for glamour lighting, which opens up faces, softens eye shadows, and smooths wrinkles. Soft lights are available in sizes ranging from 750 to 5,000 W. (See Figure 18-25.)

Fluorescent Lights　In the past, two of the problems with using fluorescent lamps for television lighting were that they did not have enough intensity and they made people look green. Several new types of fluorescent lamps have been developed that are about half the size of the fluorescent lights used in schools and offices, but they give sufficient illumination and are color-corrected for natural hues on television. They have housings similar to quartz soft lights, but use less power, and can be placed closer to the talent because

FIGURE 18-25　Soft Light.
The soft light produces the most diffused light of any floodlight. It is especially useful for glamour lighting. *(Courtesy: Kliegl Bros.)*

FLOODLIGHTS　In contrast to spots, floodlights emit a beam of soft light that produces few, if any, shadows. "Floods" use large-aperture, matte-surfaced housings to spread diffused light over broad areas. The four most common varieties of floodlights used in television are (1) scoops, (2) soft lights, (3) fluorescent lights, and (4) broads.

Scoops　Just as the fresnel is the workhorse spotlight, the scoop is the most commonly used floodlight. Aptly named for its shape, the scoop consists of a frosted lamp mounted inside a lensless, bell-shaped housing. The scoop's light is very even, which makes it an excellent fill light. The scoop is used to reduce contrast while raising the overall light level of a scene. The most commonly used scoop in television has an aperture about 18 inches in diameter and houses a 1,000- or 1,500-W lamp. (See Figure 18-24.)

Soft Lights　The soft light has a square or rectangular opening with a curved reflector surface. Soft lights produce nearly shadowless light and can be mounted either on floor stands or the grid. They are especially valuable in softening harsh,

they are cooler. The cost-savings associated with the fluorescent systems has attracted many production facilities. (See Figure 18-26.)

Broads   The broad, or pan light, is a floodlight that owes its name to its rectangular shape. Broads are the most efficient of floodlights and much smaller in overall size. At the same time, the light from a broad is somewhat harder and less diffuse than that from the larger aperture scoops or soft lights. The beam of a broad can be controlled by "trimming" with metal flaps, or "barndoors." Most broads used in television are equipped with 1,000-, 2,000-, or 5,000-watt lamps. (See Figure 18-27.)

SPECIAL-PURPOSE FLOODLIGHTS   There are two

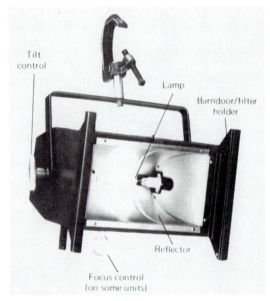

FIGURE 18-27   **Broad Light.**
The broad light is an efficient light source. Its distribution can be trimmed with barn doors. *(Courtesy: Berkey-Colortran.)*

FIGURE 18-26   **Fluorescent Light.**
Fluorescent lamps specifically designed to work with color television cameras use less power and are cooler than standard quartz-halogen lamps. They give off a soft, even light, with soft shadows. *(Courtesy: Videssence, Inc.)*

additional types of floodlights used for special-purpose lighting applications.

Strip Lights   Strip lights are long rows of broads which are used to illuminate a large area evenly. They are used most commonly to light background pieces, curtains, or cycloramas. Strip lights are available in a variety of combinations and sizes and can be hung from above or positioned on the studio floor behind a set piece. Strip lights are fitted easily with color media to produce special color effects. (See Figure 18-28.)

Cyclorama Lights   Almost all television studios are equipped with a cyclorama, a large, continuous piece of muslin or scrim material surrounding the background edge of the studio. A number of manufacturers have developed a special cyclorama (or "cyc") instrument which employs a highly efficient reflector to spread a very even beam of illumination across a wide area of the cyc. The cyc projectors are hung from the studio battens on the ceiling, and when properly focused, they provide an even wash of illumination across the entire background. Cyc lights usually are fitted with color

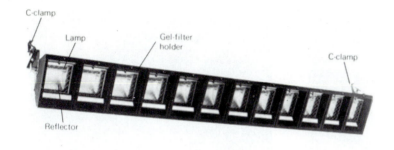

FIGURE 18-28 Strip Lights. Strip lights are commonly used to light backgrounds or cycloramas evenly.

gels to light the cyc in a variety of hues, which is very effective in color production. (See Figure 18-29.)

Hanging and Mounting Systems

All television studios are equipped with a series of battens or grids which are suspended from the

FIGURE 18-29 Cyclorama Projector. The cyc projector is usually fitted with a colored-gel filter to "paint" the cyclorama with a colored background.

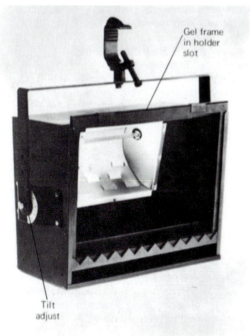

ceiling, usually in a crisscross pattern. The lighting instruments are mounted and hung from these battens. The most common type of batten is the *pipe grid,* which is a series of metal pipes hung from the studio ceiling. In some studios, the battens are on a counterweight or motor-driven system that permits them to be lowered easily to the floor for mounting instruments and then raised to any desired operating height. This is a great advantage in time savings and flexibility, since different shows often require different heights for optimum lighting. The major disadvantage of the movable batten is its increased cost over fixed-position grids. (See Figure 18-30.)

C-clamps are used to attach the lighting instruments to the pipe batten. The stem of the clamp is permanently fixed to the yoke of the lighting instrument, and the C-clamp screw is tightened onto the pipe with a crescent wrench. Since lighting instruments may weigh more than 20 pounds and are suspended 10 to 20 feet in the air, safety chains also are looped around the pipe and attached to the lighting instrument. (See Figure 18-31.) Once the C-clamp has been tightened in place, the instrument can be panned or tilted to permit focusing the light beam. (See Figure 18-32.)

TECH TIP Safety first is the most important principle of lighting. Never move a light unless you have verified that the power has been turned off. Attach the safety chain before tightening the C-clamp. Be sure barn doors are attached properly and that the focus and tilt controls work smoothly, and do not work on lighting grids directly above performers or other crew. Wear heavy gloves when handling light instruments; they become hot almost immediately after being turned on.

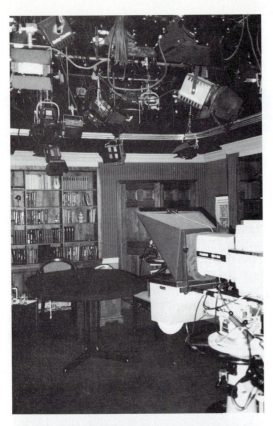

FIGURE 18-30 **Lighting Grid** (left).
A series of crossed metal pipes make up the lighting grid in most studios. *(Courtesy: C-SPAN.)*

FIGURE 18-31 **Safety Chain** (above).
Each lighting instrument must have a safety chain looped through its hanging yoke and over the pipe grid. A 20-pound instrument can smash through a skull like a sledgehammer through a melon.

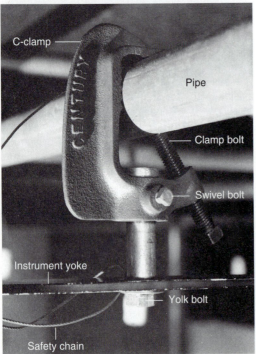

C-clamp

Pipe

Clamp bolt

Swivel bolt

Instrument yoke

Yolk bolt

Safety chain

FIGURE 18-32 **C-clamp.**
The C-clamp holds the lighting instrument to the lighting grid. For the safety of crew and performers, it must be tightened very securely.

Plugging Strips Running parallel along each pipe batten is a duct, or "power rail," containing cable that supplies electric power for each instrument. Short cables with connector plugs, called *pigtails,* hang from the plugging strips at approximately 4-foot intervals. Instruments are plugged into the pigtail to receive power. This allows each instrument to be powered independently. A number corresponding to a patch cord on the dimmer patch panel or a circuit breaker is painted above each pigtail. The numbers serve as references as the lighting director calls out each pigtail's number to the production assistant hanging the instruments. (See Figure 18-33.)

The ends of the pigtails are equipped with either three-pin connector plugs or twist-lock connectors. The male counterpart of either plug is attached to the connector cable of every lighting instrument. Twist-lock plugs are secured with a half-turn to complete the connection. To avoid the potential of a severe shock or blowing the lamp, never plug a light into a live pigtail. (See Figure 18-34.)

Auxiliary Hanging Devices Although the majority of instruments are hung directly from the studio battens with C-clamps, you may sometimes need to hang certain instruments at lower heights than a fixed grid will permit. In this case, an adjustable hanging pole is attached to the batten, and the instrument is hung at the bottom end of the pole. The length of the aluminum pole is variable and allows you to position the instrument at the necessary operating height. (See Figure 18-35.)

A commonly used, although much less effective, alternative to the telescoping pole is the *pantograph,* an accordianlike mounting device that permits an instrument or a ganged pair of instruments to be raised or lowered to a particular operating height. For a pantograph to be effective, the fixed grid must be at least 15 to 20 feet above the studio floor. Although the pantograph does permit you to raise or lower the height of the in-

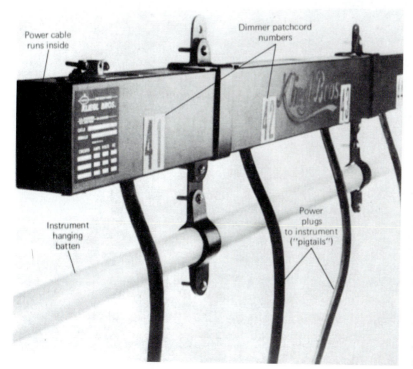

FIGURE 18-33
Plugging Strip.
The electrical cabling for lighting instruments terminates in individually labeled pigtails. The numbers along the strip refer to individual dimmer patch cords and permit each instrument to be connected to any dimmer in the lighting system. *(Courtesy: Kliegl Bros.)*

(a)

(b)

FIGURE 18-34 **Lighting Connector Plugs.**
Instruments are attached to pigtails with (*a*) the three-pin plug or (*b*) the twist-lock connector. The twist-lock connector requires a half-twist to secure or to unplug a connection.

strument relatively easily, it is heavy, cumbersome, and difficult to move from batten to batten. In addition, pantographs tend to slip, rotate, or swing, which can alter the position of a previously focused instrument. (See Figure 18-36.)

Sometimes a lighting director must position an instrument in a place where neither battens nor pantographs will serve. In this case, *a gaffer-grip clamp* can be used to fasten a lightweight instrument to sturdy set pieces or studio flats. The clamp is equipped with heavy, spring-loaded jaws that firmly grasp any solid surface. Because of their light weight and relatively high output, lensless spots are ideal instruments for clamp mounting.

There are a variety of additional hanging devices which can be employed for special lighting applications. Among these are the following: *trombones*, *set wall brackets*, and *wall sleds*. (See Figure 18-37.)

Floorstands are telescoping metal poles which usually are mounted on casters for easy movement. Floorstands are used frequently to light tabletop items or to illuminate windows or backings from behind the set, where the floorstand will not interfere with most studio operations. Soft lights can be mounted on floorstands for shadowless fill. Floorstands, or lighting tripods, are standard

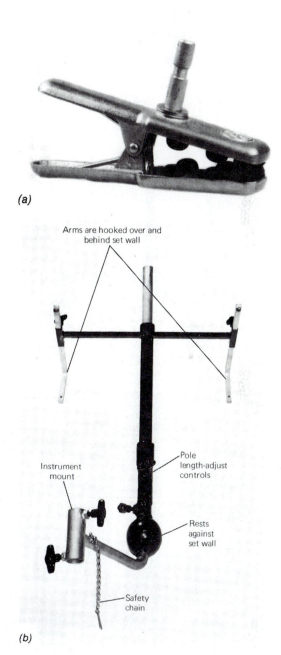

(a)

Arms are hooked over and behind set wall

Instrument mount

Pole length-adjust controls

Rests against set wall

Safety chain

(b)

FIGURE 18-35 Telescoping Hanging Light Pole. (Facing page, bottom left) The light pole can be used to extend a lighting instrument lower than the normal lighting grid allows. Once fixed, the light pole remains stationary. Unlike the pantograph, it will not sway. *(Courtesy: Mole-Richardson Corp.)*

FIGURE 18-36 Pantograph. (Facing page, bottom right) Although most studios are replacing pantographs with other hanging devices, a number of studios still use them because of their convenience.

FIGURE 18-37 Hanging Devices for Lights. (*a*) The gaffer-grip permits a lightweight instrument to be positioned anywhere necessary; (*b*) the trombone permits an instrument to be positioned over a studio set wall, allowing the set wall to support the weight of the instrument. *(Courtesy: Mole-Richardson Corp.)*

equipment in remote lighting kits. (See Figure 18-38.)

Lighting Control Equipment

One of the most important elements in effective lighting is the ability to control the light from every instrument. When we talk about *lighting control,* we refer to two distinct, but related operations: (1) controlling the distribution of light and (2) controlling the intensity of the light.

Controlling Light Distribution   There are four ways to control the distribution of light: (1) the instrument's angle of incidence, (2) barn doors and shutters, (3) beam control on the fresnel spotlight, and (4) lamp-to-subject distance.

ANGLE OF INCIDENCE   Positioning the instrument directly overhead at a 90° perpendicular angle produces the smallest circle of light distribution. As the angle of incidence flattens, the light is more broadly distributed in an ellipsoidal pattern. In addition to light distribution, the angle of incidence is related to shadow formation. (See Figure 18-39.)

BARN DOORS AND SHUTTERS   *Barn doors* are metal flaps which are attached to the fronts of fresnels, lensless spots, and some broads. Barn doors come as four-door and two-door units. Four-

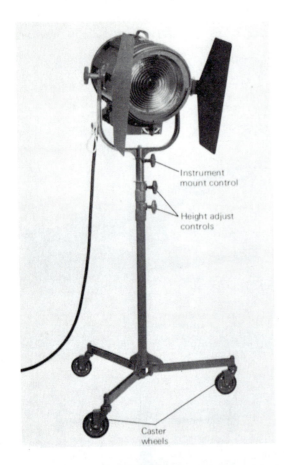

Instrument mount control

Height adjust controls

Caster wheels

FIGURE 18-38   Floorstand. Floorstand-mounted lights are easily positioned and quick to set up. When designed as aluminum tripods, floorstands are popular for remote lighting. *(Courtesy: Berkey-Colortran.)*

door units have flaps on both sides, as well as on the top and bottom of the instrument. These allow you to control the rectangle of light in all four directions. Two-door units have opposing sides that control light in only two directions at once. Barn doors are designed to rotate 360°, increasing light control. The placement of barn doors also affects light falloff, or how quickly the intensity of the light diminishes from the center of the spot where the

light is focused. Barn doors "feathered in," or angled toward the center of the light, increase the rate of falloff. Barn doors are an excellent choice for eliminating lens flare in the camera. (See Figure 18-40.)

FIGURE 18-39 Angle of Incidence.
Steeply angled lights produce a more concentrated light distribution and deeper shadows than lights positioned at shallow angles. (a) and (c) show a steep key, and (b) and (d) illustrate a shallow key.

90° angle

Minimum light distribution

(a)

45° angle

Large area of light distribution

(b)

(c)

(d)

FIGURE 18-40 Barn Doors.
Barn doors are used to direct light, control the rate of light falloff, and eliminate lens flare.

FIGURE 18-41 Flag.
A flag is placed in front of an instrument to block the light from a bright portion of the set. The flag must be positioned carefully so the edge of its shadow is not evident to the audience. *(Courtesy: Lowel-Light Mfg., Inc.)*

Shutters are built into ellipsoidal spotlights and permit the light beam to be trimmed in a variety of shapes and sizes. Manipulating the four shutters will produce different circular and rectangular light beams.

Snoots are long tubes that fit over the front of a light to concentrate the circle of light. *Flags* are rectangular pieces of metal attached to the front of a light with a flexible arm. By twisting the arm, the flag blocks part of the light. Flags are helpful for controlling light on small sections of the set, such as reducing the amount of light reaching a chrome surface. (See Figure 18-41.)

BEAM CONTROL ON THE FRESNEL SPOTLIGHT

Flooding out the beam on a fresnel spotlight enlarges the light beam's area of distribution. Spotting in the beam reduces the circle of illumination. (See Figure 18-42.)

LAMP-TO-SUBJECT DISTANCE   As the lamp-to-subject distance increases, the distribution of light widens. As the lamp is brought closer to the subject, the distribution of light narrows. (See Figure 18-43.)

Controlling Light Intensity   There are six ways to control the intensity of the light. These are (1) lamp wattage, (2) lamp-to-subject distance, (3) scrims and screens, (4) beam control on the fresnel spotlight, (5) reflectors, and (6) dimmers.

LAMP WATTAGE   The most obvious method of controlling light intensity is to select an instrument that will produce approximately the correct level of intensity when operating at full power. All things equal, the light output of lamps is proportional to their wattage. In other words, a 500-W lamp will produce one-fourth the footcandles of a 2,000-W lamp of the same design mounted in the same housing.

LAMP-TO-SUBJECT DISTANCE   The distance between the subject and the instrument is another means of controlling light intensity. The closer the lamp is to the subject, the greater is the light intensity. Conversely, the greater the distance, the less intense is the light. How much less? That is answered by the *inverse square law,* which says that the intensity is inversely proportional to the square of the change in the distance. For exam-

(a)

(b)

FIGURE 18-42 **Fresnel Spot Control.**
(a) A fresnel spotlight is flooded out; (b) the same light is spotted in. Note the difference in the circle of illumination.

FIGURE 18-43 **Lamp-to-Subject Distance and Light-Distribution Control.**
As the lamp is brought closer to the subject, the distribution of light narrows.

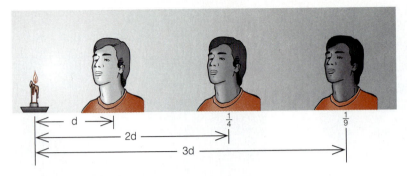

FIGURE 18-44
Inverse Square Law.
When the distance (*d*) from the light source is doubled, the intensity of the light is 1/4 (calculated $1/d^2 = 1/2^2 = 1/4$). When the distance (*d*) is tripled, the intensity of the light is 1/9 (calculated $1/d^2 = 1/3^2 = 1/9$).

ple, if the lamp-to-subject distance is doubled, the light on the subject will be one-fourth as intense. If the distance is tripled, the light intensity will be one-ninth what it was. (See Figure 18-44.) However, in television production, the results are not that exact because the inverse square law assumes that the light is uniform, not focused the way it is by fresnels and other lighting instruments. In any case, it is accurate to say that lights used at greater distances will be less intense, produce less contrast, and have softer shadows.

SCRIMS AND SCREENS A *scrim* is a translucent material made of gauze or spun glass which is placed in front of a lamp to diffuse and soften its light. Scrims decrease light intensity without reducing a lamp's color temperature. Scrims commonly are used on floodlights to increase their soft-light quality and to allow their illumination to blend smoothly with other instruments.

A *screen* is made of wire mesh and reduces light intensity without diffusing the light. For this reason, screens are used on spotlights when it is desired to reduce the spot's intensity without modifying its hard, directional quality. Screens and scrims can be placed in front of only a portion of a lamp. For example, a half-scrim can be positioned to diminish the lower half of a lamp's beam pattern to decrease light reaching a performer working close to the spot, while still throwing adequate illumination on the background. (See Figure 18-45.)

BEAM CONTROL ON THE FRESNEL SPOTLIGHT The beam control on the fresnel not only controls the size or distribution of the light, but also affects the intensity. When the beam is spotted down, the

"hot spot" produced by the instrument is about twice the intensity of a flooded-out beam from the same instrument. Most lighting directors like to work with a fresnel that is almost completely flooded out, since this will produce a relatively even spread of light across the entire subject. A

FIGURE 18-45 **Screens and Scrims.**
The screen reduces light intensity without diffusing the light beam. The scrim reduces light intensity and softens it at the same time.

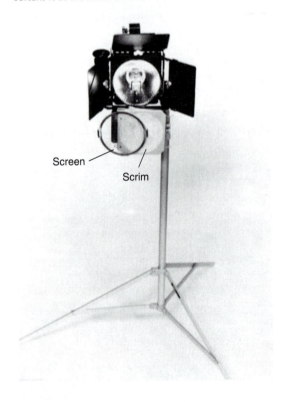

Screen

Scrim

(a)

FIGURE 18-46 Commercial Reflectors.
The instrument is aimed at (a) an umbrella or (b) a reflector panel to reduce the light intensity and soften shadows. (Courtesy: Lowel-Light Mfg., Inc.)

(b)

spotted-down beam has a very obvious hot spot with a rapid falloff, which can produce uneven lighting on a subject or area of the set. (See Figure 18-42.)

When focusing a fresnel, you should spot the beam down completely, using the hot spot to center the beam on the subject. Once the instrument has been locked firmly into place, the beam can be flooded out as far as necessary to achieve the proper light distribution and intensity level, trimming any unwanted spill light with barn doors.

REFLECTORS   Another way to control the intensity of light is to use a reflector. Commercial reflectors such as umbrellas and reflector panels are available. (See Figure 18-46.) You also can create reflectors out of inexpensive materials such as aluminum foil and Styrofoam insulation panels. (See Figure 18-47.) In each case, the lighting instrument is aimed at the reflector rather than directly at the subject. In addition to reducing the intensity of the light, reflected light will be more diffused and shadows will be softer. The same result can be achieved by bouncing the light off a light ceiling or wall.

DIMMERS   An accurate and flexible means of controlling light intensity is to use dimmer circuits. They are controlled at the *dimmer board*. (See Fig-

ure 18-48.) On the board, each lighting instrument is "assigned" to a dimmer circuit. In an older board, this is done by plugging a patch cord with the instrument's number on it into a dimmer receptacle. (See Figure 18-49.) In all modern dimmer boards, the instrument is assigned to a dimmer electronically by using a matrix that looks like a touch-tone phone. (See Figure 18-50.) More than one instrument can be assigned to a dimmer. The maximum number depends on the dimmer's rated maximum capacity, which is given in watts (W). For example, a 6,000-W (6kw) dimmer can handle any combination of lighting instruments as long as their combined wattage does not exceed 6,000 watts. That could be three 2kw-instruments (3 × 2kw = 6kw) or six 1kw-instruments (6 × 1kw = 6kw). However, on a patch panel, the number of instruments also may not exceed the number of receptacles for each dimmer.

A mid-sized board will have between twenty and thirty dimmers. Each dimmer acts as a *rheostat* placed between the source of electrical power and the instruments assigned to it, and can feed them anywhere from no power to 100 percent power. The amount of current reaching the instruments is controlled at the *dimmer fader* on the board. (See Figure 18-51.) The dimmer fader is operated just like a slide fader on an audio console. When the fader is in the "down" position, an

553

FIGURE 18-47   **Homemade Reflectors.**
Reflectors can be constructed out of inexpensive materials such as (*a*) aluminum foil or (*b*) Styrofoam insulation panels.

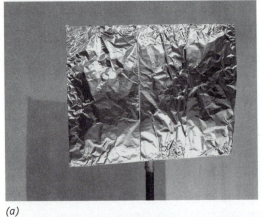

(a)   (b)

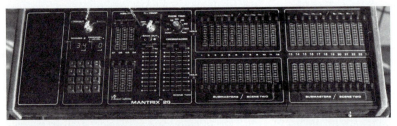

FIGURE 18-48
Dimmer Board.

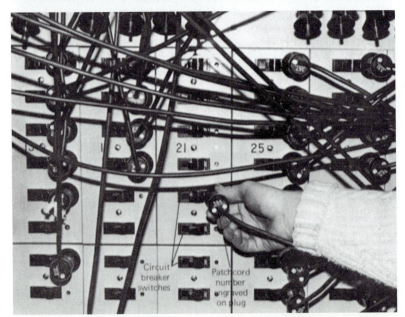

FIGURE 18-49
Lighting Patch Board.
Every pigtail connector in the studio terminates at its own numbered patch cord. Plugging the appropriate patch cord into the proper dimmer completes the electrical circuit and enables the dimmer board operator to control the light intensity of every instrument.

FIGURE 18-51 **Dimmer Fader Controls.**
When the dimmer controls are in the bottom position, no electricity reaches the instrument connected to that dimmer circuit. At the uppermost position, the instrument receives full power and the lamp glows at full intensity. Intermediate settings can be used to reduce an instrument's light output, but dimmer control settings less than 50 percent should be avoided.

instrument receives no power and is "off." As the fader is moved upward, proportionally more current flows to the instrument. Reducing the current dims the light. At full power, the lamp burns at full intensity.

TECH TIP   A word of caution about dimming: Dimming a lamp shifts its color temperature toward the red wavelength. The more the light is dimmed, the redder it becomes. If you white-balance your cameras in lighting set at full intensity, then dim one instrument, part of the set will appear too red. For this reason, in some facilities it's standard practice to use scrims on instruments rather than to use any dimming. However, shifting the color temperature could be done deliberately in special circumstances. For example, in a dramatic scene set around a campfire, dimming the light will create a red glow and contribute to the illusion that the light is coming from the fire.

Assigning each instrument to its own dimmer will give you the maximum control over the intensity of individual lights. However, it's more efficient to use fewer dimmers. When assigning more than

FIGURE 18-50 **Dimmer Assignment Matrix.**
A keypad is used to electronically assign instruments to dimmers. On this matrix, you press the instrument number, the @ key, the dimmer number, then the * key (for enter). For example, the sequence 24, @, 1, * assigns instrument #24 to dimmer #1.

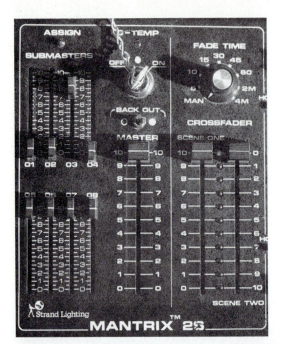

FIGURE 18-52 Scene Preset Controls.
This dimmer is able to preset and crossfade between two scenes.

one instrument to a dimmer, you should group the lights by function or by area. We will explain this when we discuss lighting techniques in the next chapter.

Most lighting control boards today are equipped with *scene preset* controls. (See Figure 18-52.) They make it possible to light more than one scene and change between them quickly and easily. For example, let's say you are lighting the set for a discussion and the director wants the show to start with the participants silhouetted in front of the background and their lights to come up after the program introduction. (NBC's weekly *Meet the Press* has used this approach for years.) This would take quite a few instruments, and controlling them individually would be difficult. Using the scene preset controls, all the background

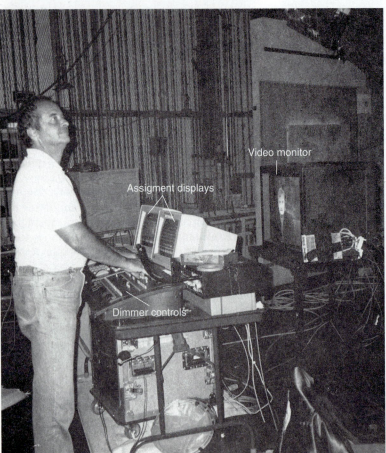

FIGURE 18-53 Computer-Assisted Lighting System. As lighting systems have become more complex, computer-controlled systems have become more common to relieve the lighting operator of difficult changes during production. *(Courtesy: Capital Cities/ABC, Inc.)*

lights could be set on scene one and all the participants' lights could be set on scene two. All it would take to make the lighting change is to fade in scene two using the crossfader control.

More sophisticated dimmer boards are equipped with computer-controlled presets that allow you to establish a number of complex lighting presets and place them in the dimmer board's memory. (See Figure 18-53.) At the appropriate time, the preset pattern is called and the lighting is reconfigured. Presets are essential for many live shows where there is no time to establish a new, complicated lighting set during production. They are also tremendously convenient when several regular sets share a studio. Once the lights have been permanently focused and hung, each lighting pattern is assigned its own preset. Then, by punching a single button, the desired lighting pattern is executed. Two additional controls on dimmer boards are the "master-fader" and the "blackout" switch, which are used to fade or to cut out all the lights simultaneously.

Today, electronic, or silicon-controlled rectifier (SCR), dimmers are the boards of choice. SCRs

employ solid state circuitry and a low pilot voltage to control the electric power. The control panel can be located in the studio or in the control room. Many units have preset memories, so that a single adjustment can control an entire gang of lights. Compared to older, autotransformer or resistance-type dimmer boards, SCRs produce almost no objectionable hum and heat during operation.

As with other areas of television production, the use of MIDI, a computer protocol that controls various activities, is influencing the most advanced lighting systems. A series of MIDI commands can flawlessly synchronize lighting changes to audio tracks, offering creative capabilities previously unavailable. Additionally, color gel "wheels" following preprogrammed MIDI instructions can revolve different colors in front of a lamp at the exact time needed. See chapters 8 and 9 for a discussion of MIDI as it relates to audio.

SUMMARY

Lighting is a fundamental part of any television production. Although the most important objective in lighting is to provide sufficient illumination for operation of the television cameras, it is also used to enhance three-dimensional perspective, direct attention to important elements in the picture, establish the mood and time of day, and contribute to the overall aesthetic composition of the shot.

The quality of light can be either hard or soft. Hard light is intense, directional, and creates strong shadows. Soft light is diffuse, spreads uniformly in all directions, and produces light shadows. Spotlights supply hard light and are used as the primary source of illumination. Soft light is supplied by large-aperture floodlights, and their diffused illumination is ideal for filling in shadows created by hard light and for blending in illumination on the set.

Light intensity is measured with a light meter. The most commonly used technique is the incident reading, which is taken from the subject's position and reads the average light that falls on the set. A more specific reading of the light available to the camera can be obtained with a reflected meter, which is aimed at the subject from the camera's position. Light readings are used to establish the proper light level for camera operation, to approximate lighting ratios, and to help determine the limits of the contrast range, which is about 30:1.

The fresnel spotlight is the workhorse television instrument. Its focusing ability and the evenness of its light beam make it ideal for illuminating performers, sets, and background areas. Other special-purpose spotlights are the ellipsoidal, lensless spots, follow spots, and PAR lights.

Floodlights such as the scoop, broad, fluorescent light, and soft light are used to provide diffuse, shadowless illumination. Special purpose instruments such as strip lights and cyc projectors are used to illuminate large areas of sets or draperies. These instruments often are fitted with color material to provide colored lighting effects.

Instruments usually are hung with C-clamps on overhead battens which are suspended from the studio ceiling. For special purpose applications, instruments can be hung from the battens on telescoping rods or pantographs, mounted on floorstands, or attached to set pieces with gaffer-grip clamps, trombones, or set wall plates.

Safety is a primary concern when hanging lights. Never plug a lamp into a live circuit, be sure to use the safety chain, and be certain barn doors and other attachments are firmly affixed to the instrument when moving it. Also, do not work on the lighting grid directly above performers or other members of the crew.

Effective lighting requires the ability to control the distribution and intensity of light accurately. Light distribution is controlled through (1) the positioning of the instrument, (2) the use of barn doors and shutters, (3) the beam control on the fresnel spotlight, and (4) varying the lamp-to-subject distance. Light intensity can be controlled through (1) selection of lamp wattage, (2) varying the lamp-to-subject distance, (3) the use of scrims and screens, (4) beam control of the fresnel spotlight, (5) reflectors, and (6) dimmers.

The distribution of electric power to each instrument is controlled through the patch panel, which enables each instrument to be assigned to a particular dimmer circuit. Some sophisticated distribution and dimmer systems incorporate a computer that memorizes instrument-dimmer circuit assignments and controls the operation of the dimmer board during production.

T E L E V I S I O N L I G H T I N G

PRODUCTION TECHNIQUES

The television image is created entirely with light. How we choose to illuminate a subject or a scene will determine how the image will appear in the videospace. When we light a scene we are painting with light to create shape and texture, highlight and shadow, accent and detail. As with other visual arts, a number of lighting guidelines and conventions have evolved over the years. In this chapter we offer them as a departure point for you to use in beginning to work with television lighting. They are not the only "solutions" to a particular lighting situation, and all successful lighting directors have broken the "rules" at one time or another to achieve a particular effect.

In the final analysis, all lighting must be evaluated by how it appears in the videospace, i.e., on the television screen. Only if the lighting complements the production's objectives, adds texture and depth to a scene, produces an aesthetically pleasing image, and provides enough illumination for the television system's operation can it be judged effective lighting.

Most television lighting tries to replicate natural lighting. One of the best ways to learn about television lighting is to observe your everyday surroundings carefully. For example, notice how the shadows, overall level of illumination, and direction of light differ in your living room during the day and in the evening. Where is the principal source of light? Are the shadows "blacker" in the evening or the day? When is the illumination more balanced? Do people look different when they sit in a chair close to a window as compared to an interior location? How would you reconstruct these differences using studio lights and a dimmer board? Could you go on location and mold the ambient light to the requirements of the television system? (See Figure 19-1.)

The point is that lighting and its effects on a subject change depending on the location, the time of day, and the principal source of illumination. Effective television lighting begins with developing an eye toward natural lighting situations. In this chapter we will work with the control afforded in the studio. In Chapter 22 we will consider the demands of remote locations in which control over lighting may be less precise. In both settings, the principles of lighting are the same and are based on the use of light and shadow to reveal a subject's form and dimensions.

LIGHT AND SHADOWS

Many beginning lighting directors are overly concerned with the appearance of shadows and try to remove them either by repositioning the instruments or by washing out the shadows with additional light. Yet it is the very presence of a shadow which helps to define space and to reveal the di-

(a)

(b)

FIGURE 19-1   Everyday Lighting.
Daylight (*a*) and incandescent light (*b*) impart an entirely different feel to a room and the production ambiance.

mensions and form of a subject. Flat, diffused, and shadowless lighting produces a very uninteresting image which lacks any depth, modeling, or "punch."

Indoor home videotapes offer a good example of the impact of shadowless lighting. These tapes often are lit with a single light attached to the camera. Although the scene is lit to a level that produces technically acceptable pictures, the lighting does little to flatter the appearance of the subjects. Without shadows and highlights, there is little to help the viewer define space and texture. (See Figure 19-2.)

The same home-movie effect would appear in television if we simply lit a scene with a bank of floodlights. We would achieve the technical level necessary for camera operation, but the pictures would appear lifeless and would convey little depth perspective. Early television often conveyed this effect because the cameras required high levels of illumination and could tolerate only a small contrast range between light and dark areas. This technical limitation forced lighting directors to light with few, if any, shadows. As the cameras became more sensitive to light and were able to accommodate a wider contrast range, lighting directors quickly took advantage of this increased sensitivity and began lighting their subjects more

realistically and with much more convincing results.

Shadows and highlights are controlled by the position, quality, and intensity of light which illuminates the subject. But you cannot set the light until you know the locations of the subject and the camera. They should appear on the *floorplan*, which we described in Chapter 17. Using the floorplan, you can work up a *lighting plot*. It should show the position of every lighting instrument that will be used. (See Figure 19-3.) When we discuss preproduction later in the chapter, we will explain in detail how to draw a lighting plot. A good starting point for your lighting plot is basic three-point lighting design.

THREE-POINT LIGHTING

Three-point lighting refers to the use of three instruments placed in three basic lighting positions. These positions are referred to by their primary functions, as follows: *key* light, *fill* light, and *back* light.

FIGURE 19-2   Positioning the Light Source.
(*a*) A subject is illuminated with a lighting instrument positioned head-on; (*b*) an offset light creates highlights and shadow, bringing out depth in the picture and producing a more flattering and interesting image.

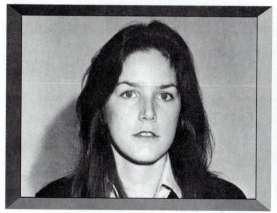

(a)   (b)

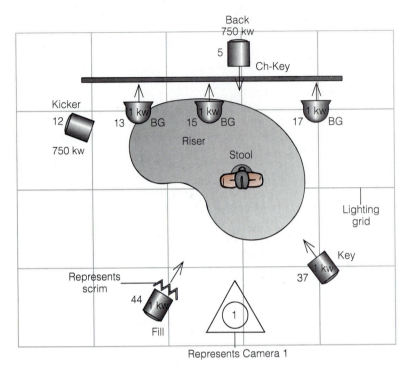

FIGURE 19-3

Basic Lighting Plot.
The lighting plot is used by the lighting director to plan the lighting design. On the basic plot: (1) The lighting grid is superimposed over the floorplan. (2) The set pieces, subject, camera, and instruments are drawn to scale. (3) Icons represent the different types and sizes of instruments. (4) The lamp size, receptacle number, and function are indicated for each instrument.

Key Light

Function The key light is the principal source of illumination for a scene. It provides the primary modeling effect, determines the basic camera lens operating level (f-stop), and acts as the reference point against which all other instruments are positioned and their light intensities balanced relative to the light level of the key.

Position The key light is positioned in front of the subject, offset to one side of the camera. (See Figure 19-4.)

The horizontal and vertical angles of the key light will vary depending on the lighting effect desired by the lighting director (LD). A good starting point is to place the key light approximately 30 to 45° to the side of the camera tilted down at a 30 to 45° vertical angle. Generally, as the key swings toward the front of the subject, modeling is reduced and the subject's features are flattened, or deaccentuated. Increasing the horizontal angle of the key, or moving it toward the side of the subject, increases modeling and, by emphasizing features and skin texture, can produce an aging effect.

Changing the key light's vertical angle also produces different shadows and highlights. At steep vertical angles, shadows begin to appear under the eyes, nose, chin, and lips of the subject. This lighting, sometimes referred to as "skull lighting," generally is unflattering. It occurs when the key is operated too close to the subject. If the angle of the key is shallow, the shadows beneath the facial features soften. At the extreme, in which the key is placed beneath the subject's face, the shadows are cast upward. Since we are accustomed to light sources striking a subject from above, underchin keys create a macabre effect and have become a convention associated with terror or supernatural programs. (See Figure 19-5.)

TECH TIP Frontal lighting reduces wrinkles (another name for skin texture) and makes subjects appear more youthful. Character lighting, created as the light swings away from the camera axis, accentuates the lines etched in the skin. Because the facial features of most people are slightly irregular, whether the key is from the left or the right side also will influence how talent appears on camera.

(a)

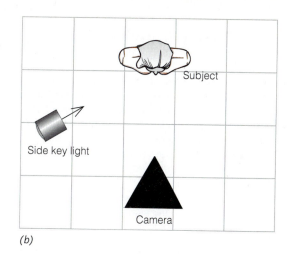

(b)

FIGURE 19-4 Key Light.
The key light serves as the principal light source on the subject. Varying the horizontal and vertical angles of the key light determines the modeling of the subject.

A key light can be either motivated or unmotivated. A *motivated* key is positioned to suggest that its illumination on a set or subject is coming from a direction or source that is part of the scene. For example, a character in a drama who walks over to a window in daylight should be lit with a key positioned from the same general direction as the window. Similarly, a subject who is sitting near a lamp or light fixture at night should have his or her key light hung from the side where the set

FIGURE 19-5 Key Light Positioned Beneath the Subject.
The upcast shadows obtained when the light is positioned beneath the subject produce an eerie and unnatural lighting effect.

(a)

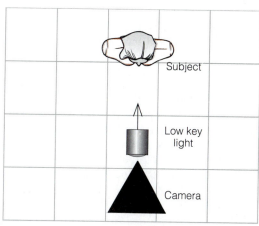

(b)

lamp is placed. Keys also can be motivated by a consideration for creating shadows that conceal. Suspense can be created when the shadows from a strategically located street light suggest the possibility of hidden danger.

Unmotivated keys are used when there is no need to consider the exact direction of the light or if a program obviously is taking place within a television studio. News programs, interview shows, and quiz programs are examples of production situations in which a motivated key is unnecessary. In such cases, the key light can be positioned on either side of the camera, although it is good practice to remain consistent in placing keys for all subjects on the same side.

Light Level   The key light will determine the relative intensities of all other instruments, which are balanced in proportion to the key's light level. Since the key will determine the basic lens operating level (f-stop), you should take a light reading to ensure that the light level produced is within the video operator's range of control. Too low a level will not provide sufficient technical illumination for camera operation. Too high a level will make it difficult to balance the remainder of the set's lighting by requiring relatively high output instruments to match the key level. Most video operators prefer a range of 125 to 200 foot candles, or about 2,000 lux.

Instruments   Fresnel spotlights almost always are used for key lights. The hard, directional light produced by the fresnel provides the necessary modeling effect on a subject by creating shadow areas. In addition, the flexibility of the flood-spot control on the fresnel and the evenness of the light beam provide the lighting director with greater control than can be obtained with any other lighting instrument. If necessary, inserting a scrim or screen will soften and reduce the intensity of the fresnel's beam. The size and wattage of the fresnel chosen for the key light depend primarily on the instrument's *throw distance,* the distance the light can be hung from the set and still provide the needed illumination. Most medium-sized studios customarily use 1- and 2-kw fresnels as their basic key lights.

Fill Light

Function   Fill light is used to lighten the shadows cast by the key light. The fill light is the second light "set," once the key has been established.

Position   The fill light must be positioned on the opposite side of the camera from the key light. While the key light often is produced by a "hard" light source, the quality of fill light should be softer and more diffuse. It should fill in the shadows made by the key light, but not create its own shadows. Fill lights should be positioned closer to the camera than the key, and at a slightly shallower angle. This often is accomplished by positioning the fill farther from the talent. The fill's greater distance reduces the angle, weakens the intensity, and softens its light relative to the key. (See Figure 19-6.)

Light Level   The intensity at which the fill light is set depends on the intended lighting effect. The relationship between the intensities of the key and fill lights greatly influences the overall feeling of a scene. This relationship is referred to as the *key-to-fill ratio.* Some programs require a very brightly lit scene with nearly transparent shadows. Other productions may favor deep shadows to create a somber or mysterious effect.

High-key lighting uses a strong fill light to lighten shadows. A high-key lighting ratio might be 2:1 or 3:1, or a ratio in which the key is two or three times more intense than the fill. High-key lighting in television usually is associated with nondramatic programs such as news, interviews, or panel programs, or with musical variety shows, where the lighting director uses light to create a sense of high energy.

Low-key lighting uses relatively weak fill as compared with the key light's intensity. As a result, shadows are deeper and more prominent. Low-key lighting falls somewhere between 3:1 and 5:1, or a ratio in which the key is between three and five times the strength of the fill. In extreme cases, the fill may be eliminated entirely. Low-key lighting is dramatic, or "theatrical." (See Figure 19-7.)

Instruments   Fill light usually uses instruments that produce softer, more diffuse light. Fresnels that are flooded out or diffused with a scrim are a good choice when the fill light's pattern must be controlled carefully. Barn doors also help shape the light distribution of the fill. Scoops and broads

(a)

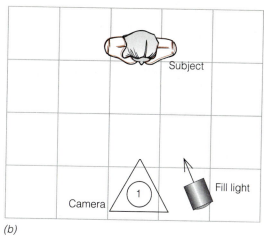

(b)

FIGURE 19-6 Fill Light.
The fill light is positioned on the side opposite the key and is used to fill in shadows created by the key light.

(a)

(b)

(c)

FIGURE 19-7 Key-to-Fill Ratio.
The quantity of fill light relative to the key light produces different contrast ratios. (a) The key and fill lights are approximately equal in intensity; (b) the fill light is much weaker than the key light; (c) the fill has been entirely eliminated, creating "hatchet" lighting.

can be used when the fill covers a rather large area and when control of the fill light distribution is not critical.

Back Light

Function   The back light is used to separate the foreground subject from the background and to increase the scene's apparent definition by providing contrast. The back light casts a rim of light that envelops a subject's shoulders and head.

Position   Ideally, the back light should be positioned directly behind the subject and at an angle that will prevent it from spilling light on the front of the subject or flaring into the camera lens. The back light should not be placed at such a steep angle that the tip of the subject's nose is illuminated. (See Figure 19-8.)

A variation of back light is called *rim lighting*. Instead of using one instrument directly behind the subject, two are placed slightly out from there and aimed at the sides of the subject's head and shoulders. This produces a nice rim of light around the subject's hair, and avoids the "hot spot" on the top of the head that you sometimes get from a single back light.

Light Level   The light level of the back light, as with all lights, is set relative to the intensity of the key. The correct level of the back light depends on the effect the lighting director is trying to create and on the lighting director's individual philosophy. While it is agreed that a rim of light across a subject's shoulders and hair will enhance foreground-background separation and provide more depth in the picture, too intense a back light can create an unnatural lighting effect that calls attention to itself. Black and white television used strong back lights to compensate for the lack of color for creating depth. Today, aided by color to establish separation, some lighting directors are of the opinion that except for certain situations—such as romantic settings or nighttime scenes—back light should be kept to a minimum.

A good rule of thumb is to start with the back-light level set at about half the key light's intensity and then to adjust the level using the television monitor for reference. Different subject and background combinations will require different key-back light ratios. For example, blondes usually need less back light than brunettes. Bald individuals often are lit with very little back light. Darker sets often suggest slightly lower back-light levels.

FIGURE 19-8   Back Light.
The back light casts a rim of light around the subject's head and shoulders to add to the image's depth dimension and to separate the subject from the background.

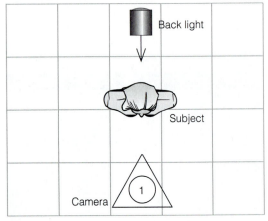

(a)

(b)

As always, the videospace represented on the monitor is your most faithful guide to how your viewer will perceive your lighting efforts.

Instruments Since back lighting requires careful control of direction and a relatively hard light, fresnels outfitted with barn doors are the best choices for back lights. To avoid hotspots, flood out the fresnel completely. Use a screen to reduce the light intensity if necessary, or choose an instrument of lower wattage.

Background Light

Once the key, back, and fill lights have been positioned and balanced, the basic three-point lighting plan is complete and the principal subject is illuminated. However, for most situations, the background area still remains to be lit.

Function Background lights are used to illuminate, accent, and model the scenery and background and to help create the overall mood of the lighting.

Position The placement of background lights is determined by the set you will be using during the

production. Whenever possible, background light should not fall on the main subject. This allows the lighting director to exercise the needed control in balancing intensities on the different areas of the set.

Use background lighting to develop texture and dimension. This increases depth and enhances the sense of realism. Naturally, a painted flat or a cyclorama has little or no depth with which a lighting director can work. In these cases, background lighting itself can introduce interest into the set through the use of color gels and projection patterns. Texture can be brought out in pleated drapes by using background lights striking the drapery at a steep angle. A frontal angle on draperies will reduce their texture when this is desired. Occasionally, lighting directors will "slash" a light across the background at a very severe angle to break up a monochrome set.

Most set backgrounds look best if certain areas are accented while other areas fall into darker shades. An overall lighting plan that mixes light and dark accents for visual variety produces the best results. (See Figure 19-9.)

FIGURE 19-9
Background Light.
The background should be illuminated to reveal depth and texture. Notice that the ceiling shows both highlight and shadow and that the background grows slowly darker as your eyes move from the performer toward the ceiling. *(Courtesy: PBS.)*

Light Level   The light level of the background lights should be adjusted only after the foreground lights are positioned and balanced. The intensity of the background lights will affect the viewers' perceptions of the foreground subject's brightness. A dark background will make a brightly lit subject stand out much more prominently than a lighter background. As a general rule, the background brightness level should be about two-thirds the brightness of the foreground subject.

Background lighting can play a major role in setting the time of day and establishing the overall mood of a particular scene. For this reason alone, the lighting director must give equal consideration to the background illumination as to the foreground lighting. A well-designed and well-executed lighting plan for the background can be a complex, but very important aspect of the total production.

Instruments   Fresnel spotlights are excellent instruments for lighting background areas. Not only does the hard, directional light cast shadows and define texture and form, but the barn doors permit accurate control of the light beam.

Ellipsoidal spots can be used in special applications to cast a projection against a cyclorama, curtain, or even a background flat. Using a cucalorus with an ellipsoidal spot is a very inexpensive and yet effective way to break up the monotony of a cyclorama or curtain. In a dramatic situation, an ellipsoidal fitted with a specially designed pattern can throw an image of a window, jail cell bars, or the like onto another portion of the background set.

Floodlights and strip lights are useful when you wish to illuminate a background area evenly. Fitting them with color media will produce a colored-light effect. With enough "wash" lights, the color of the entire background can be changed to signal transitions among scenes.

Lighting Ratios

In our discussion above, we compared the intensities of the key, fill, back, and background lights. The differences are expressed as *lighting ratios.*

FIGURE 19-10   Standard Lighting Ratios.

FUNCTION	INTENSITY (IN FOOTCANDLES)	RATIO (KEY: OTHER)
Key	200	—
Fill (high-key)	100	2:1
Fill (low-key)	50	4:1
Back	100	2:1
Background	133	2:1.3

Figure 19-10 summarizes the standard lighting ratios, given the intensity of the key as 200 fc in each ratio. Remember that these ratios are just starting points and will vary, depending on your lighting objective.

Special-Purpose Light Sources

The key, fill, back, and background light sources are the most frequently used in television lighting. However, a number of additional light sources are employed for special situations.

Side Light   The side light is placed directly to the off-key side of a subject and augments the fill light by providing accents and highlights. Side lighting increases modeling; but if it is too intense it can call attention to the light source and produce unflattering shadows. Side lighting commonly is used on dance productions, where the most important element is the outline and form of the body and not the dancer's face.

Kicker Light   A kicker is a special position for the back light. The instrument is positioned at the rear and to the side of the subject. Its purpose is to add accents to the hair. Kickers often are used for glamour effects, where the halo produced adds to the overall mood of the scene. (See Figure 19-11.)

Figure 19-12 summarizes the positions, effects, and special applications of each of the lighting functions.

Modifying the Three-Point Lighting Approach

Our discussion of three-point lighting has considered the placement of each instrument relative to *fixed* positions for one subject and one camera.

Two good questions could be asked at this point: (1) How are the key, back, and fill lights positioned for a program when there is more than one subject; and (2) What happens when the subjects or the cameras are moving? These questions illustrate an important distinction between conventional television lighting and lighting for still photography or motion pictures. Lighting for film and still photography permits the luxury of lighting for one particular camera angle at a time. However, television cannot support that approach when multiple cameras are used. Unless a program is shot single-camera style, where you can relight for each new camera position, one lighting setup must be adequate for all shots and for all angles—from a wide, establishing shot, to tight close-ups. Achieving effective lighting under these circumstances requires skill and the ability to compromise.

Multiple Subjects Television lighting directors generally light each subject with the close-up shot in mind, since the majority of shots selected will be no wider than waist shots. Less attention is paid to long shots, since the detail is less clear and the long shots make up a relatively small portion of the air time. The most effective approach is to light each major camera and subject position individually with its own key, fill, and back lights. Access to detailed shooting scripts, complete with actor blocking, is needed to accomplish this.

While this approach often requires using a greater number of instruments than alternative lighting methods, it allows the lighting director considerable control over the lighting, since individual instruments can be focused and balanced for each subject without affecting other subject-camera positions. In spite of the extra effort this approach demands, it is unquestionably the lighting technique that will consistently produce the best results.

DOUBLE-FUNCTION TECHNIQUE   An alternative approach that reduces the number of lighting instruments is to double up the functions of individual instruments. For example, sometimes a carefully positioned key light can serve as the back light for another camera's subject. (See Figure 19-13.) This approach requires less hanging and focusing of instruments, but also decreases the lighting director's flexibility. So if the back light on the one subject is too heavy, you cannot dim it without also dimming the key light on the other subject.

CROSSLIGHTING TECHNIQUE   An extension of the double-function approach is the "X Theory of Lighting," also called the "Dibie Square," after

FIGURE 19-11   **Kicker Light.**
A kicker light adds accent to a performer's hair and is frequently associated with a glamour effect. (*a*) without kicker and (*b*) with kicker.

(*a*)   (*b*)

FIGURE 19-12 Lighting Summary Chart

FUNCTION	INSTRUMENT	POSITION RELATIVE TO PRIMARY CAMERA	EFFECTS AND SPECIAL APPLICATIONS
Key	Fresnel	Approx. 30° to 45° vertical angle and to side of camera	Principal source of illumination. Basic reference for balancing intensity and position of other instruments. Positioning more frontally reduces modeling effect, steeper angle both vertically and horizontally increases modeling effect and produces more texture in subject.
Back	Fresnel	Either directly behind subject or at slight angle, vertical angle should be between 30° and 45°	Produces a rim of light around subject's head and shoulders to separate foreground subject from background and to enhance perception of depth. Heavy backlighting is used to create nighttime scenes or for special effects. Avoid too much intensity, or backlight may produce artificial effects.
Fill	Fresnel Scoop Broad Soft Light	Approx. 30° to 40° vertical angle on opposite side of key light	Used to fill in shadows which are created by key light on subject and to fill in shadow or dark areas on sets, backgrounds, and overall playing areas. Fill light intensity is set relative to the key light. A low key-to-fill ratio produces few shadows; a high key-to-fill ratio produces many shadows leading to more texture and modeling. When you are using fresnel instruments, beam should be flooded out and scrim or screen used to soften light.
Background (BG)	Fresnel Broad Scoop Ellipsoidal	Position depends upon desired effect. Frontal position flattens out background. Steeper vertical and horizontal angle increases modeling and texture on background.	Used to light backgrounds on sets, curtains, cycloramas, intensity is always balanced relative to foreground lights on subject. Lack of any background lighting creates a cameo effect. Background lights are usually the last to be focused and balanced since they depend heavily on foreground illumination. BG lights should usually attempt to bring out whatever modeling and texture exists in the background.
Side light and kicker	Fresnel	Approx. 90° angle on either side of subject.	Used to accent highlights on hair and shoulders and to outline the form of the body on such programs as dance or gymnastics. Can be used effectively to enhance nighttime lighting effects. Effect can be somewhat artificial if not properly positioned and intensity is not correctly balanced.
Cyclorama lights	Scoops Strip Lights Cyc Projection Lights	Can be hung from battens near cyc and/or placed on floor facing upward behind ground row or cyc row.	To illuminate a cyclorama. Usually, the instruments are fitted with color media to color the cyc. A number of different color effects are possible by gelling different instruments and varying intensities from the light control console.
Pattern projection	Ellipsoidal (fitted with cucalorus or other pattern)	Perpendicular frontal angle will project pattern without distortion. As the angle of instrument becomes more severe, projected pattern is distorted.	To project a pattern against a cyclorama set or other backing.

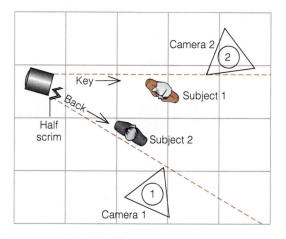

FIGURE 19-13   Combination Key/Back Lighting.
In this lighting setup, the key from one performer is used as a back light for the other performer.

lighting director George Spiro Dibie. Here's how it's done: First you imagine a square drawn around all your subjects. Then, you position a light in each corner and aim it toward the center. (See Figure 19-14.) The instruments facing away from the cameras should be scrimmed so their light is soft. The lights aimed toward the cameras should be flooded, but left uncovered. They will provide modeling for the subjects.

A variation of this four-corner technique is to replace the two lights facing away from the cameras with one fill light positioned in the center. (See Figure 19-14.) In both of these crosslighting techniques, all the instruments provide some key, fill, and back light, no matter where the cameras are

FIGURE 19-14   Crosslighting Techniques.
All the instruments provide some key, fill, and back light, no matter where the cameras are positioned. Half scrims may need to be used with the back crosslights.

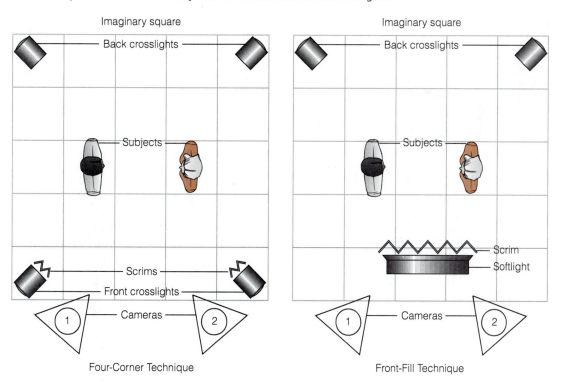

positioned. If the light on any subject is too strong, half scrims or flags can be used to cut the intensity. Using these crosslighting techniques, you do lose some control over individual instruments. However, fewer instruments need to be hung, and all 360 degrees of the set are lit fairly evenly. If you must light quickly for multiple-camera shooting, these approaches are adequate compromises, but they should never be used in place of conventional lighting approaches unless absolutely necessary.

Moving Subjects   When subjects are moving, your approach to lighting has to be modified. In this case, instead of lighting specific positions, you should light broader "playing" areas. Using the area method, the lighting director refers to the floorplan and identifies a number of major playing areas, lighting each one. You may use multiple key, fill, and back lights for each subject, covering their movement through the area, or you may use a crosslighting technique described above. (See Figure 19-15.)

While the area lighting technique usually requires fewer instruments than the individual camera and subject approach, it does have the disadvantage of reducing the lighting director's overall control. When using the area approach, it is important that multiple lights blend smoothly together. Even if three lights are used for the key, they should appear as a single key source on the monitor. Area lighting is particularly helpful in lighting musical variety programs and demonstration shows that use wide areas of studio floor and require many perspectives. Sometimes a combination of individual and area lighting is used. For example, a lead singer might be individually lit while her back-up band and vocalists would be lit with area lighting.

SPECIAL LIGHTING EFFECTS

Special studio lighting techniques are used to supplement conventional lighting techniques to provide a unique reality for the television viewer.

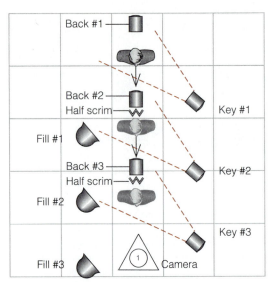

FIGURE 19-15   **Area Lighting for a Moving Subject.** The subject moving toward the camera will walk through three overlapping areas that have been lit. Half scrims have been used in two of the back lights to avoid "hot" spots as the subject passes under them.

As with other lighting effects, they rely heavily on the effective use of videospace to suggest a reality that actually does not exist inside the studio.

Lighting for Daylight

Indoor Scenes   A crucial consideration when lighting an interior set for daylight is to motivate the major source of illumination. Be certain that the main key lights are positioned to throw light from the direction of doorways or windows. Certainly, the brightest area in the background should be a window or open doorway, and a strong fresnel spotlight can throw a convincing shaft of light through the window or door to suggest sunlight. (See Figure 19-16.)

If you observe a daylit room, you will notice that walls closest to the window and at right angles to it usually receive the most light. Other wall areas often remain dark, and a lighting director should be sure to include contrasting areas of light and shadow to avoid the monotony of a uniformly bright background set.

(a)

(b)

(c)

FIGURE 19-16
(a) A living room set is illuminated with floodlights, which produces a very flat and uninteresting image. (b) The set is properly lit for a daytime look. Notice how the shadows and highlights add depth and ''punch'' to the scene. (c) The set is lit for nighttime with heavier shadows. Notice that the ''night look'' is accomplished by varying the scene's contrast, not by underlighting the scene.

573

side the television studio requires the use of hard, directional lighting and the judicious placement of shadows. Of course, you might argue that the sun produces only a single shadow while a group of instruments in the studio will result in multiple shadows which may not produce a completely realistic effect. While this is a valid argument, a single source of light will not always produce the proper modeling and depth for a subject. Multiple shadows, if they are seen by the camera at all, will appear only in long shots. The close-ups will maintain the desired effects even though the shadows may appear inconsistent on the overall set.

TECH TIP   Since many exterior sets are intercut with city panoramas or travel shots, remember to match time of day when changing locations. A high noon sun travel sequence will require steeper lighting in the studio, where late afternoon sun might require shallow angles for continuity.

Nighttime Lighting Effects

Lighting for night, whether interior or exterior scenes, requires a low-key approach to produce a high contrast ratio between light and dark areas. The lighting director must use the key to produce enough illumination for an acceptable picture while permitting dark areas to go completely black. Nighttime effects are not created simply by dimming all the set lights. This approach leads to a noisy picture that appears flat and dull without conveying the mood of nighttime.

Night effects are achieved by heavy back and rim lighting, with dark backgrounds punctuated by a few rays of light to relieve the monotony and to provide additional interest and depth perspective. While motivating the light is often an important consideration, sometimes we must cheat slightly to provide sufficient illumination for close-ups. In reality, the light from the moon streaming through a bedroom window may not be as bright as the key light we are forced to use in the studio. However, audiences tend to overlook this fact as they become absorbed in the program and the emotions expressed in the actors' faces. Be sure to illuminate your performers' faces with enough light

so that their features can be reproduced by the camera. Careful control of spill light is essential in creating an effective nighttime effect. For this reason, floodlights should be avoided, since their light cannot easily be controlled and the diffused, flat lighting they produce will wash out some of the shadows that contribute to the overall mood of the scene. (See Figure 19-16.)

An effective technique in lighting for night is to light each actor's position carefully and then let the performers walk through dark shadows with little or no fill light. Exterior night scenes are approached in much the same way. Heavy back and rim lighting will enhance the nighttime effect, and deep shadows will convey the mood and time of day to the audience. Occasionally, a light blue gel can be used to tip the quality of light toward nighttime.

Limbo and Cameo Lighting

Limbo lighting is a technique in which the foreground subject is seen against an undefined, infinite background. One of the most commonly used variations on the limbo effect is called *cameo lighting*. Cameo lighting isolates a foreground subject against a totally black background. Obtaining a cameo effect requires careful control of light distribution to keep spill light from falling on the background. Placing the foreground subject as far forward as possible will help because the angle of illumination will direct the spill toward the floor. A black velour curtain, which absorbs light, is useful for achieving the cameo effect. (See Figure 19-17.)

Spotlights are the only instruments which should be used in cameo lighting because their light distribution is the easiest to control. A bank of floodlights works well for creating neutral gray backgrounds for the infinite space of limbo lighting.

Cameo lighting often begins a scene. Then, on cue, the background lights are faded up, revealing actors and set pieces located behind the foreground performer. Scenes can be closed with the reverse of this technique; the background lights are dimmed, leaving the actors in a pool of light.

Silhouette Lighting

Silhouette lighting refers to the use of only the background and back lights to show just the forms

(a)   (b)

FIGURE 19-17 Limbo and Cameo Lighting.
(a) Limbo lighting shows talent against a neutral, undefined background; (b) cameo lighting uses a completely black background.

of performers or objects on the set. Silhouette lighting is popular for televised dance and is commonly used in mystery programs to let the audience in on the action while obscuring the identity of a character. (See Figure 19-18.)

Projecting Patterns

Projecting patterns of light onto sets, cycs, draperies, and other backgrounds can extend the versatility of the small studio. There are a great number of patterns designed to fit ellipsoidal spots for this purpose. Most are metal, but more expensive ones are made from heat resistant glass. Available patterns include stars, sunbursts, abstract designs, and clouds. Improvised patterns can be created by cutting the bottom of a pie tin with a razor knife. (See Figure 19-19.)

The size and shape of a pattern can be changed by repositioning the ellipsoidal spot. Steeper angles elongate the patterns, while more horizontal angles increase the symmetry of the pattern. A side angle creates a pattern that gradually darkens toward one side of the set and offers additional depth.

Lighting with Color

Colored light is produced with color media, commonly called "gels," attached to the face of an

instrument. The term *gels* derives from gelatin, the material once used to produce the color filters. Today, plastics, such as acetate, which resist heat and color bleaching better than gelatin are used as color media. Polyester is the most durable material used and is particularly well suited to the intense heat of television lights. A variety of trade names such as Berkey Colortran's Geletran and Roscoe's Roscolux are made of polyester.

A swatchbook containing small samples of the

FIGURE 19-18 Silhouette Lighting.
Silhouette lighting accentuates form and is commonly used in dance and mystery programs or to "reveal" talent when key and fill lights are brought up.

entire line of color material is used to select a particular color for each lighting situation. You cannot judge a particular gel simply by holding the swatch up to the light; color selection should be made by shining a light through the sample. If this is not possible, hold the material over a piece of white cardboard or, better yet, against the set material which will be used in the production.

Color media can be purchased in single sheets or large rolls. Either can be cut easily to fit any size gel frame holder, which then is attached to the instrument by three small arms. All parts of this assembly get very hot and should be handled with gloves. (See Figure 19-20.)

TECH TIP   Large rolls of gel are made available for the purpose of covering windows. Sheets of 85B gel taped to windows balance the incoming light to the color temperature of the interior studio instruments. Neutral-density gels, which reduce the overall brightness of a light source by one, two, or three stops, also are useful for creating realistic lighting effects. They are used when light coming through a window must be subdued for proper balancing.

All color media absorb some light, and some deeply saturated blues and greens can reduce light throughput by as much as 95 percent. Color-gelled instruments tend to be of higher wattage or are used closer to the background to compensate for this reduction in illumination.

Lighting Performers with Color   Under normal circumstances, color media are not used on those instruments which will illuminate performers, since their illumination will upset the color balance of the light and produce very unnatural skin tones. Some musicals, fantasies, and psychological dramas may violate this "rule." In such a case, it is important to supply a motivation for the colored light to avoid confusing the viewer.

Lighting a Cyclorama for Color   The use of colored light with a cyclorama can produce some very effective and varied lighting for color tele-

FIGURE 19-19   Pattern Projection.
Patterns can be projected onto a background to inexpensively create visual interest. Both abstract and realistic patterns are available. (*Courtesy: The Great American Market.*)

vision. To light the cyc evenly, most studios use a series of strip lights hung above the cyc on battens and another strip positioned below the cyc on the floor, hidden behind a ground row. An alternative is to use a *cyc projector*, which throws an even wash of colored light across wide areas. Regardless of which approach is used, the lights must be fitted with gels. Alternate lights may be fitted with different colors and assigned separate circuits on the dimmer board. This allows you to "paint" the cyc with different hues by adjusting the balance of the variously colored lights. Highly saturated gels are best for cyc lights. This light can be desaturated by adding light from several ungelled instruments. The color can be modified by adding light from instruments fitted with gels of complementary hues.

One of the most difficult problems in lighting a cyc is to keep the foreground illumination from spilling onto the cyc and washing out the color. This is a particularly difficult problem in smaller studios, where little space is available to separate the foreground subjects from the cyclorama. In this case, you may have to modify the positions of some foreground instruments and light with a steeper angle than usual in order to prevent as much spill as possible from hitting the cyc. A good

alternative for small studios is to use a lower-reflectance cyc—one made from material at about 60 percent gray rather than from white material, which reflects too much light and creates excess spill.

Lighting for Chroma Key

The use of electronic matting, often referred to as *chroma key,* has become increasingly popular because it provides the program director with a large measure of creative flexibility. Conventional chroma key operates by using a particular hue, usually a blue or green, as the "key" color. When the television scanning system detects this color, it electronically inserts another video source in place of the key color. A more sophisticated chroma key system called *luminance chroma key,* operates by combining brightness information and color information in producing the keying effect. This key operates by reading both the brightness of the background area and its hue. Luminance chroma keyers can be used to key in

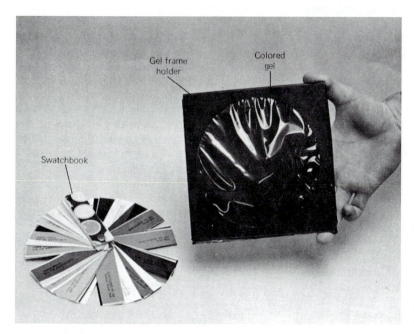

FIGURE 19-20 Color Media and Gel Frame Holder.
Color media are available in many colors. The lighting director should use a swatchbook to select the exact shade for the particular production situation.

transparent objects such as glass or the shadow of the object being keyed. We discussed chroma key in Chapter 14 and Chapter 17. However, because lighting is a fundamental part of the chroma key process, we will consider the proper lighting approach in this section.

Green and blue have been chosen as the primary key colors because they are farthest from the colors of skin tone. Since the chroma key matting operation relies on the appearance of the key color to trigger the insert circuitry, the key area must be lit evenly so shadows and spurious highlights will not interfere with the matting operation. Uneven chroma key lighting produces objectionable "crawling" or "tearing" around the edges of the insert. Contrary to popular belief, chroma key does not require excessively high brightness levels on the background area to operate properly. In fact, if the background is lit normally with the proper foreground-to-background ratio, the key should work well. The important consideration is that the background chroma key area is evenly lit.

TECH TIP   Chroma key inserts sometimes appear in the iris of blue-eyed or green-eyed performers. If unintended, this effect can be very disconcerting. The effect is eliminated by making sure the intensity of the foreground light is greater than that of the background light.

Since luminance chroma keyers read both the color and the brightness values of the background to trigger the insert circuitry, the threshold for the key operation is very narrow; a difference of approximately 10 percent brightness in the background is sufficient to trigger the insert. Therefore, it is vitally important when using a luminance chroma keyer to keep light intensity levels even across the entire background area. This can be achieved by using multiple light sources that blend well together.

The foreground subject of the key should be as far away from the background as possible for two reasons. First, greater separation decreases the likelihood of shadows falling on the background and creating tearing or bleeding in the key. Second, increased separation decreases the possibility of colored light bouncing off the background

and spilling onto the foreground subject, resulting in crawling around the edges of the key.

TECH TIP   If cramped studios make it impossible to separate the foreground and background physically, use an amber gel on the back light to minimize the light reflected from it onto the cyc. The amber gel absorbs blue light, decreasing hotspots on the cyc from reflected back light.

As producers and directors select chroma key for more production situations, the role of the lighting director becomes more complex. For example, when chroma key is used to insert an entire figure into another picture, the figure must be standing on as well as in front of chroma key material. To achieve even illumination across this entire area, very flat lighting must be used. For example, on one musical production, a group of actors spread across a wide area had to be keyed into a second camera source. The intent was to produce "heaven" with angels ethereally floating above the set. To accomplish this, 220 scoops were hung at equal intervals to illuminate the "key" set evenly. To avoid hotspots that would key unevenly, no fresnels were used. This was one situation in which the "rules" of lighting were broken to achieve the program's objectives.

Firelight

The flickering effect of fire on a subject can be simulated by attaching narrow strips of cloth to a long stick of wood. When a lamp is placed at an appropriate level (usually close to the ground and facing upward), the stick is waved gently in front of the light, producing flickering shadows on the subject. A yellow or orange gel placed in front of the light will provide the warm hue associated with firelight. Depending on the intensity and position of the instrument, you can simulate a gentle fireplace or a raging forest fire. Of course, the lighting effect will not be convincing alone. The lighting effect must be supported with appropriate sound effects and be motivated by the script. (See Figure 19-21.)

Moving Lights

Moving light, such as from a car's headlamps, can be simulated by using a fresnel spotlight mounted on a floorstand. On cue, a stagehand is instructed

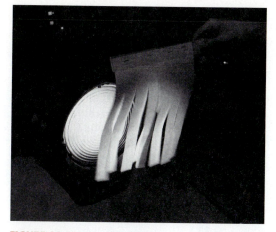

FIGURE 19-21   Firelight Effect.
Flickering light can be simulated by waving thin strips of cloth attached to a stick in front of a spotlight focused on the subject. Adding an orange gel will enhance the fire effect.

to pan the light across the set, creating the illusion of motion.

Reflected Water

A large, shallow pan of water containing several small pocket mirrors will cast the reflected ripple effect of a pool or lake. A spotlight is directed into the pan while the water is agitated. The lights dedicated to lighting the performer should be shuttered so that they do not spill on the pan of water. Otherwise, the effect will be washed out.

Lightning

The effect of a burst of lightning can be achieved by using a number of low-wattage, high-intensity lamps, such as photofloods. The lights are assigned their own dimmer and are quickly switched on and off, producing the short bursts of light. Lightning is most effective when it briefly overexposes the scene. Again, the use of sound effects coupled with the *lightning* will enhance and reinforce the overall illusion.

TECH TIP   If simulated lightning is part of the script, be sure to have plenty of spare lamps on hand. Rapidly turning lights on and off tends to burn them out. This is the reason that lights are not routinely turned off during short breaks from production. Replacing burned out lamps is an expensive and time-consuming process that breaks the rhythm of shooting.

Practical Lights

Practical lights are props and scenery such as table lamps or wall fixtures that actually function during the production. When a light is turned on as part of a scene, it should appear to add illumination to the set. Since scenes already are brightly lit, turning on a conventional lamp will produce no discernible change in illumination. For this reason, operation of a set lamp needs to be reinforced by assigning a fresnel to illuminate part of the set when the practical light is turned on. The easiest way to coordinate this is to have the dimmer board operator take a visual cue from the actions of talent during the production. If the fresnel and set lamp are not turned on at exactly the same time, the effect is destroyed.

PLANNING THE LIGHTING

Planning and executing the lighting for a program are the responsibilities of the lighting designer. All networks and most large stations and production studios employ a staff of individuals whose exclusive job is lighting. However, at smaller stations and studios, the task of lighting may be delegated to someone who must combine lighting duties with other production jobs. Often this will be a camera operator who doubles as a lighting designer. Whether your studio has someone whose sole responsibility is lighting or who combines lighting with other production functions, the basic steps in planning and executing the lighting for a television production are the same.

Preproduction Conference

As with other areas of television production, the first step in planning is the preproduction conference. Here, the lighting designer (LD) discusses the program with the director, technical director, audio technician, and set designer to plan concepts and objectives.

During the meeting, the LD will learn how the producer and program director intend to approach the program. The director and the scenic designer already should have sketched the floorplan, and a copy should be available for the LD. The program director will use the script and floorplan to indicate major actor and camera positions, and the LD should make notes on both the script and floorplan. The audio technician will discuss the best method of picking up sound—if hand, desk, or lavalier mikes will be used, there are few audio complications of concern to the lighting director. However, if a boom will be used, the LD must know its approximate position and operating range to anticipate the appearance of boom shadows.

The Lighting Plot After discussing the program objectives with the key members of the production team, the LD must use the floorplan, script, and information about the performers and camera positions to design the *lighting plot*. The LD must select the type and size of the lighting instruments, determine their function and position in the studio, supervise their hanging and focusing, balance the overall intensity of the lighting, and work out any special lighting effects. Before working in the studio, these details are considered using pencil and paper to create a lighting plot.

Working with a floorplan and lighting plot not only gives a better overall view of the set and equipment positions than you can get from standing in the middle of the studio floor, preplanning with paper and pencil also permits you to experiment with a number of different lighting approaches without wasting expensive crew and studio time. It is a lot easier to erase a mistake on the lighting plot than to reposition instruments on the lighting grid in the studio.

The lighting plot indicates the position of every instrument that will be used. Some LDs like to use tracing paper superimposed over the floorplan. This permits you to make changes on the lighting plot without obliterating the original floorplan. Others photocopy the floorplan and do preliminary work on a copy. The final lighting plot should be clean and readable and represent the working lighting plan. (See Figure 19-22.)

Studio floorplan sheets usually include the lighting grid superimposed directly on the floorplan. This gives the set designer and program director a good sense of studio size and also permits the LD to position instruments on battens which directly correspond to those in the studio. A plastic template is a convenient way of drawing in the size and type of lighting instruments. If a template is not available, devise a symbol system that indicates fresnels, scoops, strip lights, etc. The important thing is to use the symbols consistently so that the lighting crew, and others involved, will understand what each symbol means. (See Figure 19-23.)

The first step in plotting the lights is to determine which lighting approach to use: the individual performer-and-camera method or the major-area technique. Next, consider which, if any, lights must be motivated. With this information, it becomes relatively easy to locate the horizontal positioning of the lighting instruments. It is more difficult to visualize the distance each instrument should be from the set, since this determines the vertical angle and effective intensity of the instruments. Also, the placement of one instrument could cast unwanted shadows in the light thrown by another instrument. The LD should be thoroughly familiar with the studio, especially the height of the battens, before drawing the lighting plot.

TECH TIP Visualizing the effect of vertical placement of an instrument on the two-dimensional lighting plot is difficult. A good rule of thumb is that an instrument hung on a batten about 12 to 14 feet high should be placed an equal distance from the subject to achieve a 40° vertical angle, and about 16 feet away for a 35° angle.

Since the key lights are the primary lights, locate them first on the lighting plot. Select fill and back light locations that produce the desired lighting ratios and that do not obstruct the keys. After the subject's lighting is completed, place the background lights.

Lighting Inventory The *lighting inventory* contains five columns of information about the instru-

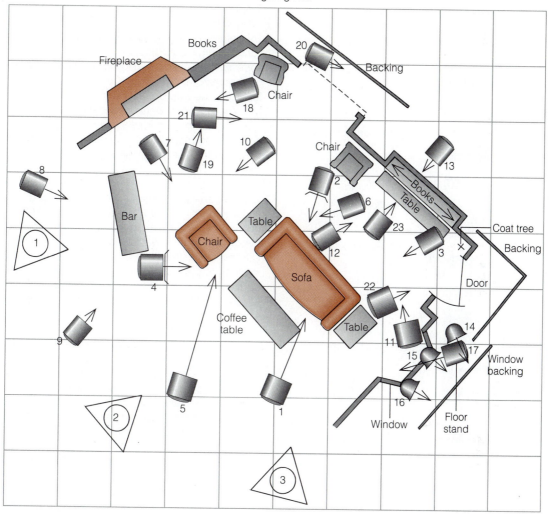

Lighting Plot

FIGURE 19-22 Lighting Plot.
Even though this set is fairly complex, the lighting plot is clear and easy to read. The lighting inventory in Figure 19-24, dimmer sheet in Figure 19-25, and cue sheet in Figure 19-26 accompany this lighting plot.

ments: (1) their numbers, (2) lamp sizes, (3) types, (4) functions, and (5) assigned dimmers. (See Figure 19-24.) The first four columns should be filled in while you design the lighting plot. Later, the dimmer assignments will be added.

As you plot the location of each instrument, place the receptacle number next to it on the light-

ing plot. This now becomes the instrument number. On the lighting inventory, which should be a separate piece of paper, write down the instrument number, and next to it the lamp size required, the type of instrument, and the function it will serve. For example, if instrument #1 is a 2,000-W fresnel that will be used to key light an actor on

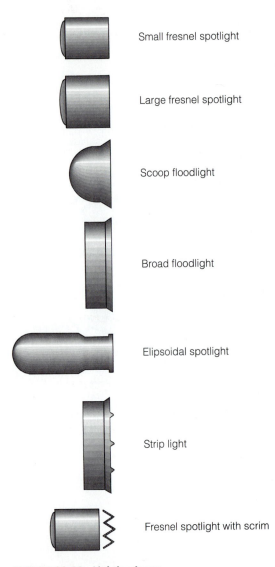

Small fresnel spotlight

Large fresnel spotlight

Scoop floodlight

Broad floodlight

Elipsoidal spotlight

Strip light

Fresnel spotlight with scrim

FIGURE 19-23   Lighting Icons.
Lighting icons are the small drawings that represent the sizes and types of lighting instruments on the lighting plot. The styles of icons will vary. The important thing is that once you decide on a style, be consistent and use it on all your lighting plots.

a sofa, write "#1; 2-kw; fresnel; John's sofa key." The complete lighting inventory list will include every light, its lamp size, its type, and its function. This information is invaluable in locating individual lights during studio setup and rehearsal. Troublesome instruments can be found quickly by looking up the instrument's function on the chart and referring to the appropriate number on the lighting plot. A carefully thought out and executed lighting inventory will pay off in enormous savings in time, energy, and money once you enter the studio to hang and focus the instruments. (See Figure 19-24.)

Dimmer and Cue Sheets   Once the lighting plot is completed, the LD must assign instruments to dimmer circuits. Keeping the number of dimmers available and their wattage capacity in mind, the LD assigns instruments to dimmers, noting each instrument assigned to every circuit by its number on the lighting inventory. Since lighting directors usually could use more dimmers than are available, the trick is to load the dimmers to achieve maximum flexibility.

For example, it is a good idea to assign a number of key lights to one dimmer, since it's rare that key lights are ever dimmed. This leaves more dimmers for back, fill, and background lights, which generally are balanced relative to the key's intensity. If special lighting effects are to be used, these instruments should be isolated on their own dimmer circuits.

The lighting director keeps track of the instruments assigned to each dimmer on a *dimmer sheet*. It should include the following information for each dimmer: (1) its number, (2) its fader control setting, (3) the numbers of the instruments assigned to each dimmer, (4) the functions of the instruments, and (5) the preset scene for each dimmer. (See Figure 19-25.) The dimmer sheets for older lighting control systems may refer to the instrument number as the "patch number," because on them the instruments are patched into the dimmer circuits, rather than being electronically assigned.

Once the LD has completed this dimmer sheet, the last step is to plan the lighting *cue sheet*. This sequences the lighting changes during a production and should specify which dimmers are involved and what the "point" setting or intensity of

INSTRUMENT NUMBER	LAMP SIZE	TYPE	FUNCTION	DIMMER
1	2K	Fresnel	SOFA KEY	1
2	1K	Fresnel	SOFA BACK (left)	2
3	1K	Fresnel	SOFA BACK (right)	2
4	2K w/screen	Fresnel	SOFA FILL	3
5	2K	Fresnel	CHAIR KEY	1
6	1K	Fresnel	CHAIR FILL	4
7	1K	Fresnel	CHAIR BACK	5
8	2K	Fresnel	BAR AREA KEY	1
9	1K	Fresnel	BAR AREA FILL	6
10	1K	Fresnel	BAR AREA BACK	7
11	2K	Fresnel	DOOR ENT. KEY	8
12	1K	Fresnel	BOOK SHELF BG	9
13	1K	Fresnel	REAR SOFA AREA BK	7
14	1500 w/scoop	Scoop	WINDOW BACKING	10
15	↓	Scoop	↓	10
16		Scoop		10
17	2K - on flr stnd	Fresnel	WINDOW LIGHT	11
18	750w	Fresnel	FIREPLACE BG	12
19	750w	Fresnel	SLASH ON F.P./BOOKS	12
20	750w	Fresnel	HALLWAY	13
21	1K	Fresnel	HALLWAY ENT. AREA	13
22	1K	Fresnel	DOORWAY ENT. AREA	14
23	750w	Fresnel	TABLE/BOOK SHLF BG	15

FIGURE 19-24
Lighting Inventory.
The lighting inventory uses the instrument number from the lighting plot to identify each instrument's lamp size, type, function, and dimmer assignment.

each should be. Information from the cue sheet can be transferred to the script to help the lighting operator time the proper light changes. If your lighting system includes memory presets, the cue sheet can be programmed into memory and recalled when needed with a push of a single button. (See Figure 19-26.)

Setup and Rehearsal

Just as the program director must plan the best way to use rehearsal and production time, so too must the lighting designer work out a schedule for rigging and focusing the lights. Compounding the problems of personnel and time limitations, another crew usually will be working on the set at the same time as the lighting crew. The LD should confer with the set designer in advance to coordinate the activities of their respective crews.

Hanging and Focusing the Lights   Using the lighting plot as a guide, the LD instructs the crew where to position each instrument. There are a variety of ways to approach hanging and focusing the instruments. Some LDs like to hang all the instruments in roughly the correct position and then go back and focus each instrument individually. Others prefer to focus each instrument as it is hung, although this slows the overall process considerably. In either case, the key lights should be hung and focused before working with the other set lights. After each instrument has been hung and plugged into the connector, another crew member at the patch panel assigns the instruments to the proper dimmer circuits.

Focusing and Balancing the Lights   Once the instruments are hung and patched, and the necessary scrims and gels are inserted into their car-

DIMMER SHEET

DIMMER #	SETTING	INSTRUMENT NUMBERS	FUNCTION	PRE SETS
1	10	368,305,329	SOFA KEY/CH KEY/BARKEY	
2	8	349,339	SOFA BK (L)/(R)	
3	8	327	SOFA FILL	
4	9½	364	CHAIR FILL	
5	10	315	CHAIR BACK	
6	8	308	BAR FILL	
7	10	313	BAR BK/REAR SOFA	
8	8	374	DOOR KEY	
9	6½	345	BOOK BG	
10	10	354,355,356	WINDOW BACKING	
11	8½	412	WINDOW LIGHT	
12	9	317,325	FIREPLACE BG/BOOK BG	
13	10	311,351	HALLWAY, DOORWAY AREA	
14	7	326	DOOR ENT.	
15	9½	335,338	TABLE/BOOK BG	

FIGURE 19-25 Dimmer Sheet.
The dimmer sheet indicates which instruments are to be patched into which dimmers. The information is used to keep track of instruments during light balancing and for production lighting cues.

FIGURE 19-26 Cue Sheet.
The cue sheet indicates each lighting cue and the dimmer settings involved. The dimmer board operator follows the cue sheet during the production to control the lighting changes.

CUE SHEET

CUE #	DIMMERS	DESCRIPTION
1	1-15@ BALANCED SETTING- NORMAL AS ON DIM PATCH SHEET	DAY
2	1 10/2 9/5 10/7 10/8 5/9 5/11 4/12 9/13 8/14 7/15 9	NIGHT/FULL
3	5 10/7 10/8 8/9 6½/11 4/14 7/15 9	NIGHT-JOHN ALONE
4	1-15 NORMAL- AS ON DIM PATCH SHEET	DAY

riers, the set is ready for the final focusing and balancing. The LD must use a light meter to set the intensities of the key lights for the standard camera operating level. A camera and studio monitor should be in place to check the effect of lighting in the videospace.

Focusing a fresnel begins by spotting the instrument down and concentrating that spot exactly where needed. Then the instrument is tightened into place and can be flooded out to even its light distribution. Barn doors are used to direct the light where needed and to trim unwanted spill. In similar manner, each of the other fresnels in use is focused. Finally, scoops and other secondary instruments are directed toward the desired areas of the set and background.

TECH TIP When focusing lights, never look directly at the instrument. Not only can this practice

severely damage your eyesight, it throws off how you perceive contrast ratios. To focus lights, look at the set and wave your hand in front of the light. This will allow you to pinpoint the hotspot. (See Figure 19-27.)

Once all the instruments have been positioned and focused, it is time to balance the illumination. The most effective way of balancing the lighting is to turn off all the lights and turn them back on one by one. As the lights are turned on in sequence, the lighting effect is "built" and the contribution of each instrument to the total image can be seen. By referring to the TV monitor, the LD adjusts the various dimmers, resetting the point level of each

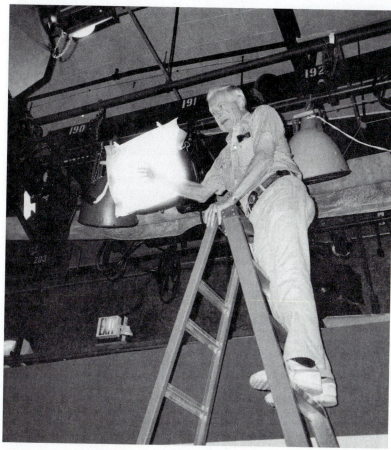

FIGURE 19-27
Aiming the Light.
The lighting designer waves his hand in front of the light and watches the shadow on the set to determine whether the light is aimed properly. (*Courtesy: KGTV-TV.*)

until the final lighting is completed. The dimmer board operator notes the final refinements so the lighting can be brought back up simply by matching dimmer settings to the information on the dimmer sheet.

Camera Rehearsal   Although the lighting may look perfect on a stationary camera, only during actual rehearsal can the LD see how the various camera shots, performers, and lighting interact. This is also when the boom operator and audio technician will be working with their equipment, and any additional problems can be discovered and resolved.

While the director works with the production crew and performers, the LD and the lighting crew will be touching up the lighting to solve whatever problems appear. An actor's hot spot can be solved by inserting a screen into the key light, slightly reducing its intensity. A background light might be dimmed to avoid overprominence of a set piece. Trimming the barn doors may help diminish the boom shadow. Lighting cues are rehearsed to improve timing. When all changes have been made, it is a good idea to take a Polaroid shot of the set to keep with the final lighting plot for future reference.

Production

By the end of camera rehearsal, the lighting should be as close to perfect as possible. During the production, some program directors will have the assistant director cue the light changes. Others will ask the LD to cue all light changes based on the script and actor movement. In those studios where an electronic dimmer board can be set up in the control room, the lighting commands can be received directly from the director or AD. Otherwise, the LD and control board operator are connected to the control room via the production intercom system.

Once the production is completed, the LD and crew must strike the lighting. Screens, scrims, and patterns should be removed and stored where they will not be damaged and can be found for the next production. Color gels that have been damaged should be discarded and replaced with new media.

COMMON LIGHTING SITUATIONS

A number of production situations are encountered frequently at all levels of television production and require fairly standard lighting approaches. This section deals with such situations and offers some ways to approach the lighting. These are offered only as starting points for the development of your own lighting plans. No two production situations are ever exactly the same, and there is never one best way of lighting any program.

News Programs

Most news sets use a desk for the newscaster and some device for incorporating graphics in the picture with the commentator. A commonly used technique for presenting graphics with news is chroma key. In this case, the LD must consider both the newscaster's illumination in the foreground and the proper lighting of the chroma key screen in the background.

First, we light the foreground subject—the newscaster. Since the newscaster invariably is lit for high key and without regard for motivating the key light, we can place the key on either side of the camera. In Figure 19-28, a 2-kw fresnel is located 30° left of the close-up camera and at a 35° vertical angle.

Fill light is handled with a 1-kw fresnel with a scrim to soften and reduce the intensity of the light. As with the key, the fill is equipped with barn doors. This is particularly important to keep spill off the chroma key panel.

The back light also will be a 1-kw fresnel with barn doors. The back light is on a separate dimmer circuit to permit adjusting the intensity depending on the hair color of the different newscasters who appear on the set.

Background lighting must be very even to support the chroma key system. A series of scoops has been equally spaced to provide a smooth wash of illumination across a broad area. The background light level is set approximately one to

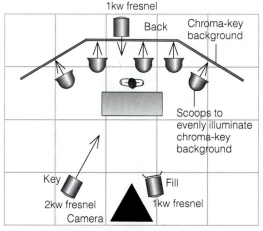

1kw fresnel
Back
Chroma-key background
Scoops to evenly illuminate chroma-key background
Key
2kw fresnel
Camera
Fill
1kw fresnel

Lighting chroma-key news set

FIGURE 19-28 **Lighting Design for a Typical News Set.**
Since the chroma key process requires an evenly lit background, scoops are used to illuminate the background.

two stops lower than talent's key light. This provides separation in both brightness and hue for proper chroma key operation and keeps the viewer's attention focused on the newscaster. (See Figure 19-28.)

Interview Programs

In an interview program, the primary focus is on the participants involved in the discussion. In most situations, each of the participants should be individually lit with key, back, and fill lights. If the format includes a panel of guests, area lighting may be a more practical approach. If area lighting is used, a half-scrim mounted sideways may be needed to keep the guest closest to the area key from being overlit relative to the guest nearer the host.

For the three-person interview illustrated in Figure 19-29, each person is individually lit. We used three 2-kw fresnels for keys, three 1-kw fresnels for back lights, and scoops for fill. Scoops were selected to blend well with the keys and because spill is not of concern here.

The background is a cyclorama, which we have lit blue. We used blue gels fitted over the cyc strips

at both the top of the cyc and along the ground row for even illumination. An ellipsoidal spot with a cucalorus throws a pattern onto the cyc. (See Figure 19-29.)

TECH TIP   When lighting the set for an interview or discussion program, remember to take into account the direction toward which the participants will be facing. Although the chairs may face forward, during conversation, most people face the person to whom they are speaking. If you light the set for the chair positions rather than how the subjects will be facing during the show, your guests may be keyed improperly.

Lighting for Charts and Demonstration Programs

When a program incorporates charts, blackboards, or weather maps, the lighting director must ensure maximum visibility and detail of the graphic. Demonstration programs invariably use close-ups, and the lighting director must consider this factor when planning the lighting.

Often, the best results are obtained by lighting the demonstrator separately from the demonstration area. Performers can be lit with conventional three-point lighting, and the demonstration area (tabletop, stove, floor, or blackboard) can be lit with diffused light from scoops or broads. The diffused light will eliminate many distracting shadows, which might interfere with the audience's view of the demonstration, and also will help to minimize specular reflections from shiny objects on the set such as cooking utensils.

Lighting for a blackboard or chart requires positioning the key light at an angle so that the shadow which is produced by the performer's body and arm will fall away from the board. Figure 19-30 illustrates how to position a key to throw the shadow behind the subject and the camera's area of interest, keeping the board and graphic free from distractions.

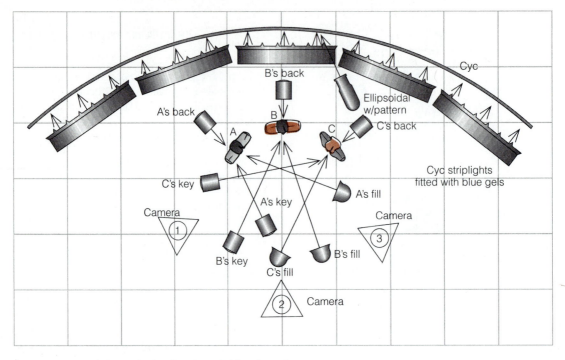

FIGURE 19-29 **Lighting Design for Three-Subject Interview.**
Each subject is lit with a separate key, back, and fill light. Scoops are used for fill, since their diffuse light will lighten shadow areas and because lighting distribution control is not critical. The background cyc is lit with a series of strip lights, which are fitted with blue gels to paint the cyc with color. A pattern is projected on the cyc with an ellipsoidal spot to add visual variety.

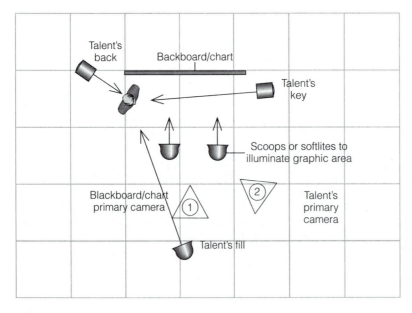

FIGURE 19-30 **Lighting Designs for Subject Using a Blackboard or Chart.**
The key light is positioned so that it will throw its shadow away from the graphic. Scoops are used to illuminate the graphic, since the scoops produce very even illumination which reduces distracting shadows.

Lighting for the Boom Microphone

Lighting for the boom microphone is one of the most difficult assignments facing the lighting designer. Just when a set appears to be lit perfectly for the camera, performers, and background, a boom shadow suddenly appears across the performer's face or against the background set. Unfortunately, there is no instant cure for boom shadow. The placement of the boom, the position of the lighting instruments, the movement of actors and camera, and the dimensions of the set all interact to create the problem.

In trying to deal with boom shadow, it is important to realize that it is almost impossible to eliminate the shadow completely. Turning off the instrument that is causing the problem is seldom an option, since that light was illuminated for some purpose. Washing the background with extreme amounts of light also is not recommended because this will ruin the lighting balance.

The best approach is to position the boom and the key light so that the boom's shadow falls outside the camera's range. Unfortunately, this is not always possible. In such a case, the background onto which the shadow falls perhaps can be darkened. As a last resort, you might consider using

shadow from a complex pattern, such as from branches thrown by a plant on the set, to camouflage the boom's shadow. (See Figure 19-31.)

Lighting for Camera Graphics

The most important consideration in lighting camera graphics or studio cards is to avoid flares or undesirable reflections. The best approach to lighting a camera graphic is to use two fresnels steeply angled toward the graphic. The steep angle directs the reflection toward the floor and away from the camera lens. A good rule of thumb is to place each fresnel about 10 feet from the art card angled at about 45° to the graphic's surface. Use scrims or the dimmer board to balance the graphic's brightness relative to the lighting of other shots taken from the studio set. This eliminates the need for a video technician to reshade the camera as it swings between graphics and the set and frees the director to cut more quickly between cameras if necessary. (See Figure 19-32.)

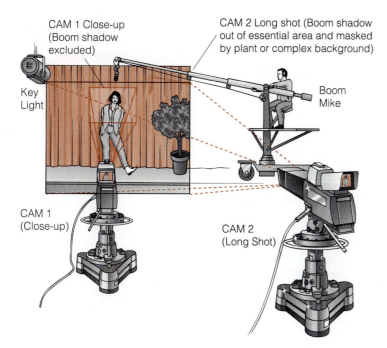

CAM 1 Close-up (Boom shadow excluded)

CAM 2 Long shot (Boom shadow out of essential area and masked by plant or complex background)

Key Light

Boom Mike

CAM 1 (Close-up)

CAM 2 (Long Shot)

FIGURE 19-31
Lighting for Boom Shadows.
The boom is positioned so that its shadow falls on a noncritical area of the scene.

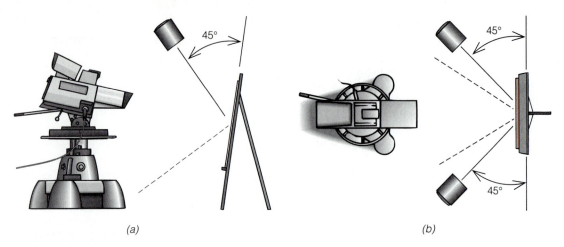

(a)   *(b)*

FIGURE 19-32 Lighting a Camera Card.
When lighting a camera card, the objective is even lighting distribution with no glare. To achieve this objective, two instruments should be positioned at steep vertical (*a*) and horizontal (*b*) angles of at least 45° to the card. In this position, any reflected light, or glare, will fall away from the camera lens. Fresnels should be used because scoops are harder to control and their light can spill over into the set area in smaller studios.

Lighting for Remote Productions

The general principles of remote lighting are the same as for studio lighting. However, lighting for remotes presents a unique set of challenges, since few locations offer the equipment and power facilities found inside the studio and which enable the LD and crew to carefully control illumination. Remote lighting demands vary widely depending on the type of production. Electronic news gath- ering (ENG) generally requires very basic lighting to supplement available light in covering news events. At the other extreme, sophisticated electronic field production (EFP) requires very complex lighting to maintain the desired realism of the remote site.

In Chapter 22 we will discuss the techniques of lighting specifically for ENG, EFP, and multi-camera remote operations.

SUMMARY

Standard television lighting uses the three-point approach—a key, fill, and back light to illuminate a subject. The key light is the principal source of illumination and serves as the reference point against which all other lights are positioned and balanced. Key lights usually are positioned at about a 30 to 45° angle to the side and above the subject. Fresnel instruments almost always are used for key lights. Fill lights, used to lighten shadow areas and blend illumination falling on the subject, are placed on the opposite side of the subject-camera axis from the key. Often, fill lights are lensless instruments with large reflector surfaces. Back lights, which separate foreground from background, usually are fresnels used with barn doors to control light distribution. Side lights, kickers, and eye lights are used for special-purpose applications in television lighting.

Television's multiple-camera approach often requires compromises from the ideals of three-point lighting. In multiple-camera situations, identify the close-up camera and design the light primarily for that shot.

Special lighting can enhance the appearance of a set and provide a special illusion for the audience. Among the most common special-effects lighting is the use of color media to produce colored light. Electronic chroma key, which relies on blue or green light evenly distributed across a background set, has become a commonly used production technique.

Preplanning the lighting is an important factor in successful lighting. During the preproduction conference, the LD will receive a copy of the script and the director's floorplan indicating basic camera and performer positions. The LD superimposes a lighting plot onto the floorplan to indicate each of the instruments and their positions on the lighting grid.

Once in studio, the LD supervises the hanging and focusing of the instruments and the electrical connection and assignment to dimmers and presets and then, using the television monitor, balances the lighting to achieve the desired effects. Dimmers, scrims, screens, and gels are all tools that can be used to modify the light to achieve the necessary objectives.

Using the full complement of tools, the LD should succeed in accentuating depth and texture, establishing the mood and time of day, providing sufficient illumination for the operation of the camera, and supporting the overall program objectives of the director. These goals are met in different ways for different program formats. Some starting points for common situations were presented.

PART SIX

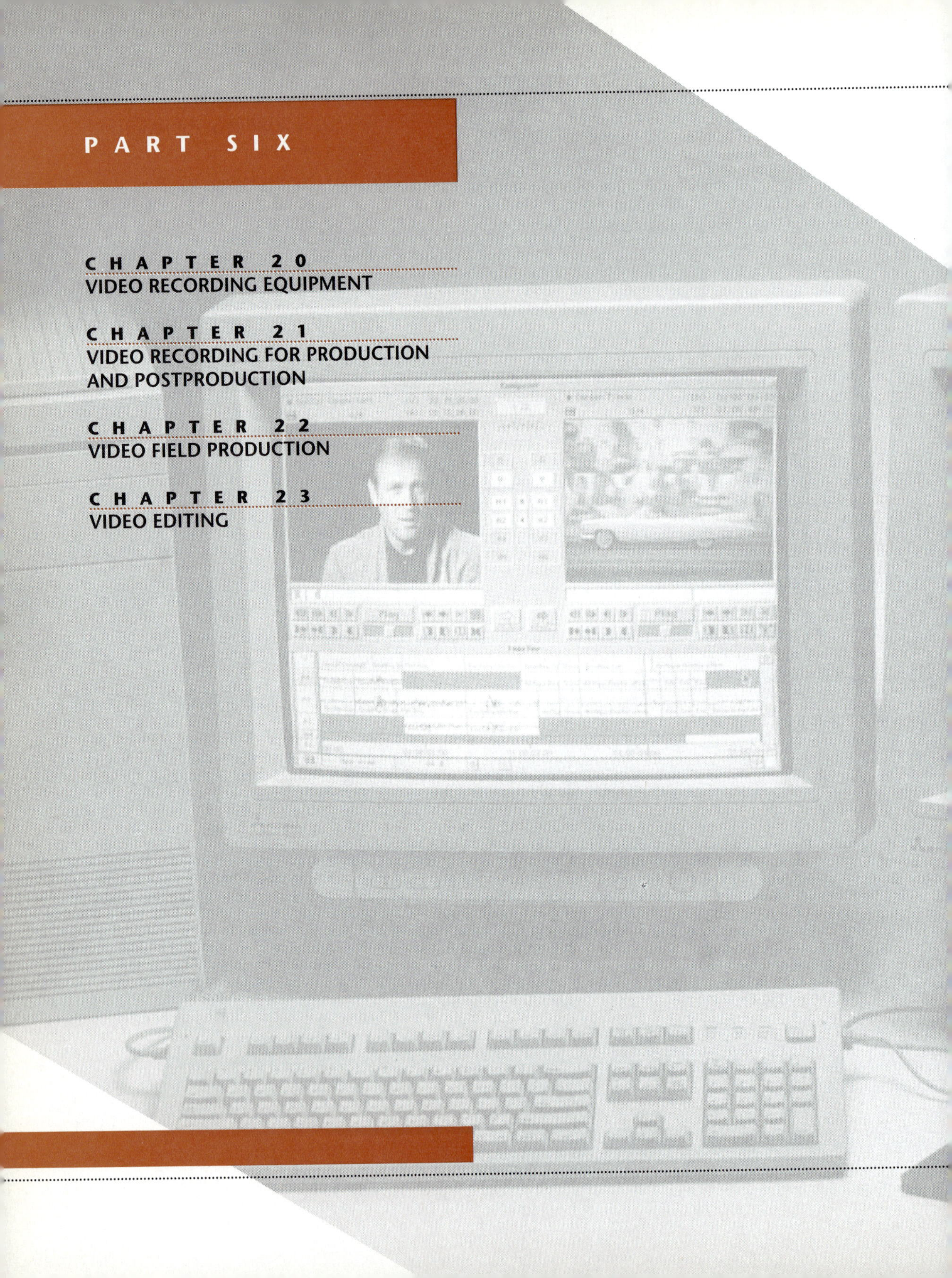

CHAPTER 20
VIDEO RECORDING EQUIPMENT

CHAPTER 21
VIDEO RECORDING FOR PRODUCTION AND POSTPRODUCTION

CHAPTER 22
VIDEO FIELD PRODUCTION

CHAPTER 23
VIDEO EDITING

As millions of California viewers tuned in the *CBS Evening News with Douglas Edwards* on November 30, 1956, few could have realized that they were watching television history being made. While the news of the day in front of the camera was fairly routine, behind the scenes, television took a giant step forward. On that day in 1956, CBS became the first network to use the new electronic videotape recorder (VTR) to delay the nightly news for the western time zone. The VTR recorded the live broadcast on the East Coast and replayed three hours later on the West Coast with quality indistinguishable from the original.

Until the development of the VTR, the only way to delay a live broadcast was to create a *kinescope* by pointing a 16-mm film camera at a television monitor and producing a reel of film. The kinescope process was clumsy and time-consuming because the film had to be developed and dried before it could be broadcast. Worse yet, the fuzzy images it produced left much to be desired. But with videotape, programming could be recorded hours, days, even weeks in advance of air time and replayed with pictures and sound quality identical to a live broadcast.

We take videotape so much for granted now that it is hard to remember a time when broadcasting live, recording a show on kinescope, or producing entirely on motion picture film were the only available production alternatives. Videotape plays such an important role in modern television that it has become a primary production tool, as essential as the camera and microphone. In addition, digital recording on videotape and videodisc formats offers a variety of new production possibilities. In Part Six, we will cover the equipment and techniques of video recording for production and postproduction, with an emphasis on video field production and video editing techniques.

VIDEO RECORDING EQUIPMENT

The basic idea behind video recording is similar to the audio recording process described in Chapter 9. However, the enormous amount of electromagnetic information needed to record and reproduce a television picture requires more complex approaches to the process. A good audiotape recorder must handle a signal with a frequency range between 20 Hz and 20,000 Hz. This is referred to as a *bandwidth* of 20,000 Hz. In contrast, a videotape recorder must process a bandwidth of about 4.2 *million* Hz to produce a color image! (See Figure 20-1.) There are many approaches to recording this large bandwidth on videotape. Each approach represents a compromise among image quality, cost, and the technology available at the time it was introduced. To help you understand the various approaches to video recording, in this chapter we will describe how video recording works and how the various videotape and videodisc formats used in television differ. We also will explain how to operate video recorders and how film is converted to video for use on television.

HOW VIDEOTAPE RECORDING WORKS

At a very basic level, videotape works much like audiotape. As with the audio system, video re-

595

200 times more information is in the video signal than in the audio signal

20 kHz Audio   4.2 MHz Video

FIGURE 20-1   Bandwidths of Audio and Video Recordings.
Videotape is required to carry 4.2 MHz of information as compared to audiotape's 20 kHz of information. This 200-fold increase in information-carrying capacity requires that the video record heads spin rather than remain stationary as with audio recording.

cording operates by storing electronic information on magnetic tape. When the video signal activates the VTR's record head, it creates a series of electromagnetic fields on the moving tape in a specific pattern which corresponds to the original video information. During playback, the tape travels past the video heads, which "read" the previously created patterns on the tape. These tiny signals are amplified by the VTR's internal circuitry and result in a duplicate of the original video signal. This is an *analog* process.

Videotape

As we already have said, the VTR must record an enormous amount of electronic information on the videotape. Therefore, means had to be found that would make it possible for a tape to hold that much

information. Two solutions involved improving the type of tape and increasing the recording speed.

Tape Type   You ought to remember from our discussion about audio that one way to improve the quality of a recording is to use a tape with a better magnetic coating. As with audiotape, videotape is made of a plastic base with a metallic oxide or pure metal coating. There are three main types of videotape used today: (1) high-density oxide, (2) metal particle, and (3) metal evaporated. The metal tapes have better signal-to-noise (S/N) ratios and better high-frequency responses. This means that these videotapes can be made thinner and narrower, and still produce the quality needed for a good television image. Today videotape comes in a number of different sizes, from 8 mm to 2 inches wide. (See Figure 20-2.) All videotapes less than 1-inch wide are housed in plastic cassettes, and you never actually touch the tape when you use them. This has led to calling video recorders that use cassettes *VCRs*, as well as VTRs.

Head-to-Tape Speed   You also should remember from our discussion of audio that another way to improve the quality of a recording is to increase the tape speed. All things being equal, the higher the speed, the better is the overall quality. This explains why, under similar recording conditions, a tape recorded at 15 inches per second (ips) will reproduce sound with better quality than one recorded at 7½ ips.

In order to record and reproduce a satisfactory video signal, engineers have determined that the effective head-to-tape velocity, or "writing speed," would have to exceed 1,000 ips. Using a stationary recording head and rapidly moving tape at about 1,000 ips, you would need almost 500,000 feet of videotape to record just one hour of programming! The solution to this problem was to move the heads as well as the tape, the approach adapted for the R-DAT digital audio recording format. The combination of rapidly rotating video heads and tape traveling past them at a much more practical speed—between 1 and 15 ips, depending on the particular VTR format—produced an effective writing speed that exceeded the minimum necessary for a technically satisfactory picture.

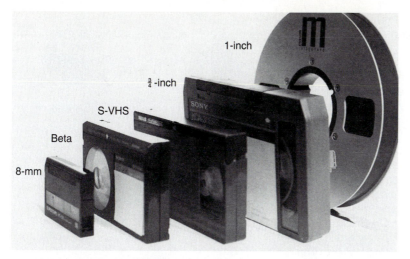

FIGURE 20-2 Videotape Formats.
Videotape comes in a number of different sizes including 2, 1, ¾, and ½ inch and 8 mm. This provides the television industry with great flexibility in meeting the demands of various production situations, but it also increases problems with compatibility across formats.

The first VTRs used in television had four rotating heads to record video *tracks* transversely, or at right angles, to the edges of 2-inch videotape. (See Figure 20-3.) This was called a "quadruplex" head system, and the VTRs became known as "quads." Quads were less than ideal for a number of reasons, such as their high cost, relative inflexibility, and demanding maintenance requirements. In addition, quads were incapable of slow-motion and still-frame operation.

FIGURE 20-3 Quadruplex Videotape Recording.
The original VTR machine which recorded the *CBS Evening News with Douglas Edwards,* the first network program ever to be videotaped, is shown on the left. *(Courtesy: Ampex Corp.)* The VTR had four rotating heads that recorded the video tracks at right angles to the edges of 2-inch videotape. This approach is called "quadruplex" recording.

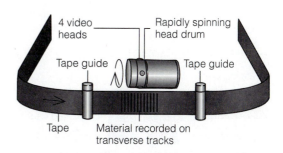

Tape Path All VTRs being manufactured today continue to use the rotating-head approach for recording video information on videotape. However, rather than moving at right angles to the video heads, the tape travels in a path shaped like a helix. Consequently, the recording process is called *helical*, or *slant-track*, recording. (See Figure 20-4.) The tape path is determined by the way the videotape is wrapped around the head drum. Figure 20-5 illustrates the two basic methods used today, called *alpha* and *omega*. On an alpha wrap VTR, the tape is wrapped completely around the head drum and resembles the Greek letter α. The omega wrap resembles the Greek letter Ω. Today all cassette-loading machines use modified omega wraps and two video heads 180° across from each other on the head drum. One-inch Type C VTRs use alpha wraps and only one video head.

Videotape Tracks

In addition to the video information, other information must be recorded on the tape, including audio and synchronization signals. The ability to record "cue" information called *SMPTE time code* offers advantages when it is time for postproduction editing. These four kinds of information are recorded on separate tracks on the videotape. (See Figure 20-6.)

FIGURE 20-4 **Helical Videotape Recording.**
All present-day analog videotape systems use helical recording in which the videotape moves across rapidly spinning video heads in a path shaped like a helix.

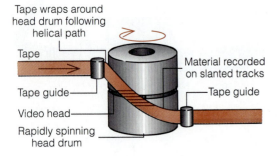

Tape wraps around
head drum following
helical path

Tape

Tape guide

Video head

Rapidly spinning
head drum

Material recorded
on slanted tracks

Tape guide

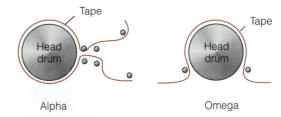

Alpha   Omega

FIGURE 20-5 **Alpha and Omega Helical Tape Wraps.**
In helical recording systems the two methods of wrapping the tape around the head drum are called *alpha* and *omega* wraps. One-inch Type C VTRs use the alpha wrap, and all cassette-loading formats use modified omega wraps. The two formats are incompatible.

Video Track Over three-fourths of the videotape's width is dedicated to recording visual information. In color television, this information consists of *luminance,* which represents the different brightness values of objects in the scene, and *chrominance,* which represents the color of the various objects seen. As we will discuss shortly, this luminance and chrominance information can be recorded in composite or component form. The National Television System Committee (NTSC) format processes 4.2 MHz of visual information.

Audio Tracks Almost all videotape formats provide at least two separate areas for recording audio information. The audio tracks can carry two monophonic audio tracks, stereo audio, or one of the audio tracks can be dedicated to SMPTE time code. Audio tracks carry between 20 to 20 kHz of information each.

TECH TIP Record the most important audio information on audio track 2. In most helical systems, audio track 2 is located on the interior of the tape and is less susceptible to damage done to the edge of the tape. However, an exception is VHS, which has audio track 1 located on the interior of the tape.

Sync (or Control) Track It is imperative that programming recorded on one machine can be played back on, edited on, and transferred to or from other machines. A series of sync pulses are

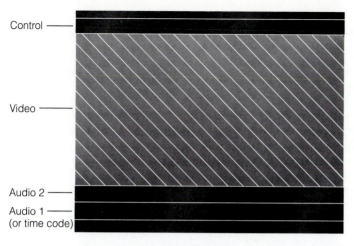

Control ——

Video ——

Audio 2 ——

Audio 1 ——
(or time code)

Composite (³/4-inch)

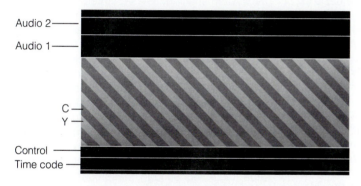

Audio 2 ——

Audio 1 ——

C ——
Y ——

Control ——
Time code ——

Component (Betacam SP, M-II)

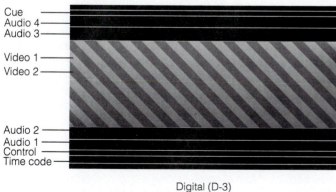

Cue ——
Audio 4 ——
Audio 3 ——

Video 1 ——
Video 2 ——

Audio 2 ——
Audio 1 ——
Control ——
Time code ——

Digital (D-3)

FIGURE 20-6
Videotape Tracks.
Videotape carries four different kinds of information: (1) video, (2) audio, (3) sync, and (4) cue (usually SMPTE time code). Different formats record this information in different ways and locate it at different physical locations on the tape.

recorded on the videotape at exact intervals of one-thirtieth of a second. All VTRs and editors incorporate control-track "readers," so that the playback speed and tension of the tape can be microscopically adjusted to keep the audio and video information passing the record/playback heads at exactly thirty frames per second. Without sync, postproduction editing would be impossible, because there would be no way to precisely coordinate the two or more machines used during the edit process.

Cue Track The cue track carries the SMPTE time code, which allows the unique identification of each frame of video. SMPTE code is the basis for all computer editing systems. It also is used to assist in producing rough cuts of material before going into the edit suite.

TECH TIP SMPTE code often is recorded as *longitudinal time code,* requiring 15 kHz of bandwidth to be recorded continuously on the cue track, which is actually an unused audio track. Besides consuming a valuable audio track, SMPTE code is unavailable in still frame. As a result, another way of recoding SMPTE time code called *vertical interval time code* (VITC) has been developed. VITC is recorded in the vertical blanking interval of the video track and therefore frees an additional audio track and is available for still-frame reviewing of the video. Both systems code frames with the identical SMPTE numbers, so tapes often have both longitudinal and VITC codes for maximum ease of postproduction.

Types of Video Signals

Color video originates as three signals, one for each of the primary colors—red, green, and blue. These are called "RGB" signals. As a group, they are referred to as the *chrominance* signal. In video recording systems, chrominance signals can be handled in one of three ways: (1) they can be kept separate; (2) they can be combined with *luminance*, or brightness, into what are called "composite" signals; and (3) chrominance and lumi-

nance can be carried as independent signals. We briefly covered these three approaches in Chapter 11, and we want to expand on them now because the type of video signal is an important consideration in choosing a video recording format.

RGB In *RGB* systems the three signals are kept separate all the way from their point of generation to their final display on a monitor. All computers produce RGB signals that may be recorded on optical videodiscs, hard disks, or floppy disks. Generally, separate signals are not recorded on videotape for television production.

Composite In *composite* video systems, the three color signals are combined, or *encoded* into one *chrominance* signal, which then is encoded with the *luminance* signal, and they flow through the system until they are separated, or *decoded*, at the color monitor or receiver. This method is the basis for the ways that both NTSC and PAL systems encode color into their signals. The original 2- and 1-inch videotape formats were designed as complete composite systems. In other words, each stage of the production process—generating the signal, passing the signal through a switcher, recording and editing the signal on tape, and playing the final tape—occurred with the video in composite form. Even though the final product was not as good as the original videotape, there was enough "headroom" (more than enough signal quality) to allow for a limited number of multiple generations without creating too many observable problems.

As tape formats became smaller, they traded away some of their resolution and color quality because the tape's reduced surface area did not provide enough magnetic particles to reproduce both high resolution and faithful color. In addition, these smaller tape formats degraded picture quality at each step of the production process. As a result, multiple-generation, small-format (½-inch and 8-mm) video was considered unacceptable for broadcast.

Component To satisfy the needs of small-format, professional videotape production, *component* video at the recording, and later the editing stages, was introduced. Put very simply, component video keeps the three color signals independent throughout the process, but not in the same way as RGB systems. There are two primary methods of recording component video. One method, sometimes referred to as the "true" component video, keeps the luminance signal (designated by the letter "Y") and two chrominance signals (R-Y and B-Y) completely separate. This is called *Y, R-Y, B-Y* component recording. The other method, called *Y/C* (or "color-under") component recording keeps the luminance (Y) signal separate, but combines the chrominance (C) signals. The way the chrominance and luminance signals are kept separate is that they are recorded in different frequency ranges on the videotape. Therefore, they can be processed independently without concern for the interference between chrominance and luminance signals that are compounded in the NTSC composite signal at every step of the production process.

Although the video signal must ultimately be translated back into a composite form for transmission, there are a number of advantages to working with component video in the program production process. The biggest benefits can be seen in video that has gone through multiple generations while being transformed into a final product. With every new generation, the sharpness and color quality of the original composite video is degraded. In component systems, many more generations of the original footage can be made before the quality becomes noticeably inferior.

The introduction of component video into cameras, record decks, and editors has allowed for broadcast-quality, small-format video. These component systems produce high quality video with equipment that weighs less and consumes less power. However, there are some costs to switching to component video. First, single cables must be replaced with multiple cables to carry the separated information. This adds complexity and potential breakdown points to the component system. As important, since every stage of the production process that occurs in component video increases the airable quality of the final product, there is pressure to have component video at the record, edit, and titling stages. However, since so much video continues to be done in the composite form and ultimately must be broadcast as composite video, a station or production house cannot simply trade in their composite editing and record

systems. Instead, they must maintain both systems to provide the necessary production flexibility.

As the ½-inch broadcast standards begin to erode the 1-inch installed equipment base, component video will continue to grow in importance. Interestingly, the growth of component video is raising the profile of the next logical extension, full digital video.

Videotape Formats

Today there are more than a dozen videotape formats being used by consumers, professionals, and a broad middle group which has been called "prosumers." Figure 20-7 lists the most popular formats and some of their key characteristics. All these designs work with the four tracks of information: video, audio, sync, and cue information. However, different formats record and play back this information in different ways on videotapes of different sizes. They also are designed to handle one type of video signal. We will now try to clarify the important differences among the various tape formats.

1-Inch Tape   One-inch tape used in the most sophisticated helical recorders sets the broadcast standard for recording and reproducing video. All 1-inch machines treat the video, audio, and sync information in a *composite* format. In addition to superior image quality, 1-inch machines provide pictures in slow motion, fast motion, and still-frame and offer flexible production and editing capabilities.

One-inch helical machines are available in either of two formats: (1) Type B and (2) Type C. A tape that is recorded in either format can only be played on another machine that uses the identical format.

TYPE B FORMAT   The Type B format uses 1-inch tape threaded in an omega wrap with a segmented recording approach. In this approach, the tape is in contact with two spinning video heads for about 190° of their rotation. In a *segmented*

FIGURE 20-7 Selected Videotape Formats.

	TAPE WIDTH	TAPE TYPE	SIGNAL TYPE	S/N Ratio (dB)		HOR. RES.	RECORD TIMES (MIN./MAX.)
				LUM.	CHROME		
VHS	½	OX	Composite	46	45	240	30/360
8-mm	8-mm	MP	Composite	46	45	260	120/240
Hi-8	8-mm	MP	Y/C	47	46	400	30/120
S-VHS	½	OX	Y/C	47	46	400	120/360
¾-Inch	¾	OX	Composite	46	46	280	10/60
¾ SP	¾	MP	Composite	47	48	340	10/60
Betacam	½	OX	Y,R-Y,B-Y	48	50	300	10/90
Betacam SP	½	MP	Y,R-Y,B-Y	51	53	344	10/90
M-II	½	ME	Y,R-Y,B-Y	52	50	344	20/90
1-Inch Type C	1	OX	Composite	52	52	360	30/90
D-1	¾	MP	Y,R-Y,B-Y	*	*	460	12/94
D-2	¾	MP	Composite	*	*	450	6/208
D-3	½	MP	Composite	*	*	450	34/208

*Not relevant in digital format.

scanning machine, the two video heads write the information sequentially on the tape so that each video frame is divided, or segmented, into a series of two packages of video lines. Although there are some exceptions, for the most part, the Type B format has become the standard in those countries using 625-line systems. (See Figure 20-8.) Type C is the most commonly used format in the 525-line countries, including the United States.

TYPE C FORMAT The Type C format uses 1-inch tape threaded in an alpha wrap and a nonsegmented recording approach, or "continuous field" format, using a single head. The primary advantage of the nonsegmented format is that each complete video field is written on every head scan of the tape. This permits accurate slow motion and freeze-framing. In addition, the single head does not need the elaborate switching circuitry necessary for the two-head segmented format, and some picture imperfections associated with multihead recording, such as "banding," are eliminated with the continuous-field approach.

Like Type B machines, Type-C VTRs are available in both studio and portable configurations. Sony and Ampex are two major manufacturers currently producing 1-inch production VTRs utilizing this format. (See Figure 20-9.)

¾-Inch Formats There are two ¾-inch formats: the original ¾-Umatic and newer ¾-SP. Available in remote and studio configurations, the ¾-inch format VCRs continue to be widely used, although the Betacam SP format has become the ENG/EFP standard, and many facilities are moving to ½-inch, 1-inch, and digital systems for studio production and postproduction.

The editing capabilities of the ¾-inch machines offer such features as high-speed search with a visible picture at up to forty times normal speed in forward or reverse, as well as conventional jogging, shuttle, and freeze-frame operations. (See Figure 20-10.)

½-Inch Formats In spite of the large number of existing ¾-inch machines, ½-inch videotape formats are rapidly replacing the ¾-inch formats.

FIGURE 20-8 Type B 1-inch VTR.
Type B 1-inch tape decks have become the standard in those countries which use a 625-line video system, such as most European countries. *(Courtesy: BTS Broadcast Systems, Inc.)*

There are two simple reasons for this: (1) the ½-inch machines are lighter and use less expensive tape, and (2) in its most sophisticated form, the ½-inch format can deliver quality that rivals, and in some ways surpasses, the 1-inch format.

VHS Originally designed for in-home use, where it remains the dominant format, the standard VHS format has been upgraded for industrial and broadcast production use as well. The most com-

mon use for the standard VHS format at this point is in primary production work at nonbroadcast industrial facilities and for use as a workprint for off-line screening and editing at more sophisticated production facilities. The major limitation of standard VHS is that by the third generation of dubbing the image quality and color reproduction have been noticeably degraded.

S-VHS S-VHS has evolved from standard VHS tape. Its most significant advantage is that it offers over 400 lines of horizontal resolution compared to standard VHS's 250 lines of resolution. Its other main advantage is that as a component video standard it can survive multiple dubbings without being degraded to an unacceptable level of resolution or color aberration. S-VHS features stereo audio with Dolby-C noise reduction.

One important feature of S-VHS is that it is "upward compatible" with standard VHS tape. This means that standard VHS tape, so dominant in the home market, can be played back on S-VHS equipment. However, this does not mean that standard VHS will appear with the resolution and color quality of material originally recorded in S-VHS. It is also worth pointing out that an S-VHS monitor is needed to derive the full benefits of viewing tapes created on S-VHS systems.

M-II M-II is a broadcast-quality tape system. Like Betacam SP, M-II is a component system that is significantly lighter and more flexible than ¾-inch, although it uses more expensive tape. As post-production suites continue to introduce ½-inch editing systems, both Betacam and M-II should proliferate.

M-II systems provide stereo audio capabilities with Dolby-C noise-reduction systems.

TECH TIP Introduced in 1976, Betamax (along with VHS) created the home video market. Unfortunately for Betamax, it lost the marketplace battle, and by the early 1990s had gone the way of other extinct videotape formats. Do not confuse Betamax with Beta*cam*, which is alive and doing extremely well.

FIGURE 20-9 Type C 1-inch VTR.
Type C 1-inch tape decks are most common in countries following the NTSC
format. Type C systems offer excellent slow motion and freeze-framing. *(Courtesy: Ampex Corp.)*

BETACAM SP This ½-inch format has rapidly evolved into the accepted professional standard and currently controls more market share than its major ½-inch competitor, M-II. Betacam SP proc-

FIGURE 20-10 ¾-inch Videocassette Recorder.
Videocassette recorders using ¾-inch tape are very popular for ENG and corporate video applications. Many cable television systems also operate on the ¾-inch format. *(Courtesy: JVC Company of America.)*

esses video in the component format, which is partly responsible for its outstanding color and resolution. Originally introduced as simply "Betacam," the "SP" was added to indicate the "Superior Performance" of the new model. The main improvements are that Betacam SP records video on a wider bandwidth, uses a higher-quality metal particle tape, and delivers high-fidelity stereo sound. Betacams were used early for remote work, such as sports and news, which benefited greatly from the small size of the integrated camera and recorder. Now, some studio work is being done in Betacam SP because it is less expensive than 1-inch Type C. (See Figure 20-11.)

8-mm Formats The smallest VCR format utilizes 8-mm (about ⅓-inch) tape inside a cassette about the size of an analog audiocassette. Because it is the smallest format, the 8-mm VCR can be utilized in an integrated camera/recorder unit that is exceptionally lightweight.

8-MM The 8-mm format was used initially in con-

FIGURE 20-11 Dockable Camera/Recorder System.
A *dockable* camera is designed to mate with various VTR formats. This dockable, Hitachi's *Z-One-B*, normally is combined with a Betacam SP VTR (as shown), but adapters are available so it may be used with M-II, S-VHS, and Hi-8 VTRs. *(Courtesy: Hitachi Denshi America, Ltd.)*

sumer camcorders marketed by Kodak in the mid-1980s. Although the camcorder did not produce professional quality video, the tape itself was made of high-quality metal particle and metal evaporated coatings. The tape had the capability to record such good video signals that it soon was adapted to other formats.

HI-8 Sony introduced the Hi-8 format in 1989. It had been developed as a "prosumer" product—one that the consumer could use as a home video recorder and the professional could use as an *acquisition format* (that is, as a format in which original footage would be shot, but not processed or edited). Sony expected that Hi-8 video would be "bumped up" to Betacam or 1-inch for editing. To assist the editing process, Sony had even built Hi-8 time code into its Y/C recording system. It did not take long for manufacturers to recognize the potential of the new format. Soon, fully professional Hi-8 camera/recorders appeared with CCD cameras, digital audio systems, and other professional features. (See Figure 20-12.) Although Betacam SP remains the camera of choice for EFP and ENG, Hi-8 has begun to make its presence felt, and even to rival S-VHS as a cost-effective

alternative to the more expensive Betacam SP format.

All the formats we have described so far record information on the videotape as analog signals. There also are formats that record the information as digital signals.

DIGITAL VIDEO

Digitizing video is accomplished using a process similar to that described in Chapter 7 for digitizing audio. Basically, the waveform of the analog signal is sampled many times per second (at twice the bandwidth) and each sample has a digital code assigned to it. Each new generation of digital video is created by regenerating video from the digital code rather than by copying the analog signal. As a result, errors are recorrected with every generation rather than being multiplied, as is the case for analog systems. Since digital video can be reproduced countless numbers of times, it is amenable to very complex editing procedures that require multiple generations of recording and

FIGURE 20-12 Hi-8 Camera/Recorder.
Professional Hi-8 camera/recorders are lightweight and extremely portable, making them valuable for EFP and ENG production. This camera/recorder, Toshiba's *TSC-200*, also has genlock capability and multiformat signal outputs, which means that it could be integrated into a studio system. *(Courtesy: Toshiba America Consumer Products, Inc.)*

rerecording. In addition, digital video signals can be processed directly by computers and digital video effects (DVE) units during postproduction. Chapter 23 presents an extended discussion of digital video in the postproduction process.

Before we discuss digital recording formats, we want to cover one digital technique, without which analog videotape could not be used in television production with the flexibility that it has today. That technique is time-base correction.

FIGURE 20-13   Time-base Correctors.
These stabilize the videotape output, cleaning up picture jitter, skew, and color breakup. The TBC is very important for synchronizing the output of many different video sources fed to a switcher or for bumping up small-format video to 1-inch for subsequent postproduction. *(Courtesy: Ampex Corp.)*

Time-Base Correction

An unsung hero in the saga of helical videotape recording is the digital technology known as *time-base correction.* Even the most expensive and technically sophisticated VTR cannot move the tape past the video heads at an absolutely precise and constant speed. Variations are to be expected in any mechanical system. In audio recording, these variations are known as *wow* and *flutter.* In video recording, the variations are called *time-base errors.* A time-base error shows up on-screen as picture jitter, "skewing," or color breakup. Digital time-base correctors, which appeared in the early 1970s, provided the correction capability necessary for helical recording.

If a time-base corrector (TBC) is used, any helical machine can produce pictures that meet the most stringent technical specifications for direct on-air broadcast or for up-dubbing to more sophisticated helical ¾-inch or 1-inch machines for editing and playback. The TBC works by converting the nonstandard output of the helical VTR into a numerical digital code which corresponds to the various picture elements in the original signal. Once the video signal has been coded, it is processed, and errors are corrected before it is reconverted to a conventional signal at the TBC output. (See Figure 20-13.)

Time-base correctors also permit ¾-inch or ½-inch program material to be integrated with sequences that were recorded in the studio on 1-inch VTRs. Frequently, a remote sequence will be recorded in the field using a ¾-inch VCR. Back

in the studio, the material is fed through the TBC and recorded in 1-inch. This is called a *bump-up* because we transfer material from a lower quality recorder to one of higher quality. By "bumping up," the director can record on the less expensive and more portable machines and then transfer the raw footage to 1-inch format without significant loss of picture quality for subsequent postproduction editing and integration with studio-recorded material.

Needless to say, a TBC cannot take a video signal from a $2,000 cassette recorder and produce a picture that rivals that of a top-quality helical 1-inch, but the TBC does permit pictures from a cassette recorder to be used on-line and enables 1-inch production VTRs to replay broadcast-quality pictures in slow motion and still-frame. It also permits the nonsynchronous signal from an inexpensive VTR to be fed into the program switcher and used along with an array of special electronic effects such as wipes, dissolves, and keys.

You may have noticed that a television program, often live sports, seems to momentarily freeze-up and then jump ever so slightly forward in the action. This is caused by a multiframe time-base corrector locking on a usable frame of video and reproducing that frame over and over again until another correctable video frame passes through the TBC. Without the TBC, the video would totally lose sync and appear as an unacceptably scrambled video image.

Tape Formats

There are three main digital videotape formats in use today: D-1, D-2, and D-3. (See Figure 20-14.)

D-1   The D-1 digital format records Y, R-Y, B-Y component signals on metal particle ¾-inch videotape and primarily is used in postproduction. The resolution and signal-to-noise ratio of D-1 signals exceed 1-inch Type C and Betacam SP, and they hold up extremely well after many generations. However, you pay for this exceptional quality, as D-1 VCRs are the most expensive on the market.

D-2   The D-2 digital format uses its own type of ¾-inch metal particle videotape, and records composite signals. Therefore, the D-2 processing circuitry is not as complex as that of D-1. Although the quality of D-2 doesn't quite match D-1, it still exceeds 1-inch Type C and Betacam SP.

D-3   The D-3 digital format uses ½-inch metal particle videotape, and records composite signals. To do this, four rotating heads record the video information, which is equal to that of D-2. In addition, four channels of digital audio can be recorded. Since D-3 VCRs use ½-inch videotape, they are lighter and more field-portable than either of the other digital formats.

Disc Formats

Before digital videotape formats existed, digital video signals were already being recorded on

FIGURE 20-14   **Digital VTR.**
The D-3 format VTR uses ½-inch videotape, which makes it lighter and more field-portable than the D-1 or D-2 digital formats, both of which use ¾-inch videotape. *(Courtesy: Panasonic Broadcast and Television Systems Company.)*

FIGURE 20-15   **Real Time Disk (RTD) Recorder.**
The RTD recorder can store digital video on a hard disk that can be accessed instantly and reproduced for use in 3D graphics, animation, and paint systems. *(Courtesy: Accom, Inc.)*

videodiscs. The first videodiscs available were "read-only," which meant that you could play what was recorded on them, but you could not erase or rerecord on the discs. Today there are two types of "rewritable," or recordable, disc formats: (1) the optical videodisc and (2) the computer disk.

Optical Videodisc   Optical videodisc recorders use laser light to record and reproduce video, audio, and synchronization signals on a flat platter. No video head physically comes into contact with the disc, which means that signals can be recorded and rerecorded many times with no deterioration of the disc. Some rewritable videodiscs are able to contain about thirty minutes of motion video or more than 57,000 still frames. Each can be randomly accessed almost instantaneously, which has advantages for use in nonlinear video editing. Videodisc recorders are able to be incorporated into RGB, composite, or component systems.

Computer Disk   The magnetic computer disk may be thought of as a data storage medium. However, once a video signal is digitized, it also can be recorded on a computer disk, as we discussed in Chapter 11. This is how the computer graphics systems work that we discussed in Chapter 16. A number of *real time disk (RTD)* recorders are on the market. (See Figure 20-15.) They are particularly useful when combined with computer-assisted editors. Recorded images can be accessed instantly, and played back at speeds as much as 100 times below or above the normal play speed. The major disadvantage of recording digital video on computer disks is that very large disk capacities are needed. While the typical RTD recorder has a capacity of only about thirty seconds, RTD units can be "chained" to increase the maximum record time to about thirty minutes.

Electronic Still Store (ESS) Systems

There is one other digital video-recording system used in television production—*electronic still store (ESS) systems.* Unlike tape systems, ESS uses a flat magnetic disk—similar to those used by data processing computers—to store and retrieve video information. The disk consists of a series of concentric circles, called *frames.* Each frame can hold a single image.

A still store system is designed to replace the use of slides and camera graphics by storing hundreds of individual images (you might think of them as individual video "slides") in its memory. Each individual image is assigned a code number and is accessible immediately at the push of a button. (See Figure 20-16.)

The still store system offers many advantages. First, as a video medium, the still store images can be recorded just before they are used so they are up-to-date. They cannot be misplaced, lost, or scratched. Nor do you need multiple copies of the same slide for different studios. For those programs where a great many still images are necessary—such as news programs, election returns, sports events, and so on—the still store disk system can hold hundreds of images, any of which can be put on the air in less than a second. The rapid access of individual frames enables the still store device also to be used to create an animation effect by playing back individual frames in a preprogrammed sequence to create the illusion of a moving image.

OPERATING THE VIDEOTAPE RECORDER

There are four operations areas that you should be familiar with: (1) inputs/outputs, (2) connectors, (3) controls, and (4) meters.

Inputs/Outputs

Whenever you use a VTR you will be using it with another piece of video equipment. Therefore, you need to know the functions of the input and output jacks on the VTR, so you can connect your equipment properly. Figure 20-17 shows a representative VTR connection area. The "line" receptacles carry separate audio and video signals to and from the video system or another VTR. Some VTRs have a "video dub" or "S-video" receptacle to use when you make dubs. Dub and S-video modes allow direct component-to-component (Y/C) transferring. The "camera" and "mic" inputs are used when you are recording directly. There also may

FIGURE 20-16   Electronic Still Store (ESS) System. ESS systems can hold hundreds of electronic "slide frames" that can be randomly accessed almost instantaneously. The ESS system shown here, called *FlashFile,* displays the stored frames in "video contact sheets" on the screen. *(Courtesy: Pinnacle Systems.)*

FIGURE 20-17   VTR Input/Output Jacks.

be a "line/camera" switch that you must set properly. On home VCRs, the "RF IN" jack is used to record the sound and picture from a television channel, and the "RF OUT" jack is used to play a videotape on a television channel.

TECH TIP "RF" stands for *radio frequency*. An RF signal combines the audio and video, then superimposes, or *modulates*, it on a frequency that can be tuned in on a television channel. VHS and other small-format VCRs have RF inputs and outputs in order to record broadcast programs off air and replay them at a later time.

Connectors

The four common video connector plugs are shown in Figure 20-18. (Audio connector plugs are shown in Figure 8-4.) BNC and S-VHS plugs are used for video line feeds; the F-type plug is used with RF cables; and the "RCA" phono plug is used with both audio and video on consumer equipment. Because many different pieces of

FIGURE 20-18 Video Connector Plugs.
BNC and S-VHS plugs are used for video line feeds. The F-type plug is used with RF cables. The "RCA" phono-type plug is used with both audio and video.

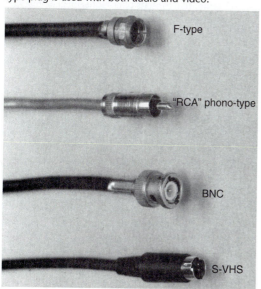

F-type

"RCA" phono-type

BNC

S-VHS

equipment will be connected in video systems, *adapters* are common. Adapters make it possible to connect equipment with dissimilar jacks, such as a BNC jack and an RCA jack. To feed several inputs from one output, it is best to use a video distribution amplifier (DA), monitor loop-through, or buffered outputs. Avoid using splitters for video because they will damage video levels.

Controls

Like the controls on audiotape recorders, the controls on VTRs should be labeled and their functions fairly obvious. Common controls you should know include record, play, pause, fast forward, rewind, and stop. Many VTRs also will have fast-forward and fast-rewind *search* controls. Two other controls are to correct "tracking" and "skewing" errors. (See Figure 20-19.) *Tracking* error appears as thin, white, horizontal lines in the picture. They result when the playback heads are not spinning exactly in the video tracks. *Skewing* error makes the top part of the picture wave back and forth like a flag. In fact, this error sometimes is called "flagging." It results when the tape is not wrapped around the head drum with the proper amount of tension. Both tracking and skewing are playback, not recording, errors. They do not indicate that anything is wrong with the recording on the tape, just that the playback needs to be adjusted.

Meters

VTRs have audio VU meters and video level meters to help you adjust recording levels. (See Figure 20-20.) However, most VTRs also have automatic gain controls for video and audio. Therefore, during field productions the meter you probably will refer to more frequently is the battery-status indicator! Another important indicator is the "warning light," which may indicate that there is a tape transport problem. You will need to keep your eye out for these possible problems that could destroy a taping session.

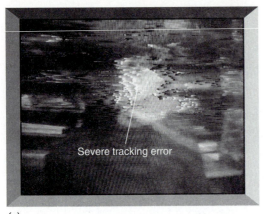
(a)

(b)

FIGURE 20-19 Tracking and Skewing Errors.
Tracking and skewing are playback, not recording, errors. (a) Tracking errors result
when the video playback heads are not spinning exactly in the prerecorded video
tracks. (b) Skewing, or flagging, errors result when the tension of the tape wrapped
around the head drum is improper. To correct either error, rotate the proper control
clockwise or counterclockwise until the picture clears up.

FIGURE 20-20 VTR Meters and Indicators.

FILM FOR TELEVISION

The flexibility, efficiency, and quality of video recording has virtually eliminated motion picture film
as a primary production vehicle for television.
However, there are still circumstances where film
is used for distribution of program material and it's
important for you to be familiar with the basic film
formats and how to utilize film within a television
production.

FIGURE 20-21 Film Formats.
As with videotape, film comes in different formats. In
general, larger film formats offer higher-quality images.

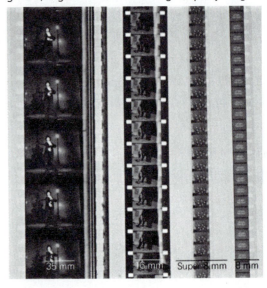

610

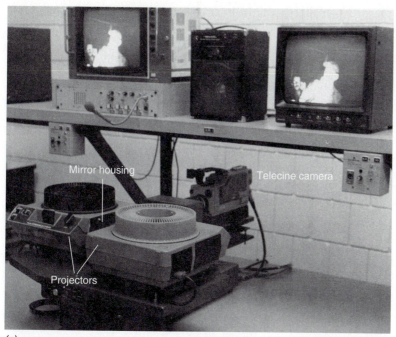

(a)

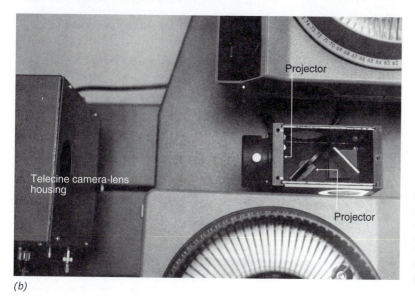

Telecine camera-lens
housing

Projector

(b)

FIGURE 20-22 Film Chain.
(a) The film chain converts
slide material to video.
(b) A mirror allows a single
"telecine" camera to
reproduce images from either
projector.

Film Formats

As with videotape, film comes in various sizes ranging from 8 mm to 70 mm in width. (See Figure 20-21.) The standard professional film format you are most likely to see is 16-mm film, which is used for distributing programming and commercials. Network-level production facilities will occasionally utilize 35-mm prints, which is the theatrical movie standard, but this equipment (and the cost of 35-mm prints) is extremely expensive and you are unlikely to come across it except under very special circumstances.

Film-to-Video Transfer

Motion picture film may be used in television production in three ways. It may be (1) incorporated as it is into a television program through a film chain; (2) transferred to videotape for inserting into a program; or (3) transferred to videotape for editing in postproduction.

A *film chain* consists of a film projector, a slide projector, a multiplexer, and a "telecine" camera. (See Figure 20-22). The film and slide projectors are the program sources. The telecine camera reproduces the film at the television rate of thirty frames per second by a scan conversion process. This does not change the speed of the motion on the screen, but does eliminate any flicker in the image. The light shining through the film stock is directed to the multiplexer, which is a mirror assembly. Depending on which way the mirror is facing, images from the film projector or the slide projector are bounced into the lens of the television camera. Just as if it were looking at a live scene, the television camera converts the light from the film or slide projector into an electronic signal that can be incorporated into the television program or sent out directly over the air.

In spite of the high quality of visuals produced on film stock, film is becoming increasingly scarce in television production studios for three reasons: First, since the advent of EFP and ENG virtually all local production is now shot on videotape. Second, most film programs and commercials are being distributed via satellite to local stations, which put them on videotape for airing later. Third, most original film for television is being transferred to video for postproduction work.

The typical film-to-video transfer process is

FIGURE 20-23 Telecine Machine.
Film-to-video transfers or original film usually are done on a telecine machine that converts the negative film to a positive image and transfers it to a broadcast quality videotape. *(Courtesy: Rank Cintel, Ltd.)*

done at a postproduction house on a *telecine machine*, usually a Rank-Cintel. (See Figure 20-23.) The film negative is converted to a positive image and transferred to a broadcast quality videotape. The tape may be any of the high-end formats, such as 1-inch Type C, D-2, or D-3, depending on what the producer wants. During the transfer process, color corrections can be made so there will be no color shifts when different scenes are edited together. The original audio, usually from an analog recorder, is dubbed to a digital format, and time code is added. Then, the audio and video are synchronized on the videotape, and the editing process can proceed. We will examine that process in Chapter 23.

SUMMARY

The videotape recorder (VTR) is a primary production tool used to (1) record programming for later replay; (2) slow down and freeze the action for instant replays and analysis; (3) incorporate previously recorded material into a production; and (4) edit a show, combining the best takes into a final edited master.

An enormous amount of electromagnetic information must be recorded on videotape to reproduce a television program. This requires (1) high quality tape and (2) a very fast head-writing speed. The three main types of videotape used today have (1) high-density oxide, (2) metal particle, or (3) metal evaporated coatings, in 2-, 1-, ¾-, ½-inch, or 8-mm widths.

The first VTRs, called quadruplex recorders, had four rotating heads to record video tracks at right angles to the edges of 2-inch videotape. All VTRs used today have rotating heads and helical, or slant-track, tape paths, which are determined by the way the videotape is wrapped around the head drum. The two basic wraps used today are *alpha* and *omega*.

Time-base correction makes it possible to incorporate helical videotapes into video productions. Two of the important and unique advantages of the helical format are its slow-motion and freeze-frame abilities.

Four kinds of information are recorded on separate tracks on videotape: (1) video, (2) audio, (3) synchronization, and (4) cue information. The approaches to recording color images on videotape depend on the way the luminance and chrominance signals are handled. The three methods are (1) RGB, (2) composite, and (3) component. Two leading component systems are called (1) *Y, R-Y, B-Y* and (2) Y/C.

Today there are more than a dozen videotape formats. Analog formats include: 1-inch Type B; 1-inch Type C; ¾-inch U-Matic; ¾-inch SP; VHS; S-VHS; M-II; Betacam SP; 8-mm; and Hi-8. Digital formats include : D-1, D-2, and D-3. There also are two types of recordable disc formats: (1) the optical videodisc and (2) the computer disk. The electronic still store (ESS) system holds hundreds of images, or electronic "slides," in its memory, each of which is instantly accessible at the push of a button.

When you operate a VTR, you should be familiar with: (1) inputs/outputs, (2) connectors, (3) controls, and (4) meters.

In spite of the high quality of visuals produced on film stock, film is becoming increasingly scarce in television. If you have the need to incorporate film into a television program, it can be done by using a film chain. A film chain consists of a film projector, a slide projector, a multiplexer, and a "telecine" camera. Today film usually is transferred to video for postproduction and editing. The typical film-to-video transfer process is done at a postproduction house on a *telecine machine*.

CHAPTER 21

VIDEO RECORDING FOR PRODUCTION AND POSTPRODUCTION

Video recording offers a wide range of enormously creative and versatile production possibilities. As with any production tool, however, it is effective only if you have carefully planned for its use. Just as the artist selects a particular paint, brush, and canvas in order to achieve a specific purpose, so too must the television producer and director select the right video recording technique for a particular production requirement.

In this chapter we will discuss the different videotape production techniques which are available to you and explain when, how, and why to use them effectively in a variety of production situations.

VIDEOTAPE PRODUCTION MODES

Once you have decided to produce your show on videotape, you must determine which videotape production mode you will use to record the show. There are four different techniques available: (1) live on tape, (2) recording in segments, (3) recording with single camera/recorder, and (4) recording with multiple cameras/multiple VTRs. Each approach has its share of advantages and disadvantages, and your decision to use a particular method or a combination of techniques will depend on the type of show you are producing, the available production and editing facilities, and the size of your production budget. Refer to Figure 21-1 as we discuss these various recording approaches.

Live on Tape

Recording a program *live on tape* means that you are, for all intents and purposes, producing a live show using multiple cameras and switching be-

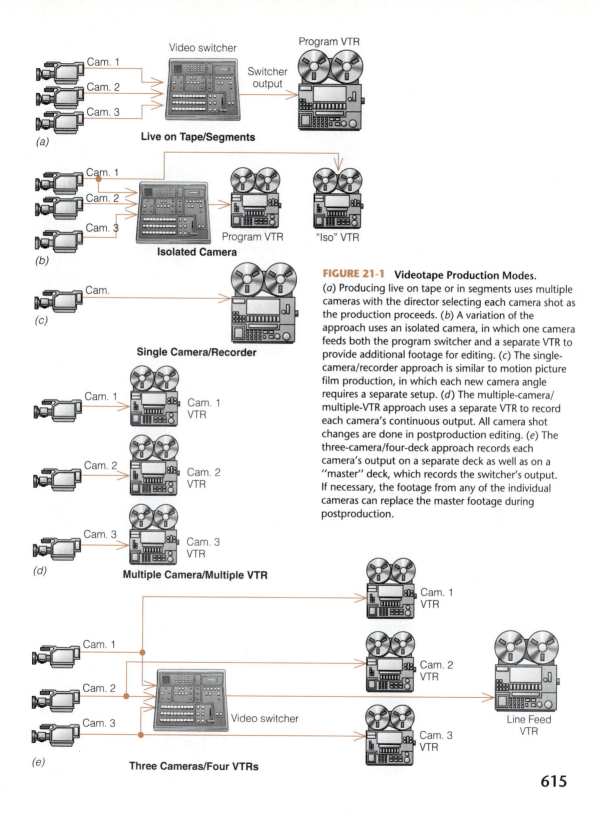

Live on Tape/Segments

(a)

Isolated Camera

(b)

Single Camera/Recorder

(c)

Multiple Camera/Multiple VTR

(d)

Three Cameras/Four VTRs

(e)

FIGURE 21-1 **Videotape Production Modes.**
(a) Producing live on tape or in segments uses multiple cameras with the director selecting each camera shot as the production proceeds. (b) A variation of the approach uses an isolated camera, in which one camera feeds both the program switcher and a separate VTR to provide additional footage for editing. (c) The single-camera/recorder approach is similar to motion picture film production, in which each new camera angle requires a separate setup. (d) The multiple-camera/multiple-VTR approach uses a separate VTR to record each camera's continuous output. All camera shot changes are done in postproduction editing. (e) The three-camera/four-deck approach records each camera's output on a separate deck as well as on a "master" deck, which records the switcher's output. If necessary, the footage from any of the individual cameras can replace the master footage during postproduction.

615

tween them from the control booth as the show proceeds. The only difference between a truly live show and a live-on-tape program is that instead of broadcasting the program as it is produced, the show is recorded on videotape for delayed broadcast. There is usually little, if any, postproduction editing on a live-on-tape show. The entire program is produced straight through, and only the most serious performance or production errors are edited after the taping is completed.

When to Use Live-on-Tape Approach   Consider the following factors in deciding whether or not to produce your show live on tape:

1   *Does the program need postproduction editing?* An interview show, for example, needs no real postproduction editing, and the flow of a live program provides the continuity necessary for an interesting and effective interview. Shooting such a program in short segments with constant starts and stops would destroy the interaction between participants. Of course, you might decide to let the interview run overtime and edit it later, cutting out irrelevant or uninteresting parts.
2   *Can the program be produced easily without editing?* Some programs are produced just as easily without postproduction editing. A game show, for example, as well as some other routine format shows, such as a daytime "home" show or some demonstration/how-to programs, usually can be produced straight through without any need for later editing.
3   *Do you have the facilities, time, and budget necessary for postproduction editing?* Editing costs money, requires available editing facilities, and takes time, delaying the production's final completion date.
4   *Is time shifting necessary?* Some programs that benefit from retaining the "live" feel are scheduled to appear at inconvenient hours for actual production. For example, The *Tonight Show with Jay Leno* airs at 11:30 P.M., although it is produced live on tape earlier in the evening for the convenience of the moderator and guests.

Recording in Segments

Recording a program in segments combines the advantages of multiple-camera production with the flexibility and creative control of postproduction editing. If this approach is used, the entire program is broken down into relatively short scenes or segments. Each segment is recorded by multiple cameras, and the director switches between them from the control room, as with any conventional program. During postproduction, the segments are edited and assembled into the composite program.

The advantage of the segment approach is that it lets you break down a large, complex production into smaller individual segments which are much easier to deal with one at a time. Since both performers and production crew concentrate on only a small piece of the larger program, they can devote their full attention to the particular segment being rehearsed and taped. Once the scene is approved by the director, everyone can turn to the next segment without concern for those sections which are already "in the can." In this way, a one-hour program becomes a series of shorter "acts," each of which is rehearsed, polished, and videotaped before the next segment is produced.

Another advantage is that scenes, or segments, can be recorded out of sequence for the convenience of the production. For instance, say you are producing a one-hour drama that begins with a courtroom scene and winds up at the end of the show on the same courtroom set. If you were broadcasting live or recording live on tape, the entire set would have to remain standing and lit so that you could use it at the end of the show. However, if you record the program in segments, you can record all the scenes involving the large courtroom set and the extras who must appear as spectators at the same time. Once all the courtroom scenes are recorded, the extras can be released and the set can be taken down to make room for other sets needed in the production. In the same way, if your program has the host and hostess open and close the show on the same set, recording both the opening and closing at the same time eliminates the need to reset and light the same area twice.

The segment approach also lets you tape many segments on one day which can be used later on a number of different shows. The long-running

PBS children's series *Sesame Street,* uses the segment approach to optimum advantage. For example, on one day the production unit may shoot a series of segments involving animals and a trainer from the local zoo. These segments are recorded, logged, and filed away where they are available for a month's worth of programs without the need to arrange for the animals to be brought to the studio on a more frequent basis. You can shoot all a program's introductions and closes on one day, all the puppet sequences the next day, and so on. Actually, the production unit never really produces an entire show from start to finish in one day. Instead, segments are continually shot—according to the program's scripts, which are written in advance—and each broadcast program is a composite of different segments assembled in postproduction.

Recording in segments can be a very efficient production approach, provided you have planned the taping sessions carefully. You must be sure that you have developed a shooting schedule well in advance and that the sequence of scenes or segments is arranged to take maximum advantage of your facilities and talent. And, of course, you must be certain that all the necessary segments have been recorded and transitions planned for later editing. It is most embarrassing to learn after you have completed production, that you forgot to record a particular segment!

Isolated (Iso) Camera   An ingenious variation on the segment approach is to use one or more of the multiple cameras as an *isolated (iso) camera.* The concept was borrowed from sports production, where it was developed to provide the viewer with another angle of the action for instant replay. Any of the cameras can be isolated, or assigned to its own VTR, while the director uses the remaining camera or cameras to cover the play. In a nonsports production, the iso camera is used in much the same way. The signal from a studio camera is split so that it feeds both the program switcher and an independent VTR, which continuously records whatever the iso camera photographs. The particular camera assigned to iso can be changed by the switcher during the program. In this way, the director cuts the show normally by switching between all the available studio cameras, while another VTR independently records the output of the designated iso camera at the same time.

The isolated technique is frequently used in situation comedy or musical programs, where its additional footage comes in handy during the postproduction editing session. It also can be used as insurance to make certain that the most important element of a program is on tape regardless of how the director cuts the show from the control booth. For example, on an interview program, the camera trained on the guest can be designated the iso camera. Regardless of how the director cuts the show from the booth, there will always be extra footage of the guest in case a camera cut is missed or to provide additional material for reaction shots. Similarly, in producing an industrial demonstration program, the camera covering the demonstration in close-up can be isolated to ensure that additional footage will be available should postproduction editing be necessary.

When to Use the Segment Approach

1   *Does the program lend itself to taping in segments?* Some shows are simply better produced straight through than in segments. Many others lend themselves more readily to the segment approach, particularly shows that do not require the continuity and flow of a complete performance from start to finish. For example, the PBS series *This Old House* works well being shot in segments because as the host moves from room to room of the remodeled home, there are natural transitions and places to start and stop the tape. If the program will not be hurt by constant starts and stops, and if segment taping is more efficient, it should be the production choice.

2   *Would it be more convenient to produce the show in segments?* The horror stories from the days of live television about performers racing across the set, changing their costumes, and just making (or missing) their next cues are no longer applicable when you tape in segments. In addition, your studio may not be large enough to accommodate all the sets you will need at the same time. Finally, it may be less expensive to produce in segments, particularly if you will need a large number of perform-

ers, extras, or musicians for only a part of the production. If you recorded the show in its on-air sequence, all the performers would have to be on hand constantly, even for those parts of the show where they were not needed. Taping in segments permits you to schedule performers only when they are actually necessary; this is a more efficient and economical use of rehearsal and production time.

Recording with Single Camera/Recorder

Unlike the two videotape techniques just discussed, which use the conventional multiple-camera approach, the single camera/recorder method is closer to film production than to most television production. This method is commonly used for electronic news gathering (ENG) and electronic field production (EFP), but it has many other production applications as well.

In this approach, a single video camera is used to shoot the entire program, shot-by-shot. Every camera shot is an individual setup with its own precisely planned lighting, audio, camera angle, and performer blocking. Since the production is concerned only with one shot at a time, the director and cast can concentrate on a specific part of the show, sometimes only a line or an actor's reaction. At the same time, the technical crew can tailor the lighting, audio, and camera movement for each individual shot without compromising, which is often necessary in multiple-camera production.

Of course, shooting a scene many times with a single camera takes longer than shooting a scene once with multiple cameras. The precision it provides both the production crew and the performers, however, makes it a very valuable technique when the situation warrants it. The production method in video is identical to the shooting technique used for motion picture film except that an electronic camera/recorder is used in place of a film camera. An obvious advantage over film is that the director, cast, and crew can immediately replay every recorded take to ensure that it is okay before proceeding to the next setup. Most field

productions are shot with this approach, since it simplifies the personnel and equipment necessary when using multiple cameras operating out of a large remote van. The single camera/recorder can be carried in a stationwagon or minivan. The smaller vehicle is unobtrusive—particularly when compared with a remote van—easy to maneuver and park, and its equipment can be unloaded, set up, broken down, and loaded back into the van or wagon in minutes, enabling the unit to shoot at a number of different locations on the same day.

Because every shot is a separate setup, each transition from shot to shot on the final master must be made with a video edit. This makes the postproduction phase quite involved. At the same time, however, complete postproduction editing brings to television the same creative control and precision once available only with film.

In order to use the single-camera technique, you must first break down the entire shooting script into small scenes and then further into individual shots or setups. You juggle the shots into the most efficient shooting sequence, which is to be followed by the director and production crew during taping.

Generally, a scene is taken first with a *master shot*. The master shot is a fairly wide angle shot that contains all the main action. The same scene must be replayed later while the camera is repositioned to shoot from a new angle, concentrating on smaller elements such as close-ups, reaction shots, and so on. Of course, if you are certain that a scene will require only one shot or setup, then the master shot is unnecessary.

Shooting shot-by-shot means you must be very conscious of *continuity*. The details in camera and actor movement, position, and the placement of sets and props must all be kept in their proper order to show the viewer a logical sequence of events once the individual shots are edited together. In other words, a cigarette should not miraculously get longer from an earlier shot to a later shot or appear first in one hand and then in another, nor should an actor be looking toward the right in one shot and toward the left in the next.

Video Pad   Whenever you are taping for editing—either in segments or with a single camera/recorder—be sure to record a *video pad* at the start and end of each take. The pad is simply an overlap of the action, which will give you more edit room during postproduction. You may find that the particular edit point you had planned to use looks wrong after you have previewed the edit. If you overlapped the action, you can use the video pad to locate a better edit point. Overlapping the action also helps performers gain the momentum necessary to reach the proper intensity level to match their preceding performance.

When to Use the Single-Camera Approach

1 *Does the production require the additional precision in setup and editing which the single-camera approach can offer?* Such productions as commercials, technical demonstrations or training tapes, and musical, dance, or dramatic shows often call for the maximum in production control. If you are working with special effects, where the proper camera position is essential to developing the most effective use of the videospace, the single-camera method is a good choice. On the other hand, the spontaneity that is automatically achieved when shooting with multiple cameras is lost in the single-camera method because each scene must be repeated for every camera angle.

2 *Is the single-camera approach more appropriate than multiple-camera methods?* Sometimes simple productions are more suited to the multiple-camera approach than to the single-camera method, particularly if you are in the studio, where multiple cameras are easily available and there are enough to cover the action. Remember that it is usually faster to shoot a scene or segment once with a number of cameras than to shoot the same scene a number of times with one camera. Also, some productions cannot be carefully controlled, started, and stopped on cue to accommodate each camera setup. Certainly a sports event is one example of a program that generally requires multiple cameras in order to be covered effectively. However, the single-camera technique requires less equipment and personnel than does the multicamera method. This added flexibility can be particularly important on remote productions. This is one reason so many commercials, documentaries, and even dramatic shows are shot with a single camera on location.

Recording with Multiple Camera/Multiple VTRs

The fourth production approach combines the flexibility and efficiency of multiple-camera shooting with the precision and accuracy of the single-camera/recorder method. Using the multiple-camera/multiple-VTR approach, you use two or more cameras on the production, but instead of feeding all the cameras into the program switcher, where each shot is selected by the director during production, each camera is connected to its own VTR. Just as with the isolated technique, each VTR continuously records everything its camera photographs. The result is simultaneous footage of the same scene from a variety of camera angles.

The approach was originally developed for film by Desi Arnaz when he and his wife, Lucille Ball, were planning the classic *I Love Lucy* series. Prior to that series, all filmed comedies were shot with a single camera and without a studio audience. The performers and director had to estimate how much time to leave between jokes for an audience "reaction," which was artificially added later as a laugh track. Arnaz and Ball wanted to film before a live audience to help the performers deliver their lines and gauge their timing to a real audience's reaction. The three-camera technique Arnaz pioneered is still used today for film-produced comedy shows and has been widely adapted for electronic recording as well.

The technique works like this: The director blocks out performer moves and camera shots as in any conventional production. During taping, the performance proceeds straight through, and each camera continuously sets up and shoots its pre-planned shots from positions marked on tape on the studio floor. Since the master-shot camera records continuously, the short period of time during which the other cameras are relocating is always covered. Usually the production is divided into acts, and each act is shot in its entirety, unless a set change is required.

Once the shooting is over, the director and editor use the footage from each camera/VTR to assemble the show. Their edit decisions are made in a comparatively pressure-free environment, which permits experimentation and improvement rather than "on the fly" decisions from the control booth during the actual production.

The advantages are obvious. The performers can develop and build their characters through an entire act without the starts and stops necessary with single camera production. The live audience is indispensable in guiding the performers' delivery and timing, yet the director and editor need not worry about editing the show until the production is completed. The disadvantage is the need for an elaborate postproduction editing process which can be both expensive and time consuming.

The production demands of videotaping soap operas on a daily basis have led to the development of another multiple-camera/multiple-VTR approach. During taping, the video from each camera is split, with one feed going to a switcher and the other going directly to an individual record deck. During taping, the director switches the show as she or he would do on any live-on-tape production. At the end of the taping, the tape from each of the cameras is synchronized with the tape recorded from the output of the switcher, called the *line feed*. If the director wants to change a shot that appeared in the line feed, it is a relatively easy task to replace the video with the footage shot by one of the other cameras. This technique saves considerable time when compared to the process of building an entire show scene-by-scene in postproduction.

Although three cameras are the usual complement for most multiple-camera/multiple-VTR productions, any number of camera/VTR systems can be used, depending on the production requirements. For example, on location, a difficult stunt or special effect might be recorded with four camera/VTR systems to ensure that the difficult-to-repeat stunt will be captured on tape from a variety of angles.

When to Use the Multiple-Camera/ Multiple-VTR Approach

1   *Do you need to cover continuous action while maintaining the capability for precision post-production editing?* Many comedy and music shows are vastly improved when performers can work in real time before an actual audience. The interaction of actor and audience can often spark a great performance, but this means that the musical number or play must run straight through with a minimum of interruptions. If your production will benefit from this continuity, the multiple-camera/multiple-VTR approach is a good choice, particularly if you will require careful editing later in post-production.

2   *Do you have the necessary technical facilities?* While the technical preparations are neither exotic nor expensive, the technique does require as many independent VTR machines as there are cameras. This may cause a scheduling problem at those facilities where the number of VTR machines is limited. In addition, your postproduction editing will be rather involved and expensive. Unless you have adequate editing facilities available and the time and money necessary to undertake the editing, you might think about an alternative technique that will require less sophisticated editing equipment and less postproduction time.

Combining Videotape Production Approaches

Although we have had to talk about each production approach individually, you should not get the idea that only one technique can be used on any show. In fact, you might find that a combination of two or more approaches is best for your production situation. For example, say you are shooting an instructional show which involves mostly interior scenes with a few location segments. You might decide to shoot all the interior studio scenes with the segment approach and the location scenes with the single-camera/recorder method.

The point is that every show presents its own unique set of production problems. Your choice of production technique should favor the one that will give you the best combination of creative control and production efficiency.

USING VIDEOTAPE IN PRODUCTION

Unlike some other production areas such as audio or lighting, where a single individual is usually responsible for the planning and execution, videotape and video recording involve a large number

TITLE: *"MASKS"*
PROD# *88-17*
DIRECTOR *YAHAGI*

DAY, DATE AND TIME	SCENE, SETUPS AND DESCRIPTION	D/N IN/EX	LOCATION AND CAST	SET PIECES/ EQUIPMENT
FRI. 6/11 8:30 AM	SCENE #3-DUEL	D/EX	HARMAN PARK JIM, PAUL, GEOFF, CLIFF	REFLECTORS/ HMI
11 AM	SCENE #26- LOVER'S GOODBYE	D/EX	HARMAN PARK JIM, MARLENE	
NOON- 1 PM	LUNCH			
1 PM	SCENE #8- PARLOR TALK	D/IN	MANSION JIM, PAUL	PARLOR PROPS #2 LIGHTS: RE: PLOT #2
4 PM	STRIKE SET			

FIGURE 21-2 **Shooting Schedule.**
A shooting schedule is used to organize the production. It should include the
location, the set, camera setups, and the talent who will appear in each scene.

of television team members. The producer and director must determine the basic production approach, the tape editor must understand how the program will be edited, and the production staff must prepare for the use of videotape. Although the actual recording and editing of a show takes place during the production and postproduction stages, the planning and preparation for the most effective use of videotape begins long before that, during the earliest stages of preproduction, and continues throughout every phase of the production process.

Preproduction Planning

As the program concept is developed and the script is prepared, the director and producer must make a number of important production decisions involving the use of videotape.

Determine the Videotape Production Approach

The first decision you must make is which production approach or combination of approaches you wish to use. The decision should be based on the various points just discussed, including the type of production, the level of precision editing re-

quired, the production budget, the technical facilities capability that you have, and the amount of production and postproduction time available. This decision should be included as part of the program treatment, since it influences so many of the other production decisions.

Shooting Schedule The shooting schedule is used to organize the sequence of taping during your production time. If you are shooting live on tape, the shooting schedule will be the same as the program's operational schedule and rundown sheet. If you will be shooting in segments or with a single camera, you must carefully develop a shooting schedule that will take into account each camera setup, the location, the set, the performers who are necessary, and the order or sequence in which you want to record them. (See Figure 21-2.)

SCENE BREAKDOWN SHEET A scene breakdown sheet is a handy way to organize the thousands of details you need to keep track of when planning your shooting schedule. On the one shown in Figure 21-3, there is a place to indicate scene and shot numbers, performers, sets, props, miscellaneous items involved in the shot, and any other

BREAKDOWN SHEET

SHEET NO. _1_

PROD NO. _6_   TITLE _THE SPREE_

LOCATION _WESTWOOD_

DAY NITE	EXT INT	NO. PAGES	SCENE NO.	DESCRIPTION	NO.	CAST	LINES	COSTUME NO.
D	I	1	1	SHOPPING SCENE		CARL	Y	1
						MARY	Y	2
						BILL	Y	1

Shot No.	1, 2, 6

SET PIECES	ATMOSPHERE	EQUIP.
PACKAGES KEY CHAIN	FESTIVE, "BUSTLING"	BETACAM FISHPOLE LIGHT PACK A

CARS LIVE STOCK	SPECIAL EFFECTS	
NONE	NONE	

FIGURE 21-3
Breakdown Sheet.
The breakdown sheet organizes all shots, talent, and props for every scene. The producer and director use breakdown sheets to plan the most efficient shooting schedule.

necessary information. Particularly if you are shooting in segments or out of sequence, organizing your script into different scenes and using the scene breakdown sheets will help to eliminate confusion and errors in production.

Some producers and directors like to write each scene and shot on a separate index card and spread the cards out on a large table or on the floor. They then shuffle the cards around in different orders to find the most efficient shooting sequence. An alternate approach is to use a self-indexing word-processing program. The word-processing software can sort each scene into shooting groups by any predetermined text item, such as an actor's name or set location. Regardless of how you develop your shooting schedule, be sure to include all the scenes and shots and to estimate the amount of production time for each as accurately as possible.

TECH TIP The benefit of self-indexing word-processing programs for creating shooting groups is that the script can be automatically reordered for distribution to the cast and crew based on the sorting program. Also, the computer-based system is not likely to overlook peripheral scenes in which an actor may have only a single line or a nonspeaking part.

VTR Scheduling Facilities You will have to be certain that someone on the production staff has scheduled VTR facilities prior to your production date. You must estimate the amount of taping time you will need, any playback facilities necessary, and the amount of recording tape you want on hand for the production. Most facilities like to record a production simultaneously on two VTRs: one serves as the master copy; the second as a protection copy in the event there are technical problems with the master recording. If you are using a protection VTR, be sure to double your tape estimate. Finally, remember to schedule the expensive and high-demand recording and playback facilities only for the times you will actually need them. You do not need recording VTRs during your camera blocking and rehearsal period, for example, so be sure to schedule them only during those times when they will actually be used.

Take Sheets   Take sheets are indispensable in production and postproduction because they identify each cut on the video recording, its running time, and whether or not it is usable footage. Prior to the production, a series of take sheets should be prepared, and a production staff member should be assigned to keeping track of all recording information on the take sheets. One copy of the take sheet should be kept in the VTR reel box, and another should be placed in the program script file. (See Figure 21-4.)

SMPTE Time Code   If you will be using SMPTE

time code, you must decide whether to use the counter to reflect *time of day,* which is the actual clock time, or *zero time,* in which the counter is started at zero at the beginning of every tape reel.

Time of day is convenient when you are recording an event in normal time, such as sports or news, where the actual time of day is used to index the action for later editing. Zero time is most useful when you are recording material that has no relation to clock time, but you want to control the time-code numbers for indexing and logging purposes. To enable you to distinguish between time-coded scenes that were recorded on different cassettes, have the hour number correspond to the tape reel number, so that 01 would mean cassette number 1, 02 would mean cassette number 2, and so on.

If you will be using time code, your take sheet should include the start and stop time code numbers for each cut. This will simplify locating the different cuts during playback and editing.

FIGURE 21-4   Take Sheet.
The take sheet numbers the takes for each scene and includes times and comments. The take sheet is especially valuable during postproduction.

TAKE SHEET

PRODUCTION TITLE *"BIOLOGY"*   VTR REEL # *60-108*

PRODUCTION NUMBER *5-32*   VTR DATE *JAN 29*

"Good" takes circled   Running time of program material   For reference during editing   Approximate starting time for each take (if using, time code)

SCENE/SHOT	TAKE	GOOD	NG	TIME	NOTES	Hr	Min	Sec	Fr	
7-A	1		X	:18	CAM OUT OF FOCUS	00	02	20	10	
	2		X	1:35	GLARE ON DEMO CLOSE-UP	00	04	15	18	
	③	X	X	1:45	ENDS ON WIDE SHOT		07	15	20	
12	①	X		2:10			10	55	25	
25	1		X	1:25	POSSIBLE CU FOR INSERT		14	15	00	
	②	X		2:38			18	30	15	

TECH TIP   Even if SMPTE time code is not available, mark each tape sheet with the VTR's footage or time counter. This simple logging system saves a great deal of time in postproduction.

Videotape Playback into the Show   Often you will need to "roll in," or play back, previously recorded tape segments into the show you are producing. To be certain that the right cut appears at the right time, prepare a cue sheet for the VTR operator which identifies each cut on the insert playback reel and its proper sequence in the show. Every segment on the reel should have been recorded with an identification slate. Using your cue sheet, the VTR operator can match the slate information with the cue sheet. This means that even if the segments are not in order on the insert reel, they will appear in the correct order during the show. Checking both the cue sheet and the ID slate will eliminate such errors as cuing the wrong take or cut, particularly on commercials or news clips, which often look alike without the slate and cue sheet information.

Setup and Rehearsal

During the studio setup, as the final touches are made before rehearsal, the VTR record and playback machines should be readied for use. If you are using a VTR to play back an insert into the show, be sure that the assistant director, director, or production assistant has gone over the playback instructions with the VTR operator to elimi-

nate confusion between the control booth and the VTR room.

The VTR room also should play back a test segment to the production control room to make certain that picture and sound levels are feeding properly. At the same time, the control room should send the recording VTR color bars and audio test tone through the switcher and audio-control console to check for outgoing levels and technical quality. It is better to learn about an incorrectly patched audio line or video problems at this stage than during production.

Production

Since the production process will vary somewhat from show to show depending on the kind of production and the production techniques being used, it is difficult to give you a single account of how the production process works. However, we can discuss a number of important functions which are standard to all recording sessions regardless of the production or production technique. These include preparing video leader, playing back recorded material into a show, and some of the common problems that can develop during a taping session.

Video Leader   Video leader contains all the technical and program information necessary to properly align the VTR machine and to identify the program or cut. The video leader includes color bars, audio test tone, identification slate, and in some instances, program-cuing information. (See Figure 21-5.)

COLOR BARS AND TEST TONE   Most VTR operators like to have at least one minute of color bars and

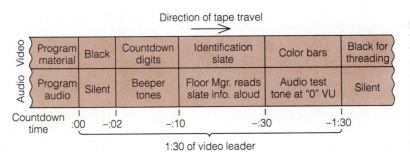

FIGURE 21-5

Videotape Leader. The tape leader should include (in order) color bars, the slate, and countdown digits prior to the programming. Note the use of black and the recommended times for each segment of the leader.

audio test tone recorded at 0 VU at the top of the tape for playback alignment purposes. The tone and "bars" should be fed through the control room switcher and audio console just before actual recording.

SLATE A visual identification slate is a must whenever you make a recording. Take sheets or box labels can be lost or mixed up, but the proper slate, recorded on the tape, is a reliable safeguard against playing back the wrong take or having a false start. The slate should contain the following information: (1) the name of the program, (2) the segment or series name and production number, (3) the recording date, (4) the air date (if known), (5) scene and take numbers, (6) director's name, and (7) any special instructions. Most production facilities use an erasable slate, and it is the floor manager's responsibility to make certain that the correct information appears on it before each recording. If you have a character generator (CG) available, you can use the CG to create the slate information electronically and leave the floor manager free to concentrate on the activities on the studio floor.

The slate is recorded immediately after the color bars and tone. To be sure that the slate is kept on screen long enough to be read, it is a good idea to have the floor manager read the slate aloud into an open mike. The aural information recorded is a double check for the VTR operator when the tape is cued for playback or editing. (See Figure 21-6.)

TECH TIP Multiple takes of a single shot often look identical, except many of them are flawed toward the middle or end of the shot. Flaws noted during taping often are missed on later playback if not previously identified. The slate is essential for flagging errors and avoiding delays in postproduction.

Program-Cuing Techniques In order to play back a videotape into an existing program precisely or to begin a program playback on time, some method of accurately cuing the tape is necessary. A common visual cue is to use electronic countdown digits. These are numbers that appear on the screen in one-second intervals from 10 to 2 seconds. At the same time that each digit appears, a 400-Hz tone—sometimes called a "beeper"—is automatically triggered and recorded on the sound track. The final two seconds are left blank and without audio to prevent accidental airing of the cue leader. Before a scene is recorded, the director calls for the digits and beepers which are recorded on the tape. Precisely at zero, the director cues talent and the segment begins.

Figure 21-7 shows the various operations that

must be done before recording a program or segments. The time column shows the approximate time before the segment begins, the video and audio columns show what is happening in each of the respective areas, and the command column shows the directions given by the program's director or assistant director in the control booth and what is heard, via the talk-back system, from the VTR room. The last column describes what is happening and why.

Remember that the cues are only as accurate as the director is in starting the program's audio and video precisely on time. If the director starts the show sooner or later than the zero mark, the cuing system will be off, and this can result in a miscue during playback.

Stop-Start Recording If you are recording in segments or with a single camera, you will naturally be stopping and starting the tape each time you begin a new take. In this case, it is very important for the take sheet and ID slate to have corresponding information. Make sure that whoever is filling out the take sheet reminds the floor manager to change the ID slate at the start of each new scene or take.

FIGURE 21-7 **Videotape Recording Procedure.**
Notice that the tape must come up to speed before the action and continue several seconds past the action to provide video pads for postproduction editing.

TIME TO START SHOW OR SEGMENT	VIDEO	AUDIO	COMMANDS	RESULTS
−2:00	Black	None	DIR: "Roll tape and record." VTR: "Tape is rolling and recording."	Instructs VTR operator to start VTR recording. Machines are recording sound and picture.
−1:30	Color Bars	0-db tone	DIR: "Bars and tone."	Color bars and audio tone are recording for approx. one min.
−0:30	Slate	FM reads slate into open mike	DIR: "Take slate."	Slate is recording as FM reads information aloud into open mike.
−0:10	Cuing Digits	Beepers	DIR: "Start digits and beepers."	Visual and audio cuing information is recorded just before program material begins.
−0:02	Black	None	DIR: "Black and ready to fade up on——. Ready to cue talent."	Two seconds of black are recorded as a safety pad to prevent cue markers from inadvertently appearing on air.
0:00	Fade in	Audio Up	DIR: "Open mike. Cue talent. Fade in—"	Segment or program begins.
At end of show or segment	Fade to black	None	DIR/AD: "Ready to stop tape . . . stop tape."	Tape is run in black for a few seconds as a safety pad. VTR should be stopped on command, and VTR operator spot-checks and OKs recording before cast and crew are released.

To make locating different cuts easier, particularly if you are not using time code numbers, have the audio technician add a tone, or "beeper," right after the floor manager reads the slate aloud. During fast forward or rewind, the tone makes a distinctive sound. By counting the number of tones, you can determine how many cuts you are into the tape.

Once you have recorded a take you *think* is usable, you may want to view it to be *sure* that it is usable before going on. Often actors and crew can improve their performance by watching the playback. However, beware of the danger of spending too much valuable studio time viewing playbacks and running out of production time at the end of the day.

TECH TIP In start-stop recording, remember to start rolling the tape at least ten seconds before taping begins and keep it rolling ten seconds after the scene has concluded even if visual continuity is not a concern. This roll-in/roll-out time is needed by the editors for synchronization in postproduction.

If you have enough tape stock available, most directors would encourage you to tape everything except the first few rehearsals. Even though the scene may not look ready, you might get that perfect performance or an unexpected shot that is a one-time occurrence. If you have it on tape, you can use it later in editing; but if it was never recorded, it is lost forever. There are some risks in extensive taping, however. Sometimes actors and crew adopt the attitude, "If I make a mistake, so what? We'll just take it again." This sort of approach can result in sloppy technical production and poor performances. Also, too many retakes can drain the cast and crew, resulting in a recorded performance that is worse than you achieved in earlier rehearsals. It is important for the director and producer to be aware of these problems and to weigh the value of taking the scene "just one more time" against the fatigue and carelessness that may result when you have honed the cast and crew past the fine edge to a dull and lifeless performance.

CONTINUITY Recording a show in segments, particularly if you are taping out of sequence,

means that you must be particularly careful about continuity problems. Costumes, props, actor positions, and set pieces must be constant so that there is a natural progression when the different shots or segments are finally edited into the composite program. Even small details which were unnoticed during the production can be ultimately distracting to the audience.

Usually the production assistant assigned the job of supervising continuity keeps a careful record of the dress and costumes, props, sets, and actor and camera positions for each shot or setup. Some production units use inexpensive Polaroid cameras to make a snapshot of each scene for continuity reference.

Completing the Recording Once you have completed recording a program or segment, go to black and continue recording for an additional fifteen or twenty seconds. This black pad serves as a safety cushion in the event the program switcher does not cut to another video source immediately after the tape playback material is finished. Finally, be sure to let the VTR operator know to stop recording. Many VTR operators are trained to let the machine continue recording, even if black is on the line, until they are given specific instructions to stop.

Videotape Playback of Recorded Material Often you will need to play back a previously recorded segment, such as a commercial, news spot, or program insert, into a production. In order to make good use of such insert material, the director, assistant director, and VTR operators must coordinate their operations so that the transition into and out of the taped segment is executed smoothly.

PREROLL CUING Since most VTRs need a certain amount of running time to lock in and stabilize picture and sound, the VTR operator must run the tape backward for a few seconds before the start of the actual program material. The amount of preroll you will need depends on the VTRs in your studio and the facility's standard operating policies.

FIGURE 21-8 **Videotape Playback Procedure.**
This procedure allows smooth videotape inserts into an ongoing program.

SCRIPT	DIRECTOR'S COMMANDS	AD'S COMMANDS	RESULTS
			VTR operator is ready.
WE'LL BE BACK WITH OUR SPECIAL GUEST ˄IN (ROLL Q) A MOMENT BUT FIRST, LET'S PAUSE FOR SOME IMPORTANT COMMERCIAL MESSAGES	Ready to roll VTR and track it Roll tape Ready to fade to black and fade up on tape	Five . . . four . . . three . . . two . . .	Floor manager gives hand signals corresponding to AD's countdown.
VTR COMML #1 (1:00) (SOT)	Fade to black Fade up on tape Track it	one . . .	Floor manager counts down to zero and give "cut" sign. Switcher fades out on picture and up on VTR, as audio engineer cuts studio mikes and brings up VTR sound track on audio console. AD begins stopwatch as VTR segment begins.
		Thirty seconds to end. Twenty seconds.	Floor manager readies studio.
	Ready on the floor Ready to cue talent and fade up on Camera 2.	Ten seconds . . . Nine . . . eight . . . seven . . . six . . . five . . . four . . . three . . . two one . . .	Floor manager begins five-zero silent hand cue.
	Fade to black Cue talent; fade up on Camera 2.		Floor manager finishes countdown and cues talent on director's command, as switcher fades to black and fades up on CAM 2. Audio engineer fades out VTR sound track and fades up studio mikes.

Each of the insert segments should already have cuing leader recorded prior to the program material. Using the leader of the VTR's tape timer, the operator will cue each cut to the agreed-on preroll time. For example, if you will use a three-second preroll cue, the tape will be rewound three seconds before the first sound and picture at the start of the program material.

If an on-camera host is going to introduce a tape clip, you can coordinate with talent where in the script to begin the roll cue. If the show is fully scripted, locate the word that is three seconds (if that is your roll-cue time) before the end of the last sentence. This becomes the roll cue, and once the word is said by the host, the director calls for the VTR operator to roll tape. The host should finish speaking three seconds later, just as the stabilized VTR playback begins the program material.

If your program is mostly ad-lib, without a fully written script, you may want to write out the tape lead-in on a cue card so that you and the talent will know precisely how long the tape introduction will run. On some very spontaneous shows, such

as news programs or sports coverage, you might use a *bumper* before the tape playback. A bumper is a still-store frame or slide that appears between the end of the talent's lead-in and the start of the pretaped segment. For example, on most sports coverage, the bumper is the game score, which is punched up prior to the tape roll. As soon as the director cuts to the bumper, the VTR operator is instructed to roll tape, and the director cuts or fades to the VTR playback as soon as the picture and sound appear. (See Figure 21-8.)

Prerolling ensures the VCR will lock up with the synchronizing electronics and produce a stable image on the screen, but many new VTRs and VCRs require no preroll and can be started from a still frame at the top of the cut, which enables the director to roll the tape instantly on cue.

SUMMARY

A program can be produced with videotape in four ways: (1) live on tape, (2) recording in segments, (3) using a single camera/recorder, and (4) recording with multiple cameras/multiple VTRs. Each of these production approaches has its own set of advantages and disadvantages, and the particular production requirements will determine which approach or combination of techniques will provide the most creative control and production efficiency.

During the preproduction phase, the director and producer must plan a shooting schedule. This is particularly important when shooting in segments or with a single camera since nonsequential shooting often can result in increased production efficiency.

During recording sessions, video leader must be laid down at the front of each tape. This usually includes color bars and an audio tone, an identification slate, and cuing information. Usually a combination of audio beepers and video countdown digits is used to roll in VTR program material accurately. Most VTRs require a preroll to run up to speed, and this must be carefully coordinated between the director, talent, and VTR operators.

VIDEO FIELD PRODUCTION

Although much of this book deals with television production inside the studio, the fact is that in today's production environment a program is as likely to be produced outside the confines of a studio as within it. In the early days of television, remote production was a difficult and expensive proposition, but the miniaturization of equipment and the development of microwave and satellite technologies have made remote production a viable alternative for almost any program.

Of course, you are most familiar with news programming, which by its very nature is shot on location where events occur. Sports, special events, and a great deal of instructional programming also are shot on location, for obvious reasons. But remote production offers a variety of options for other kinds of shows which traditionally had been shot inside a studio. Whether or not the advantages of shooting these productions outweighs the problems which a remote inevitably presents is an important production decision which must be made in the preproduction planning stage. What is important for you to understand is how to approach a remote production and how to select the best equipment and techniques to match each production situation. In this chapter we will begin with a discussion of electronic news gathering, which is a special type of remote production, since news coverage, by its very nature, offers a unique set of production challenges. Then we will discuss electronic field production (EFP) and multiple-camera remote (MCR) productions, which, although they take place outside the studio, as does ENG, utilize somewhat different production equipment and techniques.

A final word: Any remote production is, first and foremost, a television production, and as such, it uses virtually all the various techniques which we discuss in each chapter of this book. Rather than repeat what we have already said about equipment operation and production applications, we will concern ourselves in this chapter with how to apply what you already know about the equipment to the special requirements of a remote production situation. Throughout our discussion we will provide you with cross-references to the chapters in which we introduced the equipment and techniques. For more information about any specific piece of equipment and its operation, refer to the particular chapter for details.

ELECTRONIC NEWS GATHERING

Electronic news gathering (ENG) refers to the family of production hardware and techniques used to cover the news on a day-to-day basis. Although ENG production uses equipment and techniques which are, in most cases, virtually identical to those used inside the studio, the very nature of

news means that these approaches must be applied in a very special way. News coverage cannot be preplanned in advance, there is little time for equipment setup, and rehearsal is impossible owing to the spontaneous elements of a news event. An effective ENG production team combines the aesthetic and technical abilities necessary for any conventional television production with the capability to think and act quickly in response to rapidly unfolding situations. In the following sections of this chapter we will discuss the use of production equipment and techniques specifically as they apply to the coverage of news events.

ENG EQUIPMENT AND OPERATION

When we talk about *ENG production,* we are referring to single-camera production using a portable camera that is connected directly to a portable videocassette recorder, an integrated camera/recorder, or a camcorder. Since both camera and VCR are powered by batteries, the camera operator has complete mobility to cover a news event. Often, the ENG crew records program material on a videocassette in segments, and the various segments are edited later into a complete news story. Another capability of many ENG systems is to transmit live pictures and sound of an event back to the studio for immediate broadcast.

The primary goal of ENG operation is to cover fast-breaking news events, so the equipment is designed for maximum operational flexibility. Not only the camera and VCR, but also audio and lighting equipment used for ENG should be selected with portability and efficient operational capability in mind. Consequently, we usually do not demand ENG units to produce material with production values as high as we might expect from programming produced inside the studio or by EFP or large-scale remote operations. This is not to say that ENG units can produce programming that does not meet a minimum level of technical and aesthetic standards. There is no point in producing material that is so poor that it cannot be edited or broadcast or which does not enable the viewer to see and hear clearly what is taking place.

ENG Mobile Unit

At its simplest, the ENG mobile unit can be an ordinary car into which the camera operator, sound engineer, and reporter pile with their equipment and race around town. Although some smaller stations take this approach, the use of a van or minibus which has been specially designed for ENG operation offers some important advantages over a car. The van is large enough to hold all the equipment and personnel, small enough to drive, maneuver, and park easily, and able to carry a microwave system to permit both cable-free camera operation and mobile-unit-to-studio transmission for live broadcasts from the field. (See Figure 22-1.)

Power   ENG units run primarily off batteries, and the ENG van must have some way to charge the batteries while the unit is in the field. An internal generator powered by the van's engine is an effective way to make the vehicle independent of cable current. The generator supplies all the needed power whenever conventional ac power

FIGURE 22-1   ENG Mobile Unit.
ENG mobile units usually are equipped with microwave capability, on-board editing, and racks to hold the field audio and video gear. ENG vans are small enough for easy maneuverability in traffic and parking.

is unavailable. Most ENG units can be powered from standard 120-V ac, 20-A current.

Communications   A two-way radio or cellular telephone provides the necessary communications link between the ENG unit in the field and the news and engineering departments back at the studio. For on-site communications, many ENG units equip their crews with a couple of inexpensive walkie-talkie units, which permit communication over some distance between the camera crew covering the event and the engineer located inside the ENG van.

ENG Camera

We have already covered the various hand-held and shoulder-mounted cameras normally used for ENG operation in Chapter 12. The cameras selected for ENG must be battery-powered, light enough to be handled easily, and sufficiently durable and rugged in design to withstand daily operation. In addition to the camera head, the ENG unit should carry a tripod, shoulder brace, lens shade and filters, and any test equipment necessary to set up and align the camera in the field.

ENG Camera Operation   Since the introduction of camcorders and integrated camera/recorders, most ENG crews consist of a reporter and a single technician responsible for operating the camera, audio, and lighting. In a two-technician crew, more common when the camera and VTR are separate units, one person is responsible for operating the camera, while the other handles the VTR, audio, and any supplemental lighting. (See Figure 22-2.)

As soon as you arrive at the location and set up your camera, make certain you adjust the camera's white balance before you begin recording. Many ENG crews keep a white cardboard square permanently attached to the bottom of the newscaster's clipboard, so it is a simple matter to set the white balance quickly.

If you have the time, make a quick test recording of both sound and picture and replay the tape through the camera's viewfinder while you or the VCR technician listens to the audio playback. Even though you may have made perfect recordings only a few minutes earlier at another location,

(a)

Microwave uplink

ENG van

Live Action Camera

(b)

FIGURE 22-2 ENG Crews. (a) With an integrated camera/recorder, one technician is responsible for operating the camera, audio, and lighting. (b) A two-technician crew is more common when the camera and VTR are separate units.

it does not take much for the cable connecting the recorder to the VCR to break or short out, and the test recording will confirm that both camera and VCR are functioning poorly. Dockable camera/ recorders and single-unit camcorders avoid the Achilles' heel of the cable and are more rugged than component systems. On the other hand, if either the camera or record unit fails, the entire system needs replacing rather than just the VCR or camera in a stand-alone system.

We will discuss camera operation during ENG productions later in this chapter.

ENG Audio

Under most circumstances, keep ENG audio as

an interview. Removing the mike from in front of the interviewee is an effective nonverbal cue to stop talking.

simple as possible. Reporters usually use a hand-held microphone for stand-ups and interviews. On longer interviews, where sharing a single hand mike is inconvenient, you can have the reporter and subject wear lavalier microphones, and record on two audio tracks or use a portable mixer to combine the two mike inputs on one track.

Sometimes a shotgun mike is mounted atop the ENG camera to permit one operator to handle both audio and camera at the same time. This is not a particularly good idea, except in an emergency, because the resulting sound quality is never very good. A camera located far from the subject can zoom in for a close-up, but a microphone mounted on the camera must pick up the subject from too great a distance. The resulting sound is usually poor, lacking in sound presence, and includes too much extraneous noise on the track. Also, windscreens are an indispensable microphone accessory that should be permanently mounted on microphones whenever the reporter must use them outdoors.

TECH TIP   Hand-held mikes, more than lavaliers or shotgun microphones, give the reporter control of

You should always monitor the audio through a headset as you adjust levels and while you are recording the sound. This is the only way you will know exactly how the sound is being picked up by the microphone and recorded on the tape. As soon as you have finished a recording, spot-check the tape to make certain that you have recorded sound before you leave the location.

Whenever possible, try to record some "room noise" before you leave a news location. Room noise is simply the background ambience or natural sounds of a location which are recorded without anyone speaking directly into the microphone. The room noise is useful for covering audio edits or to provide some background to voice-over narration, which may be recorded later back at the studio. To record room noise, simply hold the microphone toward the general area of the event and let the VCR record the sound for ten or fifteen seconds.

ENG Videotape

The most commonly used videotape formats for ENG are ½-inch Betacam SP or M-II camera/

FIGURE 22-3   S-VHS Format Camera/Recorder.
Although integrated Betacam SP and M-II camera/recorders dominate the ENG formats, S-VHS and Hi-8 are becoming more popular because of their light weight and lower operating costs. *(Courtesy: Gossa Vision Productions.)*

recorders and the older ¾-inch videocassette. Although originally designed for high-end home use, S-VHS and Hi-8 formats also are becoming popular. (See Figure 22-3.) In addition to the VCR itself, make sure you bring along necessary tape stock, spare VCR batteries, extra cables, and a shoulder strap or backpack to permit carrying the VCR once you have arrived on location. (See Figure 22-4.)

ENG cameras enable the operator to start and stop the videotape by using controls contained on the camera itself. Before you begin recording, make certain that these controls are working properly, and make a test recording that you can play back through the camera's viewfinder.

Whenever you start a videotape recording, leave enough "video pad" time before you cue the talent for the VCR to engage the tape and to bring it up to speed. Ten seconds at the beginning of a recording and ten seconds after you have completed recording will ensure that the tape editor will have good-quality program material.

Before you start each recording session, make certain to check the battery power supply. If you have any question about how much power is remaining, replace the old batteries with a fresh unit. Weak batteries can result in camera or VCR failure at a crucial time during the recording.

It is important to label every cassette and cassette box after recording so that they do not get mixed up or inadvertently erased. The safest approach is to affix pregummed labels to *both* the cassette itself and the cassette box. If you label only the box, you might mix up cassettes and boxes, so take the extra minute to label both clearly and you will avoid possible confusion later.

ENG Lighting

Most ENG lighting is kept as simple as possible, with the primary objective to provide the necessary illumination for the camera to produce technically acceptable pictures. The best all-around lighting kit for ENG includes two open-face spotlights and a floodlight, along with aluminum light stands and a few gaffer-grip clamps for use on locations where light stands cannot be set up. Do not forget to include plenty of ac power extension cable, barn doors, and scrims in your light kit. (See Figure 22-5.)

CAMERA
Camera
Lens
Lens Shade
Battery Pack/Belt and Spares
Tripod
Lens Cleaning Tissue
White Balance Card

AUDIO
Microphones (Hand-held and Shotgun)
Microphone Cable
Headset
Portable Audio Mixer

LIGHTING
Openface Spotlights
Openface Floodlights
Portable Floorstands
Gaffer Grip Clamps
AC Power Cable
Scrims
Barndoors
Gloves
Battery for Portable Light

VCR
Videocassette Recorder
Spare Cable/VCR Cable
Batteries and Spares
Headsets
Cassettes
AC Power Adaptor

MISCELLANEOUS
Police Permits for Crew
Roadmap
Flashlight
Pads and Pens
Gaffer Tape
AC Extension Cable
Walkie-Talkies
Video Monitor/Receiver
Stopwatch

FIGURE 22-4 **ENG Equipment.**
ENG crews must carry a variety of gear in addition to the VCR and camera. Spare videotape stock, gaffers tape, extra batteries, cables, lamp bulbs, and protective rain gear are among the things that should always be available.

FIGURE 22-6 Speedlight.
A speedlight is mounted on top of the camera. While it is very convenient for fast-breaking news, the lighting effect it creates is unflattering.

DP3 Kit

DP & T Kit

Pro-visions Kit

Easy-V Kit

FIGURE 22-5 Portable Location Lighting Kit.
The basic kit includes instruments, stands, and accessories in a case. *(Courtesy: Lowel-Light Mfg., Inc.)*

Since you may have to shoot at locations where no ac power is available, a battery-powered light unit is a useful accessory to carry in the ENG van.

By its very nature, news production does not always allow you time for careful lighting, and there are times when all you can do is mount a lensless spot, called a *speedlight,* atop the camera. But it is a mistake to dismiss how important good lighting can be to quality pictures, and when the time is available, a few minutes of attention devoted to lighting can dramatically improve the quality of your tape. (See Figure 22-6.)

A single light source aimed straight at the subject creates the unflattering home-movie effect that in-studio lighting is designed to avoid. Whenever possible, try to light a subject from at least two different angles to bring out depth, texture, and detail in the picture. Using the conventional key, back, and fill positions for the instruments will produce the best lighting. If you lack the time or space for a three-instrument setup, use at least

two lights: one as a key and the other as a combination fill and kicker.

TECH TIP Light can be bounced off a wall or ceiling to create a soft, even illumination, but make sure the bounce surface is painted white. Colored areas will reflect the same color light onto the subject and will upset proper color reproduction of the subject's skin tone. (See Figure 22-7.)

FIGURE 22-7 Bouncing Light.
Bouncing the light off of white paper taped to the door increases the intensity of the base light in the room. The beam is diffuse and the shadows are softer than they would be if the light were aimed directly at the subject. *(Courtesy: WKYT-TV.)*

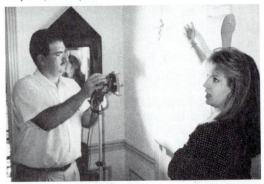

When shooting outdoors, avoid positioning a subject directly in the sun. The tremendously wide variations in brightness level between light and shadow areas will exceed the camera's acceptable contrast range and will produce a poor-quality picture. Shady areas with indirect lighting are usually ideal because their even illumination eliminates wide brightness differences on the subject. If you must shoot in the sun, set up the camera so the sun is to one side of the subject and use a reflector to fill in the other side. (See Figure 22-8.)

TECH TIP Although reflector boards are versatile, windy locations pose particular problems for their use. As the boards are blown by the wind, the fill light they cast appears to flicker and distracts the viewer. Use tripods and firmly hold the attached panels to reduce this problem.

If you are shooting outdoors at night, position the subject in front of a background that is already illuminated. If you also must light the background, have the subject stand as close to it as possible, so the subject's spill light will fall on the background area. Unless a portion of the background is sufficiently illuminated to be photographed by the camera, the subject will appear to be standing against a completely black void.

TECH TIP Avoid shooting subjects against a very white background or against an open sky. The flesh tones of the subject will turn very dark and reproduce poorly. Remember that an auto-iris always adjusts exposure for the brightest portion of the picture. This should be the principal subject, not the background area.

(a)

FIGURE 22-8 Using a Reflector in Sunlight.
(a) The reflector unit is a flexible and economical way to add fill light to lighten shadow areas when shooting outdoors. (b) In this outdoor setup, the scrim diffuses the sunlight and the reflector fills in the dark side of the subject. Sufficient illumination is provided even without additional lighting instruments. When using scrim and reflectors on stands, be sure to weigh them down with sandbags.

Scrim — Subject
Reflector
Camera

(b)

Live ENG Microwave Operation

Live ENG coverage of a news event is made possible by using microwave transmission. Microwave transmission—the point-to-point transmission of video and audio signals—has been used in television for years, mainly as a method of transmitting network programming to local affiliate stations. Technological advances in miniaturization have produced microwave units that are small enough to be installed inside an ENG van and used for news gathering operations. The microwave enables the ENG crew to cover fast-breaking news live, as the event happens, by feeding sound and picture from the remote back to the studio. The microwave system also permits ENG crews to relay videotaped segments of a news story back to the station, where it can be edited and broadcast while the ENG unit goes on to cover another assignment in the field. Microwave transmission is a line-of-sight technology, so it is limited in range to a maximum of about 25 miles unless repeater stations are available. (See Figure 22-9.)

There are two types of microwave links which

FIGURE 22-9   Microwave.
ENG vans equipped with microwave transmitters allow stories to be transmitted live from remote locations.

Retractable
microwave
tower

are useful for ENG operation: (1) mobile-unit-to-studio, and (2) camera-to-mobile unit. In both cases, the microwave system requires an uninterrupted line of sight between transmitter and receiver in order to operate.

Mobile-Unit-to-Studio Link   ENG mobile units equipped with a microwave system use the antenna atop the truck to radio signals back to the studio. Since few stations own a tower high enough to permit a line of sight between the receiving antenna at the station and the ENG mobile unit's coverage area, a *microwave relay system* is used to send signals from the field to a repeater unit atop a high-rise building and from there to the station itself. In most cities, the relay receiver dishes are mounted on the tallest, centrally located building that is available.

To help the ENG crew quickly position the truck and its microwave antenna dish for the best transmission, some stations have found it useful to develop a log book of recommended truck positions at various news locations around town. Since many stories occur in the same standard locations (city hall, downtown hotels, sports arenas), the log book saves time by informing a crew member who is unfamiliar with the location of the best place to park the mobile unit. When a direct line of sight cannot be established, such as in a downtown area surrounded by tall buildings, helicopters can carry a portable tower as part of the repeater circuit. Because of the altitude at which helicopters fly, a microwave relay carried on a helicopter can extend the microwave range to about 150 miles. As a less expensive alternative to helicopters, sometimes a signal can be bounced off one building and ricocheted to the receiving tower. (See Figure 22-10.)

Camera-to-Mobile-Unit Link   When a direct cable run from the camera to the ENG mobile unit is impossible, a small battery-operated microwave unit can be used to establish the necessary link. This makes it possible for the ENG unit to cover live events where the mobile unit cannot get as close to the action as the camera can. As with larger microwaves, a direct line of sight must be established between the camera's transmitter and the truck's receiver. Most portable units permit an operating range of about 1 mile and, depending

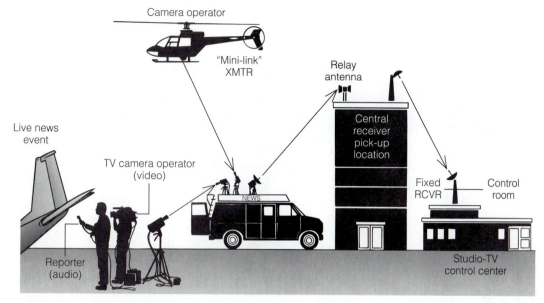

FIGURE 22-10 Microwave Links.
Here, the camera's signal is microwaved to the ENG truck and then relayed to a repeater link. The repeater links can be stationary (permanently mounted on a tall building) or mobile (in this case, on a helicopter). *(Courtesy: Farinon Electric.)*

on the size of their batteries, anywhere from four to eight hours of continuous operation. (See Figure 22-11.)

Needless to say, the same portable microwave unit can be used for other types of remote productions as well, to link cameras which are positioned where cable connections to the mobile unit are either impossible or impractical. Portable microwave units make it possible to obtain dramatic shots from a blimp or a helicopter and are indispensable in providing the type of coverage viewers have come to expect on sports, news, and entertainment remotes.

Satellite News Gathering (SNG)

In 1984, Conus Communications introduced satellite news gathering into the world of ENG. Since then, other satellite news services have begun extending the range of local news operations. A satellite news gathering truck is equipped with a satellite up-link as part of its news gathering package. With an up-link, live feeds can be sent back

to the home station when the news occurs outside microwave range (about 25 miles maximum). (See Figure 22-12.)

Just like a microwave-equipped truck, the SNG vehicle is dispatched via mobile radio or cellular phone to the news site. Upon arriving, the engineer drops the satellite transmitter's protective doors and immediately powers up the satellite transmitter. During this time, perhaps thirty minutes, the reporter and camera operator begin preparing for the news coverage. Once the power level has been obtained, the engineer uses signal-strength meters to tune in to a prearranged transponder on a satellite. (See Figure 22-13.) After the satellite has been "fixed," the engineer sends test bars and tone to the satellite. The satellite converts the up-link frequency to a different down-link frequency to avoid signal interference. The home station, and any affiliated member of the satellite network, can then lock in on the down-link.

Once the truck's signal has been linked to the home station, satellite telephone links between the truck and station are created, and an interruptible

639

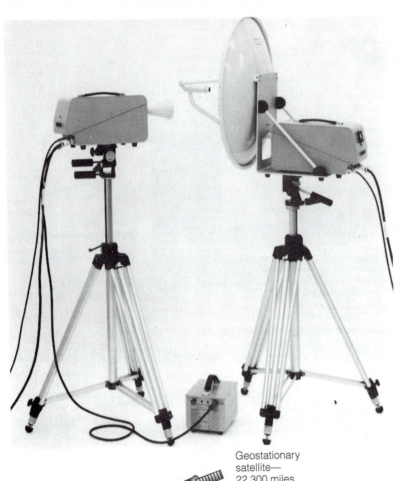

FIGURE 22-11 Portable Microwave Units.
Portable microwave units are flexible and easily set up. The horn on the left provides a 1½-mile range, while the large dish can transmit over a 26-mile distance. The battery pack on the ground powers the units. *(Courtesy: Farinon Electric.)*

FIGURE 22-12 Satellite News Gathering (SNG).
SNG has greatly extended the range of local news operations. Now stations are not limited to the 25-mile range of microwave links.

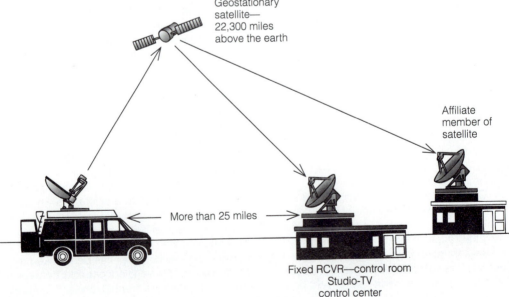

Geostationary satellite—22,300 miles above the earth

Affiliate member of satellite

More than 25 miles

Fixed RCVR—control room
Studio-TV
control center

FIGURE 22-13 **Satellite News Van.**
Satellite news gathering (SNG) trucks allow live news to be distributed nationally from any remote location. The truck is equipped with a satellite up-link. Its signal can be down-linked from the satellite to the studio. *(Courtesy: Midwest Communications Corp.)*

foldback (IFB) circuit is opened to the reporter's headset. With this IFB, the field reporter can converse "live" with the newscast's studio anchor.

In addition to the ability to transmit live programming to the station, satellite trucks provide on-board editing. This permits the videographer to shoot the story, edit it, and send it from the site of the news. Prior to SNG, the remote team would shoot the video, edit it while the ENG truck drove to within microwave range, and then send it to the station for delivery to the viewers. SNG further accelerates the immediacy of news gathering, especially for local stations with large geographic service areas.

Another area where SNG has had an enormous impact is in the coverage of international events. Today it's common to see live reports on network newscasts and Cable News Network originating from distant regions of the world. These live feeds are made possible by (1) a system of international satellites, and (2) "flyaway" satellite up-links that are small enough to be carried to remote locations in a suitcase. (See Figure 22-14.)

The growing emphasis on live microwave and SNG reports has created new demands on production personnel. Field reporters have become

much more like co-anchors than stand-ups performing on tape. Prior to the growth of live field reporting, reporters had the luxury of multiple takes and pre-scripting their stories. Increasingly today, the field reporter must be able to think on his or her feet and compose the story as it unfolds. Similarly, field editors must have good "news sense," since their edit decisions occur under time pressure in the field rather than back at the studio's edit bays.

ENG PRODUCTION

The ENG production operation works somewhat differently from other kinds of remote productions owing to the special nature of news coverage. For

FIGURE 22-14 **Flyaway Satellite Uplink.**
An up-link is an earth-to-satellite transmitter. Flyaway up-links can be transported to locations inaccessible to SNG vehicles. *(Courtesy: Mobile Telesystems, Inc.)*

this reason, it is difficult to discuss ENG production during each of the four production stages as with other kinds of remote operations. Since it is obviously impossible to predict every news event, there is little in the way of elaborate preproduction planning or rehearsal that can be directly applied to ENG operations. Also, most ENG units consist of a limited one- or two-person crew which handles all the technical operations and a reporter who functions as a producer-director on the scene.

Nevertheless, there are a number of important considerations which relate specifically to ENG production, and we can organize them into three of the production stages: preproduction planning, production, and postproduction. Since there is little rehearsal, we will not concern ourselves with that stage here.

Preproduction Planning

While it may not be possible to preplan every ENG event, there are some basic planning details which should be taken into account before the unit leaves the studio for the day's work in the field. Many ENG crews develop a standard checklist of equipment which they review prior to leaving the studio. The list in Figure 22-4 is an example of an ENG checklist.

In most towns and cities, the police department issues a "press pass," which permits reporters and crews to cross police lines in order to cover a story. Each crew member should have his or her own pass and should make certain that he or she carries it to every location.

Another indispensable item for the ENG van, which can be easily overlooked, is a complete road map of the local areas you will be covering. You never know when you will be dispatched to cover an event on a moment's notice, and you may need to consult a map to help you find your way.

Although news can happen anywhere at any time, there are usually a number of locations which the ENG unit will cover on a regular basis. City hall, the state capitol, major hotels in the area, the air-

port, the local courthouse, and major sports or events arenas are all examples of locations where news is regularly covered. Over time, ENG crews become familiar with these locations and develop routines for parking the van, setting up equipment, and so on, which makes for a more efficient operation. This information can be added to the ENG logbook, which contains essential information about regularly covered locations and which is kept on board the ENG van and is available for instant reference. Besides the previously mentioned microwave line-of-sight locations, the logbook includes information about the location of public telephones, ac power outlets that are working, names of official contacts, the best location to park the car or van, access-ways to news locations, and so on.

Whenever an ENG crew visits a new place that is not included in the logbook, the information about the new location is added so the book is continually updated. It may sound trivial, but if you have ever spent twenty minutes trying to find an open door to an enormous sports arena while the event you are supposed to cover takes place without you, you begin to appreciate how important such information can be to an efficient ENG operation.

Production

Most ENG crews consist of one or two people to handle the technical operation of camera, VCR, audio, and lighting and a reporter who also functions as a producer-director. The reporter and technical crew work closely in establishing camera positions, camera shots, and the approach that will be used to cover the event. After a certain amount of time working together, the team usually requires little formal communication between its members. This is a real advantage when breaking news events do not permit extended conversation between the reporter and technical crew. (See Figure 22-15.)

What is most important in ENG operation is for the crew to remain flexible so they can cover unexpected situations that might develop. The weakest equipment link is the cable that connects the camera to the VCR because it restricts the camera operator's movement and is subject to damage and shorting out if any stress on the cable and

FIGURE 22-15 ENG Assignment Team.
Many ENG assignments are covered with a single reporter/producer and a single camera operator/technician.

connectors develops as the camera operator's movement outdistances the VCR operator's ability to keep up. Of course, if you are working with a camera/recorder or a camcorder, the camera operator is completely self-contained and has no cable constraints on his or her movement around the scene.

Most news stories are *packages* that contain five types of footage: (1) *actuality*, which is coverage of the event as it occurs; (2) *interviews*; (3) *stand-ups*, where the reporter or correspondent talks directly to the camera; (4) *cutaways*, which are wide-angle or reverse-angle shots of the scene; and (5) *cover shots* (sometimes referred to as "B-roll") that establish the location of the overall scene. Both cutaways and cover shots can be used as transitional footage to eliminate jump cuts or audio mismatch.

The exact production sequence for an ENG package usually depends on the event that is be-

ing covered. Normally, the ENG crew will shoot the actuality first, then the interviews or statements of the major participants. However, this may be reversed, depending on the timing of events and the availability of the participants. Once the sound bites have been recorded, the news reporter will prepare stand-ups that open the package, set up the sound bites, and provide a closing summary. During the production, the camera operator should shoot a number of cutaways and cover shots which can be used to provide smooth visual transitions when editing the package.

We have described the techniques of operating cameras in Chapter 13. Everything we said there applies equally to ENG camera operation. ENG production creates additional demands on the camera operator because ENG footage usually is shot to be edited later. It is impossible to overemphasize the importance for the ENG camera operator to shoot the event with videotape editing in mind. Especially if you will not be editing the piece yourself, you must provide footage that can be edited successfully. Two areas that will be of special concern to the editor are camera movement and shot selection.

Camera Movement   The most important requirement for an ENG camera operator is to be able to react quickly to unpredictable events. However, quick responses that result in excessive camera movement or zooms are not desirable. News is exciting and the natural inclination for the camera operator is to pan and zoom about a scene much as our eyes might do normally. Although lots of camera movement may seem perfectly natural to you while you are taping the news event, once your view the footage in the edit room you will probably discover to your dismay that there is so much camera movement that it is difficult for the viewer to become oriented to what is taking place. It is difficult to edit a number of shots in which the camera is constantly moving about the scene. Therefore, the second requirement for an ENG camera operator is to keep camera movement and zooms to an absolute minimum.

Another kind of movement that also must be minimized is the natural unsteadiness of the hand-held camera caused by inevitable body movements. You should avoid the temptation to shoot all ENG footage hand-held. The camera never is as stable as when it is mounted on a tripod. You should also restrict the use of long focal-length lens settings when you use a hand-held camera because a long lens accentuates body movements, producing image shake. Of course, there are situations where a tripod cannot go where you must go to get the shot you need, but whenever you have the time and opportunity to use a tripod, the extra work is more than off-set by the improved picture quality.

TECH TIP   A body brace or a stabilization device will help you get steadier hand-held shots. But if you have neither, there are five simple things that you can do to get steadier shots when hand-holding a camera/recorder: (1) spread your feet slightly and tuck your elbows into your sides; (2) lean against a solid object such as a wall or tree; (3) use a wider focal-length lens setting and move closer to your subject; (4) sit down; and (5) practice!

Shot Selection   There are a number of ways the camera operator can help the editor through wise shot selection.

You should provide as much *cutaway footage* as possible. The editor will need cutaways to cover transitions in interviews and avoid distracting jump cuts. A cutaway can be a wide shot of the scene, a close-up of the reporter nodding to the speaker, close-ups of other cameras and reporters, and so on. You can never provide too many cutaways! Anything the editor does not use is simply erased, but it is impossible to shoot more footage once you have left the news scene.

One specific type of cutaway is called the *reverse angle* shot. Basically, a reverse angle shot is in the opposite direction of the previous shot. For example, most ENG camera operators will shoot the subject of an interview over the reporter's shoulder. The reverse angle is a shot of the reporter over the subject's shoulder. Unfortunately, using a single camera/recorder does not permit you to photograph both the reporter asking questions and the subject responding. To provide this footage, once the interview is over, position the camera in the reverse angle—over the subject's shoulder, even though the actual subject may be gone by this time—and have the reporter ask each question again while you shoot the reporter in close-up. For both journalistic and editing reasons, it is important that the reporter repeat each question identically to the way it was asked during the actual interview. The reverse angle footage enables the editor to cut in a close-up of the reporter asking each question as the news story is assembled in the edit room. (See Figure 22-16.)

When you shoot reaction shots there are several guidelines you should remember. First, observe the "axis of conversation" rule. The *axis of conversation* is a line drawn between the subject and the reporter, and the rule is that the camera should be set up on the same side of the line for each close-up. That way the subject and reporter will appear to be looking at each other when their

FIGURE 22-16 Reverse Angle Shot.
(*a*) The camera angle emphasizes the subject during the interview, but the face of the reporter cannot be seen when she asks questions. (*b*) After the interview the photographer moves to the location where the subject was standing and shoots reverse angle cutaways of the reporter. *(Courtesy: WPLG-TV.)*

close-ups are edited together. Second, keep the angle of the axis of conversation, or line of sight, matched in each shot. For example, if the subject is taller than the reporter and is looking slightly down in the frame, the reporter should be looking up at the same angle. Otherwise, it will not appear as though they are looking at each other when the close-up shots are edited together.

Likewise, the ENG camera operator should be aware of the *axis of action*, or direction of movement, in the frame. The same rule applies as with the axis of conversation. For example, if you are shooting a parade on Main Street you should remain on one side of the street, so the parade will be going in the same direction. That will make it easy to edit for continuity of motion across the screen, but will provide little flexibility in editing for visual variety. More editing options would be provided by shooting the parade from both sides of the street, as well as from the front and the back, with motion toward and away from the camera. There also will be more editing possibilities if you vary the way you shoot moving subjects. Sometimes pan with them, and other times let them move completely through the frame.

TECH TIP In unpredictable environments, ENG camera operators work with both eyes open. One eye is dedicated to the camera's eyepiece viewfinder, while the other surveys the scene to help the operator anticipate where to aim the camera next.

You should vary the *field of view* of your shots between wide shots, medium shots, and close-ups. This will provide more editing flexibility. For example, suppose you are shooting an exterior of a factory for a story on plant closings. You could shoot a continuous one-minute take like this: Start wide and hold the wide shot; zoom into a medium shot of the entrance; hold the medium shot; zoom farther into a close-up of a padlock on the entrance; hold the close-up; zoom out to the medium shot; hold the medium shot; zoom out to the original wide shot; and hold the wide shot. This sequence would give the editor many options. A sequence of cuts from the wide shot to the close-up of the padlock could be used for emphasis, creating intensity, and directing the attention of the audience to the padlock. The zoom out from the padlock to the medium shot could be used over a closing voice-over narration to represent your leaving the scene. Of course, the wide shot alone could be used as an establishing shot. The point is that the ENG camera operator, not knowing exactly how the ENG footage will be edited, should provide as many options as possible.

645

A final note: Be sure to provide plenty of "video pad" for editing. Anticipate as much as you can and start recording before the primary action occurs. At the end of a take, let the recorder roll. Although no one will ever see it in the final package, video pad is needed for the editing process. Ten seconds at the beginning and the end of a shot will make life much easier for the editor.

Live ENG Production

One of the most important capabilities of ENG is the ability to broadcast live from a remote location. In order to do this, you must establish a two-way communication link between the home studio and the ENG unit in the field. Although the two-way radio or cellular telephone is sufficient for engineering purposes, it is not useful for a live feed because it does not permit easy cuing or two-way conversations on the air between the field reporter and the anchor in the studio.

If an IFB circuit cannot be established between the studio and remote site, a battery-powered TV receiver can be employed instead. The TV monitor is simply tuned to the station's broadcast frequency and placed out of camera range, where it can be viewed by the reporter. The reporter wears an earpiece connected to the earphone jack of the receiver. By listening through the earplug and watching the television receiver, the reporter can see and hear everything that is going out over the air. As soon as the reporter hears the cue and sees the monitor picture switch to the live ENG feed, he or she commences the report. By listening to the program audio, the reporter also can engage in a two-way conversation with the anchor who is back at the studio. (See Figure 22-17.)

Postproduction Videotape Editing

Every ENG story that was videotaped in the field in segments by the single-camera/recorder approach must be edited into a completed story before it can be used. Every cut must be made by videotape editing during postproduction. In the next chapter we will describe the postproduction

Portable
television

FIGURE 22-17   Communicating on a Live Remote.
A field reporter can use a portable television to view the anchorperson during a live remote report. This improves the naturalness of the conversation.

editing process in detail. What makes ENG editing special is the fact that new footage must be edited quickly and efficiently in order to prepare the material for use on the day's news program. Also, editing often occurs on the ENG truck and is transmitted live to the station during the newscast.

Today virtually all ENG footage is recorded on helical cassettes, as was described in Chapter 20. Betacam SP has overtaken ¾-inch U-Matic as the most widely used ENG format. In either case, the news footage can be edited in its original format, and most stations actually broadcast their news segments directly from the edited master cassette by playing the VCR through a time-base corrector.

Logging the ENG Tape   Unlike commercial, corporate, or entertainment productions, where you can preview your recorded takes at a fairly leisurely pace, news production demands that quick decisions be made immediately, and often under serious time pressures. To edit ENG footage effectively, someone should provide the editor with an accurate log of each recorded cassette's contents so that the producer and tape editor can locate important cuts quickly for previewing and editing. Usually the logging is done by the field reporter while writing the story.

If you are using SMPTE time code, the time code is either recorded in the field or recorded simultaneously as the producer and/or editor screens the raw footage. By noting the time-code number for each important cut on the tape, you will be able to return to a particular segment quickly when you edit the piece. If the story is microwaved into the studio from the field, the time code is usually laid down as the microwave feed is recorded.

Many news operations prefer to use control-track time-code editing because laying down the time code requires no additional time. In this case, you should have made a log of the tape's contents, noting approximate reel times where important footage is located. For instance, if an important sound-bite interview was recorded about twelve minutes into the tape, the editor will punch 00:12:00:00 into the edit programmer, and the tape will automatically run forward. Shuttling the tape back and forth will locate the exact part of the tape where the sound bite begins. A well-prepared log is particularly important in news operations because quite often the crew and reporter who shot the story are out in the field covering other news while the editor and news program producer cut the tape for broadcast.

Editing the ENG News Story As we have mentioned already, most news packages contain actuality, sound bites from interviews, stand-ups, cutaways, and cover footage. While each news package is often slightly different, most follow a fairly basic format. First, the reporter gives a brief orientation or background to the story. This is often done as a stand-up, the reporter talking directly to the camera, or a voice-over, using the news event as a background. Next, various sound bites are used, including actuality footage or interviews. Finally, the reporter ends with another stand-up, summing up the story. Many conclude with a live handoff back to the studio anchor.

There are different approaches to editing news packages, depending on the nature of the story, the audio and video material available, the practices at your station, and simply what works best for you. In Chapter 1 we gave you a look backstage at a local news report being prepared. In that case, the reporter and editor worked as a team, compiling sound bites from interviews, voice-over narration, cover footage, cutaways, and stand-ups in a back-and-forth process that employed editing techniques such as assemble-, insert-, and split-editing, which we will describe in the next chapter. Other ENG editors like to record the sound track on the Edit Master tape first, then build the visuals to match the existing sound track using video-insert editing. Of course, you also can simply assemble the various segments, beginning with the first actuality or the reporter's stand-up and continuing through until the end of the news package. Additional voice-overs can be added later if necessary.

Since many stations are broadcasting their news packages directly from cassette, a number of ingenious and time-saving shortcuts have been developed to speed up the editing process. For example, at WSB-TV, in Atlanta, ENG footage is edited in the following sequence:

1   The editor uses the written log, which was prepared previously, to locate important scenes within the cassette tape. All editing is done using time-code numbers.
2   The producer, editor, and sometimes the reporter make the final decisions on which segments to include in the spot and their proper order.
3   A prerecorded cassette containing a ten-second countdown and video black is used for a visual cue before the actual program material. A preblacked cassette is inserted into the edit/record VTR, and the countdown and video black are transferred to the blank cassette.
4   The news story is assembled and edited according to the predetermined sequence. Sometimes the audio track is recorded first and the visuals are matched later. Other times

the sequences are assembled in order, depending on the type of story and the available footage.

5   Another cassette, which is prerecorded with video black, is used to edit-on black at the end of the story. This is a safety pad in case the program director does not punch out of the taped segment quickly enough on the air.

6   The edited tape is labeled with the story and content, date, running time, and the in and out cues. The labeled cassette then is sent by messenger to the VTR room for air.

ENG Videotape Playback   As we mentioned earlier, most operations play back the edited cassette without "bumping up" to 1-inch. To do this, the playback VCR must feed through a time-base corrector and then into the studio control room, where the playback VCR appears as one of the video inputs on the production switcher.

Since the edited tape should have been edited with some visual countdown leader, it is a simple matter of cuing up the tape and still-framing it with the pause control at the appropriate number. A three-second roll cue is common, so all you do is play back the cassette until you see the number 3 and press the pause control. The freeze-frame allows the cue leader number to appear on the VCR playback monitor in the studio control room and indicates that the tape is cued and ready. At the correct time, the director calls for the VCR operator to roll tape, and three seconds later picture and sound appear and the tape is punched up on the air.

COMMON REMOTE SITUATIONS

Any television show can be done as a remote, but there are some formats which are frequently produced in the field, such as sports remotes, indoor theatrical events, hearings and conferences, magazine-format feature stories, and corporate/institutional training programs. They are covered using electronic field production (EFP) and multi-camera remote (MCR) techniques. What distinguishes EFP and MCR production from ENG is the ability to preplan the first two and give more careful attention to the various production elements than is usually possible when covering most news events with ENG.

Every remote production—no matter how simple or complex—uses all the television production techniques we have discussed throughout the book. Shooting on remote, however, also involves a number of additional considerations that must be properly handled for an effective production. In this chapter we will discuss the various types of remote productions and how they are approached by the production team. Since remotes always involve basic television production techniques that have been dealt with in some detail elsewhere in this text, our intention here is not to repeat each of these but to discuss them within the context of the unique requirements of a remote production.

Sports Remotes

Whether a high school football championship covered by a local station or the Super Bowl covered by a national network, sports has become a regular part of television programming. Of course, not every station has the equipment and personnel resources available to the networks, but this does not mean that locally produced sports must be second-rate. It is not difficult to cover a football game with fifteen cameras and three slow-motion VTRs. The real challenge is to cover the game with only three or four cameras and still produce an exciting and entertaining show.

Quite often ingenuity and creativity can overcome certain equipment limitations. In addition, recent technological advances have drastically reduced the price of slow-motion- and still-frame-storage units, making these important sports production tools increasingly accessible. When you plan your camera positions, select strategic locations which will permit each camera to be used to the fullest extent possible. Over the years, a number of basic camera positions for various sports have been developed, and they are illustrated in Figure 22-18. Although you will have to adapt them for your own particular needs, they can provide a departure point in planning sports coverage.

Sports Director   The director of any sports event must be thoroughly familiar with the rules and the play for every event he or she is assigned to direct—not only how the game is played, but some

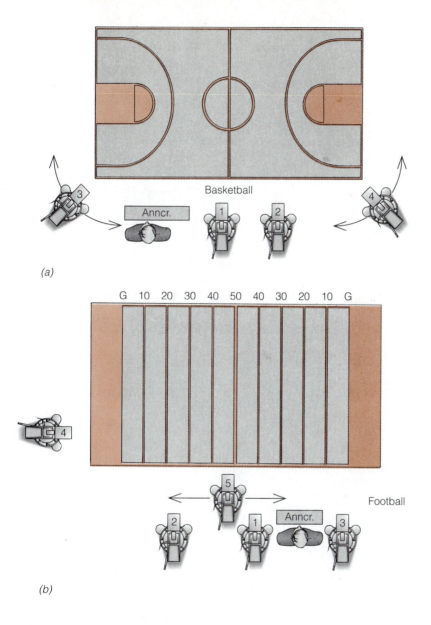

(a)

G　10　20　30　40　50　40　30　20　10　G

Football

(b)

FIGURE 22-18 **Camera Positions for Sports Events.**
Every sports event offers its own set of problems and possibilities, but the camera
positions illustrated can be used as a general guide. They must be modified,
depending on the number of cameras you have available and the production
situation. (*a*) *Basketball*. Cameras 1 and 2 are positioned above court level and
follow the action with a zoom lens. Cameras 3 and 4 are optional, but can be used
for shot variety, close-ups of foul shots, and to cover the announcer's table.
(*b*) *Football*. Cameras 1, 2, and 3 are positioned above the playing field, one on the
50-yard line and the others on the 20-yard lines. Camera 4 can be used for kicking
attempts and as an isolated camera. Camera 1 doubles as the announce booth
camera for opening and closing segments. Camera 5 is mounted on a truck or dolly
to provide a field-level view.

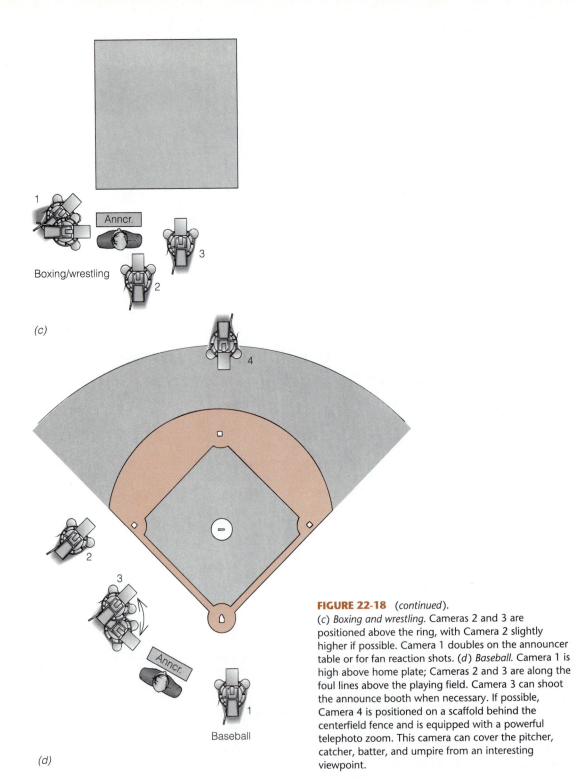

Boxing/wrestling

(c)

Baseball

(d)

FIGURE 22-18 (*continued*).
(*c*) *Boxing and wrestling.* Cameras 2 and 3 are positioned above the ring, with Camera 2 slightly higher if possible. Camera 1 doubles on the announcer table or for fan reaction shots. (*d*) *Baseball.* Camera 1 is high above home plate; Cameras 2 and 3 are along the foul lines above the playing field. Camera 3 can shoot the announce booth when necessary. If possible, Camera 4 is positioned on a scaffold behind the centerfield fence and is equipped with a powerful telephoto zoom. This camera can cover the pitcher, catcher, batter, and umpire from an interesting viewpoint.

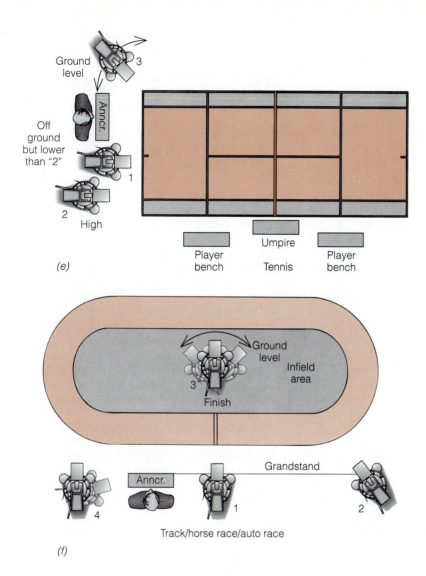

(e)

Ground level

Off ground but lower than "2"

Anncr.

1

2   High

Player bench

Umpire

Tennis

Player bench

Ground level

Infield area

3

Finish

Grandstand

Anncr.

4

1

2

Track/horse race/auto race

(f)

FIGURE 22-18 (*continued*).

(*e*) *Tennis.* Cameras 1 and 2 are positioned at one end of the court, with one camera higher than the other. Depending on the position of the announce booth, either camera can shoot the announcer when necessary. Camera 3 is at ground level and shoots close-ups of either player, as well as the umpire and player benches. (*f*) *Track events.* Events run on an oval track—such as horse racing, auto racing, or track events—can be approached in similar ways. Camera 1 is positioned high in the stands across from the finish line. Cameras 2 and 4 are at the ends of the stands and follow the racers within their fields of view. Camera 3, positioned at ground level inside the infield, can be used for closer shots as racers move along the far end of the track.

651

of the basic strategies involved. Unless you know this information, you cannot begin to determine camera positions and plan your production coverage.

The director also must do his or her homework prior to each production to learn how each team or player approaches the game and what each is likely to do in typical situations. Once these are established, the director can work out each camera's shot responsibilities based on a knowledge of the game and what is likely to occur during the particular game or match being covered.

A good sports director never loses sight of the sports contest in selecting camera shots and directing the game coverage. Yet, at the same time, realizing that there are a variety of perspectives surrounding a sports event, he or she tries to show these to the viewer as well. There is a human side to competition which takes place along the sidelines, in the dugout, on the bench, and in the stands. These can be used to increase the viewer's enjoyment of the game, as long as the atmosphere shots do not distract attention from the primary event on the playing field.

Producer   The sports producer plays a much more active role during a sports broadcast than on most scripted or preplanned productions. Usually, the producer is involved in establishing the overall game plan the director will follow, helping the director select elements to show the audience, and supervising the isolated camera and the instant-replay operation.

Mike Weisman, a former sports producer for NBC, recommends that the producer establish a definite point of view or production game plan prior to the event. This is based on the producer's research and experience with the players, coaches, and their past strategies. While the game plan must be flexible so that it can change on a moment's notice, depending on what happens on the field, it does provide a framework around which the basic coverage can be organized.

One of the producer's most important responsibilities is to coordinate the isolated cameras and the instant replays. Effective use of the isolated system requires a combination of thorough planning, good judgment, and plain luck. Based on your research and experience, you should have some idea where the key action is likely to occur for particular situations. This information is the basis for setting up the isolated-camera feed to the slow-motion VTR. A producer with only one slow-motion unit must decide whether to play it safe and feed program video or risk missing the primary action by isolating on another camera. The safe approach virtually guarantees a replay, but from the same perspective the viewer just saw. The more daring approach produces some unique viewpoints, but increases the chances that you will guess wrong and wind up without the replay of a key event. Sometimes a producer who misses the primary action on iso can salvage a replay anyway and use it to show "why the play worked" by isolating on a particular player's individual contribution. Producers communicate with the slow-motion operator via an open PL mike and with on-air talent via the IFB system.

Sports Announcers   Most sportscasts utilize two announcers: one for play-by-play and the other as an analyst or color commentator to provide insight into the game. Both announcers must keep one eye on the playing field and the other on the air monitor in the booth, which shows the game as the viewer sees it. Most announce booths are equipped with additional monitors which show the video being recorded and replayed over the isolated camera and the slow-motion unit.

Veteran ABC sportscaster Keith Jackson says the role of a television sports announcer is to "amplify, clarify, and punctuate" the action on the field. Talent must be able to watch the activity on the field, keep an eye on the air monitor, listen to the director or producer over the IFB system, and still make sense to the viewing audience.

Sportscasters are expected to prepare for each broadcast by studying the teams and players, their strategies, and whatever additional information can be obtained from team publicity offices, contacts, and press clippings. It also is important for sportscasters to be sufficiently familiar with each player's name and number that they can quickly identify them during the game. (See Figure 22-19.)

A *spotter* is often used to help the announcers

and the director identify various players and to point out significant developments. Sometimes a production will use a number of different spotters: one assigned to the announce booth to locate events for the director and another assigned to help keep statistics for the character generator to use in updating lower-third graphics.

Indoor Theatrical Events

Rock concerts, awards banquets, symphony orchestras, and stage plays are some of the common indoor theatrical events which are frequently covered as remote productions. The production approach is usually dictated by the characteristics of the event. A staged event—such as a rock concert or an awards program—offers maximum production control because the event is produced primarily for television. The appearance of camera equipment that blocks the audience's view and the production's control over the timing and sequence of the event are not problems with staged remotes. A covered event, however, presents added challenges, because the production equipment must remain unobtrusive and must not

interfere with the house audience. The television unit is invited as a guest, but it is expected to adapt to the situation and circumstances as they exist.

In either case, lighting is an important production consideration. Stage lighting is rarely sufficient for television cameras, and the lighting approach itself must be modified to produce the best television pictures. The addition of color media to the instruments, a widely used theatrical lighting approach, must be carefully planned when television will cover the event. Varying the color quality of the light can affect proper color reproduction.

In positioning cameras for an indoor theatrical remote, you may have to rope off a section of seats to provide an unrestricted view of the action area. Be careful when running cable to avoid heavily traveled aisles and doorways. Check all camera locations to make certain the camera's view will not be blocked if someone in the audience gets up during the performance.

FIGURE 22-19 Sports Announce Booth. The announcer's booth at sporting events is equipped with multiple monitors and audio sources to help the announcer accurately describe the game.

TECH TIP   When cables must cross walkways, cover the cables with flattened cardboard boxes and tape the edges of the cardboard to the floor with gaffer's tape.

Audio quality can be a real problem, especially when you must hide the microphones from the cameras. A number of directional mikes located behind the footlights will pick up the performers, but the sound quality will not be very good. Wireless microphones are becoming a standard technique for sound reinforcement and are easily adapted for television by either patching into the theater's house PA system or arranging to pick up the microphone transmitter's feed with a separate receiver.

If you are covering a symphony, opera, or ballet inside a concert hall, you may be able to record excellent audio with only one or two microphones. The mikes are located to pick up the overall sound, preserving the natural acoustical ambience of the concert hall. You will need to experiment for the best microphone placement, but once the location is determined, little, if any, mixing is necessary by the audio engineer.

Hearings and Conferences

Government hearings; educational, industrial, or civic conferences; and similar types of indoor events present special challenges for the remote production team. Usually television is permitted at these events as long as the equipment and crew remain unobtrusive and avoid interfering with or upstaging the very event they have come to cover.

Setup must be carefully planned to allow the crew enough time to prepare the equipment before the event is scheduled to begin. These events rarely accommodate television, and you may be prohibited from moving equipment around after a specified time. The event's coordinator should be contacted for a rough time schedule and sequence of the planned activities. Even so, these events have a tendency to run on their own time, and the television director should be prepared to follow whatever develops.

Lighting can present a serious problem when available light levels are too low for camera operation. The coordinator of the event may be apprehensive about approving the use of television lights, which cause heat, glare, and distractions. The best you can hope for is a compromise in which you use fewer but more efficient units which are positioned as unobtrusively as possible.

The director must learn where important participants will be located (on the panel, at the podium, in the audience) and plan to cover them for both sound and picture. If audience participation is expected, have a floor assistant on hand with a hand-held or shotgun mike to cover audience speakers. Panel speakers can be miked with either separate desk mikes or by patching into the house PA system. At least one camera should be positioned where it can photograph the audience whenever necessary.

Figure 22-20 shows a three-camera setup for a typical indoor conference of the type just described. These events frequently occur within a small, crowded room, which greatly restricts camera and crew movement. The more you learn about what is to happen, the better you can decide where to position your cameras to best cover the event's various activities. Sometimes an advance text of a speaker's address or comments can be helpful in planning the integration of graphics, visuals, and close-up shots.

Magazine-Format Feature Story

One of the most common EFP situations is the "feature story" used on magazine-format programs, on news shows, and as insert material for a variety of studio productions. Of course, every story has its own "angle," which makes it interesting and different, but there are a number of considerations which are common to such productions. An illustration of how this type of EFP can be approached is this case study of a feature story on a well-known chef which is to be produced for a local station's weekly magazine program.

The story angle concerns the chef's "no-salt gourmet diet." A few days before the production is scheduled to tape, the segment's producer visits the chef for a preinterview and to survey the location site, which is the chef's home. The producer and the chef decide that the chef will be

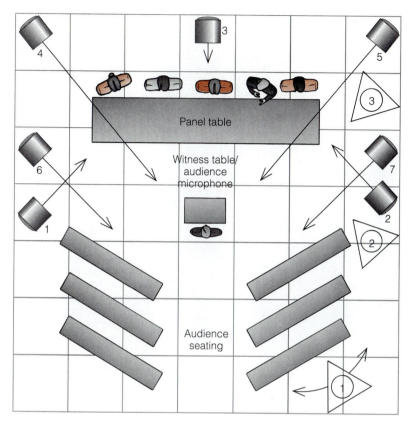

FIGURE 22-20 Camera Positions for Hearings or Conferences.
This camera setup is one standard approach to hearings or conferences. Cameras 1 and 2 are positioned to cover the speakers at the panel table. Camera 3 shoots the speaker at the witness table or the audience microphone depending on the nature of the event. Lighting instruments 1, 2, and 3 are mounted on floor stands (or if possible, hung from the ceiling with gaffer-grips) and cover the panel table. Instruments 4 and 5 illuminate the witness or audience mike areas. Instruments 6 and 7 are used to light the audience seating area. Lighting must be arranged so it will neither interfere with the participants by glaring excessively into their eyes nor create flare problems for any of the cameras.

interviewed and will also show the audience how to prepare a fish dish. This means that two different locations will be used: the living room for the interview and the kitchen for the cooking demonstration. The producer surveys both areas and determines that there is sufficient space for the camera, ample electric power for the equipment, and no serious lighting problems caused by windows, which can be closed during taping, if necessary.

Before leaving the studio, the producer meets briefly with the production crew to run down the story and how it will be shot. When the crew and the reporter arrive at the chef's home, the crew begins to set up in the living room, since the producer decided that the interview segment would be taped first. The lighting crew decides to use bounce lighting off the white ceiling primarily and takes care to spread the load of the various instruments across a number of different electric circuits to avoid overloading. (See Figure 22-21.) It is decided that rather than attempt to match the daylight color temperature outside the large living-

FIGURE 22-21
Ceiling Bounce Light.
To increase the general
illumination, bounce the light
off the ceiling. The light will
be diffused and the shadows
will be soft. If the instruments
are on stands, they must be
positioned so they are not in
the camera shots.

room windows, the crew will simply close the window shutters so that the outdoor illumination will not interfere with the interior lighting. The audio engineer attaches a lavalier microphone to the chef and to the reporter, and the interview begins.

During the interview taping, the producer takes notes on each of the subjects discussed and the approximate running time to help her later during postproduction editing.

Once the interview segment is taped, the crew strikes the equipment in the living room and sets up in the kitchen for the cooking demonstration. The producer decided earlier simply to follow the chef as he talks his way through the cooking demonstration. Once the entire preparation is complete, the crew will then shoot a number of close-up inserts of each ingredient and the close-ups will be edited into the cooking demonstration so that the audience can clearly see every ingredient before it is mixed into the final dish.

The producer also decided that she would insert a lower-third graphic caption of each ingredient as it is shown in close-up. The graphic will be inserted by a character generator during postproduction, but the camera operator must be told about this so that he can compose each close-up

and leave enough room for the lower-third insert.

The demonstration proceeds smoothly with only one hitch: The camera operator failed to get a shot of the chef as he placed the fish into the skillet, so a pickup shot is taken after the demonstration has ended, and this will be edited into the final tape to eliminate the camera error.

At the end of the shoot, the audio engineer records a few moments of "room noise" to help in postproduction editing, and the producer checks her notes to make certain that all shots necessary for editing were recorded. With nothing more needing to be done, the crew strikes and packs the equipment, returns any furniture that was moved back to its original place, and stores the production equipment inside the EFP mobile van.

During postproduction, the producer refers to her notes as she screens the raw footage. The small audiocassette recorder she had available during the interview helps her organize the screening and decide on possible sound bites. She decides to use some of the chef's interview comments as a voice-over during the cooking segment, and this is easily accomplished during postproduction. Once the final tape has been completely edited, the lower-third captions are inserted from a character generator, and the finished segment is ready to be inserted into the week's magazine show.

Corporate/Institutional Training Program

A typical corporate/institutional training program might consist of two parts: (1) a short endorsement and statement of company policy by the chief executive officer and (2) a demonstration of a particular activity important to the workplace. Since safety is a universal concern to business, industry, government, and educational institutions, a safety program will serve as a useful example. In this case, it is a tape for the university police force concerning crowd control after football games.

The producer's first task is to establish the program's objective and the amount of time available to communicate the program's message. Since it is only part of a series of training activities, the program length is limited to twenty minutes and its primary point is: Do not let the students and other crowd members get out of hand, but maintain control with a minimum show of force.

These two facts were learned during a preliminary interview with the university's chief of police. The producer prudently went "to the top" to establish contact and set the program objective. By talking with the chief, two things occurred. Most important, the cooperation of the officers was ensured. With the chief's blessing, they can take time and effort from their other obligations to assist with the production. Also, the chief can garner the cooperation of the university's president, since the demeanor of the crowd as seen on national television is known to influence the university's reputation. With the aid of the chief, our producer is penciled into the president's schedule for thirty minutes two weeks from today. After being assured that the president was comfortable making public presentations early in the morning, the producer requested the 8 A.M. slot on the calendar. With the cooperation of the university's maintenance staff, the lead-off time gives him the pre-business hours to set up the shoot in the president's office.

Before leaving the chief's office, the producer also has established a contact from his office to work with in preparing for the production. The pro-

ducer asked to meet the contact while in the chief's office, an important tactic for demonstrating the chief's commitment to the project and for sanctioning the producer's authority in the field. The producer's parting words promise a rough script of the president's message and a production schedule that once approved by the chief's office can be distributed prior to the actual day of shooting. In return, the producer is promised a series of six short interviews to be conducted with veteran officers over the next several days. To get a general feel for the issues involved in crowd control and also to make preliminary contact with the officers involved in the production, the producer asks his contact to set up a lunch in the station cafeteria for tomorrow.

Overnight, the producer formulates an initial treatment. He learned from his meeting with the chief that crowd control had become an issue after riots followed a nationally televised football game two years before. The police force had acquired copies of the news coverage and the producer's preliminary feeling was that this existing tape could provide a realistic way to establish scenarios in which officers might again find themselves. Using this footage to provide a realistic backdrop, the producer felt confident that the controlled environment of the studio could be used to tape demonstrations of recommended crowd-control procedures.

After the next day's lunch, the producer has decided to pattern the overall production after the presentation of a sports program itself. The final treatment calls for news footage to be played and then freeze-framed at the moment of confrontation. A veteran police officer provides the "color" by describing the critical elements in the confrontation. The tape then continues revealing the consequences of poor crowd control. Finally, an officer working with several students from the drama department role-play a successful defusing of the confrontation, again with the veteran officers description of the successful tactics.

The ultimate success of this project relied on safely harnessing the totally unpredictable nature of the topic while still retaining the realistic flavor of the event with the use of news footage. The superior control of lighting, audio, and background offered by the studio was legitimized by setting up the studio-taped segments as "extracts" from the rushed reality of the street. In its own way, this treatment reinforced the underlying message for crowd control: "Think before you act." A similar philosophy underlies successful remote television production.

ELECTRONIC FIELD PRODUCTION

Electronic field production (EFP) is a term that refers to a wide range of production techniques which all have one thing in common: the use of a portable camera and videocassette or videotape recorder employing the single-camera/recorder production approach. At first glance, EFP may seem quite similar to ENG, which is not surprising because EFP grew out of the technology and experience gained with ENG. However, the two are very different production approaches which have evolved in separate directions for different production applications. ENG is designed to cover fast-breaking news events, and thus must be accomplished with little preparation and a minimal ability to control events. EFP is used when immediacy is not crucial and when higher production values and better overall technical quality are important considerations. Unlike ENG, EFP offers you the ability to preplan the shoot carefully and to attend to all the aspects of the production with the same care as is if it were produced inside the studio. Thus, when we talk about EFP, we are referring not only to a production approach, but also to a production "attitude" that involves overall control of the production in ways which are impossible when dealing with news events.

EFP has become the fastest-growing area of television production because of its ability to combine flexibility and efficiency with the special flavor which only a remote can bring to a production. EFP techniques are used in the production of entertainment shows, corporate and educational programs, commercials, and the magazine-format feature programs which appear on many local stations and cable channels. The ability to apply EFP methods to a variety of production situations at every level of sophistication is one of the technique's greatest strengths. An example of a relatively simple EFP production would be an interview with the chief executive of a corporation which is taped inside his or her office by a two-person crew and edited on a basic two-VCR editing system. At the opposite end of the EFP range are commercials, training programs, or dramatic presentations which are shot in dozens of locations employing many performers, a crew of ten people or more, and a great deal of sophisticated video and audio postproduction. Using these costly resources requires careful planning.

One of the most important decisions you have to make with EFP is deciding on the level of production sophistication to use for each shoot. The ability to match precisely the amount of equipment and personnel and the level of production sophistication which are necessary to produce a particular remote will enable you to produce a program both effectively and efficiently. In this section we will discuss the equipment and techniques used in EFP and how to apply them in each of the production stages.

EFP Equipment and Operation

The wide range of production situations which employ the EFP approach result in a very wide selection of EFP equipment. For very simple EFP productions, the crew may use equipment which is virtually identical to equipment used by an ENG unit, although usually with some modifications. On the other hand, complex EFP productions may use cameras, audio equipment, lighting gear, and videotape recorders which are as sophisticated as those found inside the studio.

EFP Mobile Unit

A very simple EFP shoot may require nothing more than a conventional automobile to carry the basic equipment and crew to the production location. However, most production facilities have modified a station wagon or van to serve as the EFP mobile unit. A dedicated EFP van offers a number of important advantages. First, the van—which is usu-

FIGURE 22-22 EFP Van.
An electronic field production (EFP) van contains all equipment needed for a production. The top of the van serves as a convenient platform for high-angle shots. *(Courtesy: RCA Corp.)*

ally of the same size as an ENG van—has adequate space to securely hold a great deal of equipment and a fairly large crew. Since microwave equipment is unnecessary in EFP, the space saved can be used to store extra production equipment. Also, the roof of the van can be modified to make a convenient camera position for high-angle shots. (See Figure 22-22.)

A well-designed EFP van should have a number of built-in racks for equipment storage. The built-ins not only keep the equipment from being damaged during travel, but also keep everything neatly arranged and enable the crew to locate the equipment quickly. Also, compartmentalized storage space is highly efficient and enables the van to carry much more equipment in a relatively small space.

Electric Power   Most EFP equipment can be operated from either battery power or conventional ac. An EFP mobile unit that can hook up to an ac outlet offers increased production capability. An internal electrical generator powered off the van's engine increases its operating flexibility by permitting totally independent power operation for extended periods of time.

TECH TIP   Lighting is one of your major power concerns. As lamp cables warm up, more resis-

tance is created and power consumption increases. To avoid blowing circuits on a delayed basis, allow about 50 percent "head room" in calculating circuit load. In other words, use no more than 14 A of power (about 1600 W) on a 20-A circuit.

Communications   The EFP unit's primary communications needs are internal. Walkie-talkie units are the most useful means of establishing a communications link between crew and production team members, who may be widely separated throughout the location site.

EFP Cameras

EFP cameras are usually selected from among the high-quality, shoulder-mounted cameras or, for even better picture reproduction, the line of convertible cameras that deliver the same picture quality as their larger studio versions (see Chapter 12). Since EFP units rarely need the lightweight portability necessary for news coverage, they can afford to compromise slightly on size and weight to obtain better picture quality.

To provide for greater production flexibility, EFP camera systems are usually equipped with such accessories as special lenses, filters, and a collapsible dolly in addition to the usual tripod and shoulder mounts.

Audio

EFP audio requirements can vary from a relatively simple and straightforward hand-held or lavalier microphone to the use of a boom mike and wireless microphones for more elaborate productions. A basic audio setup should include a number of hand-held and lavalier microphones for situations where on-camera mikes are acceptable. Shotgun mikes and a fishpole boom are necessary to pick up audio when microphones cannot appear in the picture.

Since EFP often requires the use of multiple microphones, the unit should include a battery-powered audio mixer to permit the audio engineer to balance and mix a number of microphones simultaneously. For production situations where some audio playback will be necessary (such as for musical lip sync), you will have to bring an audiotape recorder, speakers, and amplifiers. For these situations, the portable mixer must have switchable line/mike levels.

Wireless microphones are becoming increasingly common on EFP shoots because of their versatility and the availability of multiple tuners which allow the wireless mikes to avoid interference with taxis, police radios, and the like. Wireless microphones produce excellent sound quality when hidden on performers, yet they avoid the problems associated with trailing cable or the need for off-camera boom microphones.

The EFP audio section should include a great deal of additional microphone cable, gaffer tape for securing cable to floors and walls, headphones for monitoring the audio pickup, and spare batteries, fuses, and so on for microphones, mixers, and recorders. Since you will often shoot outdoors, be certain to carry windscreens for all microphones.

Lighting

The higher production values expected with EFP require more than the basic lighting kit used in news productions. A standard EFP lighting package should contain lensless spotlights, floodlights, mounting devices (stands, gaffer-grips, and wall units), barn doors and screens, gels, and sufficient amounts of electric power cable. Naturally, the amount of lighting equipment you will need varies from shoot to shoot, but a standard package ought to enable the lighting director or camera operator to control the illumination effectively and to create whatever lighting effects are required.

While shooting outdoors with EFP, you may have to use booster illumination to lighten dark shadow areas on the subject. Without that additional fill light, the contrast ratio of the picture would exceed the camera's reproduction capability and result in a poor picture on screen. Re-

FIGURE 22-23 HMI PAR Lighting System.
HMI stands for "hydrogen medium-arc-length iodine." Unlike quartz lamps, HMIs are color-balanced for daylight. HMI lighting systems are very useful for illuminating large outdoor areas. The boxes at the base of the stand are the power transformers for the four lights in the system. *(Courtesy: DN Labs, Inc.)*

flector boards are the cheapest and most convenient way to produce fill light outdoors. (See Figure 22-8.) If you intend to use electrical instruments outside, be sure you use daylight-balanced HMI lights or tungsten lights outfitted with dichroic filters to convert their 3200 °K indoor light temperature to the higher 5600 °K color temperature necessary to match outdoor illumination. (See Figure 22-23.)

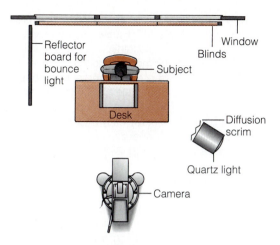

FIGURE 22-24 **Window Lighting.**
Lighting for windows is a challenge, especially when you can't avoid getting the window in the shot. In this case, you have two choices: (1) close the blinds almost completely and place a large sheet of amber gel over the window to match the daylight to your 3,200 °K quartz lights; or (2) close the window blinds completely and light the scene with quartz lights. If too much daylight is still leaking through the blinds and causing a blue halo on the subject, use a sheet of neutral density gel over the window and place blue (80B) color correction filters on the quartz lights to balance them to daylight. In either case the back light will be provided by the light coming through the window.

Windows in an interior shot can cause lighting problems, especially when you must match the brightness and color quality of outdoor light with an artificially illuminated indoor scene. The large sheets of window gel, which both color-correct outdoor light for indoors and reduce the brightness level to better match interior illumination, are very useful for these situations and should be included in the EFP lighting kit. In those instances where the natural light dominates, gels over the tungsten lamps must be used to avoid skin tones that appear yellow-orange because of the mismatched illumination. (See Figure 22-24.)

Videotape Recorders

All EFP productions are videotaped for editing later during postproduction. A commonly used EFP recorder is the ¾-inch videocassette ma-

chine which is battery-powered, highly portable, and very reliable. For those EFP productions where higher quality is required, Betacam SP and M-II VCRs have become popular because of their small size and flexible production capability. For corporate and educational uses, S-VHS and Hi-8mm provide the needed quality at affordable prices (see Chapter 20).

Battery-powered VCRs enable you to shoot your production at locations where conventional ac power is unavailable. However, batteries have limited power life and take a relatively long period of time to recharge. It is important to have a number of fresh battery packs available so you will not have to stop shooting because of rundown batteries.

TECH TIP Cold weather can reduce the useful life of a battery to one-third its normal shooting time. Keep batteries indoors as long as possible, and try to wear them next to your body under outer coats to increase shooting time.

If you will be shooting any or all of your EFP production where ac power is available, by all means use it to power the VCRs (and other equipment) whenever possible. Alternating-current power is reliable and will not run out at crucial times in production, so save the batteries for those situations where absolutely no ac power is available to you.

It goes without saying that the EFP unit should carry sufficient videotape or videocassettes for the day's shooting requirements. Always bring more stock than you think you will actually need. You can always return the unused tape, but you cannot replace the time wasted if you run out of tape before you finish shooting at the location site. You never want to find yourself in the situation of accepting a marginal tape because you are afraid you did not bring enough to finish the shoot. The videotape area on the EFP van also should have a slate for identifying each take. Pregummed labels should be affixed to every cassette or tape reel *and* to every tape box to identify the tape and its content accurately.

MULTIPLE-CAMERA REMOTE PRODUCTION

As the name suggests, *multiple-camera remote (MCR) production* uses more than one camera, enabling the director to cut between two or more cameras while the production is either recorded on tape or broadcast live. Unlike either ENG or EFP productions, which use a single-camera/recorder approach, an MCR production functions exactly like a conventional studio production, only it takes place in the field. The program director sits in a small control room situated inside the mobile van and switches between cameras as the event is covered in real time. Some MCR productions are complete programs which are broadcast live. Other MCR productions use multiple cameras to record the production in segments which are later edited into the completed show during postproduction. Although the MCR production team functions much as it would inside a studio, the fact that the production takes place in the field requires a number of additional considerations.

As with EFP production, the MCR approach offers a wide range of production capabilities. At the simplest end is a small van equipped with portable cameras (often the same as those used in an EFP unit) which are modified to feed a production switcher. Inside the minivan is a small production switcher which enables the director to cut, wipe, dissolve, and sometimes create a number of basic electronic effects. At the opposite end of the MCR range are the mammoth production vans which are literally the size of a Mack truck and contain control room and production equipment which is identical to that found inside a state-of-the-art television studio. The key element that all MCR productions have in common is the ability to cut between cameras in real time while the production is either recorded or broadcast live.

MCR Mobile Unit

The MCR mobile unit must be large enough to transport all the necessary production equipment to and from the location and, once at the site, serve as a control center during the actual production. Small-scale MCR units are often vans, minibuses, or recreational-type vehicles which have been specially modified to handle the increased weight load of the equipment and operating personnel. Large-scale MCR vans are generally trailer trucks which can run up to 45 feet in length and contain a completely equipped control room and videotape and camera control areas. (See Figures 22-25 and 22-26.)

Power   The vans are powered with utility-supplied current, which must be available at the remote site. Minivans operate from conventional 120-V, 20-A circuits, but the larger units require 220/240 V of power ranging from 50 to 200 A, depending on the size of the unit and the amount of production equipment that must be powered.

Communications   All the necessary PL communications between the control room and the production crew which are used inside the studio are duplicated in the MCR mobile van. Camera cables carry the intercom communications between the camera operators and the director. Additional intercom systems are available for the floor manager and other production personnel on large vans. On smaller vans which do not have secondary intercoms, the floor manager can plug into a nearby camera in order to communicate with the control room.

Walkie-talkies are useful for any MCR remote, but they are indispensable on those productions where the activity covered is some distance from the location where the production vans are parked.

Business telephones are an important communications link at the MCR site, especially if the unit is feeding the program back to the studio for live broadcast. Most large MCR vans carry one or more cellular phones. Those vans which rely on patching in to phone lines must notify the phone company (Telco) in advance so it can have them ready when the production van arrives.

Control Room   The control room area of the mobile van is a cramped replica of a conventional studio control room. There is a bank of monitors which display all camera and other video sources and also a production switcher that enables the director to cut between them. The size of the van determines how large a production crew the control room can accommodate and the additional equipment which can be installed. Large-scale vans have enough room for a director, switcher, and AD to sit at the production console and for a producer, character generator, and still-store unit operator to sit directly behind them. Smaller units generally can hold only three or four people inside the control area. (See Figure 22-27.)

Usually the audio-control console is located in an adjoining area which is separated from the control area by a glass window, enabling the audio engineer to monitor the program sound and communicate with the audio team without interfering with the control room operation.

Behind the control area is another area for technical operations. This is where the videotape recorder operators and their machines are located. (See Figure 22-28.) Often the camera-control units are also located in this area of the truck. Since a multiple-camera remote uses a number of cameras operating simultaneously, a technician must shade each camera as he or she would in the studio.

Transmission Facilities

If your remote production is being broadcast live, you must have a way to get the signal from your remote location to the home studio. If the production is intended for a local audience, you probably will use microwave transmission to reach the home studio. If the production is national or international, you probably will use a satellite link.

Microwave   Microwave transmission is a line-of-sight technology, which means that you must have an unobstructed path between the remote site and the microwave tower. Buildings, and even trees, can block microwave transmission. An important part of evaluating a remote site for a live broadcast is determining the series of microwave "hops," or relays between microwave towers, needed to reach the home studio where the transmitter facilities are located.

The station will have been assigned a micro-

FIGURE 22-25   Small-Scale MCR Truck.
Small-scale multiple-camera remote (MCR) trucks are often recreational vehicles modified to carry extra crew and equipment safely and securely. The truck's interior contains a control room able to handle multiple-camera shoots. *(Courtesy: Midwest Communications Corp.)*

(a)

FIGURE 22-26
Large-Scale MCR Van.
(a) Large-scale MCR trucks are
specially equipped trailer
trucks able to handle
elaborate remote productions
such as football games.
(b) The truck's interior is
divided into several
production sections.

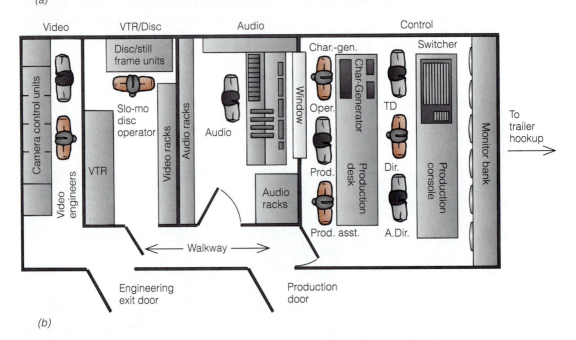

(b)

wave frequency by the Federal Communications Commission (FCC) for its use in a particular area, and the microwave relay network will be in place in most cities. The crew's responsibility is to hit the first tower with the signal to get it up on the circuit. Many stations have identified the location of the microwave towers and the direction in which to aim the remote signal from various parking places. In some areas where line of site cannot be established, the signal can be reflected off of a building. For important preplanned events, mobile microwave "towers" located in a helicopter can be dispatched to hover above the remote site as an access point to the microwave network.

FIGURE 22-28 MCR Mobile Unit Videotape Area. This MCR mobile unit is capable of recording and reproducing in 1- and ¾-inch videotape formats. *(Courtesy: Capital Cities/ABC, Inc.)*

Satellite A satellite is nothing more than a microwave tower 22,300 miles in the air. From this great height, the satellite has a line of sight that covers roughly one-third of the earth's surface. The remote signal is beamed up (up-linked) to the satellite on an assigned carrier frequency. The carrier frequency is shifted on-board the satellite so as not to interfere with the up-link and then is sent back down to an earth receive station located at the station's transmitter facilities. Because of their great line of sight and their ability to reach many earth receive stations simultaneously, satellites are ideal for transmitting television signals across long distances to multiple locations.

The current crop of communications satellites typically are equipped with twenty-four channels, known as *transponders*. Each transponder can carry a television program and is identified by number and by signal polarization, which is either *cross* or *direct*. Since satellites are extremely expensive and their number is limited by the FCC, few users, other than telephone companies, own their own satellites. Instead, a series of wholesalers known as *brokers* contract with television stations and production houses for blocks of time on particular transponders on particular satellites.

When planning a live broadcast for national or

international presentation, it is important to contract in advance for transponder availability. Since satellites use microwave frequencies, there can be conflicts between an intended satellite transmission and existing microwave services at the program origination point. Even if there are no conflicts for the use of a particular frequency, the desired transponder may be booked to another client.

In securing satellite time, reserve at least thirty minutes of setup time during which color bars and test tones are sent so that the receive station can lock in on the signal. Telephone lines between the send and receive sites allow problems that develop to be resolved. During production, extra telephone circuits can be *multiplexed,* or carried along with, the television signal.

The great distance between transmission and receive sites (a round trip of about 46,000 miles) causes some problems a production crew should anticipate. One of the most common problems involves audio, since the approximately half-second that passes between when a signal is sent and when it is received can lead to feedback problems when two-way communication, such as occurs in live interviews between a newscaster and a guest at another location, must take place. In such cases, mix-minus audio which reduces the audio problems should be used.

TECH TIP   When directing a show that includes satellite-carried conversations, stay on the speaker a split second longer than you would in a normal interview. Otherwise, the audience hears the question and then watches the interviewee hear the question a half-second later. Visually, the conversation appears stilted and the guest seems rather slow to form an opinion.

On occasion, severe weather can disrupt television transmission to the primary receive site, and a redundant link involving a different receive site should be planned. If the satellite transmission is to be handled from a portable transmitter carried on a truck, it is best to allow half a day to set up the truck and test the transmission link.

MCR Cameras

The cameras utilized on an MCR production are generally the same studio-type cameras found inside a production studio, or they are convertible cameras equipped for MCR with a large electronic viewfinder and a powerful zoom lens. In either case, the output of the camera is fed first to the CCU controls, where the picture is shaded, and then on to the production switcher located inside the control room area of the mobile van.

Newer mobile units generally use cameras which utilize triaxial cable which is one-fifth the size and weight of conventional multiconductor cable. The triaxial cable permits much longer cable runs between the camera head and the mobile unit and is easier than multicore to handle and store; thus the mobile truck can carry much more triaxial cable in a smaller space.

Camera Operation   Basically, the operation of a camera on an MCR production is the same as if the camera were being operated inside a studio. The camera operator listens to the program director over the PL headset, and a tally light indicates whenever the camera has been punched up on the air.

Of course, working a camera outside the studio adds a number of special complications to the camera operator's already difficult job. The weather can be controlled inside the studio, but it is highly unpredictable on a remote that takes place outdoors. Covering a football game in Minnesota in December or a stock car race from Florida in July are two examples of extreme weather conditions which can drastically affect a camera operator's performance. Also, many MCR productions involve sports or special events where a full rehearsal is impossible and the camera operator must be able to react quickly to the director's commands as events unfold. Finally, camera positions on a remote are often dictated by the remote location, and you may find yourself working a camera in a variety of uncomfortable or even hazardous situations. It is not uncommon to suspend a camera from a crane high above a musical concert in a park or to squeeze camera and operator into a tiny corner at the back of a theater with instructions not to disturb the audience while he or she photographs the action on stage.

Camera Mounting Equipment For most productions, the camera is mounted atop a portable tripod which is unfolded and positioned at the camera site. Unless the tripod is equipped with wheels, you will not be able to move the camera once it is positioned. While this is not always a problem, be sure you have enough tripods with wheels for those cameras which must be moved during the production. In crowd situations, the tripod must be on an elevated platform or the camera can be blocked. (See Figure 22-29.)

Hand-held cameras are often an excellent complement to a number of tripod-mounted cameras and permit the director increased camera movement. Of course, the portable camera must be cable-connected so that its picture feed runs through the production switcher inside the production truck or linked to the production van via portable microwave.

There are special situations which may require

a pedestal or a dolly unit such as a crab dolly. While these mounting devices increase your production capability, they are heavy and take up a great deal of space on the truck. They also require additional personnel to operate them.

Camera Lenses The most important question when deciding on camera lenses is the distance between the camera's position and the subject. For some remotes which take place at a sports stadium or inside an auditorium or theater, your cameras will be positioned a considerable distance from the subjects and you will need zoom lenses with a powerful telephoto capability. Range extenders are useful for increasing the telephoto power of the lens, but they also require a higher-

FIGURE 22-29 Camera Scaffolding.
Camera scaffolding provides high camera angles to peer over obstructions. Scaffolds should be sturdy and provide reliable footing for use in bad weather and high winds. *(Courtesy: Capital Cities/ABC-TV, Inc.)*

than-normal light level which may not always be available from existing illumination. Alternately, remote productions that occur within interior living spaces often require wide-angle lenses that can provide the desired images even when the camera must work in a restricted area.

Audio

An MCR production may require as many as a dozen or more individual microphone feeds. This means that the audio section of the production van must have an audio control console large enough to handle multiple audio inputs and, ideally, the ability to equalize each incoming feed to correct for acoustic problems that may occur at the location site. Most audio areas also contain the patch panels, reel-to-reel and cartridge tape machines, and audio monitoring equipment found inside a conventional studio audio-control area.

The usual complement of microphones includes lavalier, hand-held, and directional shotgun mikes, depending on the audio requirements. For sports or special-events coverage, many audio engineers and talent prefer headset mikes for better sound quality and no-hands operation. Wireless microphones are also commonly used both as hand-held mikes and to hide lavaliers on talent.

Videotape

The types of VTRs used on an MCR remote depend primarily on the size of the truck and the level of production. Smaller vans frequently use ¾-inch cassettes, although a number of facilities have installed high-quality ½-inch Betacam SP or M-II VCRs. Large vans generally use either 1-inch or ½-inch tape. The 1-inch machines usually are equipped with a slow-motion control unit enabling the director to use the slow-motion replay capability for sports and special effects.

Additional Equipment

On large-scale MCR vans used to produce an entire program, the van is equipped with a number of additional equipment items. Most vans carry a character generator to permit the director to add graphics during the production. Still-store units are also commonly used, especially in the production of sports and special-events programming.

Lighting

The lighting requirements of an MCR production depend on the particular production situation. Sometimes the unit must provide all lighting, and this can involve transporting a great deal of portable lighting equipment to the remote site. Other times the unit may be covering an existing event such as a sports event and can use the available natural or artificial illumination. For coverage of a concert or play which is being produced in front of a live audience, you may have to cover the event with existing illumination. This requires close coordination between the television lighting director and the stage lighting director to ensure that sufficient illumination is available for technical operation of the camera.

REMOTE PRODUCTION

Since both EFP and MCR production follow the same four production stages, we can discuss how the equipment and techniques are applied in each of the stages for both remote techniques at the same time.

Preproduction Planning

Preproduction planning, although important for every show, is indispensable when producing a remote. Once you are on location, you cannot run down to the supply room for some gaffer tape or pick up an extra audio cable you forgot to order. Everything your production will need must be planned in advance and brought with you to the location. Detailing the production team's needs and predicting what additional items may be necessary takes skill, experience, and a great deal of preparation.

What Kind of Remote Is It?   As with any production, your first job is to define the particular characteristics of the remote you plan to cover.

Remotes can be classified into two categories: (1) events which are *covered* and (2) events which are *staged*. A covered event occurs whether or not television is present, and the production unit has little, if any, control over the event itself. A staged event, on the other hand, offers maximum production control because it is produced specifically for television. Although a live audience might be present (as in a theater or concert hall), the spectators are themselves part of the event, which is designed and produced primarily for television.

The nature of the event also will determine the type of remote production approach you can use. A single-camera EFP approach is cheaper and more flexible than a multiple-camera remote with its large mobile unit and dozens of technicians. Yet not all events can be covered with a single camera, especially those which require multiple cameras photographing the action in real time.

Finally, the producer and director must identify the program's objectives and indicate which elements are most important to the show. Until this information is available, none of the production and engineering planning and preparation for audio, lighting, cameras, and so forth can begin.

Remote Survey

Where should the cameras be positioned? How much light is available at the location? Where do we park the mobile unit? Is there sufficient electric power for the equipment? Before you can produce at a remote location, you must run a *remote survey,* which is designed to answer these and countless other important production and engineering questions. The purpose of a remote survey is threefold: (1) to determine the location for the production, (2) to determine where all production equipment and personnel will be positioned, and (3) to determine whether all the production's needs and requirements can be handled at the remote site.

For many productions, the answer to the first question, "Where is a suitable production location?" is determined by the event itself. Wherever a sports event, parade, or conference is being held *is* the production location. But many other productions—commercials, entertainment shows, instructional programs—do not necessarily specify locations as much as an overall mood, atmos-

phere, or background. In this case, it is up to the producer and director to find a suitable location which fits the production's aesthetic needs for atmosphere and detail and meets the production's engineering and logistical requirements.

As a general rule, make your survey visit at the same time of day the event is scheduled to take place. This is especially important for outdoor remotes, since the cameras should ideally be positioned with the sun behind them. Surveying a location in the early morning, with the sun in the east, does little good if the production is scheduled to begin at 4 P.M., when the late afternoon sun is in the west. In addition to accurately estimating the sun's position, the location of shadows, the contrast between light and dark areas, and other time-related factors make it important to carefully review the site as close to the time of production as possible.

Interior locations may be immune to these problems, but they generally offer enough problems of their own. For example, a visit to a downtown hotel on a Saturday morning to survey the ballroom for an upcoming remote would likely reveal a deserted area with plenty of parking space and access for equipment. The same location during a weekday afternoon, when the remote is scheduled, can look quite different, with the parking lot full to capacity and the street clogged with pedestrians and automobile traffic that block easy access to the building. The audio environment would change in this example from the quiet of a Sunday morning to the din of rush-hour traffic.

Finally, if you have never done a program at the remote site, take nothing for granted. Are all the electrical outlets you see actually working? Does the window through which you will run cable actually open? Do you need a special key to operate the service elevator? It is better to have oversurveyed a site than to overlook an important item that can prove to be disastrous later on.

Although every remote is slightly different, here is a rundown of some of the most important production and engineering points to be considered by the survey team during their visit to the location. (See Figure 22-30.)

REMOTE SURVEY FORM

Survey Date: _____

PROGRAM: _____

PRODUCTION DATE: _____   Live/Air Time: _____ VTR _____

LOCATION SITE/ADDRESS: _____

Director: _____ Producer: _____ TD: _____

LOCATION CONTACTS

Primary Contact _____ Phone: _____

Secondary Contact _____ Phone: _____

Permits _____ Phone: _____

Parking Location _____

Credentials _____

CAMERAS (add sketch of cam positions)

	Position/Location	Lens	Cable Run
CAM #1			
CAM #2			
CAM #3			
CAM #4			

AUDIO

Mike Type	Location/Cable		Mike Type	Location/Cable
1 _____		7 _____		
2 _____		8 _____		
3 _____		9 _____		
4 _____		10 _____		
5 _____		11 _____		
6 _____		12 _____		

LIGHTING (add sketch of light plot if needed)

Available Light in fc: _____

Lighting Instr: _____
_____

FIGURE 22-30   Remote Survey Form.
The remote survey form includes important points to remember when planning a remote shoot.

PROGRAM: _____

POWER

Location Electrician Contract: _____

Power Requirements: _____

_____

AC Outlets (location/voltage/connector type) _____

_____

Special Power Instructions: _____

_____

COMMUNICATIONS

PL: #Cam Headsets _____   Special PL drops: (1) _____

(2) _____   (3) _____   (4) _____

TELEPHONE:

                              Location

Private Line: _____   _____

_____   _____

                              Location

Business Line: _____   _____

_____   _____

CONSTRUCTION:

SPECIAL INSTRUCTIONS:

Local Contacts and Clearances Always establish a local contact who can provide access, information, and help with various details. Obtain the individual's name and phone number and those of any assistants who might be helpful. Among important secondary contacts are electricians, plumbers, and maintenance people, who usually know about everything you will need for the production.

ACCESS Establish where you need access to the site, when you intend to arrive with the equipment, and who will be there to meet the crew. Setup often occurs at odd hours, and unless someone has been notified of your arrival, you may find the gates locked and no one around when your truck shows up at 4 A.M. to begin an early setup.

PERMITS Most cities require a production unit to take out a police permit either to park vehicles on the street or to shoot on public property. Be sure you have the necessary permits well before the production is scheduled, and arrange with the police for crowd or traffic control if necessary. (See Figure 22-31.)

PERMISSIONS Arrange for parking spaces for your production vehicles and for any private cars used by the cast or crew. If you must park on city streets, your police permit should indicate where and how you can position your vehicles. A parking lot next to the remote is a real convenience, but make certain that your space has been reserved by the location contact in advance.

Where to position the mobile unit is an important production and engineering consideration. There are times when you will have little choice in the matter, but if you do have an option, find a location that requires the shortest average cable run to cameras and equipment. You also will need easy access from the mobile unit to the location site, since both equipment and production personnel require unrestricted movement between the truck and the actual production area.

Cameras POSITIONS The location of your cameras is a crucial production decision that must be made during the survey. The director should already know how many cameras are available and approximately where they are to be located to cover the event. If it is to be an EFP single-camera shoot, the director must know which camera setups will be necessary and approximately where the camera will be positioned for each one.

For multicamera productions, select the best combination of positions to cover the action from a variety of perspectives. Some cameras must be located fairly high so they can provide a wide cover shot of the action. Other cameras must be located at lower levels for closer shots, as well as to photograph the various activities that surround the primary event.

Make certain you have considered screen direction by keeping all the cameras on the same side of the action axis. Otherwise, you risk inadvertently changing screen direction as you cut from one camera to another. Cameras must be positioned where they are free of shooting and movement obstructions. It does not take much skill to avoid planting a camera behind a pole or column, but beware of potential obstructions which might not be as obvious. For example, a camera positioned behind a seated theater audience might be blocked completely if someone gets up or if the audience rises to its feet during production.

Whenever possible, try to position your cameras in easily accessible locations. This is not always practical, however, and there are times when you may have to construct a special scaffold or use special equipment (such as renting a cherry-picker crane) to provide a unique camera vantage point.

Portable cameras offer much greater production flexibility than stationary cameras and can

FIGURE 22-31 **Police Permit for Remote Production.**
Police permits often are required to park mobile units on city streets and to shoot in public areas. (*Courtesy: The Mayor's Office for Film, Theatre, and Broadcast, New York City.*)

MOTION PICTURE–TELEVISION PERMIT　　　　　　　**PERMIT NO.** _____

CITY OF NEW YORK

MAYOR'S OFFICE FOR FILM, THEATRE, AND BROADCASTING

110 WEST 57TH STREET NEW YORK, N.Y. 10019

This permit is issued to the applicant to film or televise on streets or property subject to the jurisdiction of the City of New York at the times and locations designated below. The permit must be in the possession of the applicant at all times while on location. For additional assistance call the Permit Division: 489-6714. Police Unit: 592-6226.

APPLICATION NOT ACCEPTED UNLESS TYPED.

Date: _____

1. Company: _____ Production Contact: _____

2. Address: _____ Tel. No. _____

3. Locations (If more than 2 use Schedule "A") _____

_____

_____

4. Dates of filming: _____ Approx. times: _____

5. Scene to be filmed must be described accurately: _____

_____

6. Animals, firearms, special effects or unusual scene: _____

7. List production equipment: _____ # in cast & crew _____

　No. of Trucks & plate #s _____

　No. of Autos & plate #s _____

　Other vehicles & plate #s _____

8. Feature Film: ❏ TV Movie or Special: ❏ TV Series: ❏ Other: ❏ (Give title, producer, director and identify celebrities)

_____

_____

　Asst. Director: _____ Prod. Mgr. _____

9. If TV commercial name product: _____

10. Public Liability Insurance Company, Policy # and Agent: _____

　Amount: _____ Expiration date: _____

The applicant agrees to indemnify The City of New York and to be solely and absolutely liable upon any and all claims, suits and judgments against the City and/or the applicant for personal injuries and property damages arising out of or occurring during the activities of the applicant, his (its) employees or otherwise. The applicant further agrees to comply with all pertinent provisions of New York laws, rules and regulations. This permit may be revoked at any time.

VEHICLES LISTED ABOVE ARE PERMITTED TO PARK IN ANY AVAILABLE PARKING SPACES IN THE IMMEDIATE VICINITY OF THE ABOVE LISTED FILM LOCATIONS, EXCEPT: FIRE HYDRANTS.

Date	Signature of Representative	Title

DO NOT WRITE BELOW THIS LINE

The Mayor's Office Seal must be embossed on original copy.

Dated _____ 19_____　　Film Coordinator, Mayor's Office of Film, Theatre and Broadcasting

673

provide some interesting shots which literally take the viewer into the action. Their use must be carefully planned and coordinated, however. A portable camera with a cable must be positioned where the cable will not interfere with the action but will provide enough unrestricted movement. A portable microwave link completely frees the camera from cable limitations but requires additional crew members to handle the unit.

As you plan camera positions, consider what each camera is responsible for photographing during the production. For example, events which use an announce booth must have one camera positioned to cover the announcers on-camera, as well as the action itself. Other cameras may have to be located so they can easily shoot the scoreboard, the audience, backstage, graphics, and so on.

LENSES   Depending on the camera-to-subject distance and the type of shots you have planned, you will have to decide which camera lenses to use. You may have to request special lenses or range extenders to provide better shooting possibilities.

CABLE RUNS   How will you run cable from camera positions to the mobile truck? On EFP shoots where camera/recorders are used, cable runs are unnecessary. For multiple-camera productions, however, every camera must be linked to the truck by either cable or microwave. Cable runs of over 2,000 feet, using multiconductor cable, are not advisable because of possible video problems. Plan your cable runs so the cable does not interfere with the event itself, with other equipment, or with spectators or lie too close to electric power lines, which can cause serious technical problems.

Audio   Producing high-quality television audio in the studio is never easy, but the many acoustical problems, combined with the extraneous noise frequently encountered at a remote site, make the audio engineer's job that much more difficult at a remote.

Among the basic points you will need to know before surveying the site are the following: (1) Who and what must be miked? (2) Can the microphones appear in the camera shot? (3) What potential audio problems exist (cavernous sports arena, widely spaced participants at a meeting)? (4) Must any special audio arrangements be made to coordinate television coverage with the public address audio system being used at the remote site?

MIKING TALENT   Announcers, commentators, and play-by-play sportscasters usually can be miked with lavalier or hand-held microphones. A headset mike is also a good choice because it offers talent hands-free operation, reduces extraneous noise, and maintains a constant subject-to-mike distance, even as the announcer follows the action.

How much movement flexibility do the performers require? If they will remain in one location, any type of microphone or cable combination will work well. If they must be able to roam around the site, a wireless microphone provides unrestricted movement.

If the microphone must remain hidden off-camera, will a fishpole boom or a shotgun work? Sometimes hiding a lavalier under a performer's clothing will produce the best audio quality.

ATMOSPHERE SOUND   The natural sounds of an event are the subtle touches which make a production more realistic and enjoyable for the viewer. The crack of a well-hit baseball, a downcourt dribble, and the swish of a golf swing are examples of atmosphere sounds which are picked up with either a parabolic or a directional shotgun microphone. Crowds should be recorded with a microphone positioned for a very general pickup pattern. Avoid placing the microphone where it will pick up a few specific people instead of general crowd noise or too near a house PA speaker. Referee and umpire calls can be covered using either special desk mikes or shotguns or by equipping the referee or umpire with a wireless RF mike. (See Figure 22-32.)

PUBLIC ADDRESS FEEDS   Sometimes the television production uses a direct feed from the house PA system. This is often the case in governmental or

FIGURE 22-32 **Miking Natural Sound.**
The audio technician must plan for the pickup of natural sound at a remote event. Often a parabolic reflector or a shotgun microphone is held by an audio assistant outside camera range. Another approach, illustrated here, is to mount a shotgun mike on top of a camera to pick up the sound.

committee hearings, concerts, or various indoor events, where a PA is required for the house audience to hear the speakers. The use of a PA feed does not eliminate the need for additional television mikes, since announcers, crowd noise, and other audio sources are not covered by a normal PA system.

If you choose to take a PA feed, remember that the television audio technician does not control the individual microphones used by the PA system, but simply receives a single, premixed audio feed. This can be a convenience, but you also run the risk of relying on an important audio source that may not be well balanced.

CABLE RUNS   Estimate the number and lengths of audio cables necessary for every microphone position. Audio cable should be run around congested areas and away from power lines.

RECORDING ROOM NOISE   If you are recording an EFP or MCR production for later editing, remember to record some "room noise," which is simply

the natural sound of the location without anyone speaking into the microphone. The room noise will be indispensable during postproduction in helping to smooth out audio edits.

TECH TIP   The "cocktail party" phenomenon describes our ability as listeners to block out extraneous noise and concentrate on a speaker. Microphones cannot do this, and if background noise competes with a speaker, the speaker's audio will become unintelligible. As a check against competing background noise, close your eyes and slowly rotate through a 360° circle where talent will be speaking. Listen specifically for traffic, refrigeration, air conditioning, running water, etc. which might be overlooked while talent is speaking but will destroy the audio recording.

Power   Estimate the production's total power requirements, and check to see that the necessary power will be available at the remote site. In addition to noting the voltage and amperage, make certain that the wiring configuration is compatible with your equipment.

MOBILE UNIT POWER   If you will use the mobile unit to supply power to all your equipment, learn where the power source at the remote site is located and whether it is compatible in voltage, amperage, and wiring with your van. If you intend to use an internal power generator, will heat and noise present any serious problems?

POWERING INDIVIDUAL EQUIPMENT   EFP equipment is frequently powered individually. The simplest approach is battery power, but batteries limit the amount of operating time. If you will operate the equipment from power mains, make certain the correct ac outlets are accessible where you plan to shoot. Check all outlets in advance. Never assume that the presence of outlets where you intend to shoot automatically means that all the power outlets are actually working.

Check with an electrician at the remote site as to the location of the fuse or circuit breaker box. If possible, obtain the wiring schematics for the area. This way you can spread out your electrical load evenly by plugging into a number of outlets wired to different circuits. This reduces your chances of blowing a fuse or tripping a breaker and lessens the possibility of voltage fluctuations that can interfere with equipment operation.

It is often possible to tap major cable lines to provide additional power for special production requirements. However, this requires a professional electrician, and you should never attempt to rewire or tamper with electric circuits unless you are fully trained to do so.

CABLE Power cable runs must be planned for cameras, VTRs, lighting instruments, and other production equipment. Never use ordinary home extension cords, which are too thin to carry the necessary current and are susceptible to fraying or breaking. Use heavy-duty, insulated electric cable, which provides the durability, safety, and power load for a remote situation. Determine the number and the length of the cables you will need. Cable choice is particularly important in damp locations or during rainy weather.

When you plan electric cable runs, avoid leading the cable near video or audio lines, since there is a possibility of electrical interference with the program signals when video and audio lines are located too close to power cables.

Communications All the communications systems normally used for a production inside the studio must be brought to a remote location. This includes both the internal communications system for the production unit and external communications links between the remote unit in the field and the home studio.

PRODUCTION COMMUNICATIONS If you are using an MCR van with multiple cameras, the normal intercom PL system from the cameras to control room will operate once the cameras are connected to the control truck.

Additional PL lines, or "drops," for the floor manager, floor assistants, spotters, and additional production personnel must be planned during the re-

mote survey, and arrangements must be made to provide them. Determine how many headset units are needed and the length of cable necessary from control truck to each PL drop.

Commentators and announcers are usually supplied with an *interruptible foldback (IFB)* system, which permits the director and producer in the truck to talk with talent in the booth while they are on the air. An IFB system can be either wired into a dual-earpiece headset (one side contains program audio; the other IFB) or fed to a small telex earpiece worn by talent.

VIDEO AND AUDIO FEEDS During the survey, you must determine all the locations which require video or audio program feeds. Obviously, the announce booth needs a video monitor displaying the on-air picture and a feed of program audio. Other locations for video or audio feeds might include the floor manager's location—backstage, on the sidelines, or by the spotter's booth. Needless to say, separate cables must be run from the control truck to every video or audio feed.

TELEPHONES Telephones are almost always necessary, especially on live broadcasts which require a great deal of communication between the remote production site and the home studio. Internal PL telephones between areas of the remote site must be requested from the telephone company (Telco) in advance. Specify how many of these "dry pairs" you will need and their exact locations.

Business telephones are necessary for the remote unit to communicate externally. Again, the survey team must determine how many business telephones are needed and must specify their exact locations. Most large-scale remote vans already have cellular telephone units, others may require Telco to hook the phones into lines at the shoot.

PROGRAM TRANSMISSION Program video and audio for a live broadcast must be fed from the remote site back to the home station. If the remote occurs within range of the station's microwave system, this is an inexpensive way to link the remote unit to the broadcast studio. Otherwise, you must arrange for a local common carrier to transmit the program over land lines or microwave links, which they provide especially for the broadcast. Alternately, you might purchase satellite time from a broker for the transmission.

Security   Will you require any special security arrangements? This includes security for your equipment, which may stand in place all day or perhaps overnight. Crowd control also may be a problem. Does the remote location have its own security force, or will you have to make special arrangements?

Credentials and passes are often necessary to permit production personnel access to all locations at an event. Arrange for these through the location contact in advance of the production. You will need to specify how many people will require passes. This includes production staff, technical crew, and talent.

Miscellaneous   Every remote production has its own unique set of requirements. Some additional survey items you may have to take note of are these:

FOOD AND LODGING   Are you responsible for providing food for the unit? If not, are there commercial restaurants nearby where food is accessible quickly? It may be faster and easier to bring food to the location than to give everyone a lunch break and hope they all return in time.

Even if you do not have to provide a full meal, coffee and cold drinks are greatly appreciated. The cost is small, and the benefits in improved morale are worth the additional effort.

If your unit is staying overnight, you must arrange for lodging. The hotel or motel should be located as near the remote as possible to eliminate travel time.

TRANSPORTATION   Will you have to provide transportation to and from the location site? Depending on the size of your unit, this can be a relatively simple job or a major logistical operation.

CONSTRUCTION   Will any special construction be necessary? Camera platforms, the announce booth, and lighting units all may require the erection of temporary scaffolding. These should be planned for and, if possible, set up before the remote unit arrives with the equipment.

Production Meeting

Once the survey has been completed, the key team members must meet for the usual preproduction conference. The producer or director runs down the survey detailing special requirements for each of the key production areas. If the team has never done a remote at the location before, taking a few snapshots or slides of the site can help everyone who was not at the survey to visualize the overall area and specific locations.

During the meeting, the producer must plan the remote production schedule. First, the necessary arrival times for the mobile unit and technicians should be determined. If you will have to construct special platforms or lighting grids, plan to have these crews arrive early so that their jobs will be finished by the time the cameras and lights arrive at the location.

Setup will proceed much more efficiently if the entire production unit is divided into a number of smaller groups, each handling its own area of responsibility. This way one crew can unpack and mount the cameras while another group runs audio cable and connects microphones.

Setup and Rehearsal

The activities during the setup and rehearsal of every remote depend on the production approach and on the show itself. A large-scale remote requires an enormous setup compared to a single-camera EFP. In addition, the EFP unit usually sets up a single shot, rehearses it completely, and then tapes it before moving on to the next. A multiple-camera remote must completely set up the entire unit before any rehearsal or production is possible. Events which are staged for television can be carefully rehearsed, shot-by-shot if necessary. Covered events cannot be rehearsed at all, even though some of the basic format can and should be planned in advance.

With these differences in mind, let us look at setup and rehearsal procedures, focusing primarily on large-scale remote operations, which offer the most difficult challenges.

Setup Unlike a studio production, where certain elements exist from the moment you enter the studio, every remote situation must be set up from scratch. As soon as the mobile unit arrives, it should be parked and power supplied to the vehicle. The various crews which were organized in preproduction can now begin their individual assignments.

Cameras must be unpacked, carried to their planned locations, and mounted atop tripods or pedestals. Any special towers or stands for the cameras should already be in place. As the cameras are set up, another crew should be running cable from the control truck to each camera position. Once the cameras are mounted and cable runs completed, connect the cameras and switch on the power to give the camera's electronics a chance to warm up and stabilize before the engineers begin setup and alignment procedures.

The audio crew will already be unpacking their equipment, running cable to each location, and setting up the proper microphones (hand-held, lavalier, boom, and so on) at their correct positions. If necessary, label each microphone with the performer's name to avoid any confusion later on. The audio crew is usually responsible for setting up all communications systems (except telephones, which are Telco's responsibility), including IFBs and video and audio feeds.

As each microphone is positioned, run a brief sound check to make certain it has been connected, identified, and patched in properly. Equalizing and balancing microphones should wait until the audio setup is finished. Once you have checked out a particular microphone, make certain it is secured in a safe location where it will not be misplaced or damaged.

All necessary lighting instruments should be hung and focused during the setup period. Since the lights must be in position and working before the production rehearsal can begin, the lighting setup should be planned to prevent holding up the entire unit. For elaborate lighting situations, it may be advisable to have the lighting crew arrive at the location early to ensure enough time to finish the job.

Once all the equipment is set up and connected, the crew must go through a complete engineering checkout, often called the *tech rehearsal* in an MCR shoot. This is not a production rehearsal, but an engineering operation to ensure that the equipment has survived the trip in working condition and is properly set up. After the cameras are registered, audio feeds are equalized and balanced, and the other production equipment has been checked, the unit is ready for the production rehearsal.

Rehearsal The remote's rehearsal proceeds much as that for any normal studio production. EFP operations usually rehearse with the director positioned next to the camera. Each individual camera shot is set up, rehearsed, and taped until the director is satisfied and moves on to the next cycle of setup, rehearsal, and taping.

Staged productions can be carefully rehearsed by the director in exactly the same way a show would be rehearsed inside a studio. For those spontaneous events where no detailed rehearsal is possible, the director can still work out each team's individual responsibilities, based on the production plan and format.

NBC Sports director Ted Nathanson always holds a brief meeting with key production crew members prior to every broadcast. Nathanson explains what he expects each camera to cover and specifically details those shots each camera should have for a variety of expected situations. The same instructions are given to audio, to the slow-motion and VTR machine operators, and to graphics. Nathanson's approach is easily applied to any remote which cannot be completely rehearsed but follows along a preplanned sequence of events.

According to Nathanson, the top remote camera operators are the ones who constantly practice their shots before air time. Just as the players on the field practice before the game, the camera operators warm up their camera moves. It takes some time to become accustomed to a strange remote site or an awkward camera location. Practicing how far you need to zoom in or out to get certain shots, what it takes to pan quickly over to the scoreboard or to a graphic, or how much freedom of movement a portable camera operator really has can be done prior to production and will result in smoother camera work during the actual show.

Production

The production stage for a remote is usually no different from that for in-studio shows. Of course, there are always problems encountered in the field that cannot occur inside a studio that is specifically equipped for television production. For example, taping on location with a number of lighting instruments inside a small room may produce excessive heat which forces the crew to cease production periodically, turn off the lights, and allow the room temperature to cool. Otherwise, the high heat could interfere with the camera or VTR operation, not to mention the discomfort caused to both talent and crew.

TECH TIP Hot lights near the low acoustic ceiling of an office have been known to activate the office sprinkler system. Mount lights away from heat sensors to avoid this potential disaster.

Naturally, a live broadcast from an MCR van offers a special kind of excitement regardless of how much planning and rehearsal went into the show. During a live broadcast, the director must concentrate totally on the pictures and sound that are to go out over the air. He or she must rely on the AD and the producer to help with time cues, coordination, graphics, and videotape inserts or replays.

For example, on a live remote, the AD keeps an open telephone line between the production in the field and the home studio. This is necessary to cue the remote unit when to begin the show and to smoothly coordinate taped commercials and inserts which are rolled-in from the studio. An off-air monitor tuned to the local station's programming is used to show everyone inside the truck when the station has punched up the remote feed on the air.

The routine for a live remote broadcast is this:

1 Prior to air time, the AD establishes contact with the studio and synchronizes the remote's clock with the master clock at the station.
2 All time cues and coordination operations are double-checked before air time.

3 About one minute before air time, the AD readies the control room. The director tells the TD to punch up the opening shot on the line. This allows the station to confirm that the feed is reaching them and is ready to go out over the air.
4 As air time approaches, the AD simultaneously watches the clock and the off-air monitor and relays the home studio AD's countdown to the production unit.
5 The AD should hear the "go" cue over the telephone just as the air monitor switches from the station's feed to the remote's line picture. The remote production is on the air.
6 During the broadcast, the AD coordinates all commercial breaks, VTR or film rolls emanating from the home studio, and the remote's final end time.

Postproduction

Once the production is completed, the crew must strike all equipment, pack it safely, and return to the studio. A remote strike requires the same planning and coordination as the setup to do the job efficiently and effectively. After the work and effort in producing a remote, the strike is likely to be anticlimactic, but do not let the crew get careless now. It takes as much concentration and attention to detail to pack equipment as it does to set it up. Remember, the chance of damage returning to the studio is exactly the same as the chance of damage occurring on the way to the shoot, and it costs a great deal more to leave a $200 headset at a stadium than it does to leave it back at the station.

All equipment should be carefully and neatly stored away. This makes it easy to count the number of cables, headsets, microphones, and other small items which easily can be left behind. Storage space is often at a premium, and neatly coiled cable will fit better than a jumbled tangle of wire. Assign someone to make an inventory check of the equipment as it is brought back to the truck so that you can be sure you are leaving the remote site with as much equipment as you brought.

Before leaving the remote location, the producer, director, or engineering supervisor should check with the location contact to clear up any remaining business details. It may be obvious, but a production unit that leaves the location as clean as they found it and is courteous and cooperative with the location staff will find it easier the next time they must do a production at the same site.

All EFP and some MCR productions which were shot in segments will require a postproduction editing stage. We will cover videotape editing in the next chapter.

SUMMARY

A remote is any production that takes place outside the studio. Remote productions can be classified as three types: (1) electronic news gathering (ENG), (2) electronic field production (EFP), and (3) multiple camera remote (MCR) production.

Electronic news gathering production uses a portable television camera connected to a battery-operated videocassette recorder. The ENG mobile unit can be as simple as a conventional car or a specially modified van or minibus that contains all the production equipment and a microwave unit or satellite up-link which enables sound and picture to be transmitted directly back to the home station for recording or live broadcast.

The ENG camera usually is a portable camera/recorder which operates from battery-supplied power. Although ENG coverage frequently requires the camera/recorder to be hand-held, a tripod should be used when the situation permits to eliminate jitter and permit shooting at longer lens focal lengths. When shooting ENG footage, always record some cutaway footage to enable the tape editor to bridge edits.

ENG audio production is usually simple and straightforward. Hand-held or lavalier microphones are frequently used, although shotgun mikes are used when it is impossible to position the microphone directly in front of the subject. Audio recording always should be monitored through headsets to ensure quality. Before leaving a news location, the engineer should record some "room noise" to aid in audio editing of the videotape footage.

The ENG news material is recorded on either ¾-inch or ½-inch videocassettes. The VCR is battery-operated, and fresh batteries always should be kept on hand to avoid running out of power at a crucial time during recording.

ENG lighting requirements are generally straightforward, although when the situation permits, a number of portable lensless instruments should be positioned to illuminate the subject using the conventional three-instrument lighting approach.

Live sound and pictures of a news event can be transmitted back to the home station by using a portable microwave unit, which is installed in many ENG mobile vans. In addition, smaller microwave units enable the ENG camera crew to work at a distance from the mobile van without having to run cable between the camera and the mobile unit. Satellite news gathering (SNG) networks are redefining the relationships among local stations and their parent networks and making new demands on field reporters.

ENG production is somewhat different from most other television production situations owing to the nature of news coverage. Although few events can be preplanned, the ENG crew can use a logbook that includes pertinent information about each news site regularly visited by the ENG crew. During a recording, the ENG crew should remember to keep editing in mind and to shoot the event in a way that provides the editor with enough footage to assemble an effective news story. This includes the use of cutaway footage, reverse angles, and a minimum of random camera movement or zooming.

ENG footage recorded in the field must be edited into the completed news piece. The first step is to log the tape and note either the time-code or counter numbers where each important segment appears. During actual editing, the various taped cuts including sound bites, stand-ups, and cutaways must be edited and sequenced into a complete story. Most operations play back the edited cassette during production. The playback VCR is run through a time-base corrector which enables the cassette to be integrated with other video elements through the production switcher in the control room. The use of the pause control on the playback VCR makes it possible to preroll the tape to any point and freeze-frame it until called for by the program director.

Electronic field production (EFP) utilizes a single-camera/recorder production approach, but unlike ENG, it can be preplanned and permits the production crew to devote more care and attention to production details in order to produce a show with higher production values than is usually possible when covering fast-breaking news events.

Multiple-camera remotes (MCR) utilize a number of cameras which cover the event in real time, enabling the director to cut between cameras from a control room located inside the MCR mobile unit. MCR productions are either covered live or videotaped for postproduction editing later. For live coverage, the production unit must arrange for the video and audio feeds to be transmitted back to the home station for broadcast.

Planning is indispensable for a successful remote, particularly because all the usual conveniences automatically available in the studio must be specifically brought to the location site. A remote survey is conducted by the producer, director, and technical supervisor before the actual production to determine, in advance, the project's production and engineering requirements and how they can be met at the remote location.

During preproduction meetings, the survey is reviewed with the key production team members, and the usual program planning considerations are discussed. Of particular importance is whether the remote event is staged or covered. A staged event is produced specifically for television and offers maximum production control. A covered event would occur with or without the television unit at the scene and offers additional production challenges, since the remote crew must adapt to the circumstances of the event as they already exist.

Setup, rehearsal, and production operations are usually determined by the type of remote, the production approach employed, and the nature of the event itself. Postproduction involves striking and packing the equipment and restoration of the location to its original condition before the remote unit returns to the studio. In the case of EFP or an MCR production that is videotaped, postproduction editing is necessary in order to complete the program.

VIDEO EDITING

Editing has become such a key element in the production process that it is difficult to imagine any television program that does not utilize it in some way. In order to function effectively in television, you must understand how videotape is edited and the many creative production possibilities that editing offers.

VIDEOTAPE EDITING

There are a number of different ways to edit videotape, but the basic process is the same regardless of the editing system. Unlike audiotape, which can be edited by physically cutting and splicing the tape itself, all videotape editing is performed electronically. Essentially, videotape editing is an electronic transfer process in which you copy, or "dub," original "source" video material onto an "edit master" tape. As you dub the original footage, you sequence it into a completed program by using an *editing controller*, a device that operates both the playback and the edit/record VTRs and enables you to control precisely when and where the previously transferred material on the edit master tape will end, and the new material playing in from the playback (source) VTR will begin. (See Figure 23-1.) A good electronic edit will look just like a clean cut between two video sources on a switcher.

Reasons for Editing

There are many reasons for editing a program. The first and most obvious is to enable the producer or director to juxtapose various shots and

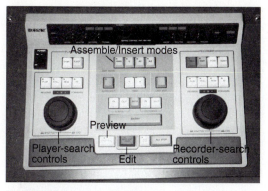

Assemble/Insert modes

Preview

Player-search controls

Edit

Recorder-search controls

FIGURE 23-1 Edit Controller.
An editing controller allows the editor to find the exact edit point on both the playback and the edit/record VTRs prior to making the edit. The editing controller has a preview capability so you can see how the transition appears before actually performing the edit.

scenes to successfully achieve the program's communications objective. It is sometimes said that a program is "made in the edit room," which refers to the power of editing to place shots and scenes in just the right sequence with the proper transitions to give the program its maximum emotional or informational impact.

Editing allows you to produce a program by shooting scenes or shots out of sequence to accommodate production schedules and then piecing the program together later in the edit room.

Editing also enables you to re-do various shots or sequences to correct mistakes which have occurred in production. The original audio and video can be separated, moved independently, and combined with new material.

Finally, editing allows you to carefully control the transitions between shows and sequences. While a good television director can cut a program between multiple cameras "on the fly," the ability to edit enables the director to precisely control when and where a cut occurs and to control the duration of a transition such as a dissolve or wipe.

Types of Edits

There are three types of edits: (1) *video-only*, (2) *audio-only*, and (3) *video-audio*. The most commonly used edit is the video-audio edit where both picture and sound are edited simultaneously. The

video-only and audio-only edits, as their names suggest, enable you to edit only picture or sound, which gives you great flexibility. For example, if you are editing a news interview, you might first assemble a video-audio sequence of the "talking-head" interview. Then, where appropriate, you can use a video-only edit to replace the interviewee's face with "B-roll" shots illustrating what she is talking about. Finally, the correspondent can lay down a narration track which you can insert over various parts of the interview and the B-roll video using audio-only edits.

To edit original material from a source videotape into a completed program on an edit master videotape, two methods of editing are used: (1) *assemble* editing and (2) *insert* editing.

Assemble and Insert Editing Methods

You should recall from Chapter 20 that four kinds of information are recorded on separate tracks on a videotape: (1) video information; (2) audio signals; (3) a control track consisting of synchronization signals; and (4) editing time code which contains cuing information. (See Figure 20-6.) The two editing methods, assemble and insert, utilize the material in the four tracks on the videotape, but they differ in the way they erase the previously transferred material and record new material in the different tracks on the edit master tape.

Assemble Editing   When the electronic editor is in the assemble mode, the new program material is added to existing program footage on the edit/record VTR beginning at the predetermined "in" edit point. Assemble edits create a new control track segment by segment as they move material from the playback to the edit/record VTR. As the edit/record VTR records, it automatically lays down new control track, and audio and video information, beginning with each new edit point. Using assemble editing, you simply add material—or assemble the program—piece by piece. In an assemble edit, both the video and audio material must be transferred in the edit.

Since the edit controller needs time to lock to

control-track information from the playback (source) and edit/record VTRs to synchronize tape movement and avoid picture breakup, there must be a control track on the edit/record VTR in the form of a recorded signal before and after the precise edit point. This extra control track can be laid down by simply letting the edit/record VTR record five to ten seconds *beyond* the "out" edit point where you want the old material to stop and the next segment of new material to begin. When the next edit is made, the playback VTR's programming is recorded over the extra information on the edit/record tape, but it will have some control track to lock onto, providing a clean edit.

Assemble edits are very convenient because you simply add segment by segment to build a show on the edit/record VTR. However, even though you have laid down additional control track at the edit point, the lack of a continuous control track, which is used like film sprocket holes to guide the VTR's operation, can result in the picture "tearing" or breaking up momentarily. (See Figure 23-2.)

Insert Editing Insert edits were originally designed to let you add video or audio to an existing program without disturbing the rest of the program material. For example, you might have recorded a scene where a character reads a letter and you want to insert a close-up of the letter which was shot after the original scene was recorded. Operating the electronic editor in the insert mode,

find the correct "in" and "out" points for the insert and make a video-only edit using your normal editing procedure. Remember, since the insert edit is being "dropped into" a previously recorded program, you must indicate both in and out points; otherwise, the insert will continue on and erase the previously recorded program material. (See Figure 23-3.)

Insert editing moves audio and/or video information from the playback unit onto a tape in the edit/record VTR which already has a continuous, undisturbed control track. A program can be constructed from start to finish using insert editing by first recording a *preblacked* tape, which is made by recording a blank tape with "black" from a studio output or a "black burst" generator. Because of this prerecording of black, the preblacked tape contains an uninterrupted control track to guide the VTR, ensuring very stable edits at all times. Using the preblacked tape, you build your program in the normal way, but instead of operating the editor in the assemble mode, you operate in the insert mode, indicating both in and out edit points. Remember to leave a video pad after each segment to help you select the best edit point for the next segment.

The key differences between assemble and insert editing are illustrated in Figure 23-4. Assemble editing is often used when long segments are being sequenced into a final program. For example, you may have taped a thirty-minute drama in three ten-minute acts using the multiple-camera/single-VTR approach, and you need to perform only two edits to assemble the program. On the other hand, if you taped the drama using the

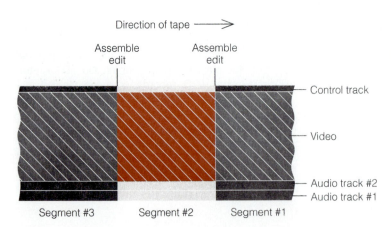

Direction of tape ⟶

Assemble edit

Assemble edit

— Control track

— Video

— Audio track #2
— Audio track #1

Segment #3   Segment #2   Segment #1

FIGURE 23-2
Assemble Editing.
In assemble editing, each segment is added to the edit master tape one after the other. The edit/record VTR lays down a new control track for each segment, along with both the audio and the video tracks. If many assemble edits of short segments are performed, the control track may become unstable.

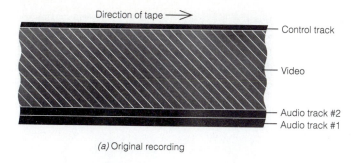

Direction of tape ⟶

Control track

Video

Audio track #2
Audio track #1

(a) Original recording

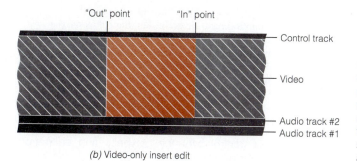

"Out" point   "In" point

Control track

Video

Audio track #2
Audio track #1

(b) Video-only insert edit

FIGURE 23-3 Insert Editing.
(a) The continuous original segment is recorded. *(b)* The video-only insert edit replaces the video track, but does not alter the control track or the audio tracks. The control track will remain stable no matter how many insert edits are performed.

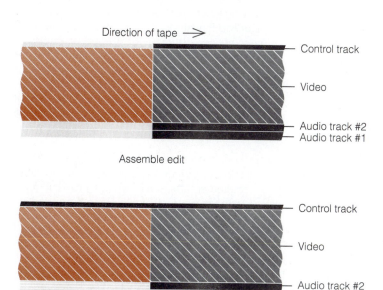

Direction of tape ⟶

Control track

Video

Audio track #2
Audio track #1

Assemble edit

Control track

Video

Audio track #2
Audio track #1

Insert edits

FIGURE 23-4 Assemble Edits versus Insert Edits.
Assemble edits may be performed on a blank tape because they record all the information needed, including a control track, but insert edits must have a control track prerecorded on the edit master tape. Assemble edits cut across all the tracks on the edit master tape, but insert edits may be video-only, audio-only, or combined video-audio edits. Insert edits never interrupt the prerecorded control track.

multiple-camera/multiple-VTR approach, you will have to perform an edit after each camera shot. In this case insert editing would be better because the control track would remain continuous and more stable. You also would have the flexibility to perform video-only and audio-only insert edits.

The only real disadvantage to the insert editing mode is the need to prepare the preblacked tape. Obviously, a one-hour tape requires you to record one hour of black before you can begin to edit. This takes one hour of real time; there is no way to speed up the recording process. Many production facilities keep a supply of preblacked tapes on hand so that emergency editing jobs or fast-breaking news can be insert edited without delay.

VIDEOTAPE EDITING CONTROL SYSTEMS

All electronic edits, whether assemble or insert edits, are made by transferring source material from a playback VTR to an edit master tape on an edit/record VTR. The method you use to control the editing operation varies, depending on the type of editing control system available to you. Each system allows the tape editor to preprogram the exact edit points on both the source and edit master tapes. The editor can then preview the edit without actually executing it. After adjusting the edit so that it is perfect, the editor leaves the preview mode and executes the actual edit. Basically there are three types of editing control systems: (1) *control track*, (2) *time code*, and (3) *computer editors*.

Control Track Editing

Control track editing is used most often for news editing and many simple editing situations. This system operates by counting television frames using the control track pulses on both the source and the edit master tapes. As each frame is counted, its precise location is displayed by a series of numbers that appear on a readout device on the editing controller. (See Figure 23-5.)

FIGURE 23-5 Edit Controller Readout.
Counting control track pulses, the edit controller displays readouts in hours, minutes, seconds, and frames for the source tape and the edit master tape. The readouts are not recorded on the tapes themselves and may be reset during editing.

Most editing controllers employ a "search knob" for each VTR. The search knob gives the tape editor control over the playback and edit/record VTRs by permitting the operator to manipulate movement of the tapes in the following ways: (1) *playing* forward or backward at normal speed; (2) *shuttling* forward or backward at slow motion or fast motion; (3) *jogging* forward or backward, moving frame by frame; (4) *still-framing*, freezing the picture completely at the exact frame where the edit is to be made. (See Figure 23-1.)

While different editing systems will have slightly different features, the editing process is basically the same:

1   Load the source and the edit master cassettes into the proper VTRs. Make sure the record button or tabs are in place on the edit master videocassette. If you will be insert editing, make sure the edit master tape is preblacked.

2   Play the source tape and set the audio levels on the edit/record VTR. You should see the source picture on the edit/record monitor. If not, make sure that the proper input is selected and that the edit/record VTR is stopped, not in "play" or "pause."

3   Select "insert-video," "insert-audio," or "assemble" on the edit controller, depending on which type of edit you want to perform.

4   Find the "in" edit point on the edit/record VTR by jogging back and forth with the search knob

or pushbutton controls until you have located the precise frame where the edit is to occur. "Freeze" this frame by pressing the "still/pause" pushbutton. This freeze-frame will be displayed on the edit/record VTR's monitor.

5 Program this frame as the "in" edit point by pressing the "edit in" and "enter" pushbuttons on the readout device. There must be at least five seconds of material prerecorded on the tape prior to the "in" point.

6 Follow the same procedure on the playback VTR to locate the frame where the new source material is to begin. The freeze-frame image will appear on the playback VTR's monitor. By looking first at the picture on the edit/record monitor and then at the picture on the playback VTR monitor, you can see how the video transition will appear.

7 Program this frame as the "in" source point by pressing the "source in" and "enter" pushbuttons on the readout device. There must be at least five seconds of video material on the tape prior to the "in" point.

8 Now you may rehearse, or "preview" the edit by pressing the "preview" button. This automatically will backroll both VTRs the same distance to synchronize precisely their preroll time, which usually is five seconds. The edit controller will roll both VTRs and electronically switch to the new material on the edit/record VTR's monitor to show you exactly how the edit will appear without actually making the edit on tape. At this time, you may adjust the audio level on the edit/record VTR. If the control track is missing from either tape for any duration during the preroll time, the editing system will not work.

9 If you want to shift either "in" point slightly, use the "trim" function. Once you have approved the preview edit, press the "edit/record" button. This will start both machines, locking them into synchronization and causing them to make the edit precisely at the programmed edit point.

In the procedure outlined above, only "in" edit points were selected. This means that the edit/record VTR would continue recording until the end of the control track on either tape or until you pressed the "end edit" button. However, it's pos-

sible to program an automatic "out" point on one of the tapes. This is especially useful when insert editing. For example, you may want to insert a video-only cutaway of a reporter to cover a jump cut during an interview. After selecting the "in" points on both tapes, you could select an "out" point three seconds later on either tape. Now the controller automatically will edit into the cutaway at the "in" points, edit out of it three seconds later, then pause both machines. Some edit controllers have a "review" button that would replay the whole sequence if pressed at that time. The "in" and "out" edits both should look like clean camera cuts.

TECH TIP If you fail to enter the edit "in" points on the readout device, the controller will assume that the freeze-frames on the source and edit master tapes are the edit "in" points and enter them automatically when you press "preview" or "edit." To edit, there must be "in" points on both the source and edit master tapes, but only *one* "out" point can be programmed. It may be on either the source or on the edit master tape.

Adding Voice-Over Tracks A common practice during ENG editing is to add a voice-over to an edited sequence. That may be done easily by following this procedure:

1 Be sure to turn down the audio on the edit/record VTR monitor to prevent audio feedback.

2 To hear the audio tracks, you will need to wear headphones.

3 Press "insert-audio" (on one track) on the edit controller. Make sure the other insert edit functions are off.

4 Press "stop" on the edit/record VTR.

5 Plug a microphone into one MIC channel on the edit/record VTR. Do a mike check and set the audio level. (See Figure 23-6.)

6 Play the edit master tape and set the "in" point.

7 Set the "out" point on the edit master.

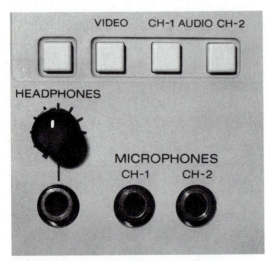

FIGURE 23-6   Edit/Record VTR Microphone Input.
Voice-over narration may be added to edit masters by plugging a mike directly into one of the MIC inputs on the edit/record VTR and performing an audio-only insert. The audio track you use will depend on whether there is time code on one of the audio tracks and whether you are recording in monaural or stereo.

8   Preview the edit. At this time, you may adjust the audio level on the edit/record VTR.
9   Perform the edit.
10   Review the edit.

Edit controllers that count each video frame in order to control the editing operation are the most commonly used editing devices owing to their versatility and low cost. However, the control-track counting system is not without its disadvantages. Since the system merely counts the video frames that exist on the tape, it is susceptible to error and is not frame-accurate. This is rarely a serious problem for most day-to-day editing requirements, and operators usually learn how to compensate for their system's minor variations and idiosyncrasies. Another disadvantage of the control-track counting system is its inability to locate automatically footage that may be anywhere along a tape. Instead, the editor must visually search through

the tape in order to locate a particular cut. Again, this is not usually a problem for most common editing situations, but on some productions which require elaborate editing of many hours of raw footage, it can be time-consuming. Finally, and most significantly, the control-track counting system does not permit the editing-control device to synchronize and control the operation of more than one playback VTR or the operation of auxiliary equipment such as multitrack audiotape recorders, switchers, and special-effects generators. In order to utilize these items to achieve more sophisticated postproduction operations, we must turn to the second type of edit controller, the time code system.

Time Code Editing

Although electronic editing will make a perfect edit exactly where programmed, locating the precise edit point can be difficult and time-consuming. In order to identify each video frame precisely and to permit much more accurate editing, a standard time code system was developed and later standardized by the Society for Motion Picture and Television Engineers (SMPTE). Since everyone standardized on the SMPTE time code, all systems—regardless of the tape format or VTR machine model—read, write, and understand the same "language." You will see time code referred to as "SMPTE/EBU" because it also has been adopted by the European Broadcasting Union (EBU).

The system works by adding an eight-digit code number to mark each video frame, in effect giving every frame its own unique "address." The time-code information is usually carried on the cue track or, on some machines, on a special time-code track. The code can be recorded either while the program is being recorded or afterward. The numbers appear on specially equipped monitors at the bottom of the picture screen and on time-code readout counters.

The eight code numbers refer to the hour, the minute, the second, and the video frame. Since there are 30 frames per second, the last two digits reach 29 before the seconds move ahead one number. (See Figure 23-7.) Although the time code itself does not function as an editing system, it is the key to all sophisticated electronic editing because it serves as the basic reference used by both conventional and computer systems to locate, cue, and edit videotape with single-frame accuracy.

TECH TIP SMPTE time code is actually an 80-bit digital "word." In addition to supplying hours, minutes, seconds, and frames, the SMPTE code specifies sync information and allows users to "write" their own information, such as the "slate code," where the shooting date or scene ID can be located.

Drop Frame versus Nondrop Frame The time code is created on the tape by a *time-code generator*, which can be run in one of two modes: (1) *drop frame* or (2) *nondrop frame*.

For certain technical reasons, if we generate the time code continuously—starting at 0:00:00:00 for the first frame and continuing for each subsequent frame on the tape—we would wind up with a discrepancy between the time code that appears on the videotape and the actual time of day or standard clock time. Consequently, the SMPTE developed an alternative generating mode called *drop frame*, which is designed to correct this discrep-

ancy. In the drop-frame mode, each minute—with the exception of every tenth minute—actually drops two frames in its time-code count. The result is a time code that precisely agrees with the actual standard clock time.

The reason this is important is because computer systems that use time code cannot function with different tapes encoded with different time codes. The different drop-frame and non-drop-frame "dialects" of time code "language" confuse the machine and inhibit its operation. This is why most production facilities have standardized on one mode—usually drop frame—for all video recording. Whichever mode you select, make certain that *all* tapes are recorded with the same time-code mode, whether it is drop frame or nondrop frame.

Drop-frame code is required because color television signals are actually processed at 29.97 frames per second rather than the 30 frames per second of black and white. As a result, about four seconds of color programming per hour must be dropped to equal one hour of "clock time."

FIGURE 23-7
SMPTE Time Code.
SMPTE time code appears as eight digits representing hours, minutes, seconds, and frame numbers, and is recorded on the videotape. The unique SMPTE frame numbers provide the basis for computer-assisted editing systems. *(Courtesy: CMX Systems, an ORROX Company.)*

Using Time Code in Production   Every video-tape to be edited must be encoded with its own unique series of ascending time codes; that is, the time code should begin with a low number and progressively increase to a higher number. In addition, it is crucial to avoid any duplication of similar time-code numbers on the same tape or on different tape reels, since the time-code reader which uses the tape as reference deals only with the eight-digit code and becomes confused if it reads two identical numbers. There are two ways you can use time code: (1) *zero start* or (2) *time of day*.

ZERO START   In *zero start,* the digits begin from zero at the start of each tape reel or recording and indicate the amount of lapsed time as the recording progresses. Most recording sessions use zero start because you can use the hour digits to designate different tape reels. The first reel would begin at 01:00:00:00, the second reel at 02:00:00:00, and so on.

TIME OF DAY   In *time of day,* the digits run synchronously with a master studio clock, and the numbers reflect the actual time of day. Time of day is a useful method when you want to use the clock time of day to log events during a recording. Recordings of news events, sports, and other productions which require you to locate events within real time are done with this method. Producers, writers, and other production personnel do not need access to the SMPTE readout digits to log events for later editing. All they have to do is refer to a studio clock, since it is identical to the time code digits on the recording tape. The disadvantage of time-of-day time code is that many computer-based editing systems work with continuous time code. If there are breaks in the time-of-day time code when the record VTR is turned off, the computer editor may have difficulty finding a particular video frame.

Recording Time Code   There are two places to record SMPTE time code on a videotape: (1) in the *vertical interval* and (2) on an *audio track.*

We discussed the vertical interval in Chapter 20. Time code is one of the signals that may be present in the vertical interval. If time code is recorded in the vertical interval, it is called *vertical interval time code*, or *VITC* (pronounced "vit-see"). The main advantage of VITC time code is that it does not take up an audio track, but a limitation is that it can only be recorded at the same time the video is being recorded.

In most videotape systems, the time code is recorded on a secondary audio track or on the VTR's cue track. This is referred to as *longitudinal time code (LTC)*. It is crucial that the time code be recorded at a sufficiently high audio level, and without distortion, for the system to read the code properly. However, if the audio level of time code is too high, it may "bleed" into the audio channels, and sound like an annoying "screech." It has been found that time code recorded at about 3 dB below zero on a VU meter provides the most satisfactory results—high enough for the system to read, but not so high that it is heard in the audio. It is definitely worth the extra few minutes it takes to make certain that the time code is being properly recorded to avoid cross-talk in the audio channels or having to completely rerecord the time code after the original recording is completed. The editing system must be able to read the time code properly or poor edits and a lack of synchronization between different machines may result.

TECH TIP   There are other types of time code, often lumped together as *RC* (*rewritable consumer*) *time code*. RC time code is generated on some consumer recording systems, but it is incompatible with SMPTE time code, and must be converted for use in professional editing.

For productions recorded inside a studio, time code is usually recorded at the same time the VTR records the program material. For remote productions recorded outside a studio on location, camera/recorders with built-in time code generators automatically lay down the time code as the original program material is recorded. This is the case with the Betacam SP, M-II, and S-VHS formats. Hi-8 camcorders record their own type of 8-mm RC time code. Some portable ¾-inch VCRs do not record time code at all. That's fine if all you are doing is control track editing. But for time code editing, the code must be added later. That can be done when the ¾-inch tape is "bumped up," or dubbed, to a one-inch format for editing. If the editing will be performed on a ¾-inch system, longitudinal time code must be added to an unused audio track on the original tape. Basically that involves doing an audio-only insert edit that records the signal from a freestanding time code generator onto one audio track.

Obviously, when handling original tapes, great care must be taken to prevent any interference with the original recording. A safer method is to dub the original tape and simultaneously add time code, either VITC or LTC. However, the trade-off is that you lose one generation on the edit master. Tapes that will be used for edit masters usually have time code recorded at the same time they are being preblacked.

Playing Back Time Code   Although the time code information is recorded and stored on a separate audio track, a time code reader is required to enable you to see the numbers during playback. The time code reader can display the figures either on the top or the bottom of the television screen along with the rest of the video image, on a separate digital clocklike readout device, or on a CRT unit.

It is also possible to "burn in" time code numbers onto a videocassette "workprint" so that you can watch the picture and see the time code on a standard VTR that is not equipped with a time code reader. This is called a burned-in "window dub" because the time code appears in a window on the screen, as in Figure 23-7. Often a window dub will be made onto a VHS cassette, which can be watched almost anywhere, and the editing planned by noting the exact time code numbers where edits are to be made. Of course, the burned-in time code can never be used on the master tape, since the playback image would include the time code numbers along with the rest of the program video.

On-Line and Off-Line Editing with Time Code
Until the development of time code, all editing was accomplished on the same mastering/high-end machines on which the programs were recorded. This is referred to as *on-line* editing. On-line editing requires more than one playback VTR, a char-

FIGURE 23-8   On-Line Editing.
On-line editing is costly because it uses expensive, high-end equipment, and requires highly-skilled technicians to operate it. *(Courtesy: Capital Cities/ ABC, Inc.)*

acter generator, graphics devices, a video switcher, and even more sophisticated hardware. On-line editing is costly because it uses expensive, high-end VTRs, and requires highly-skilled technicians to operate them. Also, machines committed to on-line editing are unavailable for other production or playback purposes. The high costs, combined with the distracting environment in the VTR tape room, often make on-line editing a pressured and difficult situation for a director and an editor. (See Figure 23-8.)

Introduction of the time code gave editors and directors an alternative: *off-line* editing. Using the off-line method, a cassette copy of the original master tape is made containing the same time code that appears on the original tape. The workprint can be recorded at the same time the master tape is recorded, or a dub can be made after the taping session is finished. (See Figure 23-9.)

The editor and director use the time code digits which appear along with the picture on the playback monitor to develop an *edit decision list*. The decision list is used later as a reference to direct the editing of the master tapes. Since all creative editing decisions are made off-line, the actual editing of the master is a straightforward and simple process of "editing by the numbers." (See Figure 23-10.)

If you wish, you can actually produce an edited

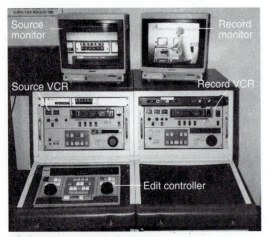

FIGURE 23-9   Off-Line Editing.
Off-line editing requires a playback VTR on which to watch the original footage to make editing decisions. An inexpensive cuts-only editing system may be used to assemble a workprint.

jobs, many directors simply use the edit number to develop the written decision list without going through the additional step of actually producing the edited workprint.

Off-line editing also can be helpful on remote productions. Many editing decisions can be made by the reporter/producer using the field record deck. Then, since almost all ENG vans offer at least assemble edit capabilities, the raw footage described by the edit decision list can be quickly assembled by the crew into a finished story and broadcast from the remote location.

Computer Editing

Computer editing systems combine the data processing capabilities of the computer with television production equipment, enabling the operator to edit efficiently and accurately. The computer controls the various playback and edit/record VTRs, and interfaces them with auxiliary production equipment such as audiotape recorders, production switchers, and special effects generators. The computer also can generate text, graphics, and special effects, and incorporate them in the finished program. (See Figure 23-11.)

The computer system uses SMPTE time code to produce an electronic *edit decision list (EDL)*—a list of every edit point, the duration of the transition (if it is a fade, dissolve, wipe, or key), and the "in"

workprint on most off-line systems. This is valuable in complex editing situations, where the editor and director need to see how the cuts actually look on the television monitor. But for most simpler editing

FIGURE 23-10   Edit Decision List.
An edit decision list sequences the various program segments into the desired order for editing. The "edit-in" and "edit-out" SMPTE time codes for each segment are listed, sometimes accompanied by a short description of the video. The edit decision list can be compiled on less expensive off-line equipment, saving time and expense prior to the actual on-line editing session.

PROGRAM: *FALL FESTIVAL AUCTION*   DATE: *12/10/94*

SEGMENT	DESCRIPTION	CASSETTE #	EDIT-IN Hr	Min.	Sec.	Fr	EDIT-OUT Hr	Min.	Sec.	Fr
1	AUCTIONEER (THOM)	1A	00	03	30	10	00	04	45	20
2	BLENDER	2A	00	01	00	00	00	01	10	00
3	AUCTIONEER (ED)	1A	00	12	10	15	00	14	20	08
4	CRUISE LINER	2A	00	02	00	00	00	02	30	00
5	THOM AND ED	1A	00	20	12	00	00	22	18	10
END										

FIGURE 23-11   Computer Editing System.
This computer editing system includes (*a*) a scene logging database and editing software on a Macintosh computer, (*b*) a Video Toaster, (*c*) VHS and ¾-inch source VTRs, and (*d*) a ¾-inch edit/record VTR. The Video Toaster functions like a combination switcher, character generator, luminance and chroma keyer, and special effects generator. *(Courtesy: Sundance Technology Group.)*

line or off-line. If you are editing on-line, you actually will be editing the master tape as you go along by making edit decisions and executing them at the same time. However, the real advantage of the computer system is the ability to work off-line, because this enables you to produce a workprint and then to have the computer automatically assemble the master footage to conform to the edited workprint.

Basically there are two types of computer editing systems: (1) *linear* and (2) *nonlinear.*

Linear Editing   All videotape editing—whether control track, time code, or computer—is a *linear* process. That is, you must program and perform the first edit, then the second, then the third, then the fourth, and so on in order until you finish. Furthermore, if you want to tighten or extend a segment in a completed program, you must also shift all the edit points following it on the edit master. (See Figure 23-12.) Likewise, if you want to drop or add a segment in a completed program, you must re-edit everything on the edit master follow-

and "out" points for each edit sequence. As you go along making your edits, the computer stores this information in its memory and uses the finished EDL as a guide for the final automatic assembly of the edit master tape.

The computer system can be used either on-

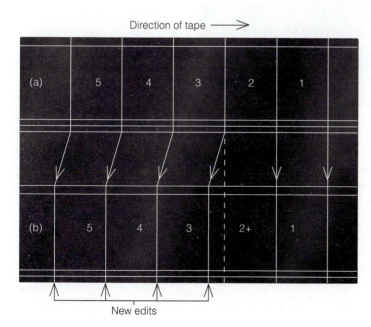

Direction of tape ⟶

New edits

FIGURE 23-12   Extending a Segment in Linear Editing.
In linear editing, if you extend or tighten one segment, all the subsequent segments must be shifted. (*a*) This original edit master has five segments. (*b*) Extending segment 2 means that segments 3–5 must be shifted by re-editing all of them at new edit points. In control track editing this must be done manually. Computer editors automatically "ripple" all the edit points following a change.

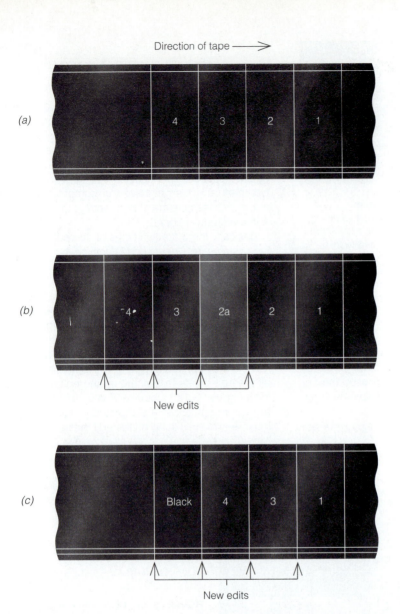

Direction of tape ⟶

(a)

4 3 2 1

(b)

4 3 2a 2 1

New edits

(c)

Black 4 3 1

New edits

FIGURE 23-13 Adding or Dropping a Segment in Linear Editing.
In linear editing, if you add or drop a segment, all the subsequent segments must
be shifted. (*a*) This original edit master has four segments. (*b*) Segment 2a has been
added; therefore, segments 3 and 4 must be re-edited onto the edit master
following segment 2a. (*c*) Segment 2 has been dropped; therefore, segments 3 and
4 must be re-edited onto the edit master following segment 1. In this case, if part of
the original edit remains visible following the re-edited segment 4, black will need to
be inserted at the end to cover up the original.

ing that segment. (See Figure 23-13.) Obviously, re-editing is inefficient and expensive.

The videotape editor has three alternatives to this time-consuming process of re-editing. The first is to record a second edit master, using the first one as the source tape, but re-editing only where needed. Although a quick solution, this approach is not desirable because the new edit master would lose a generation and program quality would suffer.

A better alternative is to use time code editing on a computer system. It provides a feature called "rippling," which works like this: When you reprogram an edit point on the edit master, the computer controller automatically shifts, or "ripples," all the following edit points exactly the same number of frames. This approach is efficient and accurate, and doesn't lose a generation. But it still is a linear process, which means that the program must be completely re-edited onto the edit master tape from beginning to end. (See Figure 23-12.)

Fortunately, there is a third alternative that has none of the limitations of the others: *nonlinear editing*.

Nonlinear Editing   Nonlinear editing is performed with a personal computer outfitted with hardware and software that enable it to digitize the video and audio and store them on computer disks. The PC is able to function like a video

switcher, special effects generator, and editing controller—all combined in one unit. (See Figure 23-14.) Nonlinear editing often is referred to as "random access editing" because it provides the editor with random access to the source material stored on computer disk. Therefore, you do not have to wait while source tapes fast forward or rewind to a desired scene. Any frame is accessible and appears almost instantaneously when called up from disk.

TECH TIP   Computer editing that uses PC-based systems often is called "desktop video." This designation comes from the fact that PCs usually sit on desk tops. Desktop video systems are capable of traditional production functions, such as titling, keying, graphics generation, time-base correction, frame synchronization, signal monitoring, and audio recording and mixing. (See Figure 23-15.)

NONLINEAR EDITING OPERATION   Unlike computer-assisted on-line tape editing, nonlinear editing is fairly easy to learn, especially if you have used PC windows-type applications. The basic operating procedure for nonlinear editing—frequently called "digital video post"—works like this:

Audio mixer
Editor display monitor
Video monitor
Edit controller
Computer keyboard
Mouse
Edit decision list
Source VCR

FIGURE 23-14
Nonlinear Editing System.
This nonlinear editing system uses the PC/MS-DOS platform and is called "Lightworks." The source video is digitized from a standard videocassette and stored on disk. All editing is performed in the computer, which automatically compiles an edit decision list that is used for the final on-line edit. *(Courtesy: Capital Cities/ ABC, Inc.)*

FIGURE 23-15 "Desktop" Computer Editing System. This "desktop" computer editing system is like a television control room in a PC. It uses PC-based software to control three source VTRs and an edit/record VTR. A user can program effects and transitions on up to five layers of video and graphics simultaneously. The video, audio, and graphic processing is digital and the recording and editing on videotape is analog. *(Courtesy: Matrox Electronic Systems.)*

1   You digitize the source video from a camera or videotape and store it on either a recordable videodisc or a hard disk. The capacity of the disk you need will be determined by (1) how much source material you digitize, and (2) whether the digitized video is low resolution (the equivalent of VHS), medium resolution (¾-inch SP), or high resolution (D-2). High-resolution video can be digitized with a lower resolution for off-line editing.

2   Compile a log of the source video as you digitize it. This will take the form of a video menu of reduced size freeze-frame stills on screens that look like photo contact sheets. These stills become the "key ID" frames for each segment and make it easy to locate segments when editing. (See Figure 23-16.) Along with these still frames, a list of their time code "addresses" will be compiled by the computer.

3   Go into the edit mode and play the source material, using the source log to find segments quickly. Depending on the nonlinear system, you will use a mouse, trackball, or keyboard to click on "in" and "out" points of the source video and audio tracks, using time-line windows for the source segments. In this way you program a sequence of stills like a storyboard, along with the types of transitions, keys, and special effects. The screen will display the source frames and the frames in a "virtual" edit master. You do not set "in" points on the edit master, because there actually is none. In nonlinear editing, as you "edit" you are not actually recording anything, you are only compiling an edit decision list of scenes and transitions. Each time you "play" your "edit," the video and audio are sequenced in real time by the computer controller. All of the shots, scenes, and transitions are reproduced in "real time" or faster or slower than normal so you can evaluate the edits and juxtaposition of shots.

4   If you don't like the timing of an edit, you can undo it. Unlike linear editing, you can tighten or extend segments without revising subsequent edit points. You also can effortlessly add, delete, and move segments around within the program.

5   When you are satisfied with your edit master, you store it on a recordable videodisc, hard disk, or videotape. Recording directly from the desktop system to a videotape (commonly called "printing to tape") requires high reso-

FIGURE 23-16   **Nonlinear Editing Monitor.**
Nonlinear systems make editing more visual by
showing still frames with their matching time code
numbers on the editing monitor. Using the computer's
mouse or keyboard, you select the frames that you
want to sequence rather than relying on the time code
numbers. The source video and edit master video are
shown in windows on the monitor. As you edit, the
computer automatically compiles an edit decision list.
(Courtesy: Capital Cities/ABC, Inc.)

lution digital video and digital-to-analog
conversion.

6   Finally, if you want to produce an edit master
on videotape, you can output your EDL, convert it to a computer-assisted tape editing format (such as CMX or Grass Valley), and perform a linear on-line auto-assemble using your
original time-coded source tapes. This is what
would be done if your digital video was low
resolution and your desktop editing was for off-
line purposes.

The advantages of nonlinear editing are: (1) it is
relatively easily learned; (2) it is suitable for both
off-line and on-line editing; (3) it can mix multiple
formats, such as NTSC and PAL; (4) it can incorporate video transitions and special effects that
formerly were available only on high-end equipment, (5) there is no quality loss in multiple generations, and (6) it is much less expensive than
high-end on-line editing systems. In addition,
nonlinear computer editing offers the significant
advantages of speed and flexibility not possible in
linear videotape editing.

The advantages of nonlinear editing have led
Emmy award-winning editor Rudy Bednar to
adopt this approach for all off-line editing of the
ABC series *Turning Point*. Bednar's assistant,
David Schisgall, has helped set up the nonlinear
system. He describes its advantages this way: "If
you can imagine linear videotape editing as a
standard typewriter, think of nonlinear computer
editing as a word processor. It allows editors to
cut and paste, make ripple-down inserts, organize
takes on the computer, and freely manipulate the
footage."

The ten-week editing process for each program
begins with preparing of logs and time-coded
transcripts of the field master tapes, from which
the producer and editor choose "selects" to digitize on the computer and store in its "gallery."
(See Figure 23-17.) Up to 22½ hours of video can
be stored in the system's hard drive memory,
along with two channels of CD-quality audio. Also,
a log consisting of the name of each shot, its time
code "in" and "out" points, a brief description, and
editorial notes are loaded into the computer. The
time spent at this point digitizing and labeling the
video and audio material speeds up the editing
process tremendously in later stages.

After the producer makes a "paper cut" of the
program using transcripts and logged footage,
the producer and editor create a "rough cut" from
the digitized video and audio material. Then a
sound designer is called in to begin composing
an original music score, which is recorded on digital audio tape with time code.

The next step is to produce an off-line "fine cut"
on the computer system. Graphics, computer-
generated animation, archival footage, and a
rough cut of the music score are incorporated in
the off-line fine cut. Cuts, dissolves, reverses,
wipes, and slow and fast motion can be performed
on the computer system, but some digital effects—such as steps, swoops, toasts, and tints—
must be produced in the on-line suite.

At this point the off-line fine cut is screened for
senior executives, and any changes agreed upon
are made. After that, the edit decision list is copied
from the computer system's hard drive to a floppy

FIGURE 23-17 Nonlinear Editing Process.
The producer and editor choose "selects" to store in the nonlinear computer editing system. The system digitizes video and audio material from a standard VCR and stores it in a "gallery" on the system's hard drive. The editor can call up a shot simply by "clicking" on its "key" frame in the gallery. *(Courtesy: Capital Cities/ ABC, Inc.)*

disk, which is taken to an on-line edit suite and used to conform the "final cut" from the original field master tapes.

The last step in the editing process is laying down the final score over the picture in the final cut, then sweetening and mixing the sound track.

POSTPRODUCTION EDITING PROCEDURES

The complexity of postproduction editing depends mainly on the production approach you used to record your program and the care you took carefully planning and documenting each shot taken during production. Shows produced live on tape or in long segments will usually need little, if any, postproduction editing. However, shows produced in short segments with a single camera or with the multiple-camera/multiple-VTR approach will require extensive postproduction edit sessions, since almost every transition must be made with a video edit.

Screening the Footage

The first step in postproduction is to screen all the material you have recorded. Using the take sheets from the production, start to view those scenes which were marked either "good" or "maybe." Those which are definitely "no good" usually need not be viewed unless you think they might contain a good shot or two which may be usable if edited into another take.

Locating the particular cut on the tape for each take or segment will go quickly if you have indicated on the take sheet either the approximate time into the tape of each cut or the SMPTE time-code numbers. In addition, the audio beeper cue tones which precede each cut make a distinctive sound as the tape is run fast forward or reverse. Counting each audio blip as you hear it will tell you how many cuts into the tape you are.

If possible, use a ½-inch copy of the original footage for previewing and screening purposes. The convenience of actually seeing each segment as you operate fast forward or reverse on the playback machine will make the viewing session go much faster, and the stop-frame and jogging capabilities of helical machines allow the director and editor to evaluate their edit decisions frame-by-frame.

If you will be editing your master tape with SMPTE time code and a computer editing system, you should have requested a cassette copy of the footage with "burned in" time code. This will permit you to screen the footage with time code numbers on any conventional VCR and monitor and not require that you tie up expensive edit decks for previewing. Noting takes or potential edit points by time code will make your on-line editing go much faster.

Once you have viewed the various takes and decided which ones you will use, watch the program material again, this time making some rough editing decisions. Many directors suggest you keep a fresh copy of the shooting script to use as an editing script, marking all edit decisions and possible alternative cuts in case the edit you planned looks wrong onscreen.

If you are working on a production where there are a number of different takes of the same scene, such as a multiple-camera/multiple-VTR show or a production that taped both the "dress" and "air" shows, as in many situation comedies, it is a great convenience to have a couple of playback decks available. This allows you to compare two different takes directly or to quickly preview edit points as you watch. If extra machines are unavailable, simply go through the script taking a few lines of dialogue or action at a time, look at all the takes you think are good, and determine which complete take or combination of different takes can be used to build the sequence.

Editing On-Line

If you will be editing on-line, that is, actually editing the master tape as you go along, you will generally start at the beginning of the program and proceed through to the end, scene-by-scene and shot-by-shot. If you have used SMPTE time code during screening, you already should have prepared a rough edit decision list indicating the various edit points and their time-code numbers. If you are working with a computer system, you will actually be making the final edits as you move along through the show. Of course, if you are editing manually—without time code or computer—you will have to preview each segment to locate and identify the edit points, using your take sheet and the VTR tape timer as a guide and watching the playback monitors for the precise edit point.

Editing Off-Line

If you are editing off-line on videotape, you will be working with a cassette copy of the original source

footage in order to prepare time-code instructions for later assembly. If you are off-lining at a non-linear editor, your source material will be digitized. In either case, there are several steps you can take to simplify the editing process.

Editing on Paper   The simplest off-line approach is to use a dub of the program video with burned-in time code and edit "on paper" by simply noting the time-code numbers for each edit point. Using the jog and pause controls, you can stop the tape in freeze-frame in order to copy the exact time-code numbers where each edit is to take place. Both the edit-in point, where the scene should begin, and the edit-out point, where the segment should end, should be noted on the edit log. Many directors find that simple editing tasks go quickly and efficiently when they use this method.

Producing a Workprint Rough-Cut   When you are dealing with a more complex production, however, such as a single-camera shoot or where multiple camera/multiple VTRs are used, the paper-and-pencil approach is usually not satisfactory because the individual shots are too short to give the director any real sense of visual continuity. In this case it is preferable to produce an edited workprint *rough-cut,* in which the individual segments are recorded in order. In a rough-cut, each segment starts a little early and ends a little late. Later, each segment is then trimmed to the exact length for proper pacing, continuity, and overall program length while editing the master tapes on-line.

Computer-Assisted Rough-Cuts   If you have a computer off-line system available, the computer will not only help you to make the rough-cut edits, but it will also keep each edit decision in its memory, eliminating the need for the director to engage in complicated bookkeeping for each time code edit point. However, you can edit footage off-line without such a computer system and still provide a completed rough-cut with the necessary time code information to guide the automatic assembly operation of the computer system during on-line assembly.

Time code editing sheet

SMPTE time code on master reels — Running time for each edit — Time code on edit VTR reel

TITLE: "SEGMENTS"
DIRECTOR:
PA:
VIDEO EDITOR:

PAGE: 3 OF 5
DATE: 3-18
ACT: OPENING

EDIT NO.	REEL NO.	PRE-EDIT HRS	MIN	SEC	FRS	DESCRIPTION	SEG TIME MIN	SEC	FRS	EDIT HRS	MIN	SEC	FRS	SEG TIME MIN	SEC	FRS	AUDIO NOTES
22	A-6	06	17	52	14	STEER WRESTLE	6	11		11	04	16	15				
		06	17	58	25						04	22	26				
23	A-6	06	02	39	00	JOHN MOUNTS UP	18	22		11	04	22	26				
			02	57	22						04	37	22				
24	A-6	06	01	18	26	JOHN ROPES STEER	10	01		11	04	37	22				
				28	27						04	46	04				
25	A-7	07	07	04	21	CLOWNS TALK	13	09		11	04	46	04				
		07	07	18	00						04	56	28				
26	A-7	07	18	53	22	CLOWNS + BULL	10	16		11	04	56	28				
		07	19	04	08						05	07	14				
27	A-6	06	32	00	25	JOHN THRU GATE	15	07		11	05	07	14				
			32	16	02						05	18	16				
28	A-6	06	47	16	26	CROWD REACTIONS	11	22		11	05	25	02				NEW CROWD NOISE
			47	28	18						05	36	09				

FIGURE 23-18 Time Code Editing Sheet.
A time code editing sheet is used to edit a show "on paper." Once the edit points are indicated by SMPTE time code numbers, the actual on-line editing of the master can proceed quickly.

To do this, all you need is a copy of the master footage with burned-in time code and a standard ½- or ¾-inch edit system such as the kind used for basic ENG editing. Once you have completed the rough-cut to your satisfaction, it is a relatively simple job to note the time code numbers for each edit point and develop the edit log which will be used to control the automatic assembly of the master tapes on-line. (See Figure 23-18.)

Conforming the edit decision list or the computer-assisted workprint to the actual master editing is a completely technical process, and quite often neither the director nor the producer is present during the on-line edit session. Often the assistant director will coordinate the master tape editing, since all creative decisions have already been made.

TECH TIP Rough-cuts can be refined with automatic trim editors. During the more carefully examined final edit, a trim editor offsets an original edit point by several frames, trimming off unneeded parts of a loose edit. The trim editor automatically calculates the new edit point by subtracting a few frames from the rough-cut edit point.

Coordination Sessions

The usual VTR editing system of a playback and an edit/record VTR limits you to cut-only edits. If

you wish to use any other type of video transition—dissolve, super, wipe, fade, or even a chroma-key insert—you must have two or more playback units and a production switcher available for postproduction editing. With this setup, postproduction proceeds much like a studio production except that the video sources are all prerecorded tapes rather than cameras. While most postproduction houses now offer multiple-playback units in separate edit *bays,* originally, the studio and its program switcher had to be scheduled for this type of editing. At that time, the postproduction process was called a *coordination session,* and the term is still used today. (See Figure 23-19.)

When using a multiple-playback system, you must be careful how your source material is arranged. For example, to execute a dissolve between two scenes, the opening scene must be on one playback deck and the following scene on a different deck.

To illustrate, let us say we want to dissolve from a comedy sketch into a close-up of a guitar as a singer begins a song. The first thing you must do is to prepare two separate playback reels: an *A* reel and a *B* reel. The *A* reel, or "roll," as it is often called, contains the last shot of the comedy

Labels on image: VCRs, Waveform monitor, Edit decision list, Program monitor, Edit controller, Laptop computer, Video switcher

FIGURE 23-19
Postproduction Edit Suites. Postproduction suites enable video editing and audio sweetening to be performed without the need for an expensive studio control room. *(Courtesy: Capital Cities/ABC, Inc.)*

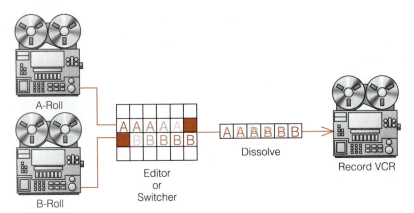

FIGURE 23-20 A/B Roll.
A- and B-roll edits are used to permit dissolves during postproduction. The first scene is set up on the *A* playback machine and the following scene is set up on the *B* playback machine. A computer-controlled or manual-controlled switcher is used to dissolve or wipe between the *A* and *B* machines.

A-Roll

B-Roll

Editor
or
Switcher

Dissolve

Record VCR

sketch, and the *B* reel contains the close-up shot of the guitar as the song begins.

Next, decide how long you want the dissolve to last. It is a lot easier if you are using time code because you can describe the length of the dissolve in terms of video frames. Say we want a dissolve that lasts about a second and a half. That would be forty-five video frames. Using time code makes it a relatively easy matter to precue both the *A* and *B* tapes so that, when they roll, there will be a forty-five-frame overlap between the end of the sketch on VTR *A* and the start of the song on VTR *B*. Both machines play through a switcher, and the edit/record VTR records the transition as you make the dissolve between the *A* and *B* machines. (See Figure 23-20.)

The same technique is used for a multiple-image effect, such as a wipe, split screen, or chroma key. The important thing is to place the scenes to be joined on separate tapes, determine how long you want both scenes to overlap, and precue the tapes so you can produce the effect through the switcher for the desired length of time.

While time code makes such edit sessions run more smoothly, it is not necessary in order to do one. If time code is unavailable, you will probably have to experiment a few times until you find the right combination of preroll cuing between the different tape machines to produce the effect you want.

Computer systems make coordination sessions relatively painless because the computer controls the entire operation—the cuing and rolling of up to six playback VTRs, the operation of the program switcher and the transition or effect, and the op-

eration of the edit/record VTR—according to the preprogrammed information in its memory.

Audio Editing with Computer Systems

Up to now you may have had the impression that videotape editing deals only with pictures. This is not really the case, however, and the use of SMPTE time code, combined with computer systems, has given directors and editors far more flexibility to deal with sound as well.

The heart of the audio editing system is, again, the SMPTE time code, which is used as a reference to keep the multitrack audio recorder operating in perfect synchronization with the video-recorders. On many complex programs, the audio is recorded directly onto a multitrack audiotape recorder (ATR). One of the ATR's tracks is assigned to record the identical time code used by the program VTR. Once the audio is recorded on the multiple tracks, the audio engineer can mix-down the sound to either monaural or stereo in a leisurely postproduction session without the pressure of an entire studio full of crew and cast members waiting around until the right audio mix is obtained. If the program requires additional sound effects, music, narration, or a laugh track, these can also be added and mixed in during the post-production phase. A major advantage of this approach—aside from the high-quality sound it can produce—is that musical performers appearing on the show can be involved in the final mixes of their own performances. This is particularly important to many rock musicians who are concerned about technical quality and want to accurately replicate their recording "sound" on television.

Once the multiple tracks are mixed-down, the final mix is transferred onto the audio tracks of the production VTR in perfect synchronization. If the program will be broadcast or distributed in stereo, the multitrack mix can be used to create two audio tracks.

Multitrack techniques are also valuable on dramatic programs, where there is a great deal of postproduction dubbing and mixing. Usually a workprint is made by off-line editing the workprint copy of the original recording. Using this as a guide, the editor, director, and audio engineer can assemble the sound track on a multitrack recorder, which, again, runs in sync with video via SMPTE time code. Sound effects, music, dialogue overdubbing, and any other audio can be added and mixed in at this time. Once all the tracks are mixed-down to a monaural or stereo version, they are laid back on the master tape for broadcast or distribution.

The SMPTE time code, along with the computer editing system, also can be helpful in smoothing out the audio after you have cut and edited a show. For example, most videotaped situation comedy shows ultimately build the broadcast show from a variety of taping sessions, each with a different audience. The edit points may naturally contain an audio mismatch, since one audience may respond differently to a joke from the way another audience did. Using time code, the audio is lifted off the master tapes, remixed, "sweetened" to smooth out rough sound transitions between edits, and laid back onto the edited master tape, producing a smooth-sounding track with a constant audio level.

What is especially important about postproduction audio mixing is the fact that it eliminates the need for the program's director to concentrate on the audio portions of the program during production. At the same time, postproduction audio mixing enables the audio technician and director to devote full attention to the studio requirements of the production without the pressure of a studio full of cameras, crew, and talent waiting while the sound mix is attended to.

For maximum postproduction audio flexibility, a multitrack audiotape recorder is necessary. Most production facilities use sixteen- or twenty-four-

track ATRs, although eight- and thirty-two-track machines are occasionally used as well. Obviously, the greater the number of audio tracks, the more flexibility the audio technician and director have to work with during postproduction. We have already discussed how the ATR is synchronized with the operation of a VTR using time code. Now we will see how to use the equipment during the postproduction mixing process.

The first step is for the program director and videotape editor to build an edited workprint using an off-line computer system and a VCR. The actual sound that was recorded during the production is used as an audio reference but with little regard at this point for how well the audio edits might sound. What is of primary concern are the video transitions, since audio problems can be corrected during the postproduction audio sessions. Once the edited video workprint is completed and approved, work can begin on the audio track by using the SMPTE time code as a reference guide.

If the original program audio was recorded only on the production VTR, the sound track must be dubbed to one of the tracks on the multichannel audio recorder. At the same time, one of the ATR's tracks is used to record SMPTE time code so that the audio track can be played back on the ATR in perfect synchronization with the video. On some productions, the original program audio may have been recorded on a multitrack recorder at the same time the videotape was recording picture. In this case, both the VTR and ATR will already have time code and can play back in perfect sync.

Now the director and the audio technician must select and assemble all the additional audio material they will need for the production. This includes voice-over narration, dialogue that is to be dubbed in place of existing audio, sound effects, and music. For each segment in the program where the director decides that additional audio is necessary, the segment must be timed to determine how much audio will be required to cover the video. For example, a car-chase sequence might need sound effects of squealing tires, sirens, an automobile engine, and music. Timing this se-

AUDIO MIX TRACK LOG

Prod. No. 31-8   Title "THIEF"   Director HENRY   Audio Eng. ALLISON

AUDIO TAPE TRACKS

1	2	3	4	5	6	7	8	9	10	11	12	13	14	15	16
ORIG. VTR AUDIO	SFX "A"	SFX "B"	SFX "C"	MUSIC "A"	MUSIC "B"	MUSIC "C"	V.O. NAR-RATOR							TIME CODE	
17:32:18 → 20:35:19	CUT #6 CAR CHASE 18:27:09 → 19:04:09	SIRENS 18:52:09 → 18:59:10	GLASS CRASH 18:55:16 → 18:57:21	"FRENZY" CUT #2 18:27:09 → 19:04:09 X	"ESCAPE IN NIGHT" CUT #5 FADE 19:00:12 → FADE OUT 20:35:19		18:27:09 → 18:59:10 19:04:09 → 20:35:19								

FIGURE 23-21 Audio-Mix Track Log.
An audio-mix track log is used with a multitrack audio recorder to identify the material on each of the audiotape recorder's tracks. The audio technician uses the information to build the final program audio. In this example, the blank tracks will be used to record intermediate mixes, which are later remixed until the final program audio is produced.

quence off the original VTR time code shows that it runs thirty-seven seconds, so at least that much audio is gathered from various sources—live recordings, sound-effects tapes, CDs, and so on—and recorded onto conventional ¼-inch audiotape or a DAT cassette.

Once all additional sounds are assembled and recorded, we are ready for the next step: the *audio laydown session.* At this point, we record, or "lay down," each of the individual sound elements onto one of the respective audio tracks on the multichannel ATR at the appropriate point in time where it will be needed during the audio mix. To do this, we must develop a *track log,* which will assign each discrete track to a particular sound function. For example, in this session we decided that Track #1 would hold the original dialogue that was dubbed from the VTR to the ATR. Tracks #2, #3, and #4 carry sound effects, Tracks #5, #6, and #7 contain music, Track #8 holds voice-over narration, and Track #15 carries the SMPTE time code signal. The reason we assign three tracks to sound-effects and music is to permit the audio technician to cross-fade from one music or sound-effects track to another. Assigning one audio source per track also makes the final audio balancing easier. We have left a number of tracks blank to permit us to record the final mix-down that will become the program's audio track. (See Figure 23-21.)

During the laydown session we use the SMPTE time code to locate the exact point on the ATR where we will need each sound sequence. Every audio segment was prepared with additional material after its time code number to provide a safety pad in case we want to fade the sound in or out. Also, we record every track at full level, since the mixing and balancing of the sound will come later.

By the end of the audio laydown session, each track contains sound material corresponding to the video action at the particular time in the program. For example, say a car-chase sequence begins at 00:18:27:09 in time code and ends thirty-seven seconds later at 00:19:04:09. On the multitrack audiotape, the sound effects and music for the chase sequence are located on their respective tracks directly between the two time code numbers.

At this point, we are ready for the final audio mix. As the director and the audio technician go through each sequence of the show, the various sound tracks are mixed and balanced. Reverberation and equalization are applied where necessary to improve the sound quality or to provide the proper sound perspective. Cross-fades are timed and executed until they deliver the exact effect desired by the director. Usually, the director and editor will work with only a short sequence at a time, perfecting the sound mix until it is just right and then recording the completed mix on one of the empty tracks of the ATR. In this way, the final audio mix for a program is assembled piece-by-piece, much like assemble editing of video. Working this way in postproduction, the director and the audio technician can concentrate on the sound and work with various mixes and sound balances to achieve the perfect combination.

The *audio cue sheet* is used to indicate the various levels for each fader on the control console and the point where fades and other audio cues should begin and end. Following the audio cue sheet, the audio technician records the final mix as the program proceeds. The output of the audio-control console is fed onto the empty track on the multitrack audiotape recorder. If a stereo mix is necessary, two tracks are used to record the stereo mix from the audio board.

Once the audio mix is recorded, the master production videotapes are first edited to match the time code of the edited workprint for video only. Then the mixed audio tracks are added, using the SMPTE time code to ensure audio and video synchronization.

Admittedly, such an elaborate postproduction audio procedure is time-consuming and expensive and requires sophisticated equipment. However, it is being increasingly used for a variety of productions because it offers enormous creative and production flexibility and ensures a top-quality final production.

SUMMARY

The ability to edit videotape is one of its most significant features. Videotape editing is an electronic process in which the original source material is transferred and edited onto an edit master tape. Editing is used to sequence shots to accomplish the program's objectives, to shift audio and video information, and to link scenes shot in different places or at different times with cuts, dissolves, or other transition techniques. The three types of edits are video-only, audio-only, and combined video-audio. Edits are executed in either assemble mode or insert mode. Insert editing produces a cleaner final product, but requires the prerecording of a preblacked tape.

There are three types of editing control systems: (1) control track, (2) time code, and (3) computer editors. The control track editing system is the simplest to operate, and uses the control tracks on the source and edit master tapes. Time code editing systems use the more precise SMPTE time code signal recorded on the tapes. The two modes of time code are drop frame and nondrop frame. Time code may be recorded in the vertical interval (VITC) or on an unused audio track (LTC) on the tapes. Time code identifies the edit points on the edit/record VTR and enables multiple source VTRs and auxiliary equipment, such as multitrack ATRs, to be synchronized with the videotape equipment. Computer editing systems combine the data processing capabilities of the computer with television production equipment, enabling the operator to edit efficiently and accurately.

During postproduction editing, the program can be edited either on-line—using production recorders and making edits as you go along—or off-line, using a workprint dubbed from the master videotape to make all editing decisions. On-line editing refers to making edits on the same high-end equipment used to record the programs. Usually on-line editing systems include high-end equipment, such as more than one playback VTR, a video switcher, character generator, and graphics devices. On-line postproduction editing is performed on computer-assisted tape systems that use SMPTE time code as a means of controlling the operation of the equipment and creating an edit decision list (EDL) that is stored in the system's memory or on a disk. Off-line editing refers to making a workprint with less costly equipment before employing expensive production machines to make the final edit master.

There are two types of computer editing systems: linear and nonlinear. In linear editing all edits must be recorded on the edit master tape in order from beginning to end. Tightening, expanding, dropping, or adding any shot in linear editing requires the shifting of all subsequent edit points on the tape. All computer-assisted videotape editing is linear.

A nonlinear editing system consists of a personal computer outfitted with hardware and software that permit it to function like a video switcher, special effects generator, and editing controller. Nonlinear editing provides random access to source material and complete flexibility in shifting elements within the final program. Nonlinear editing systems have a number of advantages over linear systems.

Postproduction editing procedures involve: (1) screening the footage, (2) editing off-line and on-line, (3) coordinating the edit sessions, and (4) mixing and sweetening the audio to improve its quality and to add sound, such as narration, music, and sound effects.

GLOSSARY

Above-the-line Budget category which includes the artistic, or creative, elements engaged in a production. Includes primarily nontechnical personnel and activities.

A-B rolling (1) Preparing film for optical printing so that each new cut is located on either the *A* or the *B* roll. (2) Utilizing two or more videotape machines and switching between them to produce a composite master.

AC Alternating current, the electrical energy found in conventional wall outlets.

Ace A 1,000-watt lighting instrument; usually refers to a 1,000-watt fresnel.

A. C. Nielsen A major research company, which provides national and regional television ratings.

Actuality News footage covering of an event as it occurs.

AD Assistant director.

ADAT format A multitrack digital audio recording format that employs the S-VHS transport system.

Additive mixing Combining proportions of the additive primaries to reproduce all hues. Color television cameras work on the principle of additive mixing. Opposite of subtractive mixing.

Additive primaries Red, blue, and green colors which, when combined in equal proportions, produce white light.

Address code Time code used to distinguish a particular location on a videotape for editing purposes. Address code indicates each frame by hour, minute, second, and frame number. See *SMPTE time code.*

Adjustable hanging pole An aluminum telescoping pole, which is used to hang lighting instruments at any desired height.

Ad-lib Dialogue or action which has not been previously rehearsed.

AFM American Federation of Musicians; a union.

AFTRA American Federation of Television and Radio Artists; a major union for television talent.

AGC Automatic gain control, a device which automatically regulates sound or video intensity to maintain the proper technical level.

Aliasing The "stairstepping," or slightly jagged edges, particularly noticeable in curved lines when an image is digitally generated.

Alpha wrap A helical-scan, VTR tape-threading configuration.

Ambience processing Digitally processing an audio signal to create artificial reverberation and sound reflections, which simulate different spatial perspectives.

Amplitude The strength or intensity of an electrical signal.

Analog The variation of an electrical signal over a continuous range to represent the original image or sound which is being processed and reproduced.

Angle of view Refers to the horizontal and vertical space seen within the frame of a camera shot. For example: wide shot, medium shot, and close-up. Also may refer to the "point of view" of the shot.

Animatics Animated storyboards.

Animation Combining individual still images to create the illusion of movement.

Aperture The opening of a lens through which the light passes. The aperture or diaphragm is usually measured in f-stops.

ARBITRON A major supplier of television rating information, mainly for local markets.

Arc Movement of a camera in an arclike, or curving, pattern.

Art director Individual responsible for designing the setting for a production and for establishing the overall visual "look," including graphics, wardrobe, and sets. Also called "scenic designer."

ASCAP American Society of Composers, Authors, and Publishers; a nonprofit, music-licensing organization.

Aspect ratio The shape of a television screen described as a numerical ratio. The standard television screen is four units wide and three units high (4:3). The standard for High Definition Television (HDTV) is sixteen units wide and nine units high (16:9).

Assemble edit Addition of new video material following program material already recorded. Does not require existing control track on the tape.

Attenuate To decrease the strength of an electrical signal. A potentiometer, or fader, permits attenuation to be continuously controlled.

Audio The sound portion of a television program.

Audio layback Process by which a multitrack audio mix is re-recorded in sync onto the original videotape.

Audio level The strength of the audio signal. "Taking an audio level" involves sampling each audio source individually.

Audio mix Balancing the levels of all audio

sources to produce the desired composite sound.

Audiospace The audience's only reference of aural reality. "Audiospace" refers to the way sound can be manipulated to produce a particular audience impression.

Audio track The particular area on audiotape or videotape which carries audio information. On multitrack machines, the tape holds a number of separate audio tracks.

Audition (1) A special audio circuit which enables the audio technician to preview or cue audio sources on a split-function audio console. (2) A try-out, in which talent is selected for a production.

Auto-Iris Automatic iris, a device which varies the aperture of a camera lens to adjust for brightness variations in the scene being photographed.

Automatic dialogue replacement (ADR) A digital audio process which is used to match audio created during postproduction to original audio recording.

Auto-transformer dimmer A lighting control dimmer, which uses a transformer to regulate the power to the lighting instruments.

Axis of action The direction of the subject's movement in the frame.

Axis of conversation The line drawn between the subject and the person speaking with the subject.

Back focus The control on a zoom lens that adjusts the distance between back of the lens and the CCD or tube face so that the image is in sharp focus when the lens is zoomed all the way out to its widest possible focal length.

Background light Illumination of the set or background. Also called a "set light."

Background music Music used under principal dialogue or program audio to establish a mood.

Backlight Illumination from behind the subject, used to separate the foreground subject from the background area. The lighting instrument is positioned above and behind the subject, usually at a 45° vertical angle.

Backtime Figuring the amount of time left in a show by subtracting the present time from the program's end time. See *Dead-roll.*

Balance (1) Refers to the overall apparent steadiness or stability of an image. Balance may be symmetrical or asymmetrical. (2) Refers to the relative loudness of the left and right audio channels in stereo.

Balanced audio cables The three-wire professional audio cable. Two wires carry the audio signal, and a third provides the ground. Balanced cables are better shielded and less susceptible to noise than unbalanced cables.

Barn doors Metal flaps which are mounted on lighting instruments and used to control light distribution.

Barrel distortion Optical distortion commonly associated with wide-angle lenses, in which the straight sides of a subject curve outward.

Base (1) Film base, the material used to make film onto which the light-sensitive emulsion is layered. (2) The metal bottom of a lamp that is inserted into the light socket.

Base station Camera-control unit for digital cameras.

Batten The metal pipes from which lighting instruments are hung.

Bayonet lock mount A type of lens mounting which does not use threads and permits rapid changing of camera lenses.

Beam splitter A device that divides the light entering a color camera through the lens into the three primary colors. The two main types of beam splitters are the prism block and the striped filter.

Beepers A series of low-frequency audio tones which are recorded prior to videotaping program material. They are used for cuing the videotape and for locating particular program segments.

Below-the-line Technical and production costs of a program, as indicated in the program budget. Includes production equipment and technical personnel.

Betacam SP A professional ½-inch videotape format. Has become the industry standard for remote productions.

Bias light Device used to boost the electrical output of television pickup tubes to permit camera operation under low light levels.

Bidirectional A microphone pickup pattern, in which the mike has two equally "live" sides.

Bit (binary digit) The fundamental code used in computer language. Each bit is designated at either a 0 or a 1.

Bit pad A computer input device that looks like a sketch pad. The artist touches locations on the bit pad with a stylus or "paintbrush" and the exact movement is reproduced as a visual image on the video monitor.

Black The darkest portion of the gray scale. In terms of program switching, "black" refers to a video source which provides sync signals but no picture.

Blast filter A microphone attachment (either external or built-in) which suppresses wind noise and breath popping. Also called a "pop filter" or "wind filter."

Bleeding When the edges of a video key or insert show the background video. Bleeding also occurs when a chroma-key insert is improperly set up.

Blocking Working out talent and camera positions for a production.

Blooming Distortion of a television picture caused by an overly high video level or an excessively bright region in the scene being photographed.

Blooping pencil A magnetic pencil used to erase the audio on a magnetic film track.

BMI Broadcast Music Incorporated; a major music-licensing organization.

Body mount Device used to mount a portable camera on the operator for steady pictures and flexible movement.

Boom microphone A microphone suspended from a long arm, which enables the mike to remain out of camera range.

Boom shadow Shadows created by a boom microphone.

Boom up; boom down (1) To raise or lower the microphone boom arm. (2) To raise or lower a camera mounted on a camera crane.

Border Edges which are electronically produced

to visually separate and distinguish wipes, split screens, or letters.

Box set A realistic television set, which consists of three walls.

Break (1) Releasing a camera to move to another position or to obtain another shot. (2) Station break; local commercials and identification between programs.

Breakaway prop A specially designed prop, which shatters harmlessly on impact.

Brightness One of the important attributes of color which determines how it will appear on a black and white gray scale. Sometimes called "value."

Broad A square or rectangular floodlight. Also called a "pan."

B-roll A film or videotape insert reel which is rolled into the program.

Budget A cost breakdown of all production elements; usually divided into above-the-line and below-the-line sections.

Bulk eraser A device which produces a strong magnetic field, used to erase quickly audio or video magnetic tapes, cartridges, and cassettes.

Bumper (1) A slide or graphic used at the beginning and end of various program segments, often before and after a commercial break. (2) Additional tape or film footage following the primary program material as a safeguard.

Bump-up Dubbing a previously recorded videotape from a smaller format to a higher one (e.g., ¾-inch to 1-inch).

Burn-in Image retention by the camera pickup tube, caused by excessively bright subject, extreme contrast, or photographing a static scene for extended period of time. Also called "sticking" or "lag."

Bus A row of buttons on the video switcher.

Bust shot Framing a subject from midchest to slightly above the head.

Byte Eight bits of information.

Calibrating the zoom Zooming to longest focal length and focusing to ensure a focused picture throughout the entire zoom range. The zoom must be calibrated whenever the camera or subject distance varies significantly.

Call sheet Schedule indicating talent, production, and technical personnel needed for rehearsal and production.

Camcorder A portable camera with a built-in videocassette recorder. They are lighter and more rugged than cameras equipped with separate record decks joined by a cable.

Cam head Camera mounting head which produces very smooth camera moves. Utilizes a series of "cams," or cylinders, to control pan and tilt.

Cameo Lighting technique in which foreground subjects appear before a completely black background.

Camera card A graphic which is photographed by a studio camera. Also called "title card," or "flip card."

Camera-control unit (CCU) Equipment containing the various controls necessary to set up, align, and regulate camera operation. Includes waveform monitor, television monitor, and shading control.

Camera head The portion of the camera chain which includes the lens system, pickup tubes, and viewfinder.

Camera imaging Converting optical energy into electrical signals by focusing light onto the photosensitive surface of an imaging device in a video camera.

Camera/recorder A camera and a recorder designed to fit together and operate as a single unit. The camera is referred to as being "dockable" with the recorder.

Cannon plug A special three-prong audio plug and connector jack which locks male and female plugs together with a small latching device. Used on all professional audio equipment.

Cans Studio headsets.

Canted angle A shot in which the subject appears tilted in the screen.

Capacitor Electronic device designed to store an electric charge. Used in condenser microphones as part of the generating element.

Capstan   The spinning shaft on an audiotape recorder that pulls the tape across the heads when the tape is pressed against the capstan by the pinch roller.

Cardioid microphone   Microphone with a heart-shaped, directional pickup pattern.

Cart   See *Cartridge*.

Cartridge   An endless loop of tape enclosed in a plastic case. The tape is played in a cartridge player and automatically recues after each use.

Cathode ray tube (CRT)   Specially designed vacuum tube in which a series of electrons are focused into a beam and strike a phosphor-coated surface, which glows to create the television image.

C-band   That portion of the spectrum between 4 and 6 gigaHertz. Popular for satellite transmission.

C-clamp   Device used to fasten lighting instruments to a lighting batten.

CD-I   Compact disc-interactive, a variation of CD-ROM.

CD-ROM   Compact disc-read only memory. A computer storage medium.

Channel assignment matrix   Can serve as a substitute for a patch panel. Allows audio sources to be electronically reassigned to inputs and outputs without physically moving audio cables. Reduces cable breakage and confusion caused by physical mispatching.

Character generator   Device which electronically produces lettering and other graphic displays directly on television screen for use in production.

Charge-coupled device (CCD)   A solid-state video transducer which is used in place of a conventional camera pickup tube.

Cheat   Repositioning a performer, camera, or object to produce a better shot.

Chroma key   Method of electronically inserting the image from one video source into the picture from another video source. The process utilizes a selected "key color," which, wherever it appears in the foreground shot, is replaced by the background image.

Chroma-key tracking   The ability of digital video manipulators to continually vary the size of the chroma-key insert, depending on the movement of the foreground subject camera. This maintains realistic visual perspective.

Chroma-key window   The area on the foreground subject set painted the "key" color, in which the background image will appear on the composite shot. Frequently used on news or instructional programs to insert graphics behind the talent.

Chrominance channels   Red, blue, and green color channels which together produce the color image. Each primary color has a separate chrominance channel in the camera.

Clapstick   Identification slate with a hinged top which, when brought down quickly, produces a loud clap, which is used to synchronize double system movie sound.

Clip   (1) The control on the video switcher which is used to regulate the intensity of a matte, key, or insert. (2) A short piece of film or videotape which is rolled into a program. (3) To cut off abruptly.

Clock time   Setting the SMPTE time code to reflect the actual time of day. Useful in cataloging tape recordings of real time events.

Close-up   A camera shot in which the principal subject is seen as relatively large and dominant in the screen.

C-mount   A threaded, screw-type lens mount.

Color bars   A standard color test signal which is generated electronically by a "color-bar generator." Used as a reference in setting up and aligning color video equipment.

Color-correction filter   Filter which changes the color temperature of the scene being photographed.

Color cycling   Refers to the ability of a computer graphic to cycle through a fixed palette of a hue, creating the illusion of motion. Commonly used in weather graphics to add motion.

Color media   See *Gel*.

Color temperature   The relative amount of reddish or bluish color quality of light. Color temperature is measured in "degrees Kelvin." Standard indoor studio lighting instruments are balanced for 3200 °K; outdoor color film and electronic cameras are balanced for approximately 5600 °K.

Colorizer   An electronic device which adds preselected colors to a monochrome image according to the gray-scale information present in the picture.

Comet-tailing   A smear of light created by an excessively bright portion of the picture. See also *Burn-in; Lag.*

Compact audio discs (CD)   The 4¾-inch plastic platters that contain digitally encoded audio. CDs offer very high fidelity and are difficult to damage.

Complementary colors   Two colors which, when added together, will produce white light. The complementary color is produced by adding two primary colors together in the proper proportions. Yellow, cyan, and magenta are the three complementary colors.

Component video   A video recording system that treats luminance and chrominance information separately. Component video is superior to composite video for postproduction editing because it allows more tape generations before noticeably degrading.

Composite signal   A complete television signal including sync pulse.

Composite video   The chrominance and luminance information in the video signal is combined and processed together. NTSC video is a composite format.

Compression   (1) The process of reducing the difference between the loudest and softest intensity of a sound signal. (2) The digital video effect in which the image is squeezed vertically and horizontally. (3) The process of digitizing audio and video signals and reducing the data required for them.

Computer platform   Refers to the combination of a computer's central processing unit (CPU) and its operating system software, which together determine how the computer processes data and performs its operations.

Condenser microphone   A microphone which uses an electronic condenser as a part of the generating element. See also *Electret condenser microphone.*

Conforming   Matching original film or videotaped footage to an edited workprint to produce the final, edited master.

Connector   The plug on the end of a cable.

Continuity   Refers to the fact that costumes, props, actor positions, and set pieces must be constant during the progression of shots. Maintaining continuity is a problem when shows are shot in segments, out of sequence.

Contrast range (contrast ratio)   The difference between the brightest and darkest portions of a picture. In television a contrast ratio of 30:1 is the widest possible brightness range which still permits accurate picture reproduction.

Control room   The area where the program's director and production personnel control the audio and video for a program.

Control track   The area of the videotape which contains information used to control and synchronize the playback and videotape editing operations.

Control-track time code   A variation on SMPTE time code, which counts control-track pulses to produce an eight-digit edit code. Does not identify frames independently, as SMPTE code does, however, but simply counts pulses from any predetermined starting point.

Cookie   See *Cucalorus.*

Coord   Short for "coordination," in which two or more videotape machines are played through a switcher to produce a composite signal, which is recorded by another VTR.

Core   Plastic hub on which audio tape or film is wound.

Countdown   (1) The numbers which appear on film or videotape before the actual program material to facilitate accurate cuing. (2) Silent hand signals delivered by the floor manager to talent to smooth the transition into, and out of, program segments.

Counterweight pedestal   Camera pedestal which uses a counterweight system to control camera height and permit smooth on-air movement of camera pedestal.

Crabbing The parallel movement of all wheels on a dolly or pedestal to permit smooth and accurate dollies, trucks, and arcs.

Cradle head A camera mounting head designed to counteract the weight of the camera during tilts, and to produce smooth pans and tilts on air.

Crane Large camera dolly in which camera and operator are mounted at the end of a long arm which permits extremely high and low camera angles, as well as very fluid on-air movement.

Crawl Credits or other graphic material moving horizontally.

Crawling Imperfections along the edges of a chroma key, in which the sides of the insert seem to move up and down.

Cross-fade The simultaneous fade-in of one audio source as another is faded out. Can also be used to vary two lighting effects. In video, the transition is called a "dissolve."

Crush To compress all blacks and dark grays in a picture in order to include white levels. Necessary when the contrast range exceeds the acceptable contrast ratio.

Crystal black A videotape which has recorded only video black. Used to lay down a continuous control track, which is necessary for "insert" editing.

Cucalorus A metal pattern which is inserted into an ellipsoidal spotlight, used to produce a shadow pattern against a set wall, curtain, or cyclorama.

Cue (1) The signal to begin a program, an action, dialogue, or other production activity. (2) To preset film, videotape, audiotape, or records, so they will be available immediately when called for by the program's director.

Cue card Large card containing dialogue which talent must deliver during the production. Held next to the camera lens by the floor manager so talent can refer to the card without making it obvious that he or she is reading.

Cue track An area on videotape reserved for additional audio information or to carry SMPTE time code information for tape editing.

Cut (1) An instantaneous change from one camera shot to another. See also *Take*. (2) A partic-ular segment in a record or tape, usually indicated by number as in "Cut #2." (3) Command which means to immediately stop talking, stop action, or stop production.

Cutaway A shot which focuses on a view other than the principal action. Used frequently to provide transitional footage or to avoid a jump cut.

Cut-in An insert from another source which is introduced into the program.

Cutoff lines Reference points on the body used to guide camera framing: the top of the head, the neck, the bust, the waist, the knee, and the toes.

Cycles per second The number of complete cycles of an electronic signal in one second. Expressed in Hertz, abbreviated as Hz.

Cyclorama (cyc) A continuous piece of canvas fabric which runs around the edges of a studio and is used to produce the illusion of infinite depth. The cyc is often "painted" with colored light for a variety of effects.

DASH Digital audio stationary head. A type of DAT recorder.

DAT Digital audiotape. The two DAT formats are: DASH and R-DAT.

dB Abbreviation for "decibel."

dc Direct current, usually provided from special electrical sources or power generators.

DCC Digital compact cassette. A recording system that uses standard-sized, high-quality audiocassettes as the storage medium. Also plays prerecorded analog cassettes.

Dead-roll To play a film, tape, or record with the pot, or fader, off and to bring up the sound or take the video at the proper time on the director's cue. Permits prerecorded material to end at a predetermined time.

Decibel A standard measure of relative intensity or power which is expressed on a logarithmic scale.

Degausser A bulk eraser.

Demographics Breaking down a viewing audience by various social and economic characteristics, such as age, sex, income, and education.

Depth of field Area in which all objects photographed by a lens and camera appear in focus. Depends on subject-to-camera distance, focal length of lens, and f-stop.

Deuce A 2,000-watt lighting instrument; usually refers to 2-kW fresnel spot.

DGA Director's Guild of America; union for directors, ADs, and stage managers.

Diaphragm (1) The adjustable opening which varies the aperture size of a lens. (2) The element in a microphone which vibrates according to the pressure variations in the air created by the sound source.

Dichroic mirror The filter in a color television camera that dissects white light into the three primary colors.

Diffusion filter A special filter which produces a fuzzy, foglike effect on the image photographed.

Digital Refers to any device in which an electronic signal is represented by computer-type binary numbers.

Digital audiotape (DAT) A digital recording process and medium which offers very high fidelity and the ability to edit through multiple generations without signal degradation.

Digital audio workstation (DAW) A system that combines computer and audio technologies.

Digital camera A camera which operates utilizing digital circuits and technology. Offers extremely stable pictures, automatic setup and picture correction, and flexibility in transmitting the picture from the camera head to the CCU (base station).

Digital scene simulation A technique which completely generates the set using a computer. No real-life objects need be photographed for a digital scene simulation.

Digital video manipulator A series of sophisticated special effects generators which utilize digital technology to manipulate and control the video image. Produces effects which are impossible utilizing analog technology.

Digital video still camera A still camera that uses high-capacity floppy disks instead of film.

Digital videotape formats D-1, D-2, and D-3 formats record video signals as digital bits of information, offering superior quality to analog video recording systems.

Digitize To convert an audio or video signal from its "analog" form into computerlike digital code numbers.

Dimmer Device used to control the amount of electric power reaching a lighting instrument and, therefore, the light output of the instrument.

Direct box A device that matches the output of an electronic instrument or synthesizer to a microphone input on the audio-control console. The instrument is recorded directly rather than miking its speaker amp. Also called "direct insertion box" or "DI box."

Director The production team member responsible for creating the sound and picture of a program.

Disc Refers to optical storage media, such as compact discs.

Disk Refers to magnetic storage media, such as computer disks.

Dissolve A simultaneous fade-in of one video source and fade-out of another. Analogous to the audio cross-fade.

Distortion Undesirable changes in the sound waveform, usually caused by electronic processes of recording and reproduction.

Diversity receiving system A special wireless microphone receiver which eliminates spurious interference or signal dropout, making RF mikes very reliable.

Dolby noise reduction An electronic process which, when used during audio recording and playback, reduces the background "noise" and produces a better quality audio signal.

Dolly (1) Camera support which permits the camera to move smoothly across the studio floor. (2) Movement of the camera on its pedestal closer to, or farther from, the subject.

Doppler radar Detects rapid changes in the speed and direction of atmospheric winds. Shows up as different color blocks, often moving, on the weather forecast.

Double reentry A sophisticated switcher which permits the output of a mix/effects system to be reentered for further video manipulation.

Double zoom A zoom lens with a continuously variable "extender" to increase the lens' focal length.

Downstream keyer A special-effects generator which enables the TD to insert or key over a composite video signal just before the video signal leaves the switcher to go over the air.

Dress rehearsal The final rehearsal of a production which is an exact duplicate of the air show.

Drop A large piece of canvas or other material used as scenery backing.

Drop-out The loss of a part of the video signal during VTR playback. A "drop-out compensator" is a device which eliminates most drop-outs by reinserting previous video information to hide the drop-out.

Dry mount press A piece of graphics equipment that uses pressure and heat to mount pictures or other graphic materials.

Dry rehearsal Rehearsal outside the studio, in which initial performer blocking is planned and run through without production facilities.

Dual redundancy Using two identical microphones to cover a sound source. In the event of mike failure, the microphone with the control pot turned off is immediately opened to continue audio without interruption.

Dub A copy of a videotape or audiotape made by recording the output of one machine on another.

Dub-down Copying a videotape from a larger tape format to a smaller one, e.g., from a ¾-inch to a VHS tape.

Dub-up See *Bump-up*.

Ducking A process that relies on an audio compressor to automatically reduce the volume of one audio source during the presence of another. For example, when an announcer speaks, the compressor automatically ducks the background music under.

DVE Digital video effects.

Dynamic microphone See *Moving-coil microphone*.

Dynamic range The range of sound level from the softest to the loudest sound that can be reproduced.

Easel card See *Camera card*.

Echo A type of reverberation. Strictly speaking, a wave which has been reflected along its transmission with sufficient difference in time and magnitude to be perceived as distinct from the original.

Edge wipe; edge key A wipe or key in which edges are electronically produced to make the key material appear more prominent on screen.

Edit decision list (EDL) A list of every edit point, the duration of transitions, the "in" and "out" points, and edit mode for each edit sequence.

Edit room Having enough space before or after the edit point to permit a clean video or audio edit.

Editing controller The device that operates the source VTRs and the edit/record VTR during the editing process.

Editing on the fly (1) Directing a multicamera production, with the director calling shots as the show progresses. (2) Editing videotape manually, which requires the edit to be timed perfectly and made as both playback and edit/record VTRs are in operation.

Effects bank The various buses on the switcher which control such electronic effects as wipes, keys, mattes, and inserts.

EFP See *Electronic field production*.

8-mm A videotape format approximately ⅓-inch in width. Popular for home video and sometimes used for ENG.

Electret condenser microphone A capacitor or condenser microphone which utilizes a precharged element, thus eliminating the need for bulky power sources.

Electron gun Device which creates the electron beam used to scan across the photosensitive element of the camera pickup tube and the phosphor-coated surface of the CRT.

Electron scanning beam The electron beam created and controlled by the electron gun and its auxiliary circuitry.

Electronic editing A postproduction operation in which videotape material is edited by dubbing from a playback machine to an edit/record VTR at the precise point where the edit is to be made.

Electronic field production (EFP) The use of a single camera with a single VTR to shoot on location in the field. EFP is distinguished from ENG by generally higher production values.

Electronic news gathering (ENG) The use of portable video cameras and portable VTRs to cover news events quickly. Most ENG units also contain a microwave, so live sound and picture can be relayed to the station for immediate broadcast.

Electronic still store (ESS) A device that can digitize a frame from a video source, store it on a disc, and reproduce the frame instantaneously. Eliminates the need for slides and camera cards.

Electronically layered sets A technique to construct a set by shooting various objects and combining them through chroma key. Digital postproduction allows for the most elaborate electronically layered sets.

Ellipsoidal spotlight Spotlight which produces hard, directional light. Internal shutters permit distribution control, and a pattern slot enables the ellipsoidal to project shadow patterns. Also called a "Leko."

Encoder Electronic device which transforms the color camera's red, blue, and green video signals into a luminance signal and a chrominance signal.

Equalizer Audio device which permits a sound signal to be manipulated by varying specific frequencies to produce a particular sound quality.

Essential area The area of the television picture which is sure to be received by all television sets. In graphics, the area where important visual and lettering information must be positioned to ensure its reception by all viewers.

Establishing shot The opening shot of a show or scene, which orients the viewer to the surroundings; usually a wide shot.

Exposure The amount of light which is allowed to enter the camera and affect the light-sensitive surface of the pickup tube or the emulsion of the film.

Fade A gradual increase or decrease of the video or audio signal. In video it is the gradual appearance of a picture from black or vice versa. In audio, it is the gradual increase in sound or vice versa.

Fader A device used to control sound, video, and lighting intensities.

Fader bar Two ganged levers on the switcher which control the output of a double bank of video sources. Fader bars are used to produce fades, dissolves, supers, split screens, and wipes.

Falloff The degree with which light goes from full intensity on a subject to black. "Rapid falloff" means there is a quick and obvious distinction between an illuminated area and a nonilluminated area. "Slow falloff" means the light intensity gradually reduces from full to none.

Fast lens A lens with a low f-stop number which permits photographing with a wide aperture and, consequently, use under low-light conditions.

FAX sheet Short for "Facilities Sheet," a listing of all production equipment necessary for a show.

Feed The transmission of a signal or a show from one point to another.

Feedback (1) Video: sending the video signal back on itself to produce a series of random streaks or patterns on the television screen. (2) Audio: sending the audio back on itself to produce an echo effect at low levels, or a loud screech when uncontrolled.

Field Half the television picture composed of either all odd or all even scanning lines. Two fields are interlaced together to produce a "frame," or complete video picture.

Field of view The area covered by a lens.

Figure-ground relationship The tendency to see the main subject in a shot as a foreground figure in front of a background (the ground).

Fill light Light used to lighten or eliminate shadows created by the key light.

Film chain Film projectors, 35-mm slide projector, multiplexer, and television film camera used to reproduce film and slides for television. Also called "telecine" or "film island."

Filter (1) Audio: device which allows some sound frequencies to pass and blocks others to manipulate sound quality. Used to simulate telephone voice, radio or TV audio, etc. (2) A glass or gelatin lens cover which is used to change the quality of the light which enters the camera.

Filter wheel A device located behind the lens on the camera that must be set properly for the color temperature of the lighting before the camera can be white balanced.

Fisheye lens An extremely wide angle lens which produces a 180° field of view.

Fishpole boom Hand-held boom, used mainly on location or where a larger boom is too unwieldy.

Fixed-focal-length lens A lens with a fixed focal length, as opposed to a zoom lens, which has a variable focal length. Also called a "primary lens."

Flagging Distortion seen on some helical VTR playbacks where straight lines at the top of the picture become wavy and fluctuate back and forth. See *Skewing error*.

Flange focus An external back focus control on a zoom lens that can be used to correct slight changes that may occur while transporting a camera.

Flare Dark or colored streaks in the picture, caused by a very bright or highly specular reflection in the scene being photographed.

Flashback; flashforward Varying the temporal order of a show by going backward or forward in time.

Flat (1) A piece of scenery used as a background set. (2) A picture lacking contrast.

Flat lighting Lighting characterized by even, diffused light without shadows or contrast.

Flip card See *Camera card*.

Flooding the beam Focusing a fresnel spotlight to "flood" position to widen the beam distribution and reduce intensity. See *Spread*.

Floodlight Wide-aperture light source which produces flat, diffused illumination over a wide area.

Floor manager Individual responsible for all activities on the studio floor and for relaying director's signals to talent during rehearsal and production. Also called "stage manager."

Floorplan A scale drawing of the studio used in planning scenery design and construction, lighting, and camera and subject blocking.

Floorstand (1) A mounting device for lighting instruments which is positioned on the studio floor. (2) An easel for holding title cards and other camera graphics.

Fluff A mistake, or error.

Fluid head A camera mounting device that uses a thick fluid in a reservoir that resists sudden movement of the camera head. This resistance results in smooth pans and tilts. Although preferable to friction heads, fluid heads are not recommended for work with very heavy cameras.

Focal length The distance from the optical center of a lens to its focal point. Expressed in millimeters (mm), it indicates the lens's image magnification.

Focal point The point where the light rays converge to produce a clear, sharp, and defined image.

Foldback Returning selected portions of an audio mix to the studio so talent can monitor it without creating a feedback loop; e.g., to foldback all musical instruments to a singer but eliminate his voice to prevent creating feedback squeal. See *Interruptible foldback*.

Follow shot A scene in which the camera follows a moving subject.

Footcandle A measure of light intensity. The amount of light produced by a candle measured one foot from the flame. One footcandle equals about 10.74 lux.

Foreground treatment Photographing certain subjects or objects in the foreground of the shot to induce depth in the picture.

Frame (1) Video: a complete television picture

consisting of two interlaced fields. There are thirty frames produced per second in NTSC television reproduction. (2) Film: a single picture in a series of pictures on motion picture film; twenty-four frames are produced each second in film. (3) The outline of the television screen which the director uses to determine which visual elements to include and which to exclude in each camera shot.

Frame buffer A computer device that digitizes video signals in real time and stores them in its own memory.

Frame-transfer CCD A three-layer charge-coupled device consisting of a photosensitive grid, storage grid, and output register. A popular CCD technology for television camera operation. Is distinct from the "interline-transfer CCD."

Framestore synchronizer A digital device which processes each television frame to correct for problems in synchronization before the video signal enters the studio system. This permits the use of wild feeds from remote sources which may not be in synchronization with the home studio.

Freeze-frame To stop the action on a single video frame. Can be produced with a slow-motion disc, an electronic still-store unit, a framestore synchronizer, or some helical VTRs.

Frequency The number of complete cycles per second of an electrical signal expressed in Hertz (Hz).

Frequency range The range of frequencies, from the lowest to the highest, that people are capable of hearing.

Frequency response The range of frequencies, from the lowest to the highest, that audio equipment can handle.

Fresnel spotlight A lighting instrument which uses a fresnel lens to produce a beam of hard, directional light, which can be varied from "spot" to "flood." The most commonly used lighting instrument in television production.

Friction head Inexpensive camera mounting device that uses a spring or pressure between two plates to control the panning or tilting. Not recommended for smooth camera movement or heavy cameras.

f-stop The numerical setting on a camera lens which indicates the size of the aperture opening. The higher the f-stop number, the smaller the opening.

Full-track recorder An audio recorder which records a monaural signal across the entire width of the audiotape.

Fundamental The tone that is the pure frequency of a pitch. For example, 440 Hz is the fundamental of middle A on the piano. In music, also called the "first harmonic." See *Harmonics.*

Gaffer-grip A strong clamp used to attach lightweight lighting instruments to scenery, doors, and other locations.

Gaffer tape Strong, all-purpose tape which is used to dress audio and video cable, secure equipment and set pieces, and for a variety of jobs around the studio and location.

Gain The amount of signal amplification for audio and video signals. "Riding gain" means varying controls to produce the proper sound level.

Gel Colored plastic or gelatin material which is mounted in front of lighting instruments to produce colored light.

Generating element The part of a microphone which transforms sound waves into electrical energy.

Generation The number of dubs away from the master original tape. As generations increase, technical quality usually decreases.

Genlock A method of synchronizing a video source not normally part of a video system to all the equipment in the system.

Geostationary satellite A satellite positioned 22,300 miles in space over the equator. The satellite rotates so that its position always is above the same location on the earth below.

Giraffe boom Tripod boom which is smaller than a large perambulator boom but provides more operating flexibility than a fishpole boom.

Glitch Picture interference or distortion which occurs momentarily.

Gobo A foreground set piece designed for the camera to shoot through.

Golden Mean Classic composition in which an image is divided into two areas so that the ratio of the small area to the large area equals the ratio of the large area to the whole. Also called the "Golden Section."

Grain Refers to the degree that the minute granules of silver, which comprise the film emulsion, appear on screen.

Graphic equalizer Divides the audio source into different frequency bands. The audio technician can use the graphic equalizer to boost or cut various frequencies in the audio spectrum.

Graphics All visuals prepared for a production. Includes camera cards, slides, electronically generated letters and symbols, computer graphics, and special graphic set pieces.

Gray scale A test pattern or chart progressing in steps from TV white to TV black. Most gray scales use either seven or ten gray scale steps.

Ground row A curved set piece positioned in front of a cyclorama to increase the perception of depth and to hide cyc strip lights from camera view.

Hand card A graphic held by talent.

Hand cue Silent hand signals given by floor manager to talent during production.

Hand prop Objects or props which are handled by performers during production.

Hard key A key or insert with distinctive borders around the edges of the key.

Hard light Light quality characterized by a strong, directional beam, which produces dark shadows. Hard light is produced by spotlights.

Hardwall flat A flat with wooden surface.

Harmonics Exact multiples of a fundamental tone. In music, called "octaves." For example, 1,760 Hz and 880 Hz are harmonics of 440 Hz. See *Overtones*.

Harmonizer An audio device which can change the key of a recorded audio signal or create a harmony track to go along with a melody track.

Harpicon A high-resolution camera pickup tube used for high definition television (HDTV).

Head (1) An electromagnet in a tape machine that erases, records, or plays back audio or video information on magnetic tape. (2) The beginning of a tape.

Headroom (1) The space left between the subject's head and the top of the screen. (2) The leeway between proper audio level and distortion.

Helical scan (helical VTR) A method of videotape recording which uses one or two video heads to scan the tape in a slanted track pattern. Also called "slant track" recording.

Hertz (Hz) A unit of frequency indicating the number of cycles per second.

Hi-8 An 8-mm videotape format that offers higher quality than standard 8 mm. Used by both consumers in home video recorders and by professionals as an acquisition format.

High band A videotape recording technique which uses high-frequency signals to produce higher-quality pictures and permit a greater number of dubs without significant reduction in picture quality.

High-definition television (HDTV) The use of specially designed video equipment capable of reproducing pictures with significantly greater resolution than is possible with conventional video equipment. HDTV uses over 1,000 video lines and 60 frames per second to create the video image as opposed to the 525-line or 625-line systems which are currently in use. HDTV aspect ratio is 16:9.

High key A lighting approach characterized by light shadows and relatively even illumination.

Highlight The brightest portion of a picture or area.

High-Z High-impedance microphone signal; rarely used in professional audio equipment.

HMI lamp A gas-filled lamp which produces a high-efficiency light output with a marked reduction in heat. The color quality of the light is daylight balanced.

Horizontal blanking interval (HBI) During the television scanning process, the period of time that the scanning beam is turned off between each scan line.

Hot Equipment is on: current is being supplied to equipment.

Hotspot An extremely bright concentration of light in one place relative to the surrounding illumination. Can create camera shading problems.

Hue The color itself of light, paint, etc. The hue is the actual color.

IATSE International Alliance of Theatrical Stage Employees; technician's union.

IBEW International Brotherhood of Electrical Workers; technician's union.

ID Short for "station identification."

Image enhancer An electronic device designed to increase picture resolution.

Image retention See *Burn-in; Comet-tailing.*

Impedance Resistance to current flow, which is especially important in matching microphones and audio equipment. Almost all professional audio microphones are low impedance (low-Z), which permits longer cable runs without a reduction in audio quality.

Incandescent lamp A lamp which produces light by heating an internal filament inside a conventional glass globe.

Incident light reading A light meter reading taken from the position of the subject with the meter facing toward the camera and light source. "Incident light" refers to the illumination which falls directly on the subject.

Input (1) The physical location at which a signal enters a system. (2) The signal entering a system.

Insert edit Electronic videotape editing in which new video, audio, or both can be inserted into a previously recorded tape without disturbing material before and after the insert. Insert editing utilizes the existing control track and produces very stable edits.

Insert key The insertion of one video image into another. See *Chroma key.*

Insert reel See *B-roll.*

Intercom Short for "intercommunication system"; the internal communication system, using telephone-type headsets, between production personnel in the control room and crew members on the studio floor. Also called "PL system."

Interlace scanning The television reproduction process in which the electron beam scans every other line as it moves, scanning all the odd lines first (odd fields), then going back and scanning all the even lines (even fields) to fill in the rest of the image.

Interline-transfer CCD A type of charge-coupled device (CCD) which interleaves the photosensitive and storage areas on a single register rather than using two separate grids. Is distinct from the other popular CCD technology used in television, which is called the "frame transfer CCD."

Interruptible foldback (IFB) device An unobtrusive earpiece worn by a performer that permits communication while on camera.

In the can A finished production which has been edited and is ready for film or videotape playback.

Inverse-square law Intensity is inversely proportional to the square of the change in the distance between a source and subject. For example: When a microphone is moved twice as far from a subject, the sound level is one-fourth as loud. When a light is moved three times as far from a subject, the intensity is one-ninth as bright.

i.p.s. Abbreviation for "inches per second." Indicates the speed of audio or videotape during recording and playback.

Iris Same as aperture.

Isolated camera A camera which feeds its own videotape machine, as well as being used in the multiple-camera video mix. Started in sports coverage but is now used for many entertainment and dramatic productions to provide additional editing footage.

Jack (1) A female socket or receptacle. (2) A stage brace used to support scenery.

Jog To slowly move helical videotape back and forth in order to locate a precise edit point.

Joystick   A hand-operated control which offers 360° positioning of the joystick. Used in switchers, to position a cutout insert, and, in some videotape edit programmers, to control the operation of the VTRs. Also used on some audio consoles to pan a sound channel when mixing in stereo.

Jump cut   A jarring transition between two camera shots, in which the subject appears to jump in the frame.

Kelvin scale   A unit of measurement used to indicate the color temperature of a light source.

Key   An electronic effect in which an image is electronically cut into another background picture. See *Matte key; Insert key; Chroma key.*

Key color   In chroma key, the color in the foreground shot that is replaced by a background image. For example, a weather forecaster standing in front of a blue wall will appear to be standing in front of a map when the map is chroma keyed into the blue key color.

Key light   The principal source of illumination on a subject or scene.

Keystone   (1) Picture distortion caused by a camera that is not at a perfect right angle to the surface of the object or graphic being photographed. (2) A piece of plywood used to reinforce the joints of a flat frame.

Kicker light   A light positioned at the rear and to the side of the subject.

Kill   To turn off a light, sound, or video feed; to cut or delete a line or portion of a program.

Kinescope   Recording a television program from a monitor using 16-mm motion picture film.

Ku-band   That portion of the spectrum between 12 and 14 gigaHertz. Becoming important for satellite transmission, especially news and business videoconferencing.

Lag   Persistence of an image on the face of the television camera pickup tube. See also *Comet-tailing; Burn-in; Image retention.*

Lavalier microphone   A small microphone designed to be worn by talent either hung from a cord or clipped to tie, lapel, or blouse.

Lead room   The space toward which a subject is looking or moving in the frame. Also called "lead space," "talk space," "nose room," or "look space."

Leko   Ellipsoidal spotlight.

Lens speed   Refers to the maximum aperture of the lens; the lowest numerical f-stop. The faster the lens, the wider the maximum aperture, and the more light-gathering capability.

Lensless spotlight   Instrument designed to produce hard, directional light without a spotlight. Lightweight and portable design makes them useful for remote production.

Level   The signal strength, or volume, of a video or audio signal.

Light meter   Meter designed to read light intensity using either reflected or incident light. Most light meters used in TV have footcandle scales.

Light plot   A floorplan showing the studio set drawn to scale, with the lighting instruments that are to be used superimposed to indicate instrument, location, and function.

Light ratio   The relative intensities of various light sources; intensity of light between key, back, and fill lights.

Limbo   (1) An area with a completely neutral background which gives the illusion of endless distance. (2) A lighting approach in which background is light gray with foreground subject prominent on screen. See also *Cameo.*

Line   (1) Line monitor: the master video monitor which shows the picture being recorded or broadcast. Also called "air monitor." (2) One of the traces of the television pickup tube scanning beam.

Linear editing   Sequential editing, usually on videotape, requiring that all edits be done in order from beginning to end. Rearranging shots is time-consuming and difficult. See *Nonlinear editing.*

Lip sync   (1) The synchronization of sound and picture. (2) Having a performer mouth words to a prerecorded sound track.

Live   (1) A program broadcast as it happens, in real time. (2) A device or piece of equipment which is turned on, e.g., "live microphone."

Live on tape A videotape production approach in which the show is produced with multiple cameras as though it were broadcast live. No postproduction editing is used.

Location A production site outside the normal studio.

Logo Symbol used to identify a station, program, sponsor, company, etc.

Long shot Camera shot of a set or subject which usually includes a wide-angle field of view. See *Establishing shot.*

Longitudinal time code (LTC) SMPTE time code recorded on a secondary audio track or on the VTR's cue track.

Loudness The perception of sound intensity or volume.

Low band Videotape recording process which uses relatively low-frequency signals to produce a video image. Provides lower-quality picture than high band VTRs.

Low key A lighting approach characterized by deep shadows, high contrast ratio, and strong use of highlight and dark areas.

Lower third Key graphic designed to appear beneath a subject in lower third of the screen. Used to identify subject, object, place.

Low-Z Low impedance; used primarily when referring to microphones. All professional mikes are low-Z because it permits longer cable runs.

Luminance channel In color television, the channel which carries the monochrome signal and provides brightness information for color receivers.

Luminance chroma key See *Soft key.*

Luminaire A lighting instrument.

Lux A measure of light intensity. One lux equals about .0931 footcandle.

M II A professional ½-inch videotape format.

Magneto-optical (MO) disc Combines the capabilities of magnetic and optical technology. Sometimes called a "floptical" disc.

Mark Tape placed on the studio floor to indicate to talent or camera operators where they should be positioned.

Masking One sound concealing another.

Master An original audiotape, videotape, or film. Used for broadcast or to produce copies. An "edit master" is the original edited copy of a program.

Master control The room where all video and audio outputs of various production studios are fed for distribution and broadcast or recording.

Master-control fader Fader on audio console which regulates the entire output of the console.

Master shot A single shot of a scene, usually a wide or long shot, which is used as the reference, or master, in editing a sequence.

Matched dissolve Dissolve from one picture to another which is closely related in appearance or shot size.

Matching transformer A device that makes it possible to connect equipment with outputs and inputs of differing impedances; for example, a high-impedance mike and a low-impedance input.

Matte key Keying a graphic or symbol over a background picture. The cut-out lettering can be electronically filled in with any desired color shade or with gray.

MDM Modular digital multitrack. An audio recording system designed to record 8-track digital audio on videocassettes.

Mechanical sound effect A sound effect which is produced through mechanical means, such as crumpling cellophane, opening and closing doors, etc. Requires a live microphone pickup to cover sound.

Microwave The line-of-sight and point-to-point transmission of video and audio signals. Commonly used to feed live and taped signals from a remote production back to the studio for taping or broadcast.

Millimeter (mm) One-thousandth of a meter; 25.4 mm = 1 inch. Measurement used to express the focal length of a lens.

Mini disc (MD) A magneto-optical disc about half the diameter of a 5-inch CD.

Mix bank A pair of buses with a fader-bar control to permit the production of fades, dissolves, and supers.

Mix/effects bank A series of buses which are connected to a fader bar and a special-effects generator to produce keys, inserts, wipes, split screens.

Modem (modulator-demodulator) A device which allows digital information to travel over analog phone lines.

Modular microphone Although the preamplifier circuits do not change, different pickup modules can be attached to the preamplifier housing. For example, a modular microphone might have a hand-held and shotgun module that could be changed for different audio requirements.

Modulation Varying the frequency, amplitude, or phase of a wave or electric current by superimposing another wave on it.

Moiré effect Spurious color patterns which appear in a television picture when certain stripes, checks, or other complex designs on fabrics or graphics interfere with the television system's scanning operation.

Monaural Single-channel audio.

Monochrome Black and white television.

Montage A rapid sequence of shots used to produce a particular impact or mood.

Morphing A digital video effect in which a subject is "stretched" into a dissimilar subject.

Motivated key Positioning the key light in a place logically determined by set elements such as a window, lamp, etc.

Moving-coil microphone Microphone designed with diaphragm connected to a moving coil which creates an electric current by its motion within a magnetic field. Also called "dynamic microphone."

M/S (mid/side) technique A stereo miking technique which places a cardioid and bipolar mike very close together creating a middle and side channel of sound.

MTS audio (multichannel television sound) This describes the audio broadcast used in stereo television.

Multiple camera/multiple VTR A videotape production approach in which each camera continuously feeds its own VTR. All editing is done in postproduction.

Multiplexer A device utilizing mirrors and prisms to enable a number of film and slide projectors to feed a single television film camera.

Multiplexing The process of "piggybacking" multiple signals on one carrier.

Multiplier Same as "range extender."

Multitrack recorder An audio recorder which permits recording signals on a number of separate tracks or channels for greater creative control in recording and mixing.

Munsell system A color scale which identifies various colors according to hue, saturation, and brightness.

Musical instrument digital interface (MIDI) MIDI is a computer instruction set which allows computer-based musical instruments to share information and be integrated into a total system.

NABET National Association of Broadcast Employees and Technicians; primarily a technicians' union.

Narrow-angle lens Long focal length lens. Produces a narrow angle of view.

Narrowcasting Directing programs toward target audiences.

Neutral-density filter Filter designed to reduce the intensity of light without affecting its color quality.

Neutral set Completely bare setting which emphasizes foreground subjects.

Noise (1) In audio, the unwanted hiss, hum, or buzz heard along with the desired sound. (2) In video, electronic interference appearing as snow or grain in the picture.

Noise gate A device that eliminates unwanted background noise between desired foreground sounds.

Noise reduction (NR) Decrease of noise in an audio reproduction.

Nonlinear editing Editing performed on a personal computer or workstation outfitted with hardware and software that enable it to digitize the video and audio, store them on computer disks, and provide the editor with almost instantaneous random access to the stored material.

Shots may be rearranged quickly and easily. See *Linear editing*.

Nonsegmented Helical recording technique using a single video head which lays down a complete video track on each pass. Permits stable freeze-frame and slow-motion operation.

Normal lens A lens with a focal length that produces the normal field of view and the spatial perspective which our eyes produce.

Normal wiring A circuit which is permanently wired into an audio console. It is broken only if a patch cord is inserted into the appropriate jack on the patch panel. See *Normalled patch panel*.

Normalled patch panel Banks of jacks that automatically connect outputs and inputs of audio equipment without patch cords as long as the normal connections are desired. Circuits are broken only when patch cords are inserted into jacks on the patch panel. See *Patch panel*.

Notch filter Removes a small wedge, or "notch," from the overall audio spectrum. Especially helpful for removing the hum from 60-Hz power.

Notes Suggestions, criticisms, and revisions given to cast and crew by director and producer after each rehearsal.

NTSC National Television Systems Committee. Devised the current television system used in the United States and Japan. The NTSC standard has 525 scan lines and thirty frames (sixty fields) per second.

Octave In music, an exact multiple of a tone. See *Harmonics*.

Off-book When talent must have dialogue memorized and not rely on script.

Off-line Editing with a workprint of original master footage. Usually SMPTE time code is used to catalogue edits, and a computer-assisted edit system is used on-line to transform workprint time codes into the final, edited master.

Ohm A measure of electrical resistance. Often expressed with symbol Ω.

Omega wrap Videotape threading configuration in which the tape on a helical VTR is wrapped around the head drum in an omega pattern.

Omnidirectional Audio pickup pattern in which microphone is designed to be equally sensitive to sounds emanating from all directions.

On-line Editing videotape using top-quality recorders, as opposed to working with inexpensive workprints of the original master tape. "On-line" also refers to a computer-assisted edit system that uses SMPTE time code from the off-line workprint to assemble the final master on large format VTRs.

1-inch Type C A professional videotape format. The standard for high-quality recording and reproduction.

Open-face spotlight Lensless spotlight.

Open set A set-design approach which uses a minimum of flats, and then only to suggest the actual environment.

Optical disc The family of technologies that use laser optic systems to read information that is prerecorded on round platters.

Oscillator An electronic device that can produce a pure tone at any frequency.

Oscilloscope A device utilizing a cathode ray tube to visually display electronic signals; used for equipment testing and setup.

Outcue The final cue of a tape or film cut; the final cue of a program.

Output (1) The physical location at which a signal leaves a source. (2) The signal leaving the source.

Overcut (1) Changing the inserted image in a key or matte picture without affecting the background picture. (2) Too much cutting between shots within a program or sequence.

Overdubbing On a multitrack audiotape recorder, recording on one track while playing prerecorded tracks in sync. See *Selective synchronization*.

Over-the-shoulder shot (O.S. shot) Camera shot in which a subject is photographed framed by another subject's shoulder in the foreground. Induces depth in the shot.

Overtones Frequencies that resonate with the fundamental tone, but are not exact multiples of it. See *Harmonics*.

PA (1) Production assistant. (2) Public address. In audio, the amplification system used to feed the audience area program sound.

Pacing The overall rhythm of the program, which is determined by the cutting, performance, and other creative aspects. Determines how the audience perceives the time of segments and the overall show.

Pad (1) A resistance placed in the audio circuit to match impedances or to cut down excessive electric power to provide greater control to the audio engineer. (2) A flexible segment in a program which can be used to stretch or shorten the running time of the show. (3) Additional video or audio on film or tape to provide protection against running out of program material.

PAL Phase alternate line. The method used to reproduce the television image in parts of Europe, South America, the Middle East, and Africa. The PAL standard has 625 scan lines and twenty-five frames (fifty fields) per second.

Paint system A digital tool for graphic artists used to shape, color, and modify visual images. An essential element in most postproduction facilities and television stations.

Pan Horizontal movement of the camera on a stationary pedestal.

Pan light Same as "broad."

Pantograph A scissor-type hanging device used to vary the height of a lighting instrument.

PAR light Short for "parabolic aluminized reflector"; a lamp with built-in reflector unit.

Parabolic reflector A large dish with a microphone mounted in the center. Used to pick up audio from large distances.

Parallel action Two or more actions or events occurring simultaneously and shown through the use of cross-cutting, flashbacks, or the use of complementary or opposing audio and video tracks.

Patch cord See *Patch panel*.

Patch panel A routing system which enables audio, lighting, and video inputs to be assigned to various control circuits and outputs. Also called a "patch bay." Provides flexibility in interconnecting equipment. Traditionally, patch panels contained a large number of jacks that could be interconnected by cables called "patch cords." Today most patch panels are computer-controlled.

Pea light A tiny Christmas tree-type light which is often used for stars in conjunction with a cyclorama.

Pedestal (1) Camera mounting device. (2) Camera operation command meaning to raise or lower the height of the camera by adjusting the pedestal column control.

Perambulator boom A large boom arm on a wheel-mounted base. A series of controls permit the microphone to be rotated and extended or retracted to cover the audio.

Performer Anyone who appears in front of the television camera or a microphone.

Persistence of vision A mental process that holds visual information in memory and integrates it with new visual information, creating the perception of continuous movement when watching a series of rapidly changing still images.

Perspective (1) Spatial relationships as they appear in a camera shot. (2) Sound perspective: the relationship of the sound quality of the visual image of the sound source.

Phase Refers to the timing of the oscillations of two identical signals and indicates the degree of synchronization between them. Frequencies are "in phase" when they begin at the same time and "out of phase" when they don't. In-phase signals result in a combined amplitude, or volume, which is greater than the individual frequencies. Out-of-phase signals reduce or eliminate some frequencies in the two signals. See *Phase cancellation*.

Phase cancellation The loss of frequencies and reduced levels when two identical audio signals are out of phase. See *Phase*.

Phi phenomenon The illusion of motion created as rows of lights turn off and on in sequence.

Photoelectric transducer Translates light (photo) into electrical impulses (electric). The television camera pickup tube and the charge-coupled device (CCD) are both photoelectric transducers.

Pickup pattern   The pattern or direction of sounds which a microphone is designed to cover. See *Polar diagram*.

Pickup tube   The vacuum tube inside the television camera head which converts light into electrical energy.

Pictorial space   A two-dimensional plane within which an art work is framed.

Pigtail   Cable and connectors running from the lighting power strip which are used to supply power to individual lighting instruments.

Pin   (1) To focus the beam of light on a fresnel down to a highly directional spot. (2) Overloading the audio level to the extent that the VU needle is driven past its maximum operating limit.

Pipe grid   Crisscrossing metal pipes suspended over the studio floor, from which lighting instruments are hung.

Pitch   The subjective perception of sound frequency.

Pixel   The smallest element of the video image. Pixels are the phosphorescent "dots" which run along each of the video lines that make up the video image. The more pixels per screen, the better the picture resolution.

PL   Short for "private line." (1) Refers to communication intercom system in a studio which enables production and crew members to talk to each other. (2) A special telephone line installed specifically for a production.

Plastics   A very general term which refers to such design elements as graphics, sets, and lighting.

Plumbicon   Camera pickup tube which utilizes a lead oxide compound as the light-sensitive element.

Points   The intensity scale used to indicate the position of a lighting dimmer fader control. Points run from zero (no power) to ten (full power).

Polar diagram   Illustration of the pickup pattern of a microphone.

Polarity reversal   Electronically reversing the gray scale of an image, so the camera's picture shows a negative image.

Polecat   Spring-loaded aluminum pole which is used to hang graphics, set pieces, lighting instruments.

Polish   A script revision or rewrite.

Polystyrene   A plastic material used in set construction and for special props. Also called "Styrofoam."

Pop filter   See *Blast filter*.

Posting   A term for "postproduction."

Postproduction   The final stage of the production process in which videotape is edited and audio is added or "sweetened" after the actual production is completed.

Pot   Short for "potentiometer"; a control operated in a clockwise or counterclockwise direction to vary the intensity of an electrical signal. Commonly refers to knob controls on audio console.

Power rail   The cable trough in which power cables for lighting instruments are run along pipe grids.

Practical lights   Set pieces, such as table lamps and chandeliers, which must actually operate during the production.

Preproduction planning   The first production stage in which the program is planned and coordinated.

Preroll   Starting a film or tape earlier than it is needed on the air to permit it to attain the proper operating speed and to stabilize. The time necessary for a preroll depends on the film or tape machines, as well as the program's script, and director and talent preference.

Pressure zone microphone (PZM)   Hears sound with equal fidelity and volume even when the sources of the sound are different distances from the microphone. A popular choice for panel discussions and audience question and answer sessions.

Preview bus   A row of video source buttons which enable the TD to look at any video picture before actually putting it on the air.

Preview monitor   The control room monitor which displays the output of the preview bus.

Primary lens   Fixed focal length lens.

Primary motion   Refers to the movement of subjects.

Primary video source Any video source which produces its own picture image, e.g., cameras, VTRs, telecine, and character generator.

Print-through A recorded signal that is slightly superimposed onto the parts of the tape that are wound against it. May occur when a tape with a recording on it is not played for some time.

Prism beam-splitter Optical device in a color camera which dissects the reflected light into the three primary colors. See *Dichroic mirror*.

Producer The production team member responsible for the entire production.

Production The third stage in the production process, when sound and picture are broadcast or recorded on tape.

Production console The long table in the control room which faces the monitor bank in which the video switcher is installed. Seated at the production console are the director, TD, AD, and other production staff members.

Production music Specially written and recorded music designed to be used as background, theme, or transitional music on a show.

Production switcher Video switcher which enables the TD to put any video source or composite picture on the air.

Program bus The master bus on a video switcher which controls the output signal of the switcher.

Program intercom PL system used to communicate directions and cues between control room and studio floor during rehearsal and production.

Program monitor Large control room monitor which displays the video output of the switcher which is being broadcast or recorded. Also called "line monitor" or "air monitor."

Progressive scanning The computer reproduction process in which the electron beam scans each line in sequence, from the top to the bottom of the screen.

Prop Short for "property"; any scenic element used to dress the set but which is not structurally a part of the background. Includes furniture, pictures, and various items used by performers. See *Hand prop*.

Protection A duplicate made of a film or tape and run simultaneously with the master machine to safeguard against technical problems during air.

Proximity effect An increase in low frequencies when a microphone is used close to a sound source.

Punch up To "take" or "cut" to a video source. Often used as a director command, e.g. "punch up" a video source, or put it on the air.

Push-off Special effect possible with a digital video manipulator unit. Effect appears as though one image literally pushes the other off the screen.

Quad split Special video effect in which four different images appear on screen simultaneously.

Quantize To convert an analog signal into a digital signal.

Quartz lamp Lamp which provides a high-intensity illumination with a constant color temperature. Also called "tungsten-halogen lamps."

Rack focus Varying the focus of a lens to change the areas which appear in and out of focus.

Radio frequency (RF) Wireless transmission of video and audio signals via various broadcast channel frequencies.

Range extender Optical device which increases the focal length of a lens.

Raster The illuminated area of the television screen which is produced by the scanning lines.

Rating A statistical estimate of a program's popularity. Expressed as a percentage of the number of households watching among all television households.

R-DAT Rotating head-digital audiotape. A digital audio recording system that uses rotating heads similar to videotape recorders.

Reaction shot A cutaway to a shot which shows the reaction of another subject. See also *Cutaway shot*.

Real time The actual time in which an event or program takes place. Used to distinguish between cutting or editing while a show's production progresses or afterwards in postproduction.

Real time disk (RTD) recorder A computer that digitizes video signals and stores them on a magnetic disk in real time.

Realistic/representational set Set design approach in which the setting is meant to appear as realistic as possible.

Recording in segments A videotape production technique in which multiple cameras are used to tape a portion of a larger program. Once all segments are recorded, they are assembled together in postproduction.

Reflected reading A light meter reading taken with the meter facing the subject and measuring the light reflected from the subject into the camera lens.

Registration The accurate alignment of the three electronic pickup tube images in a camera to produce the composite color picture.

Rehearsal The second production stage, which is often divided into two parts: (1) dry rehearsal and (2) studio rehearsal.

Release form A standard form signed by all performers before appearing on a television production.

Remote A television production produced outside the studio.

Remote survey Preliminary visit to the location site to determine all technical and creative production requirements for the show.

Resolution The degree of clarity or definition, of a picture. The higher the resolution, the sharper the image.

Reverberation The persistence of a sound which is produced either acoustically or electronically.

Reverse-angle shot A shot in the opposite direction from the previous shot. Frequently used during interviews where the reverse-angle shot is a cutaway of the reporter.

Rewritable consumer (RC) time code The time code generated on some consumer recording systems. Incompatible with SMPTE time code and must be converted for use in professional editing.

RF microphone A wireless microphone.

RGB system RGB stands for "red-green-blue" and refers to a reproduction system in which the RGB color signals are kept separate. All computers have RGB systems.

Ribbon microphone Microphone which utilizes a sensitive ribbon suspended in a magnetic field as the generating element.

Riding gain Controlling the level of a video or audio signal.

Riding levels Same as riding gain.

Rim lighting A method of backlighting in which instruments are aimed at the subject's head and shoulders from the sides, producing a rim of light around the subject's hair.

Riser A platform, usually made from plywood, which is used to elevate talent or to produce multiple levels on a studio set.

Robotic camera system Studio camera and pedestal hardware that permit remote control of camera and pedestal movements.

Roll cue The command to start a film, videotape, or audiotape.

Rolling Means that a film, videotape, or audiotape has been started and is ready for playback or recording.

Room noise Recording the ambient sound of a production location (either interior or exterior). The room noise is useful later during postproduction editing in smoothing over audio edits on audio or video tape.

Rule of Thirds Composition in which an image is divided into thirds horizontally and vertically and the center of attention is positioned at one of the intersections of the four lines separating the areas.

Rundown sheet Indicates each sequence within a program, its segment time, and the program's overall running time. Some sheets also include talent and set information which may be needed during production.

Run-through Rehearsal, usually with full facilities.

SAG Screen Actor's Guild; performers' union.

Sampler A MIDI-controlled recording device that "listens" to a sound and records it as a series of digital codes. Once a sound has been sampled, it can be manipulated in many different ways to change its quality.

Sampling The process of measuring attributes of a sound waveform thousands of times each second.

Satellite news gathering (SNG) The technique of using portable satellite up-links aimed at a satellite to deliver news via a down-link to the studio for immediate or delayed broadcast.

Saticon A Vidicon-type color pickup tube with improved operational characteristics over standard vidicons.

Saturation The strength of a color determined by its relative purity; i.e., a fully saturated color has no white light mixed in, an unsaturated color appears washed out with the addition of white light.

Scanning The television reproduction process which involves moving an electron beam across a camera pickup tube (to convert light energy into electrical impulses) and across a CRT (to reproduce the image).

Scanning area The total area scanned by the television camera and reproduced on the studio monitor.

Scene breakdown Dissecting each scene into its component parts, i.e., location, performers, sets, and props, in order to develop an efficient videotape shooting schedule.

Scenic designer Production team member responsible for designing sets and supervising set construction.

Scoop A television floodlight.

SCR dimmer Short for "silicon-controlled rectifier." A dimmer control which uses a low-level pilot voltage to control power to lighting instruments.

Scrim (1) A translucent gauze or fiberglass material used to soften and diffuse illumination from a lighting instrument. (2) A gauzelike curtain often used in conjunction with a studio cyclorama.

Script processor A computer software program that automatically formats scripts according to industry standards.

SECAM Séquentielle couleur à mémoire. Roughly translated: sequential color with memory. The method used to reproduce the television image in France, Eastern Europe, and some countries in the Middle East and Africa. Like the PAL standard, SECAM has 625 scan lines and twenty-five frames (fifty fields) per second, but its color encoding system is different from PAL.

Secondary motion Refers to camera movement.

Secondary video source The output of a mix or mix/effects bank on the video switcher, which can be reentered for additional video manipulation.

Segmented scanning A VTR recording/reproduction process in which two or more video heads are used to divide or "segment" the video track information as it is written on the videotape.

Segue To begin next sound source immediately after preceding sound without interruption.

Selective focus Utilizing depth of field to direct the viewer's attention to certain areas of the scene by varying those elements in and out of focus.

Selective synchronization The function on a multitrack audiotape recorder that makes "overdubbing" possible. Also called "sel sync." See *Overdubbing*.

Separate audio program (SAP) One of the three audio channels found in multichannel television sound (MTS). Often used for second language television.

Servostabilizer A camera mount which uses a gyroscope to provide very steady hand-held moving shots. Also used from helicopters, trains, etc. to reduce camera jitter and picture shake.

Servozoom A zoom lens which is operated via electronically controlled motors.

Setup and rehearsal The second stage of the production process, when the studio is prepared for the production, and performers and technical personnel run through their various responsibilities in order to coordinate their activities for production.

Shading Varying the video controls on a CCU to compensate for changes in scene brightness.

Shadow-keyer Chroma-keyer which can produce shadows, along with the insert image, for a more realistic composite effect.

Share Audience-measurement estimate expressed as the percentage of viewers watching a particular show among all those watching TV at the time.

Shot box Zoom lens control mounted at rear of camera, which permits the camera operator to preselect a number of specific lens focal lengths.

Shotgun microphone Highly directional microphone designed to pick up audio from large mike-to-subject distances.

Shot sheets Listings of each camera's individual shots which are given to camera operators prior to rehearsal and production.

Shot shopper Slang term for program directors who permit their camera operators freedom in selecting shots.

Show reel The edited film or videotape reel which is to be used for a production. Usually includes all cuts or segments, separated by cuing leader.

Side light Lighting instrument positioned to side of subject to emphasize body shape and form.

Signal-to-noise ratio The relationship of the strength of the video or audio signal to interfering noise. The higher the S-N ratio, the better, since this means the signal is masking the interfering noise.

Simulcast Refers to the playing of synchronized FM stereo audio along with the conventional video and audio to provide high-quality, stereo sound.

Single camera/single VTR A videotape production approach utilizing one camera and a single VTR. The camera shoots a scene from a variety of different angles, or setups, and all editing is done in postproduction.

Single system sound The process of recording both sound and picture on the same film or videotape.

16 mm A common film format.

Skewing error Results when a videotape is not wrapped around the head drum with the proper amount of tension. Appears as the top part of the picture waving back and forth like a flag. Also called "flagging."

Slant-track scanning Helical VTR recording/reproduction process in which video information is written on the tape in a slanted pattern.

Slate A blackboard or chart used to visually identify a film or videotape take according to take number, recording date, and additional identification information.

Slave Synchronizing a video or audio tape machine to a "master" machine for recording, editing, and playback operations. Commonly, a multitrack audio tape recorder is slaved to a VTR via SMPTE time code.

Slide chain 35-mm slide projector; part of the telecine.

Slip cue Method of cuing records to permit instantaneous program sound when called for by director.

Slow lens A lens with a relatively small maximum aperture; a lens with a relatively high minimum numerical f-stop which does not permit it to gather much light.

Slug A section of blank film or videotape which is inserted into the film or tape to represent additional program information which is forthcoming. The slug usually runs the exact length of the intended program material.

SMPTE Society of Motion Picture and Television Engineers.

SMPTE time code Eight-digit address code used to identify each videotape frame by hour, minute, second and frame number for precision editing.

Sneak Slowly fade in audio source.

SOF; SOT Short for "sound on film" or "sound on tape."

Soft key A chroma key in which the edges of the insert image gradually blend into the background. The soft key permits keying transparent objects and shadows into a background picture creating a more realistic key. Also called "luminance keying."

Soft light Wide aperture floodlight which produces a very diffused illumination.

Software Computer programs.

Soft wipe A wipe with edges similar to those seen in a soft key.

Solarization Video special effect in which insert key is used to produce a high-contrast image which can be colorized using the switcher SEG.

Sound bite A film or tape clip containing lip sync sound from a news story. Usually refers to a piece of an interview or a statement which is used in the news story.

Sound direction A property of sound that has become important with the increase in stereo sound reproduction. Refers to the fact that the location of a sound can be determined because our two ears hear it at slightly different times. Increases the sense of "spatialization" of sound.

Sound envelope Refers to the variation in the intensities of a sound's attack, sustain (internal dynamics), and decay.

Sound intensity The volume of the sound.

Sound perspective The relationship of the sound quality with the visual image of the sound source.

Sound presence A subjective impression of sound quality which depends upon the microphone, mike-to-subject distance, and room acoustics. More presence produces a fuller, richer, closer sounding audio.

Spaced technique Refers to a stereo miking technique that places two microphones equidistant and perpendicular to the emanating surface of the sound source.

Speaker system A device that changes audio signals into audible sound. Consists of cones called "woofers" and "tweeters." See *Transducer*.

Special-effects generator (SEG) Electronic device, usually installed in the video switcher, which is used to produce wipes, split screens, inserts, keys, and mattes.

Specular reflection Hard, intense reflection from a shiny surface.

Split edit An editing technique in which either the sound or picture is cut, then the other is cut after a slight delay. Split edits smooth out cuts-only transitions.

Split screen A wipe carried only partway through; thus, two or more images appear on screen simultaneously.

Spot down Focusing the fresnel spotlight into its spot beam; narrowing the beam distribution and increasing light intensity.

Spot meter A reflected light meter with an extremely narrow field of view to permit highly specific and accurate light readings over a limited area.

Spotlight Lighting instrument which produces a hard, directional, intense beam of light.

Spotlight effect Special video effect on many switchers which enables a portion of the screen to appear brighter in order to highlight a particular element within the shot.

Spotter A person who helps the producer, director, or talent at a remote event (usually sports) to identify participants and important action.

Spread Focusing the fresnel spotlight into its flooded beam; widening the light distribution and reducing the light intensity.

Stabilizing lens A lens with a built-in device that produces steady images. Particularly useful for hand-held camerawork.

Stage manager Same as floor manager.

Stand-up A news story delivered by a reporter on location talking directly into the camera. Also refers to the open and closing sections of a news story in which reporter talks directly to audience.

Starlight filter Special filter designed to produce a starburst effect whenever the camera photographs a high-intensity light source.

Stereo microphone A microphone system that consists of two monophonic elements inside a casing that picks up sound from two directions.

Stop down To close the aperture of a lens to permit less light to enter the camera.

Storyboard A sequence of sketches that illustrates the author's script.

Straight-up Refers to the clock time when the

seconds and minutes are both at 12, or straight-up.

Stretch (1) Director command to talent to slow dialogue or action. (2) Expanding either the white or black levels of the television camera video signal as in "stretching the whites," or "stretching the blacks."

Strike (1) To dismantle a set after the production is over. (2) To remove a prop, set piece, or item of equipment after it is no longer needed.

Striplight A row of broads attached into a strip.

Studio address (SA) Public address system which enables the director in the control room to talk to everyone on the studio floor via a loud-speaker system.

Studio plot Scale drawing of studio which is used to produce floorplan and lighting plot.

Stylized/abstract set (1) Set design approach in which the setting is designed to suggest a par-ticular environment without actually portraying it. (2) A fantasy or unreal setting.

Subjective angle Camera angle in which the camera is positioned to show the scene from a performer's point of view.

Subjective time As opposed to "real time," on-screen time in which pace is manipulated to create a desired feeling in the audience. Also called "psychological time."

Submaster A single control which enables the operator to group a number of different audio or lighting sources and to control them with one fader.

Subtractive mixing Combining colors to block some color qualities and create other colors. Equal proportions of the three primary paint colors—cyan, magenta, and yellow—result in black. The opposite of additive mixing.

Super Short for "superimposition."

Supercardioid pickup An extremely directional microphone pickup pattern.

Superimposition Combining two or more com-plete video images simultaneously using mix or mix/effects buses.

Surround-sound A process that digitally ex-pands a stereo signal during postproduction

and redirects it to five channels so the sound seems to come from a full 360 degrees.

S-VHS A professional VHS format that offers higher resolution than the standard VHS format.

Sweep reversal Electronically reversing the op-eration of the scanning beam to reverse hori-zontal or vertical placement of the image.

Sweetening Postproduction audio production to add, modify, and enhance the program audio.

Swishpan An extremely rapid pan which ap-pears as a blur on screen.

Switcher (1) Electronic device used to select the image or composite images which are either broadcast or recorded. (2) The production crew member who operates the video switcher. Also called a "technical director."

Sync generator An electronic component which produces various synchronizing pulses neces-sary for the operation of the television system.

Synthesizer A MIDI-controlled musical produc-tion instrument, usually in the form of a key-board. The synthesizer can assign different "voices" or sound qualities to music created on the keyboard. For example, the keyboard can be used to re-create the horn section of an or-chestra.

Take (1) To cut to a video source. Usually a di-rector's command, as in "Take 1." (2) Individual scenes, segments, or shots recorded on film or videotape. Each is assigned a "take number" which is used to locate and identify the seg-ments for screening and editing.

Take sheet A form used to keep track of each take. Includes take number, time, and whether it is "good" or "bad."

Talent Anyone who appears on camera or be-fore the microphone.

Tally light Lights atop the camera, inside the viewfinder, and on the control room monitors which automatically light each time the camera is punched up on the air.

Target audience The intended audience for a program. Characteristics of the target audience must be determined by the producer in prepro-duction.

TD Technical director.

Technical director The crew member who operates the video switcher during rehearsal and production.

Telecine See *Film chain*.

Telephoto lens A long-focal-length lens which produces a magnified image with a narrow horizontal field of view.

Teleprompter A prompting device which displays script copy to talent. It is usually mounted in front of the camera lens.

Television black Darkest gray-scale element, which measures approximately 3 percent reflectance but appears black onscreen.

Television white Brightest element of TV gray scale, which measures between 60 and 70 percent white reflectance but appears natural white onscreen.

Tertiary motion The illusion of movement created by changes between images.

Test tone Audio tone produced by a tone generator and used as a reference in adjusting sound levels during recording and playback.

35 mm (1) 2 × 2 inch slides used in slide chain. (2) Motion picture feature film format.

Threefold Three set flats hinged together into a single unit.

Three-point lighting Basic lighting approach which uses a key, back, and fill light to illuminate subject and create depth and texture.

¾-inch U-Matic A videotape format still widely used, but which is quickly losing ground to the professional ½-inch and 8-mm formats.

Three-shot Camera shot which includes three subjects.

Three-to-one rule In stereo audio recording with two microphones, the distance between the mikes should be at least three times the subject-to-mike distance. This eliminates the possibility of phase cancellation.

Threshold of pain The intensity at which sound becomes physically painful, usually about 120 dB.

Threshold of hearing The softest intensity at which we first begin to hear sound, given as 0 dB.

Throw focus Same as "rack focus."

Tilt Vertical movement of the camera on a stationary base.

Timbre Variations in frequencies (harmonics and overtones) that give each sound its unique quality, or tone color.

Time-base corrector (TBC) A device which corrects for technical errors in helical scan VTR formats and permits the tape to be broadcast or dubbed-up to larger tape formats.

Time code See *SMPTE time code*.

Title card See *Camera card*.

Tone Refers to a frequency. A common frequency used in audio recording and measurement is 1,000 Hz "reference" tone.

Track (1) A special area of audio or videotape which contains program information or technical control information. (2) The sound portion of a motion picture film. (3) The accuracy with which a recorded videotape plays back. (4) Director's command to key in a tape track so it is on air.

Tracking error Thin, white, horizontal lines in the picture that result when the playback heads are not spinning exactly in the prerecorded video tracks.

Tracking shot Same as a "truck."

Trade-out A practice in which advertising or television exposure is swapped for free loan of needed props, free air fare, etc.

Transducer A device used to convert energy from one form to another.

Treatment A narrative describing what will happen in a program. Usually includes descriptions of characters, the plot, action, and some dialogue.

Triaxial cable Thin, lightweight cable which is used on digital cameras. Weighs about one-fifth the amount of conventional cable. Also called "triax."

Trim (1) To adjust lighting barndoors or shutters to control extraneous light distribution falling on a subject or area. (2) To shift an edit point frame by frame.

Tripod A three-legged camera mount, sometimes attached to a dolly for maneuverability.

Most tripods are lightweight and are used for remote productions.

Trombone A special lighting hanging device which attaches over a set wall to position the instrument where necessary.

Truck Horizontal movement of the camera on its pedestal. The movement can also follow a moving subject in which case it is sometimes called a "tracking" shot.

T-stop (transmitted stop) A more reliable measure of the speed of a lens than f-stop because it takes into account how much light is absorbed by the lens' glass and measures light transmission at the back of the lens.

Tungsten-halogen lamp Specially designed lamp which utilizes a tungsten filament surrounded by halogen gas to provide constant color temperature. Sometimes referred to as a "quartz-iodine lamp."

Twofold Two set flats hinged together into a single unit.

Two-shot Camera shot including two subjects.

Unbalanced microphone cables Refers to two-wire audio cables often found on less expensive audio equipment. One wire carries the audio signal and the other wire is dedicated to ground. More susceptible to "buzz" than balanced audio cables.

Under five Refers to a category of the SAG and AFTRA contracts, which stipulate a wage difference between performers with more or less than five lines; synonym for "extra" player in a casting sheet.

Undercut Changing the background picture of a composite image key or insert without affecting the foreground picture.

Unidirectional Microphone pickup pattern in which the microphone is designed for increased sensitivity to sounds emanating from a particular direction.

Universal zoom Generally describes a lens with a wide horizontal field of view (to permit greater indoor production flexibility) and a very long telephoto focal length (for remote production coverage, especially sports). The wide zoom range permits the lens to be used in virtually every production situation.

Variable-focal-length lens Zoom lens.

Vectorscope A specially designed oscilloscope which is used to set up and align color equipment.

Velocity microphone Same as "ribbon microphone."

Vertical blanking interval (VBI) During the scanning process, the period of time that the scanning beam is turned off between fields in interlaced scanning and between frames in progressive scanning. Also referred to as "blanking."

Vertical interval switcher A television switcher which produces glitchfree transitions by switching between picture sources during the vertical interval between video frames.

Vertical interval time code (VITC) SMPTE time code recorded in the vertical interval.

VHS A consumer videotape format that is ½-inch wide and housed in a cassette.

Video The picture portion of the television signal.

Video display card A device installed inside a computer that converts its output to interlaced-scanning images for reproduction on television monitor/receivers.

Video feedback Rephotographing the output of the video switcher off a video monitor and feeding the camera's output back into the switcher to create a continuous feedback loop, which produces multiple images.

Video level The strength of the video signal; controlled by the video engineer at the CCU.

Video workstation A frame buffer controlled by a PC that can record, process, edit, and reproduce television programs. A high-end video workstation also will be able to generate digital video effects (DVE), operate paint systems, and create three-dimensional animation.

Videoconferencing Live, interactive television in which two locations are joined together via video and audio channels. "One-way videoconferences" have video originating from only one location, while "two-way videoconferences" have video being sent in both directions.

Videodiscs An optical platter read by a laser beam that contains video and audio programming. Videodiscs can be accessed very quickly and can provide high levels of viewer interaction. They are also used for postproduction editing to speed up the process.

Videospace Refers to the fact that the audience's only measure of video reality is what appears on the television screen. The videospace is the sum total of all visual elements which interact to create the video; the visual counterpart of audiospace.

Videotape recorder Electronic recording device which stores video and audio signals on magnetic tape for playback and postproduction editing.

Vidicon A type of camera pickup tube which utilizes lenses in 16-mm format.

Viewfinder The device through which the camera operator views the scene being photographed. The camera viewfinder is a miniature television monitor.

Voice coil Electromagnetic device used in dynamic microphones, as well as in loudspeaker systems.

Voice-over (V.O.) Using an announcer or performer's voice over visual material, so that the speaker is not shown on camera.

VTR Short for videotape recorder.

VU meter Audio meter which measures the intensity of sound in volume units.

Wall sled Lighting instrument mounting device which braces the weight of equipment against a set wall.

Warping A type of morphing in which the subject becomes distorted instead of stretching into another shape.

Watt A unit of electric power; used to describe the relative light output of various lamps and lighting instruments.

Waveform A graphic representation of an audio or video signal.

Waveform editing On a digital audio workstation, visually changing the waveform of the audio signal to change the sound.

Waveform monitor A specially designed oscilloscope used to graphically display a video signal.

Wedge mount Camera mounting device which enables cameras to be quickly mounted and dismounted from studio pedestals and tripods.

WGA Writer's Guild of America; writers' union.

Whip pan Same as "swish pan."

White balance A procedure that corrects a camera's color rendition by changing the pickup tube's (or CCD's) sensitivity to different portions of the light spectrum.

Wide-angle lens A camera lens with a short focal length and a wide horizontal field of view; tends to increase perception of depth and force perspective.

Wild feed A nonsynchronous video feed.

Wild sound Recording nonsynchronous sound for either film or videotape.

Windscreen Same as "blast filter."

Wing it Slang term refers to improvising or ad-libbing the production without prior rehearsal.

Wipe Video transition in which one image wipes across another to replace it.

Wireless microphone A microphone that transmits a low-power radio signal which permits cable-free operation.

Workprint (1) Film: dub of original film which is used during editing to protect the original. (2) Video: small-format dub of an original tape which is used for viewing and editing off-line.

WORM (write once, read many) recording technology Can be either video or audio. Permits the user to record a very large amount of material. However, once recorded (or written), the material cannot be changed or recorded over.

Wow and flutter Speed variations in record, tape, or film playback which distort the sound, picture, or both.

Wow in When a tape, record, or film is put on the air before it is completely up to speed. Produces a distorted sound and/or picture.

Writer's bible Information and script direction prepared by the producer about the program, objectives, characters, and other production elements which are used by the writers.

XLR connector   Cannon-type audio connector used on all professional microphones and audio equipment.

X/Y technique   Refers to a coincident stereo miking technique which crosses two microphones with their heads together but not touching.

XYZ pedestal   In a robotic camera system, a remotely-controlled camera pedestal that moves the camera left, right, forward, backward, up, and down.

Y/C recording   A method of recording component video.

Zero start   Setting SMPTE time code digits for minutes, seconds, and frames to zero before recording each new tape, with the hours set to distinguish among different tape reels. Opposite of "clock time."

Zoom lens   A variable-focal-length lens which provides a continuously changing field of view from wide angle to telephoto.

Zoom range (zoom ratio)   The range of the zoom from widest possible angle to narrowest possible angle. Often expressed as a ratio such as 10:1, 15:1, etc., the 1 referring to the shortest possible focal length.

ADDITIONAL READINGS

PART ONE IDEAS, IMAGES, AND SOUNDS

Chapter 1 Introduction to Television Production

Gayeski, D. (1991). *Corporate and Instructional Video*, 2d ed. Englewood Cliffs, N.J.: Prentice-Hall.

Hausman, C. (1991). *Institutional Video*. Belmont, Calif.: Wadsworth.

Orlik, P. B. (1988). *Critiquing Radio and Television Content*. Needham Heights, Mass.: Allyn & Bacon.

Orlik, P. B. (1992). *The Electronic Media: An Introduction to the Profession*. Needham Heights, Mass.: Allyn & Bacon.

Schihl, R. J. (1991). *Studio Drama Processes and Procedures*. Stoneham, Mass.: Focal Press.

Schihl, R. J. (1991). *Talk Show and Entertainment Program Processes and Procedures*. Stoneham, Mass.: Focal Press.

Schihl, R. J. (1991). *Television Commercial Processes and Procedures*. Stoneham, Mass.: Focal Press.

Schihl, R. J. (1991). *TV Newscast Processes and Procedures*. Stoneham, Mass.: Focal Press.

Verna, T. (1993). *Global Television: How to Create Effective Television for the 1990s*. Stoneham, Mass.: Focal Press.

Chapter 2 Aesthetics in Videospace and Audiospace

Arnheim, R. (1974). *Art and Visual Perception: A Psychology of the Creative Eye . . . The New Version*. Berkeley, Calif.: University of California Press.

Arnheim, R. (1969). *Visual Thinking*. Berkeley, Calif.: University of California Press.

Bevlin, M. E. (1977). *Design Through Discovery*. New York: Holt, Rinehart & Winston.

Cubitt, Sean (1994). *Videography: Video Media as Art and Culture*. New York: St. Martin's Press.

Eisenstein, S. (trans. by Leyda, J.) (1957). *Film Form and Film Sense*. New York: World Publishing.

Pepper, S. C. (1938). *Aesthetic Quality: A Contextualistic Theory of Beauty*. New York: Charles Scribner's Sons.

Schwartz, T. (1973). *The Responsive Chord*. New York: Anchor Books.

Shanks, B. (1976). *The Cool Fire*. New York: Norton.

Young, F. M. (1985). *Visual Studies: A Foundation for Artists and Designers*. Englewood Cliffs, N.J.: Prentice-Hall.

Zettl, H. (1990). *Sight Sound Motion: Applied Media Aesthetics*, 2d ed. Belmont, Calif.: Wadsworth.

738

Chapter 3 Writing for Television

Finn, S. (1991). *Broadcast Writing as a Liberal Art*. Englewood Cliffs, N.J.: Prentice-Hall.

International Television Association (1993). *Handbook of Treatments*. Irving, Tex.: Author.

Matrazzo, D. (1985). *The Corporate Scriptwriting Book: A Step-By-Step Guide to Writing Business Films, Videotapes, and Slide Shows*. Portland, Ore.: Communicom.

Mencher, M. (1989). *Basic News Writing*, 3d ed. Dubuque, Iowa: Wm. C. Brown.

Orlik, P. B. (1994). *Broadcast/Cable Copywriting*, 5th ed. Needham Heights, Mass.: Allyn & Bacon.

Smith, D. L. (1991). *Video Communication: Structuring Content for Maximum Program Effectiveness*. Belmont, Calif.: Wadsworth.

Strunk, W., Jr., and White, E. B. (1979). *The Elements of Style*, 3d ed. New York: Macmillan.

Walters, R. L. (1994). *Broadcast Writing: Principles and Practice*, 2d ed. New York: McGraw-Hill.

Wood, D. N. (1989). *Designing the Effective Message: Critical Thinking and Communication*. Dubuque, Iowa: Kendall/Hunt.

PART TWO   ORGANIZING, CREATING, AND INTERPRETING

Chapter 4 Producing for Television

Blumenthal, H. J. (1987). *Television Producing and Directing*. New York: Barnes & Noble.

Broughton, I. (1986). *Producers on Producing: The Making of Film and Television*. Jefferson, N.C.: McFarland and Company.

Christian, C. G. (1987). *Media Ethics: Cases and Moral Reasoning*. New York: Longman.

International Television Association (1991). *Handbook of Forms*, 2d ed. Irving, Tex.: Author.

Lindheim, R. D., and Blum, R. A. (1991). *Inside Television Producing*. Stoneham, Mass.: Focal Press.

Miller, P. (1993). *Media Law for Producers*, 2d ed. White Plains, N.Y.: Knowledge Industry Publications.

Rivers, W. L. (1988). *Ethics for the Media*. Englewood Cliffs, N.J.: Prentice-Hall.

Verna, T. (1987). *Live TV: An Inside Look at Directing and Producing*. Stoneham, Mass.: Focal Press.

Chapter 5 Directing for Television

Armer, A. A. (1990). *Directing Television and Film*. Belmont, Calif.: Wadsworth.

Crisp, M. (1993). *The Practical Director*. Stoneham, Mass.: Focal Press.

Hickman, H. R. (1991). *Television Directing*. Santa Rosa, Calif.: Cole.

Kuney, J. (1990). *Take One: Television Directors on Directing*. Westport, Conn.: Praeger.

Lewis, C., and Green, T. (1990). *The TV Director/Interpreter*. New York: Hastings House.

Chapter 6 Performing for Television

Baker, P. (1992). *Wigs and Make-up for Theater, TV and Film*. Stoneham, Mass.: Focal Press.

Bernard, I. (1993). *Film and Television Acting*. Stoneham, Mass.: Focal Press.

Blum, R. A. (1989). *Working Actors: The Craft of Television, Film and Stage Performance*. Stoneham, Mass.: Focal Press.

Hindman, J., et al. (1979). *Television Acting*. New York: Hastings House.

Hyde, S. (1991). *Television and Radio Announcing*, 6th ed. Boston: Houghton Mifflin.

Kehoe, V. J-R. (1985). *The Technique of the Professional Make-Up Artist for Film, Television and the Stage*. Stoneham, Mass.: Focal Press.

Keith, M. C. (1989). *Broadcast Voice Performance*. Stoneham, Mass.: Focal Press.

O'Donnell, L. B.; Hausman, C.; and Benoit, P. (1992). *Announcing: Broadcast Communicating Today*, 2d ed. Belmont, Calif.: Wadsworth.

PART THREE   AUDIO FOR TELEVISION PRODUCTION

Chapters 7–10   Audio Sources, Processing, Recording, and Editing

Alten, S. R. (1994). *Audio in Media*, 4th ed. Belmont, Calif.: Wadsworth.

Amyes, T. (1990). *The Technique of Audio Post-Production in Video & Film*. Stoneham, Mass.: Focal Press.

Benson, K. B., and Whitaker, J. (1990). *Television and Audio Handbook for Technicians and Engineers*. White Plains, N.Y.: Knowledge Industry Publications.

Ford, T. (1993). *Advanced Audio Production Techniques*. Stoneham, Mass.: Focal Press.

Huber, D. M. (1987). *Audio Production Techniques for Video*. Indianapolis: Howard W. Sams.

Mott, R. L. (1989). *Sound Effects: Radio, TV and Film*. Stoneham, Mass.: Focal Press.

Nisbett, A. (1989). *The Use of Microphones*, 3d ed. Stoneham, Mass.: Focal Press.

Nisbett, A. (1993). *The Sound Studio*, 5th ed. Stoneham, Mass.: Focal Press.

Pohlmann, K. C. (1989). *Principles of Digital Audio*, 2d ed. Indianapolis: Howard W. Sams.

Ratcliff, J., and Papworth, N. (1992). *Single Camera Stereo Sound*. Stoneham, Mass.: Focal Press.

Rosenbaum, M. D., and Dinges, J. (1992). *Sound Reporting: The National Public Radio Guide to Radio Journalism and Production*. Dubuque, Iowa: Kendall/Hunt.

Rossing, T. D. (1990). *The Science of Sound*, 2d ed. Reading, Mass.: Addison-Wesley.

Watkinson, J. (1993). *The Art of Digital Audio*, 2d ed. Stoneham, Mass.: Focal Press.

PART FOUR   VIDEO SYSTEMS— EQUIPMENT AND OPERATION

Chapters 11–15   Video Imaging, Processing, Cameras, and Lenses

Benson, K. B. (1986). *Television Engineering Handbook*. New York: McGraw-Hill.

Carlson, V., and Carlson, S. (1993). *Professional Cameraman's Handbook*, 4th ed. Stoneham, Mass.: Focal Press.

Hirschfeld, G. (1992). *Image Control: Motion Picture and Video Filters and Lab Techniques*. Stoneham, Mass.: Focal Press.

Inglis, A. F. (1992). *Video Engineering*. White Plains, N.Y.: Knowledge Industry Publications.

Luther, Arch C. (1991). *Digital Video in the PC Environment: Featuring DVI Technology*. New York: McGraw-Hill.

Mathias, H., and Patterson, R. (1985). *Electronic Cinematography: Achieving Photographic Control Over the Video Image*. Belmont, Calif.: Wadsworth.

Millerson, G. (1983). *Video Camera Techniques*. Stoneham, Mass.: Focal Press.

Noll, M. A. (1988). *Television Technology: Fundamentals and Future Prospects*. Norwood, Mass.: Artech House.

Ray, S. (1979). *The Photographic Lens*. Stoneham, Mass.: Focal Press.

Smith, C. (1992). *Answers to Television Technology: An Encore*. Richardson, Tex.: Newman-Smith.

Smith, C. C. (1990). *Mastering Television Technology: A Cure for the Common Video*. Richardson, Tex.: Newman-Smith.

PART FIVE   VIDEO DESIGN ELEMENTS

Chapter 16   Television Graphics

Blank, B., and Garcia, M. R. (1986). *Professional Video Graphic Design: The Art and Technology*. White Plains, N.Y.: Knowledge Industry Publications.

Hoffman, E. K. (1990). *Computer Graphics Applications: An Introduction to Desktop Publishing & Design, Presentation Graphics, Animation*. Belmont, Calif.: Wadsworth.

MacNicol, G. (1992). *Desktop Computer Anima-*

tion: *A Handbook for Low-Cost Computer Animation*. Stoneham, Mass.: Focal Press.

Merritt, D. (1993). *Graphic Design for Television*. Stoneham, Mass.: Focal Press.

Wells, M. (1990). *Desktop Video*. White Plains, N.Y.: Knowledge Industry Publications.

Chapter 17 Set and Staging Design

Arnold, R. L. (1985). *Scene Technology*. Englewood Cliffs, N.J.: Prentice-Hall.

Byrne, T. (1993). *Production Design for Television*. Stoneham, Mass.: Focal Press.

Millerson, G. (1989). *TV Scenic Design Handbook*. Stoneham, Mass.: Focal Press.

Olson, R. (1993). *Art Direction for Film and Video*. Stoneham, Mass.: Focal Press.

Sweet, H. (1990). *Handbook of Scenery, Properties and Lighting*. Boston: Allyn & Bacon.

Chapters 18 & 19 Television Lighting Equipment, Operation, and Techniques

Box, H. C. (1993). *Set Lighting Technician's Handbook: Electricity, Lighting & Safety Techniques*. Stoneham, Mass.: Focal Press.

Fitt, B., and Thornley, J. (1993). *Lighting by Design: A Technical Guide*. Stoneham, Mass.: Focal Press.

LeTourneau, T. (1987). *Lighting Techniques for Video Production: The Art of Casting Shadows*. White Plains, N.Y.: Knowledge Industry Publications.

Millerson, G. (1991). *The Technique of Lighting for Television and Motion Pictures*, 3d ed. Stoneham, Mass.: Focal Press.

PART SIX VIDEO RECORDING AND EDITING

Chapters 20–21 Video Recording

Heller, N. (1989). *Understanding Video Equipment. Design, Operation and Maintenance of Videotape Recorders and Cameras*. White Plains, N.Y.: Knowledge Industry Publications.

Robinson, J. F., and Beards, P. H. (1981). *Using Videotape*. Stoneham, Mass.: Focal Press.

Chapter 22 Video Field Production

Compesi, R., and Sherriffs, R. (1990). *Small Format Television Production*, 2d ed. Boston: Allyn & Bacon.

Gross, L. S., and Ward, L. W. (1994). *Electronic Moviemaking*, 2d ed. Belmont, Calif.: Wadsworth.

Hesketh, B., and Yorke, I. (1993). *An Introduction to Electronic News Gathering*. Stoneham, Mass.: Focal Press.

Medoff, N. J., and Tanquary, T. (1992). *Portable Video ENG and EFP*, 2d ed. White Plains, N.Y.: Knowledge Industry Publications.

Shook, F. (1989). *Television Field Production and Reporting*. New York: Longman.

Whittaker, R. (1989). *Video Field Production*. Mountain View, Calif.: Mayfield.

Chapter 23 Video Editing

Anderson, G. (1993). *Video Editing and Post-Production: A Professional Guide*, 3d ed. White Plains, N.Y.: Knowledge Industry Publications.

Browne, S. E. (1993). *Videotape Editing*, 2d ed. Stoneham, Mass.: Focal Press.

Dancyger, K. (1993). *The Technique of Film and Video Editing*. Stoneham, Mass.: Focal Press.

Ohanian, T. A. (1992). *Digital Nonlinear Editing*. Stoneham, Mass.: Focal Press.

Ratcliff, J. (1993). *Timecode: A User's Guide*. Stoneham, Mass.: Focal Press.

INDEX